THE OFFICIAL® PRICE GUIDE TO COLLECTOR PLATES

Rinker Enterprises

SEVENTH EDITION

House of Collectibles
The Ballantine Publishing Group • New York

Important Notice. All of the information, including valuations, in this book has been compiled from the most reliable sources, and every effort has been made to eliminate errors and questionable data. Nevertheless, the possibility of error, in a work of such immense scope, always exists. The publisher will not be held responsible for losses that may occur in the purchase, sale, or other transaction of items because of information contained herein. Readers who feel they have discovered errors are invited to write and inform us, so they may be corrected in subsequent editions. Those seeking further information on the topics covered in this book are advised to refer to the complete line of Official Price Guides published by the House of Collectibles.

Published by: House of Collectibles
The Ballantine Publishing Group
201 East 50th Street
New York, New York 10022

Distributed by The Ballantine Publishing Group, a division of Random House, Inc., New York, and simultaneously in Canada by Random House of Canada Limited, Toronto.

www.randomhouse.com/BB/

Manufactured in the United States of America

ISSN: 0743-8710

ISBN: 0-676-60154-5

Cover design by Dreu Pennington-McNeil
Cover photos by Harry L. Rinker

Seventh Edition: July 1999
10 9 8 7 6 5 4 3 2 1

Table of Contents

Acknowledgments

A general note of thanks to all the members of the collector plate community—artists, collectors, dealers, distributors, manufacturers, etc.—who willingly and enthusiastically provided the information found in this book.

Special thanks to: Debbi Choler of Anheuser-Busch., Inc.; Suzanne Quigley and Norma Gertsch, Executive Administrative Assistant, of Bradford Exchange; Linda Kruger of *Collectors News*; Teri Palmissano and S. Zagata-Meraz of Enesco Imports; Betty Stamatis of George Zoltan Lefton Co.; Joan McLoughlin and Fern Flamberg of Goebel; Linda Fewell, Marketing Media Relations, of Hallmark Cards; Shari Bright, President, of Incolay Studios; Tracy Brand of Islandia; Vincent T. Miscoski, a private collector who sent information about the American Express series; Lance Klass, President, of Porterfield's; Jane C. Troup of The Raymon Troup Studio; Donna Lincoln, Production Manager, of Reco International; Robert Goins of Replacements, Ltd.; Loris Crawford of Savacou Gallery; Greg Peppler of Winston Roland Ltd.; Frank Cusumano of Worldwide Collectibles; and Donald and Jennifer Zolan of Zolan Fine Arts, Ltd.

Rinker Enterprises, Inc. (5093 Vera Cruz Road, Emmaus, PA 18049) prepared the text, typeset the information, and did the page layout for this book. Dana Morykan served as project director and did the typesetting and page layout. Dena George and Kathy Williamson provided research assistance and did the electronic scanning of images. Nancy Butt assisted in the cataloging and identification of the illustrations. Harry L. Rinker reviewed, rewrote, and/or added to the introductory material. Virginia Reinbold and Richard Schmeltze also contributed.

Randy Ladenheim-Gil headed the Random House team during manuscript preparation. Timothy J. Kochuba, former General Manager of the House of Collectibles, and Alex Klapwald (production) provided their expertise. Susan Randol guided the project through its final stages of completion.

Finally, thanks to those who purchased previous editions of this title and those who are discovering the wealth of information it contains for the first time. You are the key to this book's success. We have worked hard to earn your praise. Hopefully, we have succeeded.

What Is a Collector Plate?

The limited edition plate traces its beginnings to the 1895 blue and white porcelain Christmas plate produced by Bing & Grøndahl. The concept has weathered the storms of flooded markets, wildly fluctuating economic conditions, and slipshod, opportunistic manufacturers. Today, millions of people around the globe buy collectors plates, enticed more by their subject matter and quality than investment potential.

Limited edition plates are made in every shape, size, subject matter, and material imaginable. It is the word *imagination* that suggests the key to the future of collector plates. Technology and artistic creativity continue to produce innovations in both the aesthetic and production phases.

DEFINING LIMITED EDITION COLLECTIBLES

In 1989 the Collectibles and Platemakers Guild and the National Association of Limited Edition Dealers adopted the following *Statement of Integrity* as a means of defining limited edition collectibles:

STATEMENT OF INTEGRITY

Definitions for Limited Edition Collectibles

Original — one of a kind created by the artist.

Edition Limited by Number — A reproduction of an original, the edition limited by a number pre-announced at the time the collectible is announced. Each piece may, or may not, be sequentially numbered.

Edition Limited by Firing Days — A reproduction of an original limited by number of announced firing days.

Open Edition — A reproduction of an original with no limit on time of production or the number of pieces produced and no announcement of edition size.

Sold Out or Closed — No longer available from the producer (Sold Out applies to both Editions Limited by Number and Firing Days).

Retired — No longer available from the producer and none of the pieces will ever be produced again.

Suspended — Not available from producer—production suspended.

Collectibles and Platemakers Guild Adopted Feb. 7, 1989	National Association of Limited Edition Dealers Adopted May 5, 1989

Production run information is usually recorded on the back of each plate, along with the backstamp, which is the trademark of the manufacturer. Other information often included is the name of the plate, the series title, the artist, and the date it was made. Sometimes plates are even hand-numbered in the order in which they were produced.

WHY COLLECT LIMITED EDITION PLATES?

Why do millions of people around the world collect limited edition plates? One has only to see the plates to understand their popularity. Every subject imaginable is portrayed. As new themes and styles are created, they immediately find their way to the surface of a plate.

Beautiful horses running in the wind, a child gazing adoringly at his mother, Snoopy and Charlie Brown engaged in a battle of wits—all of these and more make up the range of subject matter that appears on collector plates. Plates are produced on such a wide variety of topics in order to appeal to the collector that lurks in each of us.

A particularly popular theme is that of the world's children, in all their infinite, playful varieties. We have all been children. Seeing these touching reminders of our youth evokes pleasant sensations and memories. Even the most diehard noncollector is hard pressed not to respond to a childhood scene that parallels his own.

Manufacturers of collector plates cater to animal lovers. Almost every animal and bird has been immortalized on a plate. The depictions can vary from traditional, realistic, Audubon-like renditions to comic relief caricatures.

If you are a student of art but your budget is limited, there are plates based on the works of contemporary artists, many with collectibles in other forms such as figurines, and prints by famous fine artists. Indeed, most plate collectors display their plates as artwork and derive the same sense of pleasure and satisfaction from them that they would from original paintings.

You can also compare limited edition plates to limited edition prints. Both are aesthetically pleasing and produced by fine artists in a limited edition. However, the affordability of collector plates gives them quite an edge over prints.

Appreciation of collector plates is further enhanced by the knowledge that the price difference between a limited edition plate and an original work of art is vast. A lovely plate can be bought for $25 to $85, whereas an important painting of the same genre would run to thousands of dollars.

MAKING A CERAMIC COLLECTOR PLATE

How are ceramic collector plates produced? Few people understand the process. Obviously, the artist does not paint each plate individually. How is the original painting reproduced onto a ceramic plate?

The answer is via a ceramic decal. Before you turn up your nose, dispel any preconceived notions about decals. Ceramic decals bear no resemblance to bumper stickers or to the old-fashioned fruit and flowers with which your grandmother decorated her kitchen cabinets. The making of a ceramic decal is a very involved, highly artistic and extremely technical process that generally takes a year or two from the planning stage to the finished plate.

First, the artist meets with the producer to discuss the concept for the plate or series. The artist then produces the original painting from which the decal will be produced. To do this, he often uses a matte that precisely outlines the shape of the plate.

At this point the producer meets with the decal manufacturer. There are many key decisions to be made at this crucial stage. One of the most important is the choice of a method for making the decal. There are three basic techniques that can be used: screen printing, offset lithography, or litho/screen combination. Each of these methods has its advantages and disadvantages. It is crucial to select the process best suited to the special requirements presented by the original artwork.

Screen printing produces opaque colors, and varying the amount of color can also produce a textured look. However, extremely fine detail work and subtle shading cannot be adequately achieved using this process.

Offset multicolored lithography, on the other hand, permits extremely fine detail and tonal gradations. This is possible because of the basic premise of lithography, which is the use of tiny dots of color. The dots can vary in size and in distance from each other, thus permitting delicate shading. However, its high cost and lack of certain colors, including white, make this process less than desirable for some projects.

If neither of these processes will produce the desired results, a combination of the two is used. This is referred to as litho/screen combination printing. Screen printed colors are added to a lithographic decal when brightness is needed. An example of this would be using a silkscreen white for highlighting on a predominantly offset decal. Sometimes waves or clouds are best presented in silkscreen, which gives them a heavier appearance, a sense of depth.

Color chemists now become involved. They are experts in knowing how the various ceramic colors will fire on the different blank plates available. The color chemist is responsible for choosing the various colors that will match the original painting. Unlike the artist, he or she is restricted by the printing process chosen. When the color chemist has completed this task, the process moves to the making of the color transparency. A series of negatives is made by photographing the original artwork using various filters and screens. From these negatives the color separations are made.

Time for another decision. There are two basic approaches to color separations: four-color camera-separation and hand-separation.

The first is a process which is similar to that used in the printing of magazines. In essence, the color separation is a photographic positive of one color. The difference is that in ceramic decals the colors are not totally transparent and a true magenta is not available. As a consequence, the results are not as true to the original as they are in nonceramic printing, from the standpoint of both color and detail.

In the four-color process there are four sheets of clear acetate, each one containing a portion of the total image done in varying shades of one color, which is applied in dots. The colors used are yellow, magenta (red), cyan (blue), and black. When these sheets are layered on top of each other and precisely aligned, the desired image and colors appear. The coloration of each sheet must be perfect if the original artwork is to be faithfully reproduced. The industry has developed computerized scanners that scan the original artwork and print the color separations. The result, although not as accurate as the work of a skilled color separator, continues to show progress.

The hand-separation method is considerably more time consuming, sometimes taking several months to complete. Separate "boards" must be made for each color, from six or seven to as many as thirty or more. A "proofing" process of transferring individual color dot patterns from a metal plate to special composition paper is arduous as well. This hand-separation method produces an unparalleled richness of color but does move away somewhat from the artist's original colors.

Whether to apply only one of these processes, or to utilize a combination of the two, using additional "picked colors" to improve on the standard process, is a tough decision. For instance, skin tones of a child may be done by hand while the rest of the image is done by the camera process. This requires an expertise gained only by experience, knowing what each decision will mean when the final product goes to the oven for firing.

Printing plates are made for each color separation, regardless of the separation method used. The printing of the decal is an arduous procedure. Decals are printed on special paper that has a very shiny, smooth film on one side. This paper dissolves when dipped in water prior to transferring the decal to the blank plate for firing. Decal paper also is unique in that it always lies perfectly flat, permitting the layers of colored ceramic powder to be applied precisely.

Blank sheets of decal paper are placed in an offset printing press and are individually printed with a very thin layer of varnish, the pattern of which is determined by the color separation. The sheet then goes to a dusting machine, where the special ceramic color powder is applied. When fired, this powder "paints" the plate.

Only the varnished areas hold the powder, and only one color per day can be printed. The decals are reinserted each day, and new color is added until each decal is completed. If the plate requires twenty colors, it will take twenty days to print the decals alone. They are constantly checked throughout the printing process for correct alignment of the colored powder. The different colors must be perfectly aligned so that there will be no overlapping of color or gaps in the design on the finished plate.

When all of the colors have been applied to the decal, it is sealed with a thin top layer of clear lacquer. This lacquer is organic and dissolves without a trace during the firing of the plate. Its only job is to hold the colors in place while the decal is transferred to the blank ceramic plate.

When the decals are finished, they are sent to the plate manufacturer, for transferral to the blank, back-stamped plates for firing. Hand-decorated detail work may also be added at this time, such as the application of a gold border. If everyone along the way has done his job perfectly, the finished plate will be a true reproduction of the original painting. The process is very exacting, as some plates require several firings.

OTHER MATERIALS

Since the vast majority of limited edition plates are made from pottery or porcelain and decorated with ceramic decals, understanding this very complicated procedure gives us an added appreciation for the finished product. However, this is by no means the only method or material used.

Wedgwood makes its plates with unglazed stained jasperware, which features applied white bas-relief figures in a classical motif. Studio di Volteradici executes its sculpted plates in ivory alabaster. Incolay Studios has come up with a new material made from crushed rock with a marblelike appearance. Lalique of France uses lead crystal with etched details. The Franklin Mint, River Shore, Danbury Mint, and Reed and Barton, to name a few, produce sculpted metal plates made from gold, silver, pewter, or damascene. Another new material, tori-art, was devised by the House of Anri. It consists of wood resin that is molded and hand-painted in bright colors. One of the most unusual plates is the exquisite stained glass plate "Old Ironsides," produced by the United States Historical Society. The stained glass portion is surrounded by a polished pewter rim. It has been acclaimed by collectors and has already made a permanent place for itself in the plate world.

IN SUMMARY

The diversity of material, theme, size, shape, and price of limited edition plates is no doubt responsible for the tremendous popularity of this collectible field. Welcome to the wonderful world of collector plates.

The History of Collector Plates

Although decorative plates have fascinated people for centuries, the hobby of collecting is a fairly recent occurrence. The first elaborate designs on plates appeared in the third and fourth centuries, e.g., an ornamental plate called "The Paris Plate."

Two key discoveries laid the foundation for the production of the first collector plate. The first occurred in China, where the process for making porcelain was perfected. When the formula was brought to Europe in the seventeenth century, English and Continental manufacturers began making fine ceramic wares.

The second represented a major advance in the decorating process. In 1888 Arnold Krog, director of Royal Copenhagen, one of the oldest porcelain factories in Denmark, perfected the underglazing process. Underglazed decoration was produced by dipping an object into a transparent glaze after it had been painted in cobalt blue glaze. The two glazes fused to produce a fuzzy blue and white surface decoration.

Many European porcelain factories produced small production sets of decorative plates or commemorative pieces to honor celebrated guests visiting their country. These specimens were the forerunners of the modern collector plates.

THE BIRTH OF THE MODERN COLLECTOR PLATE

The Danish custom of the wealthy giving gifts to their servants at Christmastime was well established by the end of the nineteenth century. To celebrate the holidays, they filled plates with cakes and cookies and gave them to their servants. Over the years, the plates became more and more decorative. Eventually recipients valued the plates more highly than the treats found on them. Many were hung as wall decorations, on view throughout the year.

In 1895 Harald Bing, of Bing & Grøndahl, produced a decorative plate designed especially for this gift-giving custom. Bing also saw it as a means of testing the value of adding novelty giftware items to his product line.

This plate, which is considered the first true *collector plate*, featured a design of the Copenhagen skyline in winter. It was named "Behind the Frozen Window" and inscribed with the date 1895. Franz August Hallin designed the pattern of swishes of white against a blue background.

Although not planned initially as a series, the use of a date encouraged the company to issue another Christmas plate for 1896. Sales of these plates exceeded expectations. Bing & Grøndahl has issued an annual Christmas plate ever since. This is the oldest collector plate series and the largest in terms of the number of plates produced.

Bing & Grøndahl's success produced imitators. Most early series were short-lived. Rorstrand of Sweden began its plate series in 1904. It ended after twenty-two years. Porsgrund, a Norwegian company, issued a Christmas plate in 1909, the only one they made. Rosenthal, a German manufacturer, marketed Christmas plates between 1905 and 1909. Hutschenreuther and KPM—Berlin also produced early plates, both surviving only a few years.

In 1908 Royal Copenhagen, another Danish company, introduced a Christmas plate series that is still in production. The success of Royal Copenhagen's Christmas plate series roughly parallels that of Bing & Grøndahl.

Collector plate production slowed during World War I (1914–18) due to the scarcity of materials. The economic recession of the mid- and late 1930s, World War II, and the extended economic recovery following this war resulted in a tight market for luxury items, the category in which collector plates were classified. No one in the 1950s foresaw the complex level of buying, selling, and trading that occurs today.

BEGINNING OF THE POST-WORLD WAR II COLLECTOR PLATE PHENOMENON

Lalique, a French glassworks company, made the first post-World War II collector plate. In 1965 it announced its intention to produce an *annual* plate for collectors. Unlike earlier manufacturers, who made no special concessions to collectors, Lalique proclaimed that its first plate would be limited—not only in length of time produced but in *actual number* as well.

The contemporary collector plate was born. Lalique produced two thousand 1965 plates, a thousand of which were sold by U.S. distributors. Lalique apparently recognized that a *collector plate in limited edition* would be received more favorably in America than elsewhere. The retail price was set at $25.

The venture was a resounding success. For the next several years the porcelain trade and related industries tracked the rising growth of the American collector plate market. Lalique kept producing annual plates, as did Bing & Grøndahl and Royal Copenhagen. As early as 1968, collectors were combing the market for 1965 Lalique plates. When an example was found, it often sold for four times the initial retail price.

Secondary market values also rose on earlier plates, even though they had not been manufactured in limited quantities. The late 1960s secondary market was a paradise. Half-century-old plates, whose numbers in existence had vastly diminished over the years, were purchased for modest sums. Even bought at double or triple original retail price, the cost was a mere fraction of present day values. And this was just thirty years ago!

The 1965 Lalique plate became the subject of tremendous speculation. No other plate issued up to that time had generated so much collecting activity. Some cynical observers predicted an eventual market collapse, leaving owners holding overpriced, hard-to-sell examples. The plate eventually reached a high of $1,800. Today it books at $1,250. Some plate speculators did lose money. However, the value drop never reached the levels predicted by the critics. A $1,250 return on an initial $25 investment thirty years ago still far exceeds what one would have realized by putting the $25 in a bank savings account.

Lalique's success was not lost on other ceramic manufacturers. There was a clearly established collectors plate market. By the early 1970s dozens of manufacturers entered the limited edition plate field.

COLLECTOR PLATES IN THE 1970s

Nineteen sixty-nine was a landmark year in establishing the present-day collector plate market. Wedgwood, the most prestigious earthenware company in Great Britain, inaugurated a series of Christmas plates. Wedgwood was a legend in the industry. Nineteen sixty-nine marked Wedgwood's two-hundredth anniversary, the perfect starting date for a line of annual plates. Its first annual plate was in blue with a white sculptured likeness of Windsor Castle. It read: "Christmas 1969."

Wedgwood was collector-conscious. It planned its entry into the annual market with collectors specifically in mind. Wedgwood's approach did more in terms of drawing other companies into the collector plate field than did Lalique or any of its predecessors. Just like the 1965 Lalique plate, the Wedgwood plate's price was set at $25. Wedgwood never released the production numbers for its 1969 plate. Although not promoted as a limited edition, Wedgwood assured its customers that they would own an item of some exclusivity. After production ceased, the company destroyed the mold and thereby rendered further production, authorized or unauthorized, impossible. This was a promise that no previous manufacturer had made.

Demand soon exceeded supply. Examples appeared quickly on the secondary market. During 1970 the price rose and topped at $240. The pace of buying and selling, especially in the United States, and the rate of price increase exceeded that of the 1965 Lalique plate.

Dozens of companies soon began producing collector plates, an activity that proved beneficial to the market. As more and more plates were made, the hobbyist who not only wanted to collect, but wanted (in the early 1970s, anyway) one example of every plate produced, entered the market.

The Franklin Mint of Franklin Center, Pennsylvania, entered the collector plate market in 1970. This organization, operating since 1964, previously produced commemorative medals and other numismatic items. The Franklin Mint wanted to make a splash when it entered the collector plate market. It contracted with Norman Rockwell, America's most recognized illustrator, to design its first plate. In addition, The Franklin Mint produced the plate in sterling silver, not ceramic, thereby capturing the collector market from several angles.

With that kind of varied appeal, the 1970 Rockwell-designed plate's success was assured, even at the very high issue price of $100—the most expensive collector plate offered up to that time. Fearing that the price might place it out of reach for the average buyer and that the concept of a colorless plate would not necessarily be appealing, some gift shops hesitated to place orders. Those who did were rewarded. It sold extremely well. When it entered the secondary market, its value jumped. The Franklin Mint became one of the leaders of the plate industry, offering collectors' editions in silver, porcelain, and crystal.

The early 1970s, a period of intense activity for plate collecting, molded the hobby into its present proportions. Collector magazines and the general press ran stories about plate collecting. Specialized publications for the hobby appeared. Shows were held. Clubs and associations were founded.

The number of manufacturers issuing plates and the types of plates offered on the market multiplied at an unprecedented rate. Collector editions in glass, silver, pewter, wood, and other materials followed. Collectible ornaments and figurines arrived on the scene in the late 1980s. They quickly challenged collector plates for leadership in the limited edition marketplace.

On the secondary market, competition between hobbyists and investors drove values for some plates to astronomical heights. Prices changed so rapidly that dealers could scarcely keep track. Published advertisements became obsolete a few weeks after release. Speculation was rampant.

Manufacturers and dealers of collector plates needed to react quickly before the problems became counterproductive and caused long-term harm. Specific problems were addressed, chief among them the controversy over use of the term "limited edition."

Second, a number of lesser quality plates appeared on the market. This was the result of bandwagoning, the quick entry into the field by manufacturers whose standards of quality were lower than the initial manufacturers.

Third, the speculative fever needed to be controlled. Many felt justified in paying $300 or $400 for a plate whose issue price had been one-tenth of that amount. Waiting could mean paying an even higher figure while watching the price soar completely out of reach.

Slow growth allows time for all concerned (including the dealers) to plan their course of action. Instead, large numbers of individuals fueled by speculation fever began buying large numbers of plates. Hoards in the hundred and thousands were common. Everyone was waiting for the market to peak, at which point they would sell.

By 1973 so many plates appeared on the secondary market that supply exceeded demand. Prices decreased on a number of editions, including quality plates that did not deserve to get caught up in this tornado of speculation and profiteering. The secondary market was starting to collapse.

Some manufacturers went out of business, primarily those firms whose plates had been bought largely by investors and attracted only a minimal hobbyist following. Many plate prices dipped by 50 percent or more within one calendar year in the mid-1970s. These were editions that had little collector's appeal and whose prices had risen out of proportion to their quality, originality, or edition size.

The sudden dose of reality sent a clear message: Plate collecting was not going to be a paradise for quick-buck artists and entrepreneurs. It was shaping itself into an activity of genuine prestige, where quality and reputation carried weight and the inferior product or questionable sales approach would be recognized as such.

Several key manufacturers reevaluated their sales literature. No longer were collector plates hyped as long-term potential investments, but rather as the collectibles they are. This reorganization of the market caused pain and financial loss to many individuals, especially those from low- and middle-income families who "invested" much of their life savings into collector plates. A lesson was learned: There is no such thing as instant money.

By the end of the 1970s, the youthful exuberance of the collector plate market was ending. The phenomenal annual growth experienced by collector plates in the early and mid-1970s leveled. The secondary market saw prices decline more often than rise. The speculative bubble burst.

COLLECTOR PLATES IN THE 1980s AND 1990s

The collector plate market matured in the 1980s. Once again, the market was the provenance of manufacturers, collectors, and dealers willing to make a long-term commitment. The number of new plate issues declined sharply. This helped the market by providing collectors with more focused buying opportunities and allowing them to buy without becoming financially overextended.

Two central selling themes—artist and subject matter—dominate the collector plate market of the 1980s and 1990s. Collector plate manufacturers carefully follow several contemporary art mediums, the most important of which is limited edition prints. When an artist achieves national recognition, a collector plate series often follows. The 1980s witnessed the arrival of Ben Black and Rusty Money. Thomas Kinkade arrived in the 1990s.

In the 1980s collector plate manufacturers increased their reliance on crossover buyers, individuals who buy a plate primarily for its subject matter, e.g., a plate containing an image of a favorite movie or music star. Clearly, one of the major image shifts in the collector plate field was the arrival of the personality-driven plate image.

By the mid-1980s, the secondary collector plate market had virtually disappeared. Those who owned plates were unwilling to sell them for prices substantially below that which they paid. Best to store them and wait for the market to improve. The recession of the late 1980s and early 1990s further reinforced this approach.

If collector plates were king of the limited edition market in the 1970s, collectible figurines reign supreme in the late 1990s. While collector plates remain an important part of the contemporary collectibles market, figurines, ornaments, and prints enjoy a much stronger market share. However, what comes around, goes around. Almost thirty years have passed since the collector plate craze of the late 1960s and early 1970s. A renaissance is beginning for a select group of plates from this era, a harbinger of renewed interest in old favorites.

Contemporary Distributors and Manufacturers

BING & GRØNDAHL

In 1853 Frederick Grøndahl, a porcelain modeler who had recently left the Royal Copenhagen Porcelain Manufactory due to an artistic disagreement, and Meyer and Jacob Bing, merchant brothers, formed Bing & Grøndahl, one of today's most widely recognized companies. Within a year they began production of bisque plaques based on designs by Thorwaldsen, a well-known Danish sculptor. During the next ten years they added figurines and dinnerware to their line.

In 1886 Bing and Grøndahl introduced underglaze painting, a technique developed by Arnold Krog of Royal Copenhagen. The company made a substantial investment in securing designs from leading artists, among whom were Fanny Garde, Jean Gaugin, Effie Hegermann-Lindercrone, Kai Nielsen, Hans Tegner, and J. F. Willusmen. For years only "Copenhagen blue" was used to color porcelain wares. Other colors, e.g., black, brown, green, and flesh tones, were added as pigments were developed that could withstand the temperatures of high-gloss firing.

In 1895 Harald Bing decided to make a decorative plate for Christmas that was functional and added to an established Danish holiday custom. Traditionally, the wealthy brought gifts of plates of cakes and cookies to their servants in celebration of the holiday. The plates were kept. With the passage of time they became more and more decorative.

Bing's 1895 plate, designed by Franz August Hallin, showed the Copenhagen skyline from "Behind the Frozen Window." The swishes of white against the blue background beautifully depicted a Danish winter. Many subsequent issues picture snowy Danish landscapes associated with the Christmas holiday. In addition to Christmas plates, Bing & Grøndahl produces Mother's Day and Olympic plates and commemorative issues.

Stoneware was introduced in 1914 and soft paste porcelain in 1925. In 1949 a new plant was built for the manufacture of dinnerwares.

Today, the quality of Bing & Grøndahl products is assured to any buyer by the traditional three-tower backstamp, which depicts the towers used in the coat of arms of the city of Copenhagen.

The factory, located in the heart of the city, uses several tons of clay daily in producing its artware, dinnerware, and figurines. Some 1,300 workers skillfully monitor and produce about 10 million pieces each year. Its line of production also includes bells, cameos for jewelry, thimbles, and even high-voltage insulators.

BRADFORD GROUP AND BRADFORD EXCHANGE

Prior to founding The Bradford Exchange in 1973, J. Roderick MacArthur imported collector plates from France and sold them to collectors and dealers in the United States. Helping collectors locate and purchase hard-to-find back issues was one of his many services.

The Bradford Exchange began as a response to the need for an organized market with an exchange for the buying and selling of the most actively traded issues. Today The Exchange lists approximately 1,300 of the most widely traded plates. In addition, it handles some 5,000 over-the-counter plates that are not listed.

The Bradford Exchange also became one of the leading publishers of information about the international plate market. By the end of 1973, Bradford began publishing the Current Quotations, a.k.a. the Bradex, a report on market activity and trading prices for collector plates.

Over the years, The Bradford Exchange introduced many innovative collector plate series, continually expanding the boundaries of plate collecting. In the 1970s it offered the first movie plates depicting cinematic classics and unique medium plates featuring three-dimensional sculpting. The 1980s witnessed the arrival of the first collector plates produced in Russia and the People's Republic of China. Also introduced were plate series illustrated with nature and wildlife scenes.

In 1977, after several years at 8700 Waukegan Road, Morton Grove, Illinois, the original Bradford Exchange and its 100 employees moved to its present location at 9333 Milwaukee Avenue in Niles, a suburb on the northwest edge of Chicago. The company leased the former Sears catalog store and warehouse that was constructed in 1960. Groundbreaking for a new building, featuring the world's first architectural use of tents, was held on August 24, 1983. The building was completed in 1985. The older Sears building also was renovated to include a large skylight over a garden, fountain, and 115 foot-long bubbling stream.

J. Roderick MacArthur remained chairman of The Bradford Exchange until his death in 1984. Under his direction, The Exchange continued to innovate and grow. In 1983 computerization was introduced on the trading floor.

Bradford took its first step toward international expansion in 1979 when it opened an office in London, Ontario. Today Bradford markets collector plates in fourteen different countries in North America, Western Europe, Australia, and New Zealand. It also has sourcing offices in four Asian countries.

The Bradford Group evolved from its original unit, The Bradford Exchange of Collectors Plates. It has acquired or developed more than a dozen companies that market architectural miniatures, beer steins, collector plates, dolls, holiday ornaments, and other collectibles. Its brand names include The Ashton-Drake Galleries, Longton Crown, Hawthorne Villages, Ardleigh Elliott & Sons, The Norman Rockwell Gallery, Bradford Editions, McMemories, and Collectibles Today.

In 1976 The Bradford Museum of Collector's Plates, located in Niles, Illinois, opened to the public. It is open from 8A.M. to 4P.M., Monday through Friday; and 10A.M. to 5P.M. on Saturday and Sunday. The museum is closed on major holidays. Admission is free.

ENESCO CORPORATION

Enesco Corporation, a producer of fine gifts, collectibles, and home decor accessories, is based in Itasca, Illinois. A leader in the $9.1 billion gift and collectibles industry, the company operates the Enesco Worldwide Giftware Group with wholly owned subsidiaries in Canada, Great Britain, Germany, Scotland, and Hong Kong, as well as a network of exclusive distributors strategically located throughout the world.

Enesco was founded in 1958 as a division of N. Shure Company. Following N. Shure's sale, the import division reorganized as Enesco, formed from the phonic spellings of the prior parent company name initials—N. S. Co. Originally based in Chicago, Enesco relocated its corporate offices to Elk Grove Village in 1975 and to Itasca in 1995. The company's international showroom, warehouse, and distribution facility remains in Elk Grove Village.

The Enesco product line includes more than 12,000 gift, collectible and home accent items including the award-winning Precious Moments Collection by Enesco, one of the most popular collectibles in the world, and the Cherished Teddies Collection, currently the top-selling teddy bear collectible in the country. Other leading product categories include Beatrix Potter, Calico Kittens, From Barbie with Love, Gnomes, Mary's Moo Moos, Lucy & Me, Memories of Yesterday and Mickey & Co./Disney.

Many of Enesco's products are designed by the company's staff of sixty artists and designers, including Mary Rhyner-Nadig, creator of Mary's Moo Moos. Enesco also markets licensed gifts and collectibles from well-known artists such as Sam Butcher (Precious Moments), Priscilla Hillman (Cherished Teddies and Calico Kittens), Kim Anderson (Pretty as a Picture), David Tate and Ray Day (Lilliput Lane), Lucy Rigg (Lucy & Me) and David Winter (David Winter Cottages).

In 1978 Enesco introduced the Precious Moments Collection. Adapted from the artwork of inspirational artist Sam Butcher, the collection of teardrop-eyed children with inspirational messages is one of the nation's most popular collectibles. The Precious Moment Collectors' Club was launched in 1981 to keep collectors updated on Precious Moments events, and in 1985, the Precious Moments Birthday Club was created to introduce children to collecting.

In addition to the Precious Moments Collectors' Club and the Precious Moments Birthday Club, Enesco operates five other clubs, with a total club membership of more than 600,000.

The Cherished Teddies Club made its debut in 1994 and is Enesco's fastest growing club with more than 180,000 members. Enesco's other collectible clubs include the Memories of Yesterday Society, The David Winter Cottages Collectors' Guild and the Liliput Lane Club.

In 1983 Enesco became a wholly owned subsidiary of the Westfield, Massachusetts-based Stanhome, Inc., a multinational corporation.

In 1997 The Bradford Group entered into a long-term licensing agreement to market the product lines of Stanhome's subsidiary, Enesco Giftware Group.

In 1998 Stanhome, Inc., changed its name to Enesco Group, Inc. Today, Enesco products are distributed in more than thirty countries, including Japan, Mexico and Germany.

FENTON ART GLASS COMPANY

In 1905 two brothers, John and Frank Fenton, opened a glass-decorating business in Martins Ferry, West Virginia, called the Fenton Art Glass Company. In a short time the business, although relatively small, began to appear as a threat of competition to the companies who were supplying Fenton with glass "blanks" for decoration. Consequently, the companies soon refused to deliver any more glass. Within the next two years, the Fenton brothers decided to alleviate the problem by producing their own glass.

The plant, now located in Williamstown, West Virginia, drew skilled glassworkers—one in particular who worked with colors and helped teach other glassworkers to make carnival glass. Fenton produced many variations through the years because of the many glass treatments that were tried and perfected by craftsmen. Colors were added: caramel slag, or chocolate glass; Burmese, a greenish-yellow shade; milk glass, white and opaque; and Vasa Murrihina, a transparent glass with suspended flakes of mica that appear as silver or gold

With these innovative ideas put to practice, the company, as a natural step of succession, entered the collector plate market. Fenton had already gained a reputation for its glasswares and was being sought by collectors all over. In 1970 the first issue in the American Craftsman Series was released. The series was created to honor the craftsmen who built America. The first issue was appropriately titled "Glassmaker." Also in 1970, the Christmas in America Series began with the first issue—"Little Brown Church in the Vale"—produced in carnival, blue satin, and brown glass.

The Fenton Art Glass Company is still producing decorative plates and offers designs from its own artists in the decorating department as well as scenes from Currier & Ives. The products made today are different from those first pieces produced in 1907, but all are quality wares.

W. GOEBEL PORZELLANFABRIK

Franz Detlev and William Goebel, father and son, established a porcelain factory in Germany's Thuringia region in January 1871. After five years of producing slate pencils, chalk boards, and marbles, to appease the Duke of Coburg, the Goebel family situated their factory along the River Röden in Oeslau (now Rödental) in the heart of Germany's ceramic producing region and close to the legendary Kipfendorf clay deposits. With ready access to raw materials, easy transportation, capital, and a family "porzelliner" tradition, the Goebels shipped their first high-fired porcelain tableware and decorative items in 1879. William Goebel was largely responsible for the artistic decoration of the company. Output focused on candy dishes, dolls, figurines, lamps, religious items, and vases.

In 1889 William sent Max Louis, his son, to explore the American market. After studying the retail business in America, Max Louis Goebel (1873–1929) returned to Germany and built his own ceramics factory near Kronach. Following the death of his father in 1911, Max Louis became president of Goebel and closed down the Kronach branch. He introduced many new porcelain figurine designs and added a pottery figurine line.

Franz Goebel, son of Max Louis, and Dr. Eugene Stocke, his uncle, assumed control of the company in 1929. Franz Goebel is responsible for making arrangements to produce the company's famous Hummel figurines. During World War II, Goebel concentrated on the production of dinnerware. Following the war, the company exported large quantities of Hummels and other figurines.

Goebel introduced its first annual Hummel Christmas plate in 1972. In 1984 the first Hummel mini plate was introduced. The mini plate series lasted eight years. During the collector plate craze of the late 1970s and early 1980s, Goebel issued over a dozen plate series, including American Heritage, Charlot Byj, Mothers, Wildlife, and Winged Fantasies.

Today, various factories produce the many world-famous W. Goebel products. These include the beloved "M. I. Hummel" figurines, plates, bells, and dolls; the limited edition series figurines—Lore "Blumenkinder," Pioneer Perennials, and Eden Gallery; the lovely realistic Animals, Birds, and Wildlife Collection; figurines by international artists such as Charlot Byj, Harry Holt, Laszlo Ispanky, Phil Krackowski, Hy Levens, and Janet Robson; and other ceramic, porcelain, glass, and terra cotta products.

HAMILTON COLLECTION

The Hamilton Collection, which moved into the collector plate realm in 1978, is an international purveyor of fine limited editions, including bells, boxes, dolls, figurines, ornaments, and plates. James P. Smith, Jr., was its founder and initial CEO.

The Hamilton Collection's first plate series honored The Nutcracker Ballet. Thornton Utz's A Friend in the Sky series quickly followed.

The Hamilton Collection's staff researched and developed several new plate series. The first Japanese cloisonné and porcelain plates and the first translucent cloisonné plate are among their accomplishments.

In addition to playing a major role in creating its own innovative series, the Hamilton Collection also produced series in conjunction with some of the world's most renowned collectibles manufacturers—Boehm Studios, Hutschenreuther,

Kaiser, Maruri Studios, Pickard, Reco International, Royal Worcester, Roman, Villeroy & Boch, and Wedgwood.

The Hamilton Collection produced plates that ranged widely in theme, from entertainment including ballet, movies, opera, television, and theater, to children. Plates featuring the artwork of Bessie Pease Gutmann and Maud Humphrey are examples of the latter.

Plate artists whose artwork has appeared on Hamilton Collection plates include: Thomas Blackshear (entertainment), Sam Butcher (Precious Moments), Bob Christie (dogs), Pam Cooper (cats), Chuck DeHaan (western), Gré Gerardi (cats), John Grossman (Victorian keepsakes), Bob Harrison (cats), Jim Lamb (dogs), Rod Lawrence (bird subjects), Susie Morton (entertainment), Ron Parker (bird subjects), Gregory Perillo (American Indian), Chuck Ren (western), John Seerey-Lester (bird subjects), and David Wright (western).

In April 1997, The Bradford Group announced that it had signed a definitive agreement to acquire the Hamilton Collection, a subsidiary of Stanhome, Inc., and entered into a long-term licensing agreement to market the product lines of Stanhome's subsidiary, Enesco Giftware Group.

ISLANDIA INTERNATIONAL

Joseph Timmerman founded Sports Impressions, a marketing firm for facsimile sports autographs, in 1985. When Enesco Corporation purchased Sports Impressions in 1991, Timmerman remained as president, retaining the position until 1996.

When Timmerman started Islandia International in 1996, he found that people assumed his new company would focus on sports. Instead he identified product lines where he felt there was a hole or gap in the marketplace. "I really know everybody in the industry from manufacturing, to the artists, to design, to advertising people," he explained.

Gail Pitt's cat art and Trevor Swanson's wildlife and animal art helped launch Islandia International. Pitt's International Fat Cats plates and figures proved highly successful. Timmerman and Swanson collaborated on four collectibles series featuring wildlife and domesticated animals.

Timmerman convinced Sue Etém, Plate Artist of the Year in 1982 and 1983, to revive her role as a leading collector plate designer. Together they introduced three child-theme collector plate series. Other artists working for Islandia include: Wayne Anthony Still, who provided the artwork for the People of Africa oval plate series; Cliff Hayes, painter for Coming Home (the return of a member of the Armed Forces to family and friends) and World's Greatest (women in the workplace) series; and Robert Tannenbaum, artist for the To Have and To Hold (wedding theme) and Celebration of Life (Mother Teresa) series.

Islandia also is home to the little blue bird figurines with inspirational, scriptural messages designed by Gretchen Clasby. Timmerman himself is deeply moved by Clasby's inspirational art. He helped select the first images to appear as Islandia figurines. Clasby's Sonshine Promises collection is a high-priority line for Islandia.

PORTERFIELD'S

Lance J. Klass, an innovator and leader in the collectibles field and former president of Pemberton & Oakes, founded Porterfield's in 1994. His vision was a company that brought the finest new art to collectors in strictly limited editions and provided uncompromising standards of quality and service.

Klass was a pioneer in the development of the miniature collector plate market, a response to collectors' concerns about the amount of space required to display a substantial collection of larger format plates. Known as "Mr. Mini," he established the 3¼" plate as the industry standard. Klass also is credited for innovative packaging and display concepts, including the addition of an attractive and functional easel to display the plates.

In 1996 Klass moved Porterfield's from California to Concord, New Hampshire, prompted in part by a desire to be near portrait artist Rob Anders. Following the move, Klass worked at refining the quality of the mini collector plate. He began production of his ceramic transfers at top American facilities, exercising close control over their quality and fidelity. The production process was closely supervised.

Klass's emphasis on quality resulted in a consumer warranty that allows collectors to purchase Porterfield's mini plates completely risk free and return them for a full refund of the issue price at any time within a year and a day after purchase, no questions asked. It is billed as the longest and strongest warranty in the collectibles industry.

Porterfield's introduced Rob Anders' first heirloom miniature plate, "First Love," in March 1996. In 1998 Rob Anders and his mini plates from Porterfield's swept the "Best of Show" plate awards at the International Collectibles Exposition. Anders' "Tucked In" mini plate was voted "Best New Plate" of the year and Anders America's "Best Plate Artist." *Collector Editions Magazine* gave Anders its Award of Excellence for "Time Out" and *Collectors mart magazine* named "Cookies for Daddy" the "hottest" plate of 1997.

As of July 1998, Porterfield's had released sixteen miniature plates featuring Rob Anders' artwork. Each plate is snow-white porcelain, decorated with a 24-karat gold rim, and comes with a gift box, hand-numbered Certificate of Authenticity, information about Anders, and a free easel.

Porterfield's Internet site, www.porterfields.com, contains "The Buy 'n Sell" section, a free service to collectors that enables them to list the plates they want to buy or sell on the secondary market. It also features information about past, recent, and future releases, and artist Rob Anders.

THE RAYMON TROUP STUDIO

After years of informal releases, The Raymon Troup Studio was established in 1994 to produce and market Wm. Raymon Troup's work in prints and porcelain. It is located near Franklin, Tennessee, just south of Nashville. Troup releases collectors' plates and ornaments under his studio imprint and also produces limited edition ornaments for museums, exclusive gift shops, churches and organizations.

The first plates in The American Landmarks Series reflect Troup's love of American architecture. "The Old Mill" is a richly detailed look at a cornerstone of frontier American life. The original painting is based on a mill still operating in Pigeon Forge, Tennessee, but similar gristmills are being lovingly restored all across America. The second issue, "Ivy Green," is where Helen Keller spent her early years.

In a new series, "Star Light, Star Bright" depicts a little angel caught in a moment of wonder as a star alights upon his finger. This superb plate is executed using one of America's finest porelain, Pickard.

Wm. Raymon Troup believes that fine art should be beautiful and life-enriching, and he is constantly striving to express this philosophy. He is determined that his releases be of the finest quality and does considerable research to make his works as accurate as possible, using a magnifying glass and miniaturist's brushes to achieve many layers of detail.

RECO INTERNATIONAL CORP.

Heio W. Reich founded Reco International Corp. in 1967. His goal was to provide American collectors with a wealth of world-class collectibles in a variety of media. Initially, Reich imported plates from European manufacturers such as Crystal, Dresden, Fuerstenberg, King's, and Moser.

In 1969 Reich, inspired by the blue and white plate designs of Bing & Grøndahl and Royal Copenhagen, created his own line of blue and white plates and marketed them under the name Royale. In 1974 he established a housewares and culinary arts division.

In 1977 Reco International introduced its own limited edition collector plate series featuring full-color artwork from Jody Bergsma, Sandra Kuck, and John McClelland. Dot and Sy Barlowe and Clemente Micarelli are other artists whose work has appeared on Reco products. Over the years, Reco produced plates celebrating a diversity of subjects, e.g., ballet, children, Christmas, military, Mother's Day, nature, and wildlife.

Today Reco is shifting much of its marketing focus to giftware and home decor products. Kuck's Victorian Home Collection and Rooms with a View are two examples.

Heio Reich plays a leadership role in the Worldwide Association of Gift & Collectibles Retailers (NALED) and Collectibles & Platemakers Guild. He was a charter member of the Board of Directors of Collectors' Information Bureau. Vendor of the Year and Producer of the Year are among a long list of awards garnered by Reich and his company.

ROYAL COPENHAGEN

In the early 1770s Frantz Heinrich Muller, a Dane, founded the first porcelain factory in Denmark. Four years later, when the company was granted royal privileges, it was named Royal Copenhagen, as it is known today. In 1867 the firm lost its royal status, but this didn't stop its success. When Arnold Krog became the company's director in 1885, he began developing a technique that proved to be a great asset to the field of ceramics.

Royal Copenhagen wares are perhaps best known for a soft appearance common to many plates and figurines. This process, known as underglaze painting, was perfected by Krog in 1888. The method of dipping an object into a transparent glaze after it has been colorfully painted sparked great interest in factories all over Europe. Carving a mold to develop the artist's design in relief worked very well with the underglazed effect to create a unique design since made famous by Royal Copenhagen.

Many companies have used the underglazing process, but a highly recognizable trademark distinguishes Royal Copenhagen from the rest. It consists of three wavy blue lines. Each stands for one of the principal Danish waterways: The Sound, The Great Belt, and The Little Belt. Although there have been minor variations, the trademark has remained steady, just as has the quality of its products. Royal Copenhagen has traditionally drawn talented sculptors and artists to create the right effect for each of its products: the delicacy of porcelain, the sturdiness of stoneware, and the bright colors of faience.

Since its first Christmas plate was produced in 1908, the factory has designed collector plates for eighty years. The company employs 1,700 workers, craftsmen, and technicians. The factory's painters alone comprise 650 of these. Each person does his job in creating Christmas, Mother's Day, historical, and special issue plates. Each strives to continue the traditions that were set many years ago by the original skilled artisans of the Royal Copenhagen porcelain factory.

SAVACOU GALLERY

The "Savacou," a warrior bird in Caribbean Indian mythology, symbolizes the spirit of Savacou Gallery—a pioneer in the commercial marketing of contemporary Black Art.

As late as 1985, New York City, an international center for arts and culture, did not have a visible, full-time, commerical gallery devoted to the promotion of contemporary Black Art. Savacou Gallery was opened in October 1985 to fill this void, its mission being the promotion of established and emerging artists from the Black Diaspora, with a firm commitment to quality and value, high ethical standards, collector education and a strong community involvement.

From its inception Savacou has been at the forefront of and a leading force in the movement to popularize the art of Black artists. By working hard towards the fulfillment of its mission, the Gallery has come to occupy a respected position in the marketplace. Its owners are considered among the most knowledgeable and articulate authorities on the marketing of art by contemporary Black artists. In its effort to promote Black Art, the Gallery was responsible for the concept of an African American Art Pavilion at New York Art Expo and was largely responsible for organizing the first such pavilion in 1992; the now defunct Association of Black Owned Galleries, which was organized by Savacou Gallery in 1991.

In addition to pursuing its commercial activities, Savacou has always been active in community programs. Gallery space is opened free of charge to community groups. Events that have been hosted include book signings, poetry readings, film screenings, political roundtables, educational seminars and charity auctions.

ZOLAN FINE ARTS / WINSTON ROLAND

Zolan Fine Arts/Winston Roland are privately held companies forming a joint venture in 1996 to promote and publish Donald Zolan's award-winning artwork of early childhood throughout North America, Europe, Australia, and Africa. Offices are located in Buffalo, NY; Ontario, Canada; and Hershey, PA, the studio location.The Zolan line includes the popular miniature plates, porcelain plaques, fine art prints, canvas transfers, and lithophane lamps.

Donald Zolan is a seven-time winner of the Collector Editions Awards of Excellence for plates and prints. His other honors include being named six-time winner of the favorite Living Plate Artist of the Year, as voted for by readers of the former *Plate World* magazine, three-time winner of the Canadian Collectibles of the Year award for his miniature plates, and being a recipient of the Silver Chalice Award for Best Artist.

Zolan Fine Arts/Winston Roland is the exclusive license of The Donald Zolan Society. The Society, formed in 1997, is directed by Donald and Jennifer Zolan and managed by the Zolan Fine Arts/Winston Roland venture. Winston Roland is the exclusive distributor for the Donald Zolan/Danbury Mint collectible line.

Donald Zolan reached his twentieth year in collectibles in 1998 and remains involved in every aspect of production to guarantee that the collectibles meet the standards of the original oil paintings in quality and perfection. The complete Zolan collectible line is represented at all major gift and collectible shows throughout North America.

Gallery of Artists

ROB ANDERS

At the age of fifteen, Rob Anders left home in Michigan and went to boarding school at The Loomis School in Connecticut. It was here that he had his first inkling that his artwork was destined for greatness.

In 1967 while studying at Yale University, Anders took several art courses, including a course in oil portrait painting. Upon graduation, he entered the Navy and served two years on active combat duty in Vietnam. Following his military service, Anders attended the School of the Museum of Fine Arts in Boston, Massachusetts.

In addition to painting privately commissioned portraits since 1973, for fifteen years Anders was illustrator for the John H. Breck Company. His pastel portraits appeared in Breck Shampoo advertising and commercials. He has also been under contract with the United States Postal Service to execute portraits and illustrations for over a dozen U.S. postage stamps.

In 1976 Anders and his wife moved to Lexington. Their daughter, Lili, was born in 1978.

Since Porterfield's introduced his first heirloom miniature plate, "First Love," in 1996, Anders has risen to become one of America's leading collectibles artists. Awards include Best Plate Artist and Best New Plate at the 1998 International Collectibles Exposition and the Award of Excellence from *Collector Editions* for "Time Out."

These honors are proof positive of the enourmous appeal of Anders' art on early childhood, as well as his growing reputation nationwide for his work in collectibles.

SAM BUTCHER

Samuel J. Butcher was born in Jackson, Michigan, on New Year's Day 1939. Like many artists, Butcher was lonely as a young child and spent long hours alone, making up stories and drawing pictures to illustrate them.

At the age of ten, Butcher and his family moved to a remote community in northern California. Encouraged by teachers at his school who recognized his unique talent, he began to reach out to people with his art and discovered his drawings made others happy. When he was a high school senior in 1957, he was awarded a scholarship to the College of Arts and Crafts in Berkeley. That same year he met young Katie Cushman, who shared his interest in art. Two years later, they were married.

Following the birth of their first child in 1962, Butcher left school to work full time to support his family. In 1963 he and his family began attending a small church near their home. He accepted a job as an artist at the international Child Evangelism Fellowship in Grand Rapids, Michigan. Over the next ten years his reputation as a fine artist grew, as did his family.

In 1978 Butcher's artwork was discoverd by Enesco Chairman and CEO Eugene Freedman, who transformed the two-dimensional art into a three-dimensional figurine collection. Within a short time the new Precious Moments Collection was hailed as a "phenomenon in the giftware industry."

Sam Butcher has been honored with a multitude of awards within the collectibles industry, including: International Collectible Artist Award (1995); the Special Recognition Award by the National Association of Limited Edition Dealers (NALED, 1988); and Artist of the Year (NALED, 1992, 1995). He continues to be honored yearly with prestigious awards, including: Figurine of the Year (NALED, 1994); Ornament of the Year (NALED, 1994, 1995, 1996); and Collectible of the Year (NALED, 1992).

His devotion to his faith and to his art led to the construction of a Precious Moments Chapel near his home in Carthage, Missouri. Inspired by the Sistine Chapel, Sam painted the ceiling in a special Precious Moments scene. Giant Precious Moments murals and stained glass windows also adorn the chapel.

Sam divides his time between his home on the Chapel grounds, a residence near Chicago and the Philippines, which he regards as his second home. His affection for children has led him to set up scholarship funds for deserving students both in the United States and in the Philippines.

JOSEPH CATALANO

From the age of two, Joseph Catalano was destined to paint. His earliest training came from his grandfather Ralph Miele, a realist painter who displayed his work in Greenwich Village in the '40s and '50s. Catalano's talents blossomed under the guidance of his grandfather. Today he is regarded as one of the premier sports artists.

Catalano's professional career started at age sixteen when a portrait of John Wayne he had displayed at a school art fair led to a commission to paint a First Day Cover Stamp for a New York company. That successful project led to other covers for the governments of China, Germany, Ireland, Italy, Japan and the United States. Catalano ended up designing more than 500 portraits for the company, producing about 120 works a year.

Although Catalano had been painting sports art for several different companies since 1980, a portrait of pitcher Dwight Gooden brought the artist to the attention of Sports Impressions, a leading producer of figurines, plates and other memorabilia.

Catalano's first assignment for Sports Impressions was an illustration for a collector plate titled "Yankee Tradition" featuring New York Yankees' greats Mickey Mantle and Don Mattingly. The Gold Plate Edition became the fastest sellout in Sports Impressions' history. He followed this success with more captivating plate designs of Jose Canseco, Ted Williams, Nolan Ryan and Will Clark.

Since 1987, Catalano has designed more than 110 items for Sports Impressions including plates, mini-plates, ceramic cards, steins and lithographs. He recently created a series of plates for an NFL collection with football stars such as Joe Montana, Lawrence Taylor, Randall Cunningham and Dan Marino. Other projects feature basketball superstars Larry Bird and Michael Jordan and boxing legends Joe Louis and Rocky Marciano.

Each of Catalano's works require a meticulous eight-stage process, starting with ten to fifteen thumbnail sketches. He studies photos and film of his subjects to define features, lighting and color, and then creates a detailed drawing. Finally, he paints his composition on canvas.

Catalano has won numerous awards, including the 1990 Award of Excellence from *Collector Editions* magazine for his plate of Mickey Mantle titled "The Greatest Switch Hitter."

Catalano, who lives in Rocky Point, NY, studied at The Art Students League of New York and the Parsons School of Art and Design.

PRISCILLA HILLMAN

Priscilla Hillman is the creator of the award-winning Cherished Teddies Collection, which is distribued in more than 25 countries, including Italy, Japan and the United Kingdom.

A self-taught artist, Hillman sketched and painted as a child. After graduating from the University of Rhode Island, where she studied botany, Hillman worked at the United States Oceanographic Office for several years.

Hillman resumed her interest in art in 1965 and soon after, she began illustrating and writing children's books, including nine "Merry Mouse" books for Doubleday. The series portray mice in a variety of settings as they experience new adventures.

In the late 1980s a serious back problem kept Hillman inactive for several months. During that time she kept herself busy by looking at nostalgic photos, watching old movies and "drawing in her mind," imagining sketches of teddy bears. When she recovered, Hillman immediately went to work at her drawing board to put her teddy bears on paper, bringing Cherished Teddies to life.

In 1990 Hillman sent thirty-six original oil paintings of her teddy bears to Enesco Corporation. Enesco decided her drawings should be tranformed into three-dimensional figurines and introduced sixteen figurines in 1992. Today, the Collection has expanded to include more than six hundred figurines and accessories and is responsible for millions of dollars in retail sales.

Since its debut, Cherished Teddies has been honored with numerous awards in the gift and collectible industry, including the 1992 Teddy Bear of the Year (TOBY) Award from *Teddy Bear and Friends Magazine*, Parkwest Publication's 1993 Outstanding New Product Line, the National Association of Limited Edition Dealers (NALED) Collectible of the Year and the 1996 and 1997 NALED Miniature of the Year.

Hillman has also been recognized with prestigious accolades, including Parkwest Publications' 1993 Outstanding New Artist and NALED's 1994 Artist of the Year.

In addition to Cherished Teddies, Hillman has created three other figurine lines for Enesco: the award-winning Calico Kittens Collection, introduced in 1993; Mouse Tales, resin figurines introduced in 1995 and based on her "Merry Mouse" books; and My Blushing Bunnies, resin bunny figurines with inspirational messages introduced in 1996.

Hillman and her husband, Norman, live in a small town in New England. They have an adult son, Glenn.

THOMAS KINKADE

A unifying element infuses all of the art of Thomas Kinkade—the luminous glow of light. This mastery has earned him the title of the "Painter of Light."

Kinkade's subjects vary but for the most part they are traditional gardens, pastoral and landscape scenes, and English cottages. His first collector's plate, issued in 1991, was the award-winning "Chandler's Cottage," part of the Garden Cottages of England Series. Since then, his art work has been featured on eleven more plate series—including Home for the Holidays, Home Is Where the Heart Is, and Thomas Kinkade's Lamplight Village—winning additional awards along the way. He was one of the first artists to be selected for induction into The Bradford Exchange Plate Artist Hall of Fame in 1995.

Thomas Kinkade was born in 1958 in Placerville, California. Under the influence of his highly individualistic mother, Kinkade developed an early enthusiasm for creativity. As a teenager, he was apprenticed by Glenn Wessels, emeritus University of California art professor, who had retired to Placerville. It was during this period that Kinkade was taught the secrets of the great master painters of the world. By the age of sixteen he already was an accomplished painter in oil.

Kinkade continued his studies at the University of California at Berkeley and later at the Art Center College of Design in Pasadena. While at the Art Center he created background paintings for a motion picture—personally creating over 600 paintings for the acclaimed animated feature film "Fire and Ice." He credits this early experience for providing the foundation for his success in plate art and the other media in which he works.

In 1982 Kinkade married his childhood sweetheart, Nanette. Beginning married life on a rural ranch property, Kinkade converted a barn to his studio. His first print was published in 1984.

As a tribute to his wife and two young daughters, Kinkade hides letters and numbers signifying their birthdates, anniversaries and initials within his work. Collectors are most familiar with "N" (for his wife, Nanette), which he integrates into each work. Yet another symbol to be found in every Kinkade work is a fish—a symbol of Christianity—and the inscription "John 3:16," a reference to a Bible verse that is special to him. Occasionally he includes a likeness of himself, his wife or his daughters.

Kinkade maintains a rigorous six-day-a-week painting schedule. In addition to his work, his life revolves around his church and his family, with whom he lives in a village in the coastal foothills of Northern California.

SANDRA KUCK

Sandra Kuck burst onto the collectibles scene in 1983 with the Plate of the Year, a heartwarming portrait of two tiny girls titled "Sunday Best" and presented by Reco International. During the 1980s, Kuck reigned over the collectibles world as the winner of an unprecedented six consecutive Artist of the Year awards from the National Association of Limited Edition Dealers (NALED). Today she remains one of North America's most collected artists.

Born in East Liverpool, Ohio, Kuck and her family moved to California when she was ten years old. As a child, she drew and sketched constantly. As a student at UCLA, Kuck realized that her art professors were focused on contemporary techniques—not the Old Master discipline she found so compelling. She and a friend ventured east to New York to study at the Art Students League. There Kuck immersed herself in the classic painting methods that have helped her develop her personal style—including rich colors, faces that seem lit from within and highly realistic detail work.

Not long after her arrival in New York City, Sandra met a young police detective named John Kuck. They married when she was just 19, and soon their children, John Jr. and Evelyn, were born. The Kucks are proud grandparents of a granddaughter, Alexandra, born to John Jr. and his wife, Jennifer, on June 20, 1997. Evelyn is a recent graduate of John Marshall Law School in Chicago.

In 1979 Reco International President Heio Reich stumbled upon Sandra Kuck's work in a Long Island art gallery. Reco produced three plate series with modest results, including Kuck's first plate, "Me First," before "Sunday Best" became a nationwide sensation.

Kuck is renowned for her stunning artistic portrayals of the bond between mother and child. The emotional quality of her paintings stems from her devotion to accuracy combined with her love of children and "all things Victorian."

Although Kuck enjoys travel and acclaim, she prefers to be at home in her studio. After her workday is done, she likes nothing better than to relax with her family, especially walking in the nature preserves surrounding her Florida home. Completely unspoiled by her success, Kuck is still amazed and flattered when collectors feel they know her as if she were a family friend. She is easily overwhelmed... almost embarrassed by their praise. Her warmth and kindness—and her ability to create flawless scenes of serenity, joy and elegance—have made this Romantic Realist one of the most beloved artists in collectibles history.

LUCY RIGG

Lucy Rigg was born in Seattle on March 7, 1943. The former Lucy Weygan was the second of four girls, and has lived most of her life in Seattle. She attended Seattle public schools and the University of Washington.

Lucy has been a teddy bear collector since 1968. Her home is filled with toys and collector items, which project the warmth and joy of her artwork. She has created a special room to display the Lucy & Me Collection, which includes several hundred porcelain bisque figurines, plus many other items, including limited edition collector plates, tins, laminated bags and more—each adorned with her lovable teddy bears.

Lucy Rigg began making baker's clay teddy bear figurines in 1969 while awaiting the birth of her daughter, Noelle. She decorated the nursery with her first teddy bears, but friends and family were so enchanted with the original creations that Lucy began making them for others.

Teddy bear collectors bought her hand-painted clay dough bears, known as "Rigglets," at street fairs. To keep up with the growing demand, she imposed a quota on herself to make one hundred teddy bears per day and often stayed up until the wee hours of the morning to meet her goal.

As her teddy bears became more popular, Lucy branched into other areas. In 1977, Lucy and her friend Judi Jacobsen began a greeting card business known as Lucy & Me. The partnership ended in 1984 and each artist formed her own company.

In the late 1970s, Enesco Corporation president Eugene Freedman approached Lucy and proposed turning her handmade teddy bears into a line of porcelain bisque figurines and accessories. She was operating her growing business from a small studio, already bulging at the seams with orders for her bears. Since Enesco introduced the Lucy & Me collection in 1978, it has enjoyed steady support from collectors and teddy bear lovers.

Lucy continues to operate Lucy & Company, designing diaries, baby announcements, calendars and her "teddy bear" version of popular children's books. "Lucylocks," a beautifully illustrated variation of "Goldilocks and the Three Bears," formed the basis for the Enesco Storybook Classics series of porcelain bisque figurines.

In the last few years, Lucy has divided her time between her business and home in Seattle and extensive overseas travel. Her daughter is a senior at University of Oregon.

DONALD ZOLAN

In the life of every child there comes a special time when, through the innocence and exuberance of youth, they begin to explore the world around them with wide-eyed wonder. These magical moments of childhood are brought to life by America's premier children's artist, Donald Zolan.

Zolan was born in Brookfield, Illinois, into a family legacy of five generations of artists. This legacy of artists and sculptors began with his great-grandfather carving church altars in Germany and includes renowned artist, typographer and engraver, Rudolph Ruzicksa.

A precocious talent at an early age, Zolan completed his first watercolor at age five and his first oil painting at age eight. By age ten he attended the prestigious Chicago Art Institute on the first of several scholarships. After high school, Zolan studied at the American Academy of Art on full scholarship, completing the Academy's four-year program in just two years. Pursuing a career in fine arts for the next twenty years, Zolan exhibited his paintings at galleries and art shows throughout North America, Europe and Japan, winning numerous awards, including Best of Shows by the Salmagundi Club in New York.

In 1978 his captivating paintings of children launched his career into the collectibles industry. Selected as America's Favorite Living Plate Artist for six consecutive years, Zolan is also an eight-time winner of the annual *Collector Editions* magazine's Award of Excellence, winning more individual artist's awards than any other artist in this program. Ross Anderson, former director of the Riverside Art Museum and senior lecturer at the National Portrait Gallery in Washington, DC, describes Zolan's paintings of children as having "an unmistakable energy and uninhibited naturalness that clearly belongs to our own time... Zolan can be seen as carrying John Singer Sargent's legacy of American Impressionism into the late 20th century."

Zolan celebrates his 20th anniversary year in collectibles with the release of his 1998 miniature plate series Country Friends, the first series to bear the anniversary hallmark.

Zolan is continually inspired by his midwestern upbringing and his happy childhood. "I love little children—the way their eyes light up with excitement as they awaken to the world around them. It's a marvelous time of life filled with wonderment, a time when each new discovery is another magical moment." He and his wife and business partner, Jennifer, live in the bucolic countryside of Hershey, Pennsylvania, surrounded by rolling hills and farmland.

Collecting Tips

Many individuals buy their first collector plate to use as a decorative accent in their home or office and not with the intent to start a new hobby. Soon the joy of owning one plate creates a desire to own a second, third, and so forth. Before one realizes it, he has become a collector-plate collector. A new hobby has begun.

Collector plates also are frequently given as gifts. Many individuals are nudged along the collecting path in that fashion. No decision is made to collect, much less how to collect. The enjoyment from the gift sparks the desire to obtain more.

Many beginners experience so much satisfaction in buying plates that appeal to their aesthetic senses, that they rarely look deeper. Certainly they know about the plate hobby and that some individuals are buying in a more sophisticated way. They have heard of the various refinements of plate collecting—it would be hard to live in today's world and not have heard of them. However, not all plate owners develop into full-blown collectors. On subsequent visits to the gift shop it may be a gilt candlestick or a framed tapestry that excites their attention. They have an "eye" for decorative quality and for art. They could develop into masterful plate collectors—but they are pulled in other directions.

GETTING SERIOUS

Inevitably, some individuals develop into serious collectors. Their purchases are made with more discrimination and a sense of real direction. They acquire knowledge along with their plates. They move beyond the level of a starry-eyed child looking at an ice cream cone or methodical and precise decorator wanting a certain shade of green. They think about artists and artistic quality. Most importantly, they develop the critical judgment skills that allow them to determine if a plate is merely gift shop ware or something special and magical.

DEVELOP A COLLECTION PHILOSOPHY

Many individuals begin their collecting by buying everything they like. Pretty often counts more than manufacturing quality or reputation of the illustrator. They probably made a number of good buys along the way. Some plates probably increased in value.

However, rather than having a meaningful nucleus of a collection, the odds are quite good that their collection is nothing more than miscellaneous plates—a gift shop assortment. Once they realize this, they will undoubtedly begin reproaching themselves for not becoming more serious buyers sooner.

To the majority of collectors, developing a collection philosophy is a necessary ingredient. This is more true today when the number of available plates has increased enormously. No one can own them all, not even a tenth of them. One cannot approach the hobby like Britannia embracing the world. The best approach is to choose some aspect of the hobby that deeply excites, keep the plates that relate to it, sell or trade the balance, and move forward.

SPECIALIZE

This is called specializing. Serious collectors specialize by turning their eyes, emotions, and checkbooks toward one class of plates. The chosen group becomes, for that person, the hobby. One disciplines oneself to treat all other plates as nonexistent.

By so doing collectors create many advantages for themselves, e.g., eliminating confusion and becoming experts on one type of plate much more rapidly than they would if they tried to track the entire market. Each acquisition, regardless of price, is significant because it complements what is already owned. It fits like a piece in a puzzle.

Perhaps best of all, when (and if) the time arrives for selling, one is likely to find buyers more enthusiastic about a specialized collection as opposed to one whose examples are mixed and matched.

In choosing a suitable specialty, it is wise to take many considerations into account. Some involve the plates themselves, but most revolve around the hobbyist's personality, tastes, and financial circumstances. It is advisable that a beginner or prospective collector become thoroughly acquainted with plates before stepping into the batter's box. False starts on collections are usually made because the individual is not aware of the variety of plates that exist on the market.

This book will help. It contains a wealth of information on plate collecting and the current plate market. However, there is no substitute for the real thing. Reading about plates is not the same as handling them. An excellent approach for any beginner is to visit the shops where collector plates are sold. Browse rather than buy—do not be afraid to look around. The more shops visited before buying, the better.

SPACE AND MONEY

Two obvious considerations are money and space. One can hardly buy what one cannot afford, nor display a large collection in a confined area. Few hobbyists have unlimited budgets or vast quantities of display and storage space. Neither the lack of space nor money need pose a serious handicap. Outstanding collections of plates have been assembled by hobbyists on tight budgets and those living in cramped apartments. More and careful planning is the key. Hobbyists who must make every dollar and inch of wall space count make the best buyers. They do not spend impulsively. They put together a collection in which real pride can be taken.

It is smart at the outset to develop a budget for collector plates that becomes part of your monthly budget—a certain sum that can be set aside weekly and left to accumulate until it has grown sufficiently to make a purchase. Beginners frequently are so enthusiastic that they spend their moneys as soon as they are available—no rainy day funds and no funds for when that special buy becomes available. This is understandable.

When one starts a collection and has nothing, the natural desire is to see it grow. Each new purchase is a measure of progress. However, beware of buying addiction, a collecting disease that some collectors develop whereby they need to make a purchase every day to feel satisfied. Stop to realize that good collections are worked on for years by their owners. Acquire at a leisurely pace. Make acquisitions here and there. Enjoy and admire each acquired plate. Do not buy in a panic just to watch your collection build.

You will have dry spells in your collecting when money is needed for other purposes or, for one reason or another, time passes without any fresh acquisitions. This opportunity to slow down and reflect on what you already own should be savored.

SETS AND SERIES

Collectors have different philosophies and motivations. Some prefer working toward a specific goal—collecting sets and/or series. This is a common approach among stamp and coin collectors. It applies just as well to plates.

The most obvious, of course, is to build a set. Another is to make a collection of annual plates (which is known as a *series collection*). Collecting sets and series makes it easy to budget funds for collecting. Be flexible. Prices often change before the collection is completed.

Also, a close estimate can be made of the length of time needed to complete the collection. One can choose a short series or set in the low price range and complete it quickly or select one of the long-running annual plates and accept a greater challenge. Of course, the longer it takes to complete a collection, the more uncertainty about the total cost involved. The market could rise substantially along the way. However, this should not be regarded as a deterrent. If you build a collection whose components rise rapidly in value, you automatically own a good investment. No one expects you to regret this situation.

There is yet another factor to be weighed. In set collecting, you continually add to the set until it is complete. Series collecting is slightly different if series plates are still being manufactured. To maintain a completed series collection as truly *complete*, new releases must be added. This should be done as soon as possible. The key is to buy at the issue price.

Unfortunately, some collectors (well in the minority) can assume a negative approach toward building a set or series collection. Their attention is so firmly riveted on *completion* that they turn a hobby into a hard and cold businesslike exercise. They do not enjoy themselves. They miss the fun and satisfaction of collecting because their minds are constantly on the plates they don't own rather than the ones they do. For these individuals we would have to say that set or series collecting is unwise.

Royal Copenhagen's *Merry Christmas* is an example from a series of Christmas plates.

Gorham Collection's *Beguiling Buttercup* from the Four Seasons–Young Love series is one of a set of 4.

Photos courtesy of *Collectors News*

COLLECTING BY MANUFACTURER

Most collectors need a goal toward which to work. In the case of collector plates, it need not necessarily be completing a set or group. Another approach is to assemble a collection in which the works of as many important artists as possible are represented.

Another collecting approach is to focus on a manufacturer. This enjoys strong support among collectors. This is certainly the oldest collecting philosophy when looking at the history of collector plates. Individuals living in European towns where plates were made bought those of local manufacture. With so many companies now producing collector plates, the choice is boundless.

If you choose to focus on a large company that has issued numerous plates and continues to do so, owning one of "every" plate is not realistic. Rather, strive for a good representation of the company's works, leaning toward the issues that have special appeal to you. These may comprise the efforts of favorite artists or issues showing subjects of a topical interest.

Collecting by manufacturer is an advanced collecting approach. Yet, there is no reason why it cannot be suitable for a beginner. The *investment* aspect of such a collection is apparent. Values of collector plates tend to change *by company* much more than by individual issues. There are exceptions to this statement, but it has held true during the past decades of plate collecting. One reason is the concentration of hobbyist interest on manufacturers.

A strong sense of unity and similarity of design are the chief reasons why so many people like to collect plates from a single manufacturer. All the plates, while differing in artist, subject, and even size, have common roots. Their relationship is unmistakable. They "go together." This "going together" not only adds to their visual charm but to their cash value. When such a collection is sold, the chances for a higher resale price are increased. A specialist dealer who makes a practice of stocking the products of that company and has waiting buyers is the first place to look.

Some selectivity is required in manufacturer collecting, as in all approaches to the collector plate hobby. Select a manufacturer with a solid reputation—one whose plates are universally recognized for quality, both in respect to subject themes and execution, and whose plates are not produced in numbers that exceed the demand for them. This does not necessarily mean going automatically for companies with the highest-priced plates. Some firms whose plates are in the moderate price range are worthy of collecting.

Whether a European or American manufacturer is chosen makes little difference, as long as its products are readily available in this country. One point that the collector ought to consider is the *possible fluctuation in availability* with European manufactured plates. Occasionally, quantities of an older foreign plate reach the U.S. market and temporarily upset the domestic selling price. This is a rare occurrence, but you need to be aware that it can happen.

Also, be forewarned to avoid firms that are new or about which little is known. Manufacturers need to prove themselves both on the retail and secondary markets. Products of a brand-new firm fall within the questionable category. They represent excellent bargains if broad collecting interest develops in that firm's plates, disasters if they do not.

COLLECTING BY ARTIST

Collecting by artist is almost as popular as collecting by manufacturer. You may have a favorite artist whose works are featured on plates. If not, study the available plates and see which artist or artists catch your eye. Artist collecting is a basic and sound approach, especially as collector plates are really prints in which ceramics substitute for paper.

You need not apologize for being more interested in the artist than in the plate itself. In a sense, the artist is the plate. The artist's reputation and skills give the plate much of its value and all of its physical beauty.

W. S. George, *On Gossamer Wings,* Lena Liu

Bradford Exchange, *The Blessed Mother*, Hector Garrido

Photos courtesy of *Collectors News*

COLLECTING BY THEME

Another approach to collecting appeals to the tastes of the home decorator. Numerous individuals collect according to theme. The possibilities are endless. The walls of the family rec room might be adorned with a collection of plates immortalizing sports legends such as Mickey Mantle and Michael Jordan. For the outdoorsman, a collection based on birds of prey and animals of the wild holds special interest. Classic movies and musicals are another popular choice. Plates commemorating *The Wizard of Oz, Gone With the Wind,* and *Star Wars* are just a few examples.

The nursery presents another collecting opportunity. Disney, Peanuts, and other cartoon characters, fairy tale and nursery rhyme series, or cute and cuddly puppies and kittens are all appropriate themes.

Holiday decorating might include a series of plates celebrating the birth and life of Jesus. A more secular approach could be plates with Santa's image. The styles exhibited by different artists and manufacturers only add to the variety of interest of the subjects. With imagination and creativity, any room in the home can be enriched with the addition of collector plates.

How to Display Your Plates

One facet of collecting plates that fascinates and delights hobbyists is the seemingly endless ways to display them. A well-displayed collection adds appeal to any room and can be a source of pleasure for the collector.

Plates are one group of collectibles whose beauty is recognized and admired by all. Visitors to your home need not be collectors to be impressed with your display. Using your imagination and creative talents, you can effectively and beautifully arrange your plate collection in whatever space you have available.

ON THE WALL

There are three basic places to display a group of plates: on a wall, in a cabinet, or via individual stands on top of furniture. Displaying plates on the wall is the most popular method of display and adapts easily to either a small or large collection.

Wooden frames, metal hangers, and hanging aids can be purchased in gift shops and plate stores. Wooden frames are available in many colors, sizes, and shapes. Find one that best complements your plate's design, motif, and color scheme. A very effective way to show a series is in a shadow box frame—a wooden frame with velvet background that holds more than one plate. Some of these frames have glass fronts. The glass may help you keep your plates dust free, but some glass types can mute the plates' colors. Whatever method you choose, keeping the viewing surfaces free of dust and dirt build-up will enhance the beauty and brilliance of your collection.

There are two types of metal wall hangers. The first consists of two individual plastic or rubber-coated wires, each with a U-shape prong, that hooks the plate at the top and bottom. The two ends of each U are bent to clip over the edge and are the only part of the hanger that is visible from the front. The top and bottom wires are held in place by two springs. The hanger is attached to the plate from the back by clipping the bottom wire prongs over the edge and then stretching the springs until you can hook the top wire prongs into place. The top wire then has a slight bend, which allows you to hang the plate over a nail or hook.

The second type of hanger consists of two half-circle wires that also hook over the top and bottom of the plate. The wires, which are joined together at the center of the hanger, are shorter in length than the diameter of the plate. To attach this hanger, situate it in the center of the plate and then stretch all four ends outward until they reach the rim. Then hook the four prongs over the edges. Another wire attached to the hanger allows you to hang the plate over a nail or hook. This is the least desirable hanger because of the numerous contacts with a plate's rim.

Only buy examples that have some type of coating over the wire and/or prongs. Be very concerned about any potential damage to a plate's rim. Also, buy the correct size. A hanger that is too small puts pressure on the plate and may cause it to crack. Replace hangers every four to five years. Springs do wear out.

Many collector plates can be hung on a wall without using store-bought hangers. Some manufacturers place two holes in the foot rim on the back of the plate. Wire or string can be threaded through each hole and then tied. Be sure to allow enough slack in the wire so that it can be draped over a nail or hook. Before you place the wire over a hook, double-check that the knots are securely tied. This method is fraught with risk. Consider using a hanger even if rim holes are available.

IN THE CABINET

If your collection is fairly small and not likely to grow at a rapid pace, cabinet storage is a satisfctory method of display. If possible, use a cabinet with glass-panel doors. These are expensive when purchased new. However, if you are willing to search, you can find quality pieces at very reasonable prices on the secondhand furniture market.

A glass display cabinet with a lighting attachment, usually a fluorescent bulb placed at the top, is another possibility. These normally have glass shelves rather than wooden ones. Light travels throughout the cabinet. It is best that a display cabinet used for plates does not have wheels on its base. Wheeled cabinets move when bumped. Plates and shelves can fall. It's a disaster no one wants to experience.

When arranging items in a cabinet, don't overcrowd the shelves. Leave at least two inches of space between each plate for easier viewing. Don't trust plates to stand by propping them against the back wall. They may stand temporarily, but any slight trembling of the floor will dislodge them. Instead, use plate stands or racks. You can buy them at most gift shops and specialty plate stores.

If you use a glass-front cabinet for displaying your collection, you will have a distinct advantage over a wall display—your plates will take much longer to collect dust. Plates displayed uncovered on a wall may need to be individually wiped every week whereas only the glass front of the cabinet will need to be dusted that frequently.

ON STANDS

One type of plate stand is made of twisted wire about the thickness of coat-hanger wire. When using these, be very careful that you don't scratch the plate. Put a small piece of felt between the plate edge and the stand.

A second type of plate stand is made of molded plastic and has a groove to hold the bottom of the plate. They are inexpensive and serve the purpose perfectly.

If you buy holders in quantity, you may even be able to purchase them at a discount. They can also be bought secondhand at flea markets or garage sales.

In addition to their use in a cabinet, metal or plastic stands also can be used to display plates on tables, mantels, or any flat surface. Plate stands can be very decorative, complementing and enhancing a plate's design, or clear plastic and plain, allowing every part of the plate to be visible with nothing to distract from its beauty. If you display your plates on stands, consider how susceptible they are to damage resulting from children or pets. Most plate stands are not designed to be pushed and shoved about.

MIX AND MATCH

Once you've decided where you want to display your collection, the fun begins. The possibilities of combinations for displays are endless. Here are a few suggestions to consider. Use your imagination and enjoy!

You may want to accent your collection or just a few plates with other items that correspond in topic, basic design, or artistic style. If Hummel annuals and anniversary issues are in your collection, try accenting them with other items made by Goebel, such as figurines and wall plaques. If you own one of the candleholders, lamp bases, or music boxes, this will also add variety to your display and may be just perfect for a baby's room.

Schmid, *A Gift from Heaven*

Bing & Grøndahl, *The Carousel*

Photos courtesy of *Collectors News*

If you collect topically, accent possibilities abound. Ceramic puppies, puppies on hooked rugs, tapestries, and even paintings can make an attractive display to go along with a theme collection of collector plates with puppy images. If flowers are your hobby, try arranging vases of homegrown flowers to match the floral artwork on your plates. Use dried or silk flowers to add variety. Consider placing your favorite teddy bear on a table next to your plates that depict children playing with *their* favorite toys.

If you have nonplate items by the same manufacturer as your plates, e.g., Bing & Grøndahl figurines have the same color scheme as Bing & Grøndahl plates, display them together. Collector plates of jasperware can be attractively shown in a china or curio cabinet with the many other wares made by Wedgwood. Royal Copenhagen has a Mother and Child Series in plates as well as in figurines. The design of the first plate, a mother and baby robin, was taken directly from one of the company's figurines. Both have the same soft look from the underglazed design and create a very impressive combination.

Another way to add variety to your display is to supplement it with works in other media by the same artist. This might prove costly if the artist is nationally or internationally famous. Many who collect an artist's work acquire paintings, lithographs, or serigraphs first. Later they are attracted to plates by finding the same designs on these ceramic masterpieces that they found in the other media.

GET STARTED

Take time to choose the right colors and styles for you. Coordinate your favorite pieces to create a display that any collector would be proud of. Then share you decorated rooms with others, but most of all, *enjoy them yourself!*

Caring for Your Plates

Collector plates require minimum care and attention. There are only a few basic rules to learn. It is true that plates, like all ceramic objects, will break if dropped. Aside from this they are quite sturdy in terms of resistance to deterioration and will endure for a very, very long time.

Proof of the long-term endurance of ceramics is found in art museums where pottery three thousand and four thousand years old is displayed. Many of these pieces, uncovered through archeological digs, were buried beneath the ground for ages. Yet they remain intact. Some 17th and 18th century ceramic examples appear almost as though they were made yesterday.

GENERAL CONSIDERATIONS

Your objective is to maintain your plates in exactly the same condition as when you acquired them. Some thought and preventive maintenance is all that is necessary.

The way plates are stored plays a major role in their preservation. With safe storage there is virtually no need to do anything other than an occasional cleaning to remove the inevitable accumulation of dust.

If it becomes necessary to wash a plate do this only for plates with a glazed surface. A simple wiping with a damp cloth should remove surface dust if it has not been allowed to build up too long. Rub gently. Do it a second or third time since dust sometimes takes a while to loosen. Wiping surfaces that are not glazed only rubs the dirt into the porous surface. Over time, the result is a plate whose surface appears dull, dirty or even stained. Use a feather duster to clean the surfaces of bisque plates. Do it often. At least once a month. Built-up dirt is the enemy.

Glazed surface collector plates can be washed in lukewarm water with mild soap. Do not use hot water and ordinary dish detergent. The latter may be too harsh and might remove some of the delicate surface banding or highlights. For wiping, use a soft cloth. Do not wipe hard. Take care that your fingernails don't come into contact with the plate. It is also wise to remove rings and other jewelry before washing a plate.

Do not wash collector plates under running water. Use a basin. Wash them first in soapy water and rinse them in a separate clear water bath. It may be necessary to rinse them several times. Make certain all soap film is removed. Wash the backs as well as the fronts and edges.

Be extremely careful when washing plates with gold highlights and banding. Often gilding is on the surface, not under the glaze. It can rub off. Better to have a regular feather dusting routine than to rely on washing for this type of plate.

After washing, dry your plate with another soft cloth, one that will not leave lint particles. You may want to use thick paper towels to prevent lint remnants. Discard each towel as soon as it becomes saturated with water.

Some common grease stains can be successfully removed. The procedure is to use soap and water as outlined above but concentrate wiping in the area of the stain. Periodic checks must be made during the cleaning procedure to measure your progress. Do not wipe longer than is necessary.

Grease stains that appear to have vanished in the washing process sometimes reappear after the plate is dry. The water camouflages them. Rather than wiping too much, it is best to dry the plate and check the results of your efforts. Wash again if necessary.

PACKING FOR SHIPMENT

The dread of every plate collector is the need to move his collection. Plates must be taken down and packed. Concern mounts. How will the plates survive the move?

There is little danger in transporting plates or even in shipping them through the mail provided simple precautions are taken. Dealers mail plates regularly and seldom encounter breakage. When sending plates by mail or by any commercial carrier, pack one plate per container. The original box in which the plate came is often the best shipping container. You can pack more than one in a container, but this increases the risk of breakage and damage.

Assuming you are packing one plate per container, you will want to begin with a sturdy box that is at least three inches larger on all sides than the plate. In other words, for a plate ten inches in diameter, the ideal box would measure sixteen inches by sixteen inches. The box should be about two inches deep and preferably closed on the top and bottom, with a flap-type opening on one end. This is better than a box on which the lid is removable. In any event, the box must be good and strong. If it's flexible at all, it may not be safe enough to do the job.

Wrap the plate in several layers of tissue paper or bubble wrap, securing it with tape. Then wrap in layers of newspapers, again sealing with tape. This provides a cushion to protect against scraping. Next step is to place a sheet of very heavy cardboard (about the same thickness as the walls of the box) on each side of the plate. These sheets of cardboard should be nearly as large as the box so that they will fit inside tightly. Having done this, tape the edges of the cardboard sheets together to form a sandwich, enclosing the plate inside them. Use regular packing tape to do this. Stuff the box with newspaper or add styrofoam peanuts so that there is no movement. Seal the box flap shut with strong tape. The plate should travel safely.

It is smart to insure the parcel. Obtain a receipt. Mark the parcel "Fragile."

INSURANCE

Are my collector plates covered by my household insurance? If you are a collector and have not asked this question, you should. Even a small collection of twenty-five plates can have a replacement value that exceeds $2,500.

Check your household insurance policy. Many policies now include the following statement in their "PROPERTY NOT ELIGIBLE" section: "Property listed below is not eligible for replacement cost settlement. Any loss will be settled at actual cash value at time of loss but not more than the amount required to repair or replace. / a. antiques, fine arts, paintings and similar articles of rarity or antiquity which cannot be replaced / b. memorabilia, souvenirs, collectors items and similar articles whose age or history contributes to their value." Collector plates fall into the "b" group.

If your household policy does cover your collector plates, make certain of two things. First, you want replacement, not cash value for your collection. Collector plates are appreciating, not depreciating personal property. Second, coverage should include breakage as well as the traditional coverage for fire, theft, etc.

Schedule a policy review with your insurance carrier. Before the meeting, make a list of the plates in your collection. Information should include name of manufacturer, title of plate, size, year of issue, name of artist, series identification, purchase cost, date of purchase, and current value. Make two copies. Keep one with your collection and the other at a location away from your collection. The list does you no good if it is destroyed along with your collection.

Photograph your collection. The ideal approach is to photograph each plate individually. If this is not practical, take a group photograph. Some collectors videotape their collection, incorporating a verbal description of each plate as part of the videotaping process. Again, make a duplicate copy and store it at an alternate location. Review your videotape every three to five years. Videotapes do deteriorate.

If your collection is not adequately covered under your homeowner's policy, you need to buy a fine arts rider, a form of Marine Inland insurance. Do not hesitate to ask for quotes from more than one company. Rates fluctuate between companies. Make certain you know exactly what type of coverage is quoted. Most companies provide only one price quote. It may or may not cover breakage. Insist on two quotes, one for breakage and one for other types of loss. You do not have to take both. You may wish to "self insure" for breakage.

A per loss deductible of $250 or $500 greatly reduces the cost of coverage. The insurance company wants to avoid nuisance claims. Also ask for portal to portal coverage, that each plate in the collection is covered from the time you buy it until the time you sell it.

Some insurance companies require that your collection be appraised. The appraiser must be a neutral party, never the owner of the collection nor the dealer who sold a large portion of it.

The mid-1990s witnessed the arrival of several insurance companies, agents, and groups specializing in insuring collections. The International Collectors

Insurance Agency (PO Box 6991, Warwick, RI 02887) is one such group. The company specializes in covering ceramics and glass.

The National Association of Collectors (PO Box 2782, Huntersville, NC 28070; 1-800-287-7127) offers a program whereby when you join the Society (an annual fee of $20) you become eligible to buy up to $50,000 of unscheduled insurance at extremely favorable rates. Coverage is on a replacement cost base and is "all risk," covering fire, windstorm, vandalism, theft, vehicle overturn, accidental breakage, and other perils. The program was designed specifically by collectors for collectors. Unlike the program of the International Collectors Insurance Agency that limits its coverage only to ceramic and glass items, the NAC policy covers all antiques and collectibles found in the home.

Investing in Collector Plates

Investment in contemporary collectibles, especially collector plates, reached record proportions in the mid- and late 1970s. Plates attracted more attention than most collectibles because of their limited edition status and the rapid advance in the price of some plates, more the result of speculation fever than common sense. This speculation fever caused disruption and uncertainty in the market. Many buyers with little market knowledge tried to ride the wave. The result was disastrous.

In 1973 a number of the speculators sold off their plates. The market quickly flooded. Prices on some issues dropped dramatically. The market was in a state of shock. The market stabilized in the late 1970s and it has been stable ever since. Today, most buyers recognize that investment is a long-term proposition.

Current investors are more selective in their buying and are holding longer before selling. This is healthy for the market because it takes plates out of circulation for an extended period of time. It allows desire and scarcity to develop on their own. A good investment is one that stands the test of time.

Can you *invest* in collector plates and make a profit? You can. It is work. And, it is risky. Knowledge of plates, the plate market, and basic investment principles is essential. It is not as simple as going out and buying a random selection of plates and putting them away for a certain length of time. Some plates have better investment potential than others.

First, when buying for profit, one must understand what constitutes *profit*. Selling for more than you paid does not necessarily result in a profit. The length of holding time must be taken into account. For example, assume you buy a plate for $70 today and sell it for $100 five years later. It appears that you made a profit, but you did not. Inflation reduces the dollar's buying power each year. The $100 you receive may not buy as much as the $70 you originally spent. You might have actually lost money.

This is why merchants and dealers favor a quick turnaround of their capital. The longer something takes to sell, the more it must be sold for in order to realize a good return. If your plate is not rising in value faster than the rate of inflation, it is not a profitable investment.

Also, you bought at retail and will most likely sell at wholesale when you cash in your investment. In selling to a dealer, you do not expect to obtain full retail price. Therefore, your plates need to register a very dramatic price increase, in the neighborhood of 25 percent per year or more, to be sold profitably. Some plates do this well; many do not.

As an investor, you have the option of purchasing newly issued editions as they come out and paying the issue price. You also can buy older plates that are now selling for more than their issue price. There is less speculation involved in buying older plates, especially those with an established secondary market. The key is to buy right, i.e., keep a good working margin.

If a plate has moved up 20 percent to 30 percent in price within six months of being sold out, it has a fair chance of doing as well or better over the next several years. Public reaction is difficult to forecast. Even the most knowledgeable experts misjudge the popularity of plates on some occasions. There have been many instances of editions that drew little attention when they first came on the market but rose rapidly in value thereafter. Likewise, there are those that showed all of the favorable signs for investment but just did not catch on as expected.

There are some basic guidelines that apply when attempting to forecast future price movement. Remember, these are guidelines, not absolutes:

1. Since many collectors buy their plates by artist, a new series of plates by an artist with an established collector following is usually considered favorable for investment. If the artist's work has saturated the market, avoid the plate.
2. Edition size plays a role in investment potential, if other qualities are favorable. A low-edition plate by an unknown artist would not generally be considered attractive for investment.
3. Topical themes of popular interest can affect a plates's investment potential.

THE REAL INVESTMENT

The real investment in collector plates is the joy and satisfaction of ownership and the pleasures you receive each time you look at and/or handle them. It is the wise collector who values his plates for their decorative and nostalgic value and not for their potential as an investment.

Fall in love with the plates you buy. Plan on keeping and enjoying them for a lifetime. There is no finer investment than this.

Buying and Selling Collector Plates

What are your collector plate objectives? Do you want to collect, invest, or deal in collector plates? The advice that follows applies to one or more groups, but not always universally. Pick and choose the advice that best serves your needs. Ignore what does not apply; think about what does.

You *can* make a profit buying and selling collector plates. If profit is your chief motivation, your approach is different from that of the hobbyist or "fan" of collector plates. As a seller, you may have to pass on plates that appeal to you personally but do not have mass sales appeal. The reverse is also true. If you buy for profit, you may acquire some editions that are not among your personal favorites. Most importantly, you need to be a tough buyer. In order to meet your expenses and make a profit, you need to buy at a net cost of twenty to thirty cents on your potential retail dollar. Plates likely to remain in inventory for an extended period must be purchased for even less.

Circumstances in the market at the time you buy and sell are a key factor in determining value. The market for antiques, collectibles and contemporary items is trendy. Tastes can change rapidly. What is hot today can be cool tomorrow. Certain types of collections and/or inventory are more apt to return a profit than others. This has little to do with their size or the sum total of capital invested. If the potential buyer likes a plate it will sell well.

Collections focusing on popular editions by major plate manufacturers always fall within the favorable category in respect to resale. They can be sold for a higher percentage of their current retail value than plates produced by less popular manufacturers. There is magic in a name. Manufacturers such as Lalique and Wedgwood have carefully cultivated their market image. Not every manufacturer stands the test of time. Many 1970s collector plate manufacturers are no longer in business. Manufacturers are responsible for much of the public relations hype behind their plate series. When the hype ends, interest often wanes. The old adage of sticking with winners applies with the proviso of focusing on long-term, not short-term winners.

Theme collector plates with strong crossover collecting appeal increase the likelihood of an easy sell. If you collect plates in which cats are a major image focus, you have a very appealing collection. Collector plate manufacturers have identified a number of universal generic themes from childhood to animals and other natural subjects to classic movies and movie stars. Crossover collectors, those attracted to the plate because of the image on its surface rather than the fact

Enesco, *Barbie as Eliza Doolittle*

Sports Impressions, *1927 Yankees*
Photo courtesy of *Collectors News*

that it is a collector plate, play an important role in sustaining the market for many collector plates. When a plate has crossover appeal to collectors from three or more collecting categories, its future is secure.

A "hot" artist, especially a recent award recipient, is a selling plus. Often a company will feature the designs of one artist for a complete series. Chances are great that the artist did plates and/or series designs for another company. If your collection is a mix and match group focusing on the work of one individual, it is called a "miscellaneous" collection. Most dealers welcome the opportunity to buy a collection based on the works of a popular artist. They already may have standing orders from their customers for some of the plates. Beware. Artist popularity is trendy. An artist who is in today may be out tomorrow.

Rob Anders' *Time Out*

Donald Zolan's *Waiting to Play*

Photos courtesy of *Collectors News*

SOURCES OF SUPPLY

The major sources of supply for collector plates are specialist dealers, general gift shops, and manufacturers, many of whom sell directly to the public. Recent editions of the Collectors' Information Bureau's *Collectibles Market Guide & Price Index* (available from Collectors' Information Bureau, 5065 Shoreline Road, Suite 200, Barrington, IL 60010) contain a "Directory to Secondary Market Dealers." Additional dealer listings can be found in David Maloney Jr.'s *Maloney's Antiques and Collectibles Resource Directory* (available from Antique Trader Books, PO Box 1050, Dubuque, IA 52004). Collector plates also are found in a variety of other sale environments: secondhand shops, antiques shows, auctions, flea markets, garage sales, and advertisements in the collector publications and local newspapers.

Begin your quest to acquire collector plates in your own locale. Supplement the local selection through telephone and mail-order purchases.

Obviously, you will encounter differences buying from one type of source rather than from another. Prices will vary and so will the selection. Dealers offering the best selections tend to charge full market prices or very close to them. Bargains frequently turn up in locations where just a few plates are found.

Collector plate collectors have a distinct advantage over many other hobbyists. Bargains *are* bargains. If a coin collector or an antiques enthusiast finds an item selling for half or less of book, there is a strong possibility the item is a reproduction or fake. Fakes are a minor problem in the world of collector plates. This is not to say that buying should be done haphazardly without proper examination. While authenticity is not in question, there are other points to consider—the plate's physical condition and whether it has been correctly identified.

Some plates are very similar to each other, yet from different series. The same artist may be featured in different series with art bearing nearly identical titles. Obviously, these differences can and do influence value. This is why the often-repeated saying, "The back of a plate tells more about it than the front," is worth remembering. Check the back of every plate for the manufacturers' marks, series, title, artist and edition size. You do not want to be surprised after you get the plate home.

Bargains are most often found at off-the-beaten-path sources. In some cases, the sellers are not aware of current market values and have acquired collector plates from individuals who likewise were unaware of their values. This happens with collector plates more frequently than most collectible items. If a noncollector received a plate as a gift in the early 1970s when the hobby was just becoming established, he may think of it more as a decorative gift than an object with potential long-term value. When selling the plate, the individual may be perfectly satisfied to accept $5 or $10 for an item actually worth $100 or more.

Finding bargains is exciting. However, if you have specific collecting goals, such as completing an artist collection or assembling a full set of one manufacturer's series, bargains need to be supplemented with purchases from within the regular plate marketplace. It can be exasperating to continually look for a plate and not find it. Yes, bargains save money. However, when you find a plate you need at full retail, you should consider buying it, especially if you have been hunting it for several years. If you want it now, and some collectors do, pay the full retail value and order the plate from a well-stocked supplier.

In the final analysis, take whatever buying approach that suits you the best. Some collectors have a more adventurous spirit than others and more free time and mobility. They enjoy the hunt as much as the capture. Others make buying as painless as possible. Their enjoyment comes from continually admiring the plates that they own.

Buying Direct from the Manufacturer

Some manufacturers sell their plates directly to the public. They advertise in magazines and mail to customer lists they assembled or acquired. Many now have their own Internet web site. If you respond to a manufacturer's magazine ad, you will be placed on its mailing list and receive announcements of future editions. You also are likely to receive announcements from manufacturers with whom you have never done business.

Manufacturers frequently sell their mailing lists. The result is that a name from one maker's list gradually gets on almost every maker's list. Few collectors object to this. They want to receive these announcements because it keeps them fully informed on every new issue.

Obviously, you cannot buy every plate offered to you. But, save all literature received from the manufacturers even if you have no intention of buying their plates. Maintain a filing system for manufacturers' announcements and brochures. This material will prove useful in the future for dating and tracking the value of a particular plate.

The most important step in buying from a manufacturer is to know exactly what you are ordering. Read the description carefully. Pay close attention to the size, material, type of decoration, and other pertinent information. Plates pictured in brochures are not usually shown in actual size. You should find a precise statement of the diameter in the promotional text.

Keep in mind that sales brochures and announcements are sometimes printed before the plate is actually manufactured. The photograph or photographs in the brochure are not the final plate design but a master or "dummy" model that has been prepared strictly for use in advertising. While the actual plate should be very nearly identical to the photograph, sometimes there are minor variations. Rarely, but it happens, the change is major.

As far as the colors are concerned, these will not reproduce 100 percent accurately in the photograph. Even if the photograph is excellent in quality, which most of those in plate brochures are, it will not catch every nuance or subtle tonal quality of the colors appearing on the plate. Be alert for imperfections in a plate. If there is a problem, contact the company, return the plate immediately, and request a replacement.

When you order a plate from a manufacturer, there may be a slight delay, particularly if you order within a "time deadline" announcement. Veteran collectors have learned to be patient and not start watching the mail a week after posting their orders. If you have not received the plate you ordered after six to eight weeks and you have received no announcement from the company about a change in the mailing date, write and ask about the current status of your order.

When your plate is received, save the box. This adds to a plate's value. Also save all literature that accompanies the plate.

Buying from Plate Dealers

The focus here is on dealers who either specialize only in the sale of collector plates or for whom plates make up a large portion of their stock and trade. They include plate dealers and gift shops, some of whom deal exclusively in newly issued plates and some of whom sell new plates in addition to those no longer available from the manufacturer.

Selling plates that are no longer being produced is the lifeblood of the specialized plate dealer. This is the famed secondary market. Dealers try to triple and quadruple their initial investment. When the value is high, doubling is acceptable. The secondary market has far more risk than the current production market, but also offers a greater profit potential if all goes well.

A merchant selling a plate currently in production tries to sell as close to the manufacturer's announced price as possible. Often he sells for somewhat less than the suggested retail price in order to compete with other dealers. Having bought the plate at the established wholesale level, this leaves only a modest profit margin.

Secondary market plates present more flexibility. The dealer buys them not from a wholesaler charging a set price but from the public. The price is negotiated sale by sale. Thus, dealers have more leeway in buying and selling. If the plate is in demand, they sell it at a price well above its initial issue retail price. Because there is no fixed price, dealers try for the best price possible. They succeed more often than they fail.

Dealers try to maintain as comprehensive a stock as possible, especially for plates from the most popular editions and series. The flow of material makes it impossible to have one of every plate in stock. A dealer may be slightly overstocked on a plate at one time and out of stock at another. As more and more are produced, the task of keeping "something for everybody" grows increasingly more challenging. Some dealers specialize. If you are looking for a plate issued by one of the smaller or more obscure manufacturers, you may need to contact several dealers before finding one who has the plate you are seeking.

Browsing in a plate shop, especially one that is well-stocked, is a treat for any collector. In most cases, the selling price will be marked on a card alongside each plate. This refers to only to that plate. After reaching the secondary market, many plates from the same series sell for different prices. One or two plates, usually the first edition from the series, become more popular than the rest.

Just as prices vary in a given shop on plates of the same series, they also vary throughout the trade. Learn to compare prices between shops. Trade periodicals and price guides help you keep up with the market. Do not expect the seller to do this homework for you.

If you want a certain plate and do not find it displayed in the shop, ask for it. In many shops, only a portion of the stock is on display. The dealer may have many other plates in a back room or cellar. Possibly a consignment has just arrived and is in the process of being cataloged and priced. The plate you want may go on display the very next day.

When dealers do not have the plate you want, they may be willing to take your name and address and hunt for it for you. With the connections most dealers have, they locate almost any plate in a very short time. Of course, it might not be at the price you are willing to pay. Therefore, it is essential when asking a dealer to locate a plate for you that you honestly tell him what you are prepared to pay. Once committed, honor your pledge.

If the dealer issues a list, pick one up before you leave and study it at home. It may be obsolete by the time it's in your hands. Chances are some of the plates already have been sold. Any such list is useful for comparing the dealer's prices to those found in advertisements of other dealers to see just how the prices compare.

If you order a plate from a dealer, when it arrives, examine it for scratches or other damage before paying. If a plate is in a sealed box, open the box and make your inspection *in the shop,* not at home. It may not be easy or even possible to return a plate once you remove it from the shop.

Buying by Mail Order

Collector plates are sold by mail by large specialist dealers (often the very same ones who operate shops), general dealers in collector's items, and private collectors. Plate and antiques trade publications contain page after page of advertisements by individuals willing to sell through the mail. Many advertisements list available plates and the asking prices. Others ask you to send your want list and an SASE (self-addressed, stamped envelope).

There are those who list their available plates, but do not price them. Instead, they ask for offers. This form of selling is actually an auction in disguise. Avoid buying from these individuals. If you want to buy at auction, go through traditional auction channels.

Buying via mail is a very satisfactory way of adding to your collection. It gives you a far greater choice of what you buy and from whom. Any slight disadvantages that may be involved, e.g., delays in the mail, are offset by positive factors.

One big plus of mail-order buying is that the selling vehicle often contains advertisements from dozens of dealers, many of whom are offering the same plate. You can compare prices. Find the best deal.

Unless the plate you are seeking is scarce, two or more dealers will offer it at the same time. The prices will differ from one seller to the next. One seller may be a private collector, another an investor, and another a regular dealer. Their cost of merchandise is different, thus making their selling prices different.

Check out the terms of sale. They also can differ: one seller may pay postage, another may not. The seller offering the lowest price is not automatically the one offering the best buy.

Always read the advertisement and review its listings carefully before placing an order. A well-prepared ad or list gives the name of the manufacturer as well as the series and plate name. It also may provide information on the artist, the year of issue and the size. To save space, some dealers provide only the very basic information. In extreme cases, everything is omitted except the title. The assumption is that the buyer knows what he is buying.

The less information an advertisement provides, the more careful you need to be when buying. This is particularly true if the stated price is far different from the book or trade price at which the plate normally sells. It might be the same scene by the same artist but in a smaller size. There may be unspecified damage. There is absolutely no way of knowing for certain unless you contact the seller and ask for specifics.

Do not pay attention to the promotional verbage in advertisements. Dealers may honestly believe that their price is the lowest for a particular plate or series when several other ads on the same page confirm that it is not. There is no way they can know what prices were going to be quoted *at the same time* by other dealers. The more ads you read and the more lists you receive, the better will be your capability of judging the really good buys.

Buying at Flea Markets and Secondhand Shops

Collector plates do turn up at flea markets and secondhand (thrift) locations—perhaps not in quite the same quantity as they did a few years ago, but they are certainly available. If you comb flea markets and thrift shops you will definitely encounter many, many bargains.

The basic problem with plates sold at thrift shops and flea markets is that they are rarely found in the original box. They may be scratched or damaged in some other way. This is why it is absolutely critical that you take extra time to examine plates at thrift shops and flea markets. There is no bargain in buying a collector plate with problems. Avoid purchasing any plate that is not in fine condition or better.

Buying at Auction

Collector plates appear at all types of auctions ranging from on-site and mail auctions containing only collector plates to general auctions held at small auction barns or someone's front yard. Auction buying appeals to many plate collectors. The competition and the showlike atmosphere of auctions are exhilarating. If you fail to get a desired plate, you leave the auction feeling entertained. Auctions are more fun than browsing in a shop.

The great attraction of auction sales is that they have the allure of buying below normal retail prices. Anyone bidding at an auction, whether mail-bid or floor-sale, might get lucky and buy a $100 plate for $50 or $60. This does happen. In a typical auction where there are hundreds of plates offered, several dozen will sell below market price.

Auction results are not predictable. Best guesstimates are wrong more often than they are right. Even auctioneers have difficulty forecasting prices. There are dozens of variables that affect price, e.g., who is present, level of competition, weather conditions, economy, etc.

The level of competition changes with each lot. One lot may attract dozens of bidders, another only two or three. One bidder restricts his bids to the plates of a specific manufacturer. Another is a topical collector who bids only on the half dozen railroad theme plates included in the sale. Yet another is a Rockwell collector. One needs a certain Hummel Christmas plate to complete a collection. Some bidders are dealers executing orders for customers or buying for their own stock. The list never ends.

When two determined bidders clash on a lot, the price balloons far above the plate's normal retail value. The successful bidder may or may not have second thoughts afterward, but there are auction buyers who willingly pay more than the book value. Most dealers and collectors discount this event. However, if the same plate begins to top its book value regularly when sold at auction, market price adjusts upward to reflect the auction prices realized.

Dealers keep a careful watch on auction sale results. Most of the plate collecting trends first become apparent at auction. To say that the auctions make the market is much more accurate than to say the market makes the auctions. Hence, it is very important for collectors to track the auction scene, just as dealers do.

Every collector plate appears at an auction sooner or later. The more recent and common ones are auctioned repeatedly, sometimes with several examples in the same auction. Dealers often sell slower moving stock at auction. This allows new collectors to enter the collector plate field at a modest cost. Dealers know that auction bidders like to get bargains and that without bargains there would be very little appeal for auction sales.

At a public auction you have the opportunity to examine the lots before bidding on them. Every auction has a presale exhibit during which the lots are placed on view and can be handled. Always examine any collector plate upon which you plan to bid. Mark the items upon which you wish to bid in the catalog. Note the maximum price you are willing to pay. Deciding on your bid limits *before* the sale is a wise move. You have the chance to deliberate coolly and calmly before the auction begins. Avoid auction fever at all costs.

How much should you bid? The usual advice is: "Bid what the lot is worth to you." This should probably be amended to read, "Bid what the lot is worth to you, in light of the alternatives." First, would you really be happy owning a $50 plate for which you paid $100? Second, what are the chances of finding it on the regular retail market? When found, how much is the price likely to be? If you have established a good rapport with several dealers, you know you can buy virtually any plate you want if you are willing to pay the dealer's price. Use auctions as a method to acquire plates below dealer retail.

Never bid above retail unless the plate is extremely scarce. Even then, exercise control. Collector plates are mass-produced items. Most serious collectors, those who have experience in auction buying and are confident of the actions, limit their bidding to 60 percent to 70 percent of book value, approximately two-thirds of the normal retail value. Rarely do they exceed 80 percent of book. This is a perfectly logical bidding practice. If they lose a plate, what have they really lost? They can always buy the plate from a dealer at retail.

See how the sale is organized. Pay close attention to the terms and conditions. Is there a buyer's penalty? If so, how much? Some lots may have a reserve or minimum bid. This is more apt to be the case in a mail-bid sale than at a public auction. If a minimum bid is stated, you are at liberty to bid that amount if you wish. There is no obligation to bid higher. However, the chances are good that someone else also will bid the minimum bid. If you really want the item, it would be wise to bid slightly more.

Cataloged auctions often provide a low and high estimate for each lot. These estimates aid bidders who are unsure about values. It is not unusual for prices to fall outside estimates—high and low. Experienced collectors do not allow estimates to influence them. They know what the plate is worth to them. This is the only value that really counts. If they are smart, this is what they bid and not a penny more.

When bidding in person, you can adjust your bids based on your success or failure in bidding on other lots. For example, say there are ten lots in a sale that interest you. If you bid on the first five that come up and get them all, your finances may require you to cease bidding at that point.

Read the catalog descriptions carefully to be sure you know exactly what you're bidding on. Description quality varies from auction to auction. Add your own notes made during the preview.

Buying from Other Collectors

You can often buy below market values by dealing directly with other collectors or private individuals who own plates. There are expenses involved. Unless you know of individuals with plates to sell, they may not be easily found without running advertisements. Ads can be placed in your local newspaper and/or in regional trade publications.

Hometown ads are often very effective, especially in localities where there are no plate shops. Anyone in these areas who has plates to sell is glad to find a willing buyer nearby.

Swapping with other collectors is another way to get the collector plates you desire. Plate hobbyists do not swap as much as stamp and coin collectors do. Duplicates are uncommon. Most collectors only buy one example of a plate. Swapping often occurs when a collector's interest shifts. He swaps plates in which he has lost interest for examples that meet his current passion. Swapping is generally done on a wholesale cost basis.

SELLING YOUR PLATES

There are a number of methods available through which one can sell collector plates. Some result in a minimal price received, others offer the potential for a higher return. Each requires hard work, persistence, and flexibility.

Selling to a Dealer

Dealers buy plates to replenish their stock. They prefer to buy from private sellers more than from any other source of supply. In fact, it is largely the general public selling to dealers that keeps the secondary market going.

Condition is critical. If your plates have any damage, i.e., chips, cracks, fading, surface defects, etc., they will not find a buyer. The plate needs to be in fine to excellent condition. In addition, the plate should have its original box and all supporting literature. If not, deduct 25 percent from what you expect to get. Finally, the more recent the plate, the less you are likely to receive for it. Plates made before 1980 do best on the secondary market.

Since plates have established market values, the buyer and seller usually have a fair idea of what they are worth. Actually, this makes it much easier to arrive at a mutually satisfactory price. Haggling is kept to a minimum.

Investors carefully plan the sale of their plates. They usually will not sell unless they see a substantial profit. Many investors were badly burned in the late 1970s and early 1980s. As a result many are still holding and hoping. A fast or forced sale made because cash is needed usually results in a loss, with plates often realizing only ten to twenty cents on the dollar of the initial purchase price.

Whether or not you make a profit on your plates when selling them to a dealer depends on the current market value. If you bought a plate at $90 when it was issued and the average retail price has now reached $300, you will have no trouble profiting. A dealer will pay around $125 to $150 for the plate, possibly more if it's a really hot item for which he gets many requests. On the other hand, if your plate has not advanced much in value, a dealer's buying price probably will result in a loss for you. Dealers do not base their buying prices on the original issue prices but on current secondary market values. Everything depends on how much the dealer feels he can get when he sells the plates and how long it will take him to sell.

A dealer who is overstocked on a particular plate will either decline to purchase it or offer a lower sum than usual. Dealers do not accumulate large stocks of any single plate unless they believe the value will rise in the near future. If the dealer is totally out of stock on the plate or plates you want to sell, he might pay a bit more. This is why it pays to talk with several dealers before accepting an offer. The offers you receive will vary from one dealer to the next.

Dealers' advertisements in specialized plate and trade publications often state buying prices. In fact, some advertisements show the buying and selling price. You may be surprised at the comparatively small spread, sometimes as little as twenty percent, between a dealer's buying and selling price. Do not assume this applies to the dealer's entire inventory. The advertised plates are usually those in which the dealer specializes. They sometimes will pay sixty percent of the normal retail price for plates that are on their "most wanted" list. Otherwise, buy offers are at one-third or less of book value. When a dealer makes a low offer, it is usually because he feels a plate is overpriced on the current market and is anticipating a decrease in value. Another dealer may feel differently and be willing to pay more.

A plate that has just recently gone out of production has less interest to a dealer. The market value at that point will probably be 25 percent to 35 percent of the issue price—no more. Some dealers may refuse to buy even at these prices because they have ample inventory. It may take fifteen to twenty years before the situation changes.

You can sell to a dealer by mail or take your plates to his shop. When selling by mail, send the dealer a list of the plates you want to sell and wait for a reply. Do not ship to him on approval. On your list, state the manufacturer, artist, series name, individual plate titles, and sizes. Include your asking price—for each individual plate and the entire lot.

A critical phase in selling by mail is to pack your plates securely for shipment, and insure them for their full value. If the value exceeds the limit for postal insurance, use a commercial delivery service such as United Parcel Service.

Selling at Auction

Many auctioneers will accept your plates for inclusion in their sales. Some may not if they feel they cannot secure a good price. Be appreciative of such an auctioneer.

You can often do better selling by auction than selling outright. Of course, there is no guarantee of this. Auction selling involves some uncertainty. There is the chance of doing very well, obtaining the full retail value, or experiencing a disappointing sale.

Some auctioneers will let you place minimum selling prices on your plates to prevent them from going for ridiculously low prices. A reserve should not exceed 40 percent of initial retail value. Expect to pay a fee to the auctioneer if your plates do not sell. The auctioneer cannot afford to work for free.

Whether to sell by auction or to a dealer is a choice the individual must make based on his circumstances. When cash is needed in a hurry, selling to a dealer is the best route. The auction process can take weeks or months from the time your plates are consigned for sale until the date payment is received.

Material sold on consignment is auctioned on a commission basis. The auction house receives a certain percentage of the price on each lot. Most houses work with a percentage of around 25 percent, though some charge as much as 35 percent. Usually the company's overhead costs determine the size of percentage. An auctioneer who publishes illustrated catalogs charges a higher commission rate. This is not unfair. Large auction houses with attractive catalogs often realize better prices for the items they sell. Even though you are paying a commission that is 5 percent or 10 percent higher, your end return may still be higher.

When items are accepted for sale by an auctioneer, you and the auctioneer sign a contract. The contract carries all of the terms involved in the sale. It specifies the date on which your plates will be sold, the rate of commission, the date on which you can expect to receive payment (usually thirty days after the auction), and other details. Read the contract thoroughly before signing. Ask questions about anything that is not clear. Keep your copy of the contract until you receive payment for your merchandise.

Private Sales

There is a great deal of work and some risk involved in selling your plates privately. The reward is a higher rate of return. Only you can decide if you have the time, money, and patience required for selling privately.

Here is a general rule to help you decide if a private sale approach makes sense. If you have extremely common collector plates, i.e., plates that are readily available in the marketplace, a private sale makes no sense. Hard-to-find and scarce plates are the best candidates for private sale.

When selling privately, think sixty to seventy cents on the retail dollar. If a person wanted to pay full price for a plate, he would buy it from a dealer or at a shop. Individuals who buy privately expect to save money.

Begin by placing a classified advertisement in *Collector's mart magazine, Collectors News,* or *Antique Trader Weekly*. You will find their addresses in the "Publications, Museums, and Factory Tours" chapter. While advertising in your local newspaper is likely to be expensive, the cost to advertise in your local shopper (penny press) is not.

Keep your advertisement short and concise. Cost is per word. Consider listing a telephone number and e-mail address instead of a street address. If you have a large number of plates, ask potential buyers to send an SASE (self-addressed, stamped envelope) for a full listing of your plates.

When selling privately, insist on payment in advance. Never send plates on approval. Wait four to five days between the time you deposit a check and the time you send the package just in case the check you received is bad.

When shipping plates you have sold, consider photographing them prior to shipping. This establishes the condition of the plates when they left your hands. Plates are damaged in shipment. Buyers have been known to substitute a bad plate for a good one and then return it claiming the plate was misrepresented.

Who pays for shipping? If the sale totals in the hundreds of dollars, the seller pays. If it is only one or two plates, the buyer. Make certain that you insure any package you ship. A return receipt is a good idea.

Selling to The Bradford Exchange and/or Replacements, Ltd.

The Bradford Exchange (9333 North Milwaukee Avenue, Niles, IL 60714 / 1-800-323-5577) is the world's largest trading center for limited-edition collector's plates, conducting more than 13,000 primary and secondary market transactions each business day. Replacements, Ltd. (1089 Knox Road, Greensboro, NC 27420 / 1-800-737-5223) is the world's largest retailer of discontinued and active china, crystal, flatware, and collectibles.

Both buy collector plates for resale on the secondary market. As buyers, they pay approximately 35 to 50 percent of the current secondary market retail value of a plate—more if they have a waiting list, less if the plate is likely to remain in inventory for an extended period of time. Each buys only those plates for which they have or anticipate a market. Although they occasionally will buy single plates, they much prefer to buy in quantity.

Make a complete list of the plates you wish to sell. Organize the list by: (1) maker, (2) series, and (3) title. When describing each individual plate, make certain to include the name of the illustrator, number of plates in the edition if it is limited, if the period shipping carton and/or all the paperwork that accompanied the plate, e.g., the guarantee, is present, and the condition of the plate, box, and paperwork. If you have multiples of the same plate, include that information.

When your list is complete, send it to one or both business. Do not list a selling price. Both prefer to make offers, i.e., quote a purchase price for those plates they wish to purchase. You can make their job easier by leaving a large margin on the left or right side of the page in which they can write their offer. When your list is returned, do not be surprised by the lack of a quote on every plate. Remember, each buys selectively. Neither has the desire or space to create a back inventory of unsalable plates.

Read the terms of the offer carefully. How long is the offer good? Generally, you have two or more weeks to decide if you wish to sell or not. If you are waiting for a second offer, this time passes more quickly than you think. Who pays for shipping? The seller pays for shipping. Before accepting one offer over another, check to determine packing, shipping, and insurance costs. They tend to be higher than most individuals expect. You need to deduct them to determine the true amount you will receive for selling your plates.

What about the plates they do not want? Make a new list of the remaining plates, send it to those secondary market dealers found in the *Collectibles Market Guide & Price Index or Maloney's Antiques & Collectibles Resource Directory*. Indicate that you want to sell the collection as a unit and are not looking for individual quotes. Taking the balance of your collection to a local auctioneer and telling him to sell them for whatever they will bring is an alternate approach.

Selling on the Internet

Direct sale or auction are two basic methods to sell on the Internet. Both are in their infancy and experiencing growing pains. Each has pluses and minuses.

Selling on the Internet requires three basic pieces of equipment—hardware (computer, monitor, etc.), software (operating program), and scanner and/or electronic camera. Although it is possible to sell on the Internet without a supporting image, it is not advisable. Internet sales are image driven.

Placing classified advertisements and establishing a store front are the two most frequent direct sale methods used on the Internet. Check these four web sites: www.buycollectibles.com; www.collectoronline.com; www.tias.com; and www.csmonline.com. Each offers the ability to establish a store front or sell individually within a general store (classified advertisement) environment.

As the 1990s comes to a close, the Internet auction is the clear favorite among sellers of individual items. Check these sites: www.auctionuniverse.com; www.ebay.com; and www.ontique.com. Ebay's success is the envy of the industry. It seems as though each week sees an announcement from yet another company that they are creating an Internet auction site. This is one instance where it pays to stick with proven winners. Only use an auction site that has an established track record of two or more years.

Internet auction costs are low, often less than two dollars per item. Most auction sites allow you to suggest an opening bid, actually an announced reserve, or to set a undisclosed reserve, a value the object must reach before it is considered sold. These two approaches allow the seller to establish a minimum price at which he is willing to sell.

The ideal approach, providing you are willing to take the risk, is to auction without a suggested opening bid or reserve. When auctioning a plate that has sold well before on the Internet, the risk is minimal. When there is no established sales record, the risk of receiving a lower bid than you expect is higher.

The glamour of selling on the Internet ends when a sale is made. Usually several e-mails and/or telephone calls are exchanged before a seller has secured a buyer's mailing address and agreement is reached on shipping and handling costs. There is a wait, ideally days and sometimes weeks for payment to arrive. Clearly stating payment policies and shipping costs in a sale or auction advertisement avoids delay and problems.

It is the seller's responsibility to pack items for shipment. The breakage potential is high for collector plates. Most buyers are willing to pay for insurance coverage. Consider paying it yourself when encountering a buyer who refuses.

Establish and clearly state your return policy. Anticipate complaints. Kudos to those Internet sellers offering a "money back, no questions asked" guarantee. More and more buyers are refusing to deal with sellers who have a *caveat emptor* (let the buyer beware) policy.

Finally, do not be discouraged if you attempted to sell or auction on the Internet and no buyers materialize. As this book goes to press, the percentage of individuals buying on the Internet is very small. It will increase exponentially in the years ahead. What does not sell today is very likely to sell tomorrow.

Fakes and Imitations

The hobby of collecting, no matter what you choose to collect, is plagued by fakes and counterfeits. The limited edition plate collector, however, is luckier than most. While the markets for stamps, coins, and antiques are rife with fakes and reproductions, the collector plate field remains relatively pure. Actual fakes are very rare on the U.S. market despite rising prices and the corresponding increase in temptation for counterfeiters.

This does not mean, however, that the inexperienced buyer should not be cautious. Certain pitfalls exist. With a little insight and know-how, you will become informed enough to avoid them.

Any manufactured object of quality that proves successful on the market will draw inexpensive imitations. This is true of cars, clothing, anything. Plates are no exception. The public's rush to buy a plate issued for $50 creates a great incentive for a manufacturer to produce a lesser quality plate with a selling price of $5 or $10. The assumption is that many purchasers of collector plates are not connoisseurs or even *collectors*. They are simply charmed by the physical qualities of the plate. Could they not be just as charmed by a less expensive imitation produced in vast quantities? Unfortunately, the answer is often yes.

Gift shops are being inundated with plates that, while appearing to be collector plates, are nothing more than facsimiles. They seldom carry the designs of noted artists. Those that do are poorly reproduced. Overall workmanship is well below the standard of collector plates. The edition is not limited. In fact, quite the opposite is true. Production is overwhelmingly high and quality is very low.

If you are a novice in this field of collecting, be aware that not every plate in a gift shop is a collector plate. When attractively displayed among collector plates, imitations may be deceiving. They may be the same size. They may be just as colorful. When you handle them, they may feel about the same. If you want a true collector plate, don't be fooled. Be prepared.

Become familiar with the names of companies that make collector plates and with their identifying backstamps. Learn to recognize the styles and signatures of your favorite artists. Backstamps and signatures are two important assurances that what you buy is authentic and not an imitation.

Many imitations originate in Hong Kong or Japan. Their designs are similar to themes found on collector plates. However, they are produced and imported in quantities large enough to saturate the market. These plates, while not limited in production, obviously sell. Otherwise, the producers and distributors would not profit.

The issue is not whether a plate is a forgery. As mentioned earlier, fakes are virtually nonexistent. The question is whether you want to collect limited edition plates or just hang a pretty plate on your wall for decoration. If you are interested only in collector plates, then your best protection is to restrict your buying to shops that specialize in limited edition collectibles. By dealing with reputable professionals you will save yourself a lot of problems.

Do not expect to find a valuable collector plate in a dime store or large discount store. These plates may be decorative, but they will not be limited in edition with the potential to appreciate in value. The key is to view collecting plates as you would view collecting fine art. You would never expect to purchase quality artwork at bargain basement prices. You get what you pay for.

It is of the utmost importance to educate yourself in this field. Subscribe to the various collector plate periodicals. They are a treasure trove of invaluable information to both the novice and the advanced collector.

Once you have learned to spot designers' styles and manufacturers' hallmarks, you can easily avoid imitation.

State-of-the-Market Report

The State-of-the-Market Report in the previous edition of this book began: "The collector plate market is alive and well. It survived the speculative craze of the early 1970s, over-production by manufacturers in the middle and late 1970s, the flooding of the secondary market in the late 1970s and early 1980s, and the recession of the late 1980s and early 1990s. Although relatively quiet for the past fifteen years, there are signs that the collector plate market is about to enjoy a collecting renaissance. The signs are early, and they may be misleading. The answer will be obvious in another two or three years."

Those three years have passed. While the jury is still out, rumors abound that their ruling will be favorable. The secondary market for collector plates is the best it has been in the last two decades.

Alas, the market has not made a full recovery, nor is this likely. Secondary market buyers are highly selective. More 1970s and 1980s collector plates are priced near or above their initial retail price in this edition than its predecessor. However, the percent is small, less than 5 percent.

The vast majority of collector plates from the 1970s and 1980s have not stood the test of time. They still sell on the secondary market well below their initial retail price. This does not mean they should be discarded. Today's collecting market is extremely trendy. What is in one moment can be out the next.

Crossover collectors, those individuals who buy something because its surface image reflects their collecting interest, still outnumber pure collector plate collectors as buyers. This is why so many contemporary plate series are theme, e.g., cats, or licensed, e.g., NASCAR, driven. Rather than look down on these individuals, thank them for keeping the secondary collector plate market as strong as it is.

Market flooding continues as large collections of collector plates find their way into auctions and flea markets as individuals who collected them or more likely their heirs offer them for sale. Rather than discard or destroy a plate, individuals are willing to sell them to a new owner for pennies on the dollar. Condition, scarcity, and desirability are the three collecting keys of the twenty-first century. Most collector plates survive in fine or better condition. Unfortunately, most are common, not scarce, and desirability is spotty.

Cheerleaders contribute to a successful market. Hype fuels collecting in both the primary and secondary market. Compared to the rest of the sectors within the contemporary collectibles market, now estimated to be a ten-billion-dollar-a-year business, collector plate hype takes a back seat to cottages, figurines, and ornaments. Full page advertisements still appear in household periodicals and Sunday newspaper supplements. Several artists and manufacturers have organized collectors' clubs to promote their specific offerings. Anheuser-Busch and Coca-Cola are examples of companies whose expanded licensing programs are impacting positively on the collectibles market.

As the 1990s comes to a close, the loudest cheers are being heard from the secondary market. Krause Publications and Replacements, Ltd., have added their voices to those of The Collectors' Information Bureau and *Collectors News* in touting the secondary collector plate market. This is more than a shot in the arm. It is an adrenaline rush.

Krause (700 East State Street, Iola, WI 54990) acquired *Collector's mart magazine,* launched its *Collector's mart magazine Price Guide to Limited Edition Collectibles*, and became actively involved in the management of contemporary collectibles shows. Although Krause's commitment is to the contemporary collectibles market as a whole, its efforts should result in a significant growth bounce in the secondary collector plate market.

Replacements, Ltd. (1089 Knox Road, Greensboro, NC 27420) continues to be more aggressive in acquiring than marketing out-of-production collector plates. Replacements' breadth of inventory offers a formidable challenge to that of The Bradford Exchange, especially when a collector is seeking a plate from a lesser known manufacturer whose production runs were low. Look for a major market bounce when Replacements' collectibles division finally launches an aggressive sale marketing campaign.

Contemporary collector plates are holding their own in specialized gift shops, such as Hallmark stores. Most stores devote two or more free-standing shelves to them. While the decline in shelf space has ceased, there is no sign of growth. This sales market sector continues its "wait and see" attitude.

The Internet is the big unknown. The vast majority, probably 90 percent or more, of the objects sold direct or via auction on the Internet, are from the post-1945 era. The number of collector plates being offered for sale on the Internet increases each month. So does the percentage of those sold and the price being paid per unit. As might be expected, collector plates attracting the most interest are those with crossover characteristics.

Finally, the truth sometimes hurts. This price guide honestly reports prices. Plates that sell substantially below or near, but still below, their initial retail value are clearly identified. Unlike some other guides that refuse to list a plate's secondary market value below the initial retail price, this book tells it like it is. If collector plates are going to enjoy a secondary market, the available information presented must be accurate and trustworthy.

List of Manufacturers

Anheuser-Busch, Inc., 2700 South Broadway, St. Louis, MO 63118; (800) 325-9656; Fax: (314) 577-9656; http://www.budweiser.com

Anna-Perenna Porcelain, Inc., 35 River Street, New Rochelle, NY 10801; (914) 633-3777; Fax: (914) 633-8727

Artists of the World, 2915 North 67th Place, Scottsdale, AZ 85251; (602) 946-6361; Fax: (602) 941-8918

The B & J Company, PO Box 67, Georgetown, TX 78626; (512) 863-8318; Fax: (512) 863-0833

Bradford Exchange, 9333 North Milwaukee Avenue, Niles, IL 60714; (800) 323-5577; http://www.bradex.com; http://www.collectiblestoday.net

Cast Art Industries, Inc., 1120 California Avenue, Corona, CA 91719; (800) 932-3020; Fax: (909) 371-0674; http://www.castart.com

Cavanaugh Group International, 1000 Holcomb Woods Parkway, Suite 400B, Roswell, GA 30076; (770) 643-1175; Fax: (770) 643-1172

Christopher Radko, PO Box 725, Ardsley, NY 10501; (914) 693-3952; Fax: (914) 693-3770

Cross Gallery, Inc., 180 North Cedar, PO Box 4181, Jackson, WY 83001; (307) 733-2200; Fax: (307) 733-1414

C.U.I., Inc. / Classic Carolina Collections / Dram Tree, 1502 North 23rd Street, Wilmington, NC 28405; (910) 251-1110

The Danbury Mint, 47 Richards Avenue, Norwalk, CT 06857; (800) 426-0373

Department 56, Inc., PO Box 44456, Eden Prairie, MN 55344; (800) 548-8696; http://www.department56.com; http://www.dept56.com; http://www.d56.com

DianaArt, 3152 Eutaw Forest Drive, Waldorf, MD 20603; (800) 742-2248; Fax: (301) 645-7054

Duncan Royale, 1141 South Acacia Avenue, Fullerton, CA 92631; (714) 879-1360; Fax: (714) 879-4611

Edna Hibel Studio, PO Box 9967, Riviera Beach, FL 33419; (561) 848-9633; Fax: (561) 848-9640

Enesco Corporation, 225 Windsor Drive, Itasca, IL 60143; (800) 4-ENESCO; Fax: (630) 875-5352; http://www.enesco.com

Fenton Art Glass Company, 700 Elizabeth Street, Williamstown, WV 26187; (304) 375-6122; Fax: (304) 375-6459

Fitz and Floyd, 13111 North Central Expressway, Dallas, TX 75243; (972) 918-0098; Fax: (972) 454-1208

Flambro Imports, Inc., 1530 Ellsworth Industrial Drive, Atlanta, GA 30318; (404) 352-1381; Fax: (404) 352-2150

The Franklin Mint, U.S. Route 1, Franklin Center, PA 19091; (800) 843-6468; Fax: (610) 459-6880

Gartlan USA, Inc., 575 Route 73 North, Suite A-6, West Berlin, NJ 08091; (609) 753-9229; Fax: (609) 753-9280

Georgetown Collection, PO Box 9730, Portland, ME 04104; (800) 626-3330

Goebel of North America (Hummel), Goebel Plaza, North Route 31, Pennington, NJ 08534; (609) 737-1980; Fax: (609) 737-1545

Dave Grossman Creations, Inc., 1608 North Warson Road, St. Louis, MO 63132; (800) 325-1655; Fax: (314) 423-7620

H & G Studios, Inc., 5660 Corporate Way, West Palm Beach, FL 33407; (800) 777-1333; Fax: (561) 615-8400

Hadley House, 11001 Hampshire Avenue South, Bloomington, MN 55438; (800) 927-0880

Hallmark Cards, Inc., PO Box 419580, Kansas City, MO 64141; (800) 425-5627; Fax: (816) 274-5061

Incolay Studios, Inc., 520 Library Street, San Fernando, CA 91340; (800) 462-6529; Fax: (818) 365-9599

Islandia International, 78 Bridge Road, Islandia, NY 11722; (516) 234-9817; Fax: (516) 234-9183

Lalique, 499 Veterans Boulevard, Carlstadt, NJ 07072; (800) CRISTAL

Geo. Zoltan Lefton Company, 3622 South Morgan Street, Chicago, IL 60609; (773) 254-4344; Fax: (773) 254-4545

Lenox Collections / Gorham, 100 Lenox Drive, Lawrenceville, NJ 08648; (609) 844-1467; Fax: (609) 844-1580

Lightpost Publishing, 521 Charcot Avenue, San Jose, CA 95131; (800) 366-3733

Lladró USA, Inc., 1 Lladro Drive, Moonachie, NJ 07074; (800) 634-9088

Marty Bell Fine Art, Inc., 9550 Owensmouth Avenue, Chatsworth, CA 91311; (800) 637-4537; Fax: (818) 709-7668

Maruri USA Corporation, 21510 Gledhill Street, Chatsworth, CA 91311; (800) 562-7874

Miss Martha Originals, PO Box 5038, Glencoe, AL 35905; (205) 492-0221; Fax: (205) 492-0261

Norman Rockwell Galleries, 9333 North Milwaukee Avenue, Niles, IL 60714; (800) 451-8451

Orrefors of Sweden, 140 Bradford Drive, Berlin, NJ 08009; (609) 768-5400; Fax: (609) 768-9762

Parkhurst Enterprises, 130 Main Street, Seal Beach, CA 90740; (310) 832-1076; Fax: (310) 493-0996

Pickard, Inc., 782 Pickard Avenue, Antioch, IL 60002; (708) 395-3800

Porsgrund USA, Inc., 2920-3000 Wolff Street, Racine, WI 53404; (414) 632-3433

Porterfield's, 12 Chestnut Pasture Road, Concord, NH 03301; (800) 660-8345; Fax: (603) 228-1888

The Raymon Troup Studio, 1590 Lewisburg Pike, Franklin, TN 37064; Tel/Fax: (615) 794-3498

RECO International Corporation, 150 Haven Avenue, Port Washington, NJ 11050; (516) 767-2400; Fax: (516) 767-2409

Roman, Inc., 555 Lawrence Avenue, Roselle, IL 60172; (630) 529-3000; Fax: (630) 529-1121

Rosenthal USA, 355 Michelle Place, Carlstadt, NJ 07072; (201) 804-8000

Rowe Pottery Works, 404 England Street, Cambridge, WI 53523; (800) 356-7687

Royal Copenhagen, Inc. / Bing & Grøndahl, 41 Madison Avenue, New York, NY 10010; (800) 431-1992; Fax: (212) 685-7995

Royal Doulton USA, Inc., 701 Cottontail Lane, Somerset, NJ 08873; (732) 356-7880; Fax: (732) 764-4974

Sarah's Attic, PO Box 448, Chesaning, MI 48616; (800) 437-4363; Fax: (517) 845-3477

Savacou Gallery, 240 East 13th Street, New York, NY 10003; (800) 258-4385; Fax: (212) 220-8446

Seymour Mann, Inc., 225 Fifth Avenue, New York, NY 10010; (212) 683-7262; Fax: (212) 213-4920

U.S. Historical Society, First and Main Streets, Richmond, VA 23219; (804) 648-4736

Waterford Wedgwood, 1330 Campus Parkway, PO Box 1454, Wall, NJ 07719; (732) 938-5800; Fax: (732) 938-7768

Willitts Designs International, 1129 Industrial Avenue, Petaluma, CA 94952; (707) 778-7211; Fax: (707) 769-0304

Wild Wings, 2101 South Highway 61, Box 451, Lake City, MN 55041; (800) 445-4833; Fax: (612) 345-2981

Winston Roland Limited, 85 River Rock Drive, Unit 201, Buffalo, NY 14207; (800) 265-1020; Fax: (519) 659-2923

Zolan Fine Arts, 29 Cambridge Drive, Hershey, PA 17033; (717) 534-2446; Fax: (717) 534-109

Publications, Museums and Factory Tours

PUBLICATIONS

Antique Trader Weekly, PO Box 1050, Dubuque, IA 52004. Weekly tabloid newspaper since 1957. Covers a wide range in the antiques and collectibles field. There are brief, incomplete listings on new plate issues and some occasional editorial on the subject. Contains classifieds for all types of collector items.

Collectors' Bulletin, Rosie Wells Enterprises, Inc., 22341 East Wells Road, Canton, IL 61520. Published six times per year—February/March, April/May, June/July, August/September, October/November, and December/January. Covers the full scope of limited edition collectibles, including plates, dolls, prints, figurines, teddy bears, and ornaments.

Collector's mart magazine, Krause Publications, 700 East State Street, Iola, WI 54990. Published seven times per year—February, April, June, August, September, October, and December. Covers a wide range of limited edition collectibles, including plates, dolls, prints, figurines, and teddy bears.

Collectors News, PO Box 156, Grundy Center, IA 50638. Weekly tabloid newspaper with a section each week on collector plates. Most editorial content appears to be press releases from plate manufacturers.

MUSEUMS AND FACTORY TOURS

The Bradford Museum of Collector's Plates, 9333 North Milwaukee Avenue, Niles, IL 60714; (847) 966-2770
Hours: Monday through Friday, 8:00A.M.–4:00P.M.; Saturday and Sunday, 10:00A.M.–5:00P.M.; closed major holidays
Admission: Free

Department 56 Showroom Tour of One Village Place, 6436 City West Parkway Eden Prairie, MN 55344; (800) 548-8696
Hours: May through August, Fridays, 9:00A.M.–3:00P.M.
Admission: Free; reservations should be made one week in advance

Fenton Art Glass Company, 420 Caroline Avenue., Williamstown, WV 26187; (304) 375-7772
Factory Tour Hours: Monday through Friday, 8:00A.M.–2:00P.M.
Closed Saturday, Sunday, major holidays, and the first two weeks in July
Museum & Gift Shop Hours: January through March, Monday through Saturday, 8:00A.M.–5:00P.M.; Sunday 12:15P.M.–5:00P.M.; April through December, Monday through Friday, 8:00A.M.–8:00P.M.; Saturday, 8:00A.M.–5:00P.M.; Sunday, 12:15P.M.–5:00P.M.
Admission: Free

Franklin Mint Museum, U.S. Route 1, Franklin Center, PA 19091 (five miles south of Media, PA); (610) 459-6168
Hours: Monday through Saturday, 9:30A.M.–4:30P.M.; Sunday 1:00P.M.–4:30P.M.; closed major holidays
Admission: Free

Frankoma Pottery Tour, 2400 Frankoma Road., Sapulpa, OK 74067; (800) 331-3650
Factory Tour Hours: Monday through Friday, 9:30A.M.–2:00P.M.
Gift Shop Hours: Monday through Saturday, 9:00A.M.–5:00P.M.; Sunday 1:00P.M.–5:00P.M.
Admission: Free

Hibel Museum of Art, 150 Royal Poinciana Plaza, Palm Beach, FL 33480; (561) 833-6870
Hours: Tuesday through Saturday, 10:00A.M.–5:00P.M.; Sunday 1:00P.M.–5:00P.M.
Admission: Free

The Hummel Museum, Inc., 199 Main Plaza, New Braunfels, TX 78131; (210) 625-5636
Hours: Monday through Saturday, 10:00A.M.–5:00P.M.; Sunday 12P.M.–5:00P.M.; closed major holidays
Admission: $5.00 adults, $4.50 senior citizens, $3.00 groups of 10 or more and students ages 6 to 18, children under 5 free

Lladró Museum and Galleries, 43 West 57th Street, New York, NY 10019; (212) 838-9341
Hours: Tuesday through Saturday, 10:00A.M.–5:30P.M.
Admisison: Free

The Norman Rockwell Museum, Route 183, Stockbridge, MA 01262; (413) 298-4100
Hours: May through October, 10:00A.M.–5:00P.M. daily; November through April, weekdays, 10:00A.M.–4:00P.M.; weekends, 10:00A.M.–5:00P.M.
Admission: $9.00 adults, $2.00 under 18

Glossary

Alabaster — a fine-grained, somewhat translucent kind of gypsum stone or a mottled kind of calcite that is found in marble. (see also Ivory Alabaster.)

Annual — a term used to describe an item issued once a year, or yearly. When used as a series name, annual usually means the series is not a commemorative or a holiday issue.

Art Deco — a classical style of art that emphasized symmetrical and rectilinear shapes, such as the cylinder and the rectangle. It was popular from the 1920s to the 1940s in Europe and the United States.

Art Nouveau — a style of art popular in the 1890s and until about 1920. It emphasized decoration rather than form, expressing this often in a whiplash curve and lines of floral and leaflike designs.

Backstamp — a printed or incised symbol or logo, usually found on the underside of an object, that gives some or all of the information on the object's origin, such as the name of the producer, sponsor, or artist, the title, issue date, number of sequence, and artist's signature.

Banding — a term used to describe hand application of metals, such as gold and silver, to the rim of an item.

Baroque — a French word meaning an irregular shape. It was used to describe a style of art popular in the seventeenth and eighteenth centuries. Baroque art was characteristically displayed by dynamic movements, exaggerated ornamentation, bold contrasts, and massive forms.

Basalt — a dense, fine-grained black volcanic stone. Wedgwood introduced black basalts for ornamental and useful wares.

Bas-Relief — a method of decoration on an object in which the design is raised above a background. This is produced either by pouring a liquid mixture into a mold or by applying to a background an already formed design.

Bisque or Biscuit — a name applied to any pottery item that has been fired in a kiln once but has not been glazed.

Body — the clay or mixture of substances combined to make pottery ware.

Bone Ash — the powder produced when animal bones, usually those of oxen, are crushed and ground. It is an ingredient in bone china that makes it appear whiter and more translucent.

Bone China or Bone Porcelain — ceramic wares that are pure white due to added bone ash. It is softer than hard-paste porcelain but more durable than soft-paste porcelain.

Camber — a shape that has a slightly convex surface. The first camber-shaped collector plate was issued in 1982 by Royal Doulton.

Cameo — a carving in relief that has a color contrasting with its background.

Carnival Glass — inexpensively produced glass made primarily from 1900 to 1925. Items made of carnival glass were originally used as fair prizes. This glass is iridescent and is produced in many colors.

Ceramic — any ware or work of a potter or object made from baked clay.

Certificate of Authenticity — a written statement received when an object is bought that assures the origin and sequence number of an edition.

China — a term originally used for all wares produced in China. It is now used in reference to any hard, vitreous, or glassy ceramic consisting of kaolin, ball clay, china stone, feldspar, and flint.

Cinnabar — a bright red mineral found in hydrothermal deposits of volcanic regions. It is the principal ore of mercury and mercuric sulfide.

Cobalt — a steel-gray metallic element used as a pigment in tin-enamels and glazes. The most common use is in cobalt blue glaze.

Crazing — a mesh of cracks in the glaze on a piece of pottery; also called crackle if found in Chinese porcelains.

Crystal — a very clear, brilliant glass of fine quality, well suited for prism cuts by refracting light. Full lead crystal contains at least 24 percent lead.

Damascene — a method of decorating by filling inlaid designs with gold or copper, perfected by Reed & Barton.

Delftware — tin-glazed earthenware that was originally developed in Delft, Holland.

Dresden — a term often used as synonymous with Meissen porcelain. Dresden and Meissen were two cities in eastern Germany that produced porcelain. The first porcelain produced outside China was discovered by Johann Friedrich Bottger in the Dresden factory in 1709.

Earthenware — any pottery that is not vitrified. It is the largest kind of pottery, including delftware, faience, and majolica.

Edition — the total number produced of one design in a series.

Electroplating — method of covering one metal with another by electrolysis.

Embossing — a method of decoration with raised designs, produced either in a mold or with a stamp.

Enamel — a glassy substance with mineral oxides fused to a surface for decoration.

Engraving — a method of decoration produced by cutting into a surface with tools or acids.

Etching — a method of decoration produced by using acid to cut a design. The surface to be decorated is first covered with a wax; then the acid eats into the areas left bare or carved out with a needle.

Faience — a type of earthenware covered in a tin glaze. Faience is increasingly being used to mean the same as delftware and majolica. The difference is that the Delft faience uses a more refined clay. The name comes from an Italian town called Faenza.

Feldspar — a kind of crystalline rock from which kaolin, one of the main components of porcelain and china, is formed when the rock decomposes.

Fire — the process of heating a piece of clay to high temperatures, transforming it into porcelain or pottery.

Flow Blue — the name given to pottery blue underglaze designs because of the slight fuzziness resulting from glazing over the color blue.

Glaze — a liquid compound that, when fired on a ceramic piece, becomes a glasslike surface. It is used to seal the surface so that it is nonabsorbent.

Glost Fire — a process of firing in a kiln to fuse the glaze.

Hallmark — a stamped or incised mark identifying the manufacturer.

Hard-Paste Porcelain — a vitreous ceramic made primarily of kaolin, or china clay, and petuntse, which is china stone. It is somewhat translucent and when tapped should ring. When chipped, it will have a shell-like or conchoidal shape to the chip.

Incising — a method of cutting designs or inscriptions into the surface of an object for decoration.

Incolay Stone — a material from which Incolay Studios produces art objects that look like cameos. The process for making it is kept secret by the Studio, but it is known that it contains some quartzlike minerals.

Inlaid — a kind of decoration produced by etching into a surface and then filling the etched-out areas with another substance, usually silver or gold.

Iridescence — the intermingling of colors as in a rainbow or as seen in mother-of-pearl. This may be produced by alkaline glazes on ceramic wares.

Ivory Alabaster — a type of fine-grained nontranslucent gypsum, which may acquire a patina with age.

Jasperware — a hard, unglazed stoneware produced by Wedgwood originally in 1775. Color is added to a naturally white body by mixing in metallic oxides. Pale blue is the most common.

Kaolin — a fine white clay used to produce china and porcelain.

Kiln — an oven in which ceramic pieces are fired.

KPM — the abbreviation for Koenigliche Porzellan Manufacture.

Lead Crystal — (see Crystal).

Limited Edition — a term used to describe an item that is produced for a specific period of time or in a specified amount previously decided upon by the manufacturer.

Luster — a film covering an item made of silver, copper, gold, or platinum pigment reduced from an oxide for decoration.

Majolica — any tin-glaze earthenware from Italy.

Mold — the form that shapes ceramic pieces of art. The object is formed either by pressing clay into the mold or by pouring a liquid clay formula into the mold, and the excess water is absorbed, leaving a hardened shape.

Overglaze — an enameled design painted on top of a fired glaze and then fired again at a lower temperature for permanence.

Parian — a hard-paste porcelain named after parian marble. It is a vitrified china that can be fired at a lower temperature, allowing for a greater variety of possible colors for designs.

Pentuntse — a fusible component of hard-paste porcelain.

Porcelain — a fine, hard, white, vitrified material that is generally fired at about 1400 degrees Celsius. Its chief components are kaolin and pentuntse, and when fired they produce a translucent material that will ring when tapped.

Pottery — a general name given to all ceramic wares. In the present market, it sometimes refers only to earthenware, not including porcelain or any ceramic with a vitrified surface.

Queen's Ware — an earthenware developed by Wedgwood for Queen Charlotte of England in 1765. It is cream in color and is also called white ware.

Relief Decoration — a design that is raised above a background. This is produced either by pouring a liquid clay mixture into a mold or by applying an already formed design to an object.

Satin Glass — art glass made with a matte finish rather than a polished finish.

Soft-Paste Porcelain — a porcelain made of white firing clay and silicate, a ground-up mass of glass, sand, or broken china. This very translucent material is also called artificial porcelain and is generally fired at about 1100 degrees Celsius.

Stoneware — a name that applies to all vitrified and nonporous pottery, except porcelain.

Terra Cotta — the name used for clay fired without glaze. This type of clay is more often formed by a potter than by a sculptor, who produces earthenware.

Tin Glaze — a dense lead glaze that is colored white and made opaque by adding ashes of tin. It may also be colored by adding metallic oxides.

Toriart — a method of molding wood shavings into a solid form, perfected by the House of Anri. The forms may then be carved to carry a design or may already have a relief design from the mold.

Translucence — a property of some ceramics in which light can be seen through an object that is not transparent.

Triptych — a set of three paintings with a common theme, usually religious, connected together and often used as an altarpiece.

Underglaze — a method in which colors are painted on ceramic bisque, which is then dipped in glaze and fired a second time.

Vitreous or Vitrification — the condition of a ceramic object when fired that results in a glassy and impermeable surface.

How to Use This Book

This book is designed to be a teaching tool, a checklist, and a pricing aid. It offers a more realistic look at the collector plate market—indicating those plates that are attracting collector interest and those that are not—than is available from any other source.

TEACHING TOOL

Take the time to read the chapters in the front of the book. "The History of Collector Plates" offers a detailed look at the origin of the collector plate, how it evolved, and its current role within the world of contemporary collectibles. Several brief manufacturer histories and artist biographies are provided. Knowing about a collector plate's maker and artist adds to the personal value of the plate.

Collecting requires a commitment to understanding the hows and whys of any collecting category. This understanding is essential if you wish to become a savvy collector. You will find everything you need to know and more in the chapters preceding the checklist/price guide portion of this book.

Finally, information about periodicals, museums, factory tours, terms (glossary), and names and addresses of manufacturers appears in the front of this book rather than as appendices in the back. This is information to which the collector plate collector continually refers. Including it in the front matter makes it easier to find and use.

CHECKLIST

You would be making a mistake if you think of this book only as a price guide. It has been designed to serve as a collector plate checklist. The listings for each manufacturer are as complete as possible. With rare exceptions, e.g., Danbury Mint, collector plate manufacturers cooperated fully with this project.

The checklist is organized alphabetically by manufacturer. Use the page heads as a guide to locating the manufacturer in which you are interested. Be creative in your search. For example, Edna Hibel Studios will be found under "H" not "E." We have tried our best to select the key word in a company's title for alphabetizing purposes.

When checking or collecting a specific series, be aware that different plates can have identical or near identical titles. While accuracy is our goal, occasionally manufacturers, wholesalers, retailers, dealers, and other listing sources provide a slightly different title for the same plate. We found title differences between catalog advertisements and the information listed on the back of the plate. Which title is correct? We have tried hard to make the right selection. Hopefully, we have.

PRICE GUIDE

It is time for price honesty in respect to collector plates. In today's market, there frequently is a major difference, down as well as up, between the **ISSUE** (initial issue retail price) and the **CURRENT** (current secondary market value). The purpose of this book is not to prop the collector plate market. If a plate that initially sold for $25 is now worth $10, you need to know this.

Due to the tremendous price fluctuation at the low end of the collector plate market, we have created four codes for use in this book. They are:

RI = **Recent Issue**. This is a plate that has been issued in the last five years. Any value above its initial retail value is highly speculative. Be forewarned against paying two and three times the retail price for a plate so young. These plates are infants in the market. Their only reliable value is what they sold for initially.

NR = **Near Retail**. This is a value assigned to a plate that sells within plus or minus $5 of its initial retail price. It is a plate that is on its way up. It has found collector favor, but has not yet joined the ranks of those plates whose secondary market values significantly exceed their initial retail prices.

BR = **Below Retail**. This indicates plates that are selling for prices that are more than $5 below their initial retail value. In many cases, the plate's value is less than $10. As you review the plates with a **BR** designation, keep in mind the following—the longer a plate falls within this **BR** price range, the less likely it is to ever achieve a profitable status. The one thing that can change this is if its surface image suddenly becomes of interest to crossover collectors.

NA = **Not Available.** Because this book serves as a checklist as well as a price guide, we have included listings for plates even if their date of issue, initial retail price or current secondary market value could not be determined. When any of this information was unavailable, it is noted with the **NA** designation. A dash in both of the price columns signifies that a plate series is being sold only as a set, not as individual plates.

Prices in this book are retail, i.e., what you would have to pay if you wanted to buy a plate. If you are selling your plates to a dealer expect between twenty-five and thirty cents on the dollar. Hopefully sales via auction will bring a higher figure and a private sale even more. The only individual likely to get full retail is a dealer or specialized shop owner.

Finally, prices in this book are for collector plates in fine or better condition with their period boxes and all supporting literature. If the box is missing, deduct 10 percent. Subtract another 5 percent for missing literature. If the plate is damaged in any way, its value diminishes by 60 to 75 percent or more.

INDEXES

The book contains two indexes, each designed to make it a simple task to locate the collector plates you own or wish to buy. The **Artist Index** allows you to locate the full range of work by your favorite artist. The **Series Index** provides a quick reference point to a complete list of plates in any series.

COMMENTS INVITED

The Official Price Guide to Collector Plates is a major effort to deal with a complex field. You are encouraged to send your comments and suggestions to: Collector Plates, c/o Rinker Enterprises, Inc., 5093 Vera Cruz Road, Emmaus, PA 18049.

Collector Plate Listings

ACCENT ON ART UNITED STATES

Mother Goose

		ISSUE	CURRENT
1978	JACK AND JILL, Oscar Graves, 5,000	59.50	80.00

Nobility of the Plains

		ISSUE	CURRENT
1978	THE COMANCHE, Oscar Graves, 12,500	80.00	NR
1979	MOVING DAY, Oscar Graves, 3,500	80.00	NR

ACE PRODUCT MANAGEMENT GROUP

Good Times Together

1995	ROAD TRIP, B. Otero, 10,000	32.00	RI

Harley-Davidson Christmas

1984	1909 V-TWIN, 8,500	19.95	NR
1985	PERFECT TREE, 8,500	22.50	NR
1986	MAIN STREET, 8,500	24.95	NR
1987	JOY OF GIVING, 8,500	24.95	NR
1988	HOME FOR THE HOLIDAYS, 8,500	29.95	NR
1989	29 DAYS TILL XMAS, 8,500	34.95	NR
1990	RURAL DELIVERY, 8,500	34.95	NR
1991	SKATING PARTY, 8,500	34.95	NR
1992	A SURPRISE VISIT, 9,500	38.00	NR
1993	CHRISTMAS VACATION, 9,500	38.00	RI

Harley-Davidson Pewter

1988	WINTER GATHERING, 3,000	74.95	NR
1989	1989 PLATE, 3,000	89.95	NR
1990	SPRING RACES, 3,000	99.95	NR
1990	SUMMER TRADITION, 3,000	99.95	NR

Harley-Davidson Pewter Decade

1992	BIRTH OF LEGEND—1900's, 3,000	120.00	NR
1993	GROWTH OF SPORT—1910's, 3,000	125.00	RI
1994	ROARING INTO THE 20's—1920's, 3,000	130.00	RI
1995	GROWING STRONGER WITH TIME—1930's, 3,000	132.00	RI
1997	TO WAR ONCE MORE—1940's, 3,000	130.00	RI

Holiday Memories Christmas

1994	UNDER THE MISTLETOE, B. Otero, 15,000	38.00	RI
1995	LATE ARRIVAL, B. Otero, 15,000	38.00	RI
1996	AFTER THE PAGEANT, B. Otero, 15,000	38.00	RI
1997	ROADSIDE REVELATION, B. Otero, 15,000	38.00	RI

COUNT AGAZZI ITALY

Children's Hour

		ISSUE	CURRENT
1970	OWL, 2,000	12.50	NR
1971	CAT, 2,000	12.50	NR
1972	PONY, 2,000	12.50	NR
1973	PANDA, 2,000	12.50	NR

Easter

1971	PLAYING THE VIOLIN, 600	12.50	NR
1972	AT PRAYER, 600	12.50	NR
1973	WINGED CHERUB, 600	12.50	NR

Famous Personalities

1968	FAMOUS PERSONALITIES, 600	8.00	NR
1970	FAMOUS PERSONALITIES, 1,000	12.50	NR
1973	FAMOUS PERSONALITIES, 600	15.00	NR

Father's Day

1972	FATHER'S DAY, 144	35.00	NR
1973	FATHER'S DAY, 288	19.50	NR

Mother's Day

1972	MOTHER'S DAY, 144	35.00	NR
1973	MOTHER'S DAY, 720	19.50	NR

Single Issues

1969	APOLLO II, 1,000	17.00	NR
1973	PEACE, 720	12.50	NR

ALLISON AND COMPANY UNITED STATES

Late to Party

1982	PIECE OF CAKE, Betty Allison, 12,500	35.00	NR
1983	CHEESE PLEASE, Betty Allison, 12,500	35.00	NR
1983	TOAST TO A MOUSE, Betty Allison, 12,500	35.00	NR

Nature's Beauty

1981	WINTER'S PEACE, Betty Allison, 7,500	70.00	NR
1982	SUMMER'S JOY, Betty Allison, 7,500	70.00	NR

AMERICAN ARTISTS UNITED STATES

(Modern Masters)

Cats for Cat Lovers

1987	ROMEO AND JULIET, Susan Leigh	29.50	NR

		ISSUE	CURRENT

Family Treasures (Modern Masters)

1981	CORA'S RECITAL, Richard Zolan, 15,000	39.50	NR
1982	CORA'S TEA PARTY, Richard Zolan, 15,000	39.50	NR
1983	CORA'S GARDEN PARTY, Richard Zolan, 15,000	39.50	NR

Famous Fillies

1987	LADY'S SECRET, Fred Stone, 9,500	65.00	NR
1988	RUFFIAN, Fred Stone, 9,500	65.00	90.00
1988	GENUINE RISK, Fred Stone, 9,500	65.00	NR
1992	GO FOR THE WAND, Fred Stone, 9,500	65.00	85.00

Feathered Friends

1982	PARAKEETS, Linda Crouch, 19,500	29.50	NR

Flower Fantasies

1985	SPRING BLOSSOMS, Donald Zolan, 15 days	24.50	NR

Fred Stone Classics

1987	THE SHOE—8,000 WINS, Fred Stone, 9,500	75.00	85.00
1987	THE ETERNAL LEGACY, Fred Stone, 9,500	75.00	95.00
1988	FOREVER FRIENDS, Fred Stone, 9,500	75.00	85.00
1989	ALYSHEBA, Fred Stone, 9,500	75.00	NR

Gold Signature

1990	SECRETARIAT FINAL TRIBUTE, Fred Stone, sgd, 4,500	150.00	375.00
1990	SECRETARIAT FINAL TRIBUTE, Fred Stone, 7,500	75.00	100.00
1991	OLD WARRIORS, Fred Stone, sgd, 4,500	150.00	425.00
1991	OLD WARRIORS, Fred Stone, 7,500	75.00	100.00

Gold Signature II

1991	NORTHERN DANCER, Fred Stone, dbl signature, 1,500	175.00	250.00

Forever Friends
Photo courtesy of *Collectors News*

Northern Dancer
Photo courtesy of *Collectors News*

		ISSUE	CURRENT
1991	NORTHERN DANCER, Fred Stone, sgd, 3,000	150.00	NR
1991	NORTHERN DANCER, Fred Stone, 7,500	75.00	NR
1991	KELSO, Fred Stone, dbl signature, 1,500	175.00	NR
1991	KELSO, Fred Stone, sgd, 3,000	150.00	NR
1991	KELSO, Fred Stone, 7,500	75.00	NR

Gold Signature III

1992	DANCE SMARTLY—PAT DAY, UP, Fred Stone, dbl signature, 1,500	175.00	NR
1992	DANCE SMARTLY—PAT DAY, UP, Fred Stone, sgd, 3,000	150.00	NR
1992	DANCE SMARTLY—PAT DAY, UP, Fred Stone, 7,500	75.00	NR
1993	AMERICAN TRIPLE CROWN—1937–1946, Fred Stone, sgd, 2,500	195.00	RI
1993	AMERICAN TRIPLE CROWN—1937–1946, Fred Stone, 7,500	75.00	RI
1993	AMERICAN TRIPLE CROWN—1948–1978, Fred Stone, sgd, 2,500	195.00	RI
1993	AMERICAN TRIPLE CROWN—1948–1978, Fred Stone, 7,500	75.00	RI
1994	AMERICAN TRIPLE CROWN—1919–1935, Fred Stone, sgd, 2,500	95.00	RI
1994	AMERICAN TRIPLE CROWN—1919–1935, Fred stone, 7,500	150.00	RI

Gold Signature IV

1995	JULIE KRONA, Fred Stone, dbl signature, 2,500	150.00	RI
1995	JULIE KRONA, Fred Stone, 7,500	75.00	RI

Horses of Fred Stone

1981	PATIENCE, Fred Stone, 9,500	55.00	NR
1982	ARABIAN MARE AND FOAL, Fred Stone, 9,500	55.00	NR
1982	SAFE AND SOUND, Fred Stone, 9,500	55.00	75.00
1983	CONTENTMENT, Fred Stone, 9,500	55.00	125.00

Mares and Foals

1985	WATER TROUGH, Fred Stone, 12,500	49.50	100.00
1985	TRANQUILITY, Fred Stone, 12,500	49.50	65.00
1986	PASTURE PEST, Fred Stone, 12,500	49.50	100.00
1987	ARABIANS, Fred Stone, 12,500	49.50	NR

Mares and Foals II

1989	THE FIRST DAY, Fred Stone, open	35.00	NR
1989	DIAMOND IN THE ROUGH, Fred Stone, retrd.	35.00	NR

Mares and Foals—Miniature

1986	TRANQUILITY, Fred Stone, 12,500, 6½"	25.00	NR
1991	PATIENCE, Fred Stone, 19,500, 6½"	25.00	NR
1992	KIDNAPPED, Fred Stone, 19,500, 6½"	25.00	NR
1992	PASTURE PEST, Fred Stone, 19,500, 6½"	25.00	NR
1992	WATER TROUGH, Fred Stone, 19,500, 6½"	25.00	NR
1993	ARABIAN MARE AND FOAL, Fred Stone, 19,500, 6½"	25.00	RI
1993	CONTENTMENT, Fred Stone, 19,500, 6½"	25.00	RI

Mother and Child Cats

1983	KITTY LOVE, Phyllis Hollands-Robinson, 19,500	29.50	NR

Noble Tribes

1983	ALGONQUIN, Donald Zolan, 19,500	49.50	65.00
1984	SIOUX, Donald Zolan, 19,500	49.50	65.00

		ISSUE	CURRENT

Racing Legends

		ISSUE	CURRENT
1989	PHAR LAP, Fred Stone, 9,500	75.00	NR
1989	SUNDAY SILENCE, Fred Stone, 9,500	75.00	NR
1990	JOHN HENRY—SHOEMAKER, Fred Stone, 9,500	75.00	NR

Saturday Evening Post Covers

		ISSUE	CURRENT
1983	SANTA'S COMPUTER, Scott Gustafson, 15 days	29.50	NR

Sport of Kings

		ISSUE	CURRENT
1984	MAN O' WAR, Fred Stone, 9,500	65.00	75.00
1984	SECRETARIAT, Fred Stone, 9,500	65.00	100.00
1985	JOHN HENRY, Fred Stone, 9,500	65.00	75.00
1986	SEATTLE SLEW, Fred Stone, 9,500	65.00	NR

Stallions

		ISSUE	CURRENT
1983	BLACK STALLION, Fred Stone, 9,500	49.50	150.00
1983	ANDALUSIAN, Fred Stone, 9,500	49.50	150.00

Zoe's Cats

		ISSUE	CURRENT
1985	THE SNIFFER, Zoe Stokes, 12,500	29.50	NR
1985	WAITING, Zoe Stokes, 12,500	29.50	NR
1985	SUNSHINE, Zoe Stokes, 12,500	29.50	NR
1985	TARZAN, Zoe Stokes, 12,500	29.50	NR

Single Issues

		ISSUE	CURRENT
1984	GOING TO GRANDMA'S HOUSE, Donald Zolan, 15,000	29.50	NR
1984	GIFT FOR GRANDMA, Donald Zolan, 15,000	29.50	NR
1986	MAY QUEEN, Zoe Stokes, 21 days	29.95	NR
1987	THE SHOE, Fred Stone, 9,500	75.00	NR

AMERICAN COMMEMORATIVE UNITED STATES

Southern Landmarks

		ISSUE	CURRENT
1973	MONTICELLO, 9,800	43.00	95.00
1973	WILLIAMSBURG, 9,800	43.00	95.00
1974	BEAUVOIR, 9,800	43.00	90.00
1974	GABILDO, 9,800	43.00	90.00
1975	HERMITAGE, 9,800	43.00	90.00
1975	OAK HILL, 9,800	43.00	90.00
1976	GOVERNOR TRYON'S PLACE, 9,800	43.00	70.00
1976	MONTPELIER, 9,800	43.00	70.00
1977	ELMSCOURT, 9,800	43.00	60.00
1977	ASHLAND, 9,800	43.00	60.00
1978	MT. VERNON, 9,800	43.00	60.00
1978	WHITE HOUSE, 9,800	43.00	NR
1979	CUSTIS LEE, 9,800	43.00	NR
1979	DRAYTON HALL, 9,800	43.00	NR
1980	FT. HILL, 9,800	43.00	NR
1980	LIBERTY HALL, 9,800	43.00	NR

AMERICAN CRYSTAL UNITED STATES

Christmas

		ISSUE	CURRENT
1970	CHRISTMAS	17.50	NR
1971	CHRISTMAS	12.00	NR
1972	CHRISTMAS	12.00	NR
1973	CHRISTMAS	17.00	NR

Mother's Day

1971	MOTHER'S DAY	8.00	NR
1972	MOTHER'S DAY, 2,000	12.00	NR
1973	MOTHER'S DAY	23.00	NR

Single Issue

1969	ASTRONAUT	17.50	NR

AMERICAN EXPRESS COMPANY UNITED STATES

(Lenox)

American Trees of Christmas

1976	DOUGLAS FIR, 1 year	60.00	NR
1977	SCOTCH PINE, 1 year	60.00	NR

Birds of North America

1978	SAW-WHET OWLS, 9,800	38.00	NR
1978	BOB-WHITE QUAIL, 9,800	38.00	NR
1978	OCTOBER CARDINALS, 9,800	38.00	NR
1978	LONG-EARED OWL, 9,800	38.00	NR
1978	EASTERN BLUEBIRDS, 9,800	38.00	NR
1978	AMERICAN WOODCOCK, 9,800	38.00	NR
1978	RUFFED GROUSE, 9,800	38.00	NR
1978	HOUSE WREN, 9,800	38.00	NR

Four Freedoms

1976	FREEDOM OF WORSHIP, 1 year	37.50	NR
1976	FREEDOM FROM WANT, 1 year	37.50	NR
1976	FREEDOM FROM FEAR, 1 year	37.50	NR
1976	FREEDOM OF SPEECH, 1 year	37.50	NR

Great Leaders of the World (Lenox)

1972	POPE PIUS 1ST	75.00	NR
1972	BILLY GRAHAM	75.00	NR
1972	DOUGLAS MACARTHUR	75.00	NR
1972	HARRY TRUMAN	75.00	NR
1972	LYNDON B. JOHNSON	75.00	NR
1972	DWIGHT D. EISENHOWER	75.00	NR
1972	RICHARD M. NIXON	75.00	NR
1972	WINSTON CHURCHILL	75.00	NR
1972	ADLAI STEVENSON	75.00	NR
1972	ALBERT SCHWEITZER	75.00	NR

Bobolink
Photo courtesy of Vincent T. Miscoski

Scarlet Tanager
Photo courtesy of Vincent T. Miscoski

Songbirds of Roger Tory Peterson (Porcelaine Georges Boyer, Limoges)

		ISSUE	CURRENT
1982	BOBOLINK, Roger Tory Peterson, 1 year	48.00	NR
1982	BLUEBIRD, Roger Tory Peterson, 1 year	48.00	NR
1982	MOCKINGBIRD, Roger Tory Peterson, 1 year	48.00	NR
1982	SCARLET TANAGER, Roger Tory Peterson, 1 year	48.00	NR
1982	ROBIN, Roger Tory Peterson, 1 year	48.00	NR
1982	BLUE JAY, Roger Tory Peterson, 1 year	48.00	NR
1982	CARDINAL, Roger Tory Peterson, 1 year	48.00	NR
1982	WOOD THRUSH, Roger Tory Peterson, 1 year	48.00	NR
1982	BALTIMORE ORIOLE, Roger Tory Peterson, 1 year	48.00	NR
1982	ROSE-BREASTED GROSBEAK, Roger Tory Peterson, 1 year	48.00	NR
1982	BARN SWALLOW, Roger Tory Peterson, 1 year	48.00	NR
1982	FLICKER, Roger Tory Peterson, 1 year	48.00	NR

AMERICAN GREETINGS UNITED STATES

Holly Hobbie

NA	A SMILE REFLECTS A HAPPY HEART	NA	18.00

Holly Hobbie Mother's Day

1973	MILLIONS OF STARS IN THE HEAVENS ABOVE	NA	16.00
1975	A MOTHER'S LOVE JUST GROWS AND GROWS	NA	16.00

AMERICAN HERITAGE UNITED STATES

Africa's Beauties

1983	KILIMANJARA (ELEPHANT FAMILY), Douglas Van Howd, 5,000	65.00	NR
1984	KENYA DESIGN (ZEBRA FAMILY), Douglas Van Howd, 5,000	65.00	NR

		ISSUE	CURRENT
American Sail			
1983	DOWN EASTER IN A SQUALL, Edward Ries, 5,000	39.50	NR
1983	YOUNG AMERICA, Edward Ries, 5,000	39.50	NR
America's Heritage of Flight			
1983	KITTY HAWK, Allen Adams, 5,000	39.50	NR
Battle Wagons			
1982	GENERAL QUARTERS, Edward Ries, 5,000	39.50	NR
1983	LAST CRUISE, Edward Ries, 5,000	39.50	NR
Celebrity Clowns			
1982	EMMETT, Jon Helland, 12,500	50.00	NR
1982	JUDY, Jon Helland, 12,500	50.00	NR
1982	JIMMY, Jon Helland, 12,500	50.00	NR
1982	THE SHARK, Jon Helland, 12,500	50.00	NR
Craftsman Heritage			
1983	DECOY MAKER, Ray Orosz, 5,000	39.50	NR
1983	SAILMAKER, Ray Orosz, 5,000	39.50	NR
Equestrian Love			
1983	ARABIAN DESTINY, 5,000	39.50	NR
Lil' Critters			
1982	INQUISITIVE, Allen Adams, 10,000	40.00	NR
Sawdust Antics			
1983	EMMETT'S EIGHT BALL, Jon Helland, 5,000	50.00	NR
1983	EMMETT WITH A BANG, Jon Helland, 5,000	50.00	NR
Vanishing West			
1982	HELLBENT, David Miller, 7,500	60.00	NR
1983	COLD TRAIL, David Miller, 5,000	60.00	NR

Emmett With a Bang
Photo courtesy of *Collectors News*

AMERICAN HOUSE UNITED STATES

Single Issues

		ISSUE	CURRENT
1972	LANDING OF COLUMBUS, 1,500	100.00	NR
1972	LANDING OF COLUMBUS, 1,000	250.00	NR

AMERICAN LEGACY UNITED STATES

Children to Love

1982	WENDY, Sue Etem, 10,000	60.00	125.00
1982	JAKE, Sue Etem, 10,000	60.00	NR
NA	JED, Sue Etem, 10,000	60.00	NR

Holidays Around the World

1984	ELYSA'S CHRISTMAS, Ignacio Gomez, 12,500	39.50	NR

Penni Anne Cross

1979	CROW BABY, Penni Anne Cross, 7,500	55.00	NR
1981	PAIUTE PALS, Penni Anne Cross, 7,500	55.00	NR
1981	BIG SISTER'S BUCKSKINS, Penni Anne Cross, 7,500	55.00	NR

Special Heart

1982	REACHING TOGETHER, Sue Etem, 40,000	35.00	NR
1983	LOVE IN YOUR HEART, Sue Etem, 40,000	35.00	NR

Walter Brennan

1983	GRAMPA, Walter Brennan, Jr., 10,000	60.00	NR
1984	TO KISS A WINNER, Walter Brennan, Jr., 10,000	45.00	NR

Single Issues

1979	REVE DE BALLET, Julian Ritter, 7,500	55.00	NR
1980	NAVAJO MADONNA, Olaf Wieghorst, 7,500	65.00	NR
1984	NAVAJO NANNY, Penni Anne Cross, 7,500	55.00	NR

Navajo Nanny
Photo courtesy of *Collectors News*

		ISSUE	CURRENT
NA	SWEET DREAMS, Jim Daly, 7,500	55.00	NR
NA	UNDER SURVEILLANCE, Frank McCarthy, 10,000	65.00	NR
NA	PROMISED LAND, Joe Beeler, 10,000	65.00	NR
NA	WINTER SONG, Michael Coleman, 7,500	65.00	NR
NA	THE DINNEH, R. Browne McGrew, 7,500	65.00	NR
NA	BUFFALO SCOUT, Olaf Wieghorst, 7,500	65.00	NR

AMERICAN RAILS & HIGHWAYS

Corvette

1994	1964/94 MUSTANG, P. Adams	40.00	RI
1995	1978 CORVETTE, P. Adams	40.00	RI
1982	CORVETTE, P. Adams	40.00	RI
1995	35TH CORVETTE, P. Adams	40.00	RI
1995	40TH ANNIVERSARY THUNDERBIRD, P. Adams	40.00	RI
1995	40TH CORVETTE, P. Adams	40.00	RI
1995	VIPER GTS-RT/10, P. Adams	40.00	RI
1995	VIPER GTS-R	40.00	RI
1995	1995 75TH INDY PACE CAR, R. Pedersen	40.00	RI
1996	VIPER 1996 INDY PACE CAR, B. Hubbock	40.00	RI
1996	GRAND SPORT CORVETTE	40.00	RI

Train

1993	G6-1, P. Adams	33.00	RI
1994	HIAWATHA, P. Adams	33.00	RI
1994	N.Y. CENTRAL, P. Adams	33.00	RI
1995	BLACK JACK, P. Adams	33.00	RI
1995	K-4, P. Adams	33.00	RI
1995	MAPLE LEAF, P. Adams	33.00	RI
1995	B & O CHESSIE, R. Pedersen	33.00	RI
1995	CHIEF, R. Pedersen	33.00	RI
1995	SANTA FE SUPER CHIEF, R. Pedersen	33.00	RI
1995	UNION PACIFIC, E-9, R. Pedersen	33.00	RI
1996	ERIE F-8, R. Pedersen	33.00	RI
1996	NEW HAVEN, R. Pedersen	33.00	RI

AMERICAN ROSE SOCIETY UNITED STATES

All-American Roses

1975	OREGOLD, 9,800	39.00	140.00
1975	ARIZONA, 9,800	39.00	140.00
1975	ROSE PARADE, 9,800	39.00	140.00
1976	YANKEE DOODLE, 9,800	39.00	135.00
1976	AMERICA, 9,800	39.00	135.00
1976	CATHEDRAL, 9,800	39.00	135.00
1976	SEASHELL, 9,800	39.00	135.00
1977	DOUBLE DELIGHT, 9,800	39.00	115.00
1977	PROMINENT, 9,800	39.00	115.00
1977	FIRST EDITION, 9,800	39.00	115.00
1978	COLOR MAGIC, 9,800	39.00	105.00
1978	CHARISMA, 9,800	39.00	100.00

		ISSUE	CURRENT
1979	PARADISE, 9,800	39.00	70.00
1979	SUNDOWNER, 9,800	39.00	80.00
1979	FRIENDSHIP, 9,800	39.00	80.00
1980	LOVE, 9,800	49.00	80.00
1980	HONOR, 9,800	49.00	70.00
1980	CHERISH, 9,800	49.00	80.00
1981	BING CROSBY, 9,800	49.00	75.00
1981	WHITE LIGHTNIN', 9,800	49.00	65.00
1981	MARINA, 9,800	49.00	70.00
1982	SHREVEPORT, 9,800	49.00	60.00
1982	FRENCH LACE, 9,800	49.00	65.00
1982	BRANDY, 9,800	49.00	70.00
1982	MON CHERI, 9,800	49.00	NR
1983	SUN FLARE, 9,800	49.00	70.00
1983	SWEET SURRENDER, 9,800	49.00	NR
1984	IMPATIENT, 9,800	49.00	NR
1984	OLYMPIAD, 9,800	49.00	NR
1984	INTRIGUE, 9,800	49.00	NR
1985	SHOWBIZ, 9,800	49.50	NR
1985	PEACE, 9,800	49.50	NR
1985	QUEEN ELIZABETH, 9,800	49.50	NR

ANHEUSER-BUSCH, INC. UNITED STATES

Archive Plates

1992	1893 COLUMBIAN EXPOSITION N3477, D. Langeneckert, 25 days	27.50	BR
1992	GANYMEDE, D. Langeneckert, 25 days	27.50	BR
1995	BUDWEISER'S GREATEST TRIUMPH, N5195, 25 days	27.50	RI
1995	MIRROR OF TRUTH, N5196, 25 days	27.50	RI

Civil War

1992	GENERAL GRANT N3478, D. Langeneckert, 25 days	45.00	BR
1993	GENERAL ROBERT E. LEE N3590, D. Langeneckert, 25 days	45.00	RI
1993	PRESIDENT ABRAHAM LINCOLN N3591, D. Langeneckert, 25 days	45.00	RI

Holiday Plates

1989	WINTER'S DAY N2295, B. Kemper, retrd	30.00	45.00
1990	AN AMERICAN TRADITION N2767, S. Sampson, retrd	30.00	BR
1991	THE SEASON'S BEST N3034, S. Sampson, 25 days	30.00	BR
1992	A PERFECT CHRISTMAS N3440, S. Sampson, 25 days	27.50	BR
1993	SPECIAL DELIVERY N4002, N. Koerber, 25 days	27.50	RI
1994	HOMETOWN HOLIDAY, N4572, B. Kemper, 25 days	27.50	RI
1995	LIGHTING THE WAY HOME, N5215, T. Jester, 25 days	27.50	RI
1996	BUDWEISER CLYDESDALES, N5778, J. Raedeke, 25 days	27.50	RI
1997	HOME FOR THE HOLIDAYS, N5779, H. Droog, 25 days	27.50	RI

Man's Best Friend

1990	BUDDIES N2615, M. Urdahl, retrd	30.00	45.00
1990	SIX PACK N3005, M. Urdahl, retrd	30.00	NR
1992	SOMETHING'S BREWING N3147, M. Urdahl, 25 days	30.00	NR
1993	OUTSTANDING IN THEIR FIELD N4003, M. Urdahl, 25 days	27.50	RI

		ISSUE	CURRENT

1992 Olympic Team

1991	1992 OLYMPIC TEAM WINTER PLATE N3180, 25 days	35.00	BR
1992	1992 OLYMPIC TEAM SUMMER PLATE N3122, 25 days	35.00	BR

ANNADOR TRADING COMPANY CANADA

Single Issue

1987	THE APPRENTICE, Nori Peter, 7,500	45.00	NR

ANNA-PERENNA GERMANY

American Silhouettes I—The Children

1981	FIDDLERS TWO, Pat Buckley Moss, 5,000	75.00	400.00
1982	MARY WITH THE LAMBS, Pat Buckley Moss, 5,000	75.00	125.00
1982	RING AROUND THE ROSIE, Pat Buckley Moss, 5,000	75.00	175.00
1982	WAITING FOR TOM, Pat Buckley Moss, 5,000	75.00	200.00

American Silhouettes II—The Family

1982	FAMILY OUTING, Pat Buckley Moss, 5,000	75.00	150.00
1982	JOHN AND MARY, Pat Buckley Moss, 5,000	75.00	125.00
1982	HOMEMAKERS A-QUILTING, Pat Buckley Moss, 5,000	75.00	85.00
1984	LEISURE TIME, Pat Buckley Moss, 5,000	75.00	85.00

American Silhouettes III—Valley Life

1982	FROSTY FROLIC, Pat Buckley Moss, 5,000	75.00	250.00
1982	HAYRIDE, Pat Buckley Moss, 5,000	75.00	85.00
1983	SUNDAY RIDE, Pat Buckley Moss, 5,000	75.00	85.00
1984	MARKET DAY, Pat Buckley Moss, 5,000	75.00	120.00

Arctic Spring

1983	PATIENCE, Nori Peter, 9,500	75.00	NR
NA	PROUD MOTHER, Nori Peter	75.00	NR
NA	WE LIKE IT, Nori Peter	75.00	NR

Bashful Bunnies

1981	SPRING'S SURPRISE, Mary Ellen Wehrli, 15,000	62.50	NR
1982	SUMMER'S SUNSHINE, Mary Ellen Wehrli, 15,000	62.50	NR
1982	FALL'S FROLIC, Mary Ellen Wehrli, 15,000	62.50	NR
1983	WINTER'S WONDER, Mary Ellen Wehrli, 15,000	62.50	NR

Birds of Fancy

1978	FIREBIRD, Dr. Irving Burgues, 5,000	110.00	BR

Capricious Clowns

1981	CLOWNS AND UNICORNS, Margaret Kane, 9,800	95.00	BR
1981	MASQUERADE PARTY, Margaret Kane, 9,800	95.00	BR

Celebration

1986	WEDDING JOY, Pat Buckley Moss, 5,000	100.00	200.00

		ISSUE	CURRENT
1987	THE CHRISTENING, Pat Buckley Moss, 5,000	100.00	150.00
1988	THE ANNIVERSARY, Pat Buckley Moss, 5,000	100.00	NR
1989	FAMILY REUNION, Pat Buckley Moss, 5,000	100.00	125.00

Children of Mother Earth

1983	SPRING, Norval Morrisseau, 2,500	250.00	NR
1983	SUMMER, Norval Morrisseau, 2,500	250.00	NR
1983	AUTUMN, Norval Morrisseau, 2,500	250.00	NR
1983	WINTER, Norval Morrisseau, 2,500	250.00	NR

Christmas Magic

1984	NOEL, NOEL, Pat Buckley Moss, 5,000	67.50	325.00
1985	HELPING HANDS, Pat Buckley Moss, 5,000	67.50	200.00
1986	NIGHT BEFORE CHRISTMAS, Pat Buckley Moss, 5,000	67.50	100.00
1987	CHRISTMAS SLEIGH, Pat Buckley Moss, 5,000	75.00	125.00
1988	CHRISTMAS JOY, Pat Buckley Moss, 7,500	75.00	NR
1989	CHRISTMAS CAROL, Pat Buckley Moss, 7,500	80.00	NR
1990	CHRISTMAS EVE, Pat Buckley Moss, 7,500	80.00	NR
1991	THE SNOWMAN, Pat Buckley Moss, 7,500	80.00	NR
1992	CHRISTMAS WARMTH, Pat Buckley Moss, 7,500	85.00	NR
1993	JOY TO THE WORLD, Pat Buckley Moss, 7,500	85.00	RI
1994	CHRISTMAS NIGHT, Pat Buckley Moss, 5,000	85.00	RI
1995	CHRISTMAS AT HOME, Pat Buckley Moss, 5,000	85.00	RI
1996	MISTLETOE MAGIC, Pat Buckley Moss, 5,000	85.00	RI

We Like It
Photo courtesy of *Collectors News*

Christmas Sleigh
Photo courtesy of *Collectors News*

Enchanted Gardens

1978	JUNE DREAM, Carol Burgues, 5,000	75.00	BR
1978	SUMMER DAY, Carol Burgues, 5,000	95.00	NR

Floral Fantasies

1978	EMPRESS GOLD, Carol Burgues, 5,000	110.00	BR

Flowers of Count Lennart Bernadotte (Hamilton Collection)

		ISSUE	CURRENT
1982	IRIS, Count Lennart Bernadotte/Garie Von Schunk, 17,800	75.00	95.00
1983	CARNATION, Count Lennart Bernadotte/Garie Von Schunk, 17,800	75.00	95.00
1983	LILY, Count Lennart Bernadotte/Garie Von Schunk, 17,800	75.00	NR
1983	FREESIA, Count Lennart Bernadotte/Garie Von Schunk, 17,800	75.00	NR
1984	ORCHID, Count Lennart Bernadotte/Garie Von Schunk, 17,800	75.00	NR
1984	ROSE, Count Lennart Bernadotte/Garie Von Schunk, 17,800	75.00	NR
1984	TULIP, Count Lennart Bernadotte/Garie Von Schunk, 17,800	75.00	95.00
1984	CHRYSANTHEMUM, Count Lennart Bernadotte/Garie Von Schunk, 17,800	75.00	NR

Grandparent Diptych

		ISSUE	CURRENT
1990	HELLO GRANDMA, Pat Buckley Moss, 9,500	75.00	NR
1990	HELLO GRANDPA, Pat Buckley Moss, 9,500	75.00	NR

Happy Village

		ISSUE	CURRENT
1983	SPRING—SPRING PICNIC, Elke Sommer, 5,000	55.00	NR
1983	SUMMER—ON THE POND, Elke Sommer, 5,000	55.00	NR
1983	AUTUMN—HARVEST DANCE, Elke Sommer, 5,000	55.00	NR
1983	WINTER—SNOW KIDS, Elke Sommer, 5,000	55.00	NR

Iris
Photo courtesy of *Collectors News*

Autumn—Harvest Dance
Photo courtesy of *Collectors News*

Heartland

		ISSUE	CURRENT
1989	THE BLACKSMITH, Pat Buckley Moss, open	90.00	NR
1991	SUNDAY OUTING, Pat Buckley Moss, open	90.00	NR
1992	PRAIRIE WINTER, Pat Buckley Moss, open	90.00	NR
1993	THE SCHOOLHOUSE, Pat Buckley Moss, open	90.00	RI

International Mother Love

		ISSUE	CURRENT
1979	GESA UND KINDER, Edna Hibel, 5,000	195.00	NR
1980	ALEXANDRA UND KINDER, Edna Hibel, 5,000	195.00	NR

Joyful Children

		ISSUE	CURRENT
1992	PURPLE UMBRELLA, Pat Buckley Moss, 5,000	70.00	125.00
1993	DANCE OF THE BUTTERFLIES, Pat Buckley Moss, 5,000	70.00	RI
1994	THE DOLL'S HOUSE, Pat Buckley Moss, 5,000	70.00	RI
1994	THE MEDICS, Pat Buckley Moss, 5,000	70.00	RI

Joys of Motherhood

1979	GESA AND CHILDREN, 5,000	165.00	NR
1980	ALEXANDRA AND CHILDREN, 5,000	175.00	NR

Masquerade Fantasies

1981	THE MASQUERADE PARTY, Margaret Kane, 9,800	95.00	NR
1981	CLOWNS AND UNICORNS, Margaret Kane, 9,800	95.00	NR

Mother's Love

1991	TENDER HANDS, Pat Buckley Moss, 5,000	85.00	NR
1992	MOTHER'S LOVE, Pat Buckley Moss, 5,000	85.00	NR
1993	MOTHER'S WORLD, Pat Buckley Moss, 5,000	80.00	RI
1994	MOTHER'S JOY, Pat Buckley Moss, 5,000	80.00	RI
1995	THE NEWBORN, Pat Buckley Moss, 5,000	80.00	RI
1996	TREASURED BABE, Pat Buckley Moss, 5,000	80.00	RI
1997	MOTHER'S DAY, Pat Buckley Moss, 5,000	80.00	RI
1998	A PRECIOUS MOMENT, Pat Buckley Moss, 5,000	80.00	RI

Oriental Tranquility

1978	CHUN LI AT POND, Dr. Irving Burgues, 5,000	100.00	BR
1979	MING TAO ON PATH OF FAITH, Dr. Irving Burgues, 5,000	110.00	BR

Reflection of Youth

1984	THE SWIMMERS, Ken Danby, 9,500	75.00	NR

Rhythm and Dance

1983	BALLROOM, Al Hirschfield, 5,000	29.50	NR
1983	PAS DE DEUX, Al Hirschfield, 5,000	29.50	NR
1983	SWING, Al Hirschfield, 5,000	29.50	NR
1983	JAZZ, Al Hirschfield, 5,000	29.50	NR
1983	AEROBICS, Al Hirschfield, 5,000	29.50	NR
1983	CAKE WALK, Al Hirschfield, 5,000	29.50	NR
1983	CHARLESTON, Al Hirschfield, 5,000	29.50	NR
1983	STRUT, Al Hirschfield, 5,000	29.50	NR

Romantic Love

1979	ROMEO AND JULIET, Frank Russell and Gertrude Barrer, 7,500	95.00	NR
1980	LANCELOT AND GUINEVERE, Frank Russell and Gertrude Barrer, 7,500	95.00	NR
1981	HELEN AND PARIS, Frank Russell and Gertrude Barrer, 7,500	95.00	NR
1982	LOVERS OF TAJ MAHAL, Frank Russell and Gertrude Barrer, 7,500	95.00	NR

Treasured Friends

1995	LEARNED PAIR, Pat Buckley Moss, 5,000	85.00	RI
1995	LORDS OF THE REALM, Pat Buckley Moss, 5,000	85.00	RI
1996	NOBLE FILLY, Pat Buckley Moss, 5,000	85.00	RI

Triptych Series

		ISSUE	CURRENT
1978	BYZANTINE TRIPTYCH, Frank Russell and Gertrude Barrer, 5,000	325.00	BR
1980	JERUSALEM TRIPTYCH, Frank Russell and Gertrude Barrer, 5,000	350.00	BR

Uncle Tad's Cat

		ISSUE	CURRENT
1979	OLIVER'S BIRTHDAY, Thaddeus Krumeich, 5,000	75.00	150.00
1980	PEACHES AND CREAM, Thaddeus Krumeich, 5,000	75.00	85.00
1981	PRINCESS AURORA, QUEEN OF THE NIGHT, Thaddeus Krumeich, 5,000	80.00	NR
1981	WALTER'S WINDOW, Thaddeus Krumeich, 5,000	80.00	NR

Uncle Tad's Golden Oldies

		ISSUE	CURRENT
1985	MY MERRY OLDSMOBILE, Thaddeus Krumeich	39.50	55.00
1985	DOWN BY THE OLD MILL STREAM, Thaddeus Krumeich	39.50	50.00
1986	RAMONA, Thaddeus Krumeich	39.50	NR
1987	PADDLIN' MADELINE HOME, Thaddeus Krumeich	39.50	60.00

Uncle Tad's Holiday Cats

		ISSUE	CURRENT
1982	JINGLE BELLS, Thaddeus Krumeich, 9,800	75.00	NR
1983	POLLYANNA, Thaddeus Krumeich, 9,800	75.00	NR
1984	PUMPKIN, Thaddeus Krumeich, 9,800	75.00	NR
1985	PERRY, BUTTERCUP AND BLACKEYED SUSAN, Thaddeus Krumeich, 9,800	75.00	NR

Uncle Tad's Tick Tock

		ISSUE	CURRENT
1982	HICKORY, DICKORY, Thaddeus Krumeich, 5,000	150.00	NR

Single Issue

		ISSUE	CURRENT
1993	SUMMER WEDDING, Pat Buckley Moss, 5,000	100.00	RI
1994	SCHOOL DAYS, Pat Buckley Moss, 5,000	85.00	RI
1994	VISITING NURSE, Pat Buckley Moss, 5,000	85.00	RI
1995	FRIENDS FOREVER, Pat Buckley Moss, 5,000	85.00	RI
1995	THE MUSEUM, Pat Buckley Moss, 5,000	40.00	RI
1995	SKATING JOY, Pat Buckley Moss, 5,000	40.00	RI
1996	WEDDING DAY, Pat Buckley Moss, 5,000	45.00	RI

ANRI ITALY

(Schmid)

Christmas

		ISSUE	CURRENT
1971	ST. JAKOB IN GRODEN, J. Malfertheiner, 10,000	37.50	65.00
1972	PIPERS AT ALBEROBELLO, J. Malfertheiner, 1 year	45.00	75.00
1973	ALPINE HORN, J. Malfertheiner, 1 year	45.00	390.00
1974	YOUNG MAN AND GIRL, J. Malfertheiner, 1 year	50.00	95.00
1975	CHRISTMAS IN IRELAND, J. Malfertheiner, 1 year	60.00	NR
1976	ALPINE CHRISTMAS, J. Malfertheiner, 1 year	65.00	190.00
1977	LEGEND OF HELIGENBLUT, J. Malfertheiner, 6,000	65.00	90.00
1978	KLOCKLER SINGERS, J. Malfertheiner, 6,000	80.00	90.00
1979	MOSS GATHERERS, 6,000	135.00	175.00
1980	WINTRY CHURCHGOING, 6,000	170.00	NR
1981	SANTA CLAUS IN TYROL, 6,000	165.00	200.00
1982	THE STAR SINGERS, 6,000	165.00	NR

		ISSUE	CURRENT
1983	UNTO US A CHILD IS BORN, Haral Schmalzl, 6,000	165.00	310.00
1984	YULETIDE IN THE VALLEY, 6,000	165.00	NR
1985	GOOD MORNING, GOOD CHEER, J. Malfertheiner, 6,000	165.00	NR
1986	A GRODEN CHRISTMAS, J. Malfertheiner, 6,000	165.00	200.00
1987	DOWN FROM THE ALPS, J. Malfertheiner, 6,000	195.00	250.00
1988	CHRISTKINDLE MARKT, J. Malfertheiner, 6,000	220.00	230.00
1989	FLIGHT INTO EGYPT, J. Malfertheiner, 6,000	275.00	NR
1990	HOLY NIGHT, J. Malfertheiner, 6,000	300.00	NR

Disney Four Star Collection

1989	MICKEY MINI PLATE, Disney Studios, 5,000	40.00	65.00
1990	MINNIE MINI PLATE, Disney Studios, 5,000	40.00	95.00
1991	DONALD MINI PLATE, Disney Studios, 5,000	50.00	NR

Father's Day

1972	ALPINE FATHER AND CHILDREN, 5,000	35.00	100.00
1973	ALPINE FATHER AND CHILDREN, 5,000	40.00	100.00
1974	CLIFF GAZING, 5,000	50.00	90.00
1975	SAILING, 5,000	60.00	100.00

Ferràndiz Annual

1984	PASTORAL JOURNEY, Juan Ferràndiz, 2,000	170.00	NR
1985	A TENDER TOUCH, Juan Ferràndiz, 2,000	170.00	NR

Ferràndiz Christmas (Schmid)

1972	CHRIST IN THE MANGER, Juan Ferràndiz, 4,000	35.00	200.00
1973	CHRISTMAS, Juan Ferràndiz, 4,000	40.00	225.00
1974	HOLY NIGHT, Juan Ferràndiz, 4,000	50.00	100.00
1975	FLIGHT INTO EGYPT, Juan Ferràndiz, 4,000	60.00	95.00
1976	TREE OF LIFE, Juan Ferràndiz, 4,000	60.00	85.00
1976	GIRL WITH FLOWERS, Juan Ferràndiz, 4,000	65.00	185.00
1978	LEADING THE WAY, Juan Ferràndiz, 4,000	77.50	180.00
1979	THE DRUMMER, Juan Ferràndiz, 4,000	120.00	175.00

Unto Us a Child Is Born
Photo courtesy of *Collectors News*

Peace Attend Thee
Photo courtesy of *Collectors News*

		ISSUE	CURRENT
1980	REJOICE, Juan Ferràndiz, 4,000	150.00	160.00
1981	SPREADING THE WORD, Juan Ferràndiz, 4,000	150.00	NR
1982	THE SHEPHERD FAMILY, Juan Ferràndiz, 4,000	150.00	NR
1983	PEACE ATTEND THEE, Juan Ferràndiz, 4,000	150.00	NR

Ferràndiz Mother's Day

1972	MOTHER SEWING, Juan Ferràndiz, 3,000	35.00	200.00
1973	ALPINE MOTHER AND CHILD, Juan Ferràndiz, 3,000	40.00	150.00
1974	MOTHER HOLDING CHILD, Juan Ferràndiz, 3,000	50.00	150.00
1975	DOVE GIRL, Juan Ferràndiz, 3,000	60.00	150.00
1976	MOTHER KNITTING, Juan Ferràndiz, 3,000	60.00	200.00
1977	ALPINE STROLL, Juan Ferràndiz, 3,000	65.00	125.00
1978	THE BEGINNING, Juan Ferràndiz, 3,000	75.00	100.00
1979	ALL HEARTS, Juan Ferràndiz, 3,000	120.00	170.00
1980	SPRING ARRIVALS, Juan Ferràndiz, 3,000	150.00	165.00
1981	HARMONY, Juan Ferràndiz, 3,000	150.00	NR
1982	WITH LOVE, Juan Ferràndiz, 3,000	150.00	NR

Ferràndiz Wooden Birthday (Schmid)

1972	BOY, Juan Ferràndiz, 1 year	15.00	100.00
1972	GIRL, Juan Ferràndiz, 1 year	15.00	160.00
1973	BOY, Juan Ferràndiz, 1 year	20.00	200.00
1973	GIRL, Juan Ferràndiz, 1 year	20.00	150.00
1974	BOY, Juan Ferràndiz, 1 year	22.00	160.00
1974	GIRL, Juan Ferràndiz, 1 year	22.00	160.00

Ferràndiz Wooden Wedding

1972	BOY AND GIRL EMBRACING, Juan Ferràndiz, 1 year	40.00	100.00
1973	WEDDING SCENE, Juan Ferràndiz, 1 year	40.00	150.00
1974	WEDDING, Juan Ferràndiz, 1 year	48.00	150.00
1975	WEDDING, Juan Ferràndiz, 1 year	60.00	150.00
1976	WEDDING, Juan Ferràndiz, 1 year	60.00	90.00

Mother's Day

1972	ALPINE MOTHER AND CHILDREN, 5,000	35.00	50.00
1973	ALPINE MOTHER AND CHILDREN, 5,000	40.00	50.00
1974	ALPINE MOTHER AND CHILDREN, 5,000	50.00	NR
1975	ALPINE STROLL, 5,000	60.00	NR
1976	KNITTING, 5,000	60.00	NR

Sarah Kay Annual

1984	A TIME FOR SECRETS, Sarah Kay, 2,500	120.00	NR
1985	CAROUSEL MAGIC, Sarah Kay, 2,500	120.00	NR

ANTIQUE TRADER UNITED STATES

Bible Series

1973	DAVID AND GOLIATH, 2,000	10.75	NR
1973	MOSES AND GOLDEN IDOL, 2,000	10.75	NR
1973	NOAH'S ARK, 2,000	10.75	NR
1973	SAMSON, 2,000	10.75	NR

		ISSUE	CURRENT
Christmas			
1971	CHRIST CHILD, 1,500	10.95	NR
1972	FLIGHT INTO EGYPT, 1,500	10.95	NR
C. M. Russell			
1971	BAD ONE, C. M. Russell, 2,000	11.95	NR
1971	DISCOVERY OF LAST CHANCE GULCH, C. M. Russell, 2,000	11.95	NR
1971	DOUBTFUL VISITOR, C. M. Russell, 2,000	11.95	NR
1971	INNOCENT ALLIES, C. M. Russell, 2,000	11.95	NR
1971	MEDICINE MAN, C. M. Russell, 2,000	11.95	NR
Currier & Ives			
1969	BASEBALL, 2,000	9.00	NR
1969	FRANKLIN EXPERIMENT, 2,000	9.00	NR
1969	HAYING TIME, 2,000	9.00	NR
1969	WINTER IN COUNTRY, 2,000	9.00	NR
Easter			
1971	CHILD AND LAMB, 1,500	10.95	NR
1972	SHEPHERD WITH LAMB, 1,500	10.95	NR
Father's Day			
1971	PILGRIM FATHER, 1,500	10.95	NR
1972	DEER FAMILY, 1,000	10.95	NR
Mother's Day			
1971	MADONNA AND CHILD, 1,500	10.95	NR
1972	MOTHER CAT AND KITTENS, 1,000	10.95	NR
Thanksgiving			
1971	PILGRIMS, 1,500	10.95	NR
1972	FIRST THANKSGIVING, 1,000	10.95	NR

ARABIA OF FINLAND FINLAND

Christmas Annual			
1978	INLAND VILLAGE SCENE, 1 year	49.00	NR
1979	FOREST VILLAGE SCENE, 1 year	72.00	NR
1980	SEASIDE VILLAGE SCENE, 1 year	79.00	NR
1981	CHRISTMAS PLATE, 1 year	87.00	NR
1982	CHRISTMAS PLATE, 1 year	95.00	NR
Kalevala Series			
1976	VAINOMOINEN'S SOWING SONG, Raija Uosikkinen, 1,996	30.00	230.00
1977	AINO'S FATE, Raija Uosikkinen, 1,008	30.00	NR
1978	LEMMINKAINEN'S CHASE, Raija Uosikkinen, 2,500	39.00	NR
1979	KULLERVO'S REVENGE, Raija Uosikkinen, 1 year	39.50	NR
1980	VAINOMOINEN'S RESCUE, Raija Uosikkinen, 1 year	45.00	60.00
1981	VAINOMOINEN'S MAGIC, Raija Uosikkinen, 1 year	49.50	NR
1982	JOUKAHAINEN SHOOTS THE HORSE, Raija Uosikkinen, 1 year	55.50	NR

		ISSUE	CURRENT
1983	LEMMINKAINEN'S ESCAPE, Raija Uosikkinen, 1 year	60.00	85.00
1984	LEMMINKAINEN'S MAGIC FEATHERS, Raija Uosikkinen, 1 year	49.50	90.00
1985	LEMMINKAINEN'S GRIEF, Raija Uosikkinen, 1 year	60.00	NR
1986	OSMATAR CREATING ALE, Raija Uosikkinen, 1 year	60.00	85.00
1987	VAINOMOINEN TRICKS ILMARINEN, Raija Uosikkinen, 1 year	65.00	90.00
1988	HEARS VAINOMOINEN WEEP, Raija Uosikkinen, 1 year	69.00	115.00
1989	FOUR MAIDENS, Raija Uosikkinen, 1 year	75.00	85.00
1990	ANNIKKA, Raija Uosikkinen, 1 year	85.00	105.00
1991	LEMMINKAINEN'S MOTHER SAYS DON'T/WAR, Raija Uosikkinen, 1 year	85.00	NR

ARCADIAN PEWTER, INC.

Red Oak II

1995	RED OAK II, N. Lindblade, open	74.95	RI

ARIZONA ARTISAN UNITED STATES

Christmas

1974	MEXICAN CHRISTMAS, 1 year	20.00	NR
1975	NAVAJO CHRISTMAS, 1 year	20.00	NR

Thanksgiving

1975	NAVAJO THANKSGIVING, 1 year	15.00	NR

ARLINGTON MINT UNITED STATES

Christmas

1972	HANDS IN PRAYER, 1 year	125.00	BR

ARMSTRONG'S / CROWN PARIAN UNITED STATES

(FAIRMONT, Waterford-Wedgwood)

American Folk Heroes

1983	JOHNNY APPLESEED, Gene Boyer, 50 days	35.00	NR
1984	DAVY CROCKETT, Gene Boyer, 50 days	35.00	NR
1985	BETSY ROSS, Gene Boyer, 50 days	35.00	NR

Beautiful Cats of the World

1979	SHEENA, Douglas Van Howd, sgd, 5,000	60.00	80.00
1979	SHEENA'S CUBS, Douglas Van Howd, sgd, 5,000	60.00	NR
1980	ELISHEBA, Douglas Van Howd, sgd, 5,000	60.00	NR
1980	ELISHEBA'S CUBS, Douglas Van Howd, sgd, 5,000	65.00	NR
1981	ATARAH, Douglas Van Howd, sgd, 5,000	60.00	NR
1982	ATARAH'S CUBS, Douglas Van Howd, sgd, 5,000	60.00	NR

Buck Hill Bears

1986	TIDDLYWINK AND PIXIE, Robert Pearcy, 10,000	29.50	NR
1986	REBECCA AND FRIEND, Robert Pearcy, 10,000	29.50	NR

Commemorative Issues

		ISSUE	CURRENT
1983	70 YEARS YOUNG, Red Skelton, 15,000, 10½"	85.00	NR
1984	FREDDIE THE TORCHBEARER, Red Skelton, 15,000, 8½"	62.50	NR
1994	RED & HIS FRIENDS, Red Skelton, 165, 12¼"	700.00	RI

Elisheba
Photo courtesy of *Collectors News*

Freddie the Torchbearer
Photo courtesy of *Collectors News*

Companions

1986	ALL BARK AND NO BITE, Robert Pearcy, 10,000	29.50	NR

Constitution

1987	U.S. *CONSTITUTION* VS. *GUERRIERE*, Alan D'Estrehan, 10,000	39.50	NR
1987	U.S. *CONSTITUTION* VS. *TRIPOLI*, Alan D'Estrehan, 10,000	39.50	NR
1987	U.S. *CONSTITUTION* VS. *JAVA*, Alan D'Estrehan, 10,000	39.50	NR
1987	U.S. *CONSTITUTION* IN THE GREAT CHASE, Alan D'Estrehan, 10,000	39.50	NR

Eyes of the Child (Waterford-Wedgwood)

NA	LITTLE LADY LOVE, Peter Fromme-Douglas, 15,000	65.00	NR
NA	MY BEST FRIEND, Peter Fromme-Douglas, 15,000	65.00	NR
NA	I WISH UPON A STAR, Peter Fromme-Douglas, 15,000	65.00	NR
NA	IN A CHILD'S THOUGHT, Peter Fromme-Douglas, 15,000	65.00	NR
NA	PUPPY LOVE, Peter Fromme-Douglas, 15,000	65.00	NR

Faces of the World

1988	ERIN (IRELAND), Lisette DeWinne, 14 days	24.50	NR
1988	CLARA (BELGIUM), Lisette DeWinne, 14 days	24.50	NR
1988	LUISA (SPAIN), Lisette DeWinne, 14 days	24.50	NR
1988	TAMIKO (JAPAN), Lisette DeWinne, 14 days	24.50	NR
1988	COLETTE (FRANCE), Lisette DeWinne, 14 days	24.50	NR
1988	HEATHER (ENGLAND), Lisette DeWinne, 14 days	24.50	NR
1988	GRETA (AUSTRIA), Lisette DeWinne, 14 days	24.50	NR
1988	MARIA (ITALY), Lisette DeWinne, 14 days	24.50	NR

		ISSUE	CURRENT

Freddie the Freeloader (Crown Parian)

1979	FREDDIE IN THE BATHTUB, Red Skelton, 10,000	55.00	225.00
1980	FREDDIE'S SHACK, Red Skelton, 10,000	55.00	120.00
1981	FREDDIE ON THE GREEN, Red Skelton, 10,000	60.00	NR
1982	LOVE THAT FREDDIE, Red Skelton, 10,000	60.00	NR

Freddie's Adventure (Crown Parian)

1982	CAPTAIN FREDDIE, Red Skelton, 15,000	60.00	NR
1982	BRONCO FREDDIE, Red Skelton, 15,000	62.50	NR
1983	SIR FREDDIE, Red Skelton, 15,000	62.50	NR
1984	GERTRUDE AND HEATHCLIFFE, Red Skelton, 15,000	62.50	NR

Freedom Collection of Red Skelton

1990	THE ALL AMERICAN, Red Skelton, sgd, 1,000	195.00	300.00
1990	THE ALL AMERICAN, Red Skelton, 9,000	62.50	NR
1991	INDEPENDENCE DAY?, Red Skelton, sgd, 1,000	195.00	NR
1991	INDEPENDENCE DAY?, Red Skelton, 9,000	62.50	NR
1992	LET FREEDOM RING, Red Skelton, sgd, 1,000	195.00	NR
1992	LET FREEDOM RING, Red Skelton, 9,000	62.50	NR
1993	FREDDIE'S GIFT OF LIFE, Red Skelton, sgd, 1,000	195.00	RI
1993	FREDDIE'S GIFT OF LIFE, Red Skelton, 9,000	62.50	RI

Golden Memories

1995	THE DONUT DUNKER, Red Skelton, sgd, 1,000	375.00	RI
1996	CLEM & CLEMENTINE, Red Skelton, sgd, 1,000	385.00	RI
1996	SAN FERNANDO RED, Red Skelton, sgd, 1,000	385.00	RI
1997	JR., THE MEAN WIDDLE KID, Red Skelton, sgd, 1,000	385.00	RI

Happy Art (Crown Parian)

1981	WOODY'S TRIPLE SELF-PORTRAIT, Walter Lantz, 10,000	39.50	NR
1981	WOODY'S TRIPLE SELF-PORTRAIT, Walter Lantz, sgd, 1,000	100.00	200.00
1983	GOTHIC WOODY, Walter Lantz, 10,000	39.50	NR
1983	GOTHIC WOODY, Walter Lantz, sgd, 1,000	100.00	200.00
1984	BLUE BOY WOODY, Walter Lantz, 10,000	39.50	NR
1984	BLUE BOY WOODY, Walter Lantz, sgd, 1,000	100.00	200.00

Huggable Puppies

1984	TAKE ME HOME, Robert Pearcy, 10,000	29.50	NR
1985	OH HOW CUTE, Robert Pearcy, 10,000	29.50	NR
1985	PUPPY PALS, Robert Pearcy, 10,000	29.50	NR
1986	WHO, ME?, Robert Pearcy, 10,000	29.50	NR

Infinite Love

1987	A PAIR OF DREAMS, Sue Etem, 14 days	24.50	NR
1987	THE EYES SAY "I LOVE YOU," Sue Etem, 14 days	24.50	NR
1987	ONCE UPON A SMILE, Sue Etem, 14 days	24.50	NR
1987	KISS A LITTLE GIGGLE, Sue Etem, 14 days	24.50	NR
1988	LOVE GOES FORTH IN LITTLE FEET, Sue Etem, 14 days	24.50	NR
1988	BUNDLE OF JOY, Sue Etem, 14 days	24.50	NR
1988	GRINS FOR GRANDMA, Sue Etem, 14 days	24.50	NR
1989	A MOMENT TO CHERISH, Sue Etem, 14 days	24.50	NR

U.S. Constitution *vs.* Guerriere

Oh How Cute

Once Upon a Smile

Purr-swayed

Buckles

Master Lambton

Photos courtesy of *Collectors News*

		ISSUE	CURRENT

Lovable Kittens

1983	THE CAT'S MEOW, Robert Pearcy, 10,000	29.50	NR
1984	PURR-SWAYED, Robert Pearcy, 10,000	29.50	NR
1985	THE PRINCE OF PURRS, Robert Pearcy, 10,000	29.50	NR
1986	PET, AND I'LL PURR, Robert Pearcy, 10,000	29.50	NR

Mischief Makers

1986	PUDDLES, Sue Etem, 10,000	39.95	NR
1986	BUCKLES, Sue Etem, 10,000	39.95	NR
1987	TRIX, Sue Etem, 10,000	39.95	NR
1988	NAP, Sue Etem, 10,000	39.95	NR

Moments of Nature

1980	CALIFORNIA QUAIL, John Ruthven, 5,000	39.50	NR
1981	CHICKADEE, John Ruthven, 5,000	39.50	NR
1981	SCREECH OWLS, John Ruthven, 5,000	39.50	NR

North American Birds

1984	CALIFORNIA QUAIL, Jon Roberton, 7,500	60.00	NR

Portraits of Childhood

1983	MISS MURRAY, Sir Thomas Lawrence, 7,500	65.00	NR
1984	MASTER LAMBTON, Sir Thomas Lawrence, 7,500	65.00	NR

Reflections of Innocence

1984	ME AND MY FRIEND, Miguel Paredes, 10,000	37.50	NR
1985	MY RAINBEAU, Miguel Paredes, 10,000	37.50	NR
1986	ROWBOAT RENDEZVOUS, Miguel Paredes, 10,000	37.50	NR
1987	HATCHING A SECRET, Miguel Paredes, 10,000	37.50	NR

Signature Collection

1986	ANYONE FOR TENNIS?, Red Skelton, 9,000	62.50	NR
1986	ANYONE FOR TENNIS?, Red Skelton, sgd, 1,000	125.00	450.00
1987	IRONING THE WAVES, Red Skelton, 9,000	62.50	NR
1987	IRONING THE WAVES, Red Skelton, sgd, 1,000	125.00	300.00
1988	THE CLIFFHANGER, Red Skelton, 9,000	62.50	NR
1988	THE CLIFFHANGER, Red Skelton, sgd, 1,000	150.00	300.00
1988	HOOKED ON FREDDIE, Red Skelton, 9,000	62.50	NR
1988	HOOKED ON FREDDIE, Red Skelton, sgd, 1,000	175.00	250.00

Songs of Caroline

NA	AUTUMN'S PRAYER OF THANKSGIVING, Penni Anne Cross, 5,000	35.00	NR

Sporting Dogs (Wildlife Internationale)

1985	DECOY (LABRADOR RETRIEVER), John Ruthven, 5,000	55.00	100.00
1985	RUMMY (ENGLISH SETTER), John Ruthven, 5,000	55.00	NR
1985	DUSTY (GOLDEN RETRIEVER), John Ruthven, 5,000	55.00	80.00
1985	SCARLETT (IRISH SETTER), John Ruthven, 5,000	55.00	100.00

Sports

1985	PETE ROSE, Rod Schenken, sgd, 1,000, 10¼"	100.00	NR

		ISSUE	CURRENT
1985	PETE ROSE, Rod Schenken, 10,000, 10¼"	45.00	NR

Statue of Liberty

1985	THE DEDICATION, Alan D'Estrehan, 10,000	39.50	NR
1986	IMMIGRANTS, Alan D'Estrehan, 10,000	39.50	NR
1986	INDEPENDENCE, Alan D'Estrehan, 10,000	39.50	NR
1986	RE-DEDICATION, Alan D'Estrehan, 10,000	39.50	NR

Three Graces

1985	THALIA, Michael Perham, 7,500	49.50	NR
1986	AGLAIA, Michael Perham, 7,500	49.50	NR
1987	EUPHROSYNE, Michael Perham, 7,500	49.50	NR

Wells Fargo

1979	UNDER SURVEILLANCE, McCarty, 10,000	65.00	NR
1979	PROMISED LAND, McCarty, 10,000	65.00	NR
1982	WINTERSONG, McCarty, 10,000	65.00	NR
1983	TURNING THE LAND, McCarty, 10,000	65.00	NR

Single Issues

1978	AFFECTION, Rosemary Calder, 7,500	60.00	NR
1982	BUON NATALE, Valentino Garavani, 7,500	300.00	NR

ARTA AUSTRIA

Christmas

1973	NATIVITY—IN MANGER, 1,500	50.00	70.00

Mother's Day

1973	FAMILY WITH PUPPY, 1,500	50.00	70.00

ARTAFFECTS

(Curator Collection, March of Dimes, Signature Collection, Vague Shadows)

Adventures of Peter Pan

1990	FLYING OVER LONDON, Tom Newsom, 14 days	29.50	40.00
1990	LOOK AT ME, Tom Newsom, 14 days	29.50	40.00
1990	THE ENCOUNTER, Tom Newsom, 14 days	29.50	40.00
1990	NEVER LAND, Tom Newsom, 14 days	29.50	40.00

American Blues—Winter Mindscape

1989	PEACEFUL VILLAGE, Rob Sauber, 14 days	29.50	55.00
1989	SNOWBOUND, Rob Sauber, 14 days	29.50	NR
1990	PAPA'S SURPRISE, Rob Sauber, 14 days	29.50	NR
1990	WELL-TRAVELED ROAD, Rob Sauber, 14 days	29.50	NR
1990	FIRST FREEZE, Rob Sauber, 14 days	29.50	NR
1990	COUNTRY MORNING, Rob Sauber, 14 days	29.50	NR
1990	SLEIGH RIDE, Rob Sauber, 14 days	29.50	NR
1990	JANUARY THAW, Rob Sauber, 14 days	29.50	NR

		ISSUE	CURRENT

America's Indian Heritage

		ISSUE	CURRENT
1987	CHEYENNE NATION, Gregory Perillo, 10 days	24.50	35.00
1988	ARAPAHO NATION, Gregory Perillo, 10 days	24.50	45.00
1988	KIOWA NATION, Gregory Perillo, 10 days	24.50	45.00
1988	SIOUX NATION, Gregory Perillo, 10 days	24.50	35.00
1988	CHIPPEWA NATION, Gregory Perillo, 10 days	24.50	35.00
1988	CROW NATION, Gregory Perillo, 10 days	24.50	45.00
1988	NEZ PERCE NATION, Gregory Perillo, 10 days	24.50	45.00
1988	BLACKFOOT NATION, Gregory Perillo, 10 days	24.50	35.00

American Blues Special Occasions

		ISSUE	CURRENT
1992	HAPPILY EVER AFTER (WEDDING), Rob Sauber	35.00	NR
1992	THE PERFECT TREE (CHRISTMAS), Rob Sauber	35.00	NR
1992	MY SUNSHINE (MOTHERHOOD), Rob Sauber	35.00	NR

American Maritime Heritage

		ISSUE	CURRENT
1987	U.S.S. *CONSTITUTION*, Kipp Soldwedel, 14 days	35.00	NR

Angler's Dream (Signature Collection)

		ISSUE	CURRENT
1983	BROOK TROUT, John Eggert, 9,800	55.00	NR
1983	CHINOOK SALMON, John Eggert, 9,800	55.00	NR
1983	LARGEMOUTH BASS, John Eggert, 9,800	55.00	NR
1983	STRIPED BASS, John Eggert, 9,800	55.00	NR

Baby's Firsts

		ISSUE	CURRENT
1989	VISITING THE DOCTOR, Rob Sauber, 14 days, 6½"	21.50	NR
1989	BABY'S FIRST STEP, Rob Sauber, 14 days, 6½"	21.50	NR
1989	FIRST BIRTHDAY, Rob Sauber, 14 days, 6½"	21.50	NR
1989	CHRISTMAS MORN, Rob Sauber, 14 days, 6½"	21.50	NR
1989	PICTURE PERFECT, Rob Sauber, 14 days, 6½"	21.50	NR

Backstage

		ISSUE	CURRENT
1990	THE RUNAWAY, Barry Leighton-Jones, 14 days	29.50	NR
1990	THE LETTER, Barry Leighton-Jones, 14 days	29.50	NR
1990	BUBBLING OVER, Barry Leighton-Jones, 14 days	29.50	NR

Baker Street (Signature Collection)

		ISSUE	CURRENT
1983	SHERLOCK HOLMES, Mitchell Hooks, 9,800	55.00	NR
1983	WATSON, Mitchell Hooks, 9,800	55.00	NR

Becker Babies (Curator Collection)

		ISSUE	CURRENT
1983	SNOW PUFF, Charlotte Becker, limited	29.95	45.00
1984	SMILING THROUGH, Charlotte Becker, limited	29.95	45.00
1984	PALS, Charlotte Becker, limited	29.95	45.00

Bessie's Best

		ISSUE	CURRENT
1984	OH! OH! A BUNNY, Bessie Pease Gutmann, open	29.95	65.00
1984	THE NEW LOVE, Bessie Pease Gutmann, open	29.95	65.00
1984	MY BABY, Bessie Pease Gutmann, open	29.95	65.00

			ISSUE	CURRENT
1984	LOOKING FOR TROUBLE, Bessie Pease Gutmann, open		29.95	65.00
1984	TAPS, Bessie Pease Gutmann, open		29.95	65.00

Bring unto Me the Children

1994	A LITTLE LOVE SONG, Gregory Perillo, closed	29.50	RI
1994	THE BAPTISM, Gregory Perillo, closed	29.50	RI
1994	COMMUNION, Gregory Perillo, closed	29.50	RI
1994	HEAVENLY EMBRACE, Gregory Perillo, closed	29.50	RI
1994	THE LORD'S PRAYER, Gregory Perillo, closed	29.50	RI
1994	LOVE'S BLESSING, Gregory Perillo, closed	29.50	RI
1994	SWEET DREAMS, Gregory Perillo, closed	29.50	RI
1994	SWEET SERENITY, Gregory Perillo, closed	29.50	RI

Carnival (Signature Collection)

1983	KNOCK 'EM DOWN, Tom Newsom, 19,500	39.95	NR
1983	CAROUSEL, Tom Newsom, 19,500	39.95	NR
1983	FORTUNE TELLER, Tom Newsom, 19,500	39.95	NR
1983	RING THE BELL, Tom Newsom, 19,500	39.95	NR

Childhood Delights (Signature Collection)

1983	AMANDA, Rob Sauber, 7,500	45.00	75.00

Children of the Prairie

1993	TENDER LOVING CARE, Gregory Perillo	29.50	RI
1993	DAYDREAMERS, Gregory Perillo	29.50	RI
1993	PLAY TIME, Gregory Perillo	29.50	RI
1993	THE SENTINEL, Gregory Perillo	29.50	RI
1993	BEACH COMBER, Gregory Perillo	29.50	RI
1993	WATCHFUL WAITING, Gregory Perillo	29.50	RI
1993	PATIENCE, Gregory Perillo	29.50	RI
1993	SISTERS, Gregory Perillo	29.50	RI

Looking For Trouble
Photo courtesy of *Collectors News*

Bring to Me the Children
Photo courtesy of *Collectors News*

Christian Classics (Curator Collection)

		ISSUE	CURRENT
1987	BRING TO ME THE CHILDREN, Alton S. Tobey	35.00	NR
1987	WEDDING FEAST AT CANA, Alton S. Tobey	35.00	NR
1987	THE HEALER, Alton S. Tobey	35.00	NR

Christmas Celebrations of Yesterday

1993	CHRISTMAS ON MAIN STREET, Martha Leone	27.00	RI
1993	CHRISTMAS ON THE FARM, Martha Leone	27.00	RI
1993	CHRISTMAS EVE, Martha Leone	27.00	RI
1993	WREATH MAKER, Martha Leone	27.00	RI
1993	CHRISTMAS PARTY, Martha Leone	27.00	RI
1993	TRIMMING THE TREE, Martha Leone	27.00	RI
1993	CHRISTMAS BLESSINGS, Martha Leone	27.00	RI
1993	HOME FOR CHRISTMAS, Martha Leone	27.00	RI

Classic American Cars

1989	DUESENBERG, Jim Deneen, 14 days	35.00	NR
1989	CADILLAC, Jim Deneen, 14 days	35.00	NR
1989	CORD, Jim Deneen, 14 days	35.00	NR
1989	RUXTON, Jim Deneen, 14 days	35.00	NR
1990	LINCOLN, Jim Deneen, 14 days	35.00	NR
1990	PACKARD, Jim Deneen, 14 days	35.00	NR
1990	HUDSON, Jim Deneen, 14 days	35.00	NR
1990	PIERCE-ARROW, Jim Deneen, 14 days	35.00	NR

Classic American Trains

1988	HOMEWARD BOUND, Jim Deneen, 14 days	35.00	50.00
1988	A RACE AGAINST TIME, Jim Deneen, 14 days	35.00	60.00
1988	MIDDAY STOP, Jim Deneen, 14 days	35.00	50.00
1988	THE SILVER BULLET, Jim Deneen, 14 days	35.00	65.00
1988	TRAVELING IN STYLE, Jim Deneen, 14 days	35.00	50.00
1988	ROUND THE BEND, Jim Deneen, 14 days	35.00	50.00
1988	TAKING THE HIGH ROAD, Jim Deneen, 14 days	35.00	45.00
1988	COMPETITION, Jim Deneen, 14 days	35.00	NR

Classic Circus (Curator Collection)

1983	THE FAVORITE CLOWN, 17,500	39.95	NR

Club Member Limited Edition Redemptions

1992	THE PENCIL, Gregory Perillo, 1 year	35.00	75.00
1992	STUDIES IN BLACK AND WHITE, Gregory Perillo, 1 year, set of 4	75.00	100.00
1993	WATCHER OF THE WILDERNESS, Gregory Perillo, 1 year	60.00	RI

Colts

1985	APPALOOSA, Gregory Perillo, 5,000	40.00	NR
1985	PINTO, Gregory Perillo, 5,000	40.00	55.00
1985	ARABIAN, Gregory Perillo, 5,000	40.00	55.00
1985	THOROUGHBRED, Gregory Perillo, 5,000	40.00	55.00

Council of Nations (Hamilton Collection)

1992	STRENGTH OF THE SIOUX, Gregory Perillo, 14 days	29.50	NR

		ISSUE	CURRENT
1992	PRIDE OF THE CHEYENNE, Gregory Perillo, 14 days	29.50	40.00
1992	DIGNITY OF THE NEZ PERCE, Gregory Perillo, 14 days	29.50	NR
1992	COURAGE OF THE ARAPAHO, Gregory Perillo, 14 days	29.50	NR
1992	POWER OF THE BLACKFOOT, Gregory Perillo, 14 days	29.50	NR
1992	NOBILITY OF THE ALGONQUIN, Gregory Perillo, 14 days	29.50	NR
1992	WISDOM OF THE CHEROKEE, Gregory Perillo, 14 days	29.50	40.00
1992	BOLDNESS OF THE SENECA, Gregory Perillo, 14 days	29.50	NR

Gift Edition (Curator Collection)

1982	THE WEDDING, Rob Sauber	37.50	NR
1984	HAPPY BIRTHDAY, Rob Sauber	37.50	NR
1985	ALL ADORE HIM, Rob Sauber	37.50	NR
1985	HOME SWEET HOME, Rob Sauber	37.50	NR
1986	THE ANNIVERSARY, Rob Sauber	37.50	NR
1986	SWEETHEARTS, Rob Sauber	37.50	NR
1986	THE CHRISTENING, Rob Sauber	37.50	NR
1987	MOTHERHOOD, Rob Sauber	37.50	NR
1987	FATHERHOOD, Rob Sauber	37.50	NR
1987	SWEET SIXTEEN, Rob Sauber	37.50	NR

Good Sports

1989	PURRFECT GAME, S. Miller-Maxwell, 14 days, 6½"	22.50	NR
1989	ALLEY CATS, S. Miller-Maxwell, 14 days, 6½"	22.50	NR
1989	TEE TIME, S. Miller-Maxwell, 14 days, 6½"	22.50	NR
1989	TWO/LOVE, S. Miller-Maxwell, 14 days, 6½"	22.50	NR
1989	WHAT'S THE CATCH?, S. Miller-Maxwell, 14 days, 6½"	22.50	NR
1989	QUARTERBACK SNEAK, S. Miller-Maxwell, 14 days, 6½"	22.50	NR

Great American Trains

1992	THE ALTON LIMITED, Jim Deneen, 75 days	27.00	NR
1992	THE CAPITOL LIMITED, Jim Deneen, 75 days	27.00	NR
1992	THE MERCHANTS LIMITED, Jim Deneen, 75 days	27.00	NR
1992	THE BROADWAY LIMITED, Jim Deneen, 75 days	27.00	NR
1992	THE SOUTHWESTERN LIMITED, Jim Deneen, 75 days	27.00	NR
1992	THE BLACKHAWK LIMITED, Jim Deneen, 75 days	27.00	NR
1992	THE SUNSHINE SPECIAL LIMITED, Jim Deneen, 75 days	27.00	NR
1992	THE PANAMA SPECIAL LIMITED, Jim Deneen, 75 days	27.00	NR

Great Trains (Curator Collection)

1985	SANTA FE, Jim Deneen, 7,500	35.00	80.00
1985	TWENTIETH CENTURY LTD., Jim Deneen, 7,500	35.00	80.00
1986	EMPIRE BUILDER, Jim Deneen, 7,500	35.00	80.00

Heavenly Angels

1992	HUSH-A-BYE, MaGo, 75 days	27.00	NR
1992	HEAVENLY HELPER, MaGo, 75 days	27.00	NR
1992	HEAVENLY LIGHT, MaGo, 75 days	27.00	NR
1992	THE ANGEL'S KISS, MaGo, 75 days	27.00	NR
1992	CAUGHT IN THE ACT, MaGo, 75 days	27.00	NR
1992	MY ANGEL, MaGo, 75 days	27.00	NR
1992	SLEEPY SENTINEL, MaGo, 75 days	27.00	NR

How Do I Love Thee? (Signature Collection)

		ISSUE	CURRENT
1983	ALAINA, Rob Sauber, 19,500	39.95	NR
1983	TAYLOR, Rob Sauber, 19,500	39.95	NR
1983	RENDEZVOUS, Rob Sauber, 19,500	39.95	NR
1983	EMBRACE, Rob Sauber, 19,500	39.95	NR

Indian Bridal

		ISSUE	CURRENT
1990	YELLOW BIRD, Gregory Perillo, 14 days, 6½"	25.00	NR
1990	AUTUMN BLOSSOM, Gregory Perillo, 14 days, 6½"	25.00	NR
1990	MISTY WATERS, Gregory Perillo, 14 days, 6½"	25.00	NR
1990	SUNNY SKIES, Gregory Perillo, 14 days, 6½"	25.00	NR

Lands Before Time

		ISSUE	CURRENT
1994	IMPERIAL DYNASTY, A. Chesterman	29.50	RI
1994	KNIGHTS IN SHINING ARMOR, A. Chesterman	29.50	RI
1994	PHARAOH'S RETURN, A. Chesterman	29.50	RI
1994	ROMAN HOLIDAY, A. Chesterman	29.50	RI

Life of Jesus

		ISSUE	CURRENT
1992	THE LAST SUPPER, L. Marchetti, 25 days	27.00	NR
1992	THE SERMON ON THE MOUNT, L. Marchetti, 25 days	27.00	NR
1992	THE AGONY IN THE GARDEN, L. Marchetti, 25 days	27.00	NR
1992	THE BLESSING OF THE CHILDREN, L. Marchetti, 25 days	27.00	NR
1992	THE RESURRECTION, L. Marchetti, 25 days	27.00	NR
1992	THE HEALING OF THE SICK, L. Marchetti, 25 days	27.00	NR
1992	THE DESCENT FROM THE CROSS, L. Marchetti, 25 days	27.00	NR

Living in Harmony

		ISSUE	CURRENT
1991	PEACEABLE KINGDOM, Gregory Perillo, 75 days	29.50	NR

Magical Moments (Curator Collection)

		ISSUE	CURRENT
1981	HAPPY DREAMS, Bessie Pease Gutmann, <1 year	29.95	80.00
1981	HARMONY, Bessie Pease Gutmann, <1 year	29.95	75.00
1982	HIS MAJESTY, Bessie Pease Gutmann, <1 year	29.95	45.00
1982	WAITING FOR DADDY, Bessie Pease Gutmann, <1 year	29.95	45.00
1982	THANK YOU GOD, Bessie Pease Gutmann, <1 year	29.95	45.00
1983	THE LULLABYE, Bessie Pease Gutmann, <1 year	29.95	45.00

MaGo's Motherhood

		ISSUE	CURRENT
1990	SERENITY, MaGo, 14 days	60.00	BR

Maidens

		ISSUE	CURRENT
1985	SHIMMERING WATERS, Gregory Perillo, 5,000	50.00	100.00
1985	SNOW BLANKET, Gregory Perillo, 5,000	60.00	100.00
1985	SONG BIRD, Gregory Perillo, 5,000	60.00	100.00

Melodies of Childhood (Signature Collection)

		ISSUE	CURRENT
1983	TWINKLE, TWINKLE LITTLE STAR, Hector Garrido, 19,500	35.00	NR
1983	ROW, ROW, ROW YOUR BOAT, Hector Garrido, 19,500	35.00	NR
1983	MARY HAD A LITTLE LAMB, Hector Garrido, 19,500	35.00	NR

Mother's Love

		ISSUE	CURRENT
1984	DADDY'S HERE, Bessie Pease Gutmann, limited	29.95	50.00
1988	FEELINGS, Gregory Perillo, 1 year	35.00	55.00
1989	MOONLIGHT, Gregory Perillo, 1 year	35.00	65.00
1990	PRIDE AND JOY, Gregory Perillo, 1 year	39.50	50.00
1991	LITTLE SHADOW, Gregory Perillo, 1 year	39.50	NR

Mother's Love (Curator Collection)

1984	CONTENTMENT, Norman Rockwell, 7,500	35.00	NR

Native American Christmas

1993	THE LITTLE SHEPHERD, Gregory Perillo, 1 yr	35.00	RI
1994	JOY TO THE WORLD, Gregory Perillo, 1 yr	45.00	RI

North American Wildlife

1989	MUSTANG, Gregory Perillo, 14 days	29.50	NR
1989	WHITE-TAILED DEER, Gregory Perillo, 14 days	29.50	NR
1989	MOUNTAIN LION, Gregory Perillo, 14 days	29.50	NR
1990	AMERICAN BALD EAGLE, Gregory Perillo, 14 days	29.50	NR
1990	TIMBER WOLF, Gregroy Perillo, 14 days	29.50	NR
1990	POLAR BEAR, Gregory Perillo, 14 days	29.50	NR
1990	BUFFALO, Gregory Perillo, 14 days	29.50	NR
1990	BIGHORN SHEEP, Gregory Perillo, 14 days	29.50	NR

Nursery Pair (Curator Collection)

1983	IN SLUMBERLAND, Charlotte Becker, open	25.00	40.00
1983	THE AWAKENING, Charlotte Becker, open	25.00	40.00

Old-Fashioned Christmas

1993	UP ON THE ROOFTOP, Rob Sauber	29.50	RI
1994	THE TOY SHOPPE, Rob Sauber	29.50	RI
1994	CHRISTMAS DELIGHT, Rob Sauber	29.50	RI
1994	CHRISTMAS EVE, Rob Sauber	29.50	RI

On the Road (Curator Collection)

1984	PRIDE OF STOCKBRIDGE, Norman Rockwell, open	35.00	55.00
1984	CITY PRIDE, Norman Rockwell, open	35.00	55.00
1984	COUNTRY PRIDE, Norman Rockwell, open	35.00	55.00

Perillo Christmas

1987	SHINING STAR, Gregory Perillo, 1 year	29.50	70.00
1988	SILENT LIGHT, Gregory Perillo, 1 year	35.00	65.00
1989	SNOW FLAKE, Gregory Perillo, 1 year	35.00	NR
1990	BUNDLE UP, Gregory Perillo, 1 year	39.50	65.00
1991	CHRISTMAS JOURNEY, Gregory Perillo, 1 year	39.50	NR

Perillo's Favorites

1994	BUFFALO AND THE BRAVE, Gregory Perillo	45.00	RI
1994	HOME OF THE BRAVE AND FREE, Gregory Perillo	35.00	RI

Appaloosa

The Alton Limited

City Pride

Curiosity

Protector of the Plains

The Proposal

Photos courtesy of *Collectors News*

Perillo's Four Seasons

		ISSUE	CURRENT
1991	SUMMER, Gregory Perillo, 14 days, 6½"	25.00	NR
1991	AUTUMN, Gregory Perillo, 14 days, 6½"	25.00	NR
1991	WINTER, Gregory Perillo, 14 days, 6½"	25.00	NR
1991	SPRING, Gregory Perillo, 14 days, 6½"	25.00	NR

Playful Pets (Curator Collection)

1982	CURIOSITY, John Henry Dolph, 7,500	45.00	60.00
1982	MASTER'S HAT, John Henry Dolph, 7,500	45.00	60.00

Portraits (Curator Collection)

1986	CHANTILLY, John Eggert, 14 days	24.50	35.00
1986	DYNASTY, John Eggert, 14 days	24.50	35.00
1986	VELVET, John Eggert, 14 days	24.50	35.00
1986	JAMBALAYA, John Eggert, 14 days	24.50	35.00

Portraits by Perillo—Miniature

1989	SMILING EYES, Gregory Perillo, 9,500, 4¼"	19.50	NR
1989	BRIGHT SKY, Gregory Perillo, 9,500, 4¼"	19.50	NR
1989	RUNNING BEAR, Gregory Perillo, 9,500, 4¼"	19.50	NR
1989	LITTLE FEATHER, Gregory Perillo, 9,500, 4¼"	19.50	NR
1990	PROUD EAGLE, Gregory Perillo, 9,500, 4¼"	19.50	NR
1990	BLUE BIRD, Gregory Perillo, 9,500, 4¼"	19.50	NR
1990	WILDFLOWER, Gregory Perillo, 9,500, 4¼"	19.50	NR
1990	SPRING BREEZE, Gregory Perillo, 9,500, 4¼"	19.50	NR

Portraits of American Brides (Curator Collection)

1986	CAROLINE, Rob Sauber, 10 days	29.50	45.00
1986	JACQUELINE, Rob Sauber, 10 days	29.50	NR
1987	ELIZABETH, Rob Sauber, 10 days	29.50	69.00
1987	EMILY, Rob Sauber, 10 days	29.50	75.00
1987	MEREDITH, Rob Sauber, 10 days	29.50	75.00
1987	LAURA, Rob Sauber, 10 days	29.50	45.00
1987	SARAH, Rob Sauber, 10 days	29.50	45.00
1987	REBECCA, Rob Sauber, 10 days	29.50	65.00

Proud Young Spirits

1990	PROTECTOR OF THE PLAINS, Gregory Perillo, 14 days	29.50	NR
1990	WATCHFUL EYES, Gregory Perillo, 14 days	29.50	55.00
1990	FREEDOM'S WATCH, Gregory Perillo, 14 days	29.50	NR
1990	WOODLAND SCOUTS, Gregory Perillo, 14 days	29.50	NR
1990	FAST FRIENDS, Gregory Perillo, 14 days	29.50	NR
1990	BIRDS OF A FEATHER, Gregory Perillo, 14 days	29.50	NR
1990	PRAIRIE PALS, Gregory Perillo, 14 days	29.50	NR
1990	LOYAL GUARDIAN, Gregory Perillo, 14 days	29.50	NR

Reflections of Youth

1988	JULIA, MaGo, 14 days	29.50	50.00
1988	JESSICA, MaGo, 14 days	29.50	NR
1988	SEBASTIAN, MaGo, 14 days	29.50	NR

		ISSUE	CURRENT
1988	MICHELLE, MaGo, 14 days	29.50	NR
1988	ANDREW, MaGo, 14 days	29.50	NR
1988	BETH, MaGo, 14 days	29.50	NR
1988	AMY, MaGo, 14 days	29.50	NR
1988	LAUREN, MaGo, 14 days	29.50	NR

Rockwell Americana (Curator Collection)

1981	SHUFFLETON'S BARBERSHOP, Norman Rockwell, 17,500	75.00	125.00
1982	BREAKING HOME TIES, Norman Rockwell, 17,500	75.00	100.00
1983	WALKING TO CHURCH, Norman Rockwell, 17,500	75.00	100.00

Rockwell Trilogy (Curator Collection)

1981	STOCKBRIDGE IN WINTER 1, Norman Rockwell, <1 year	35.00	45.00
1982	STOCKBRIDGE IN WINTER 2, Norman Rockwell, <1 year	35.00	45.00
1983	STOCKBRIDGE IN WINTER 3, Norman Rockwell, <1 year	35.00	50.00

Romantic Cities of Europe

1989	VENICE, L. Marchetti, 14 days	35.00	60.00
1989	PARIS, L. Marchetti, 14 days	35.00	45.00
1990	LONDON, L. Marchetti, 14 days	35.00	45.00
1990	MOSCOW, L. Marchetti, 14 days	35.00	NR

Rose Wreaths

1993	SUMMER'S BOUNTY, Knox/Robertson	27.00	RI
1993	VICTORIAN FANTASY, Knox/Robertson	27.00	RI
1993	GENTLE PERSUASION, Knox/Robertson	27.00	RI
1993	SUNSET SPLENDOR, Knox/Robertson	27.00	RI
1994	SWEETHEARTS DELIGHT, Knox/Robertson	27.00	RI
1994	SWEET SUNSHINE, Knox/Robertson	27.00	RI
1994	FLORAL FASCINATION, Knox/Robertson	27.00	RI
1994	LOVE'S EMBRACE, Knox/Robertson	27.00	RI

Sailing Through History (Curator Collection)

1986	FLYING CLOUD, Kipp Soldwedel, 14 days	29.50	45.00
1986	SANTA MARIA, Kipp Soldwedel, 14 days	29.50	45.00
1986	MAYFLOWER, Kipp Soldwedel, 14 days	29.50	45.00

Simpler Times (Curator Collection)

1984	LAZY DAZE, Norman Rockwell, 7,500	35.00	55.00
1984	ONE FOR THE ROAD, Norman Rockwell, 7,500	35.00	55.00

Songs of Stephen Foster (Signature Collection)

1984	OH! SUSANNAH, Rob Sauber, 3,500	60.00	70.00
1984	I DREAM OF JEANIE / LIGHT BROWN HAIR, Rob Sauber, 3,500	60.00	70.00
1984	BEAUTIFUL DREAMER, Rob Sauber, 3,500	60.00	70.00

Special Occasions (Curator Collection)

1981	BUBBLES, Frances Tipton Hunter, <1 year	29.95	40.00
1982	BUTTERFLIES, Frances Tipton Hunter, <1 year	29.95	40.00

Spirits of Nature

		ISSUE	CURRENT
1993	PROTECTOR OF THE NATIONS, Gregory Perillo, 3,500	60.00	RI
1993	DEFENDER OF THE MOUNTAIN, Gregory Perillo, 3,500	60.00	RI
1993	SPIRIT OF THE PLAINS, Gregory Perillo, 3,500	60.00	RI
1993	GUARDIAN OF SAFE PASSAGE, Gregory Perillo, 3,500	60.00	RI
1993	KEEPER OF THE FOREST, Gregory Perillo, 3,500	60.00	RI

Studies in Black and White—Collector's Club Miniatures

		ISSUE	CURRENT
1992	DIGNITY, Gregory Perillo, 1 year	—	—
1992	DETERMINATION, Gregory Perillo, 1 year	—	—
1992	DILIGENCE, Gregory Perillo, 1 year	—	—
1992	DEVOTION, Gregory Perillo, 1 year	—	—
	Set of 4	75.00	NR

Studies of Early Childhood

		ISSUE	CURRENT
1990	CHRISTOPHER AND KATE, MaGo, 150 days	34.90	BR
1990	PEEK-A-BOO, MaGo, 150 days	34.90	NR
1990	ANYBODY HOME?, MaGo, 150 days	34.90	NR
1990	THREE-PART HARMONY, MaGo, 150 days	34.90	55.00

Tender Moments

		ISSUE	CURRENT
1985	SUNSET, Gregory Perillo, 2,000	—	—
1985	WINTER ROMANCE, Gregory Perillo, 2,000	—	—
	Set of 2	150.00	250.00

Timeless Love

		ISSUE	CURRENT
1989	THE PROPOSAL, Rob Sauber, 14 days	35.00	NR
1989	SWEET EMBRACE, Rob Sauber, 14 days	35.00	NR
1990	AFTERNOON LIGHT, Rob Sauber, 14 days	35.00	NR
1990	QUIET MOMENTS, Rob Sauber, 14 days	35.00	NR

Times of Our Lives

		ISSUE	CURRENT
1982	THE WEDDING, Rob Sauber, limited, 10¼"	37.50	NR
1984	HAPPY BIRTHDAY, Rob Sauber, limited, 10¼"	37.50	NR
1985	ALL ADORE HIM, Rob Sauber, limited, 10¼"	37.50	NR
1985	HOME SWEET HOME, Rob Sauber, limited, 10¼"	37.50	NR
1986	SWEETHEARTS, Rob Sauber, limited, 10¼"	37.50	NR
1986	THE ANNIVERSARY, Rob Sauber, limited, 10¼"	37.50	NR
1987	MOTHERHOOD, Rob Sauber, limited,10¼"	37.50	NR
1987	FATHERHOOD, Rob Sauber, limited, 10¼"	37.50	NR
1987	SWEET SIXTEEN, Rob Sauber, limited, 10¼"	37.50	NR
1988	THE WEDDING, Rob Sauber, limited, 6½"	19.50	NR
1988	HAPPY BIRTHDAY, Rob Sauber, limited, 6½"	19.50	NR
1988	ALL ADORE HIM, Rob Sauber, limited, 6½"	19.50	NR
1988	HOME SWEET HOME, Rob Sauber, limited, 6½"	19.50	NR
1988	SWEETHEARTS, Rob Sauber, limited, 6½"	19.50	NR
1988	THE ANNIVERSARY, Rob Sauber, limited, 6½"	19.50	NR
1988	MOTHERHOOD, Rob Sauber, limited, 6½"	19.50	NR
1988	FATHERHOOD, Rob Sauber, limited, 6½"	19.50	NR

		ISSUE	CURRENT
1988	THE CHRISTENING, Rob Sauber, limited, 6½"	19.50	NR
1989	VISITING THE DOCTOR, Rob Sauber, 14 days, 10¼"	39.50	NR
1990	MOTHER'S JOY, Rob Sauber, limited, 6½"	22.50	NR
1990	MOTHER'S JOY, Rob Sauber, limited, 10¼"	39.50	NR

Tribal Images

1994	BLACKFOOT CHIEFTAINS, Gregory Perillo, closed	35.00	RI
1994	CHEYENNE CHIEFTAINS, Gregory Perillo, closed	35.00	RI
1994	CROW CHIEFTAINS, Gregory Perillo, closed	35.00	RI
1994	SIOUX CHEIFTAINS, Gregory Perillo, closed	35.00	RI

Tribute

1982	I WANT YOU, James Montgomery Flagg, limited	29.95	40.00
1982	GEE, I WISH, Howard Chandler Christy, limited	29.95	40.00
1983	SOLDIER'S FAREWELL, Norman Rockwell, limited	29.95	40.00

Unicorn Magic (Signature Collection)

1983	MORNING ENCOUNTER, Jeffrey Ferreson, 7,500	50.00	NR
1983	AFTERNOON OFFERING, Jeffrey Ferreson, 7,500	50.00	NR

War Ponies of the Plains

1992	NIGHTSHADOW, Gregory Perillo, 75 days	27.00	NR
1992	WINDCATCHER, Gregory Perillo, 75 days	27.00	NR
1992	PRAIRIE PRANCER, Gregory Perillo, 75 days	27.00	NR
1992	THUNDERFOOT, Gregory Perillo, 75 days	27.00	NR
1992	PROUD COMPANION, Gregory Perillo, 75 days	27.00	NR
1992	SUN DANCER, Gregory Perillo, 75 days	27.00	NR
1992	FREE SPIRIT, Gregory Perillo, 75 days	27.00	NR
1992	GENTLE WARRIOR, Gregory Perillo, 75 days	27.00	NR

Young Chieftains

1985	YOUNG SITTING BULL, Gregory Perillo, 5,000	50.00	75.00
1985	YOUNG JOSEPH, Gregory Perillo, 5,000	50.00	75.00
1985	YOUNG RED CLOUD, Gregory Perillo, 5,000	50.00	75.00
1985	YOUNG GERONIMO, Gregory Perillo, 5,000	50.00	75.00
1985	YOUNG CRAZY HORSE, Gregory Perillo, 5,000	50.00	75.00

Young Emotions

1986	TEARS, Gregory Perillo, 5,000	—	—
1986	SMILES, Gregory Perillo, 5,000	—	—
	Set of 2	75.00	250.00

Special Issues

1983	INDIAN STYLE, Gregory Perillo, 17,500	50.00	NR
1984	THE LOVERS, Gregory Perillo, limited	50.00	100.00
1987	WE THE PEOPLE, Howard Chandler Christy, limited	35.00	NR
1989	GOD BLESS AMERICA, Rob Sauber, 14 days, 6½"	19.50	NR
1989	GOD BLESS AMERICA, Rob Sauber, 14 days, 10¼"	39.50	NR
1994	DIVINE INTERVENTION, MaGo	35.00	RI

ARTISTS OF THE WORLD UNITED STATES

(Fairmont China, Gorham, Sportscast)

Anthony Sidoni Series

		ISSUE	CURRENT
1982	THE LITTLE YANKEE, Anthony Sidoni, 15,000	35.00	NR
1983	LITTLE SATCHMO, Anthony Sidoni, 15,000	40.00	NR

Celebration

		ISSUE	CURRENT
1993	THE LORD'S CANDLE, Ted DeGrazia, 5,000	39.50	RI
1993	PIÑATA PARTY, Ted DeGrazia, 5,000	39.50	RI
1993	HOLIDAY LULLABY, Ted DeGrazia, 5,000	39.50	RI
1993	CAROLING, Ted DeGrazia, 5,000	39.50	RI

Children (Fairmont China, Gorham)

		ISSUE	CURRENT
1976	LOS NIÑOS, Ted DeGrazia, 5,000	35.00	1,100.00
1976	LOS NIÑOS, Ted DeGrazia, sgd, 500	100.00	1,500.00
1977	WHITE DOVE, Ted DeGrazia, 5,000	40.00	200.00
1977	WHITE DOVE, Ted DeGrazia, sgd, 500	100.00	450.00
1978	FLOWER GIRL, Ted DeGrazia, 9,500	45.00	250.00
1978	FLOWER GIRL, Ted DeGrazia, sgd, 500	100.00	450.00
1979	FLOWER BOY, Ted DeGrazia, 9,500	45.00	250.00
1979	FLOWER BOY, Ted DeGrazia, sgd, 500	100.00	450.00
1980	LITTLE COCOPAH GIRL, Ted DeGrazia, 9,500	50.00	195.00
1980	LITTLE COCOPAH GIRL, Ted DeGrazia, sgd, 500	100.00	450.00
1981	BEAUTIFUL BURDEN, Ted DeGrazia, 9,500	50.00	195.00
1981	BEAUTIFUL BURDEN, Ted DeGrazia, sgd, 500	100.00	450.00
1981	MERRY LITTLE INDIAN, Ted DeGrazia, 9,500	55.00	195.00
1981	MERRY LITTLE INDIAN, Ted DeGrazia, sgd, 500	100.00	450.00
1983	WONDERING, Ted DeGrazia, 10,000	60.00	160.00
1984	PINK PAPOOSE, Ted DeGrazia, 10,000	65.00	125.00
1985	SUNFLOWER BOY, Ted DeGrazia, 10,000	65.00	125.00

Children—Miniature

		ISSUE	CURRENT
1980	LOS NIÑOS, Ted DeGrazia, 5,000	15.00	300.00
1981	WHITE DOVE, Ted DeGrazia, 5,000	15.00	100.00
1982	FLOWER GIRL, Ted DeGrazia, 5,000	15.00	50.00
1982	FLOWER BOY, Ted DeGrazia, 5,000	15.00	55.00
1983	LITTLE COCOPAH GIRL, Ted DeGrazia, 5,000	15.00	70.00
1983	BEAUTIFUL BURDEN, Ted DeGrazia, 5,000	15.00	55.00
1984	MERRY LITTLE INDIAN, Ted DeGrazia, 5,000	15.00	65.00
1984	WONDERING, Ted DeGrazia, 5,000	15.00	50.00
1985	PINK PAPOOSE, Ted DeGrazia, 5,000	15.00	40.00
1985	SUNFLOWER BOY, Ted DeGrazia, 5,000	15.00	25.00

Children at Play

		ISSUE	CURRENT
1985	MY FIRST HORSE, Ted DeGrazia, 15,000	65.00	100.00
1986	GIRL WITH SEWING MACHINE, Ted DeGrazia, 15,000	65.00	150.00
1987	LOVE ME, Ted DeGrazia, 15,000	65.00	100.00
1988	MERRILY, MERRILY, MERRILY, Ted DeGrazia, 15,000	65.00	150.00
1989	MY FIRST ARROW, Ted DeGrazia, 15,000	65.00	100.00
1990	AWAY WITH MY KITE, Ted DeGrazia, 15,000	65.00	100.00

My First Horse

Girl with Little Brother

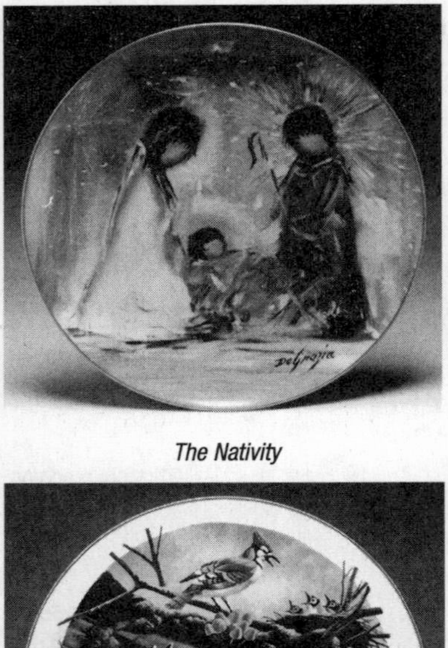

The Nativity

Freedom's Companion—Golden Eagle

No Peace in Paradise

DeGrazia and His Mountain

Photos courtesy of *Collectors News*

		ISSUE	CURRENT

Children of Aberdeen

		ISSUE	CURRENT
1979	GIRL WITH LITTLE BROTHER, Kee Fung Ng, 1 year	50.00	BR
1980	THE SAMPAN GIRL, Kee Fung Ng, 1 year	50.00	BR
1981	GIRL WITH LITTLE SISTER, Kee Fung Ng, 1 year	55.00	BR
1982	GIRL WITH SEASHELLS, Kee Fung Ng, 1 year	60.00	BR
1983	GIRL WITH SEABIRDS, Kee Fung Ng, 1 year	60.00	NR
1984	BROTHER AND SISTER, Kee Fung Ng, 1 year	60.00	NR

Children of Don Ruffin

		ISSUE	CURRENT
1980	FLOWERS FOR MOTHER, Don Ruffin, 5,000	50.00	NR
1981	LITTLE EAGLE, Don Ruffin, 5,000	55.00	NR
1982	THE LOST MOCCASINS, Don Ruffin, 7,500	60.00	NR
1982	SECURITY, Don Ruffin, 7,500	60.00	NR
1984	AMERICANS ALL, Don Ruffin, 7,500	60.00	NR

Children of the Sun

		ISSUE	CURRENT
1987	SPRING BLOSSOMS, Ted DeGrazia, 150 days	34.50	50.00
1987	MY LITTLE PINK BIRD, Ted DeGrazia, 150 days	34.50	50.00
1987	BRIGHT FLOWERS OF THE DESERT, Ted DeGrazia, 150 days	37.90	75.00
1988	GIFTS FROM THE SUN, Ted DeGrazia, 150 days	37.90	75.00
1988	GROWING GLORY, Ted DeGrazia, 150 days	37.90	50.00
1988	THE GENTLE WHITE DOVE, Ted DeGrazia, 150 days	37.90	75.00
1988	SUNFLOWER MAIDEN, Ted DeGrazia, 150 days	37.90	50.00
1989	SUN SHOWERS, Ted DeGrazia, 150 days	37.90	50.00

Don Ruffin Series

		ISSUE	CURRENT
1976	NAVAJO LULLABY, Don Ruffin, 9,500	40.00	90.00
1976	NAVAJO LULLABY, Don Ruffin, 500	100.00	230.00
1977	THROUGH THE YEARS, Don Ruffin, 5,000	45.00	150.00
1978	CHILD OF THE PUEBLO, Don Ruffin, 5,000	45.00	75.00
1979	COLIMA MADONNA, Don Ruffin, 5,000	50.00	NR
1980	SUN KACHIMA, Don Ruffin, 5,000	50.00	NR
1981	INNER PEACE, Don Ruffin, 5,000	55.00	NR
1982	MADONNA OF THE CROSS, Don Ruffin, 5,000	60.00	NR
1983	NAVAJO PRINCESS, Don Ruffin, 5,000	60.00	NR
1983	SECURITY, Don Ruffin, 7,500	60.00	NR
1984	AMERICANS ALL, Don Ruffin, 7,500	60.00	NR

Endangered Birds

		ISSUE	CURRENT
1976	KIRTLAND'S WARBLER, 5,000	195.00	NR
1976	AMERICAN EAGLE, 5,000	195.00	NR
1977	PEREGRINE FALCON, 5,000	200.00	NR

Fiesta of the Children

		ISSUE	CURRENT
1990	WELCOME TO THE FIESTA, Ted DeGrazia, 150 days	34.50	BR
1990	CASTANETS IN BLOOM, Ted DeGrazia, 150 days	34.50	NR
1991	FIESTA FLOWERS, Ted DeGrazia, 150 days	34.50	NR
1991	FIESTA ANGELS, Ted DeGrazia, 150 days	34.50	NR

Floral Fiesta

		ISSUE	CURRENT
1994	LITTLE FLOWER VENDOR, Ted DeGrazia, 5,000	39.50	RI

		ISSUE	CURRENT
1994	FLOWERS FOR MOTHER, Ted DeGrazia, 5,000	39.50	RI
1995	FLORAL INNOCENCE, Ted DeGrazia, 5,000	39.50	RI
1995	FLORAL BOUQUET, Ted DeGrazia, 5,000	39.50	RI
1996	FLORAL CELEBRATION, Ted DeGrazia, 5,000	39.50	RI
1996	FLORAL FIESTA, Ted DeGrazia, 5,000	39.50	RI

Holiday (Fairmont China)

1976	FESTIVAL OF LIGHTS, Ted DeGrazia, 9,500	45.00	375.00
1976	FESTIVAL OF LIGHTS, Ted DeGrazia, sgd, 500	100.00	600.00
1977	BELL OF HOPE, Ted DeGrazia, 9,500	45.00	200.00
1977	BELL OF HOPE, Ted DeGrazia, sgd, 500	100.00	450.00
1978	LITTLE MADONNA, Ted DeGrazia, 9,500	45.00	200.00
1978	LITTLE MADONNA, Ted DeGrazia, sgd, 500	100.00	500.00
1979	THE NATIVITY, Ted DeGrazia, 9,500	50.00	275.00
1979	THE NATIVITY, Ted DeGrazia, sgd, 500	100.00	500.00
1980	LITTLE PIMA DRUMMER, Ted DeGrazia, 9,500	50.00	125.00
1980	LITTLE PIMA DRUMMER, Ted DeGrazia, sgd, 500	100.00	450.00
1981	A LITTLE PRAYER—CHRISTMAS ANGEL, Ted DeGrazia, 9,500	100.00	125.00
1981	A LITTLE PRAYER—CHRISTMAS ANGEL, Ted DeGrazia, sgd, 500	100.00	450.00
1982	BLUE BOY, Ted DeGrazia, 10,000	60.00	125.00
1982	BLUE BOY, Ted DeGrazia, sgd, 96	100.00	500.00
1983	HEAVENLY BLESSINGS, Ted DeGrazia, 10,000	65.00	130.00
1984	NAVAJO MADONNA, Ted DeGrazia, 10,000	65.00	95.00
1985	SAGUARO DANCE, Ted DeGrazia, 10,000	65.00	125.00

Holiday—Miniature

1980	FESTIVAL OF LIGHTS, Ted DeGrazia, 5,000	15.00	200.00
1981	BELL OF HOPE, Ted DeGrazia, 5,000	15.00	95.00
1982	LITTLE MADONNA, Ted DeGrazia, 5,000	15.00	95.00
1982	THE NATIVITY, Ted DeGrazia, 5,000	15.00	95.00
1983	LITTLE PIMA DRUMMER, Ted DeGrazia, 5,000	15.00	25.00
1983	LITTLE PRAYER, Ted DeGrazia, 5,000	20.00	NR
1984	BLUE BOY, Ted DeGrazia, 5,000	20.00	NR
1984	HEAVENLY BLESSINGS, Ted DeGrazia, 5,000	20.00	NR
1985	NAVAJO MADONNA, Ted DeGrazia, 5,000	20.00	50.00
1985	SAGUARO DANCE, Ted DeGrazia, 5,000	20.00	75.00

Prowlers of the Clouds

1981	FIRST LIGHT—GREAT HORNED OWL, Larry Toschik, 5,000	55.00	NR
1981	HIS GOLDEN THRONE—SCREECH OWL, Larry Toschik, 5,000	55.00	NR
1982	FREEDOM'S SYMBOL—BALD EAGLE, Larry Toschik, 5,000	60.00	NR
1982	FREEDOM'S COMPANION—GOLDEN EAGLE, Larry Toschik, 5,000	60.00	NR

Special Release

1996	WEDDING PARTY, Ted DeGrazia, 5,000	49.50	RI

Sports Announcers (Sportscast)

NA	HARRY CARAY, Aaron Hicks, sgd	97.50	NR

Sweetheart Series

1984	WE BELIEVE, Rusty Money, 10,000	40.00	NR

Vel Miller Series

		ISSUE	CURRENT
1982	MAMA'S ROSE, Vel Miller, 15,000	35.00	NR
1983	PAPA'S BOY, Vel Miller, 15,000	40.00	NR

Western Series

1986	MORNING RIDE, Ted DeGrazia, 5,000	65.00	100.00
1987	BRONCO, Ted DeGrazia, 5,000	65.00	100.00
1988	APACHE SCOUT, Ted DeGrazia, 5,000	65.00	100.00
1989	ALONE, Ted DeGrazia, 5,000	65.00	100.00

Woodland Friends

1983	SPRING OUTING—WHITETAIL DEER, Larry Toschik, 5,000	60.00	NR
1984	NO REST FOR THE NIGHT SHIFT, Larry Toschik, 5,000	60.00	NR
1984	SPRING OUTING, Larry Toschik, 5,000	60.00	NR
1985	NO PEACE IN PARADISE, Larry Toschik, 5,000	60.00	NR

World of Game Birds

1977	MALLARDS—WHISTLING IN, Larry Toschik, 5,000	45.00	80.00
1978	MAYTIME—GAMBEL QUAIL, Larry Toschik, 5,000	45.00	NR
1979	AMERICAN AUTUMN—RING-NECKED PHEASANT, Larry Toschik, 5,000	50.00	NR
1980	NOVEMBER JOURNEY—CANADA GEESE, Larry Toschik, 5,000	50.00	NR

Single Issues

1977	THE STATESMAN, Don Ruffin, 3,500	65.00	BR
1977	THE CLOWN ALSO CRIES, Don Ruffin, 7,500	65.00	BR

Special Issues

1983	DEGRAZIA AND HIS MOUNTAIN, Larry Toschik, 15,000	65.00	NR
1984	LITTLE GIRL PAINTS DEGRAZIA, Ted DeGrazia, 12,500	65.00	NR

ART WORLD OF BOURGEAULT UNITED STATES

English Countryside

1981	THE COUNTRY SQUIRE, Robert Bourgeault, 1,500	70.00	250.00
1981	THE WILLOWS, Robert Bourgeault, 1,500	85.00	250.00
1982	ROSE COTTAGE, Robert Bourgeault, 1,500	90.00	250.00
1983	THATCHED BEAUTY, Robert Bourgeault, 1,500	95.00	250.00

English Countryside, Single Issues

1984	THE ANNE HATHAWAY COTTAGE, Robert Bourgeault, 500	150.00	500.00
1986	SUFFOLK PINK, Robert Bourgeault, 50	220.00	250.00
1988	STUART HOUSE, Robert Bourgeault, 50	325.00	500.00
1989	LARK RISE, Robert Bourgeault, 50	450.00	500.00

Royal Gainsborough

1990	THE LISA-CAROLINE, Robert Bourgeault	75.00	NR
1991	A GAINSBOROUGH LADY, Robert Bourgeault	NA	NA

Royal Literary Series

1986	JOHN BUNYAN COTTAGE, Robert Bourgeault, 4,500	60.00	75.00

		ISSUE	CURRENT
1987	THOMAS HARDY COTTAGE, Robert Bourgeault, 4,500	65.00	80.00
1988	JOHN MILTON COTTAGE, Robert Bourgeault, 4,500	65.00	80.00
1989	ANNE HATHAWAY COTTAGE, Robert Bourgeault, 4,500	65.00	80.00

Where Is England?

1990	FORGET-ME-NOT, Robert Bourgeault, 50	525.00	600.00
1991	THE FLEECE INN, Robert Bourgeault, 50	525.00	600.00
1992	MILBROOK HOUSE, Robert Bourgeault, 50	525.00	NR
1993	COTSWOLD BEAUTY, Robert Bourgeault, 50	525.00	RI

Where Is Scotland?

1991	EILEAN DONAN CASTLE, Robert Bourgeault, 50	525.00	600.00

Single Issues

1986	ROSE COTTAGE, Robert Bourgeault, 1,500	150.00	NR
1986	ANNE HATHAWAY COTTAGE, Robert Bourgeault, 500	250.00	NR

ARZBERG PORCELAIN GERMANY

Birds of the Country Year

1983	JANUARY, Martin Camm	NA	NA
1983	FEBRUARY, Martin Camm	NA	NA
1983	MARCH, Martin Camm	NA	NA
1983	APRIL, Martin Camm	NA	NA
1984	MAY, Martin Camm	NA	NA
1984	JUNE, Martin Camm	NA	NA
1984	JULY, Martin Camm	NA	NA
1984	AUGUST, Martin Camm	NA	NA
1985	SEPTEMBER, Martin Camm	NA	NA
1985	OCTOBER, Martin Camm	NA	NA
1985	NOVEMBER, Martin Camm	NA	NA
1985	DECEMBER, Martin Camm	NA	NA

AVONDALE UNITED STATES

Annual Christmas

1978	...AND THE HEAVENS REJOICED, Frances Taylor Williams, 6,500	90.00	NR
1982	...AND THERE CAME THE WISEMEN, Frances Taylor Williams, 6,500	90.00	NR
1983	THE SHEPHERD, Frances Taylor Williams, 6,500	90.00	NR

Artistry of Almazetta Casey

1979	PRIMA BALLERINA, Almazetta Casey, 15,000	70.00	NR
1979	COURT JESTERS, Almazetta Casey, 10,000	70.00	NR

Cameos of Childhood

1978	MELISSA, Frances Taylor Williams, 23,050	65.00	NR
1979	FIRST BORN, Frances Taylor Williams, 12,000	70.00	NR
1980	MELISSA'S BROTHER, Frances Taylor Williams, 8,400	70.00	NR
1981	DADDY AND I, Frances Taylor Williams, 10,000	75.00	NR

Melissa's Brother
Photo courtesy of *Collectors News*

Maiden of the Sea
Photo courtesy of *Collectors News*

		ISSUE	CURRENT
Growing Up			
1982	A RIBBON FOR HER HAIR, Frances Taylor Williams, 6,500	75.00	NR
Mother's Day			
1984	JUST LIKE MOTHER, Frances Taylor Williams, 6,500	75.00	NR
Myths of the Sea			
1979	POSEIDON, Gregg Appleby, 15,000	70.00	NR
1981	MAIDEN OF THE SEA, Gregg Appleby, 15,000	75.00	NR

AYNSLEY GREAT BRITAIN

A Christmas Carol			
1979	MR. FEZZIWIG'S BALL, 1 year	30.00	NR
1980	MARLEY'S GHOST, 1 year	36.00	NR
Single Issues			
1969	PRINCE OF WALES, 1,000	50.00	NR
1970	THE MAYFLOWER, 1,000	35.00	NR
1973	1,000 YEARS OF ENGLISH MONARCHY, 1,000	30.00	NR

B & J ART DESIGNS UNITED STATES

Old-Fashioned Christmas			
1983	CAROL, Jan Hagara, 15,000	45.00	NR
Old-Fashioned Country			
1984	CHRISTINA, Jan Hagara, 20,000	39.00	NR
1985	LAUREL, Jan Hagara, 15,000	42.50	NR

Carol
Photo courtesy of *Collectors News*

Adrianne and the Bye-Lo Doll
Photo courtesy of *Collectors News*

Yesterday's Children

		ISSUE	CURRENT
1978	LISA AND THE JUMEAU DOLL, Jan Hagara, 5,000	60.00	95.00
1979	ADRIANNE AND THE BYE-LO DOLL, Jan Hagara, 5,000	60.00	90.00
1980	LYDIA AND THE SHIRLEY TEMPLE DOLL, Jan Hagara, 5,000	60.00	75.00
1981	MELANIE AND THE SCARLETT O'HARA DOLL, Jan Hagara, 5,000	60.00	NR

BARANYK DESIGN UNITED STATES

Hart

1997	HART—ONE, Johnny Hart, 100 days	25.00	RI
1997	HART—TWO, Johnny Hart, 100 days	25.00	RI

BAREUTHER GERMANY

Bareuther Christmas (Worldwide Collectibles)

1996	SLEDDING PARTY, open	67.50	RI
1997	JOY OF CHRISTMAS EVE, 1 year	67.50	RI

Bareuther Mother's Day (Worldwide Collectibles)

1997	MOTHER'S HAPPINESS, Hans Schiffmann, 1 year	67.50	RI

Christmas

1967	STIFTSKIRCHE, Hans Mueller, 10,000	12.00	85.00
1968	KAPPLKIRCHE, Hans Mueller, 10,000	12.00	25.00
1969	CHRISTKINDLEMARKT, Hans Mueller, 10,000	12.00	20.00
1970	CHAPEL IN OBERNDORF, Hans Mueller, 10,000	12.50	20.00
1971	TOYS FOR SALE, Hans Mueller, from drawing by Ludwig Ricter, 10,000	12.75	25.00
1972	CHRISTMAS IN MUNICH, Hans Mueller, 10,000	14.50	25.00
1973	SLEIGH RIDE, Hans Mueller, 10,000	15.00	35.00
1974	BLACK FOREST CHURCH, Hans Mueller, 10,000	19.00	NR
1975	SNOWMAN, Hans Mueller, 10,000	21.50	30.00

		ISSUE	CURRENT
1976	CHAPEL IN THE HILLS, Hans Mueller, 10,000	23.50	NR
1977	STORY TIME, Hans Mueller, 10,000	24.50	40.00
1978	MITTENWALD, Hans Mueller, 10,000	27.50	NR
1979	WINTER DAY, Hans Mueller, 10,000	35.00	NR
1980	MITTENBERG, Hans Mueller, 10,000	37.50	NR
1980	WALK IN THE FOREST, Hans Mueller, 10,000	39.50	NR
1982	BAD WIMPFEN, Hans Mueller, 10,000	39.50	NR
1983	NIGHT BEFORE CHRISTMAS, Hans Mueller, 10,000	39.50	NR
1984	ZEIL ON THE RIVER MAIN, Hans Mueller, 10,000	42.50	NR
1985	WINTER WONDERLAND, Hans Mueller, 10,000	42.50	55.00
1986	CHRISTMAS IN FORCHHEIM, Hans Mueller, 10,000	42.50	70.00
1987	DECORATING THE TREE, Hans Mueller, 10,000	42.50	85.00
1988	ST. COLOMAN CHURCH, Hans Mueller, 10,000	52.50	65.00
1989	SLEIGH RIDE, Hans Mueller, 10,000	52.50	80.00
1990	THE OLD FORGE IN ROTHENBURG, Hans Mueller, 10,000	52.50	NR
1991	CHRISTMAS JOY, Hans Mueller, 10,000	56.50	NR
1992	MARKET PLACE IN HEPPENHEIM, Hans Mueller, 10,000	59.50	NR
1993	WINTER FUN, Hans Mueller, 10,000	59.50	RI
1994	COMING HOME FOR CHRISTMAS, Hans Mueller, 10,000	59.50	RI

Danish Church

1968	ROSKILDE CATHEDRAL, 1 year	12.00	25.00
1969	RIBE CATHEDRAL, 1 year	12.00	25.00
1970	MARMOR KIRKEN, 1 year	13.00	NR
1971	EJBY CHURCH, 1 year	13.00	NR
1972	KALUNDBORG KIRKEN, 1 year	13.00	20.00
1973	GRUNDTVIG KIRKEN, 1 year	15.00	NR
1974	BROAGER KIRKEN, 1 year	15.00	NR
1975	ST. KNUDS KIRKEN, 1 year	20.00	NR
1976	OSTERLAS KIRKEN, 1 year	20.00	NR
1977	BUDOLFI KIRKEN, 1 year	20.00	NR
1978	HADERSLAV CATHEDRAL, 1 year	20.00	NR
1979	HOLMENS CHURCH, 1 year	20.00	NR

Esteban Murillo Series

1972	FRUIT VENDORS COUNTING MONEY, Bartolomé Esteban Murillo	12.00	45.00
1972	BOYS EATING PASTRY, Bartolomé Esteban Murillo	12.00	45.00
1972	BEGGAR BOYS PLAYING DICE, Bartolomé Esteban Murillo	42.00	NR
1972	BOYS EATING MELONS AND GRAPES, Bartolomé Esteban Murillo	42.00	NR

Father's Day

1969	CASTLE NEUSCHWANSTEIN, Hans Mueller, 1 year	10.50	55.00
1970	CASTLE PFALZ, Hans Mueller, 1 year	12.50	20.00
1971	CASTLE HEIDELBERG, Hans Mueller, 1 year	12.75	25.00
1972	CASTLE HOHENSCHWANGAN, Hans Mueller, 1 year	14.50	25.00
1973	CASTLE KATZ, Hans Mueller, 1 year	15.00	30.00
1974	WURZBURG CASTLE, Hans Mueller, 1 year	19.00	50.00
1975	CASTLE LICHTENSTEIN, Hans Mueller, 1 year	21.50	35.00
1976	CASTLE HOHENZOLLERN, Hans Mueller, 1 year	23.50	30.00
1977	CASTLE ELTZ, Hans Mueller, 1 year	24.50	30.00
1978	CASTLE FALKENSTEIN, Hans Mueller, 1 year	27.50	NR
1979	CASTLE REINSTEIN, Hans Mueller, 2,500	35.00	NR
1980	CASTLE COCHEM, Hans Mueller, 2,500	37.50	NR

		ISSUE	CURRENT
1981	CASTLE GUTENFELS, Hans Mueller, 2,500	39.50	NR
1982	CASTLE ZWINGERBERG, Hans Mueller, 2,500	39.50	NR
1983	CASTLE LAUNSTEIN, Hans Mueller, 2,500	39.50	NR
1984	CASTLE NUENSTEIN, Hans Mueller, 2,500	42.50	NR

Mother's Day

1969	MOTHER AND CHILDREN, Ludwig Richter, 5,000	10.50	75.00
1970	MOTHER AND CHILDREN, Ludwig Richter, 5,000	12.50	30.00
1971	MOTHER AND CHILDREN, Ludwig Richter, 5,000	12.75	20.00
1972	MOTHER AND CHILDREN, Ludwig Richter, 5,000	15.00	NR
1973	MOTHER AND CHILDREN, Ludwig Richter, 5,000	15.00	NR
1974	MUSICAL CHILDREN, Ludwig Richter, 5,000	19.00	35.00
1975	SPRING OUTING, Ludwig Richter, 5,000	21.50	NR
1976	ROCKING THE CRADLE, Ludwig Richter, 5,000	23.50	NR
1977	NOON FEEDING, Ludwig Richter, 5,000	24.50	NR
1978	BLIND MAN'S BLUFF, Ludwig Richter, 5,000	27.50	NR
1979	MOTHER'S LOVE, Ludwig Richter, 5,000	37.50	NR
1980	THE FIRST CHERRIES, Ludwig Richter, 5,000	37.50	NR
1981	PLAYTIME, Ludwig Richter, 5,000	39.50	NR
1982	SUPPERTIME, Ludwig Richter, 5,000	39.50	NR
1983	ON THE FARM, Ludwig Richter, 5,000	39.50	NR
1984	VILLAGE CHILDREN, Ludwig Richter, 5,000	42.50	NR

Thanksgiving

1971	FIRST THANKSGIVING, 2,500	13.50	35.00
1972	HARVEST, 2,500	14.50	20.00
1973	COUNTRY ROAD IN AUTUMN, 2,500	15.00	NR
1974	OLD MILL, 2,500	19.00	NR
1975	WILD DEER IN FOREST, 2,500	21.50	NR
1976	THANKSGIVING ON FARM, 2,500	23.50	NR
1977	HORSES, Hans Mueller, 2,500	24.50	NR
1978	APPLE HARVEST, Hans Mueller, 2,500	27.50	NR
1979	NOONTIME, Hans Mueller, 2,500	35.00	NR
1980	LONGHORNS, Hans Mueller, 2,500	37.50	NR
1981	GATHERING WHEAT, Hans Mueller, 2,500	39.50	NR
1982	AUTUMN, Hans Mueller, 2,500	39.50	NR
1983	HARROW, Hans Mueller, 2,500	39.50	NR
1984	FARMLAND, Hans Mueller, 2,500	42.50	NR

BARTHMANN GERMANY

Christmas

1977	MARY WITH CHILD, 300	326.00	NR
1978	ADORATION OF CHILD, 500	326.00	NR
1979	HOLY MOTHER OF KASANSKAJA, 500	361.00	NR
1980	HOLY MOTHER BY KYKOS, 500	385.00	NR

BAYEL OF FRANCE FRANCE

Bicentennial

1974	LIBERTY BELL, 500	50.00	NR

		ISSUE	CURRENT
1975	INDEPENDENCE HALL, 500	60.00	NR
1976	SPREAD EAGLE, 500	60.00	NR

Eagle

1974	EAGLE HEAD, 300	50.00	NR
1974	EAGLE IN FLIGHT, 300	50.00	NR

Flowers

1972	ROSE, 300	50.00	NR
1973	LILIES, 300	50.00	NR
1973	ORCHID, 300	50.00	NR

BEACON PLATE MANUFACTURING UNITED STATES

Pace Setters

1987	FREDERICK DOUGLASS, 2,500	53.50	NR

BELLEEK POTTERY GREAT BRITAIN

Christmas

1970	CASTLE CALDWELL, 7,500	25.00	80.00
1971	CELTIC CROSS, 7,500	25.00	50.00
1972	FLIGHT OF THE EARLS, 7,500	30.00	NR
1973	TRIBUTE TO YEATS, 7,500	38.50	NR
1974	DEVENISH ISLAND, 7,500	45.00	175.00
1975	THE CELTIC CROSS, 7,500	48.00	75.00
1976	DOVE OF PEACE, 7,500	55.00	NR
1977	WREN, 7,500	55.00	NR

Holiday Scenes in Ireland

1991	TRAVELING HOME, 7,500	75.00	NR
1992	BEARING GIFTS, 7,500	75.00	RI

Irish Wildlife

1978	A LEAPING SALMON	55.00	70.00
1979	HARE AT REST	58.50	65.00
1980	THE HEDGEHOG	66.50	NR
1981	RED SQUIRREL	78.00	NR
1982	IRISH SEAL	78.00	NR
1983	RED FOX	85.00	NR

St. Patrick's Day

1986	ST. PATRICK BANISHING THE SNAKES FROM IRELAND, Fergus Cleary, 10,000	75.00	NR

BENGOUGH CANADA

Christmas

1972	CHARLES DICKENS CHRISTMAS CAROL, 490	125.00	NR

		ISSUE	CURRENT

Northwest Mounted Police

		ISSUE	CURRENT
1972	1898 DRESS UNIFORM, 1,000	140.00	NR
1972	FIRST UNIFORM, 1,000	140.00	NR
1976	CHAPEL IN THE HILLS, Hans Mueller, 10,000	23.50	NR
1977	STORY TIME, Hans Mueller, 10,000	24.50	40.00
1978	MITTENWALD, Hans Mueller, 10,000	27.50	NR
1979	WINTER DAY, Hans Mueller, 10,000	35.00	NR
1980	MITTENBERG, Hans Mueller, 10,000	37.50	NR

Royal Canadian Police

1972	ORDER DRESS, 1,000	140.00	NR

BERLIN DESIGN GERMANY

Christmas

1970	CHRISTMAS IN BERNKASTEL, 4,000	14.50	125.00
1971	CHRISTMAS IN ROTHENBURG, 20,000	14.50	40.00
1972	CHRISTMAS IN MICHELSTADT, 20,000	15.00	50.00
1973	CHRISTMAS IN WENDELSTEIN, 20,000	20.00	45.00
1974	CHRISTMAS IN BREMEN, 20,000	25.00	40.00
1975	CHRISTMAS IN DORTLAND, 20,000	30.00	NR
1976	CHRISTMAS IN AUGSBURG, 20,000	32.00	50.00
1977	CHRISTMAS IN HAMBURG, 20,000	32.00	NR
1978	CHRISTMAS IN BERLIN, 20,000	36.00	75.00
1979	CHRISTMAS IN GREETSIEL, 20,000	47.50	60.00
1980	CHRISTMAS IN MITTENBERG, 20,000	50.00	NR
1981	CHRISTMAS EVE IN HAHNENKLEE, 20,000	55.00	NR
1982	CHRISTMAS EVE IN WASSERBERG, 20,000	55.00	NR
1983	CHRISTMAS IN OBERNDORF, 20,000	55.00	NR
1984	CHRISTMAS IN RAMSAU, 20,000	55.00	NR
1985	CHRISTMAS IN BAD WIMPFEN, 20,000	55.00	NR
1986	CHIRSTMAS EVE IN GELNHAUS, 20,000	65.00	NR
1987	CHRISTMAS EVE IN GOSLAR, 20,000	65.00	NR
1988	CHRISTMAS EVE IN RUHPOLDING, 20,000	65.00	NR
1989	CHRISTMAS EVE IN FRIEDECHSDADT, 20,000	80.00	NR
1990	CHRISTMAS EVE IN PARTENKIRCHEN, 20,000	80.00	NR
1991	CHRISTMAS EVE IN ALLENDORF, 20,000	80.00	NR

Father's Day

1971	BROOKLYN BRIDGE ON OPENING DAY, 12,000	14.50	20.00
1972	CONTINENT SPANNED, 3,000	15.00	35.00
1973	LANDING OF COLUMBUS, 2,000	18.00	40.00
1974	ADORN'S BALLOON, 1 year	25.00	35.00

Historical

1975	WASHINGTON CROSSING THE DELAWARE, 1 year	30.00	NR
1976	TOM THUMB, 1 year	32.00	NR
1977	ZEPPELIN, 1 year	32.00	NR
1978	BENZ MOTOR CAR MUNICH, 10,000	36.00	NR
1979	JOHANNES GUTENBERG AT MAINZ, 10,000	47.50	NR

		ISSUE	CURRENT

Holiday Week of the Family Kappelmann

1984	MONDAY, limited	33.00	NR
1984	TUESDAY, limited	33.00	NR
1985	WEDNESDAY, Detlev Nitschke, limited	33.00	NR
1985	THURSDAY, limited	35.00	NR
1985	FRIDAY, limited	35.00	NR
1986	SATURDAY, limited	35.00	NR
1986	SUNDAY, limited	35.00	BR

Mother's Day

1971	GREY POODLES, 20,000	14.50	25.00
1972	FLEDGLINGS, 10,00	15.00	25.00
1973	DUCK FAMILY, 5,000	16.50	40.00
1974	SQUIRRELS, 6,000	22.50	40.00
1975	CATS, 6,000	30.00	40.00
1976	DEER, 6,000	32.00	NR
1977	STORKS, 6,000	32.00	NR
1978	MARE AND FOAL, 6,000	36.00	NR
1979	SWANS WITH CYGNETS, 6,000	47.50	NR
1980	GOAT FAMILY, 6,000	55.00	NR
1981	DACHSHUND AND PUPPIES, 1 year	50.00	NR

BETOURNE STUDIOS FRANCE

Jean-Paul Loup Christmas

1971	NOEL, Jean-Paul Loup, 300	125.00	1,000.00
1972	NOEL, Jean-Paul Loup, 300	150.00	700.00
1973	NOEL, Jean-Paul Loup, 300	175.00	500.00
1974	NOEL, Jean-Paul Loup, 400	200.00	500.00
1975	NOEL, Jean-Paul Loup, 250	250.00	500.00
1976	NOEL, Jean-Paul Loup, 150	300.00	600.00

Mother's Day

1974	MOTHER AND CHILD, 500	250.00	1,200.00
1975	MOTHER'S DAY, 400	285.00	300.00
1976	MOTHER AND CHILD, 250	300.00	600.00

BIEDERMANN & SONS

Single Issues

1993	FOUR CALLING BIRDS, 250	17.50	RI
1994	DRUMMER BOY, 250	20.00	RI

BING & GRØNDAHL DENMARK

American Christmas Heritage

1996	THE STATUE OF LIBERTY, C. Magadini, 1 year	47.50	RI
1997	CHRISTMAS EVE AT THE LINCOLN MEMORIAL, C. Magadini, 1 year	47.50	RI

		ISSUE	CURRENT

Bicentennial

1976	E PLURIBUS UNUM, 1 year	50.00	NR

Carl Larsson Miniature

1986	THE FLOWER WINDOW, Carl Larsson, 15,000	15.00	NR
1986	LUNCH UNDER THE BIRCH TREE, Carl Larsson, 15,000	15.00	NR
1986	WINTER AND THE OLD BARN, Carl Larsson, 15,000	15.00	NR
1986	MAMA'S ROOM, Carl Larsson, 15,000	15.00	NR
1986	IDUNA'S NEW DRESS, Carl Larsson, 15,000	15.00	NR
1986	WORKING IN THE WOODS, Carl Larsson, 15,000	15.00	NR
1986	HARVEST, Carl Larsson, 15,000	15.00	NR
1986	POTATO HARVEST, Carl Larsson, 15,000	15.00	NR
1986	FISHING, Carl Larsson, 15,000	15.00	NR
1986	OPENING DAY OF THE CRAYFISH SEASON, Carl Larsson, 15,000	15.00	NR
1986	AZALEA, Carl Larsson, 15,000	15.00	NR
1986	APPLE HARVEST, Carl Larsson, 15,000	15.00	NR

Carl Larsson Series

1977	FLOWERS ON WINDOWSILL, Carl Larsson, 7,500, set of 4	150.00	NR
1977	BREAKFAST UNDER BIG BIRCH, Carl Larsson, 7,500, set of 4	150.00	NR
1977	YARD AND WAREHOUSE, Carl Larsson, 7,500, set of 4	150.00	NR
1977	KITCHEN, Carl Larsson, 7,500, set of 4	150.00	NR
1978	FIRST BORN, Carl Larsson, 7,500, set of 4	150.00	NR
1978	ROOM FOR MOTHER AND CHILDREN, Carl Larsson, 7,500, set of 4	150.00	NR
1978	PORTRAIT OF INGA-MARIA THIEL, Carl Larsson, 7,500, set of 4	150.00	NR
1978	IDUNA, Carl Larsson, 7,500, set of 4	150.00	NR
1979	FORESTRY, Carl Larsson, 7,500, set of 4	150.00	NR
1979	CUTTING GRASS, Carl Larsson, 7,500, set of 4	150.00	NR
1979	POTATO HARVEST, Carl Larsson, 7,500, set of 4	150.00	NR
1979	FISHERY, Carl Larsson, 7,500, set of 4	150.00	NR

Cat Portraits

1987	MANX AND KITTENS, L. Alice Hanbey, 14,500	39.50	NR

Manx and Kittens
Photo courtesy of *Collectors News*

A Joyful Flight
Photo courtesy of *Collectors News*

		ISSUE	CURRENT
1987	PERSIAN AND KITTENS, L. Alice Hanbey, 14,500	39.50	NR
1987	SOMALI AND KITTENS, L. Alice Hanbey, 14,500	39.50	NR
1987	BURMESE AND KITTENS, L. Alice Hanbey, 14,500	39.50	NR

Centennial Anniversary Commemoratives

1995	CENTENNIAL PLAQUETTES, Series of ten 5" plates featuring Bing & Grøndahl motifs: 1895, 1905, 1919, 1927, 1932, 1945, 1954, 1967, 1974, 1982, 1 year	250.00	RI
1995	CENTENNIAL PLATE: BEHIND THE FROZEN WINDOW, Franz A. Hallin, 10,000	39.50	RI
1995	CENTENNIAL PLATTER: TOWERS OF COPENHAGEN, Jørgen Nielsen, 7,500	195.00	RI

Centennial Collection

1991	CROWS ENJOYING CHRISTMAS, Dahl Jensen, 1 year	59.50	NR
1992	COPENHAGEN CHRISTMAS, Hans Flugenring, 1 year	59.50	NR
1993	CHRISTMAS ELF, Henry Thelander, 1 year	59.50	RI
1994	CHRISTMAS IN CHURCH, Henry Thelander, 1 year	59.50	RI
1995	BEHIND THE FROZEN WINDOW, Franz August Hallin, 1 year	59.50	RI

Children's Day

1985	THE MAGICAL TEA PARTY, Carole Roller, 1 year	24.50	BR
1986	A JOYFUL FLIGHT, Carole Roller, 1 year	26.50	BR
1987	THE LITTLE GARDENERS, Carole Roller, 1 year	29.50	NR
1988	WASH DAY, Carole Roller, 1 year	34.50	NR
1989	BEDTIME, Carole Roller, 1 year	37.00	NR
1990	MY FAVORITE DRESS, Sven Vestergaard, 1 year	37.00	NR
1991	FUN ON THE BEACH, Sven Vestergaard, 1 year	39.50	60.00
1992	A SUMMER DAY IN THE MEADOW, Sven Vestergaard, 1 year	39.50	NR
1993	THE CAROUSEL, Sven Vestergaard, 1 year	39.50	RI
1994	THE LITTLE FISHERMAN, Sven Vestergaard, 1 year	39.50	RI
1995	MY FIRST BOOK, Sven Vestergaard, 1 year	39.50	RI
1996	THE LITTLE RACERS, Sven Vestergaard, 1 year	39.50	RI
1997	BATH TIME, Sven Vestergaard, 1 year	39.50	RI

Christmas

1895	BEHIND THE FROZEN WINDOW, Franz August Hallin, 1 year	.50	6,000.00
1896	NEW MOON OVER SNOW-COVERED TREES, Franz August Hallin, 1 year	.50	2,250.00
1897	CHRISTMAS MEAL OF THE SPARROWS, Franz August Hallin, 1 year	.75	1,000.00
1898	CHRISTMAS ROSES AND CHRISTMAS STAR, Fanny Garde, 1 year	.75	950.00
1899	THE CROWS ENJOYING CHRISTMAS, Dahl Jensen, 1 year	.75	1,250.00
1900	CHURCH BELLS CHIMING IN CHRISTMAS, Dahl Jensen, 1 year	.75	850.00
1901	THE THREE WISE MEN FROM THE EAST, S. Sabra, 1 year	1.00	600.00
1902	INTERIOR OF A GOTHIC CHURCH, Dahl Jensen, 1 year	1.00	500.00
1903	HAPPY EXPECTATION OF CHILDREN, Margrethe Hyldahl, 1 year	1.00	350.00
1904	VIEW OF COPENHAGEN FROM FREDERIKSBERG HILL, Cathinka Olsen, 1 year	1.00	100.00
1905	ANXIETY OF THE COMING CHRISTMAS NIGHT, Dahl Jensen, 1 year	1.00	150.00
1906	SLEIGHING TO CHURCH ON CHRISTMAS EVE, Dahl Jensen, 1 year	1.00	125.00
1907	THE LITTLE MATCH GIRL, Ingeborg Plockross, 1 year	1.00	100.00
1908	ST. PETRI CHURCH OF COPENHAGEN, Povl Jorgensen, 1 year	1.00	150.00
1909	HAPPINESS OVER THE YULE TREE, Aarestrup, 1 year	1.50	75.00
1910	THE OLD ORGANIST, C. Ersgaard, 1 year	1.50	100.00
1911	FIRST IT WAS SUNG BY ANGELS TO SHEPHERDS, Harald Moltke, 1 year	1.50	100.00
1912	GOING TO CHURCH ON CHRISTMAS EVE, Einar Hansen, 1 year	1.50	70.00
1913	BRINGING HOME THE YULE TREE, T. Larsen, 1 year	1.50	90.00

		ISSUE	CURRENT
1914	ROYAL CASTLE OF AMALIENBORG, COPENHAGEN, T. Larsen, 1 year	1.50	80.00
1915	DOG GETTING DOUBLE MEAL ON CHRISTMAS EVE, Dahl Jensen, 1 year	1.50	150.00
1916	CHRISTMAS PRAYER OF THE SPARROWS, J. Bloch Jorgensen, 1 year	1.50	90.00
1917	ARRIVAL OF THE CHRISTMAS BOAT, Achton Friis, 1 year	1.50	75.00
1918	FISHING BOAT RETURNING HOME FOR CHRISTMAS, Achton Friis, 1 year	1.50	100.00
1919	OUTSIDE THE LIGHTED WINDOW, Achton Friis, 1 year	2.00	60.00
1920	HARE IN THE SNOW, Achton Friis, 1 year	2.00	60.00
1921	PIGEONS IN THE CASTLE COURT, Achton Friis, 1 year	2.00	75.00
1922	STAR OF BETHLEHEM, Achton Friis, 1 year	2.00	90.00
1923	ROYAL HUNTING CASTLE, THE ERMITAGE, Achton Friis, 1 year	2.00	60.00
1924	LIGHTHOUSEIN DANISH WATERS, Achton Friis, 1 year	2.50	95.00
1925	THE CHILD'S CHRISTMAS, Achton Friis, 1 year	2.50	95.00
1926	CHURCHGOERS ON CHRISTMAS DAY, Achton Friis, 1 year	2.50	75.00
1927	SKATING COUPLE, Achton Friis, 1 year	2.50	90.00
1928	ESKIMO LOOKING AT VILLAGE CHURCH IN GREENLAND, Achton Friis, 1 year	2.50	70.00
1929	FOX OUTSIDE FARM ON CHRISTMAS EVE, Achton Friis, 1 year	2.50	90.00
1930	YULE TREE IN TOWN HALL SQUARE, COPENHAGEN, Hans Flugenring, 1 year	2.50	80.00
1931	ARRIVAL OF THE CHRISTMAS TRAIN, Achton Friis, 1 year	2.50	85.00
1932	LIFE BOAT AT WORK, Hans Flugenring, 1 year	2.50	80.00
1933	THE KORSOR-NYBORG FERRY, Hans Flugenring, 1 year	3.00	70.00
1934	CHURCH BELL IN TOWER, Immanuel Tjerne, 1 year	3.00	100.00
1935	LILLEBELT BRIDGE CONNECTING FUNEN WITH JUTLAND, Ove Larsen, 1 year	3.00	100.00
1936	ROYAL GUARD OUTSIDE AMALIENBORG CASTLE, Ove Larsen, 1 year	3.00	75.00
1937	ARRIVAL OF CHRISTMAS GUESTS, Ove Larsen, 1 year	3.00	80.00
1938	LIGHTING THE CANDLES, Immanuel Tjerne, 1 year	3.00	150.00
1939	OLE LOCK-EYE, THE SANDMAN, Immanuel Tjerne, 1 year	3.00	175.00
1940	DELIVERING CHRISTMAS LETTERS, Ove Larsen, 1 year	4.00	165.00
1941	HORSES ENJOYING CHRISTMAS MEAL IN STABLE, Ove Larsen, 1 year	4.00	250.00
1942	DANISH FARM ON CHRISTMAS NIGHT, Ove Larsen, 1 year	4.00	225.00
1943	THE RIBE CATHEDRAL, Ove Larsen, 1 year	5.00	165.00
1944	SORGENFRI CASTLE, Ove Larsen, 1 year	5.00	130.00
1945	THE OLD WATER MILL, Ove Larsen, 1 year	5.00	200.00
1946	COMMEMORATION CROSS—DANISH SAILORS, Margrethe Hyldahl, 1 year	5.00	80.00
1947	DYBBOL MILL, Margrethe Hyldahl, 1 year	5.00	150.00
1948	WATCHMAN, SCULPTURE OF TOWN HALL, Margrethe Hyldahl, 1 year	5.50	75.00
1949	LANDSOLDATEN, DANISH SOLDIER, Margrethe Hyldahl, 1 year	5.50	75.00
1950	KRONBORG CASTLE AT ELSINORE, Margrethe Hyldahl, 1 year	5.50	120.00
1951	*JENS BANG,* NEW PASSENGER BOAT RUNNING BETWEEN COPENHAGEN AND AALBORG, Margrethe Hyldahl, 1 year	6.00	125.00
1952	OLD COPENHAGEN CANALS AT WINTERTIME WITH THORVALDSEN MUSEUM IN BACKGROUND, Borge Pramvig, 1 year	6.00	100.00
1953	ROYAL BOAT IN GREENLAND WATERS, Kjeld Bonfils, 1 year	7.00	100.00
1954	BIRTHPLACE OF HANS CHRISTIAN ANDERSEN, WITH SNOWMAN, Borge Pramvig, 1 year	7.50	125.00
1955	KAULUNDBORG CHURCH, Kjeld Bonfils, 1 year	8.00	140.00
1956	CHRISTMAS IN COPENHAGEN, Kjeld Bonfils, 1 year	8.50	200.00
1957	CHRISTMAS CANDLES, Kjeld Bonfils, 1 year	9.00	125.00
1958	SANTA CLAUS, Kjeld Bonfils, 1 year	9.50	100.00
1959	CHRISTMAS EVE, Kjeld Bonfils, 1 year	10.00	120.00
1960	DANISH VILLAGE CHURCH, Kjeld Bonfils, 1 year	10.00	120.00
1961	WINTER HARMONY, Kjeld Bonfils, 1 year	10.50	60.00
1962	WINTER NIGHT, Kjeld Bonfils, 1 year	11.00	50.00
1963	THE CHRISTMAS ELF, Henry Thelander, 1 year	11.00	90.00
1964	THE FIR TREE AND HARE, Henry Thelander, 1 year	11.50	35.00

Christmas in Church

The Old Water Mill

Christmas Tale

Christmas in Woods

Christmas in the Old Town

Christmas Eve at the Farmhouse

Photos courtesy of *Collectors News*

		ISSUE	CURRENT
1965	BRINGING HOME THE CHRISTMAS TREE, Henry Thelander, 1 year	12.00	45.00
1966	HOME FOR CHRISTMAS, Henry Thelander, 1 year	12.00	35.00
1967	SHARING THE JOY OF CHRISTMAS, Henry Thelander, 1 year	13.00	25.00
1968	CHRISTMAS IN CHURCH, Henry Thelander, 1 year	14.00	20.00
1969	ARRIVAL OF CHRISTMAS GUESTS, Henry Thelander, 1 year	14.00	20.00
1970	PHEASANTS IN THE SNOW AT CHRISTMAS, Henry Thelander, 1 year	14.50	NR
1971	CHRISTMAS AT HOME, Henry Thelander, 1 year	15.00	BR
1972	CHRISTMAS IN GREENLAND, Henry Thelander, 1 year	16.50	BR
1973	COUNTRY CHRISTMAS, Henry Thelander, 1 year	19.50	BR
1974	CHRISTMAS IN THE VILLAGE, Henry Thelander, 1 year	22.00	NR
1975	THE OLD WATER MILL, Henry Thelander, 1 year	27.50	NR
1976	CHRISTMAS WELCOME, Henry Thelander, 1 year	27.50	BR
1977	COPENHAGEN CHRISTMAS, Henry Thelander, 1 year	29.50	BR
1978	A CHRISTMAS TALE, Henry Thelander, 1 year	32.00	BR
1979	WHITE CHRISTMAS, Henry Thelander, 1 year	36.50	BR
1980	CHRISTMAS IN THE WOODS, Henry Thelander, 1 year	42.50	NR
1981	CHRISTMAS PEACE, Henry Thelander, 1 year	49.50	BR
1982	THE CHRISTMAS TREE, Henry Thelander, 1 year	54.50	NR
1983	CHRISTMAS IN THE OLD TOWN, Henry Thelander, 1 year	54.50	BR
1984	THE CHRISTMAS LETTER, Edvard Jensen, 1 year	54.50	BR
1985	CHRISTMAS EVE AT THE FARMHOUSE, Edvard Jensen, 1 year	54.50	BR
1986	SILENT NIGHT, HOLY NIGHT, Edvard Jensen, 1 year	54.50	NR
1987	THE SNOWMAN'S CHRISTMAS EVE, Edvard Jensen, 1 year	59.50	NR
1988	IN THE KING'S GARDEN, Edvard Jensen, 1 year	59.50	BR
1989	CHRISTMAS ANCHORAGE, Edvard Jensen, 1 year	59.50	NR
1990	CHANGING OF THE GUARDS, Edvard Jensen, 1 year	64.50	80.00
1991	COPENHAGEN STOCK EXCHANGE, Edvard Jensen, 1 year	69.50	100.00
1992	CHRISTMAS AT THE RECTORY, Edvard Jensen, 1 year	69.50	100.00
1993	FATHER CHRISTMAS IN COPENHAGEN, Edvard Jensen, 1 year	69.50	RI
1994	A DAY AT THE DEER PARK, Edvard Jensen, 1 year	72.50	RI
1995	THE TOWERS OF COPENHAGEN, Jørgen Nielsen, 1 year	74.50	RI
1996	WINTER AT THE OLD MILL, Jørgen Nielsen, 1 year	74.50	RI
1997	COUNTRY CHRISTMAS, Jørgen Nielsen, 1 year	69.50	RI

Christmas Around the World (Royal Copenhagen)

1995	SANTA IN GREENLAND, Hans Henrik Hansen, 1 year	74.50	RI
1996	SANTA CLAUS IN THE ORIENT, Hans Henrik Hansen, 1 year	74.50	RI
1997	SANTA CLAUS IN RUSSIA, Hans Henrik Hansen, 1 year	69.50	RI

Christmas in America

1986	CHRISTMAS EVE IN WILLIAMSBURG, Jack Woodson, 1 year	29.50	150.00
1987	CHRISTMAS EVE AT THE WHITE HOUSE, Jack Woodson, 1 year	34.50	NR
1988	CHRISTMAS EVE AT ROCKEFELLER CENTER, Jack Woodson, 1 year	34.50	60.00
1989	CHRISTMAS IN NEW ENGLAND, Jack Woodson, 1 year	37.00	55.00
1990	CHRISTMAS EVE AT THE CAPITOL, Jack Woodson, 1 year	39.50	55.00
1991	CHRISTMAS EVE AT INDEPENDENCE HALL, Jack Woodson, 1 year	45.00	60.00
1992	CHRISTMAS IN SAN FRANCISCO, Jack Woodson, 1 year	47.50	NR
1993	COMING HOME FOR CHRISTMAS, Jack Woodson, 1 year	47.50	RI
1994	CHRISTMAS EVE IN ALASKA, Jack Woodson, 1 year	47.50	RI
1995	CHRISTMAS EVE IN MISSISSIPPI, Jack Woodson, 1 year	47.50	RI

Christmas in America Anniversary Plate

1991	CHRISTMAS EVE IN WILLIAMSBURG, Jack Woodson, 1 year	69.50	80.00

Christmas Eve in Williamsburg

Christmas in New England

Chopin

Alexandra and Amy

Home Is Best

Bird and Chicks

Photos courtesy of *Collectors News*

		ISSUE	CURRENT
1995	THE CAPITOL, Jack Woodson, 1 year	74.50	RI

Christmas in Denmark (Royal Copenhagen)

1995	CHRISTMAS TALES, Hans Henrik Hansen, 1 year	74.50	RI

Composers of Classical Music

1979	BEETHOVEN, 1 year	37.50	NR
1980	BACH, 1 year	37.50	NR
1981	BRAHMS, 1 year	37.50	NR
1982	CHOPIN, 1 year	37.50	NR
1983	HAYDN, 1 year	37.50	NR
1984	EDVARD GRIEG	37.50	NR

Gentle Love

1985	JOANNA AND JON, Adeline Heesen Cooper, 9,500	45.00	NR
1985	ALEXANDRA AND AMY, Adeline Heesen Cooper, 9,500	45.00	NR
1985	INGRID AND LISA, Adeline Heesen Cooper, 9,500	45.00	NR
1985	ELIZABETH AND DAVID, Adeline Heesen Cooper, 9,500	45.00	NR

Hans Christian Andersen (Ghent Collection)

1979	THUMBELINA, 7,500	42.50	NR
1980	EMPEROR'S NEW CLOTHES, 7,500	42.50	NR
1980	LITTLE MERMAID, 7,500	42.50	NR
1980	NIGHTINGALE, 7,500	42.50	NR

Heritage

1976	NORSEMAN, 5,000	30.00	NR
1977	NAVIGATORS, 5,000	30.00	NR
1978	DISCOVERY, 5,000	39.50	NR
1979	EXPLORATION, 5,000	39.50	NR
1980	HELMSMAN, 5,000	45.00	NR

Jubilee Five-Year Christmas

1915	FROZEN WINDOW, Franz August Hallin, 1 year	3.00	200.00
1920	CHURCH BELLS, Fanny Garde, 1 year	4.00	60.00
1925	DOG OUTSIDE WINDOW, Dahl Jensen, 1 year	5.00	180.00
1930	THE OLD ORGANIST, C. Ersgaard, 1 year	5.00	210.00
1935	LITTLE MATCH GIRL, Ingeborg Plockross, 1 year	6.00	450.00
1940	THREE WISE MEN, S. Sabra, 1 year	10.00	1,800.00
1945	ROYAL GUARD AMALIENBORG CASTLE, T. Larsen, 1 year	10.00	90.00
1950	ESKIMOS, Achton Friis, 1 year	15.00	90.00
1955	DYBBOL MILL, Margarethe Hyldahl, 1 year	20.00	210.00
1960	KRONBORG CASTLE, Margarethe Hyldahl, 1 year	25.00	90.00
1965	CHURCHGOERS, Achton Friis, 1 year	25.00	NR
1970	AMALIENBORG CASTLE, T. Larsen, 1 year	30.00	BR
1975	HORSES ENJOYING MEAL, Ove Larsen, 1 year	40.00	BR
1980	HAPPINESS OVER YULE TREE, Aarestrup, 1 year	60.00	BR
1985	LIFEBOAT AT WORK, Hans Flugenring, 1 year	65.00	BR
1990	THE ROYAL YACHT DANNEBROG, Kjeld Bonfils, 1 year	95.00	BR
1995	CENTENNIAL PLATTER, Jørgen Nielsen, 7,500	195.00	RI
1996	LIFEBOAT AT WORK, Hans Flugenring, 1,000 (released a year late)	95.00	RI

Moments of Truth

		ISSUE	CURRENT
1984	HOME IS BEST, Kurt Ard, limited	29.50	BR
1984	THE ROAD TO VIRTUOSITY, Kurt Ard, limited	29.50	BR
1985	FIRST THINGS FIRST, Kurt Ard, limited	29.50	BR
1985	UNFAIR COMPETITION, Kurt Ard, limited	29.50	BR
1986	BORED SICK, Kurt Ard, limited	29.50	BR
1986	FIRST CRUSH, Kurt Ard, limited	29.50	BR

Mother's Day

1969	DOGS AND PUPPIES, Henry Thelander, 1 year	9.75	300.00
1970	BIRD AND CHICKS, Henry Thelander, 1 year	10.00	20.00
1971	CAT AND KITTEN, Henry Thelander, 1 year	11.00	NR
1972	MARE AND FOAL, Henry Thelander, 1 year	12.00	NR
1973	DUCK AND DUCKLINGS, Henry Thelander, 1 year	13.00	20.00
1974	BEAR AND CUBS, Henry Thelander, 1 year	16.50	NR
1975	DOE AND FAWNS, Henry Thelander, 1 year	19.50	NR
1976	SWAN FAMILY, Henry Thelander, 1 year	22.50	NR
1977	SQUIRREL AND YOUNG, Henry Thelander, 1 year	23.50	NR
1978	HERON, Henry Thelander, 1 year	24.50	NR
1979	FOX AND CUBS, Henry Thelander, 1 year	27.50	BR
1980	WOODPECKER AND YOUNG, Henry Thelander, 1 year	29.50	NR
1981	HARE AND YOUNG, Henry Thelander, 1 year	36.50	NR
1982	LIONESS AND CUBS, Henry Thelander, 1 year	39.50	NR
1983	RACCOON AND YOUNG, Henry Thelander, 1 year	39.50	BR
1984	STORK AND NESTLINGS, Henry Thelander, 1 year	39.50	BR
1985	BEAR AND CUBS, Henry Thelander, 1 year	39.50	NR
1986	ELEPHANT WITH CALF, Henry Thelander, 1 year	39.50	50.00
1987	SHEEP WITH LAMBS, Henry Thelander, 1 year	42.50	75.00
1988	CRESTED PLOVER AND YOUNG, Henry Thelander, 1 year	47.50	80.00
1988	LAPWING MOTHER WITH CHICKS, Henry Thelander, 1 year	49.50	90.00
1989	COW WITH CALF, Henry Thelander, 1 year	49.50	60.00
1990	HEN WITH CHICKS, L. Jensen, 1 year	49.50	85.00
1991	NANNY GOAT AND HER TWO FRISKY KIDS, L. Jensen, 1 year	54.50	BR
1992	PANDA WITH CUBS, L. Jensen, 1 year	59.50	70.00
1993	ST. BERNARD DOG AND PUPPIES, A. Therkelsen, 1 year	59.50	RI
1994	CAT WITH KITTENS, A. Therkelsen, 1 year	59.50	RI
1995	HEDGEHOG WITH YOUNG, A. Therkelsen, 1 year	59.50	RI
1996	KOALA AND YOUNG, A. Therkelsen, 1 year	59.50	RI
1997	GOOSE AND GOSLINGS, Les Didier, 1 year	59.50	RI

Mother's Day Five-Year Jubilee

1979	DOG AND PUPPIES, Henry Thelander, 1 year	55.00	NR
1984	SWAN WITH CYGNETS, Henry Thelander, 1 year	65.00	NR
1989	MARE AND COLT, Henry Thelander, 1 year	95.00	NR
1994	WOODPECKER AND YOUNG, Henry Thelander, 1 year	95.00	RI

Olympic Games

1972	MUNICH, GERMANY, 1 year	20.00	NR
1976	MONTREAL, CANADA, 1 year	29.50	55.00
1980	MOSCOW, RUSSIA, 1 year	43.00	90.00
1984	LOS ANGELES, USA, 1 year	45.00	65.00
1988	SEOUL, KOREA, 1 year	60.00	75.00
1992	BARCELONA, SPAIN, 1 year	74.50	85.00

		ISSUE	CURRENT

Places of Enchantment

		ISSUE	CURRENT
1997	VENICE, Sven Vestergaard, 7,500	69.50	RI

Santa Claus Collection

		ISSUE	CURRENT
1989	SANTA'S WORKSHOP, Hans Henrik Hansen, 1 year	59.50	115.00
1990	SANTA'S SLEIGH, Hans Henrik Hansen, 1 year	59.50	90.00
1991	SANTA'S JOURNEY, Hans Henrik Hansen, 1 year	69.50	120.00
1992	SANTA'S ARRIVAL, Hans Henrik Hansen, 1 year	74.50	BR
1993	SANTA'S GIFTS, Hans Henrik Hansen, 1 year	74.50	RI
1994	CHRISTMAS STORIES, Hans Henrik Hansen, 1 year	74.50	RI

Seasons Remembered

		ISSUE	CURRENT
1983	THE WILDFLOWERS OF SUMMER, Verner Münch, 10,000	35.00	NR
1983	AUTUMN SHOWERS, Verner Münch, 10,000	35.00	NR
1983	THE PROMISE OF SPRING, Verner Münch, 10,000	35.00	NR
1983	THE WINTER OF THE SNOWMAN, Verner Münch, 10,000	35.00	NR
1984	THE WILDFLOWERS OF SUMMER, Verner Münch, 7,500	35.00	NR
1984	AUTUMN SHOWERS, Verner Münch, 7,500	35.00	NR
1984	THE PROMISE OF SPRING, Verner Münch, 7,500	35.00	NR
1984	THE WINTER OF THE SNOWMAN, Verner Münch, 7,500	35.00	NR

Statue of Liberty

		ISSUE	CURRENT
1985	STATUE OF LIBERTY, 10,000	60.00	75.00

Summer at Skagen

		ISSUE	CURRENT
1986	SUMMER EVENING, limited	34.50	NR
1987	LUNCHEON AT KROYER'S, limited	34.50	NR

Windjammers

		ISSUE	CURRENT
1980	DANMARK, James Mitchell, 10,000	95.00	NR
1980	EAGLE, James Mitchell, 10,000	95.00	NR
1981	GLADAN, James Mitchell, 10,000	95.00	NR
1981	GORDON/FOCK, James Mitchell, 10,000	95.00	NR
1982	AMERIGO VESPUCCI, James Mitchell, 10,000	95.00	NR
1982	CHRISTIAN RADICH, James Mitchell, 10,000	95.00	NR

Young Adventurer Plate

		ISSUE	CURRENT
1990	THE LITTLE VIKING, Sven Vestergaard, 1 year	52.50	60.00

Single Issues

		ISSUE	CURRENT
1978	MADONNA, 10,000	45.00	NR
1978	SEAGULL, 7,500	75.00	NR
1980	VIKING, 10,000	65.00	NR

BLUE DELFT NETHERLANDS

Christmas

		ISSUE	CURRENT
1970	DRAWBRIDGE NEAR BINNEHOF, 1 year	12.00	25.00
1971	ST. LAUREN'S CHURCH, 1 year	12.00	25.00
1972	CHURCH AT BIERKADE, 1 year	12.00	NR

		ISSUE	CURRENT
1973	ST. JAN'S CHURCH, 1 year	12.00	NR
1974	DINGERADEEL, 1 year	13.00	NR
1975	MAASSLUIS, 1 year	13.00	NR
1976	MONTELBAANSTOWER, 1 year	15.00	NR
1977	HARBOUR TOWER OF HOORN, 1 year	19.50	NR
1978	BINNENPOORT GATE, 1 year	21.00	NR

Christmas Story

1982	THE ANGEL GABRIEL FOREBODING MARIA	35.00	NR

Father's Day

1971	FRANCESCO LANA'S AIRSHIP, 1 year	12.00	30.00
1972	DR. JONATHAN'S BALLOON, 1 year	12.00	30.00

Mother's Day

1971	MOTHER AND DAUGHTER OF THE 1600s, 1 year	12.00	NR
1972	MOTHER AND DAUGHTER OF THE ISLE OF URK, 1 year	12.00	NR
1973	REMBRANDT'S MOTHER, 1 year	12.00	NR

Single Issues

1972	OLYMPIAD	12.00	NR
1972	APOLLO II	6.00	NR

BLUE RIVER MILL UNITED STATES

Once Upon a Barn

1986	MAIL POUCH BARN, Ray Day, 5,000	45.00	NR
1986	ROCK CITY BARN, Ray Day, 5,000	45.00	NR
1987	MERAMEC CAVERNS BARN, Ray Day, 5,000	45.00	NR
1987	COCA-COLA BARN, Ray Day, 5,000	45.00	NR

Mail Pouch Barn
Photo courtesy of *Collectors News*

LINDA BOEHM

Egyptian Treasures of Tutankhamen

		ISSUE	CURRENT
1977	THE HEADDRESS, 5,000	50.00	NR
1978	THE MUMMY COLLAR, 5,000	50.00	NR

BOEHM STUDIOS, EDWARD MARSHALL GREAT BRITAIN

(Hamilton/Boehm, Hamilton Collection)

Award-Winning Roses (Hamilton/Boehm)

1979	PEACE ROSE, Boehm Studio Artists, 15,000	45.00	100.00
1979	WHITE MASTERPIECE ROSE, Boehm Studio Artists, 15,000	45.00	75.00
1979	TROPICANA ROSE, Boehm Studio Artists, 15,000	45.00	65.00
1979	ELEGANCE ROSE, Boehm Studio Artists, 15,000	45.00	65.00
1979	QUEEN ELIZABETH ROSE, Boehm Studio Artists, 15,000	45.00	65.00
1979	ROYAL HIGHNESS ROSE, Boehm Studio Artists, 15,000	45.00	65.00
1979	ANGEL FACE ROSE, Boehm Studio Artists, 15,000	45.00	65.00
1979	MR. LINCOLN ROSE, Boehm Studio Artists, 15,000	45.00	65.00

Banquet of Blossoms and Berries

1982	WINTER HOLIDAY BOUQUET, Boehm Studio Artists, 15,000	62.50	NR
1982	THANKSGIVING BOUQUET, Boehm Studio Artists, 15,000	62.50	NR
1982	SCHOOL DAYS BOUQUET, Boehm Studio Artists, 15,000	62.50	NR
1982	INDIAN SUMMER BOUQUET, Boehm Studio Artists, 15,000	62.50	NR
1982	MID-SUMMER BOUQUET, Boehm Studio Artists, 15,000	62.50	NR
1982	AUTUMN BOUQUET, Boehm Studio Artists, 15,000	62.50	NR

Butterflies of the World

1978	MONARCH AND DAISY, 5,000	62.00	NR
1978	RED ADMIRAL AND THISTLE, 5,000	62.00	NR

Butterfly

1975	BLUE MOUNTAIN SWALLOWTAILS, 100	450.00	NR
1975	JEZABELS, 100	450.00	NR
1976	COMMA WITH LOOPS, 100	450.00	NR
1976	AFRICAN BUTTERFLIES, 100	450.00	NR
1976	SOLANDRAS MAXIMA, 100	450.00	NR

Egyptian Commemorative

1978	TUTANKHAMEN, 5,000	125.00	170.00
1978	TUTANKHAMEN, hand painted, 225	975.00	NR

European Birds

1973	SWALLOW, 4,319	50.00	NR
1973	CHAFFINCH, 4,319	50.00	NR
1973	COAL TIT, 4,319	50.00	NR
1973	TREE SPARROW, 4,319	50.00	NR
1973	KINGFISHER, 4,319	50.00	NR
1973	GOLD CREST, 4,319	50.00	NR
1973	BLUE TIT, 4,319	50.00	NR

		ISSUE	CURRENT
1973	LINNET, 4,319	50.00	NR

Fancy Fowl

1974	PAIR, 85	2,000.00	NR

Favorite Florals

1978	CLEMATIS, 2,500	58.00	NR
1978	RHODODENDRON, 2,500	58.00	NR
1979	BOEHM ORCHID, 2,500	58.00	NR
1979	YELLOW ROSE, 2,500	58.00	NR
1980	SPIDER ORCHID, 2,500	58.00	NR
1980	DAHLIA, 2,500	58.00	NR

Flower Series

1975	LILIES, 100	450.00	490.00
1975	PASSION FLOWERS, 100	450.00	490.00
1975	DOUBLE CLEMATIS, 100	450.00	490.00

Gamebirds of North America (Hamilton/Boehm)

1984	RING-NECKED PHEASANT, Boehm Studio Artists, 15,000	62.50	NR
1984	BOB-WHITE QUAIL, Boehm Studio Artists, 15,000	62.50	NR
1984	AMERICAN WOODCOCK, Boehm Studio Artists, 15,000	62.50	NR
1984	CALIFORNIA QUAIL, Boehm Studio Artists, 15,000	62.50	NR
1984	RUFFED GROUSE, Boehm Studio Artists, 15,000	62.50	NR
1984	WILD TURKEY, Boehm Studio Artists, 15,000	62.50	NR
1984	WILLOW PARTRIDGE, Boehm Studio Artists, 15,000	62.50	NR
1984	PRAIRIE GROUSE, Boehm Studio Artists, 15,000	62.50	NR

Hard Fruits

1975	PLUMS, 100	450.00	NR
1975	PEARS, 100	450.00	NR
1975	PEACHES, 100	450.00	NR
1975	APPLES, 100	450.00	NR

Honor America

1974	AMERICAN BALD EAGLE, 12,000	85.00	NR

Hummingbird Collection (Hamilton/Boehm)

1980	CALLIOPE, Boehm Studio Artists, 15,000	62.50	80.00
1980	BROADBILLED, Boehm Studio Artists, 15,000	62.50	NR
1980	BROADTAIL, Boehm Studio Artists, 15,000	62.50	NR
1980	RUFOUS FLAME BEARER, Boehm Studio Artists, 15,000	62.50	80.00
1980	STREAMERTAIL, Boehm Studio Artists, 15,000	62.50	80.00
1980	BLUE THROATED, Boehm Studio Artists, 15,000	62.50	80.00
1980	CRIMSON TOPAZ, Boehm Studio Artists, 15,000	62.50	NR
1980	BRAZILIAN RUBY, Boehm Studio Artists, 15,000	62.50	80.00

Judaic Commemorative

1978	ROSE/GOLD, 75	555.00	NR
1979	BLUE, 1,500	45.00	NR

Life's Best Wishes (Hamilton Collection)

		ISSUE	CURRENT
1982	LONGEVITY, Boehm Studio Artists	75.00	NR
1982	HAPPINESS, Boehm Studio Artists	75.00	NR
1982	FERTILITY, Boehm Studio Artists	75.00	NR
1982	PROSPERITY, Boehm Studio Artists	75.00	NR

Miniature Roses (Hamilton Collection)

		ISSUE	CURRENT
1982	TOY CLOWN, Boehm Studio Artists, 28 days	39.50	45.00
1982	RISE 'N' SHINE, Boehm Studio Artists, 28 days	39.50	45.00
1982	CUDDLES, Boehm Studio Artists, 28 days	39.50	45.00
1982	PUPPY LOVE, Boehm Studio Artists, 28 days	39.50	45.00

Musical Maidens of the Imperial Dynasty

		ISSUE	CURRENT
1984	THE FLUTE, 15,000	65.00	NR

Oriental Birds

		ISSUE	CURRENT
1975	BLUEBACKED FAIRY BLUEBIRDS, 100	400.00	NR
1975	AZURE-WINGED MAGPIES, 100	400.00	NR
1976	GOLDEN-FRONTED LEAFBIRD, 100	400.00	NR
1976	GOLDEN-THROATED BARBET, 100	400.00	NR

Owl Collection (Hamilton/Boehm)

		ISSUE	CURRENT
1980	BOREAL OWL, Boehm Studio Artists, 15,000	45.00	95.00
1980	SNOWY OWL, Boehm Studio Artists, 15,000	45.00	95.00
1980	BARN OWL, Boehm Studio Artists, 15,000	45.00	80.00
1980	SAW-WHET OWL, Boehm Studio Artists, 15,000	45.00	75.00
1980	GREAT HORNED OWL, Boehm Studio Artists, 15,000	45.00	75.00
1980	SCREECH OWL, Boehm Studio Artists, 15,000	45.00	75.00
1980	SHORT-EARED OWL, Boehm Studio Artists, 15,000	45.00	75.00
1980	BARRED OWL, Boehm Studio Artists, 15,000	45.00	75.00

Panda

		ISSUE	CURRENT
1982	PANDA, HARMONY, 5,000	65.00	NR
1982	PANDA, PEACE, 5,000	65.00	NR

Roses of Excellence

		ISSUE	CURRENT
1981	THE LOVE ROSE, Boehm Studio Artists, 1 year	62.00	85.00
1982	WHITE LIGHTNIN', Boehm Studio Artists, 1 year	62.00	NR
1983	BRANDY, Boehm Studio Artists, 1 year	62.00	NR
1983	SUN FLARE, Boehm Studio Artists, 1 year	62.00	NR

Seashells

		ISSUE	CURRENT
1975	VIOLET SPIDER CONCH, 100	450.00	NR
1975	ROOSTER TAIL CONCH, 100	450.00	NR
1976	ORANGE SPIDER CONCH, 100	450.00	NR
1976	CHERAGRA SPIDER CONCH, 100	450.00	NR

Soft Fruits

		ISSUE	CURRENT
1975	LOGANBERRIES, 100	450.00	NR
1976	CHERRIES, 100	450.00	NR
1976	STRAWBERRIES, 100	450.00	NR

		ISSUE	CURRENT
1976	GRAPES, 100	450.00	NR

Tribute to Award-Winning Roses

1983	IRISH GOLD, Boehm Studio Artists, 15,000	62.50	NR
1983	HANDEL, Boehm Studio Artists, 15,000	62.50	NR
1983	QUEEN ELIZABETH, Boehm Studio Artists, 15,000	62.50	NR
1983	ELIZABETH OF GLAMIS, Boehm Studio Artists, 15,000	62.50	NR
1983	ICEBERG, Boehm Studio Artists, 15,000	62.50	NR
1983	MOUNTBATTEN, Boehm Studio Artists, 15,000	62.50	NR
1983	SILVER JUBILEE, Boehm Studio Artists, 15,000	62.50	NR
1983	PEACE, Boehm Studio Artists, 15,000	62.50	NR

Tribute to Ballet (Hamilton Collection)

1982	NUTCRACKER, Boehm Studio Artists, 15,000	62.50	NR
1982	FIREBIRD, Boehm Studio Artists, 15,000	62.50	NR
1982	DON QUIXOTE, Boehm Studio Artists, 15,000	62.50	NR
1982	LA BAYADERE, Boehm Studio Artists, 15,000	62.50	NR

Water Birds (Hamilton/Boehm)

1981	CANADA GEESE, Boehm Studio Artists, 15,000	62.50	NR
1981	WOOD DUCK, Boehm Studio Artists, 15,000	62.50	NR
1981	HOODED MERGANSER, Boehm Studio Artists, 15,000	62.50	NR
1981	ROSS'S GEESE, Boehm Studio Artists, 15,000	62.50	NR
1981	COMMON MALLARD, Boehm Studio Artists, 15,000	62.50	NR
1981	CANVAS BACK, Boehm Studio Artists, 15,000	62.50	NR
1981	GREEN-WINGED TEAL, Boehm Studio Artists, 15,000	62.50	NR
1981	AMERICAN PINTAIL, Boehm Studio Artists, 15,000	62.50	NR

Woodland Birds of America

1984	DOWNY WOODPECKER WITH FLOWERING CHERRY BLOSSOMS	75.00	NR

BOHEMIA CZECHOSLOVAKIA

Mother's Day

1974	MOTHER'S DAY, 500	130.00	155.00
1975	MOTHER'S DAY, 500	140.00	160.00
1976	MOTHER'S DAY, 500	150.00	160.00

BOMAR STUDIO UNITED STATES

Liberace Signature Collection

1984	MR. SHOWMANSHIP, 30,000	95.00	NR

BONITA MEXICO

Mother's Day

1972	MOTHER WITH BABY, Raul Anguiano, 4,000	75.00	85.00

BORSATO

Masterpiece Series

		ISSUE	CURRENT
1978	SERENITY, 5,000	75.00	BR
1978	TITIAN, 5,000	75.00	BR

Plaques

		ISSUE	CURRENT
1973	GOLDEN YEARS, 750	1,450.00	1,750.00
1974	TENDER MUSINGS, 250	1,650.00	1,900.00

BRADFORD EXCHANGE CANADA

Big League Dreams

		ISSUE	CURRENT
1993	HEY, BATTER BATTER, Stewart Sherwood	29.90	RI
1994	THE WIND UP, Stewart Sherwood	29.90	RI
1994	SAFE!!!, Stewart Sherwood	32.90	RI
1994	A DIFFERENCE OF OPINION, Stewart Sherwood	32.90	RI
1994	I GOT IT, I GOT IT!, Stewart Sherwood	32.90	RI
1994	VICTORY, Stewart Sherwood	32.90	RI

BRADFORD EXCHANGE PEOPLES REPUBLIC OF CHINA

Dream of the Red Chamber

		ISSUE	CURRENT
1994	PAO-CHOI: PRECIOUS CLASP	29.90	RI
1994	HSIANG-YUN: LITTLE CLOUD	29.90	RI
1994	YUAN-CHUN: BEGINNING OF SPRING	29.90	RI
1994	HSI-FENG: PHOENIX	29.90	RI
1994	TAI-YU: BLACK JADE	29.90	RI
1994	TAN-CHUN: TASTE OF SPRING	29.90	RI

BRADFORD EXCHANGE RUSSIA

Nutcracker

		ISSUE	CURRENT
1993	MARIE'S MAGICAL GIFT, Natalia Zaitseva, closed	39.87	RI
1993	DANCE OF SUGAR PLUM FAIRY, Natalia Zaitseva, closed	39.87	RI
1994	WALTZ OF THE FLOWERS, Natalia Zaitseva, closed	39.87	RI
1994	BATTLE WITH THE MICE KING, Natalia Zaitseva, closed	39.87	RI
1994	HEAVENLY HERALDS, Natalia Zaitseva, closed	29.87	RI
1994	DIVINE CHORUS, Natalia Zaitseva, closed	29.87	RI
1995	SPRINGTIME DUET, Natalia Zaitseva, closed	32.87	RI
1995	MYSTICAL CHIMES, Natalia Zaitseva, closed	32.87	RI

BRADFORD EXCHANGE UNITED STATES

(W. S. George, Edwin M. Knowles, Roman, Inc.)

100 Acre Wood Holiday

		ISSUE	CURRENT
1997	A SINGING SORT OF HOLIDAY, 95 days	29.95	RI

		ISSUE	CURRENT

Aladdin

1993	MAGIC CARPET RIDE, Disney Studios, 95 days	29.90	RI
1993	A FRIEND LIKE ME, Disney Studios, 95 days	32.90	RI
1994	ALADDIN IN LOVE, Disney Studios, 95 days	32.90	RI
1994	TRAVELING COMPANIONS, Disney Studios, 95 days	32.90	RI
1994	MAKE WAY FOR PRINCE ALI, Disney Studios, 95 days	32.90	RI
1994	ALADDIN'S WISH, Disney Studios, 95 days	32.90	RI
1995	BEE YOURSELF, Disney Studios, 95 days	32.90	RI
1995	GROUP HUG, Disney Studios, 95 days	32.90	RI

Alice in Wonderland

1993	THE MAD TEA PARTY, Scott Gustafson, closed	32.90	RI
1993	THE CHESHIRE CAT, Scott Gustafson, closed	32.90	RI
1994	CROQUET WITH THE QUEEN, Scott Gustafson, closed	32.90	RI
1994	ADVICE FROM A CATERPILLAR, Scott Gustafson, closed	32.90	RI

America's Triumph in Space

1993	THE EAGLE HAS LANDED, Robert Schaar, 95 days	29.90	RI
1993	THE MARCH TOWARD DESTINY, Robert Schaar, 95 days	29.90	RI
1994	FLIGHT OF GLORY, Robert Schaar, 95 days	32.90	RI
1994	BEYOND THE BOUNDS OF EARTH, Robert Schaar, 95 days	32.90	RI
1994	CONQUERING THE NEW FRONTIER, Robert Schaar, 95 days	32.90	RI
1994	RENDEZVOUS WITH VICTORY, Robert Schaar, 95 days	32.90	RI
1994	THE NEW EXPLORERS, Robert Schaar, 95 days	32.90	RI
1994	TRIUMPHANT FINALE, Robert Schaar, 95 days	32.90	RI

America the Beautiful

1996	OH BEAUTIFUL FOR SPACIOUS SKIES, Larry K. Martin	NA	RI

Ancient Seasons

1995	EDGE OF NIGHT, M. Silversmith, 95 days	29.90	RI
1995	JOURNEY THROUGH MIDNIGHT, M. Silversmith, 95 days	29.90	RI
1995	MID-WINTER PASSAGE, M. Silversmith, 95 days	29.90	RI
1995	WINTER SOJOURN, M. Silversmith, 95 days	29.90	RI
1995	WINTER STORM, M. Silversmith, 95 days	29.90	RI

Angelic Visions from Lena Liu

1997	ON PEACEFUL WINGS, Lena Liu, 95 days	29.95	RI

Autumn Encounters

1995	WOODLAND INNOCENTS, Cynthie Fisher, 95 days	29.90	RI

Babe Ruth Centennial

1994	THE 60TH HOMER, P. Heffernan, closed	34.90	RI
1995	RUTH'S PITCHING DEBUT, P. Heffernan, closed	29.90	RI
1995	THE FINAL HOME RUN, P. Heffernan, closed	29.90	RI
1995	BARNSTORMING DAYS, P. Heffernan, closed	29.90	RI

Baseball Record Breakers

1996	CAL RIPKEN, Jason Walker, 95 days, 8¹/₈"	29.95	RI

Baskets of Love

		ISSUE	CURRENT
1993	ANDREW AND ABBY, Alexei Isakov, closed	29.90	RI
1993	CODY AND COURTNEY, Alexei Isakov, closed	29.90	RI
1993	EMILY AND ELLIOTT, Alexei Isakov, closed	32.90	RI
1993	HEATHER AND HANNAH, Alexei Isakov, closed	32.90	RI
1993	JUSTIN AND JESSICA, Alexei Isakov, closed	32.90	RI
1993	KATIE AND KELLY, Alexei Isakov, closed	34.90	RI
1994	LOUIE AND LIBBY, Alexei Isakov, closed	34.90	RI
1994	SAMMY AND SARAH, Alexei Isakov, closed	34.90	RI

Battles of American Civil War

		ISSUE	CURRENT
1994	GETTYSBURG, James Griffin, 95 days	29.90	RI
1995	VICKSBURG, James Griffin, 95 days	29.90	RI

Bear Essentials of Life

		ISSUE	CURRENT
1996	LOVE, D. Kingston Baker, 95 days	29.90	RI

Beary Merry Christmas

		ISSUE	CURRENT
1996	A MOMENT TO TREASURE, Stewart Sherwood, 95 days	29.95	RI
1996	A ROMANTIC RIDE, Stewart Sherwood, 95 days	29.95	RI

Beatitudes

		ISSUE	CURRENT
1996	BLESSED ARE THE PURE IN HEART	NA	RI

Blessed Mother

		ISSUE	CURRENT
1996	THE ANNUNCIATION, Hector Garrido, 95 days	29.95	RI

Bunny Tales

		ISSUE	CURRENT
NA	FOOTLOOSE, Vivi Crandall	29.95	RI
NA	I'M ALL EARS, Vivi Crandall	29.95	RI

Bunny Workshop

		ISSUE	CURRENT
1995	MAKE TODAY EGGSTRA SPECIAL, Jane Maday, 95 days	19.95	RI

Bygone Days

		ISSUE	CURRENT
1994	SODA FOUNTAIN, Lee Dubin, closed	29.90	RI
1995	SAM'S GROCERY STORE, Lee Dubin, closed	29.90	RI
1995	SATURDAY MATINEE, Lee Dubin, closed	29.90	RI
1995	THE CORNER NEWS STAND, Lee Dubin, closed	29.90	RI
1995	MAIN STREET SPLENDOR, Lee Dubin, 95 days	29.90	RI
1995	THE BARBER SHOP, Lee Dubin, 95 days	29.90	RI

Cabbage Rose Corners

		ISSUE	CURRENT
1996	ROSE PETAL GIFT SHOPPE, L. Burns, 95 days	29.90	RI

Cabins of Comfort River

		ISSUE	CURRENT
1995	COMFORT BY CAMPLIGHT'S FIRE, F. Buchwitz, 95 days	29.90	RI

Carousel Daydreams

		ISSUE	CURRENT
1994	SWEPT AWAY, Mr. Tseng, closed	39.90	RI

		ISSUE	CURRENT
1995	WHEN I GROW UP, closed	39.90	RI
1995	ALL ABOARD, closed	44.90	RI
1995	HOLD ONTO YOUR DREAMS, closed	44.90	RI
1995	FLIGHT OF FANCY, closed	44.90	RI
1995	BIG HOPES, BRIGHT DREAMS, 95 days	49.90	RI
1995	VICTORIAN REVERIE, 95 days	49.90	RI
1995	WISHFUL THINKING, 95 days	49.90	RI
1995	DREAMS OF DESTINY, 95 days	49.90	RI
1995	MY FAVORITE MEMORY, 95 days	49.90	RI

Charles Wysocki's American Frontier

1993	TIMBERLINE JACK'S TRADING POST, Charles Wysocki, 95 days	29.90	RI
1994	DR. LIVINGWELL'S MEDICINE SHOW, Charles Wysocki, 95 days	29.90	RI
1994	BUSTLING BOOMTOWN, Charles Wysocki, 95 days	29.90	RI
1994	KIRBYVILLE, Charles Wysocki, 95 days	29.90	RI
1994	HEARTY HOMESTEADERS, Charles Wysocki, 95 days	29.90	RI
1994	OKLAHOMA OR BUST, Charles Wysocki, 95 days	29.90	RI

Charles Wysocki's Folktown

1996	BIRDIE'S PERCH COFFEE SHOP, Charles Wysocki, 95 days	29.90	RI
1996	CHIPS AND FELTS, Charles Wysocki, 95 days	29.90	RI
1996	QUILT LADIES SOCIAL CLUB, Charles Wysocki, 95 days	29.90	RI
1996	STOOLPIGEON GOSSIP SHOP, Charles Wysocki, 95 days	29.90	RI
1996	SWEET SHOP, Charles Wysocki, 95 days	29.90	RI
1996	TOWN FLORIST, Charles Wysocki, 95 days	29.90	RI

Charles Wysocki's Hometown Memories

1994	SMALL TALK AT BIRDIE'S PERCH, Charles Wysocki, 95 days	29.90	RI
1995	TRANQUIL DAYS/RAVENSWHIP COVE, Charles Wysocki, 95 days	29.90	RI
1995	SUMMER DELIGHTS, Charles Wysocki, 95 days	29.90	RI
1995	CAPTURING THE MOMENT, Charles Wysocki, 95 days	29.90	RI
1995	A FAREWELL KISS, Charles Wysocki, 95 days	29.90	RI
1995	JASON SPARKIN' THE LIGHTHOUSE KEEPER'S DAUGHTER, Charles Wysocki, 95 days	29.90	RI

Charles Wysocki's Peppercricket Grove

1993	PEPPERCRICKET FARMS, Charles Wysocki, 95 days	24.90	RI
1993	GINGERNUT VALLEY INN, Charles Wysocki, 95 days	24.90	RI
1993	BUDZEN'S FRUITS AND VEGETABLES, Charles Wysocki, 95 days	24.90	RI
1993	PUMPKIN HOLLOW EMPORIUM, Charles Wysocki, 95 days	24.90	RI
1993	LIBERTY STAR FARMS, Charles Wysocki, 95 days	24.90	RI
1993	OVERFLOW ANTIQUE MARKET, Charles Wysocki, 95 days	24.90	RI
1993	BLACK CROW ANTIQUE SHOPPE, Charles Wysocki, 95 days	24.90	RI

Cherished Traditions

1995	THE WEDDING RING, Mary Ann Lasher, 95 days	29.90	RI
1995	THE STAR, Mary Ann Lasher, 95 days	29.90	RI

Cherubs of Innocence

1994	THE FIRST KISS, William A. Bouguereau, 95 days	29.90	RI
1995	LOVE AT REST, William A. Bouguereau, 95 days	29.90	RI
1995	THOUGHTS OF LOVE, William A. Bouguereau, 95 days	32.90	RI

		ISSUE	CURRENT
1995	LOVING GAZE, Zatzka, 95 days	32.90	RI

Choir of Angels

1995	SONG OF JOY, Peggy L. Toole, 95 days	29.90	RI
1996	SONG OF HARMONY, Peggy L. Toole, 95 days	29.90	RI
1996	SONG OF HOPE, Peggy L. Toole, 95 days	29.90	RI
1996	SONG OF PEACE, Peggy L. Toole, 95 days	34.90	RI

Chosen Messengers

1993	THE PATHFINDERS, Gale Running Wolf, closed	29.90	RI
1993	THE OVERSEERS, Gale Running Wolf, closed	29.90	RI
1994	THE PROVIDERS, Gale Running Wolf, closed	32.90	RI
1994	THE SURVEYORS, Gale Running Wolf, closed	32.90	RI

A Christmas Carol

1993	GOD BLESS US EVERYONE, Lloyd Garrison, closed	29.90	RI
1993	GHOST OF CHRISTMAS PRESENT, Lloyd Garrison, closed	29.90	RI
1994	A MERRY CHRISTMAS TO ALL, Lloyd Garrison, closed	29.90	RI
1994	A VISIT FROM MARLEY'S GHOST, Lloyd Garrison, closed	29.90	RI
1994	REMEMBERING CHRISTMAS PAST, Lloyd Garrison, closed	29.90	RI
1994	A SPIRIT'S WARNING, Lloyd Garrison, closed	29.90	RI
1994	THE TRUE SPIRIT OF CHRISTMAS, Lloyd Garrison, closed	29.90	RI
1994	A MERRY CHRISTMAS, BOB, Lloyd Garrison, closed	29.90	RI

Christmas in the Village

1995	THE VILLAGE TOY SHOP, Renee McGinnis, closed	29.95	RI
1995	LITTLE CHURCH IN THE VALE, Renee McGinnis, closed	29.95	RI
1995	THE VILLAGE CONFECTIONARY, Renee McGinnis, closed	29.95	RI
1995	THE VILLAGE INN, Renee McGinnis, closed	29.95	RI
1995	GOODNIGHT DEAR FRIENDS, Renee McGinnis, closed	29.95	RI
1995	A NEW FALLEN SNOW, Renee McGinnis, closed	29.95	RI

Christmas Memories

1993	WINTER'S TALE, J. Tanton, closed	29.90	RI
1993	FINISHING TOUCHES, J. Tanton, closed	29.90	RI
1994	WELCOME TO OUR HOME, J. Tanton, closed	29.90	RI
1994	A CHRISTMAS CELEBRATION, J. Tanton, closed	29.90	RI

Civil War: 1861–1865

1996	GETTYSBURG: TRIUMPH & TRAGEDY, T. Taylor, closed	29.90	RI

Classic Cars

1993	1957 CORVETTE, D. Everhart, closed	54.90	RI
1993	1956 T-BIRD, D. Everhart, closed	54.90	RI
1994	1957 BEL AIR, D. Everhart, closed	54.90	RI
1994	1965 MUSTANG, D. Everhart, closed	54.90	RI

Classic Melodies from *The Sound of Music*

1995	SING ALONG WITH MARIA, Michael Hampshire, closed	29.90	RI
1995	A DROP OF GOLDEN SUN, Michael Hampshire, closed	29.90	RI
1995	THE VON TRAPP FAMILY SINGERS, Michael Hampshire, closed	29.90	RI
1995	ALPINE REFUGE, Michael Hampshire, closed	29.90	RI

Classic Roses

		ISSUE	CURRENT
1996	BEAUTY IN BLOOM, Lynn Moser, open	34.95	RI
1996	MAGIC IN MAUVE, Lynn Moser, open	34.95	RI
1996	PRECIOUS IN PURPLE, Lynn Moser, open	34.95	RI
1996	PRETTY IN PINK, Lynn Moser, open	34.95	RI

Corinthian Angels

1996	LOVE IS PATIENT, open	34.95	RI

Costuming of a Legend: Dressing *Gone with the Wind*

1993	THE RED DRESS, Douglas Klauba, closed	29.90	RI
1993	THE GREEN DRAPERY DRESS, Douglas Klauba, 95 days	29.90	RI
1994	THE GREEN SPRIGGED DRESS, Douglas Klauba, 95 days	29.90	RI
1994	BLACK AND WHITE BENGALINE DRESS, Douglas Klauba, 95 days	29.90	RI
1994	WIDOW'S WEEDS, Douglas Klauba, 95 days	29.90	RI
1994	THE COUNTRY WALKING DRESS, Douglas Klauba, 95 days	29.90	RI
1994	PLAID BUSINESS ATTIRE, Douglas Klauba, 95 days	29.90	RI
1994	ORCHID PERCALE DRESS, Douglas Klauba, 95 days	29.90	RI
1994	THE MOURNING GOWN, Douglas Klauba, 95 days	29.90	RI
1994	FINAL OUTTAKE: THE GREEN MUSLIN DRESS, Douglas Klauba, 95 days	29.90	RI

Country Wonderland

1995	THE QUIET HOUR, Wilhelm Goebel, 95 days	29.90	RI

Cow-Hide

1995	INCOWGNITO, Diana Casey, 95 days	29.90	RI
1995	INCOWSPICUOUS, Diana Casey, 95 days	29.90	RI
1996	COWMMOOFLAGE, Diana Casey, 95 days	34.95	RI
1996	COWPANIONS, Diana Casey, 95 days	34.95	RI

Currier & Ives Christmas

1995	AMERICAN HOMESTEAD WINTER	34.95	RI
1995	AMERICAN WINTER SCENES	34.95	RI
1995	EARLY WINTER	34.95	RI
1996	WINTER MOON/FEEDING CHICKENS	34.95	RI

Deer Friends at Christmas

1994	ALL A GLOW, Joe Thornbrugh, closed	29.90	RI
1994	A GLISTENING SEASON, Joe Thornbrugh, closed	29.90	RI
1994	HOLIDAY SPARKLE, Joe Thornbrugh, closed	29.90	RI
1995	WOODLAND SPLENDOR, Joe Thornbrugh, closed	29.90	RI
1995	STARRY NIGHT, Joe Thornbrugh, closed	29.90	RI
1995	RADIANT COUNTRYSIDE, Joe Thornbrugh, closed	29.90	RI

Desert Rhythms

1994	PARTNER WITH THE BREEZE, Melinda Cowdery, 95 days	29.90	RI
1994	WIND DANCER, Melinda Cowdery, 95 days	29.90	RI
1994	RIDING ON AIR, Melinda Cowdery, 95 days	29.90	RI

Diana: Queen of Our Hearts

1997	THE PEOPLE'S PRINCESS, Jean Monte, 95 days, oval	29.95	RI

		ISSUE	CURRENT
Dick Tracy: America's Favorite Detective			
1996	THE CRIME STOPPER	29.90	RI
Disneyland's 40th Anniversary			
1995	SLEEPING BEAUTY CASTLE, Disney Studios	29.95	RI
1995	DISNEYLAND RAILROAD, Disney Studios	29.95	RI
1996	MAIN STREET, U.S.A., Disney Studios	29.95	RI
1996	FLIGHT TO NEVERLAND, Disney Studios	32.95	RI
1996	HAUNTED MANSION, Disney Studios	32.95	RI
1996	IT'S A SMALL WORLD, Disney Studios	32.95	RI
1996	MATTERHORN, Disney Studios	32.95	RI
1996	MICKEY'S TOONTOWN, Disney Studios	32.95	RI
1996	PIRATES OF THE CARIBBEAN, Disney Studios	32.95	RI
1996	WELCOME TO WONDERLAND, Disney Studios	32.95	RI
Disney's Musical Memories			
1995	THE FAIREST ONE OF ALL, Disney Studios, 95 days	29.90	RI
1995	CINDERELLA'S WISH COME TRUE, Disney Studios, 95 days	29.90	RI
1996	ALADDIN'S MAGICAL NEW WORLD, Disney Studios, open	32.90	RI
Divine Light			
1995	SAVIOUR IS BORN, R. McCausland, open	34.95	RI
1996	BIRTH OF A KING, R. McCausland, open	34.95	RI
1996	BLESSED IS THE CHILD, R. McCausland, open	34.95	RI
1996	WE SHALL PRAISE HIM, R. McCausland, open	34.95	RI
Dog Days			
1993	SWEET DREAMS, Jerry Gadamus, closed	29.90	RI
1993	PIER GROUP, Jerry Gadamus, closed	29.90	RI
1993	WAGON TRAIN, Jerry Gadamus, closed	32.90	RI
1993	FIRST FLUSH, Jerry Gadamus, closed	32.90	RI
1993	LITTLE RASCALS, Jerry Gadamus, closed	32.90	RI
1993	WHERE'D HE GO?, Jerry Gadamus, closed	32.90	RI
Elvis: Young and Wild			
1993	THE KING OF CREOLE, Bruce Emmett, 95 days	29.90	RI
1993	KING OF THE ROAD, Bruce Emmett, 95 days	29.90	RI
1994	TOUGH BUT TENDER, Bruce Emmett, 95 days	32.90	RI
1994	WITH LOVE, ELVIS, Bruce Emmett, 95 days	32.90	RI
1994	THE PICTURE OF COOL, Bruce Emmett, 95 days	32.90	RI
1994	KISSING ELVIS, Bruce Emmett, 95 days	34.90	RI
1994	THE PERFECT TAKE, Bruce Emmett, 95 days	34.90	RI
1994	THE ROCKIN' REBEL, Bruce Emmett, 95 days	34.90	RI
Emmitt Smith: Run to Daylight			
1997	SUPER BOWL XXX, Danny Day, 95 days	29.95	RI
Enchanted Charms of Oz			
1996	CAN'T EVEN SCARE A CROW, Michael Dudash, open	32.90	RI
1996	FRESH FROM BRUSH UP SHOP, Michael Dudash, open	32.90	RI
1996	THERE'S NO PLACE LIKE HOME, Michael Dudash, open	32.90	RI

		ISSUE	CURRENT
1996	WONDERFUL WIZARD OF OZ, Michael Dudash, open	32.90	RI

Escape to the Country

1996	COUNTRY CORNUCOPIA, David Henderson, open	29.95	RI
1996	COUNTRY WELCOME, David Henderson, open	29.95	RI
1996	COUNTY LINE FARMER'S MARKET, David Henderson, open	29.95	RI

Faces of the Wild

1995	THE WOLF, Donna Parker, 1 year	39.90	RI
1995	THE WHITE WOLF, Donna Parker, 1 year	39.90	RI
1995	THE COUGAR, Donna Parker, 95 days	44.90	RI
1995	THE BOBCAT, Donna Parker, 95 days	44.90	RI
1995	THE BEAR, Donna Parker, 95 days	44.90	RI
1995	THE FOX, Donna Parker, 95 days	44.90	RI
1995	THE BISON, Donna Parker, 95 days	44.90	RI
1995	THE LYNX, Donna Parker, 95 days	44.90	RI

Fairyland

1994	TRAILS OF STARLIGHT, Mimi Jobe, 95 days	29.90	RI
1994	TWILIGHT TRIO, Mimi Jobe, 95 days	29.90	RI
1994	FOREST ENCHANTMENT, Mimi Jobe, 95 days	32.90	RI
1995	SILVERY SPLASHER, Mimi Jobe, 95 days	32.90	RI
1995	MAGICAL MISCHIEF, Mimi Jobe, 95 days	32.90	RI
1995	FAREWELL TO THE NIGHT, Mimi Jobe, 95 days	34.90	RI

Family Affair

1995	DEN MOTHER, Carl Brenders, 95 days	29.90	RI
1995	CLOSE TO MOM, Carl Brenders, 95 days	29.90	RI
1995	FULL HOUSE, Carl Brenders, 95 days	29.90	RI
1995	SHADOWS IN THE GRASS, Carl Brenders, 95 days	29.90	RI
1995	UNDER MOTHER'S WATCHFUL EYE, Carl Brenders, 95 days	29.90	RI
1995	ROCKY CAMP, D. L. Rust, 95 days	29.90	RI

Family Circles

1993	GREAT GRAY OWL FAMILY, D. L. Rust, closed	29.90	RI
1993	GREAT HORNED OWL FAMILY, D. L. Rust, closed	29.90	RI
1994	BARRED OWL FAMILY, D. L. Rust, closed	29.90	RI
1994	SPOTTED OWL FAMILY, D. L. Rust, closed	29.90	RI

Family's Love

1996	GIVING THANKS, S. Wheeler	29.95	RI

Field Pup Follies

1994	SLEEPING ON THE JOB, Cliff Jackson, closed	29.90	RI
1994	HAT CHECK, Cliff Jackson, closed	29.90	RI
1994	FOWL PLAY, Cliff Jackson, closed	29.90	RI
1994	TACKLING LUNCH, Cliff Jackson, closed	29.90	RI

Fierce and Free: The Big Cats

1995	BLACK LEOPARD, J. Beecham	39.90	RI
1995	COUGAR, J. Beecham	39.90	RI
1995	JAGUAR, J. Beecham	39.90	RI

		ISSUE	CURRENT
1995	SNOW LEOPARD, J. Beecham	39.90	RI
1996	AFRICAN LION, J. Beecham	39.90	RI
1996	THE TIGER, J. Beecham	39.90	RI

Fleeting Encounters

1995	AUTUMN RETREAT, M. Budden, 95 days	29.90	RI

Floral Frolics

1994	SPRING SURPRISES, Glenna Kurz, closed	29.90	RI
1994	BEE CAREFUL, Glenna Kurz, closed	29.90	RI
1995	FUZZY FUN, Glenna Kurz, closed	32.90	RI
1995	SUNNY HIDEOUT, Glenna Kurz, closed	32.90	RI

Floral Greetings

1994	CIRCLE OF LOVE, Lena Liu, 95 days	29.90	RI
1994	CIRCLE OF ELEGANCE, Lena Liu, 95 days	29.90	RI
1994	CIRCLE OF HARMONY, Lena Liu, 95 days	32.90	RI
1994	CIRCLE OF JOY, Lena Liu, 95 days	32.90	RI
1994	CIRCLE OF ROMANCE, Lena Liu, 95 days	34.90	RI
1995	CIRCLE OF INSPIRATION, Lena Liu, 95 days	34.90	RI

Footsteps of the Brave

1993	NOBLE QUEST, H. Schaare, 95 days	24.90	RI
1993	AT STORM'S PASSAGE, H. Schaare, 95 days	24.90	RI
1993	WITH BOUNDLESS VISION, H. Schaare, 95 days	27.90	RI
1993	HORIZONS OF DESTINY, H. Schaare, 95 days	27.90	RI
1993	PATH OF HIS FOREFATHERS, H. Schaare, 95 days	27.90	RI
1993	SOULFUL REFLECTION, H. Schaare, 95 days	29.90	RI
1993	THE REVERENT TRAIL, H. Schaare, 95 days	29.90	RI
1994	AT JOURNEY'S END, H. Schaare, 95 days	34.90	RI

Forever Glamorous Barbie

1995	ENCHANTED EVENING, C. Falberg, 1 year	49.90	RI
1995	SOPHISTICATED LADY, C. Falberg, 1 year	49.90	RI
1995	SOLO IN THE SPOTLIGHT, C. Falberg, 1 year	49.90	RI
1995	MIDNIGHT BLUE, C. Falberg, 1 year	49.90	RI

Fracé's Kingdom of the Great Cats: Signature Collection

1994	MYSTIC REALM, Charles Fracé, 95 days	39.90	RI
1994	SNOW LEOPARD, Charles Fracé, 95 days	39.90	RI
1994	EMPEROR OF SIBERIA, Charles Fracé, 95 days	39.90	RI
1994	HIS DOMAIN, Charles Fracé, 95 days	39.90	RI
1994	AMERICAN MONARCH, Charles Fracé, 95 days	39.90	RI

Freshwater Game Fish of North America

1994	RAINBOW TROUT, Ed Totten, 95 days	29.90	RI
1995	LARGEMOUTH BASS, Ed Totten, 95 days	29.90	RI
1995	BLUE GILLS, Ed Totten, 95 days	29.90	RI
1995	NORTHERN PIKE, Ed Totten, 95 days	29.90	RI
1995	BROWN TROUT, Ed Totten, 95 days	29.90	RI

Friendship in Bloom

		ISSUE	CURRENT
1994	PAWS IN THE POSIES, Lily Chang, 95 days	34.90	RI
1995	COZY PETUNIA PATCH, Lily Chang, 95 days	34.90	RI
1995	PATIENCE & IMPATIENCE, Lily Chang, 95 days	34.90	RI

Gallant Men of the Civil War

1994	ROBERT E. LEE, John Paul Strain, 95 days	29.90	RI
1995	STONEWALL JACKSON, John Paul Strain, 95 days	29.90	RI
1995	NATHAN BEDFORD FOREST, John Paul Strain, 95 days	29.90	RI
1995	JOSHUA CHAMBERLAIN, John Paul Strain, 95 days	29.90	RI
1995	JOHN HUNT MORGAN, John Paul Strain, 95 days	29.90	RI

A Garden of Little Jewels (6-plate Palladian window display)

1998	PRECIOUS TREASURES, Larry K. Martin, fan shaped	34.95	RI
1998	2nd RELEASE, Larry K. Martin, fan shaped	34.95	RI
1998	3rd RELEASE, Larry K. Martin, square	34.95	RI
1998	4th RELEASE, Larry K. Martin, square	34.95	RI
1998	5th RELEASE, Larry K. Martin, square	34.95	RI
1998	6th RELEASE, Larry K. Martin, square	34.95	RI

Gardens of Innocence

1994	HOPE, Donna Richardson, 95 days	29.90	RI
1994	CHARITY, Donna Richardson, 95 days	29.90	RI
1994	JOY, Donna Richardson, 95 days	32.90	RI
1994	FAITH, Donna Richardson, 95 days	32.90	RI
1994	GRACE, Donna Richardson, 95 days	32.90	RI
1995	SERENITY, Donna Richardson, 95 days	34.90	RI
1995	PEACE, Donna Richardson, 95 days	34.90	RI
1995	PATIENCE, Donna Richardson, 95 days	34.90	RI

Getting Away from It All

1995	MOUNTAIN HIDEAWAY, D. L. Rust, 95 days	29.90	RI

Glory of Christ

1995	CHRIST FEEDS THE MULTITUDES, Robert T. Barrett, 95 days	29.90	RI
1995	CHRIST WALKS ON WATER, Robert T. Barrett, 95 days	29.90	RI
1996	CHRIST BEFORE THE APOSTLES, Robert T. Barrett, 95 days	29.90	RI
1996	RAISING OF LAZARUS, Robert T. Barrett, 95 days	29.90	RI
1996	WEDDING AT CANA, Robert T. Barrett, 95 days	29.90	RI
1996	THE ASCENSION, Robert T. Barrett, 95 days	29.90	RI

Gone with the Wind: Cameo Memories

1997	STEEL MAGNOLIA, Chris Notarile, 5 days	34.95	RI

Gone with the Wind: Musical Treasures

1994	TARA: SCARLETT'S TRUE LOVE, A. Jenks, 95 days	29.90	RI
1994	SCARLETT: BELLE OF 12 OAKS BBQ, A. Jenks, 95 days	29.90	RI
1995	CHARITY BAZAAR, A. Jenks, 95 days	32.90	RI
1995	THE PROPOSAL, A. Jenks, 95 days	32.90	RI

A Garden of Little Jewels Collection

The Last Supper Collection

		ISSUE	CURRENT

Gone with the Wind: Portrait in Stained Glass

		ISSUE	CURRENT
1995	SCARLETT RADIANCE, M. Phalen, closed	39.90	RI
1995	RHETT'S BRIGHT PROMISE, M. Phalen, closed	39.90	RI
1995	ASHLEY'S SMOLDERING FIRE, M. Phalen, closed	39.90	RI
1995	MELANIE LIGHTS HIS WORLD, M. Phalen, 95 days	39.90	RI

Great Moments in Baseball

		ISSUE	CURRENT
1993	JOE DIMAGGIO: THE STREAK, Stephen Gardner, 95 days	29.90	RI
1993	STAN MUSIAL: 5 HOMER DOUBLE HEADER, Stephen Gardner, 95 days	29.90	RI
1994	BOBBY THOMSON: SHOT HEARD ROUND THE WORLD, Stephen Gardner, 95 days	32.90	RI
1994	BILL MAZEROSKI: WINNING HOME RUN, Stephen Gardner, 95 days	32.90	RI
1994	DON LARSEN: PERFECT SERIES GAME, Stephen Gardner, 95 days	32.90	RI
1994	J. ROBINSON: SAVED PENNANT, Stephen Gardner, 95 days	34.90	RI
1994	SATCHEL PAIGE: GREATEST GAMES, Stephen Gardner, 95 days	34.90	RI
1994	BILLY MARTIN: THE RESCUE CATCH, Stephen Gardner, 95 days	34.90	RI
1994	DIZZY DEAN: THE WORLD SERIES SHUTOUT, Stephen Gardner, 95 days	34.90	RI
1995	CARL HUBBELL: THE 1934 ALL STATE, Stephen Gardner, 95 days	36.90	RI

Great Superbowl Quarterbacks

		ISSUE	CURRENT
1995	JOE MONTANA: KING OF COMEBACKS, Rick Brown, 95 days	29.90	RI
1995	JOE NAMATH: THE GUARANTEE, Rick Brown, 95 days	29.90	RI
1995	BART STARR: WINNING THE FIRST SUPERBOWL, Rick Brown, 95 days	29.90	RI
1995	JOHNNY UNITAS: CHAMPION, Rick Brown, 95 days	29.90	RI
1995	LEN DAWSON: MOST VALUABLE, Rick Brown, 95 days	29.90	RI
1996	BOB GRIESE, Rick Brown, 95 days	29.90	RI
1996	KEN STABLER: THE SNAKE STRIKES, Rick Brown, 95 days	29.90	RI

Guidance from Above

		ISSUE	CURRENT
1994	PRAYER TO THE STORM, B. Jaxon, closed	29.90	RI
1995	APPEAL TO THUNDER, B. Jaxon, closed	29.90	RI
1995	BLESSING THE FUTURE, B. Jaxon, closed	32.90	RI
1995	SHARING THE WISDOM, B. Jaxon, closed	32.90	RI

Happy Hearts

		ISSUE	CURRENT
1995	CONTENTMENT, Jim Daly, 95 days	29.90	RI
1995	PLAYMATES, Jim Daly, 95 days	29.90	RI
1995	CHILDHOOD FRIENDS, Jim Daly, 95 days	32.90	RI
1995	FAVORITE GIFT, Jim Daly, 95 days	32.90	RI

Heart of Cat Country

		ISSUE	CURRENT
1996	ALL ABOARD, R. Nanini, 95 days	29.95	RI

Heart of the Rockies (4-plate rectangular panorama)

		ISSUE	CURRENT
1998	THE EAGLES CALL IN WELCOME, Harold Roe	39.95	RI
1998	2nd RELEASE, Harold Roe	39.95	RI
1998	3rd RELEASE, Harold Roe	39.95	RI
1998	4th RELEASE, Harold Roe	39.95	RI

Heart Strings

		ISSUE	CURRENT
1996	FAMILY TIES, Judy Gibson, 95 days	34.95	RI

		ISSUE	CURRENT
1996	GIFT OF FRIENDSHIP, Judy Gibson, 95 days	34.95	RI

Heart to Heart

1995	THINKING OF YOU, Raphael-inspired, 95 days	29.90	RI
1995	SPEAKING OF LOVE, Raphael-inspired, 95 days	29.90	RI
1995	TALES OF FANCY, Fiorentino-inspired, 95 days	29.90	RI
1995	ECHOES OF AFFECTION, Maratta-inspired, 95 days	29.90	RI
1995	WHISPERS IN ROMANCE, Maratta-inspired, 95 days	29.90	RI
1996	FEELINGS OF ENDEARMENT, E. Steinbruck, open	29.90	RI

Heavenly Chorus

1995	ANGELS WE HAVE HEARD ON HIGH, Roger Akers, closed	39.90	RI
1995	HARK THE HERALD ANGELS SING, Roger Akers, closed	39.90	RI
1996	O COME ALL YE FAITHFUL, Roger Akers, closed	39.90	RI

Heaven on Earth

1994	I AM THE LIGHT OF THE WORLD, Thomas Kinkade, 95 days	29.90	RI
1995	I AM THE WAY, Thomas Kinkade, 95 days	29.90	RI
1995	THY WORD IS A LAMP, Thomas Kinkade, 95 days	29.90	RI
1995	FOR THOU ART MY LAMP, Thomas Kinkade, 95 days	29.90	RI
1995	IN HIM WAS LIFE, Thomas Kinkade, 95 days	29.90	RI
1995	BUT THE PATH OF JUST, Thomas Kinkade, 95 days	29.90	RI

Heaven Sent

1994	SWEET DREAMS, Lee Bogle, 95 days	29.90	RI
1994	PUPPY DOG TAILS, Lee Bogle, 95 days	29.90	RI
1994	TIMELESS TREASURE, Lee Bogle, 95 days	32.90	RI
1995	PRECIOUS GIFT, Lee Bogle, 95 days	32.90	RI

Heaven's Little Sweethearts

1996	AN ANGEL'S KINDNESS, Donna Brooks	29.95	RI
1996	AN ANGEL'S LOVE, Donna Brooks	29.95	RI
1996	AN ANGEL'S CARING, Donna Brooks	29.95	RI
1996	AN ANGEL'S DEVOTION, Donna Brooks	29.95	RI
1996	AN ANGEL'S TOUCH, Dona Gelsinger	29.95	RI

Heirloom Memories

1993	PORCELAIN TREASURES, A. Pech, closed	29.90	RI
1994	RHYTHMS IN LACE, A. Pech, closed	29.90	RI
1994	PINK LEMONADE ROSES, A. Pech, closed	29.90	RI
1994	VICTORIAN ROMANCE, A. Pech, closed	29.90	RI
1994	TEA TIME TULIPS, A. Pech, closed	29.90	RI
1994	TOUCH OF THE IRISH, A. Pech, closed	29.90	RI

Heirlooms and Lace

1994	TOUCH OF THE IRISH, A. Pech, closed	29.90	RI

Hidden Garden

1993	CURIOUS KITTEN, Todd Clausnitzer, closed	29.90	RI
1994	THROUGH THE EYES OF BLUE, Todd Clausnitzer, closed	29.90	RI
1994	AMBER GAZE, Todd Clausnitzer, closed	29.90	RI
1994	FASCINATING FIND, Todd Clausnitzer, closed	29.90	RI

Hidden World

		ISSUE	CURRENT
1993	TWO BY THE NIGHT, TWO BY THE LIGHT, D. L. Rust, closed	29.90	RI
1993	TWO BY STEAM, TWO IN DREAM, D. L. Rust, closed	29.90	RI
1993	TWO ON SLY, TWO WATCH NEARBY, D. L. Rust, closed	32.90	RI
1993	HUNTER GROWLS, SPIRITS PROWL, D. L. Rust, closed	32.90	RI
1993	IN MOONGLOW ONE DRINKS, D. L. Rust, closed	32.90	RI
1993	SINGS AT THE MOON, SPIRITS SING IN TUNE, D. L. Rust, closed	34.90	RI
1994	TWO CUBS PLAY AS SPIRIT SHOWS THE WAY, D. L. Rust, closed	34.90	RI
1994	YOUNG ONES HOLD ON TIGHT AS SPIRITS STAY IN SIGHT, D. L. Rust, closed	34.90	RI

Hideaway Lake

1993	RUSTY'S RETREAT, D. L. Rust, closed	34.90	RI
1993	FISHING FOR DREAMS, D. L. Rust, closed	34.90	RI
1994	SUNSET CABIN, D. L. Rust, closed	34.90	RI
1994	ECHOES OF MORNING, D. L. Rust, closed	34.90	RI

Home in the Heartland

1995	BARN RAISING, Martha Leone, 95 days	34.95	RI
1996	THE APPLE BLOSSOM FESTIVAL, Martha Leone, 95 days	34.95	RI
1996	COUNTRY FAIR, Martha Leone, 95 days	34.95	RI

Honoring the Spirit

1997	THE OFFERING, Julie Kramer, 95 days	39.95	RI

Hunchback of Notre Dame

1996	TOUCHED BY LOVE, Disney Studios	29.95	RI

Hunters of the Spirit

1995	PROVIDER, R. Docken, 95 days	29.90	RI
1995	DEFENDER, R. Docken, 95 days	29.90	RI
1995	GATHERER, R. Docken, 95 days	29.90	RI
1995	SEEKER, R. Docken, 95 days	29.90	RI
1996	THE HUNTER, R. Docken, 95 days	29.90	RI

Illusions of Nature

1995	A TRIO OF WOLVES, M. Bierlinski, 95 days	29.90	RI
1995	RUNNING DEER, M. Bierlinski, 95 days	29.90	RI
1995	AUTUMN ILLUSION, Janene Grende, 95 days	29.90	RI

Immortals of the Diamond

1994	THE SULTAN OF SWAT, Cliff Jackson, closed	39.90	RI
1994	PRIDE OF THE YANKEES, Cliff Jackson, closed	39.90	RI
1995	THE GEORGIA PEACH, Cliff Jackson, closed	39.90	RI
1995	THE WINNINGEST PITCHER, Cliff Jackson, closed	39.90	RI

It's a Wonderful Life

1995	AN ANGEL GETS HIS WINGS, Diane Sivavec, open	34.95	RI
1995	WELCOME HOME, Diane Sivavec, open	34.95	RI
1996	BY THE LIGHT OF THE MOON, Diane Sivavec, open	34.95	RI
1996	I'M THE ANSWER TO YOUR PRAYER, Diane Sivavec, open	34.95	RI

		ISSUE	CURRENT
Jim Hautman's Classic Waterfowl			
1996	MALLARDS: ON THE WING, Jim Hautman, 95 days	29.90	RI
Joe Montana: Ticket to Glory			
1997	SUPER BOWL XVI, Dan Smith, 95 days, rectangular	34.95	RI
Keepsakes of the Heart			
1993	FOREVER FRIENDS, Corinne Layton, closed	29.90	RI
1993	AFTERNOON TEA, Corinne Layton, closed	29.90	RI
1993	RIDING COMPANIONS, Corinne Layton, closed	29.90	RI
1994	SENTIMENTAL SWEETHEARTS, Corinne Layton, closed	29.90	RI
Kindred Moments			
1995	SISTERS ARE BLOSSOMS, Chantal Poulin, 95 days	19.95	RI
1996	FOREVER FRIENDS, Chantal Poulin, 95 days	19.95	RI
1996	CLOSE AT HEART, Chantal Poulin, 95 days	19.95	RI
Kindred Spirits			
1996	SPIRIT OF THE WOLF, Chantal Poulin	29.95	RI
Kindred Thoughts			
1995	SISTERS, Chantal Poulin, 95 days	29.90	RI
Kingdom of Enchantment			
1996	MOONBEAM TRAILS, Mimi Jobe	29.95	RI
1996	MOONLIGHT WONDER, Mimi Jobe	29.95	RI
Kingdom of the Unicorn			
1993	THE MAGIC BEGINS, M. Ferraro, closed	29.90	RI
1993	IN CRYSTAL WATERS, M. Ferraro, closed	29.90	RI
1993	CHASING A DREAM, M. Ferraro, closed	29.90	RI
1994	THE FOUNTAIN OF YOUTH, M. Ferraro, closed	29.90	RI
Kitten Expeditions			
1996	BY THE LILY POND, Jürgen Scholz, 98 days	29.95	RI
1996	AT THE GARDEN FENCE, Jürgen Scholz, 98 days	29.95	RI
Land of Oz: New Dimension			
1995	STEP INTO THE EMERALD CITY, D. Cherry, 95 days	34.90	RI
1995	WIZ LENTICULAR, D. Cherry, 95 days	34.90	RI
Last Supper (3-plate rectangular panorama)			
NA	THIS IS MY BODY, Christopher Nick	39.95	RI
NA	2nd RELEASE, Christopher Nick	39.95	RI
NA	3rd RELEASE, Christopher Nick	39.95	RI
Legendary Jackie Robinson			
1997	BREAKING BARRIERS, Brent Benger, 95 days	34.95	RI

			ISSUE	CURRENT
Legend of the White Buffalo				
1995	MYSTIC SPIRIT, D. Stanley, 95 days		29.90	RI
1995	CALL OF THE CLOUDS, D. Stanley, 95 days		29.90	RI
1995	VALLEY OF THE SACRED, D. Stanley, 95 days		29.90	RI
1996	BUFFALO SPIRIT OF THE VILLAGE, D. Stanley, 95 days		29.90	RI
1996	SPIRIT OF THE BUFFALO SHAMAN, D. Stanley, 95 days		29.90	RI
1996	WHITE BUFFALO CALF WOMAN, D. Stanley, 95 days		29.90	RI
Legend of the Moon				
1996	MOON OF RUNNING WOLVES, W. Terry		34.95	RI
Legends: World Record Whitetails				
1996	THE JORDAN BUCK, Ron Van Gilder		29.95	RI
Lena Liu's Beautiful Gardens—Inspired by Lena Liu				
1994	IRIS GARDEN, closed		34.00	RI
1994	PEONY GARDEN, closed		34.00	RI
1994	ROSE GARDEN, closed		39.00	RI
1995	LILY GARDEN, closed		39.00	RI
1995	TULIP GARDEN, closed		39.00	RI
1995	ORCHID GARDEN, closed		44.00	RI
1995	POPPY GARDEN, closed		44.00	RI
1995	CALLA LILY GARDEN, closed		44.00	RI
1995	MORNING GLORY GARDEN, closed		44.00	RI
1995	HIBISCUS GARDEN, 95 days		47.00	RI
1995	CLEMATIS GARDEN, 95 days		47.00	RI
1995	GLADIOLA GARDEN, 95 days		47.00	RI
Lena Liu's Country Accents				
1995	GARDEN DELIGHTS, Lena Liu, 95 days, oval		29.95	RI
1995	GARDEN PLEASURES, Lena Liu, 95 days, oval		29.95	RI
Lena Liu's Floral Cameos				
1997	REMEMBRANCE, Lena Liu, 95 days		29.95	RI
NA	ENCHANTMENT, Lena Liu		29.95	RI
NA	CHERISHED, Lena Liu		32.95	RI
Life of Christ				
1994	THE PASSION IN THE GARDEN, Robert T. Barrett, closed		29.90	RI
1994	JESUS ENTERS JERUSALEM, Robert T. Barrett, closed		29.90	RI
1994	JESUS CALMS THE WATERS, Robert T. Barrett, closed		32.90	RI
1994	SERMON ON THE MOUNT, Robert T. Barrett, closed		32.90	RI
1994	THE LAST SUPPER, Robert T. Barrett, closed		32.90	RI
1994	THE ASCENSION, Robert T. Barrett, closed		34.90	RI
1994	THE RESURRECTION, Robert T. Barrett, closed		34.90	RI
1994	THE CRUCIFIXION, Robert T. Barrett, closed		34.90	RI
Light of the World				
1995	THE LAST SUPPER, Christopher Nick, 95 days		29.90	RI
1995	BETRAYAL IN THE GARDEN, Christopher Nick, 95 days		29.90	RI
1995	FACING HIS ACCUSERS, Christopher Nick, 95 days		29.90	RI

		ISSUE	CURRENT
1996	JESUS GOES BEFORE PILATE, Christopher Nick, 95 days	29.90	RI
1996	PRAYER IN THE GARDEN, Christopher Nick, 95 days	29.90	RI
1996	WAY OF THE CROSS, Christopher Nick, 95 days	29.90	RI

Lincoln's Portraits of Valor

1993	THE GETTYSBURG ADDRESS, Robert A. Maguire, 95 days	29.90	RI
1993	EMANCIPATION PROCLAMATION, Robert A. Maguire, 95 days	29.90	RI
1993	THE LINCOLN-DOUGLAS DEBATES, Robert A. Maguire, 95 days	29.90	RI
1993	THE SECOND INAUGURAL ADDRESS, Robert A. Maguire, 95 days	29.90	RI

Lion King

1994	THE CIRCLE OF LIFE, Disney Studios, 95 days	29.90	RI
1995	LIKE FATHER, LIKE SON, Disney Studios, 95 days	29.90	RI
1995	COURTING THE FUTURE KING, Disney Studios, 95 days	29.90	RI
1995	HAKUNA MATATA, Disney Studios, 95 days	29.90	RI
1995	I'M GONNA BE KING, Disney Studios, 95 days	29.90	RI
1995	KING WITHIN, Disney Studios, 95 days	29.90	RI
1995	WE'LL ALWAYS BE FRIENDS, Disney Studios, 95 days	29.90	RI
1995	BEST FRIENDS, Disney Studios, 95 days	29.90	RI
1995	A CRUNCHY FEAST, Disney Studios, 95 days	32.90	RI

Litter Rascal

1996	SNEAKING SECONDS, Carolyn Jagodits	29.95	RI

Little Bandits

1993	HANDLE WITH CARE, Carolyn Jagodits, closed	29.90	RI
1993	ALL TIED UP, Carolyn Jagodits, closed	29.90	RI
1993	EVERYTHING'S COMING UP DAISIES, Carolyn Jagodits, closed	32.90	RI
1993	OUT OF HAND, Carolyn Jagodits, closed	32.90	RI
1994	PUPSICLES, Carolyn Jagodits, closed	32.90	RI
1994	UNEXPECTED GUESTS, Carolyn Jagodits, closed	32.90	RI

Lords of Forest and Canyon

1994	MOUNTAIN MAJESTY, Greg Beecham, 95 days	29.90	RI
1995	PROUD LEGACY, Greg Beecham, 95 days	29.90	RI
1995	GOLDEN MONARCH, Greg Beecham, 95 days	29.90	RI
1995	FOREST EMPEROR, Greg Beecham, 95 days	29.90	RI

Loving Hearts

1995	UNSELFISH AND GIVING, Renee McGinnis, 95 days	29.95	RI
1995	PATIENT AND KIND, Renee McGinnis, 95 days	29.95	RI
1996	BEAUTY AND SPLENDOR, Renee McGinnis, 95 days	29.95	RI

Majestic Patriots

1996	MY COUNTRY TIS OF THEE, Gene Dieckhoner, 95 days	29.90	RI

Majestic Trains of Yesteryear

1996	THE INYO V & T, G. Wilmott	29.90	RI

Marilyn by Milton H. Greene: Up Close and Personal

1997	FOREVER, MARILYN, Milton H. Greene	34.95	RI

		ISSUE	CURRENT
1997	BODY AND SOUL, Milton H. Greene	34.95	RI

Marilyn: The Golden Collection

1995	SULTRY YET REGAL, Michael Deas, 95 days	29.90	RI
1995	GRACEFUL BEAUTY, Michael Deas, 95 days	29.90	RI

Mary's Moo Moos

1995	PASTURE BEDTIME, Mary Rhyner-Nadig	29.95	RI

Masters of Land and Sky

1995	NOBLE BOND, Strongin	29.90	RI
1996	ENDURING PRESENCE, Strongin	29.90	RI
1996	SOVEREIGN UNITY, Strongin	29.90	RI

Me and My Shadow

1994	EASTER PARADE, Jennifer R. Welty, closed	29.90	RI
1994	A GOLDEN MOMENT, Jennifer R. Welty, closed	29.90	RI
1994	PERFECT TIMING, Jennifer R. Welty, closed	29.90	RI
1994	GIDDIYAP, Jennifer R. Welty, closed	29.90	RI

Mewsic for the Holidays

1997	FROSTY THE SNOWCAT, Randy Spangler, 95 days	34.95	RI

Michael Jordan: Breaking Records

1997	BREAKING THE RECORDS, <3 years	49.95	RI

Michael Jordan: A Legend for All Time

1995	SOARING STAR, A. Katzman, closed	79.95	RI
1996	RIM ROCKER, A. Katzman, 95 days	79.95	RI

Mickey and Minnie Through the Years

1995	MICKEY'S BIRTHDAY PARTY, 1942, Disney Studios, 95 days	29.90	RI
1995	BRAVE LITTLE TAILOR, Disney Studios, 95 days	29.90	RI
1995	MICKEY MOUSE CLUB, Disney Studios, 95 days	29.90	RI
1995	STEAMBOAT WILLIE, Disney Studios, 95 days	29.90	RI

Mickey Mantle Collection

1996	500TH HOME RUN CLUB, Stephen Gardner	39.95	RI
1996	BRONX BOMBER, Stephen Gardner	39.95	RI
1996	TRIPLE CROWN SEASON, Stephen Gardner	39.95	RI

M. I. Hummel (Studio Hummel)

NA	APPLE TREE BOY, M.I. Hummel, 15,000	49.95	RI
NA	APPLE TREE GIRL, M.I. Hummel, 15,000	49.95	RI

Miracle of Christmas

1996	ONCE UPON A HOLY NIGHT, Jennifer R. Welty	34.95	RI

Moments in the Garden

1995	RUBY TREASURES, Cynthie Fisher	29.95	RI

		ISSUE	CURRENT
1996	LUMINOUS JEWELS, Cynthie Fisher	29.95	RI
1996	LUSTROUS SAPPHIRE, Cynthie Fisher	29.95	RI
1996	RADIANT GEMS, Cynthie Fisher	29.95	RI
1996	SHIMMERING SPLENDOR, Cynthie Fisher	29.95	RI

Moments of Serenity

1994	MORNING REFLECTIONS, Bruce Langton	29.90	RI

Mother's Love

1995	REMEMBRANCE, Jan Anderson, 95 days	29.90	RI

Musical Carousels

1993	SWEET STANDER, Roger Akers	49.00	RI
1993	JOYFUL JUMPER, Roger Akers	49.00	RI

Musical Tribute to Elvis the King

1994	ROCKIN' BLUE SUEDE SHOES, Bruce Emmett, 95 days	29.90	RI
1994	HOUND DOG BOP, Bruce Emmett, 95 days	29.90	RI
1995	RED, WHITE & GI BLUES, Bruce Emmett, 95 days	32.90	RI
1995	AMERICAN DREAM, Bruce Emmett, 95 days	32.90	RI
1995	FALLING IN LOVE WITH THE KING, Bruce Emmett, 95 days	32.90	RI
1995	GOSPEL IN HIS SOUL, Bruce Emmett, 95 days	32.90	RI
1995	YOUR FUN LOVIN' TEDDY BEAR, Bruce Emmett, 95 days	32.90	RI
1996	LOVE: THE GREATEST GIFT, Bruce Emmett, 95 days	34.90	RI

Mysterious Case of Fowl Play

1994	INSPECTOR CLAWSEAU, B. Higgins Bond, closed	29.90	RI
1994	GLAMOURPUSS, B. Higgins Bond, closed	29.90	RI
1994	SOPHISTICAT, B. Higgins Bond, closed	29.90	RI
1994	KOOL CAT, B. Higgins Bond, closed	29.90	RI
1994	SNEAKERS AND HIGH-TOP, B. Higgins Bond, closed	29.90	RI
1994	TUXEDO, B. Higgins Bond, closed	29.90	RI

Mystic Guardians

1993	SOUL MATES, Sandra Hill, 95 days	29.90	RI
1993	MAJESTIC MESSENGER, Sandra Hill, 95 days	29.90	RI
1993	COMPANION SPIRITS, Sandra Hill, 95 days	32.90	RI
1994	FAITHFUL FELLOWSHIP, Sandra Hill, 95 days	32.90	RI
1994	SPIRITUAL HARMONY, Sandra Hill, 95 days	32.90	RI
1994	ROYAL UNITY, Sandra Hill, 95 days	32.90	RI

Mystic Spirits

1995	MOON SHADOWS, Vivi Crandall, 95 days	29.90	RI
1995	MIDNIGHT SNOW, Vivi Crandall, 95 days	29.90	RI
1995	ENTRANCING GLANCE, Vivi Crandall, 95 days	29.90	RI
1995	KEEPER OF THE NIGHT, Vivi Crandall, 95 days	29.90	RI
1995	SILENT ENCOUNTER, Vivi Crandall, 95 days	29.90	RI
1995	ARCTIC NIGHTS, Vivi Crandall, 95 days	32.90	RI
1996	SILENT NIGHT, Vivi Crandall, 95 days	32.90	RI

Native American Legends: Chiefs of Destiny

1994	SITTING BULL, Cliff Jackson, closed	39.90	RI

		ISSUE	CURRENT
1994	CHIEF JOSEPH, Cliff Jackson, closed	39.90	RI
1995	RED CLOUD, Cliff Jackson, closed	44.90	RI
1995	CRAZY HORSE, Cliff Jackson, closed	44.90	RI
1995	GERONIMO, Cliff Jackson, closed	44.90	RI
1995	TECUMSEH, Cliff Jackson, closed	44.90	RI

Native Beauty

1994	THE PROMISE, Lee Bogle, 95 days	29.90	RI
1994	AFTERGLOW, Lee Bogle, 95 days	29.90	RI
1994	WHITE FEATHER, Lee Bogle, 95 days	29.90	RI
1995	FIRST GLANCE, Lee Bogle, 95 days	29.90	RI
1995	MORNING STAR, Lee Bogle, 95 days	29.90	RI
1995	QUIET TIME, Lee Bogle, 95 days	29.90	RI
1995	WARM THOUGHTS, Lee Bogle, 95 days	29.90	RI

Native Visions

1994	BRINGERS OF THE STORM, Julie Kramer Cole, 95 days	29.90	RI
1994	WATER VISION, Julie Kramer Cole, 95 days	29.90	RI
1994	BROTHER TO THE MOON, Julie Kramer Cole, 95 days	29.90	RI
1995	SON OF THE SUN, Julie Kramer Cole, 95 days	29.90	RI
1995	MAN WHO SEES FAR, Julie Kramer Cole, 95 days	29.90	RI
1995	LISTENING, Julie Kramer Cole, 95 days	29.90	RI
1996	THE RED SHIELD, Julie Kramer Cole, 95 days	29.90	RI
1996	TOPONAS, Julie Kramer Cole, 95 days	29.90	RI

Nature's Little Treasures

1994	GARDEN WHISPERS, Larry K. Martin, 95 days	29.90	RI
1994	WINGS OF GRACE, Larry K. Martin, 95 days	29.90	RI
1994	DELICATE SPLENDOR, Larry K. Martin, 95 days	32.90	RI
1994	PERFECT JEWELS, Larry K. Martin, 95 days	32.90	RI
1994	MINIATURE GLORY, Larry K. Martin, 95 days	32.90	RI
1994	PRECIOUS BEAUTIES, Larry K. Martin, 95 days	34.90	RI
1994	MINUTE ENCHANTMENT, Larry K. Martin, 95 days	34.90	RI
1994	RARE PERFECTION, Larry K. Martin, 95 days	34.90	RI
1995	MISTY MORNING, Larry K. Martin, 95 days	36.90	RI

Nature's Nobility

1996	THE BUCK, Donna Parker, <1 year, 8¼"	39.95	RI
1996	THE WOLF, Donna Parker, <1 year, 8¼"	39.95	RI
1996	DALL SHEEP, Donna Parker, <1 year, 8¼"	39.95	RI

Nesting Neighbors

1998	OUR GINGERBREAD COTTAGE, sculpted	39.95	RI
1998	OUR SWEET HIDEAWAY, sculpted	39.95	RI

New Horizons

1993	BUILDING FOR A NEW GENERATION, Robert R. Copple, 95 days	29.90	RI
1994	THE POWER OF GOLD, Robert R. Copple, 95 days	29.90	RI
1994	WINGS OF SNOWY GRANDEUR, Robert R. Copple, 95 days	32.90	RI
1994	MASTER OF THE CHASE, Robert R. Copple, 95 days	32.90	RI
1995	COASTAL DOMAIN, Robert R. Copple, 95 days	32.90	RI
1995	MAJESTIC WINGS, Robert R. Copple, 95 days	32.90	RI

NFL 75th Anniversary All-Time Team

		ISSUE	CURRENT
1995	FOREST GREGG / JOE GREEN, M. Corning	34.95	RI
1995	MIKE WEBSTER / RAY NITSCHKE, M. Corning	34.95	RI
1996	GALE SAYERS / JACK LAMBERT, M. Corning	34.95	RI
1996	JOHNNY UNITAS / BOB LILY, M. Corning	34.95	RI

Nightsongs: The Loon

1994	MOONLIGHT ECHOES, Jim Hansel, closed	29.90	RI
1994	EVENING MIST, Jim Hansel, closed	29.90	RI
1994	NOCTURNAL GLOW, Jim Hansel, closed	32.90	RI
1994	TRANQUIL REFLECTIONS, Jim Hansel, closed	32.90	RI
1994	PEACEFUL WATERS, Jim Hansel, closed	32.90	RI
1994	SILENTLY NESTLED, Jim Hansel, closed	34.90	RI
1994	NIGHT LIGHT, Jim Hansel, closed	34.90	RI
1995	PEACEFUL HOMESTEAD, Jim Hansel, closed	34.90	RI
1995	SILENT PASSAGE, Jim Hansel, closed	34.90	RI
1995	TRANQUIL REFUGE, Jim Hansel, closed	36.90	RI
1995	SERENE SANCTUARY, Jim Hansel, closed	36.90	RI
1995	MOONLIGHT CRUISE, Jim Hansel, closed	36.90	RI

Nightwatch: The Wolf

1994	MOONLIGHT SERENADE, Don Ningwance, closed	29.90	RI
1994	MIDNIGHT GUARD, Don Ningwance, closed	29.90	RI
1994	SNOWY LOOKOUT, Don Ningwance, closed	29.90	RI
1994	SILENT SENTRIES, Don Ningwance, closed	29.90	RI
1994	SONG TO THE NIGHT, Don Ningwance, closed	29.90	RI
1994	WINTER PASSAGE, Don Ningwance, closed	29.90	RI

Northern Companions

1995	MIDNIGHT HARMONY, K. Weisberg, 95 days	29.90	RI

Northwoods Spirit

1994	TIMELESS WATCH, D. Wenzel, 95 days	29.90	RI
1994	WOODLAND RETREAT, D. Wenzel, 95 days	29.90	RI
1994	FOREST ECHO, D. Wenzel, 95 days	29.90	RI
1995	TIMBERLAND GAZE, D. Wenzel, 95 days	29.90	RI
1995	EVENING RESPITE, D. Wenzel, 95 days	29.90	RI

Nosy Neighbors

1994	CAT NAP, Persis Clayton Weirs, 95 days	29.90	RI
1994	SPECIAL DELIVERY, Persis Clayton Weirs, 95 days	29.90	RI
1995	HOUSE SITTING, Persis Clayton Weirs, 95 days	29.90	RI
1995	OBSERVATION DECK, Persis Clayton Weirs, 95 days	32.90	RI
1995	SURPRISE VISIT, Persis Clayton Weirs, 95 days	32.90	RI

Old Fashioned Christmas with Thomas Kinkade

1993	ALL FRIENDS ARE WELCOME, Thomas Kinkade, 95 days	29.90	RI
1993	WINTER'S MEMORIES, Thomas Kinkade, 95 days	29.90	RI
1993	A HOLIDAY GATHERING, Thomas Kinkade, 95 days	32.90	RI
1994	CHRISTMAS TREE COTTAGE, Thomas Kinkade, 95 days	32.90	RI
1995	THE BEST TRADITION, Thomas Kinkade, 95 days	32.90	RI

		ISSUE	CURRENT

Once Upon a Time

1997	GOLDILOCKS AND THE THREE BEARS, Scott Gustafson, 95 days	34.95	RI

Our Heavenly Mother

1996	ADORATION, Hector Garrido, 95 days	34.90	RI
1996	FAITHFULNESS, Hector Garrido, 95 days	34.90	RI
1996	HEAVENLY DEVOTION, Hector Garrido, 95 days	34.90	RI
1996	CONSTANCY, Hector Garrido, 95 days	34.90	RI

Panda Bear Hugs

1993	ROCK-A-BYE, Will Nelson, closed	39.90	RI
1993	LOVING ADVICE, Will Nelson, closed	39.90	RI
1993	A PLAYFUL INTERLUDE, Will Nelson, closed	39.90	RI
1993	A TASTE OF LIFE, Will Nelson, closed	39.90	RI

Pathways of the Heart

1993	OCTOBER RADIANCE, Jesse Barnes, 95 days	29.90	RI
1993	DAYBREAK, Jesse Barnes, 95 days	29.90	RI
1994	HARMONY WITH NATURE, Jesse Barnes, 95 days	29.90	RI
1994	DISTANT LIGHTS, Jesse Barnes, 95 days	29.90	RI
1994	A NIGHT TO REMEMBER, Jesse Barnes, 95 days	29.90	RI
1994	PEACEFUL EVENING, Jesse Barnes, 95 days	29.90	RI

Paws in Action

1995	PLAYFUL DREAMS, M. Rien	29.90	RI
1995	SWEET SLUMBER, M. Rien	29.90	RI
1996	NESTLED WRESTLE, M. Rien	29.90	RI

Peaceable Kingdom

1994	NOAH'S ARK, M. Harvey, closed	29.90	RI

Peace on Earth

1993	WINTER LULLABY, Duane Geisness, closed	29.90	RI
1994	HEAVENLY SLUMBER, Duane Geisness, closed	29.90	RI
1994	SWEET EMBRACE, Duane Geisness, closed	32.90	RI
1994	WOODLAND DREAMS, Duane Geisness, closed	32.90	RI
1994	SNOWY SILENCE, Duane Geisness, closed	32.90	RI
1994	DREAMY WHISPERS, Duane Geisness, closed	32.90	RI

Picked from an English Garden

1994	INSPIRED BY ROMANCE, W. Von Schwarzbek, closed	32.90	RI
1995	LASTING TREASURES, W. Von Schwarzbek, closed	32.90	RI
1995	NATURE'S WONDERS, W. Von Schwarzbek, closed	32.90	RI
1995	SUMMER RHAPSODY, W. Von Schwarzbek, closed	32.90	RI

Pinegrove Winter Cardinals

1994	EVENING IN PINEGROVE, Sam Timm, 95 days	29.90	RI
1994	PINEGROVE'S SUNSET, Sam Timm, 95 days	29.90	RI
1994	PINEGROVE'S TWILIGHT, Sam Timm, 95 days	29.90	RI
1994	DAYBREAK IN PINEGROVE, Sam Timm, 95 days	29.90	RI
1994	PINEGROVE'S MORNING, Sam Timm, 95 days	29.90	RI

		ISSUE	CURRENT
1994	AFTERNOON IN PINEGROVE, Sam Timm, 95 days	29.90	RI
1994	MIDNIGHT IN PINEGROVE, Sam Timm, 95 days	29.90	RI
1994	AT HOME IN PINEGROVE, Sam Timm, 95 days	29.90	RI

Pocahontas

1996	LOVE'S EMBRACE, Disney Studios, 95 days	29.95	RI

Pooh's Hunnypot Adventures

1996	IT'S JUST A SMALL PIECE OF WEATHER, Disney Studios	39.95	RI
NA	HIP HIP POOHRAY, Disney Studios	39.95	RI

Popeye: The One and Only

1996	POPEYE THE SAILORMAN, E. C. Segar	NA	RI

Portraits of Majesty

1994	SNOWY MONARCH, Dominique Brand, 95 days	29.90	RI
1995	REFLECTION OF KINGS, Dominique Brand, 95 days	34.90	RI
1995	EMPEROR OF HIS REALM, Dominique Brand, 95 days	34.90	RI
1995	SOLEMN SOVEREIGN, Dominique Brand, 95 days	34.90	RI

Postcards from Thomas Kinkade

1995	SAN FRANCISCO, Thomas Kinkade, 95 days	34.90	RI
1995	PARIS, Thomas Kinkade, 95 days	34.90	RI
1995	NEW YORK CITY, Thomas Kinkade, 95 days	34.90	RI

Practice Makes Perfect

1994	WHAT'S A MOTHER TO DO?, Lynn Kaatz, closed	29.90	RI
1994	THE ONES THAT GOT AWAY, Lynn Kaatz, closed	29.90	RI
1994	POINTED IN THE WRONG DIRECTION, Lynn Kaatz, closed	32.90	RI
1994	FISHING FOR COMPLIMENTS, Lynn Kaatz, closed	32.90	RI
1994	A DANDY DISTRACTION, Lynn Kaatz, closed	32.90	RI
1995	MORE THAN A MOUTHFUL, Lynn Kaatz, closed	34.90	RI
1995	ON THE RIGHT TRACK, Lynn Kaatz, closed	34.90	RI
1995	MISSING THE POINT, Lynn Kaatz, closed	34.90	RI

Precious Visions

1994	BRILLIANT MOMENT, Janene Grende, 95 days	29.90	RI
1995	BRIEF INTERLUDE, Janene Grende, 95 days	29.90	RI
1995	TIMELESS RADIANCE, Janene Grende, 95 days	29.90	RI
1995	ENDURING ELEGANCE, Janene Grende, 95 days	32.90	RI

Proud Heritage

1994	MYSTIC WARRIOR: MEDICINE CROW, M. Amerman, closed	34.90	RI
1994	GREAT CHIEF: SITTING BULL, M. Amerman, closed	34.90	RI
1994	BRAVE LEADER: GERONIMO, M. Amerman, closed	34.90	RI
1995	PEACEFUL DEFENDER: CHIEF JOSEPH, M. Amerman, closed	34.90	RI

Purrfectly at Home

1996	HOME SWEET HOME, Merri Roderick	39.95	RI
1996	KITTY CORNER, Merri Roderick	39.95	RI

Quiet Moments

		ISSUE	CURRENT
1994	TIME FOR TEA, Kevin Daniel, 95 days	29.90	RI
1995	A LOVING HAND, Kevin Daniel, 95 days	29.90	RI
1995	KEPT WITH CARE, Kevin Daniel, 95 days	29.90	RI
1995	PUPPY LOVE, Kevin Daniel, 95 days	29.90	RI

Radiant Messengers

		ISSUE	CURRENT
1994	PEACE, Larry K. Martin, 95 days	29.90	RI
1994	HOPE, 95 days	29.90	RI
1994	BEAUTY, 95 days	29.90	RI
1994	INSPIRATION, 95 days	29.90	RI

Reflections of Marilyn

		ISSUE	CURRENT
1994	ALL THAT GLITTERS, Chris Notarile, 95 days	29.90	RI
1994	SHIMMERING HEAT, Chris Notarile, 95 days	29.90	RI
1994	MILLION DOLLAR STAR, Chris Notarile, 95 days	29.90	RI
1995	A TWINKLE IN HER EYE, Chris Notarile, 95 days	29.90	RI

Remembering Elvis

		ISSUE	CURRENT
1995	THE KING, Nate Giorgio, 95 days	29.90	RI
1995	THE LEGEND, Nate Giorgio, 95 days	29.90	RI

Royal Enchantments

		ISSUE	CURRENT
1994	THE GIFT, J. Penchoff, <1 year	39.90	RI
1995	THE COURTSHIP, J. Penchoff, <1 year	39.90	RI
1995	THE PROMISE, J. Penchoff, <1 year	39.90	RI
1995	THE EMBRACE, J. Penchoff, <1 year	39.90	RI

Sacred Circle

		ISSUE	CURRENT
1993	BEFORE THE HUNT, Kirk Randle	29.90	RI
1993	SPIRITUAL GUARDIAN, Kirk Randle	29.90	RI
1993	GHOST DANCE, Kirk Randle	32.90	RI
1994	DEER DANCE, Kirk Randle	32.90	RI
1994	WOLF DANCE, Kirk Randle	32.90	RI
1994	PAINTED HORSE, Kirk Randle	34.90	RI
1994	TRANSFORMATION DANCE, Kirk Randle	34.90	RI
1994	ELK DANCE, Kirk Randle	34.90	RI

Santa's Little Helpers

		ISSUE	CURRENT
1994	STOCKING STUFFERS, B. Higgins Bond, closed	24.90	RI
1994	WRAPPING UP THE HOLIDAYS, B. Higgins Bond, closed	24.90	RI
1994	NOT A CREATURE WAS STIRRING, B. Higgins Bond, closed	24.90	RI
1995	COZY KITTENS, B. Higgins Bond, closed	24.90	RI
1995	HOLIDAY MISCHIEF, B. Higgins Bond, closed	24.90	RI
1995	TREATS FOR SANTA, B. Higgins Bond, closed	24.90	RI

Santa's on His Way

		ISSUE	CURRENT
1994	CHECKING IT TWICE, Scott Gustafson, closed	29.90	RI
1994	UP, UP & AWAY, Scott Gustafson, closed	29.90	RI
1995	SANTA'S FIRST STOP, Scott Gustafson, closed	32.90	RI
1995	GIFTS FOR ONE AND ALL, Scott Gustafson, closed	32.90	RI

		ISSUE	CURRENT
1995	A WARM SEND-OFF, Scott Gustafson, closed	32.90	RI
1995	SANTA'S REWARD, Scott Gustafson, closed	34.90	RI

Seasons of Love

1996	A CHERISHED MOMENT, M. Sarnat	29.95	RI

Seasons on the Open Range

1996	SEASON OF GOLD, L. Zabel	29.95	RI

Signs of Spring

1994	A FAMILY FEAST, Joe Thornbrugh, 95 days	29.90	RI
1995	HOW FAST THEY GROW, Joe Thornbrugh, 95 days	29.90	RI
1995	OUR FIRST HOME, Joe Thornbrugh, 95 days	29.90	RI
1995	AWAITING NEW ARRIVALS, Joe Thornbrugh, 95 days	29.90	RI

Silent Journey

1994	WHERE PATHS CROSS, Diana Casey, 95 days	29.90	RI
1994	ON EAGLE'S WINGS, Diana Casey, 95 days	29.90	RI
1994	SEEING THE UNSEEN, Diana Casey, 95 days	29.90	RI
1995	WHERE THE BUFFALO ROAM, Diana Casey, 95 days	29.90	RI
1995	UNBRIDLED MAJESTY, Diana Casey, 95 days	29.90	RI
1995	WISDOM SEEKER, Diana Casey, 95 days	29.90	RI
1995	JOURNEY OF THE WILD, Diana Casey, 95 days	29.90	RI

Small Blessings

NA	NOW I LAY ME DOWN TO SLEEP, Corinne Layton	NA	30.00

Soft Elegance

1994	PRISCILLA IN PEARLS, R. Iverson, 95 days	29.90	RI
1995	TABITHA ON TAFFETA, R. Iverson, 95 days	29.90	RI
1995	EMILY IN EMERALDS, R. Iverson, 95 days	29.90	RI
1995	ALEXANDRA IN AMETHYSTS, R. Iverson, 95 days	29.90	RI

Where Paths Cross
Photo courtesy of *Collectors News*

The Lovers
Photo courtesy of *Collectors News*

		ISSUE	CURRENT

Solid Gold Elvis

1996	JAILHOUSE ROCK, Nate Giorgio, 95 days	29.95	RI

Some Beary Nice Places

1994	WELCOME TO THE LIBEARY, J. Tanton, closed	29.90	RI
1994	WELCOME TO OUR COUNTRY KITCHEN, J. Tanton, closed	29.90	RI
1995	BEARENNIAL GARDEN, J. Tanton, closed	32.90	RI
1995	WELCOME TO OUR MUSIC CONSERBEARTORY, J. Tanton, closed	32.90	RI

Someone to Watch over Me

1995	GUIDING THE WAY	29.90	RI
1995	GUIDED JOURNEY	29.90	RI
1995	HELPING HAND ON HIGH	29.90	RI
1995	NURTURING INNOCENCE	29.90	RI
1995	PROTECTED SLEEP	29.90	RI
1995	SAFE AT PLAY	29.90	RI
1996	BY MY SIDE	29.90	RI
1996	FAITHFUL CARE	29.90	RI

Soul Mates

1995	THE LOVERS, Lee Bogle, 95 days	29.90	RI
1995	THE AWAKENING, Lee Bogle, 95 days	29.90	RI
1995	THE EMBRACE, Lee Bogle, 95 days	29.90	RI

Soul of the Wilderness

1995	CHANCE OF FLURRIES, B. Parrish	34.95	RI
1995	ONE LAST LOOK, B. Parrish	34.95	RI
1995	SILENT WATCH, B. Parrish	34.95	RI
1996	WINTER SOLSTICE, B. Parrish	34.95	RI
1996	WINTER WHITES, B. Parrish	34.95	RI

Sovereigns of the Sky

1994	SPIRIT OF FREEDOM, Gene Dieckhoner, closed	39.00	RI
1994	SPIRIT OF PRIDE, Gene Dieckhoner, closed	39.00	RI
1994	SPIRIT OF VALOR, Gene Dieckhoner, closed	44.00	RI
1994	SPIRIT OF MAJESTY, Gene Dieckhoner, closed	44.00	RI
1994	SPIRIT OF GLORY, Gene Dieckhoner, closed	44.00	RI
1995	SPIRIT OF COURAGE, Gene Dieckhoner, closed	44.00	RI
1995	SPIRIT OF BRAVERY, Gene Dieckhoner, closed	44.00	RI
1995	SPIRIT OF HONOR, Gene Dieckhoner, closed	44.00	RI

Sovereigns of the Wild

1993	THE SNOW QUEEN, D. Grant	29.90	RI
1994	LET US SURVIVE, D. Grant	29.90	RI
1994	COOL CATS, D. Grant	29.90	RI
1994	SIBERIAN SNOW TIGERS, D. Grant	29.90	RI
1994	AFRICAN EVENING, D. Grant	29.90	RI
1994	FIRST OUTING, D. Grant	29.90	RI

Spirit Journeys

1996	SUMMONED SPIRITS, Julie Kramer Cole, 95 days	29.95	RI

		ISSUE	CURRENT

Spirit of the Wilderness

1996	EBONY CHIEF, Eddie LePage	34.90	RI

Study of a Champion

1995	DEVOTED PARTNER, Bruce Langton	29.90	RI
1995	LOYAL COMPANION, Bruce Langton	29.90	RI
1995	TRUSTED FRIEND, Bruce Langton	29.90	RI
1996	FAITHFUL BUDDY, Bruce Langton	29.90	RI

Sunflower Serenade

1996	GOLDEN SUNSHINE, Y. Lantz	NA	RI

Superstars of Baseball

1994	WILLIE "SAY HEY" MAYS, Ted Sizemore, closed	29.90	RI
1995	CARL "YAZ" YASTRZEMSKI, Ted Sizemore, closed	29.90	RI
1995	FRANK "ROBBY" ROBINSON, Ted Sizemore, closed	32.90	RI
1995	BOB GIBSON, Ted Sizemore, closed	32.90	RI
1995	HARMON KILLEBREW, Ted Sizemore, closed	32.90	RI
1995	DON DRYSDALE, Ted Sizemore, closed	34.90	RI
1995	AL KALINE, Ted Sizemore, closed	34.90	RI
1995	MAURY WILLS, Ted Sizemore, closed	34.90	RI

Superstars of Country Music

1993	DOLLY PARTON: I WILL ALWAYS LOVE YOU, Nate Giorgio	29.90	RI
1993	KENNY ROGERS: SWEET MUSIC MAN, Nate Giorgio	29.90	RI
1994	BARBARA MANDRELL, Nate Giorgio	32.90	RI
1994	GLEN CAMPBELL: RHINESTONE COWBOY, Nate Giorgio	32.90	RI

Tale of Peter Rabbit and Benjamin Bunny

1994	A POCKET FULL OF ONIONS, Roger Akers, closed	39.00	RI
1994	BESIDE HIS COUSIN, Roger Akers, closed	39.00	RI
1995	ROUND THAT CORNER, Roger Akers, closed	39.00	RI
1995	SAFELY HOME, Roger Akers, closed	44.00	RI
1995	MR. MCGREGOR'S GARDEN, Roger Akers, closed	44.00	RI
1995	ROSEMARY TEA AND LAVENDER, Roger Akers, closed	44.00	RI
1995	AMONGST THE FLOWERPOTS, Roger Akers, closed	44.00	RI
1995	FRIENDS ARE FOR FUN, Roger Akers, closed	44.00	RI
1995	UPON THE SCARECROW, Roger Akers, closed	44.00	RI

Tea for Two

1996	SPRING ROSE TEAPOT, Jean Monte	34.95	RI

Teddy Bear Dreams

1995	CATCH A FALLING STAR, Donna Parker, <1 year, oval, 7³/₈"	49.95	RI

That's What Friends Are For

1994	FRIENDS ARE FOREVER, Alexei Isakov, closed	29.90	RI
1994	FRIENDS ARE COMFORT, Alexei Isakov, closed	29.90	RI
1994	FRIENDS ARE LOVING, Alexei Isakov, closed	29.90	RI
1995	FRIENDS ARE FOR FUN, Alexei Isakov, closed	29.90	RI

Lamplight Brooke
Photo courtesy of
Collectors News

		ISSUE	CURRENT
Thomas Kinkade's End of a Perfect Day (3-plate rectangular panorama)			
1997	AUTUMN SERENITY, Thomas Kinkade	39.95	RI
1997	2nd RELEASE, Thomas Kinkade	39.95	RI
1997	3rd RELEASE, Thomas Kinkade	39.95	RI
Thomas Kinkade's Guiding Lights			
1997	THE LIGHT OF PEACE, Thomas Kinkade, oval	29.95	RI
1997	BEACON OF HOPE, Thomas Kinkade, oval	29.95	RI
Thomas Kinkade's Illuminated Cottages			
1994	THE FLAGSTONE PATH, Thomas Kinkade, closed	34.90	RI
1995	THE GARDEN WALK, Thomas Kinkade, closed	34.90	RI
1995	CHERRY BLOSSOM HIDEAWAY, Thomas Kinkade, closed	34.90	RI
1995	THE LIGHTED GATE, Thomas Kinkade, closed	37.90	RI
Thomas Kinkade's Inspirations			
1997	SERENITY PRAYER, Thomas Kinkade, 95 days	29.95	RI
Thomas Kinkade's Lamplight Village			
1995	LAMPLIGHT BROOKE, Thomas Kinkade, 95 days	29.90	RI
1995	LAMPLIGHT LANE, Thomas Kinkade, 95 days	29.90	RI
1995	LAMPLIGHT INN, Thomas Kinkade, 95 days	29.90	RI
Thomas Kinkade's Lamplight Village (3-plate rectangular panorama)			
1997	LAMPLIGHT BROOKE, Thomas Kinkade	39.95	RI
1997	LAMPLIGHT LANE, Thomas Kinkade	39.95	RI
1997	LAMPLIGHT INN, Thomas Kinkade	39.95	RI
Thomas Kinkade's Scenes of Serenity			
1996	HOPE'S COTTAGE, Thomas Kinkade, 95 days, 8½"	29.95	RI
1997	HOPE'S COTTAGE, Thomas Kinkade, oval	29.95	RI
Those Who Guide Us			
1995	ST. FRANCIS OF ASSISI, Hector Garrido	29.90	RI

		ISSUE	CURRENT
1995	ST. JOSEPH, Hector Garrido	29.90	RI
1996	ST. ANTHONY, Hector Garrido	29.90	RI
1996	ST. JUDE, Hector Garrido	29.90	RI

Through a Child's Eyes

1994	LITTLE BUTTERFLY, Karen Noles, closed	29.90	RI
1995	WOODLAND ROSE, Karen Noles, closed	29.90	RI
1995	TREETOP WONDER, Karen Noles, closed	29.90	RI
1995	LITTLE RED SQUIRREL, Karen Noles, closed	32.90	RI
1995	WATER LILY, Karen Noles, closed	32.90	RI
1995	PRAIRIE SONG, Karen Noles, closed	32.90	RI

Thundering Waters

1994	NIAGARA FALLS, F. Miller	34.90	RI
1994	LOWER FALLS, YELLOWSTONE, F. Miller	34.90	RI
1994	BRIDAL VEIL FALLS, F. Miller	34.90	RI
1995	HAVISU FALLS, F. Miller	34.90	RI

Thunder in the Sky

1996	D-DAY, THE AIRBORN ASSAULT, R. Taylor	29.95	RI
1996	THE MIGHTY 8TH, COMING HOME, R. Taylor	29.95	RI

Timberland Secrets

1995	GENTLE AWAKENING, Linda Daniels	29.90	RI
1995	GOOD DAY TO PLAY, Linda Daniels	29.90	RI
1995	SWEET DREAMS, Linda Daniels	29.90	RI
1996	A MOMENT'S PAUSE, Linda Daniels	29.90	RI
1996	TRANQUIL RETREAT, Linda Daniels	29.90	RI
1996	WINTRY WATCH, Linda Daniels	29.90	RI

To Soar with Eagles

1995	THROUGH THE CRYSTAL MIST, Koller	32.95	RI
1996	ABOVE THE TURBULENT TIDE, Persis Clayton Weirs	32.95	RI
1996	SOARING TO GREATER HEIGHTS, Persis Clayton Weirs	32.95	RI
1996	CASCADING INSPIRATION, Persis Clayton Weirs, 95 days	29.95	RI

Toy Story

1996	FRIENDS AT LAST, Disney Studios	NA	RI

Trail of the Whitetail

1996	HOMEWARD BOUND, Michael Sieve	34.95	RI
1996	AFTER THE STORM, Michael Sieve	34.95	RI
1996	FAST BREAK, Michael Sieve	34.95	RI
1996	MAPLE RUSH, Michael Sieve	34.95	RI
1996	SECOND SEASON, Michael Sieve	34.95	RI

Trains of the Great West

1993	MOONLIT JOURNEY, Kirk Randle	29.90	RI
1993	MOUNTAIN HIDEAWAY, Kirk Randle	29.90	RI
1993	EARLY MORNING ARRIVAL, Kirk Randle	29.90	RI
1994	THE SNOWY PASS, Kirk Randle	29.90	RI

Tranquil Retreats

		ISSUE	CURRENT
1996	DAY'S END, Judy Gibson	NA	RI
1996	DAYBREAK, Judy Gibson	NA	RI

Treasured Ducks of Canada

1993	DAWN LIGHT: PINTAIL, Ken Ferris	29.90	RI
1993	EARLY SPRING: HOODED MERGANSER, Ken Ferris	29.90	RI
1993	GENTLE REFLECTIONS: GREENTEAL, Ken Ferris	29.90	RI
1993	QUIET WATERS: MALLARD, Ken Ferris	29.90	RI

Treasure from the Vatican

1996	BIRTH OF CHRIST	NA	RI

Treasures of Russian Tradition

1996	COBALT MAJESTY, I. Makarova	NA	RI
1996	GOLDEN PEARESCENCE, I. Makarova	NA	RI
1996	LAPIS RADIANCE, I. Makarova	NA	RI
1996	SAPPHIRE SPLENDOUR, I. Makarova	NA	RI

Treasures of the Moon (Wedgwood)

1998	CHRYSANTHEMUM, Haruyo Morita	NA	RI
1998	ORCHID, Haruyo Morita	NA	RI
1998	PEONIES, Haruyo Morita	NA	RI
1998	WISTERIA AND MAGNOLIA, Haruyo Morita	NA	RI

Tribute to Selena

1996	SELENA FOREVER, Bruce Emmett, 95 days	29.95	RI

Tribute to the Armed Forces

1995	PROUD TO SERVE, Dodge	NA	RI

Selena Forever
Photo courtesy of *Collectors News*

Miracle of Life
Photo courtesy of *Collectors News*

		ISSUE	CURRENT

Triumph in the Air

1994	CHECKMATE!, H. Krebs, 95 days	34.90	RI
1994	ONE HECK OF A DEFLECTION SHOT, H. Krebs, 95 days	34.90	RI
1994	HUNTING FEVER, H. Krebs, 95 days	34.90	RI
1995	STRUCK BY THUNDER, H. Krebs, 95 days	34.90	RI

Twilight Memories

1995	WINTER'S TWILIGHT, Jesse Barnes, 95 days	29.90	RI
1995	HOLIDAY HOMECOMING, Jesse Barnes, 95 days	29.90	RI

Two's Company

1994	GOLDEN HARVEST, S. Eide, 95 days	29.90	RI
1995	BROTHERLY LOVE, S. Eide, 95 days	29.90	RI
1995	SEEING DOUBLE, S. Eide, 95 days	29.90	RI
1995	SPRING SPANIELS, S. Eide, 95 days	29.90	RI

Under a Snowy Veil

1995	WINTER'S WARMTH, Carl Sams, 95 days	29.90	RI
1995	SNOW MATES, Carl Sams, 95 days	29.90	RI
1995	WINTER'S DAWN, Carl Sams, 95 days	29.90	RI
1995	FIRST SNOW, Carl Sams, 95 days	29.90	RI

Under Mother's Wing

1995	ECHOES ALONG THE RIVER, Desmond McCaffrey	29.90	RI
1995	MONARCH'S LIGHT, Desmond McCaffrey	29.90	RI
1996	RUNNING WITH THE LIGHT, Desmond McCaffrey	29.90	RI

Under the Northern Lights

1996	CATCHING THE ELUSIVE LIGHT, Desmond McCaffrey	29.90	RI

Untamed Spirits

1993	WILD HEARTS, Persis Clayton Weirs	29.90	RI
1994	BREAKAWAY, Persis Clayton Weirs	29.90	RI
1994	FOREVER FREE, Persis Clayton Weirs	29.90	RI
1994	DISTANT THUNDER, Persis Clayton Weirs	29.90	RI

Untamed Wilderness

1995	UNEXPECTED ENCOUNTER, Persis Clayton Weirs, 95 days	29.90	RI
1995	LONESOME BULL, Persis Clayton Weirs, 95 days	29.90	RI
1995	PAUSE FROM THE JOURNEY, Persis Clayton Weirs, 95 days	29.90	RI
1995	WHITETAIL CROSSING, Persis Clayton Weirs, 95 days	29.90	RI
1996	FLEETING SPLENDOR, Persis Clayton Weirs, 95 days	29.90	RI
1996	SILENT BEAUTY, Persis Clayton Weirs, 95 days	29.90	RI

Vanishing Paradises

1993	THE RAINFOREST, Gene Dieckhoner	29.90	RI
1994	THE PANDA'S WORLD, Gene Dieckhoner	29.90	RI
1994	SPLENDORS OF INDIA, Gene Dieckhoner	29.90	RI
1994	AN AFRICAN SAFARI, Gene Dieckhoner	29.90	RI

		ISSUE	CURRENT
Victorian Garden Jewels			
1995	PRIMROSE PATCH / ROSE ARBOUR	NA	RI
Visions Beneath the Sea			
1996	MIRACLE OF LIFE, Christian Riese Lassen, 95 days	29.95	RI
1996	DIAMOND HEAD DAWN, Christian Riese Lassen, 95 days	29.95	RI
1996	MAUI WHALE SONG, Christian Riese Lassen, 95 days	29.95	RI
1996	MOTHER'S LOVE, Christian Riese Lassen, 95 days	29.95	RI
Visions from Eagle Ridge			
1995	ASSEMBLY OF PRIDE, Diana Casey, 95 days	29.90	RI
1996	LEGACY OF LIBERTY, Diana Casey, 95 days	29.90	RI
Visions of Faith			
1997	BE NOT AFRAID, Greg Olson, 95 days	29.95	RI
Visions of Glory			
1995	IWO JIMA, D. Cook, closed	29.90	RI
1995	FREEING OF PARIS, D. Cook, closed	29.90	RI
Visions of Our Blessed Mother			
1997	OUR LADY OF PEACE, 95 days	44.95	RI
Visions of the Sacred			
1994	SNOW RIDER, D. Stanley, 95 days	29.90	RI
1994	SPRING'S MESSENGER, D. Stanley, 95 days	29.90	RI
1994	THE CHEYENNE PROPHET, D. Stanley, 95 days	32.90	RI
1995	BUFFALO CALLER, D. Stanley, 95 days	32.90	RI
1995	JOURNEY OF HARMONY, D. Stanley, 95 days	32.90	RI
1995	CELEBRATION OF SPIRIT, D. Stanley, 95 days	34.90	RI
1995	COUNCIL OF ANIMALS, D. Stanley, 95 days	34.90	RI
1995	THUNDERBIRD, D. Stanley, 95 days	34.90	RI
1996	APACHE WAR WOMAN, D. Stanley, 95 days	36.90	RI
1996	THE GATHERER, D. Stanley, 95 days	36.90	RI
Visions of the West			
1995	HEALER, D. Stanley, 95 days	32.90	RI
Visit from St. Nick			
1995	TWAS THE NIGHT BEFORE CHRISTMAS, Cliff Jackson, 95 days	49.00	RI
1995	UP TO THE HOUSETOP, Cliff Jackson, 95 days	49.00	RI
1995	A BUNDLE OF TOYS, Cliff Jackson, 95 days	54.00	RI
1995	THE STOCKINGS WERE FILLED, Cliff Jackson, 95 days	54.00	RI
1995	VISIONS OF SUGARPLUMS, Cliff Jackson, 95 days	54.00	RI
1995	TO MY WONDERING EYES, Cliff Jackson, 95 days	59.00	RI
1995	A WINK OF HIS EYE, Cliff Jackson, 95 days	59.00	RI
1995	HAPPY CHRISTMAS TO ALL, Cliff Jackson, 95 days	59.00	RI
Visit to Brambly Hedge			
1994	SUMMER STORY, Jill Barklem, closed	39.90	RI
1994	SPRING STORY, Jill Barklem, closed	39.90	RI

		ISSUE	CURRENT
1994	AUTUMN STORY, Jill Barklem, closed	39.90	RI
1995	WINTER STORY, Jill Barklem, closed	39.90	RI

Warm Country Moments

1994	MABEL'S SUNNY RETREAT, Mary Ann Lasher, 95 days	29.90	RI
1994	ANNABELLE'S SIMPLE PLEASURES, Mary Ann Lasher, 95 days	29.90	RI
1994	HARRIET'S LOVING TOUCH, Mary Ann Lasher, 95 days	29.90	RI
1994	EMILY AND ALICE IN A JAM, Mary Ann Lasher, 95 days	29.90	RI
1995	HANNA'S SECRET GARDEN, Mary Ann Lasher, 95 days	29.90	RI

Warmth of Home at Christmas

1995	WARM WINTER'S EVE, Loque	NA	RI

Welcome to the Neighborhood

1994	IVY LANE, B. Mock, closed	29.90	RI
1994	DAFFODIL DRIVE, B. Mock, closed	29.90	RI
1995	LILAC LANE, B. Mock, closed	34.90	RI
1995	TULIP TERRACE, B. Mock, closed	34.90	RI

When All Hearts Come Home

1993	OH CHRISTMAS TREE, Jesse Barnes, 95 days	29.90	RI
1993	NIGHT BEFORE CHRISTMAS, Jesse Barnes, 95 days	29.90	RI
1993	COMFORT AND JOY, Jesse Barnes, 95 days	29.90	RI
1993	GRANDPA'S FARM, Jesse Barnes, 95 days	29.90	RI
1993	PEACE ON EARTH, Jesse Barnes, 95 days	29.90	RI
1993	NIGHT DEPARTURE, Jesse Barnes, 95 days	29.90	RI
1993	SUPPER AND SMALL TALK, Jesse Barnes, 95 days	29.90	RI
1993	CHRISTMAS WISH, Jesse Barnes, 95 days	29.90	RI

When Dreams Blossom

1994	DREAMS TO GATHER, Renee McGinnis, 95 days	29.90	RI
1994	WHERE FRIENDS DREAM, Renee McGinnis, 95 days	29.90	RI
1994	THE SWEETEST OF DREAMS, Renee McGinnis, 95 days	32.90	RI
1994	DREAMS OF POETRY, Renee McGinnis, 95 days	32.90	RI
1995	A PLACE TO DREAM, Renee McGinnis, 95 days	32.90	RI
1995	DREAMING OF YOU, Renee McGinnis, 95 days	32.90	RI

When I Grow Up

1994	ON THE COUNT OF THREE, Christopher Nick	NA	RI

When Stories Come Alive

1994	AT THE ROUND-UP, Tiritilli	NA	RI

Where Eagles Soar

1994	ON FREEDOM'S WING, Frank Mittelstadt, 95 days	29.90	RI
1994	ALLEGIANCE WITH THE WIND, Frank Mittelstadt, 95 days	29.90	RI
1995	PRIDE OF THE SKY, Frank Mittelstadt, 95 days	29.90	RI
1995	WINDWARD MAJESTY, Frank Mittelstadt, 95 days	29.90	RI
1995	NOBLE LEGACY, Frank Mittelstadt, 95 days	29.90	RI
1995	PRISTINE DOMAINS, Frank Mittelstadt, 95 days	29.90	RI
1995	SPLENDOR IN FLIGHT, Frank Mittelstadt, 95 days	29.90	RI
1995	ROYAL ASCENT, Frank Mittelstadt, 95 days	29.90	RI

		ISSUE	CURRENT
1995	LAKESIDE EAGLES, Frank Mittelstadt, 95 days	29.90	RI
1995	LIGHTHOUSE EAGLES, Frank Mittelstadt, 95 days	29.90	RI

Where Paths Join

1997	SHARED WORLDS, Diana Casey, 95 days	29.95	RI

Where Paths Meet

1996	NATIVE HARMONY, Diana Casey, 95 days	29.95	RI

Whispering Wings

1996	MORNING GLORY, Janene Grende	29.95	RI
1996	PERFECT HARMONY, Janene Grende	29.95	RI

Whispers on the Wind

1995	ANNA'S HUMMINGBIRD, K. O'Malley	44.95	RI
1995	RUBY THROATED HUMMINGBIRD, K. O'Malley	44.95	RI
1996	ALLEN'S HUMMINGBIRD, K. O'Malley	44.95	RI
1996	RUFOUS WITH FOXGLOVES, K. O'Malley	44.95	RI

Wild Pageantry

1995	FLIGHT OF THE PHEASANT, Frank Mittelstadt	NA	RI
1995	THUNDERING WINGS: RUFFLED GROUSE	NA	RI

Wildflower Legacy

1995	NATURE'S LEGACY, Renee McGinnis	NA	RI

Windows on a World of Song

1993	THE LIBRARY: CARDINALS, Kevin Daniel, closed	34.90	RI
1993	THE DEN: BLACK-CAPPED CHICKADEES, Kevin Daniel, closed	34.90	RI
1993	THE BEDROOM: BLUEBIRDS, Kevin Daniel, closed	34.90	RI
1994	THE KITCHEN: GOLDFINCHES, Kevin Daniel, closed	34.90	RI

Wings of Glory

1995	PRIDE OF AMERICA, J. Spurlock, closed	32.90	RI
1995	SPIRIT OF FREEDOM, J. Spurlock, closed	32.90	RI
1996	PORTRAIT OF LIBERTY, J. Spurlock, closed	32.90	RI
1996	PARAGON OF COURAGE, J. Spurlock, closed	32.90	RI

Winnie the Pooh and Friends

1995	TIME FOR A LITTLE SOMETHING, Cliff Jackson, 95 days	39.90	RI
1995	BOUNCING'S WHAT TIGGERS DO BEST, Cliff Jackson, 95 days	39.90	RI
1995	YOU'RE A REAL FRIEND, Cliff Jackson, 95 days	44.90	RI
1995	SILLY OLD BEAR, Cliff Jackson, 95 days	44.90	RI
1995	RUMBLY IN MY TUMMY, Cliff Jackson, 95 days	44.90	RI
1995	MANY HAPPY RETURNS OF THE DAY, Cliff Jackson, 95 days	49.90	RI
1996	T IS FOR TIGGER, Cliff Jackson, 95 days	49.90	RI
1996	NOBODY UNCHEERED WITH BALLOONS, Cliff Jackson, 95 days	49.90	RI
1996	DO YOU THINK IT'S A WOOZLE?, Cliff Jackson, 95 days	49.90	RI
1996	FINE DAY TO BUZZ WITH THE BEES, Cliff Jackson, 95 days	49.90	RI
1996	POOH STICKS, Cliff Jackson, 95 days	49.90	RI
1996	THREE CHEERS FOR POOH, Cliff Jackson, 95 days	49.90	RI

Time for a Little Something
Photo courtesy of *Collectors News*

Winter's Calm
Photo courtesy of *Collectors News*

Winnie the Pooh: Honey of a Friend

		ISSUE	CURRENT
1997	SWEET AS HONEY, 95 days	29.95	RI

Winnie the Pooh Storybook Collection

		ISSUE	CURRENT
1997	TOO MUCH HONEY, 295 days	39.95	RI

Winter Evening Reflections

		ISSUE	CURRENT
1996	AS TWILIGHT FALLS, S. Kozar	39.95	RI
1996	DAY FADES TO MEMORY, S. Kozar	39.95	RI
1996	DOWN BY THE STREAM, S. Kozar	39.95	RI
1996	SHADOWS GROW LONGER, S. Kozar	39.95	RI

Winter Garlands

		ISSUE	CURRENT
1996	CRISP MORNING CALL, Sam Timm	34.95	RI
1996	FROSTY SEASON, Sam Timm	34.95	RI
1996	JEWELS IN THE SNOW, Sam Timm	34.95	RI

Winter Retreat

		ISSUE	CURRENT
1996	WHITETAILS PAUSE, Persis Clayton Weirs	NA	RI

Winter Shadows

		ISSUE	CURRENT
1995	CANYON MOON, Nancy Glazier, 95 days	29.90	RI
1995	SHADOWS OF GRAY, Nancy Glazier, 95 days	29.90	RI
1995	BROKEN WATCH, Persis Clayton Weirs, 95 days	29.90	RI
1995	MOONLIGHT SHADOWS, Persis Clayton Weirs, 95 days	29.90	RI
1995	TRACKERS, Persis Clayton Weirs, 95 days	29.90	RI
1995	VIGILANT COMPANIONS, Persis Clayton Weirs, 95 days	29.90	RI
1996	ICY SHADOWS, Persis Clayton Weirs, 95 days	29.90	RI

Wish You Were Here

		ISSUE	CURRENT
1994	END OF A PERFECT DAY, Thomas Kinkade, 95 days	29.90	RI
1994	A QUIET EVENING/RIVERLODGE, Thomas Kinkade, 95 days	29.90	RI

		ISSUE	CURRENT
1994	SOFT MORNING LIGHT, Thomas Kinkade, 95 days	29.90	RI

With Watchful Eyes

1994	WINTER WHITE, Morten E. Solberg	29.90	RI

Wizard of Oz

1995	THERE'S NO PLACE LIKE HOME, Michael Dudash	29.95	RI

Wolf Pups: Young Faces of the Wilderness

1995	MORNING INNOCENTS, Linda Daniels, 95 days	29.95	RI
1995	NEW ADVENTURE, Linda Daniels, 95 days	29.95	RI
1995	TOMORROW'S PRIDE, Linda Daniels, 95 days	29.95	RI
1996	CASS TO THE FUTURE, Linda Daniels, 95 days	29.95	RI
1996	EARLY ASPIRATIONS, Linda Daniels, 95 days	29.95	RI
1996	ONE TO ONE, Linda Daniels, 95 days	29.95	RI
1996	ROSY BEGINNINGS, Linda Daniels, 95 days	29.95	RI

Woodland Tranquility

1994	WINTER'S CALM, Greg Alexander, 95 days	29.90	RI
1995	FROSTY MORN, Greg Alexander, 95 days	29.90	RI
1995	CROSSING BOUNDARIES, Greg Alexander, 95 days	29.90	RI
1995	BROKEN SILENCE, Greg Alexander, 95 days	29.90	RI
1995	SNOWY VEIL, Greg Alexander, 95 days	29.90	RI
1996	RIVER REFLECTIONS, Greg Alexander, 95 days	29.90	RI
1996	SUNSET AT CORNUCOPIA, Greg Alexander, 95 days	34.90	RI
1996	TWILIGHT APPROACH, Greg Alexander, 95 days	34.90	RI

Woodland Wings

1994	TWILIGHT FLIGHT, Jim Hansel, closed	34.90	RI
1994	GLIDING ON GILDED SKIES, Jim Hansel, closed	34.90	RI
1994	SUNSET VOYAGE, Jim Hansel, closed	34.90	RI
1995	PEACEFUL JOURNEY, Jim Hansel, closed	34.90	RI

World Beneath the Waves

1995	SEA OF LIGHT, D. Terbush, 95 days	29.90	RI
1995	ALL GOD'S CHILDREN, D. Terbush, 95 days	29.90	RI
1995	HUMPBACK WHALES, D. Terbush, 95 days	29.90	RI
1994	CIRCLE OF LOVE, D. Terbush, 95 days	29.90	RI
1995	FOLLOW YOUR HEART, D. Terbush, 95 days	29.90	RI
1995	LONG BEFORE MAN, D. Terbush, 95 days	29.90	RI
1995	REACH FOR YOUR DREAMS, D. Terbush, 95 days	29.90	RI
1995	SHARE THE LOVE, D. Terbush, 95 days	29.90	RI
1996	ALL THE MIRACLES TO SEA, D. Terbush, 95 days	29.90	RI

World of the Eagle

1993	SENTINEL OF THE NIGHT, Jim Hansel	29.90	RI
1994	SILENT GUARD, Jim Hansel	29.90	RI
1994	NIGHT FLYER, Jim Hansel	32.90	RI
1994	MIDNIGHT DUTY, Jim Hansel	32.90	RI

World of Wildlife: Celebrating Earth Day

1995	A DELICATE BALANCE, Todd Clausnitzer, 95 days	29.90	RI

		ISSUE	CURRENT
1995	AFRICA: EXQUISITE TRANQUILITY, Todd Clausnitzer, 95 days	29.90	RI
1995	EUROPE: IN NATURAL HARMONY, Todd Clausnitzer, 95 days	29.90	RI
1995	NORTH AMERICA: A DELICATE BALANCE, Todd Clausnitzer, 95 days	29.90	RI
1996	SOUTH AMERICA: EXOTIC KINGDOM, Todd Clausnitzer, 95 days	29.90	RI

WWII: 50th Anniversary

1994	1941: A WORLD AT WAR	NA	RI
1994	1941: TAKING A STAND	NA	RI

WWII: A Remembrance

1994	D-DAY, James Griffin, 95 days	29.90	RI
1994	THE BATTLE OF MIDWAY, James Griffin, 95 days	29.90	RI
1994	THE BATTLE OF THE BULGE, James Griffin, 95 days	32.90	RI
1995	BATTLE OF THE PHILIPPINES, James Griffin, 95 days	32.90	RI
1995	DOOLITTLE'S RAID OVER TOKYO, James Griffin, 95 days	32.90	RI

Single Issue

1991	KOALA, Charles Fracé	27.50	NR
1991	BABY SEALS, Mike Jackson	27.50	NR
1991	WHALES, Anthony Casay	32.50	NR
1991	A MOTHER'S CARE, Joyce Bridgett	27.50	NR
1991	FLEETING ENCOUNTER, Charles Fracé	27.50	NR
1991	ASIAN ELEPHANT, Will Nelson	30.50	NR
1993	A TABBY'S VIEW, Todd Clausnitzer	29.90	RI
1994	BEARER OF LOVE, Carolyn Jagodits	29.90	RI
1994	SILVER SCOUT, Eddie LePage	29.90	RI
1994	MR. HOCKEY: GORDIE HOWE, Rob MacDougall	29.90	RI
1994	BABY BLUES, Audrey Casey	29.90	RI
1994	MEDICINE HAT OF THE SACRED DOGS, Julie Kramer Cole	29.90	RI
1995	UNITED IN SPIRIT	29.90	RI
1995	1991 CHAMPIONSHIP, Chuck Gillies	29.90	RI
1995	THE COMEBACK, Chuck Gillies	29.90	RI
1995	HOME IS WHERE YOU HANG YOUR HEART, Katherine Salentine	29.95	RI
1995	EYES OF THE WOLF, Diana Casey	29.95	RI
1995	OH BEAUTIFUL FOR SPACIOUS SKIES	29.95	RI
1995	SOLITUDE: JAGUAR, Jeffrey R. Farmer	29.95	RI
1995	SERENITY: THE COUGAR, Nate Giorgio	29.95	RI
1995	THE LORD'S PRAYER, Christopher Nick	29.95	RI
1995	GEM LIGHT, GEM BRIGHT, Mimi Jobe	29.90	RI
1995	MINKA UNDER COVER, Wolfgang Kaiser	29.95	RI
1995	AUTUMN MIRAGE, Janene Grende	29.95	RI
1995	ON STAGE IN HAWAII, sculpted	59.95	RI
1996	GENTLE EMBRACE, Lee Bogle	29.95	RI
1996	ON STAGE IN HAWAII, sculpted	59.95	RI
1996	JEWEL OF THE SOUTH, Chris Notarile	34.95	RI
1996	THUNDERING HOOVES, Chuck DeHaan	29.95	RI
1996	CELEBRATION OF LOVE, limited, heart shaped	39.95	RI
1996	THE GIFT, Lee Bogle	29.95	RI
1996	REJOICE, Lena Liu	29.95	RI
1996	HOPES OF ST. NICHOLAS, Chuck Gillies	34.95	RI
1996	U.S.S. ENTERPRISE	59.95	RI
1996	THE PASSAGE, Craig Tennant	34.95	RI

		ISSUE	CURRENT
1996	ROSE-COLORED DAWN, Lena Liu	39.95	RI
1996	RECORD 72 WINS, Glen Green	34.95	RI
1996	HOLLYWOOD REBEL, Michael Deas	34.95	RI
1996	THE LITTLE DRUMMER BOY, Jennifer R. Welty, musical	34.95	RI
1996	BRETT FAVRE—LEADER OF THE PACK, Rick Brown, limited, oval	29.95	RI
1996	HOLLYWOOD REBEL, Michael Deas	34.95	RI
1996	ON THE WARPATH, Sam Bass	35.00	RI
1996	READY TO RACE, Mark Lacourciere	35.00	RI
1996	MARCH 23, 1994—HISTORIC "802ND," Glen Green	34.95	RI
1996	DETROIT RED WINGS, David Craig, rectangular	34.95	RI
1996	THE INTIMIDATOR, Sam Bass	35.00	RI
1997	51,636 AND COUNTING, Diane Sivavec, rectangular	34.95	RI
1997	L.A. AT LAST, Morgan Weistling, limited	35.00	RI
1997	LUKE SKYWALKER	35.00	RI
1997	SUPER BOWL CHAMPION, Rick Brown	29.95	RI
1997	TWILIGHT COTTAGE, Thomas Kinkade	34.95	RI
1998	DIANA, A ROSE EVERLASTING, Collin Bogle, musical	34.95	RI
1998	DIANA, ENGLAND'S ROSE, William Chambers, sculpted	39.95	RI
NA	ALWAYS MY DAUGHTER, Mary Ann Lasher	29.95	RI
NA	ALWAYS MY MOTHER, Mary Ann Lasher	29.95	RI
NA	ANGEL OF HOPE, sculpted, oval	39.95	RI
NA	BASKET OF LOVE, Lily Chang	29.95	RI
NA	BEDTIME PRAYERS, Edgar Jerins, oval	29.95	RI
NA	BLUSHING BEAUTY, Michael Gerry	34.95	RI
NA	CHERISH YOUR FAMILY, Glenna Kurz	29.95	RI
NA	DELIVERANCE, Chuck Ren	39.95	RI
NA	DO NOT DISTURB, sculpted	39.95	RI
NA	EYES FOR YOU, Kayomi, oval	34.95	RI
NA	THE FIREST OF THEM ALL, Peter Fryer	29.95	RI
NA	GARDEN JEWELS, Lena Liu	34.95	RI
NA	HEAVENLY HIBISCUS, sculpted	29.95	RI
NA	KINDNESS	29.90	RI
NA	MIDNIGHT MAGIC, Peter Kull	34.95	RI
NA	MOONLIT TRAIL, Joyce Patti	29.95	RI
NA	MY MORNING FRIEND, Zula Kenyon	39.95	RI
NA	RENEWAL, Ernie Cselko	34.95	RI
NA	SEALED WITH A KISS, Anthony Casay	29.95	RI
NA	SERENITY'S SONG, Nadezhda Strelkina, octagnal	29.95	RI
NA	SISTERS SHARE A SPECIAL WARMTH, Chantal Poulin	29.95	RI
NA	SLEEPING BEAUTY CASTLE, Disney Studios	29.95	RI
NA	SOUL MATES, Lee Cable, oval	34.95	RI
NA	SPRING'S AWAKENING, Steve Hardock	39.95	RI
NA	SPRINGTIME BLUES, Terry Isaac	39.95	RI
NA	STARLIGHT SERENADE, Cynthie Fisher	29.95	RI
NA	STARLIT PRANCER, sculpted, oval	49.95	RI
NA	SWEET SLUMBER, Bessie Pease Gutmann, heart shaped	29.95	RI
NA	SWEET SPLENDOR, Glynda Turley	29.95	RI
NA	TENDER HEARTS, Lena Liu, heart shaped	29.95	RI
NA	TIME OUT, Bessie Pease Gutmann, oval	34.95	RI
NA	UNBRIDLED BEAUTY, D. E. Kucera	34.95	RI
NA	VISION OF THE PACK, Diana Casey	29.95	RI
NA	WINTER SOLSTICE, Steve Hardock	39.95	RI

BRANTWOOD COLLECTION UNITED STATES

		ISSUE	CURRENT
Howe Christmas			
1978	VISIT FROM SANTA, Howe, 1 year	45.00	NR
John Falter Christmas			
1979	CHRISTMAS MORNING, John Falter, 5,000	25.50	NR
Little Clowns			
1979	GOING TO CIRCUS, 5,000	29.50	NR
Marien Carlsen Mother's Day			
1978	JENNIFER AND JENNY FUR, Marien Carlsen, 1 year	45.00	NR
1979	FOOTBALL BROTHERS, Marien Carlsen, 5,000	45.00	NR
Rockwell Mother's Day			
1979	HOMECOMING, Norman Rockwell, 20,000	39.50	NR
Single Issue			
1978	TRIBUTE TO ROCKWELL, 1 year	35.00	NR

BRAYMER HALL UNITED STATES

American Folk Art			
1982	SPRING CELEBRATION, Fred Wallin, 10,000	24.50	NR
1982	SUMMER BOUNTY, Fred Wallin, 10,000	24.50	NR
Childhood Sonatas			
1981	SERENADE, Frank Palmieri, 15,000	28.50	NR
1982	PRELUDE, Frank Palmieri, 15,000	28.50	NR
1983	CAPRICE, Frank Palmieri, 15,000	28.50	NR

Caprice
Photo courtesy of *Collectors News*

		ISSUE	CURRENT

Yesterday Dreams

		ISSUE	CURRENT
1983	SWING QUARTET, Jack Appleton, 5,000	50.00	NR
1984	SLEIGH BELLES, Jack Appleton, 5,000	50.00	NR

Single Issue

		ISSUE	CURRENT
1982	HOW DO I LOVE THEE?, Rob Sauber, 19,500	39.95	NR

BRENTWOOD FINE ARTS UNITED STATES

Nostalgic Memories

		ISSUE	CURRENT
1984	FIRST GAME, Marilyn Zapp, 12,500	39.50	NR

PAUL BRIANT AND SONS UNITED STATES

Christmas

		ISSUE	CURRENT
1971	FRUITS OF SPIRIT, 350	125.00	BR
1972	LABOUR OF LOVE, 700	100.00	NR
1973	ANNUNCIATION	100.00	NR

Easter

		ISSUE	CURRENT
1972	THE LAST SACRIFICE, 500	85.00	NR

Seven Sacraments

		ISSUE	CURRENT
1982	THE GIFT OF THE SPIRIT, Terry Clark, 2,000	110.00	NR

BRIARCREST UNITED STATES

Toys from the Attic

		ISSUE	CURRENT
1982	THIS OLE BEAR CHAUNCEY JAMES, James Tuck, 10 days	45.00	NR

BRIMARK LTD. UNITED STATES

Yetta's Holidays

		ISSUE	CURRENT
1986	CHRISTMAS BLOCKS, Carol-Lynn Rossel Waugh	29.50	NR

BRINDLE FINE ARTS UNITED STATES

Expressions

		ISSUE	CURRENT
1979	QUIET EYES, Claude Hulce, 3,000	60.00	NR

Fantasy in Motion

		ISSUE	CURRENT
1978	LITTLE BLUE HORSE, Lenore Béran, 3,000	75.00	NR
1979	HORSE OF A DIFFERENT COLOR, Lenore Béran, 3,000	75.00	NR

		ISSUE	CURRENT

Lenore Béran Special

1980	HOMAGE, Lenore Béran, 2,500	125.00	NR

Moods of the Orient

1978	SOFTLY, THE SUN SETS, Lenore Béran, 4,000	75.00	NR
1980	TRANQUIL MORN, Lenore Béran, 3,000	75.00	NR

Those Precious Years

1980	LITTLE CURT AND FRIEND, 3,000	60.00	NR

BYDGO

Christmas

1969	SHEPHERDESS AND SHEEP, 5,000	10.00	NR
1970	CLUMSY HANS, 5,000	10.00	NR
1971	THE FLYING TRUNK, 5,000	10.00	NR
1972	CHINESE NIGHTINGALE, 5,000	10.00	NR

BYLINY PORCELAIN RUSSIA

Flights of Fancy: Ornamental Art of Old Russia

1991	ENCHANTMENT, Sergei P. Rogatov	29.87	NR
1991	RHAPSODY, Sergei P. Rogatov	29.87	BR
1991	SPLENDOR, Sergei P. Rogatov	32.87	NR
1991	RAPTURE, Sergei P. Rogatov	32.87	NR
1991	FANTASIE, Sergei P. Rogatov	32.87	45.00
1991	REVERIE, Sergei P. Rogatov	32.87	55.00

Jewels of the Golden Ring

1990	ST. BASIL'S, MOSCOW	29.87	BR
1991	TRINITY MONASTERY, ZAGORSK	29.87	BR
1991	ROSTOV THE GREAT	32.87	BR
1991	NIKITSKY MONASTERY	32.87	NR
1991	BORIS AND GLEB MONASTERY	32.87	NR
1991	YAROSLAVI KREMLIN	34.87	NR
1991	SUZDAL, PEARL OF THE GOLDEN RING	34.87	NR
1991	THE GOLDEN GATES OF VLADIMIR	34.87	NR

Legend of the Scarlet Flower

1991	THE ENCHANTED GARDEN	29.87	NR
1991	THE VOICE OF KINDNESS	29.87	NR
1992	THE SPIRIT OF LOVE	29.87	40.00
1992	THE SCARLET FLOWER	32.87	55.00
1992	THE MAGIC RING	32.87	55.00
1992	MERCHANT'S FAREWELL	32.87	65.00

Legend of Tsar Saltan

1991	THE ARRIVAL OF TSAR SALTAN, Galina Zhiryakova, 195 days	39.87	NR
1991	THE MAGIC LAND OF PRINCE GUIDON, Galina Zhiryakova, 195 days	39.87	60.00

			ISSUE	CURRENT
1991	THE SWAN PRINCESS, Galina Zhiryakova, 195 days		39.87	45.00
1991	THE MAGIC SQUIRREL, Galina Zhiryakova, 195 days		39.87	75.00

Russian Fairy Tale Princesses

1992	LUDMILLA	35.87	NR
1992	THE SNOWMAIDEN	35.87	NR
1992	SLEEPING BEAUTY	35.87	60.00
1992	VASILISA THE BEAUTIFUL	35.87	85.00

Russian Seasons

1992	WINTER MAJESTY	29.87	NR
1992	SPRINGTIME SPLENDOR	29.87	NR
1992	SUMMERTIME SERENADE	32.87	NR
1992	AUTUMN FANTASIE	32.87	80.00
1992	WINTER IDYLL	32.87	60.00
1993	SPRINGTIME REJOICE	34.87	RI
1993	SUMMERTIME BOUNTY	34.87	RI
1993	AN AUTUMN MEDLEY	34.87	RI

Tale of Father Frost

1992	FOR ALL BOYS AND GIRLS	29.87	45.00
1992	THROUGH FORESTS OF SNOW	29.87	NR
1992	TREE TRIMMING TIME	32.87	100.00
1992	THE CIRCLE DANCE	32.87	90.00
1993	A SNOWY PLAYLAND	32.87	RI
1993	ON THIS COLD AND WINTRY NIGHT	32.87	RI

Village Life of Russia

1990	A WINTER SLEIGH RIDE, Natalya V. Leonova	35.87	BR
1990	BRINGING HOME THE HARVEST, Natalya V. Leonova	35.87	BR
1991	A CELEBRATION OF FRIENDSHIP, Natalya V. Leonova	38.87	BR
1991	A VILLAGE WEDDING, Natalya V. Leonova	38.87	NR
1991	COUNTRY PEDDLER, Natalya V. Leonova	38.87	NR

Splendor
Photo courtesy of *Collectors News*

The Merry Musicians
Photo courtesy of *Collectors News*

		ISSUE	CURRENT
1991	VILLAGE COBBLER, Natalya V. Leonova	40.87	NR
1991	TO THE SPRING FESTIVAL, Natalya V. Leonova	40.87	BR
1991	THE MERRY MUSICIANS, Natalya V. Leonova	40.87	NR

CABOCHON / CONTEMPORARY ORIGINALS, INC. UNITED STATES

Nancy Doyle's Candy Girls

1983	REBECCA, Nancy Doyle, 15,000	50.00	NR

CALHOUN'S COLLECTORS SOCIETY

(Royal Cornwall)

Creation (Charter Release)

1977	IN THE BEGINNING, Yiannis Koutsis, 19,500	29.50	155.00
1977	IN HIS IMAGE, Yiannis Koutsis, 19,500	29.50	120.00
1978	ADAM'S RIB, Yiannis Koutsis, 19,500	29.50	100.00
1978	BANISHEED FROM EDEN, Yiannis Koutsis, 19,500	29.50	90.00
1978	NOAH AND THE ARK, Yiannis Koutsis, 19,500	29.50	90.00
1980	TOWER OF BABEL, Yiannis Koutsis, 19,500	29.50	80.00
1980	SODOM AND GOMORRAH, Yiannis Koutsis, 19,500	29.50	80.00
1980	JACOB'S WEDDING, Yiannis Koutsis, 19,500	29.50	80.00
1980	REBEKAH AT THE WELL, Yiannis Koutsis, 19,500	29.50	80.00
1980	JACOB'S LADDER, Yiannis Koutsis, 19,500	29.50	80.00
1980	JOSEPH'S COAT OF MANY COLORS, Yiannis Koutsis, 19,500	29.50	80.00
1980	JOSEPH INTERPRETS PHARAOH'S DREAM, Yiannis Koutsis, 19,500	29.50	80.00

Four Seasons (Charter Release)

1978	WARMTH (WINTER), Gunther Granget, 17,500	50.00	NR
1978	VOICES OF SPRING (SPRING), Gunther Granget, 17,500	50.00	NR
1978	THE FLEDGLING (SUMMER), Gunther Granget, 17,500	50.00	NR
1978	WE SURVIVE (FALL), Gunther Granget, 17,500	50.00	NR

Single Issue

1985	LITTLE JESTER, Rosemary Calder, 1 year	29.50	NR

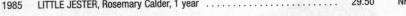

Little Jester
Photo courtesy of *Collectors News*

CALIFORNIA PORCELAIN, INC. UNITED STATES

		ISSUE	CURRENT
Best of Sascha			
1979	FLOWER BOUQUET, Sascha Brastoff, 7,500	65.00	NR
Now Is the Moment			
1984	BE STILL, Carolyn Blish, 12,500	35.00	NR
Seed of the People			
1984	KEENAH, THE STRONG ONE, Carolyn Blish, 10,000	29.95	NR
Vanishing Animals			
1979	ASIAN MONARCH, Gene Dieckhoner, 7,500	40.00	NR
1979	SNOW LEOPARDS, Gene Dieckhoner, 7,500	45.00	NR
1980	PANDAS, Gene Dieckhoner, 7,500	45.00	NR
1981	POLAR BEARS, Gene Dieckhoner, 7,500	50.00	NR
Single Issue			
1983	KOALA, Gene Dieckhoner, 5,000	29.95	NR

N. C. CAMERON & SONS LTD. CANADA

Single Issue			
1997	SANTA'S TIME OUT, James Lumbers, 95 days	39.95	RI
1998	SHORELINE ENCOUNTER, Brent Townsend, 96 days	49.95	RI

CANADIAN COLLECTOR PLATES CANADA

Children of the Classics			
1982	ANNE OF GREEN GABLES, Will Davies, 15,000	78.00	NR
1983	TOM SAWYER, Will Davies, 15,000	78.00	NR

Anne of Green Gables
Photo courtesy of *Collectors News*

		ISSUE	CURRENT
Days of Innocence			
1982	BUTTERFLIES, Will Davies, 15,000	78.00	NR
1983	HE LOVES ME, Will Davies, 15,000	78.00	NR
Discover Canada			
1979	SAWMILL—KINGS LANDING, James Keirstead, 10,000	98.00	350.00
1980	QUEBEC WINTER, Krieghoff, 10,000	125.00	150.00
1982	BEFORE THE BATH, Paul Peel, 10,000	125.00	NR
1982	THE GRIST MILL, DELTA, James Keirstead, 10,000	125.00	NR
1982	ANGLICAN CHURCH AT MAGNETAWAN, A. J. Casson, 10,000	125.00	NR
1983	MAJESTIC ROCKIES, 10,000	125.00	NR
1983	HABITANTS DRIVING THE SLEIGH, 10,000	125.00	NR
1984	AUTUMN MEMORIES, 10,000	125.00	NR
1984	AFTER THE BATH, Paul Peel, 10,000	125.00	NR

CAPO DI MONTE ITALY

Christmas			
1972	CHERUBS, 500	55.00	90.00
1973	BELLS AND HOLLY, 500	55.00	NR
1974	CHRISTMAS, 1,000	60.00	NR
1975	CHRISTMAS, 1,000	60.00	NR
1976	CHRISTMAS, 250	65.00	NR
Mother's Day			
1973	MOTHER'S DAY, 500	55.00	70.00
1974	MOTHER'S DAY, 500	60.00	70.00
1975	MOTHER'S DAY, 500	60.00	70.00
1976	MOTHER'S DAY, 500	65.00	NR

CARMEL COLLECTION UNITED STATES

Country Friends			
1983	MEETING AT THE FENCE, Helen Rampel, 15,000	45.00	NR

Meeting at the Fence
Photo courtesy of *Collectors News*

		ISSUE	CURRENT

Famous Parades

1983	MACY'S THANKSGIVING PARADE, Melanie Taylor Kent, 1 year	39.50	NR

First Performers

1983	DARLING DIANA, Elizabeth Maxwell, 19,500	39.50	NR

Joy of Christmas

1983	CHRISTMAS DELIGHT, Jerome Walczak, 19,500	39.50	NR

Memories of the Heart

1984	PETALS, Elizabeth Maxwell, 15,000	28.50	NR

CARSON MINT UNITED STATES

(B & J Art Designs)

America Has Heart (B & J Art Designs)

1980	MY HEART'S DESIRE, Jan Hagara, 1 year	24.50	135.00
1981	HEARTS AND FLOWERS, Jan Hagara, 1 year	24.50	40.00
1982	THE HEARTY SAILOR, Jan Hagara, 1 year	28.50	NR
1983	SHANNON'S SWEETHEART, Jan Hagara, 1 year	28.50	NR

Bear Feats

1983	TEDDY BEAR PICNIC, Susan Anderson, 15,000	37.50	NR
1984	ON THE BEACH, Susan Anderson, 15,000	37.50	NR

Big Top

1981	THE WHITE FACE, Edward J. Rohn, 60 days	28.50	NR
1982	THE TRAMP, Edward J. Rohn, 60 days	28.50	NR

Hollywood Squares

1979	PETER MARSHALL, 100 days	28.50	NR
1980	GEORGE GOBEL, 100 days	28.50	NR

The Littlest

1982	THE LITTLEST STOCKING, June Colbert, 12,500	29.50	NR
1983	LITTLEST SANTA, June Colbert, 12,500	29.50	NR

Magic Afternoons

1980	ENCHANTED GARDEN, Jo Anne Mix, 5,000	39.50	NR
1981	THE DELIGHTFUL TEA PARTY, Jo Anne Mix, 5,000	39.50	NR

Moments in Time

1979	FREEDOM FLIGHT, 5,000	55.00	NR

Nature's Children

1982	CANDICE, Don Price, 12,500	29.50	NR
1983	CORY, Don Price, 12,500	29.50	NR

My Heart's Desire
Photo courtesy of *Collectors News*

Daisies for Mommie
Photo courtesy of *Collectors News*

Old Fashioned Mother's Day (B & J Art Designs)

		ISSUE	CURRENT
1979	DAISIES FROM MARY BETH, Jan Hagara, 1 year	38.00	80.00
1980	DAISIES FROM JIMMY, Jan Hagara, 1 year	37.50	80.00
1981	DAISIES FROM MEG, Jan Hagara, 1 year	37.50	NR
1982	DAISIES FOR MOMMIE, Jan Hagara, 1 year	37.50	NR

To Mom with Love

1983	A BASKET OF LOVE, Cynthia Knapton, 15,000	37.50	NR

CARTIER FRANCE

Cathedral

1972	CHARTRES CATHEDRAL, 12,500	50.00	70.00
1974	CHARTRES MILLOUS, 500	130.00	160.00

CASA DI ZACCHINI UNITED STATES

Three-Dimensional

1997	DUE DENTI, Hugo Zacchini, 1,300	75.00	RI

Single Issue

1997	FAGIOLINO, Olympia Zacchini, based on art of Hugo Zacchini, 1,300	75.00	RI

CAST ART INDUSTRIES UNITED STATES

Dreamsicles Holiday Collection

1995	FINISHING TOUCHES, DS200, 1 year	30.00	RI
1996	SANTA IN DREAMSICLE LAND, DS215, 1 year	30.00	RI
1997	STAR OF WONDER, 10144, 1 year	30.00	RI

Dreamsicles Sculpted Plates

		ISSUE	CURRENT
1996	THE BEST GIFT OF ALL, DC339, Kristin Haynes, open	37.00	RI
1996	BLESS US ALL, DC338, Kristin Haynes, open	37.00	RI
1996	HEAVEN'S LITTLE HELPER, DC336, Kristin Haynes, open	37.00	RI
1996	A HUG FROM THE HEART, DC337, Kristin Haynes, open	37.00	RI
1997	A LOVE LIKE NO OTHER, 10079, Kristin Haynes, open	37.00	RI

CASTLETON CHINA UNITED STATES

Aviation (American Historical)

1972	AMELIA EARHART, 3,500	40.00	60.00
1972	CHARLES LINDBERGH, 3,500	40.00	NR

Bicentennial (Shenango)

1972	A NEW DAWN, 7,600	60.00	NR
1972	TURNING POINT, 7,600	60.00	NR
1973	SILENT FOE, 7,600	60.00	NR
1973	THE STAR-SPANGLED BANNER, 7,600	60.00	NR
1973	U.S.S. *CONSTITUTION*, 7,600	60.00	NR
1974	ONE NATION, 7,600	60.00	NR
1974	WESTWARD HO, 7,600	60.00	NR

Natural History (American Historical)

1973	PAINTED LADY, 1,500	40.00	NR
1973	ROSEATE SPOONBILL, 1,500	40.00	NR

Single Issue

1976	GENERAL DOUGLAS MACARTHUR, 1,000	30.00	NR

CATALINA PORCELAIN UNITED STATES

Escalera's Christmas

1982	SPECIAL DELIVERY, Rudy Escalera, 19,500	32.50	NR
1982	ESPECIALLY FOR YOU, Rudy Escalera, 19,500	35.00	NR

CAVANAGH GROUP INTERNATIONAL UNITED STATES

Coca-Cola American Life Heritage Collection

1996	CALENDAR GIRL, Hilda Clark, 8,000	60.00	RI
1996	BOY FISHING, Norman Rockwell, 5,000	60.00	RI

Coca-Cola Santa Claus Heritage Collection

1994	SANTA AT HIS DESK, 5,000	60.00	RI
1995	BOY FISHING, Norman Rockwell, 5,000	60.00	RI
1995	GOOD BOYS AND GIRLS, Haddon Sundblom, 2,500	60.00	RI
1995	HILDA CLARK WITH ROSES, 5,000	60.00	RI
1996	TRAVEL REFRESHED, Haddon Sundblom, open	60.00	RI

Boy Fishing

Good Boys and Girls

Dolly Parton

Mike Tyson

Photos courtesy of *Collectors News*

CELEBRITY IMPRESSIONS

(Enesco, Sports Impressions)

That's My Dog

		ISSUE	CURRENT
1988	SCHNAUZER, Jim Killen, 10,000	39.50	NR
1988	BLACK POODLE, Jim Killen, 10,000	39.50	NR
1988	COLLIE, Jim Killen, 10,000	39.50	NR
1988	GERMAN SHEPHERD, Jim Killen, 10,000	39.50	NR

Single Issues

		ISSUE	CURRENT
1987	CLINT EASTWOOD, Glenice, 5,000, 10¼"	49.50	NR
1987	CLINT EASTWOOD, Glenice, 4¼"	19.95	NR
1987	DOLLY PARTON, Glenice, 5,000, 8½"	39.50	NR
1987	KENNY ROGERS, Glenice, 5,000, 8½"	39.50	NR
1987	THE DUKE, Glenice, 5,000, 10¼"	49.50	NR

		ISSUE	CURRENT
1987	THE DUKE, Glenice, 4¼"	19.95	NR
1987	MIKE TYSON, Glenice, 5,000, 8½"	39.50	NR
1987	HULK HOGAN, Glenice, 5,000	39.50	NR

CERTIFIED COLLECTIBLES

Smitten by Kittens

1997	CLEO, Mia Love, 5,000	29.95	RI

CERTIFIED RARITIES UNITED STATES

(Master Engravers of America)

Indian Dancers (Master Engravers of America)

1979	EAGLE DANCER, Don Ruffin, 2,500	300.00	320.00
1980	HOOP DANCER, Don Ruffin, 2,500	300.00	320.00

Postal Artists

1978	COLIAS EURYDICE, Stanley Galli, 15,000	60.00	NR
1979	EUYPHYDRYAS PHAETON, Stanley Galli, 7,500	60.00	NR

Renaissance Masters

1978	ALBA MADONNA, 15,000	55.00	BR
1979	PIETA, 5,000	55.00	NR

CHILMARK UNITED STATES

Family Christmas

1978	TRIMMING THE TREE, 10,000	65.00	NR

Holy Night

1979	WISEMEN, 10,000	65.00	NR

In Appreciation

1978	FLOWERS OF FIELD, 10,000	65.00	NR

CHINESE FINE ARTS CO., INC. UNITED STATES

Eight Immortals

1979	LI T'IEH-KUAI—POVERTY, sgd and dated by sculptor, 300	175.00	NR

CHING-T'AI-LAN PEOPLES REPUBLIC OF CHINA

Winged Jewels: Chinese Cloisonné Birds and Flowers

1991	AZURE-WINGED MAGPIE	95.00	BR
1991	LONG-TAILED TITMOUSE	95.00	NR
1991	ROSY MINIVET	100.00	NR

Azure-Winged Magpie
Photo courtesy of *Collectors News*

		ISSUE	CURRENT
1991	KINGFISHER	100.00	NR
1992	ORIOLE	100.00	NR
1992	FLOWERPECKER	105.00	NR
1992	PEKING ROBIN	105.00	140.00
1992	SHRIKE	105.00	140.00

CHRISTIAN BELL PORCELAIN CANADA

Age of Steam

1981	SYMPHONY IN STEAM, Theodore A. Xaras, 15,000	65.00	200.00
1982	BRIEF ENCOUNTER, Theodore A. Xaras, 15,000	65.00	80.00
1983	NO CONTEST, Theodore A. Xaras, 15,000	65.00	115.00
1984	TIMBER COUNTRY, Theodore A. Xaras, 15,000	65.00	BR
1985	WHITE PASS IN YUKON, Theodore A. Xaras, 15,000	65.00	NR

American Steam

1982	HIAWATHA, Theodore A. Xaras, 15,000	65.00	NR
1983	HITTIN' THE DIAMOND, Theodore A. Xaras, 15,000	65.00	NR
1984	MORNING AT THE DEPOT, Theodore A. Xaras, 15,000	65.00	NR
1984	WINTER ON THE BOSTON & MAINE, Theodore A. Xaras, 15,000	65.00	NR
1985	ON THE HORSESHOE CURVE, Theodore A. Xaras, 15,000	65.00	NR

Canadian Pacific Last Spike Centennial (Two-Plate Series)

1986	BIG HILL, Theodore A. Xaras, 7,500	—	—
1986	FIELD HILL, Theodore A. Xaras, 7,500	—	—
	Set of 2	135.00	145.00

Copeland Remembers

1986	POSSESSION IS..., Eric Copeland	65.00	NR

Great Atlantic Liners

1987	H.M.S. *QUEEN MARY*, Theodore A. Xaras	NA	NA

No Contest
Photo courtesy of *Collectors News*

Sugarbush
Photo courtesy of *Collectors News*

Men of the Rails

		ISSUE	CURRENT
1982	ENGINEER, Theodore A. Xaras, <1 year	39.50	NR
1983	PULLMAN PORTER, Theodore A. Xaras, <1 year	39.50	NR
1983	CONDUCTOR, Theodore A. Xaras, <1 year	39.50	NR
1983	NIGHT OPERATOR, Theodore A. Xaras, <1 year	39.50	NR

Preserving a Way of Life

1980	MAKING WAY FOR CARS, 5,000	60.00	NR
1980	ATOP HAY WAGON, 5,000	60.00	NR
1982	SUGARBUSH, Peter Etril Snyder, hand numbered, 10,000	65.00	NR
1982	FISHING FOR REDFIN, Peter Etril Snyder, 10,000	65.00	NR
1982	WHEAT HARVEST, Peter Etril Snyder, 10,000	65.00	NR
1982	RETURNING FROM THE VILLAGE, Peter Etril Snyder, 10,000	65.00	NR
1984	RECESS TIME, Peter Etril Snyder, 10,000	65.00	NR
1986	THE NEW HORSE, Peter Etril Snyder, 10,000	65.00	NR

Vanishing Africa

1983	THE SENTINEL, Douglas Manning, 15,000	75.00	NR

Wild North

1983	EMPEROR OF THE NORTH, Douglas Manning, 15,000	75.00	NR

Single Issue

1984	ROYAL HUDSON '2860'—FIRST LADY OF STEAM, Theodore A. Xaras, 25,000	NA	NA

CHRISTIAN FANTASY COLLECTIBLES UNITED STATES

Christian Fantasy

1985	THE LEGEND OF THE PRAYER BEAR I, Tim Hildebrandt, 5,100	50.00	NR
1986	THE LEGEND OF THE PRAYER BEAR II, Tim Hildebrandt, 5,100	50.00	NR
1987	THE LEGEND OF THE PRAYER BEAR III, Tim Hildebrandt, 5,100	50.00	NR

Ice Palace of the Fairies
Photo courtesy of *Collectors News*

Fantasy Cookbook

		ISSUE	CURRENT
1986	PICNIC IN THE WOODS, Tim Hildebrandt, 7,100	50.00	NR
1987	THE MAGICAL LAGOON, Tim Hildebrandt, 7,100	50.00	NR
1987	A DWARF CELEBRATION, Tim Hildebrandt, 7,100	50.00	NR
1987	THE WIZARD'S MAGICAL FEAST, Tim Hildebrandt, 7,100	50.00	NR
1987	A STEW POT, Tim Hildebrandt, 7,100	50.00	NR
1987	THE MERMAID'S HIDDEN WATERFALL, Tim Hildebrandt, 7,100	50.00	NR
1987	TINY CELEBRATION, Tim Hildebrandt, 7,100	50.00	NR
1987	THE ENCHANTED REALM OF ZIR, Tim Hildebrandt, 7,100	50.00	NR

Realms of Wonder I

1986	WIZARD'S GLADE, Tim Hildebrandt, 9,100	50.00	NR
1987	MERMAID'S GROTTO, Tim Hildebrandt, 9,100	50.00	NR
1987	ICE PALACE OF THE FAIRIES, Tim Hildebrandt, 9,100	50.00	NR
1987	MUSHROOM VILLAGE OF THE ELVES, Tim Hildebrandt, 9,100	50.00	NR
1987	FOREST OF THE UNICORN, Tim Hildebrandt, 9,100	50.00	NR
1987	THE ELVEN FORTRESS (PEGASUS), Tim Hildebrandt, 9,100	50.00	NR
1987	THE WATER NIXIE, Tim Hildebrandt, 9,100	50.00	NR
1987	DWARVES, Tim Hildebrandt, 9,100	50.00	NR

Realms of Wonder II

1987	WIZARD'S STEED, Tim Hildebrandt, 9,100	50.00	NR
1987	SEA LORD OF LAMURIA, Tim Hildebrandt, 9,100	50.00	NR
1987	COUNCIL OF THE ELVES, Tim Hildebrandt, 9,100	50.00	NR
1987	FAIRIES II, Tim Hildebrandt, 9,100	50.00	NR

Santa's Night Out

1986	SANTA DAYDREAMS, Tim Hildebrandt, 9,100	50.00	NR

CHRISTIAN SELTMANN GERMANY

Luekel's Idyllic Village Life

1986	BLACKSMITH, Luekel	24.50	NR

		ISSUE	CURRENT
1986	THE ARRIVAL OF THE STAGECOACH, Luekel	24.50	BR
1986	STOP AT THE VILLAGE INN, Luekel	27.50	BR
1986	IN THE FIELDS AT HARVEST TIME, Luekel	27.50	NR
1987	ON THE WAY TO THE MARKET, Luekel	27.50	NR
1987	AT THE VILLAGE FOUNTAIN, Luekel	27.50	NR
1987	THE FISHERMAN, Luekel	29.50	NR
1987	DAYTRIP IN THE SUMMERTIME, Luekel	29.50	NR
1987	THE FARMER'S WEDDING, Luekel	29.50	NR
1988	ANGLER'S PLEASURE, Luekel	29.50	NR

Velvet Paws

1991	PLAYMATES	29.00	NR
1991	GYMNASTICS	29.00	40.00
1991	THE MISHAP	32.00	45.00
1992	FRIEND OR FOE?	32.00	NR
1992	UNEXPECTED VISIT	32.00	NR
1992	HIDE AND SEEK	34.00	NR
1992	WATER SPORTS	34.00	NR
1992	IN THE GARDEN	34.00	NR
1992	SWINGING EXERCISE	34.00	50.00
1992	DOLL'S PRAM EXPRESS	36.00	150.00
1992	PLAYING WITH SOAP BUBBLES	36.00	NR
1993	BIKE CHAMPIONS	36.00	RI
1993	CARNIVAL OF CATS	36.00	RI

CLARISSA'S CREATIONS

Single Issues

1990	LITTLE BALLERINA, C. Johnson, 14 days	48.00	NR
1994	MEMORIES, C. Johnson, 25,000	48.00	RI

CLEVELAND MINT UNITED STATES

Da Vinci Series

1972	LAST SUPPER, Leonardo da Vinci, 5,000	150.00	BR

COLLECTOR'S WEEKLY UNITED STATES

American Series

1971	MISS LIBERTY, 500	12.50	NR
1972	MISS LIBERTY, 900	12.50	NR
1973	EAGLE, 900	9.75	NR

COMMAND PERFORMANCE

Single Issue

1998	NEIL DIAMOND, sgd, 1,000	225.00	RI

CONTINENTAL MINT UNITED STATES

Tom Sawyer

		ISSUE	CURRENT
1976	TAKING HIS MEDICINE, 5,000	60.00	NR
1977	PAINTING FENCE, 5,000	60.00	NR
1978	LOST IN CAVE, 5,000	60.00	NR
1979	SMOKING PIPE, 5,000	60.00	NR

Single Issue

1979	BUTTER GIRL, 5,000	60.00	NR

CREATIVE WORLD UNITED STATES

Aesop's Fables

1979	THE FOX AND THE GRAPES, 9,750	85.00	NR

Four Seasons

1972	FALL, silver plate, 2,000	75.00	NR
1972	FALL, sterling silver, 2,000	125.00	NR
1973	SPRING, silver plate, 2,300	75.00	NR
1973	SPRING, sterling silver, 750	125.00	NR
1973	WINTER, silver plate, 2,000	75.00	NR
1973	WINTER, sterling silver, 2,250	125.00	NR
1974	SUMMER, silver plate, 300	75.00	NR
1974	SUMMER, sterling silver, 750	125.00	NR

Help My Friends

NA	CORKY'S DREAM, Murray Karn, limited	NA	NA

Immortals of Early American Literature

1978	VILLAGE SMITHY, Roger Brown, 15,000	50.00	BR

Corky's Dream
Photo courtesy of *Collectors News*

Eriko and Noriko
Photo courtesy of *Collectors News*

		ISSUE	CURRENT
1979	RIP VAN WINKLE, Roger Brown, 15,000	55.00	NR

Living Dolls

1982	ERIKO AND NORIKO, David Smiton, 9,500	49.50	NR
1983	INGRID AND INGEMAR, David Smiton, 9,500	49.50	NR

Prize Collection

1982	FAMILY CARES, 12,500	45.00	NR
1983	WIND IN THE FROLIC, 12,500	45.00	NR

Rockwell Series

1978	LOOKING OUT TO SEA, Roger Brown, 15,000	50.00	65.00
1978	YANKEE DOODLE, Roger Brown, 15,000	50.00	BR
1979	GIRL AT THE MIRROR, Roger Brown, 15,000	55.00	NR

Wags to Riches

1982	BENJI THE MOVIE STAR, Murray Karn, 19,500	29.50	NR
1982	BENJI AND TIFFANY, Murray Karn, 19,500	29.50	NR
1983	MERRY CHRISTMAS BENJI, Murray Karn, 19,500	29.50	NR
1984	BENJI'S BARBER SHOP BLUES, Murray Karn, 19,500	35.00	NR

CRESTLEY COLLECTION

Backyard Buddies

1994	APRIL OUTING, S. Woods	19.95	RI
1994	DECEMBER CUDDLE, S. Woods	19.95	RI
1994	JULY JUBILEE, S. Woods	19.95	RI
1994	JUNE DELIGHT, S. Woods	19.95	RI
1994	MAY DAY, S. Woods	19.95	RI
1994	OCTOBER HARVEST, S. Woods	19.95	RI
1995	JANUARY JINGLE, S. Woods	19.95	RI

Christmas at Primrose Hill

1994	BE IT EVER SO HUMBLE, S. Wheeler	19.95	RI

Coral Kingdoms

1994	AFTERNOON FROLIC, Anthony Casay	NA	RI
1994	DAYBREAK DELIGHT, Anthony Casay	NA	RI
1994	MOONLIGHT DISCOVERY, Anthony Casay	NA	RI
1994	MORNING ENCHANTMENT, Anthony Casay	NA	RI
1994	SUNSET SERENADE, Anthony Casay	NA	RI
1994	TWILIGHT WONDER, Anthony Casay	NA	RI

Friends Forever

1994	BUDDING FRIENDSHIP, Whitten	NA	RI
1994	CUDDLE UP, Whitten	NA	RI
1994	DRINKIN' BUDDIES, Whitten	NA	RI
1994	PUPPY LOVE, Whitten	NA	RI
1994	SHARING THE WONDER, Whitten	NA	RI
1994	TIGHT-KNIT FRIENDS, Whitten	NA	RI

Heavenly Hearts

		ISSUE	CURRENT
1994	FAITH AND CHARITY, T. Cathey	19.95	RI
1994	GOODNESS AND HOPE, T. Cathey	19.95	RI
1994	JOY, T. Cathey	19.95	RI
1994	LIBERTY AND PEACE, T. Cathey	19.95	RI
1994	PATIENCE, T. Cathey	19.95	RI
1994	PRUDENCE, T. Cathey	19.95	RI
1994	SWEETNESS AND GRACE, T. Cathey	19.95	RI
1995	INSPIRATION, T. Cathey	19.95	RI

Native Beauty

1994	DANCE IN THE SUN, Lakofka	NA	RI

Native Sky

1994	ONE WITH THE SKY, Lakofka	NA	RI
1994	SPIRIT OF THE FULL MOON, Lakofka	NA	RI
1994	WHEN LIGHTNING CASTS SHADOWS, Lakofka	NA	RI

Picture Purrfect Cats

1994	EVERYONE NEEDS A TEDDY	19.95	RI
1994	FLUFF AND FLOWERS	19.95	RI
1994	PEEK-A-BOO KITTY	19.95	RI
1994	PERFECTLY POISED	19.95	RI
1994	TEATIME TABBY	19.95	RI
1995	IN THE PINK	19.95	RI
1995	KITTEN ON THE KEYS	19.95	RI

Prayers to the Great Spirit

1994	PRAYER TO THE DAWN, B. Jaxon	NA	RI
1994	PRAYER TO THE FOREFATHERS, B. Jaxon	NA	RI

Primrose Hill

1993	LOVE'S A GIFT FROM THE HEART, S. Wheeler	NA	RI
1994	GOD BLESS OUR HOME, S. Wheeler	NA	RI
1994	HOME IS WHERE THE HEART IS, S. Wheeler	NA	RI
1994	LET HEAVEN AND NATURE SING, S. Wheeler	NA	RI
1994	SENDING SMILES ACROSS MILES, S. Wheeler	NA	RI

Profiles of Bravery

1993	THE BOLD AND THE FREE, S. Evans	19.95	RI
1993	THE NOBLE AND THE PROUD, S. Evans	19.95	RI
1994	THE FIERCE AND THE MIGHTY, S. Evans	19.95	RI
1994	THE STRONG AND THE BRAVE, S. Evans	19.95	RI
1994	THE WILD AND THE WISE, S. Evans	19.95	RI

Teddy Bear Fair

1994	AND AWAY WE GO, T. Dubois	19.95	RI
1994	HERE WE GO 'ROUND, T. Dubois	19.95	RI
1994	JUST THE TWO OF US, T. Dubois	19.95	RI
1994	THE POWER OF LOVE, T. Dubois	19.95	RI
1994	SITTING ON TOP OF THE WORLD, T. Dubois	19.95	RI

		ISSUE	CURRENT
1994	SWEETEST OF ALL, T. Dubois	19.95	RI
1994	YOUR HEART'S DESIRE, T. Dubois	19.95	RI
1994	BEAR HUGS AND HONEY PIES, T. Dubois	19.95	RI

Tribute to Roy Rogers

1994	HOME ON THE RANGE, C. Johnson	19.95	RI
1994	HAPPY TRAILS TO YOU, C. Johnson	19.95	RI

Trolls

1993	MONDAY'S TROLL, T. Dubois	19.95	RI
1993	TUESDAY'S TROLL, T. Dubois	19.95	RI
1993	WEDNESDAY'S TROLL, T. Dubois	19.95	RI
1994	THURSDAY'S TROLL, T. Dubois	19.95	RI
1994	FRIDAY'S TROLL, T. Dubois	19.95	RI
1994	SATURDAY'S TROLL, T. Dubois	19.95	RI
1994	SUNDAY'S TROLL, T. Dubois	19.95	RI

Vision Quest

1993	EAGLE DANCE, L. Kendricks	19.95	RI
1993	SHARING THE SPIRIT, L. Kendricks	19.95	RI
1994	CALLING THE STORM, L. Kendricks	19.95	RI
1994	A HIGHER POWER, L. Kendricks	19.95	RI
1994	SEEKING THE DAWN, L. Kendricks	19.95	RI
1994	SOARING SPIRIT, L. Kendricks	19.95	RI
1994	VALLEY OF THE SPIRIT, L. Kendricks	19.95	RI

Young and Restless

1993	NIKKI'S WORLD, Gray	NA	RI
1994	CRICKET'S TRAILS, Gray	NA	RI
1994	JILL'S ESCAPADES, Gray	NA	RI
1994	KATHERINE'S LEGACY, Gray	NA	RI
1994	VICTOR'S EMPIRE, Gray	NA	RI

CRISTAL D'ALBRET FRANCE

Four Seasons

1972	SUMMER, 1,000	65.00	110.00
1973	AUTUMN, 1,000	75.00	95.00
1974	SPRING, 1,000	75.00	170.00
1975	WINTER, 1,000	88.00	155.00

Single Issue

1972	BIRD OF PEACE, 3,700	88.00	155.00

CROWN DELFT NETHERLANDS

Christmas

1969	MAN BY FIRE, 1 year	10.00	30.00
1970	TWO SLEIGH RIDERS, 1 year	10.00	20.00
1971	CHRISTMAS TREE, 1 year	10.00	NR

		ISSUE	CURRENT
1972	BAKING FOR CHRISTMAS, 1 year	10.00	NR

Father's Day

1970	FATHER'S DAY, 1 year	10.00	NR
1971	FATHER'S DAY, 1 year	10.00	NR
1972	FATHER'S DAY, 1 year	10.00	NR
1973	FATHER'S DAY, 1 year	10.00	NR

Mother's Day

1970	SHEEP, 1 year	10.00	NR
1971	STORK, 1 year	10.00	NR
1972	DUCKS, 1 year	10.00	NR
1973	MOTHER'S DAY, 1 year	10.00	NR

CUI—CAROLINA COLLECTION—DRAM TREE UNITED STATES

Christmas

1991	CHECKIN' IT TWICE EDITION I, CUI, 4,950	39.50	NR

Classic Cars

1992	1957 CHEVY, G. Geivette, 28 days	40.00	NR

Coors Factory

1992	COORS FACTORY FIRST EDITION	29.50	NR
1993	COORS FACTORY SECOND EDITION	29.50	RI

Coors Winterfest

1992	SKATING PARTY, T. Stortz, 45 days	29.50	NR

Corvette

1992	1953 CORVETTE, G. Geivette, 28 days	40.00	NR

Environmental

1991	RAIN FOREST MAGIC EDITION I, C. L. Bragg, 4,950	39.50	NR
1992	FIRST BREATH, M. Hoffman, 4,950	40.00	NR

First Encounter

1993	STAND OFF, R. Cruwys, closed	29.50	RI
1994	CLASS CLOWN, R. Cruwys, closed	29.50	RI

Girl in the Moon

1991	MILLER GIRL IN THE MOON EDITION I, CUI, 9,950	39.50	NR

Great American Sporting Dogs

1992	BLACK LAB EDITION I, Jim Killen, 20,000	40.00	NR
1993	GOLDEN RETRIEVER EDITION II, Jim Killen, 28 days	40.00	RI
1993	SPRINGER SPANIEL EDITION III, Jim Killen, 28 days	40.00	RI
1993	YELLOW LABRADOR EDITION IV, Jim Killen, 28 days	40.00	RI
1993	ENGLISH SETTER EDITION V, Jim Killen, 28 days	40.00	RI

		ISSUE	CURRENT
1993	BRITTANY SPANIEL EDITION VI, Jim Killen, 28 days	40.00	RI

Native American

1991	HUNT FOR THE BUFFALO EDITION I, P. Kethley, 4,950	39.50	NR
1992	STORY TELLER, P. Kethley, 4,950	40.00	NR

DANBURY MINT UNITED STATES

(Anna-Perenna, Pickard, Rosenthal, Winston Roland)

American Countryside

NA	AUTUMN VILLAGE, Eric Sloane	NA	NA
NA	WINTER BRIDGE, Eric Sloane	NA	NA
NA	SUMMER BARN, Eric Sloane	NA	NA
NA	WINTER MORNING, Eric Sloane	NA	NA
NA	HILL FARM, Eric Sloane	NA	NA
NA	FISHING, Eric Sloane	NA	NA
NA	END OF SUMMER, Eric Sloane	NA	NA
NA	MAPLE SUGAR, Eric Sloane	NA	NA
NA	SPRING HOUSE, Eric Sloane	NA	NA
NA	OCTOBER GLORY, Eric Sloane	NA	NA

American Farm

1991	DOWN ON THE FARM, Lowell Davis	NA	NA

Bicentennial Silver

1973	BOSTON TEA PARTY, 7,500	125.00	NR
1974	FIRST CONTINENTAL CONGRESS, 7,500	125.00	NR
1975	PAUL REVERE'S RIDE, 7,500	125.00	NR
1976	DECLARATION OF INDEPENDENCE, 7,500	125.00	NR
1977	WASHINGTON AT VALLEY FORGE, 7,500	125.00	NR
1978	MOLLY PITCHER, 7,500	125.00	NR
1979	*BON HOMME RICHARD*, 7,500	125.00	NR

Blessed Are Ye

1992	LIFE'S BLESSING, Ruth J. Morehead	NA	NA

Boys Will Be Boys

1993	CLEAN AS A WHISTLE, Jim Daly	NA	RI
1993	FAVORITE READER, Jim Daly	NA	RI
1993	HER HERO, Jim Daly	NA	RI
1993	KEPT IN, Jim Daly	NA	RI
1993	SHOESHINE BOY, Jim Daly	NA	RI
1993	SLINGSHOT PAL, Jim Daly	NA	RI
1993	THE THIEF, Jim Daly	NA	RI
1993	TRANQUIL MOMENT, Jim Daly	NA	RI

Cats and Flowers

1989	HOW SWEET IT IS, Irene Spencer	NA	NA
1989	ONE DAY IN MAY, Irene Spencer	NA	NA
1989	NOSE BLOOM, Irene Spencer	NA	NA
1989	BEAUTY AND THE BEES, Irene Spencer	NA	NA

		ISSUE	CURRENT
1989	GARDEN OF WEEDIN, Irene Spencer	NA	NA
1989	FAUX PAW, Irene Spencer	NA	NA
1989	BIRD'S-EYE VIEW, Irene Spencer	NA	NA

Century Plate

1993	WE WISH YOU THE BEST, Berta Hummel	NA	RI
1994	TELL THE WORLD, Berta Hummel	NA	RI

Champion Thoroughbreds

1997	SECRETARIAT, Susie Morton, 75 days	29.90	RI

Christmas

1975	SILENT NIGHT, <1 year	24.50	NR
1976	JOY TO THE WORLD, <1 year	27.50	NR
1977	AWAY IN THE MANGER, <1 year	28.50	NR
1978	THE FIRST NOEL, <1 year	29.50	NR

Currier & Ives Silver

1972	THE ROAD WINTER, 7,500	125.00	NR
1973	CENTRAL PARK WINTER, 7,500	125.00	NR
1974	WINTER IN THE COUNTRY, 7,500	125.00	NR
1975	AMERICAN HOMESTEAD, 7,500	125.00	NR
1976	AMERICAN WINTER EVENING, 7,500	125.00	135.00
1977	WINTER MORNING, 7,500	125.00	135.00

David Maass Pheasant Plate Collection

1997	A WINTER RAINBOW, David Maass, 75 days	29.90	RI

Day with Garfield

1978	THERE IS SO MUCH TO ADMIRE, Jim Davis	NA	NA
1978	SLEEP, THE PERFECT EXERCISE, Jim Davis	NA	NA
1978	CATS CAN HAVE FUN TOO, Jim Davis	NA	NA
1978	SIMPLE MINDS, SIMPLE PLEASURES, Jim Davis	NA	NA
1978	DREAMS CAN TAKE YOU ANYWHERE, Jim Davis	NA	NA
1978	AND NOW FOR DESSERT, Jim Davis	NA	NA
1978	BREAKFAST SURE LOOKS FRESH, Jim Davis	NA	NA
1978	FRIENDS ARE FOREVER, Jim Davis	NA	NA
1978	I GOT UP FOR THIS, Jim Davis	NA	NA
1978	I DENY EVERYTHING, Jim Davis	NA	NA
1978	I'LL RISE BUT WON'T SHINE, Jim Davis	NA	NA
1978	IT'S NOT THE HAVING, IT'S THE GETTING, Jim Davis	NA	NA

Dear Diary: Garfield

1990	NINE LIVES, Jim Davis	NA	NA
1990	GOD LEAVES, Jim Davis	NA	NA
1990	NEW CONDO, Jim Davis	NA	NA
1990	CHARMING CAT, Jim Davis	NA	NA
1990	I COMPOSED MYSELF, Jim Davis	NA	NA
1990	ART PROJECT, Jim Davis	NA	NA
1990	WHAT A NIGHT, Jim Davis	NA	NA
1990	UNCLE ED, Jim Davis	NA	NA

		ISSUE	CURRENT
Ducks Taking Flight			
1988	HAZY ASCENT, David Maass	NA	NA
1988	MISTY MORNING, David Maass	NA	NA
1988	FOLLOW THE LEADER, David Maass	NA	NA
1988	RIPPLED LANDING, David Maass	NA	NA
1988	FEEDING FLIGHT, David Maass	NA	NA
1988	MIGRANTS, David Maass	NA	NA
1988	IN TO FEED, David Maass	NA	NA
1988	LAST OF THE SEASON, David Maass	NA	NA
Fantasyland			
1993	MYSTIC GUARDIAN, Ken Barr	NA	RI
1993	ENCHANTED FOREST, Ken Barr	NA	RI
Farming the Heartland			
1992	BEATING THE STORM, E. Kaye	NA	NA
1992	BOUNTIFUL HARVEST, E. Kaye	NA	NA
1992	HARVESTING AT LAST, E. Kaye	NA	NA
1993	BAILING THE HAY, E. Kaye	NA	RI
1993	TAKING A BREAK, E. Kaye	NA	RI
1993	WELL DESERVED BREAK, E. Kaye	NA	RI
Flags of America—National Flag Association (Pickard)			
NA	BRITISH UNION FLAG / UNION JACK 1606	NA	NA
NA	FIRST STARS AND STRIPES / BETSY ROSS FLAG 1777	NA	NA
NA	BUNKER HILL FLAG FLOWN AT LEXINGTON AND CONCORD 1775	NA	NA
NA	GREEN MOUNTAIN BOYS FLAG CARRIED BY ETHAN ALLEN 1775	NA	NA
NA	RATTLESNAKE FLAG / FIRST NAVY JACK 1776	NA	NA
NA	FORT MOULTRIE FLAG CARRIED IN DEFENDING SOUTH CAROLINA 1776	NA	NA
NA	ROYAL STANDARD OF SPAIN FLOWN BY CHRISTOPHER COLUMBUS 1492	NA	NA
NA	PHILADELPHIA LIGHT HORSE CARRIED IN KEY AMERICAN VICTORIES 1775	NA	NA
Friends of the Forest			
NA	WHITE-TAILED DEER	NA	NA
Gentle Friends			
1991	FAVORITE PET, M. I. Hummel	NA	NA
1991	FARM BOY, M. I. Hummel	NA	NA
1991	FEEDING TIME, M. I. Hummel	NA	NA
1991	FRIENDS, M. I. Hummel	NA	NA
1991	GOOSE GIRL, M. I. Hummel	NA	NA
1991	LET'S SING, M. I. Hummel	NA	NA
1991	GOAT HERDER, M. I. Hummel	NA	NA
1991	PLAYMATES, M. I. Hummel	NA	NA
1991	FEATHERED FRIENDS, M. I. Hummel	NA	NA
1991	CINDERELLA, M. I. Hummel	NA	NA
1991	LAST SHEEP, M. I. Hummel	NA	NA
1991	STROLLING ALONG, M. I. Hummel	NA	NA
Great American Sailing Ships (Rosenthal)			
NA	THE *EAGLE*	NA	NA
NA	THE *COLUMBIA*	NA	NA

		ISSUE	CURRENT
NA	THE *CHARLES W. MORGAN*	NA	NA
NA	USS *CONSTITUTION*	NA	NA
NA	THE *AMERICA*	NA	NA
NA	THE *LIGHTNING*	NA	NA
NA	THE *ALFRED*	NA	NA
NA	THE *BON HOMME RICHARD*	NA	NA
NA	THE *FLYING CLOUD*	NA	NA
NA	THE *SEA WITCH*	NA	NA
NA	THE *ANN MCKIM*	NA	NA

Great Art Masterpieces Silver

1975	MONA LISA, 7,500	125.00	NR
1975	THE LAST SUPPER, 7,500	135.00	NR
1976	SUNFLOWER, 7,500	135.00	NR
1976	BLUE BOY, 7,500	135.00	NR

High Fashion Barbie

NA	1959 BARBIE	NA	NA
NA	1960 EVENING	NA	NA
NA	1960 SOLO	NA	NA
NA	1963 LADY	NA	NA
NA	1963 PROM	NA	NA
NA	1965 DANCE	NA	NA
NA	1965 BLUE	NA	NA
NA	1966 DEBUTANTE	NA	NA

Journey of a Dream

NA	BUDDIES	NA	NA
NA	THE FOAL	NA	NA
NA	THE PARADE	NA	NA
NA	SMALL TALK	NA	NA
NA	PIED PIPER	NA	NA
NA	JUST LIKE ME	NA	NA
NA	SWEET MISS	NA	NA
NA	SMALL TALK	NA	NA
NA	DAISY CHAIN	NA	NA
NA	DREAM CASTLE	NA	NA
NA	FLIGHT	NA	NA

Kitten Cousins

1990	PLAYFUL COMPANIONS, Ruanne Manning	NA	NA
1990	DOUBLE TROUBLE, Ruanne Manning	NA	NA
1990	BAG O' FUN, Ruanne Manning	NA	NA
1990	REGAL SIAMESE, Ruanne Manning	NA	NA
1990	BUTTERFLY, Ruanne Manning	NA	NA
1990	QUIET MEMORY, Ruanne Manning	NA	NA
1990	STUFFED FRIEND, Ruanne Manning	NA	NA
1990	CUP OF TROUBLE, Ruanne Manning	NA	NA

Legends in Gray

NA	LEE AFTER THE BATTLE, Mort Künstler	NA	NA
NA	UNTIL WE MEET AGAIN, Mort Künstler	NA	NA

		ISSUE	CURRENT
NA	PLANNING THE ATTACK, Mort Künstler	NA	NA
NA	LEE AT FREDERICKSBURG, Mort Künstler	NA	NA
NA	GENTLE TEARS, Mort Künstler	NA	NA
NA	STONEWALL JACKSON AT HARPER'S FERRY, Mort Künstler	NA	NA
NA	THERE STANDS JACKSON LIKE A STONEWALL, Mort Künstler	NA	NA
NA	THE GENERALS WERE BROUGHT TO TEARS, Mort Künstler	NA	NA

Little Companions

1991	APPLE TREE BOY AND GIRL, M. I. Hummel	NA	NA
1991	BUDDING SCHOLARS, M. I. Hummel	NA	NA
1991	COME BACK SOON, M. I. Hummel	NA	NA
1991	COUNTRY CROSSROAD, M. I. Hummel	NA	NA
1991	HELLO DOWN THERE, M. I. Hummel	NA	NA
1991	LITTLE EXPLORERS, M. I. Hummel	NA	NA
1991	LITTLE MUSICIANS, M. I. Hummel	NA	NA
1991	PRIVATE PARADE, M. I. Hummel	NA	NA
1991	SQUEAKY CLEAN, M. I. Hummel	NA	NA
1991	STORMY WEATHER, M. I. Hummel	NA	NA
1991	SURPRISE, M. I. Hummel	NA	NA
1991	TENDER LOVING CARE, M. I. Hummel	NA	NA

Little Women

1990	AMY, Elaine Gignilliat	NA	NA
1990	LAURIE'S PROPOSAL, Elaine Gignilliat	NA	NA
1990	WEDDING DAY, Elaine Gignilliat	NA	NA
1990	MARMEE AND BETH, Elaine Gignilliat	NA	NA
1990	BETH, Elaine Gignilliat	NA	NA
1990	JO, Elaine Gignilliat	NA	NA
1990	THE PROFESSOR'S PROPOSAL, Elaine Gignilliat	NA	NA

Magic Moments of Childhood

NA	BUILDING SANDCASTLES, Liz Mayes	NA	NA
NA	WELCOME BABY, Liz Mayes	NA	NA
NA	NEW PUPPY, Liz Mayes	NA	NA
NA	FIRST KISS, Liz Mayes	NA	NA
NA	CHRISTMAS MORNING, Liz Mayes	NA	NA
NA	BRIDESMAID, Liz Mayes	NA	NA
NA	CATCHING BUTTERFLIES, Liz Mayes	NA	NA
NA	BIRTHDAY WISH, Liz Mayes	NA	NA
NA	BEDTIME STORY, Liz Mayes	NA	NA
NA	PAINTING A PICTURE, Liz Mayes	NA	NA
NA	SHARING SECRETS, Liz Mayes	NA	NA

Michelangelo Crystal

1977	PIETA, <1 year	75.00	NR
1978	HOLY FAMILY, <1 year	75.00	NR
1978	MOSES, <1 year	75.00	NR
1979	CREATION OF ADAM, <1 year	75.00	NR

Michelangelo Silver

1973	PIETA, 7,500	125.00	140.00
1973	HOLY FAMILY, 7,500	125.00	140.00

		ISSUE	CURRENT
1973	MOSES, 7,500	125.00	140.00
1973	CREATION OF ADAM, 7,500	125.00	140.00

Old Time Country Winter

1990	WHAT A RIDE, C. J. Sternberg	NA	NA
1990	SNOWY FRIENDS, C. J. Sternberg	NA	NA
1990	TAPPING THE SUGAR MAPLES, C. J. Sternberg	NA	NA
1990	SNOW FORTS, C. J. Sternberg	NA	NA
1990	THE RACE THROUGH TOWN, C. J. Sternberg	NA	NA
1990	SKATING ON THE POND, C. J. Sternberg	NA	NA
1990	CHITTENDON'S PLACE, C. J. Sternberg	NA	NA
1990	TREE LIGHTING, C. J. Sternberg	NA	NA

On the Wing

1990	ABRUPT DESCENT, David Maass	NA	NA
1992	OVER WATER, David Maass	NA	NA
1992	SETTLING IN, David Maass	NA	NA

Pewter

1977	CHRISTMAS CAROL, Jan Hagara	27.50	NR

Pigs in Bloom

1997	HAMMING IT UP, Joan Wright, 75 days	29.90	RI
1997	SNOOZING SWINE, Joan Wright, 75 days	29.90	RI
1997	HOGWASH, Joan Wright, 75 days	29.90	RI
1997	PIGGING OUT, Joan Wright, 75 days	29.90	RI
1997	SQUEALBARROW, Joan Wright, 75 days	29.90	RI
1997	GARDEN PARTY, Joan Wright, 75 days	29.90	RI
1997	HOG HARVEST, Joan Wright, 75 days	29.90	RI
1997	PIGMENTATION, Joan Wright, 75 days	29.90	RI

Squealbarrow
Photo courtesy of *Collectors News*

Stag Falls
Photo courtesy of *Collectors News*

Porcelain Plates

		ISSUE	CURRENT
1977	OFFICIAL AMERICA'S CUP, <1 year	20.00	NR
1977	TALL SHIPS, <1 year	21.00	NR
1977	QUEEN'S SILVER JUBILEE, <1 year	85.00	NR

Pride of the Wilderness

1993	FALL RETREAT, Bob Travers, 75 days	29.90	RI
1993	FULL ALERT, Bob Travers, 75 days	29.90	RI
1993	SNOWBOUND, Bob Travers, 75 days	29.90	RI
1997	WINTER STAG, Bob Travers, 75 days	29.90	RI

Puppy Pals

1989	TIME OUT, Ruane Manning	NA	NA
1991	PLEASANT DREAMS, Ruane Manning	NA	NA
1991	HIDE-AND-SEEK, Ruane Manning	NA	NA
1991	DECOY DELIGHT, Ruane Manning	NA	NA
1991	BONNET BOW, Ruane Manning	NA	NA

Scenes from a Wooded Glen

NA	NUTHATCH, Jo Polseno	NA	NA
NA	CHIPMUNK, Jo Polseno	NA	NA
NA	FAWN, Jo Polseno	NA	NA

Sportsmen

1992	THREE'S A CROWD, Phillip Crowe	NA	NA
1992	GOLDEN MEMORIES, Phillip Crowe	NA	NA
1992	TEXAS TWOS, Phillip Crowe	NA	NA
1992	TAILGATE PARTY, Phillip Crowe	NA	NA
1992	JUST MISSED, Phillip Crowe	NA	NA

Tall Ships

NA	ENGLAND	NA	NA
NA	SPAIN	NA	NA
NA	NETHERLANDS	NA	NA
NA	WEST GERMANY	NA	NA
NA	PORTUGAL	NA	NA
NA	UNITED STATES	NA	NA
NA	JAPAN	NA	NA
NA	FRANCE	NA	NA
NA	SWEDEN	NA	NA
NA	NORWAY	NA	NA
NA	ITALY	NA	NA
NA	DENMARK	NA	NA

Underwater Paradise

1993	DISCOVERY OFF ANAHOLA, Robert Lyn Nelson	NA	RI
1994	CALIFORNIA SPIRITS, Robert Lyn Nelson	NA	RI
1994	CHEZ PAUL, Robert Lyn Nelson	NA	RI
1994	HAWAIIAN MUSES, Robert Lyn Nelson	NA	RI
1994	HONOLUA: BAY OF PIILANI, Robert Lyn Nelson	NA	RI

		ISSUE	CURRENT
1994	LA LE'S SACRED PRINCESS, Robert Lyn Nelson	NA	RI
1994	LAHAINA SEA FLIGHT, Robert Lyn Nelson	NA	RI
1994	MOONLIT MOMENT, Robert Lyn Nelson	NA	RI
1994	NEW MOON OVER WINGWORD OHU, Robert Lyn Nelson	NA	RI
1994	SEARCH FOR HARMONY, Robert Lyn Nelson	NA	RI
1994	SERENITY OF WAIPIO, Robert Lyn Nelson	NA	RI
1994	SUNLIT GOLD, Robert Lyn Nelson	NA	RI

White House China

NA	JAMES MADISON	NA	NA
NA	JOHN QUINCY ADAMS	NA	NA
NA	ABRAHAM LINCOLN	NA	NA
NA	FRANKLIN PIERCE	NA	NA
NA	U.S. GRANT	NA	NA
NA	JAMES MONROE	NA	NA
NA	ANDREW JACKSON	NA	NA
NA	JAMES POLK	NA	NA
NA	BENJAMIN HARRISON	NA	NA
NA	ZACHARY TAYLOR	NA	NA
NA	MILLARD FILMORE	NA	NA
NA	GEORGE WASHINGTON	NA	NA

Whitetail Splendor

NA	NOVEMBER FROST, Larry Zach, 75 days	29.90	RI
1997	BROKEN SOLITUDE, Larry Zach, 75 days	29.90	RI

Wilderness Reflections

1997	STAG FALLS, John Van Straalen, 75 days	29.90	RI

Winged Treasures

NA	FIRE AND SNOW, Derk Hansen	NA	NA

Young Innocence

1992	BEDTIME PRAYERS, Rod Lawrence	NA	NA

D'ARCEAU LIMOGES FRANCE

Cambier Mother's Day

1983	MICHÈLE ET SYLVIE, Guy Cambier	32.84	45.00
1984	MARIE ET JACQUELINE, Guy Cambier	32.84	NR
1985	MONIQUE ET FRANÇOIS, Guy Cambier	32.84	NR
1986	MARIANNE ET THERESE, Guy Cambier	32.84	NR

Collection Le Patrimoine de Lafayette (The Lafayette Legacy)

1973	THE SECRET CONTRACT, André Restieau	14.82	NR
1973	THE LANDING AT NORTH ISLAND, André Restieau	19.82	NR
1974	THE MEETING AT CITY TAVERN, André Restieau	19.82	NR
1974	THE BATTLE OF BRANDYWINE, André Restieau	19.82	NR
1975	THE MESSAGES TO FRANKLIN, André Restieau	19.82	NR
1975	THE SIEGE AT YORKTOWN, André Restieau	19.82	NR

Marie et Jacqueline
Photo courtesy of *Collectors News*

L'Imperatrice Joséphine
Photo courtesy of *Collectors News*

		ISSUE	CURRENT

French Country Landscapes

1987	ALONG THE RIVERSIDE, Julien	NA	NA
1987	HARVEST IN CHAMPAGNE, Julien	NA	NA
1987	SUNDAY IN A VILLAGE, Julien	NA	NA
1988	FLOCK OF SHEEP IN AUVERGNE, Julien	NA	NA
1988	HARBOUR SCENE IN PROVENCE, Julien	NA	NA
1988	OLD WATER MILL IN ALSACE, Julien	NA	NA
1988	PICNIC ON THE GRASS, Julien	NA	NA
1989	PROMENADE IN THE ALPS, Julien	NA	NA

Gigi

1985	GIGI, Jean-Claude Guidou	NA	NA
1985	NIGHT THEY INVENTED CHAMPAGNE, Jean-Claude Guidou	NA	NA
1986	GIGI IN LOVE, Jean-Claude Guidou	NA	NA
1986	I REMEMBER IT WELL, Jean-Claude Guidou	NA	NA

Joséphine et Napoléon

1984	L'IMPERATRICE JOSÉPHINE, limited	29.32	NR
1984	NAPOLÉON, limited	29.32	NR
1984	THE MEETING, limited	29.32	NR

La Belle Epoque

1986	LIANE DE POUGY, Brenot	NA	NA
1986	SARAH BERNHARDT, Brenot	NA	NA
1987	ANNA PAVLOVA, Brenot	NA	NA

Les Douze Sites Parisiens de Louis Dali (The Twelve Parisian Places of Louis Dali)

1980	L'ARC DE TRIOMPHE, Louis Dali	22.94	NR
1981	LA CATHEDRALE NOTRE-DAME, Louis Dali	24.94	30.00
1981	LA PLACE DE LA CONCORDE, Louis Dali	24.94	30.00
1981	L'ÉGLISE SAINT-PIERRE ET LE SACRÉ-COEUR DE MONTMARTRE, Louis Dali	26.83	30.00
1982	LE MARCHÉ AUX FLEURS ET LA CONCIERGERIE, Louis Dali, 1 year	26.83	NR

		ISSUE	CURRENT
1982	LA POINTE DU VERT GALANT ET LE PONT NEUF, Louis Dali, 1 year	26.83	NR
1983	LE JARDIN DES TUILERIES, Louis Dali, 1 year	26.83	NR
1983	LE MOULIN ROUGE, Louis Dali, 1 year	26.83	NR
1983	LE PONT ALEXANDRE III, Louis Dali, 1 year	26.83	NR
1983	L'OPÉRA, Louis Dali, 1 year	26.83	NR
1983	LA TOUR EIFFEL, Louis Dali, 1 year	26.83	NR
1983	L'HÔTEL DE VILLE DE PARIS, Louis Dali, 1 year	26.83	NR

Les Femmes du Siècle (The Women of the Century)

1976	SCARLET EN CRINOLINE, François Ganeau	17.67	40.00
1976	SARAH EN TOURNURE, François Ganeau	22.74	30.00
1976	COLETTE, François Ganeau	22.74	30.00
1976	LEA, François Ganeau	22.74	30.00
1977	ALBERTINE, François Ganeau, 1 year	22.74	NR
1977	EDITH, François Ganeau	22.74	NR
1977	DAISY, François Ganeau, 1 year	22.74	NR
1977	MARLÈNE, François Ganeau, 1 year	22.74	NR
1978	HÉLÈNE, François Ganeau, 1 year	22.74	NR
1978	SOPHIE, François Ganeau, 1 year	22.74	50.00
1979	FRANÇOISE EN PANTALON, François Ganeau, 1 year	22.74	50.00
1979	BRIGITTE EN MINI-JUPE, François Ganeau, 1 year	22.74	50.00

Les Jeunes Filles des Saisons (The Girls of the Seasons)

1978	LA JEUNE FILLE D'ETÉ, Guy Cambier, 15,000	105.00	120.00
1979	LA JEUNE FILLE D'HIVER, Guy Cambier, 15,000	105.00	NR
1980	LA JEUNE FILLE DU PRINTEMPS, Guy Cambier, 15,000	105.00	NR
1981	LA JEUNE FILLE D'AUTOMNE, Guy Cambier, 15,000	105.00	125.00

Les Noels de France

1986	THE MAGICAL WINDOW, Jean-Claude Guidou, 150 days	28.47	50.00
1988	NOËL EN ALSACE, Jean-Claude Guidou, 150 days	28.47	NR

L'Arc de Triomphe

Noël en Alsace
Photo courtesy of *Collectors News*

Les Très Riches Heures (The Very Rich Hours)

		ISSUE	CURRENT
1979	JANVIER, Jean Dutheil, 1 year	75.48	NR
1980	AVRIL, Jean Dutheil, 1 year	75.48	NR
1981	AOÛT, Jean Dutheil, 1 year	75.48	NR
1982	JUIN, Jean Dutheil, 1 year	75.48	NR
1984	MAI, Jean Dutheil, 1 year	75.48	NR

Noël Vitrail (Stained-glass Christmas)

1975	LA FUITE EN EGYPTE, André Restieau	24.32	35.00
1976	DANS LA CRÈCHE, André Restieau	24.32	30.00
1977	LE REFUS D'HÈBERGEMENT, André Restieau	24.32	30.00
1978	LA PURIFICATION, André Restieau, 1 year	26.81	NR
1979	L'ADORATION DES ROIS, André Restieau, 1 year	26.81	40.00
1980	JOYEUSE NOUVELLE, André Restieau, 1 year	28.74	NR
1981	GUIDES PAR L'ETOILE, André Restieau, 1 year	28.74	NR
1982	L'ANNUNCIATION, André Restieau, 1 year	30.74	45.00

Mai
Photo courtesy of *Collectors News*

Guides par l'Etoile

DAUM FRANCE

Art Nouveau

1979	WATER LILIES, 4,000	125.00	NR
1980	LILY POND, 4,000	150.00	NR
1981	SWAN, 4,000	170.00	NR

Famous Musicians

1971	BACH, 2,000	75.00	NR
1971	BEETHOVEN, 2,000	75.00	NR
1971	MOZART, 2,000	75.00	NR

		ISSUE	CURRENT
1971	WAGNER, 2,000	75.00	NR
1972	DEBUSSY, 2,000	75.00	NR
1972	GERSHWIN, 2,000	75.00	NR

Four Seasons

1970	AUTUMN, Raymond Corbin, 2,000	150.00	NR
1970	WINTER, Raymond Corbin, 2,000	150.00	NR
1970	SPRING, Raymond Corbin, 2,000	150.00	NR
1970	SUMMER, Raymond Corbin, 2,000	150.00	NR

Nymphea

1979	WATER LILIES, 4,000	125.00	140.00
1980	LILY POND, 4,000	150.00	170.00

Salvador Dali

1970	CECI N'EST PAS UNE ASSIETTE, 2,000	475.00	NR
1970	TRIOMPHALE, 2,000	475.00	NR

DAVENPORT POTTERY GREAT BRITAIN

Attwell's Silver Linings

1988	THANK GOD FOR FIDO, Mabel Lucie Attwell	24.50	NR
1988	RAINBOWS, Mabel Lucie Attwell	24.50	30.00
1988	HOW GOOD OF GOD, Mabel Lucie Attwell	24.50	30.00
1988	A BIT OF LOVE, Mabel Lucie Attwell	24.50	55.00

Cottages of Olde England

1991	HOLLYHOCK COTTAGE, Ian Fraser	75.00	NR
1991	LILAC COTTAGE, Ian Fraser	75.00	85.00
1991	WILD ROSE COTTAGE, Ian Fraser	75.00	125.00
1991	CATTAIL COTTAGE, Ian Fraser	75.00	130.00

Lilac Cottage
Photo courtesy of *Collectors News*

Falstaff
Photo courtesy of *Collectors News*

Gardens of Victoria

		ISSUE	CURRENT
1989	THE QUEEN VICTORIA ROSE	60.00	NR
1989	THE CROWN ORCHID	60.00	75.00
1990	THE EMPRESS OF INDIA	65.00	NR
1990	THE ROYAL CARNELIA	65.00	75.00
1990	THE REGAL CLEMATIS	65.00	100.00
1991	THE SOVEREIGN POPPY	65.00	100.00

Toby Plate Collection

1984	TOBY FILLPOT, Wilfred Blandford	35.00	NR
1984	FALSTAFF, Douglas Tootle	35.00	BR
1985	JACK TAR, Douglas Tootle	40.00	NR
1986	MR. PICKWICK, Douglas Tootle	40.00	BR
1986	FRIAR TUCK, Douglas Tootle	40.00	NR
1986	LONG JOHN SILVER	40.00	BR

Treasury of Classic Children's Verse

1986	ALL THINGS BRIGHT AND BEAUTIFUL	29.00	NR
1986	PIRATE STORY	29.00	NR
1987	THE STAR	29.00	35.00
1987	ANIMAL CRACKERS	32.00	NR
1987	TARTARY	32.00	50.00
1987	LOOKING-GLASS RIVER	32.00	40.00
1988	THE KITE	34.00	50.00
1988	AT THE ZOO	34.00	55.00

World of Beatrix Potter

1991	TALE OF PETER RABBIT, Beatrix Potter	59.00	90.00
1992	TALE OF TOM KITTEN, Beatrix Potter	59.00	110.00
1992	TALE OF JEMIMA PUDDLEDUCK, Beatrix Potter	64.00	145.00
1992	TALE OF TWO BED MICE, Beatrix Potter	64.00	85.00
1992	TALE OF JEREMY FISHER, Beatrix Potter	64.00	145.00
1993	TALE OF BENJAMIN BUNNY, Beatrix Potter	69.00	RI
1993	TALE OF MRS. TIGGY-WINKLE, Beatrix Potter	69.00	RI
1993	TALE OF THE TAILOR OF GLOUCHESTER, Beatrix Potter	69.00	RI

LOWELL DAVIS FARM CLUB

Davis Cat Tales

1982	RIGHT CHURCH WRONG PEW, Lowell Davis, 12,500	37.50	90.00
1982	COMPANY'S COMING, Lowell Davis, 12,500	37.50	90.00
1983	ON THE MOVE, Lowell Davis, 12,500	37.50	90.00
1983	FLEW THE COOP, Lowell Davis, 12,500	37.50	90.00

Davis Christmas Annual

1983	HOOKER AT MAILBOX WITH PRESENT, Lowell Davis, 7,500	45.00	130.00
1984	COUNTRY CHRISTMAS, Lowell Davis, 7,500	45.00	125.00
1985	CHRISTMAS AT FOXFIRE FARM, Lowell Davis, 7,500	45.00	150.00
1986	CHRISTMAS AT RED OAK, Lowell Davis, 7,500	45.00	100.00
1987	BLOSSOM'S GIFT, Lowell Davis, 7,500	45.00	100.00
1988	CUTTING THE FAMILY CHRISTMAS TREE, Lowell Davis, 7,500	47.50	75.00

Country Christmas
Photo courtesy of *Collectors News*

Blacksmith Shop
Photo courtesy of *Collectors News*

		ISSUE	CURRENT
1989	PETER AND THE WREN, Lowell Davis, 7,500	47.50	75.00
1990	WINTERING DEER, Lowell Davis, 7,500	47.50	NR
1991	CHRISTMAS AT RED OAK II, Lowell Davis, 7,500	55.00	75.00
1992	BORN ON A STARRY NIGHT, Lowell Davis, 7,500	55.00	NR
1993	WAITING FOR MR. LOWELL, Lowell Davis, 7,500	55.00	RI
1994	VISIONS OF SUGARPLUMS, Lowell Davis, 7,500	55.00	RI
1995	BAH HUMBUG, Lowell Davis, 7,500	55.00	RI

Davis Country Pride

1981	SURPRISE IN THE CELLAR, Lowell Davis, 7,500	35.00	200.00
1981	PLUM TUCKERED OUT, Lowell Davis, 7,500	35.00	115.00
1981	DUKE'S MIXTURE, Lowell Davis, 7,500	35.00	190.00
1982	BUSTIN' WITH PRIDE, Lowell Davis, 7,500	35.00	100.00

Davis Pen Pals (Schmid)

1993	THE OLD HOME PLACE, 25800, Lowell Davis, closed	50.00	RI

Davis Red Oak Sampler

1986	GENERAL STORE, Lowell Davis, 5,000	45.00	110.00
1987	COUNTRY WEDDING, Lowell Davis, 5,000	45.00	125.00
1989	COUNTRY SCHOOL, Lowell Davis, 5,000	45.00	110.00
1990	BLACKSMITH SHOP, Lowell Davis, 5,000	52.50	110.00

Davis Special Edition Plates

1983	THE CRITICS, Lowell Davis, 12,500	45.00	95.00
1984	GOOD OLE DAYS PRIVY SET II, Lowell Davis, 5,000	60.00	185.00
1986	HOME FROM MARKET, Lowell Davis, 7,500	55.00	145.00

DAYBRAKE MARKETING CANADA

Single Issue

1984	ERNIE'S FARM FRIENDS, Tammy Laye, 7,500	50.00	NR

DELOS APOLLO GREECE

Great Love Stories of Greek Mythology

		ISSUE	CURRENT
1988	APHRODITE AND ADONIS	65.00	BR
1989	EROS AND PSYCHE	65.00	BR
1989	DAPHNE AND APOLLO	65.00	BR
1989	PYGMALION AND GALATEA	65.00	BR

DELPHI UNITED STATES

Adventures of Indiana Jones: The Last Crusade

1989	INDIANA JONES, Victor Gadino, 150 days	24.75	NR
1989	INDIANA JONES AND HIS DAD, Victor Gadino, 150 days	24.75	40.00
1990	INDIANA JONES/DR. SCHNEIDER, Victor Gadino, 150 days	27.75	NR
1990	A FAMILY DISCUSSION, Victor Gadino, 150 days	27.75	NR
1990	YOUNG INDIANA JONES, Victor Gadino, 150 days	27.75	40.00
1991	INDIANA JONES/THE HOLY GRAIL, Victor Gadino, 150 days	27.75	60.00

Beatles

1991	THE BEATLES, LIVE IN CONCERT, Nate Giorgio, 150 days	24.75	45.00
1991	HELLO AMERICA, Nate Giorgio, 150 days	24.75	50.00
1991	A HARD DAY'S NIGHT, Nate Giorgio, 150 days	27.75	55.00
1992	BEATLES '65, Nate Giorgio, 150 days	27.75	65.00
1992	HELP, Nate Giorgio, 150 days	27.75	50.00
1992	THE BEATLES AT SHEA STADIUM, Nate Giorgio, 150 days	29.75	NR
1992	RUBBER SOUL, Nate Giorgio, 150 days	29.75	NR
1992	YESTERDAY AND TODAY, Nate Giorgio, 150 days	29.75	NR

Beatles '67–'70

1992	SGT. PEPPER THE 25TH ANNIVERSARY, Diane Sivavec, 150 days	27.75	NR
1992	ALL YOU NEED IS LOVE, Diane Sivavec, 150 days	27.75	NR
1993	ABBEY ROAD, Diane Sivavec, 150 days	27.75	RI
1993	HEY JUDE, Diane Sivavec, 150 days	27.75	RI
1993	LET IT BE, Diane Sivavec, 150 days	27.75	RI
1993	MAGICAL MYSTERY TOUR, Diane Sivavec, 150 days	27.75	RI

Classic Diners

1993	TWILIGHT AT THE GALAXY, Herring	NA	RI

Commemorating the King

1993	THE ROCK AND ROLL LEGEND, Mark Stutzman, 95 days	29.75	RI
1993	LAS VEGAS, LIVE, Mark Stutzman, 95 days	29.75	RI
1993	BLUES AND BLACK LEATHER, Mark Stutzman, 95 days	29.75	RI
1993	PRIVATE PRESLEY, Mark Stutzman, 95 days	29.75	RI
1993	GOLDEN BOY, Mark Stutzman, 95 days	29.75	RI
1993	SCREEN IDOL, Mark Stutzman, 95 days	29.75	RI
1993	OUTSTANDING YOUNG MAN, Mark Stutzman, 95 days	29.75	RI
1993	THE TIGER: FAITH, SPIRIT AND DISCIPLINE, Mark Stutzman, 95 days	29.75	RI

Dream Machines

1988	'56 T-BIRD, P. Palma, 150 days	24.75	NR

		ISSUE	CURRENT
1989	'57 CORVETTE, P. Palma, 150 days	24.75	NR
1989	'58 BIARRITZ, P. Palma, 150 days	27.75	NR
1989	'56 CONTINENTAL, P. Palma, 150 days	27.75	NR
1989	'57 BEL AIR, P. Palma, 150 days	27.75	NR
1989	'57 CHRYSLER 300C, P. Palma, 150 days	27.75	NR

Elvis on the Big Screen

1992	ELVIS IN LOVING YOU, Bruce Emmett, 150 days	29.75	50.00
1992	ELVIS IN G.I. BLUES, Bruce Emmett, 150 days	29.75	75.00
1992	VIVA LAS VEGAS, Bruce Emmett, 150 days	32.75	95.00
1993	ELVIS IN BLUE HAWAII, Bruce Emmett, 150 days	32.75	RI
1993	ELVIS IN JAILHOUSE ROCK, Bruce Emmett, 150 days	32.75	RI
1993	ELVIS IN SPINOUT, Bruce Emmett, 150 days	34.75	RI
1993	ELVIS IN SPEEDWAY, Bruce Emmett, 150 days	34.75	RI
1993	ELVIS IN HARUM SCARUM, Bruce Emmett, 150 days	34.75	RI

Indiana Jones

'57 Corvette

Jailhouse Rock

Babe Ruth: The Called Shot

Photos courtesy of *Collectors News*

Elvis Presley Hit Parade

		ISSUE	CURRENT
1992	HEARTBREAK HOTEL, Nate Giorgio, 150 days	29.75	NR
1992	BLUE SUEDE SHOES, Nate Giorgio, 150 days	29.75	NR
1992	HOUND DOG, Nate Giorgio, 150 days	32.75	NR
1992	BLUE CHRISTMAS, Nate Giorgio, 150 days	32.75	NR
1992	RETURN TO SENDER, Nate Giorgio, 150 days	32.75	NR
1993	TEDDY BEAR, Nate Giorgio, 150 days	34.75	RI
1993	ALWAYS ON MY MIND, Nate Giorgio, 150 days	34.75	RI
1993	MYSTERY TRAIN, Nate Giorgio, 150 days	34.75	RI
1993	BLUE MOON OF KENTUCKY, Nate Giorgio, 150 days	34.75	RI
1993	WEAR MY RING AROUND YOUR NECK, Nate Giorgio, 150 days	36.75	RI
1993	SUSPICIOUS MINDS, Nate Giorgio, 150 days	36.75	RI
1993	PEACE IN THE VALLEY, Nate Giorgio, 150 days	36.75	RI

Elvis Presley: In Performance

1990	'68 COMEBACK SPECIAL, Bruce Emmett, 150 days	24.75	55.00
1991	KING OF LAS VEGAS, Bruce Emmett, 150 days	24.75	85.00
1991	ALOHA FROM HAWAII, Bruce Emmett, 150 days	27.75	60.00
1991	BACK IN TUPELO, 1956, Bruce Emmett, 150 days	27.75	55.00
1991	IF I CAN DREAM, Bruce Emmett, 150 days	27.75	50.00
1991	BENEFIT FOR THE U.S.S. *ARIZONA*, Bruce Emmett, 150 days	29.75	50.00
1991	MADISON SQUARE GARDEN 1972, Bruce Emmett, 150 days	29.75	55.00
1991	TAMPA 1955, Bruce Emmett, 150 days	29.75	55.00
1991	CONCERT IN BATON ROUGE 1974, Bruce Emmett, 150 days	29.75	70.00
1992	ON STAGE IN WICHITA 1974, Bruce Emmett, 150 days	31.75	75.00
1992	IN THE SPOTLIGHT: HAWAII '72, Bruce Emmett, 150 days	31.75	70.00
1992	TOUR FINALE: INDIANAPOLIS 1977, Bruce Emmett, 150 days	31.75	NR

Elvis Presley: Looking at a Legend

1988	ELVIS AT GATES OF GRACELAND, Bruce Emmett, 150 days	24.75	70.00
1989	JAILHOUSE ROCK, Bruce Emmett, 150 days	24.75	70.00
1989	THE MEMPHIS FLASH, Bruce Emmett, 150 days	27.75	50.00
1989	HOMECOMING, Bruce Emmett, 150 days	27.75	55.00
1990	ELVIS AND GLADYS, Bruce Emmett, 150 days	27.75	40.00
1990	A STUDIO SESSION, Bruce Emmett, 150 days	27.75	NR
1990	ELVIS IN HOLLYWOOD, Bruce Emmett, 150 days	29.75	50.00
1990	ELVIS ON HIS HARLEY, Bruce Emmett, 150 days	29.75	50.00
1990	STAGE DOOR AUTOGRAPHS, Bruce Emmett, 150 days	29.75	NR
1991	CHRISTMAS AT GRACELAND, Bruce Emmett, 150 days	32.75	70.00
1991	ENTERING SUN STUDIO, Bruce Emmett, 150 days	32.75	50.00
1991	GOING FOR THE BLACK BELT, Bruce Emmett, 150 days	32.75	40.00
1991	HIS HAND IN MINE, Bruce Emmett, 150 days	32.75	70.00
1991	LETTERS FROM FANS, Bruce Emmett, 150 days	32.75	60.00
1991	CLOSING THE DEAL, Bruce Emmett, 150 days	34.75	50.00
1992	ELVIS RETURNS TO THE STAGE, Bruce Emmett, 150 days	34.75	50.00

Fabulous Cars of the Fifties

1993	'57 RED CORVETTE, G. Angelini, closed	24.75	RI
1993	'57 WHITE T-BIRD, G. Angelini, closed	24.75	RI
1993	'57 BLUE BELAIR, G. Angelini, closed	27.75	RI
1993	'59 PINK CADILLAC, G. Angelini, closed	27.75	RI
1994	'56 LINCOLN PREMIER, G. Angelini, closed	27.75	RI
1994	'59 RED FORD FAIRLANE, G. Angelini, closed	27.75	RI

In the Footsteps of the King (Bradford Exchange)

		ISSUE	CURRENT
1993	GRACELAND: MEMPHIS, TENNESSEE, Diane Sivavec, closed	29.75	RI
1994	ELVIS' BIRTHPLACE: TUPELO, MISSISSIPPI, Diane Sivavec, closed	29.75	RI
1994	ELVIS' DAY JOB: MEMPHIS, TENNESSEE, Diane Sivavec, closed	32.75	RI
1994	FLYING CIRCLE G RANCH: WALLS, MISSISSIPPI, Diane Sivavec, closed	32.75	RI
1994	THE LAUDERDALE COURTS, Diane Sivavec, closed	32.75	RI
1994	PATRIOTIC SOLDIER: BAD NAUHEIM, WEST GERMANY, Diane Sivavec, closed	34.75	RI

Legends of Baseball

1992	BABE RUTH: THE CALLED SHOT, Brent Benger, 150 days	24.75	NR
1992	LOU GEHRIG: THE LUCKIEST MAN, Jeff Barson, 150 days	24.75	NR
1993	CHRISTY MATHEWSON, Jeff Barson, 150 days	24.75	RI
1993	CY YOUNG: THE PERFECT GAME, Jeff Barson, 150 days	24.75	RI
1993	HONUS WAGNER: FLYING DUTCHMAN, Jeff Barson, 150 days	29.75	RI
1993	JIMMIE FOX: THE BEAST, Jeff Barson, 150 days	29.75	RI
1993	MEL OTT: MASTER MELVIN, Jeff Barson, 150 days	29.75	RI
1993	ROGER HORNSBY: 424 SEASON, Jeff Barson, 150 days	29.75	RI
1993	TRIS SPEAKER: THE GRAY EAGLE, Jeff Barson, 150 days	29.75	RI
1993	TY COBB: THE GEORGIA PEACH, Jeff Barson, 150 days	29.75	RI
1993	WALTER JOHNSON: THE SHUTOUT, Jeff Barson, 150 days	29.75	RI
1994	LEFTY GROVE, Jeff Barson, 150 days	29.75	RI
1994	LEFTY GROVE: HIS GREATEST, Jeff Barson, 150 days	31.75	RI
1994	MICKEY COCKRANE: BLACK MIKE, Jeff Barson, 150 days	31.75	RI
1994	PIE TRAYNOR: PITTSBURGH CHAMPION, Jeff Barson, 150 days	31.75	RI
1994	SHOELESS JOE JACKSON: TRIPLES, Jeff Barson, 150 days	31.75	RI
1995	GROVER ALEXANDER, Jeff Barson, 150 days	31.75	RI

Magic of Marilyn

1992	FOR OUR BOYS IN KOREA 1954, Chris Notarile, 150 days	24.75	30.00
1992	OPENING NIGHT 1954, Chris Notarile, 150 days	24.75	30.00
1993	RISING STAR 1954, Chris Notarile, 150 days	27.75	RI
1993	STOPPING TRAFFIC, Chris Notarile, 150 days	27.75	RI
1993	STRASBERG'S CLASS, Chris Notarile, 150 days	27.75	RI
1993	PHOTO OPPORTUNITY, Chris Notarile, 150 days	27.75	RI
1993	SHINING STAR, Chris Notarile, 150 days	27.75	RI
1993	CURTAIN CALL, Chris Notarile, 150 days	27.75	RI

Marilyn Monroe Collection

1989	MARILYN MONROE/*SEVEN-YEAR ITCH*, Chris Notarile, 150 days	24.75	65.00
1990	MARILYN MONROE/DIAMONDS/GIRLS BEST FRIEND, Chris Notarile, 150 days	24.75	60.00
1991	MARILYN MONROE/RIVER OF NO RETURN, Chris Notarile, 150 days	27.75	65.00
1992	*HOW TO MARRY A MILLIONAIRE*, Chris Notarile, 150 days	27.75	70.00
1992	THERE'S NO BUSINESS/SHOW BUSINESS, Chris Notarile, 150 days	27.75	70.00
1992	MARILYN MONROE IN *NIAGARA*, Chris Notarile, 150 days	29.75	75.00
1992	MY HEART BELONGS TO DADDY, Chris Notarile, 150 days	29.75	75.00
1992	MARILYN MONROE/CHERIE IN *BUS STOP*, Chris Notarile, 150 days	29.75	60.00
1992	MARILYN MONROE IN *ALL ABOUT EVE*, Chris Notarile, 150 days	29.75	60.00
1992	MARILYN MONROE IN *MONKEY BUSINESS*, Chris Notarile, 150 days	31.75	60.00
1992	MARILYN MONROE IN *DON'T BOTHER TO KNOCK*, Chris Notarile, 150 days	31.75	60.00
1992	MARILYN MONROE/WE'RE NOT MARRIED, Chris Notarile, 150 days	31.75	60.00

		ISSUE	CURRENT

Michael Jackson

1990	BILLIE JEAN, Nate Giorgio	NA	NA

Portraits of the King

1991	LOVE ME TENDER, David Zwierz, 150 days	27.75	35.00
1991	ARE YOU LONESOME TONIGHT?, David Zwierz, 150 days	27.75	50.00
1991	I'M YOURS, David Zwierz, 150 days	30.75	75.00
1991	TREAT ME NICE, David Zwierz, 150 days	30.75	65.00
1992	THE WONDER OF YOU, David Zwierz, 150 days	30.75	NR
1992	YOU'RE A HEARTBREAKER, David Zwierz, 150 days	32.75	NR
1992	JUST BECAUSE, David Zwierz, 150 days	32.75	NR
1992	FOLLOW THAT DREAM, David Zwierz, 150 days	32.75	40.00

Take Me Out to the Ballgame

1993	WRIGLEY FIELD: FRIENDLY CONFINES, David Henderson, 95 days	29.75	RI
1993	YANKEE STADIUM: HOUSE OF BABE RUTH, David Henderson, 95 days	29.75	RI
1993	BRIGGS STADIUM: HOME OF THE TIGERS, David Henderson, 95 days	32.75	RI
1993	COMISKEY PARK: HOME OF THE WHITE SOX, David Henderson, 95 days	32.75	RI
1993	FENWAY PARK: HOME OF THE GREEN MONSTER, David Henderson, 95 days	32.75	RI
1993	MEMORIAL STADIUM: HOME OF THE ORIOLES, David Henderson, 95 days	34.75	RI
1994	CLEVELAND STADIUM: CLEVELAND INDIANS, David Henderson, 95 days	34.75	RI
1994	COUNTY STADIUM, David Henderson, 95 days	34.75	RI
1994	EBBETS FIELD: HOME OF THE DODGERS, David Henderson, 95 days	34.75	RI
1994	SHIBE PARK: PHILADELPHIA HOME, David Henderson, 95 days	34.75	RI
1995	FORBES FIELD: PITTSBURGH PIRATES, David Henderson, 95 days	34.75	RI
1995	POLO GROUNDS: NEW YORK GIANTS, David Henderson, 95 days	34.75	RI

DEPARTMENT 56 UNITED STATES

A Christmas Carol

1991	THE CRATCHITS' CHRISTMAS PUDDING, 5706-1, R. Innocenti, 18,000	60.00	BR
1992	MARLEY'S GHOST APPEARS TO SCROOGE, 5721-5, R. Innocenti, 18,000	60.00	BR
1993	THE SPIRIT OF CHRISTMAS PRESENT, 5722-3, R. Innocenti, 18,000	60.00	RI
1994	VISIONS OF CHRISTMAS PAST, 5723-1, R. Innocenti, 18,000	60.00	RI

Dickens' Village

1987	DICKENS' VILLAGE PORCELAIN PLATES, 5917-0, closed, set of 4	140.00	NR

DE PAUW STUDIOS UNITED STATES

Single Issue

1976	BICENTENNIAL LINCOLN, 2,400	30.00	70.00

DERBY COLLECTION

Wild Innocence

NA	MY BUDDY, Doris Scott Nelson, limited	29.95	NR

DEVONSHIRE USA UNITED STATES

Single Issue

		ISSUE	CURRENT
1987	A TIMELESS TRADITION, Carlo Beninati, 30 days	29.50	NR

DIANA ART UNITED STATES

Backyard Birds

		ISSUE	CURRENT
1996	MOUNTAIN LAUREL CARDINAL, Ron Holyfield, 5,000	30.00	RI
1997	APPLE BLOSSOM TIME, Ron Holyfield, 5,000	30.00	RI
1997	GOLD IN THE DOGWOOD, Ron Holyfield, 5,000	30.00	RI
1997	JEWELS IN THE ORCHARD, Ron Holyfield, 5,000	30.00	RI

Christmas Collection

		ISSUE	CURRENT
1996	DOWN THE CHIMNEY HE GOES, Denise Calisti, 25 days	34.95	RI

Ducks for all Seasons

		ISSUE	CURRENT
1997	AUTUMN'S JEWELS, Robin Naomi Rogers, 5,000	30.00	RI
1997	SPRING SPLENDOR, Robin Naomi Rogers, 5,000	30.00	RI
1997	SUMMER SWIM, Robin Naomi Rogers, 5,000	30.00	RI
1997	WINTER VISITORS, Robin Naomi Rogers, 5,000	30.00	RI

Endangered Species

		ISSUE	CURRENT
1997	FROLICKING DOLPHINS, Linda Thompson, 5,000	30.00	RI
1997	LAST REFUGE MANATEES, Linda Thompson, 5,000	30.00	RI
1997	WHALE OF A TIME, Linda Thompson, 5,000	30.00	RI
1997	WOLF DEN, Linda Thompson, 5,000	30.00	RI

Exotic Animals

		ISSUE	CURRENT
1996	ELEPHANT COUNTRY, Grant Hacking, 25 days	30.00	RI
1996	GIRAFFES, Grant Hacking, 25 days	30.00	RI
1996	TIGER REFLECTION, Grant Hacking, 25 days	30.00	RI
1996	YOUNG SILVERBACK, Grant Hacking, 25 days	30.00	RI

Farm Animals

		ISSUE	CURRENT
1996	GOOD MOOOOD!, Denise Calisti, 15 days	29.95	RI
1997	PIGGY'S PICNIC, Denise Calisti, 15 days	29.95	RI

Single Issues

		ISSUE	CURRENT
1997	KITTY'S QUILT, Sandra Williams, 15 days	29.95	RI

RICHARD DISILVIO STUDIO

Pantheon of Composers

		ISSUE	CURRENT
1992	GIACOMO PUCCINI, Richard DiSilvio, 1 year	29.95	NR
1992	GIOACCHINO ROSSINI, Richard DiSilvio, 1 year	29.95	NR
1992	LUDWIG VAN BEETHOVEN, Richard DiSilvio, 1 year	29.95	NR
1992	WOLFGANG A. MOZART, Richard DiSilvio, 1 year	29.95	NR
1993	FRANZ LISZT, Richard DiSilvio, 1 year	29.95	RI

		ISSUE	CURRENT
1993	GIUSEPPE VERDI, Richard DiSilvio, 1 year	29.95	RI
1993	PETER TCHAIKOVSKY, Richard DiSilvio, 1 year	29.95	RI
1993	RICHARD WAGNER, Richard DiSilvio, 1 year	29.95	RI

Wedding Collection

1993	KISS OF ETERNAL LOVE, Richard DiSilvio, 10,000	29.95	RI

Single Issue

1992	COLUMBUS DISCOVERY OF AMERICA, Richard DiSilvio, 2,000	29.95	NR

DOMINION CHINA, LTD CANADA

(Edwin M. Knowles)

Be My Baby

1994	BABY BLUES	29.90	RI
1995	SAFETY IN NUMBERS	29.90	RI
1995	WAITING FOR SUPPER	29.90	RI
1995	BEACH BUMS	29.90	RI

Birds of the North

1990	GOLDEN FLIGHT: CANADA GEESE, Darrell Bush	34.80	BR
1990	WINTER WINGS: SNOW GEESE, Darrell Bush	34.80	BR
1990	TRANQUIL BEAUTY: TRUMPETER SWANS, Darrell Bush	37.80	NR
1991	MORNING LIGHT: COMMON LOONS, Darrell Bush	37.80	NR
1991	ROCKY PERCH: HOMED PUFFINS, Darrell Bush	37.80	NR
1991	BARROW'S GOLDEN EYE, Darrell Bush	37.80	NR
1991	FLYING IN: KING ELDER DUCKS, Darrell Bush	39.80	NR
1991	ON THE WING: BLUEBILLS, Darrell Bush	39.80	50

Heartfelt Traditions

1992	JOY TO THE WORLD	34.80	70.00
1992	COME ALL YE FAITHFUL	34.80	45.00
1993	A MIDNIGHT CLEAR	34.80	RI
1993	WE GATHER TOGETHER	34.80	RI

On the Wing: Bluebills
Photo courtesy of *Collectors News*

Joys of Childhood

		ISSUE	CURRENT
1992	YOU'LL PLAY GOALIE!	29.80	45.00
1992	TOASTY WARM	29.80	70.00
1992	MAKING A FRIEND	32.80	75.00
1992	LUNCHTIME	32.80	60.00
1992	SNOW ANGELS	32.80	75.00
1993	BEDTIME STORY	34.80	RI
1993	LET'S GO!	34.80	RI
1993	TIME TO GO HOME	34.80	RI

Lords of the Wilderness

1992	HIS DOMAIN: MOOSE	34.80	50.00
1992	MOUNTAIN KINGDOM: GRIZZLY	34.80	70.00
1992	PRINCELY REALM: WHITE-TAILED DEER	37.80	NR
1992	ROYAL PRESENCE: ELK	37.80	60.00

Moments of Serenity

1994	WHISPERING WATERS	29.90	RI
1994	TWILIGHT HARMONY	32.90	RI
1995	PEACEFUL CROSSING	32.90	RI
1995	TRANQUIL RETREAT	32.90	RI
1995	EVENING RESPITE	32.90	RI

Portraits of the Wild

1991	READY: WHITE-TAILED DEER	29.80	NR
1991	NOT THIS YEAR: MULE DEER	29.80	40.00
1992	CHANGING DIRECTION: ELK	32.80	NR
1992	FROSTY MORNING: BUFFALO	32.80	40.00
1992	GRAND VIEW: JASPER RAMS	32.80	45.00
1992	BELOW THE PEAK: ANTELOPE	34.80	55.00
1992	ABOVE AND BEYOND: MOUNTAIN GOATS	34.80	60.00
1992	PROUD DOMAIN: MOOSE	34.80	50.00

Proud Passage

1992	THE RETURN HOME	29.80	50.00
1993	SPRING LANDING	29.80	RI
1993	AT THE NEST	32.80	RI
1993	FAMILY PORTRAIT	32.80	RI
1993	LEARNING TO FLY	32.80	RI
1993	TAKING OFF	32.80	RI

Reflections of Canadian Childhood

1987	DREAMS OF GLORY	24.80	BR
1987	QUIET MOMENT	24.80	BR
1987	PICK OF THE CROP	27.80	BR
1988	WISHFUL THINKING	27.80	BR
1988	SUNDAY BEST	27.80	BR
1988	PEACEMAKER	27.80	NR
1988	AUTUMN YEARNING	29.80	NR
1989	WINNING WAYS	29.80	NR

"The Loon" Voice of the North (Bradford Exchange)

		ISSUE	CURRENT
1991	KEEPING THEM SAFE, Donald Li-Leger	29.80	NR
1991	EARLY START, Donald Li-Leger	34.80	50.00
1992	REGAL WINGS, Donald Li-Leger	37.80	NR
1992	TIME TO FLY, Donald Li-Leger	37.80	NR
1992	QUIET REPAST, Donald Li-Leger	37.80	55.00
1992	SILENT SNOW, Donald Li-Leger	39.80	NR
1992	TAKE TO THE AIR, Donald Li-Leger	39.80	NR
1992	KEPT WITH CARE, Donald Li-Leger	39.80	55.00

Treasures of the Arctic

1990	KINGS OF THE HILL	29.80	BR
1991	SPIRITS OF THE WILD	29.80	NR
1991	SPRING ON THE MOUNTAIN	32.80	BR
1991	MOTHER'S WATCHFUL EYE	32.80	NR
1991	A RESTING PLACE	32.80	NR
1991	ON THE TRAIL	32.80	45.00

Victorian Christmas

1989	COMING HOME	39.80	BR
1990	SKATING ON THE POND	39.80	BR
1991	TRIMMING THE TREE	44.80	BR
1992	JOYFUL CAROLERS	44.80	NR
1993	WINDOW SHOPPING	44.80	RI
1994	A WINTER PASTIME	46.80	RI

Wild and Free: Canada's Big Game

1988	THE GRIZZLY BEAR	29.80	NR
1989	THE MOOSE	29.80	NR
1989	THE BIGHORN SHEEP	32.80	NR
1989	THE WHITE-TAILED DEER	32.80	BR
1990	THE ELK	32.80	BR
1990	THE POLAR BEAR	32.80	BR
1990	THE PRONGHORN	34.80	BR
1990	THE CINNAMON BEAR	34.80	BR

Wings upon the Wind (Edwin M. Knowles)

1986	THE LANDING, Donald Pentz, 150 days	21.80	NR
1986	THE NESTING, Donald Pentz, 150 days	21.80	60.00
1986	THE COURTSHIP, Donald Pentz, 150 days	24.80	NR
1987	THE FAMILY, Donald Pentz, 150 days	24.80	BR
1987	SOUTHWARD BOUND, Donald Pentz, 150 days	24.80	NR
1987	WINTER HOME, Donald Pentz, 150 days	24.80	NR

DRESDEN GERMANY

(Reco International)

Christmas

1971	SHEPHERD SCENE, factory artist, 3,500	15.00	50.00
1972	NIKLAS CHURCH, factory artist, 6,000	15.00	25.00
1973	SCHWANSTEIN CHURCH, factory artist, 6,000	18.00	35.00

		ISSUE	CURRENT
1974	VILLAGE SCENE, factory artist, 5,000	20.00	30.00
1975	ROTHENBURG SCENE, factory artist, 5,000	24.00	30.00
1976	VILLAGE CHURCH, factory artist, 5,000	26.00	35.00
1977	OLD MILL, factory artist, 5,000	28.00	NR

Mother's Day

1972	DOE AND FAWN, Hans Waldheimer, 8,000	15.00	20.00
1973	MARE AND COLT, Hans Waldheimer, 6,000	16.00	25.00
1974	TIGER AND CUB, Hans Waldheimer, 5,000	20.00	25.00
1975	DACHSHUND FAMILY, Hans Waldheimer, 5,000	24.00	30.00
1976	OWL AND OFFSPRING, Hans Waldheimer, 5,000	26.00	NR
1977	CHAMOIS, Hans Waldheimer, 5,000	28.00	NR

DUNCAN ROYALE UNITED STATES

History of Santa Claus I

1985	MEDIEVAL, Susie Morton, 10,000	40.00	75.00
1985	KRIS KRINGLE, Susie Morton, 10,000	40.00	75.00
1985	PIONEER, Susie Morton, 10,000	40.00	NR
1986	RUSSIAN, Susie Morton, 10,000	40.00	75.00
1986	SODA POP, Susie Morton, 10,000	40.00	NR
1986	CIVIL WAR, Susie Morton, 10,000	40.00	75.00
1986	THOMAS NAST SANTA, Thomas Nast, 10,000	40.00	65.00
1987	ST. NICK, Susie Morton, 10,000	40.00	NR
1987	DEDT MOROZ, Susie Morton, 10,000	40.00	75.00
1987	BLACK PETER, Susie Morton, 10,000	40.00	60.00
1987	VICTORIAN, Susie Morton, 10,000	40.00	NR
1987	WASSAIL, Susie Morton, 10,000	40.00	NR

History of Santa Claus II

1986	LORD OF MISRULE, T. Holter Bruckner, 10,000	80.00	NR

EBELING AND REUSS UNITED STATES

Christmas

1982	A TIME OF SONG AND CAROLING, Joan Walsh Anglund, 7,500	15.00	NR

ELEGANCE OF BRONZE

Knapp Series

1978	NAVAJO MADONNA, 2,500	285.00	NR

ENCHANTICA

Dragon Collection

1992	WINTER DRAGON—GRAWLFANG, 2200, 15,000	50.00	NR
1992	SPRING DRAGON—GORGOYLE, 2201, 15,000	50.00	NR

		ISSUE	CURRENT
1993	SUMMER DRAGON—ARANGAST, 2202, 15,000	50.00	NR
1993	AUTUMN DRAGON—SNARLGARD, 2203, 15,000	50.00	NR

ENESCO UNITED STATES

Barbie—Arabian Knights—Miniature

1997	ARABIAN KNIGHTS SCHEHERAZADE / KING SHAHRIAR 1964, 171069	12.50	RI

Barbie—Bob Mackie

1996	QUEEN OF HEARTS BARBIE, 157678, open	25.00	RI
1997	GODDESS OF THE SUN, 260215, 7,500	35.00	RI
1997	MOON GODDESS, 260231, 7,500	35.00	RI

Barbie—Bob Mackie JC Penny Exclusive

1995	QUEEN OF HEARTS BARBIE, J1276, 7,500	30.00	RI
1996	GODDESS OF THE SUN, J8768, 7,500	30.00	RI
1997	MOON GODDESS, 260266, 5,000	30.00	RI

Barbie—Cinderella—Miniature

1997	CINDERELLA 1964, 171042	12.50	RI

Barbie—Elite Dealer Exclusive

1997	GODDESS OF THE SUN/MOON GODDESS, Set 270539, 2,500	125.00	RI
1997	BARBIE AS DOROTHY/KEN AS LION/KEN AS SCARECROW, KEN AS TIN MAN, Set 284335, 2,500	150.00	RI

Barbie—FAO Schwarz Exclusive

1994	SILVER SCREEN BARBIE, 128805, 3,600	30.00	RI
1995	CIRCUS STAR BARBIE, 150339, 3,600	30.00	RI

Barbie—Glamour

1994	35TH ANNIVERSARY BARBIE, 655112, 5,000	30.00	RI
1995	BARBIE SOLO IN THE SPOTLIGHT, 1959, 5,000	30.00	RI
1995	BARBIE ENCHANTED EVENING, 1960, 175587, 10,000	30.00	RI
1996	HERE COMES THE BRIDE, 1966, 170984, open	30.00	RI
1996	HOLIDAY DANCE, 1965, 188794, 10,000	30.00	RI
1997	WEDDING DAY, 1959, 260282, 7,500	30.00	RI

Barbie—Great Eras

1996	GIBSON GIRL BARBIE, 174769, 10,000	30.00	RI
1996	1920's FLAPPER BARBIE, 174777, 10,000	30.00	RI
1997	1850's SOUTHERN BELLE, 174785, 7,500	30.00	RI
1997	EGYPTIAN QUEEN, 174793, 7,500	30.00	RI
1997	ELIZABETH QUEEN BARBIE, 17815, 7,500	30.00	RI
1997	MEDIEVAL LADY BARBIE, 174807, 7,500	30.00	RI

Barbie—Guinevere—Miniature

1997	A ROYAL SURPRISE GUINEVERE / KING ARTHUR 1964, 171050	12.50	RI

		ISSUE	CURRENT

Barbie—Happy Holidays

1994	HAPPY HOLIDAYS BARBIE, 1994, 115088, 5,000	30.00	RI
1995	HAPPY HOLIDAYS BARBIE, 1995, 143154, 1 year	30.00	RI
1995	HAPPY HOLIDAYS BARBIE, 1988, 154180, 1 year	30.00	RI
1996	HAPPY HOLIDAYS BARBIE, 1989, 188859, 1 year	30.00	RI
1996	HAPPY HOLIDAYS BARBIE, 1996, 188816, 1 year	30.00	RI
1997	HAPPY HOLIDAYS BARBIE, 1997, 274259, 1 year	30.00	RI
1997	HAPPY HOLIDAYS BARBIE, 1990, 274232, 1 year	30.00	RI

Barbie—Hollywood Legends

1996	BARBIE AS SCARLETT O'HARA IN GREEN VELVET, 171093, 10,000	35.00	RI
1997	BARBIE AS SCARLETT O'HARA IN RED VELVET, 260169, 7,500	35.00	RI
1997	BARBIE AS DOROTHY, 260193, 7,500	35.00	RI
1997	BARBIE AS DOROTHY/KEN AS LION/KEN AS SCARECROW/KEN AS TIN MAN, 284327, 7,500	35.00	RI
1997	BARBIE AS GLINDA THE GOOD WITCH, 274275, 7,500	35.00	RI

Barbie—Litte Red Riding Hood—Miniature

1997	LITTLE RED RIDING HOOD 1964, 171077	12.50	RI

Barbie—*My Fair Lady*

1997	BARBIE AS ELIZA DOOLITTLE, 270512, 7,500	30.00	RI
1997	BARBIE AS ELIZA DOOLITTLE, 274291, 7,500	35.00	RI

Best Loved Cottages of Lilliput

1996	PARADISE LODGE, David Tate, open	55.00	RI

Calico Kittens

1997	FRIENDSHIP IS HEAVENLY, Priscilla Hillman, dated, 5,000	35.00	RI
1998	WAGON AND KITTIES, Priscilla Hillman, sculpted, oval	35.00	RI

Cherished Teddies—Baby

1998	SWEET LITTLE ONE, 203726, Priscilla Hillman, 1 year	35.00	RI

Cherished Teddies—Cherished Seasons

1997	SPRING BRINGS A SEASON OF BEAUTY, 203386, Priscilla Hillman, open	35.00	RI
1997	SUMMER BRINGS A SEASON OF WARMTH, 203394, Priscilla Hillman, open	35.00	RI
1997	AUTUMN BRINGS A SEASON OF THANKSGIVING, 203408, Priscilla Hillman, open	35.00	RI
1997	WINTER BRINGS A SEASON OF JOY, 203416, Priscilla Hillman, open	35.00	RI

Cherished Teddies—Christmas

1995	THE SEASON OF JOY, 141550, Priscilla Hillman, dated, 1 year	35.00	RI
1996	THE SEASON OF PEACE, 176060, Priscilla Hillman, dated, 1 year	35.00	RI
1997	THE SEASON TO BELIEVE, 272183, Priscilla Hillman, dated, 1 year	35.00	RI
1998	THE SEASON OF MAGIC, 352748, Priscilla Hillman, dated, 1 year	35.00	RI

Cherished Teddies—Easter

1996	SOME BUNNY LOVES YOU, 156590, Priscilla Hillman, dated, 1 year	35.00	RI
1997	SPRINGTIME HAPPINESS, 203009, Priscilla Hillman, dated, 1 year	35.00	RI

Happy Holidays Barbie, 1997

Friendship Is Heavenly

Look Out—Something Good Is Coming Your Way

We're Steppin' Out

Merry Christmas Deer

Autumn's Praise

Photos courtesy of *Collectors News*

		ISSUE	CURRENT

Cherished Teddies—Heaven Has Blessed This Day

1998	BOY WITH PRAYER BOOK, 303186, Priscilla Hillman, 1 year	10.00	RI
1998	GIRL WITH PRAYER BOOK, 303186, Priscilla Hillman, 1 year	10.00	RI

Cherished Teddies—Mother's Day

1996	A MOTHER'S HEART IS FULL OF LOVE, 156493, Priscilla Hillman, dated, 1 year	35.00	RI
1997	OUR LOVE IS EVER-BLOOMING, 203025, Priscilla Hillman, dated, 1 year	35.00	RI
1998	MOM—MAKER OF MIRACLES, 303046, Priscilla Hillman, dated, 1 year	35.00	RI

Cherished Teddies—Nursery Rhymes

1995	JACK AND JILL / OUR FRIENDSHIP WILL NEVER TUMBLE, 114901, Priscilla Hillman, open	35.00	RI
1995	MARY HAD A LITTLE LAMB / I'LL ALWAYS BE BY YOUR SIDE, 128902, Priscilla Hillman, open	35.00	RI
1995	OLD KING COLE / YOU WEAR YOUR KINDNESS LIKE A CROWN, 135437, Priscilla Hillman, open	35.00	RI
1996	LITTLE MISS MUFFET / I'M NEVER AFRAID WITH YOU AT MY SIDE, 145033, Priscilla Hillman, open	35.00	RI
1996	LITTLE JACK HORNER / I'M PLUM HAPPY YOU'RE MY FRIEND, 151998, Priscilla Hillman, open	35.00	RI
1996	LITTLE BO PEEP / LOOKING FOR A FRIEND LIKE YOU, 164658, Priscilla Hillman, open	35.00	RI
1996	WEE WILLIE WINKIE / GOOD NIGHT, SLEEP TIGHT, 170941, Priscilla Hillman, open	35.00	RI
1996	MOTHER GOOSE & FRIENDS / HAPPILY EVER AFTER WITH FRIENDS, 170968, Priscilla Hillman, open	35.00	RI

Cherished Teddies—'Tis the Season

1996	ANGEL IN RED COAT, 176303, Priscilla Hillman	12.50	RI
1996	BABY'S FIRST CHRISTMAS, 176346, Priscilla Hillman	12.50	RI
1996	GIRL IN RED COAT, 176117, Priscilla Hillman	12.50	RI
1996	GIRL WITH GREEN COAT, 176281, Priscilla Hillman	12.50	RI
1996	OUR FIRST CHRISTMAS, 176311, Priscilla Hillman	12.50	RI
1996	SANTA WITH TREE AND TOYS, 176338, Priscilla Hillman	12.50	RI

Cherished Teddies—Spring Time

1998	FAITH, 104140, Priscilla Hillman	10.00	RI
1998	HOPE, 104140, Priscilla Hillman	10.00	RI
1998	CHARITY, 104140, Priscilla Hillman	10.00	RI
1998	LOVE, 104140, Priscilla Hillman	10.00	RI

Cherished Teddies—Thanksgiving

1998	WE BEAR THANKS, 272426, Priscilla Hillman	35.00	RI

Eras of Coke Years

1996	1940–1950, 169870, 4" d	7.50	RI
1996	1970–1980, 169889, 4" d	7.50	RI
1996	1920–1930, 169862, 4" d	7.50	RI
1996	1970–1980, 188735, 8" d	30.00	RI
1996	1940–1950, 188581, 8" d	30.00	RI

		ISSUE	CURRENT
1996	1920–1930, 188565, 8" d	30.00	RI

Kinka Collector Plaque

1989	KINKA, 119601, Kinka, open	10.00	NR

Little Bible Friends

1981	THE NATIVITY, Lucas, 25,000	40.00	NR
1982	FLIGHT INTO EGYPT, Lucas, 25,000	40.00	NR
1982	THE LAST SUPPER, Lucas, 25,000	40.00	NR

Lucy & Me Christmas Collection

1988	NUTCRACKER SUITE, Lucy Rigg	17.00	NR
1997	CHRISTMAS PAGEANT, Lucy Rigg, dated, 1 year, with easel	20.00	NR

Mary's Moo Moos

1997	IT'S BUTTER TO GIVE THAN TO RECEIVE, Mary Rhyner-Nadig, dated, 1 year	35.00	RI

Mary's Moo Moos Mooey Christmas

1996	WHEEE ARE MOVIN!, Mary Rhyner-Nadig, 1 year	17.50	RI

Memories of Yesterday

1993	LOOK OUT—SOMETHING GOOD IS COMING YOUR WAY!, 530298, Samuel Butcher, 1 year	50.00	RI
1994	PLEASANT DREAMS AND SWEET REPOSE, 528102, Mabel Lucie Attwell, 1 year	50.00	RI
1995	JOIN ME FOR A LITTLE SONG, 134880, Mabel Lucie Attwell, 1 year	50.00	RI

Mickey & Co.

1996	WE'RE STEPPIN' OUT, platter	45.00	RI
1996	MERRY MICKEY CHRISTMAS!, plaque	40.00	RI
1997	THE SPIRIT OF CHRISTMAS, plaque	40.00	RI

Precious Moments Beauty of Christmas

1994	YOU'RE AS PRETTY AS A CHRISTMAS TREE, 530409, Samuel Butcher, open	50.00	RI
1995	HE COVERS THE EARTH WITH HIS BEAUTY, 142670, Samuel Butcher, open	50.00	RI
1996	PEACE ON EARTH...ANYWAY, 183377, Samuel Butcher, open	50.00	RI
1997	CANE YOU JOIN US FOR A MERRY CHRISTMAS, 272701, Samuel Butcher, open	50.00	RI

Precious Moments Christmas Blessings

1990	WISHING YOU A YUMMY CHRISTMAS, 523801, Samuel Butcher, 1 year	50.00	NR
1991	BLESSINGS FROM ME TO THEE, 523680, Samuel Butcher, 1 year	50.00	NR
1992	BUT THE GREATEST OF THESE IS LOVE, 527742, Samuel Butcher, 1 year	50.00	NR
1993	WISHING YOU THE SWEETEST CHRISTMAS, 530204, Samuel Butcher, 1 year	50.00	RI

Precious Moments Christmas Collection

1981	COME LET US ADORE HIM, E5646, Biel and Butcher, 15,000	40.00	NR
1982	LET HEAVEN AND NATURE SING, E2347, Biel and Butcher, 15,000	40.00	NR
1983	WEE THREE KINGS, E9256, Biel and Butcher, 15,000	40.00	NR
1984	UNTO US A CHILD IS BORN, E5395, Samuel Butcher, 15,000	40.00	NR

		ISSUE	CURRENT

Precious Moments Christmas Love

		ISSUE	CURRENT
1986	I'M SENDING YOU A WHITE CHRISTMAS, 101834, Samuel Butcher, 1 year	45.00	NR
1987	MY PEACE I GIVE UNTO THEE, 102954, Samuel Butcher, 1 year	45.00	NR
1988	MERRY CHRISTMAS DEER, 520284, Samuel Butcher, 1 year	50.00	NR
1989	MAY YOUR CHRISTMAS BE A HAPPY HOME, 523003, Samuel Butcher, 1 year	50.00	NR

Precious Moments Easter

		ISSUE	CURRENT
1993	MAKE A JOYFUL NOISE, Samuel Butcher, 1 year	18.50	RI

Precious Moments Four Seasons

		ISSUE	CURRENT
1985	VOICE OF SPRING, 12106, Samuel Butcher, 1 year	40.00	50.00
1985	SUMMER'S JOY, 12114, Samuel Butcher, 1 year	40.00	50.00
1986	AUTUMN'S PRAISE, 12122, Samuel Butcher, 1 year	40.00	NR
1986	WINTER'S SONG, 12130, Samuel Butcher, 1 year	40.00	NR

Precious Moments Holly-Day Greetings

		ISSUE	CURRENT
1996	PEACE ON EARTH, 3½" d	10.00	RI
1997	MERRY CHRISTMAS, 3½" d	10.00	RI
1997	HAPPY HOLLY-DAYS, 3½" d	10.00	RI
1997	HOLLY-DAY WISHES, 3½" d	10.00	RI
1997	CHRISTMAS WISHES, 3½" d	10.00	RI
1997	JOYOUS HOLIDAY, 3½" d	10.00	RI

Precious Moments Inspired Thoughts

		ISSUE	CURRENT
1980	LOVE ONE ANOTHER, E5215, Samuel Butcher, 15,000	40.00	NR
1981	MAKE A JOYFUL NOISE, E7174, Samuel Butcher, 15,000	40.00	NR
1982	I BELIEVE IN MIRACLES, E9257, Samuel Butcher, 15,000	40.00	NR
1984	LOVE IS KIND, E2847, Samuel Butcher, 15,000	40.00	NR

Precious Moments Joy of Christmas

		ISSUE	CURRENT
1982	I'LL PLAY MY DRUM FOR HIM, E2357, Samuel Butcher, 1 year	40.00	NR
1983	CHRISTMASTIME IS FOR SHARING, E0505, Samuel Butcher, 1 year	40.00	NR
1984	THE WONDER OF CHRISTMAS, E5396, Samuel Butcher, 1 year	40.00	NR
1985	TELL ME THE STORY OF JESUS, 15237, Samuel Butcher, 1 year	40.00	NR

Precious Moments Mother's Day

		ISSUE	CURRENT
1994	THINKING OF YOU IS WHAT I REALLY LIKE TO DO, 531766, Samuel Butcher, 1 year	50.00	RI
1995	HE HATH MADE EVERYTHING BEAUTIFUL IN HIS TIME, 129151, Samuel Butcher, open	50.00	RI
1996	OF ALL THE MOTHERS I HAVE KNOWN THERE'S NONE AS PRECIOUS AS MY OWN, 163716, Samuel Butcher, 1 year	50.00	RI

Precious Moments Mother's Love

		ISSUE	CURRENT
1981	MOTHER SEW DEAR, E5217, Samuel Butcher, 15,000	40.00	NR
1982	THE PURR-FECT GRANDMA, E7173, Samuel Butcher, 15,000	40.00	NR
1983	THE HAND THAT ROCKS THE FUTURE, E9256, Samuel Butcher, 15,000	40.00	NR
1984	LOVING THY NEIGHBOR, E2848, Samuel Butcher, 15,000	40.00	NR

Precious Moments Open Editions

		ISSUE	CURRENT
1981	THE LORD BLESS YOU AND KEEP YOU, E5216, Samuel Butcher	30.00	40.00

		ISSUE	CURRENT
1982	REJOICING WITH YOU, E7172, Samuel Butcher	30.00	40.00
1982	JESUS LOVES ME—GIRL WITH TEDDY BEAR, E9276, Samuel Butcher	30.00	45.00
1983	OUR FIRST CHRISTMAS TOGETHER, E2378, Samuel Butcher	30.00	45.00
1983	JESUS LOVES ME—BOY HOLDING TEDDY BEAR, E9275, Samuel Butcher	30.00	45.00
1994	BRING THE LITTLE ONES TO JESUS, 531359, Samuel Butcher, 1 year	50.00	RI
1997	LOVE ONE ANOTHER, 186406, Samuel Butcher, open	35.00	RI
1997	GOOD FRIENDS ARE FOREVER, 186457, Samuel Butcher, open	35.00	RI

Pretty as a Picture

1997	I KNOW HOW TO WIN A HEART, Kim Anderson, open	20.00	RI

Spirit of Santa, sculpted

1997	MERRY CHRISTMAS TO ALL, Mary Rhyner-Nadig, 1 year	35.00	RI

Star Trek

1996	CAPTAIN JAMES T. KIRK U.S.S. *ENTERPRISE*, 109703, 8½" d	30.00	RI
1996	U.S.S. *ENTERPRISE*, 109797, 8½" d	30.00	RI
1996	THE CREW, 771481, 8½" d	30.00	RI
1996	CAPTAIN JAMES T. KIRK U.S.S. *ENTERPRISE*, 109878, 4½" d	7.50	RI
1996	THE CREW, 110302, 4½" d	7.50	RI
1996	U.S.S. *ENTERPRISE*, 110256, 4½" d	7.50	RI

Star Trek: The Next Generation

1996	THE CREW, 771619, 8½" d	30.00	RI
1996	CAPTAIN JEAN-LUC PICARD U.S.S. *ENTERPRISE*, 109045, 8½" d	30.00	RI
1996	U.S.S. *ENTERPRISE*, 109053, 8¼" d	30.00	RI
1996	THE CREW, 109274, 4¼" d	7.50	RI
1996	U.S.S. *ENTERPRISE*, 109088, 4¼" d	7.50	RI
1996	CAPTAIN JEAN-LUC PICARD U.S.S. *ENTERPRISE*, 109061, 4¼" d	7.50	RI
1996	U.S.S. *ENTERPRISE*, 913243, 4" d	7.50	RI
1996	THE CREW, 913251, 4" d	7.50	RI

Teddy Tompkins Collection

1997	A HARVEST OF FUN AND FRIENDSHIP, Tim Tompkins, 5,000	30.00	RI

R. J. ERNST ENTERPRISES UNITED STATES

(Porter & Price, Viletta China)

Bare Innocence

1986	FREE AT LAST, Glen Banse, 10 days	24.50	NR

Beautiful World

1981	TAHITIAN DREAMER, Susie Morton, 27,500	27.50	NR
1982	FLIRTATION, Susie Morton, 27,500	27.50	NR
1983	ELKE OF OSLO, Susie Morton, 27,500	27.50	NR

Busy Bears

1986	HEADING SOUTH, Simon Devoche, 100 days	19.50	NR
1986	BREAKFAST BREAK, Simon Devoche, 100 days	19.50	NR
1986	FALL FUN, Simon Devoche, 100 days	19.50	NR

Free at Last

Elke of Oslo

Flying Low

John Lennon

Look at Me, Daddy

Night Rose

Photos courtesy of *Collectors News*

		ISSUE	CURRENT
1986	FLYING LOW, Simon Devoche, 100 days	19.50	NR

Children of the Past

1986	BOY WITH HOOP, Peter Quidley, 90 days	29.50	NR

Classy Cars

1982	THE 26T, Scott Kuhnly, 20 days	24.50	40.00
1982	THE 31A, Scott Kuhnly, 20 days	24.50	40.00
1983	THE PICKUP, Scott Kuhnly, 20 days	24.50	40.00
1983	THE PANEL VAN, Scott Kuhnly, 20 days	24.50	40.00

Commemoratives

1981	JOHN LENNON, Susie Morton, 30 days	39.50	145.00
1982	ELVIS PRESLEY, Susie Morton, 30 days	39.50	90.00
1982	MARILYN MONROE, Susie Morton, 30 days	39.50	125.00
1983	JUDY GARLAND, Susie Morton, 30 days	39.50	65.00
1983	JOHN WAYNE, Susie Morton, 2,500	39.50	110.00

Country Cousins

1986	YEP THAT'S IT, William Powell, 30 days	24.50	NR
1986	SHE'S ALL YOURS, William Powell, 30 days	24.50	NR

Daddy's Little Girl

1986	LOOK AT ME, DADDY, John Letostak, 90 days	29.50	NR

Elvira

1986	NIGHT ROSE, Susie Morton, 90 days	29.50	45.00
1988	RED VELVET, Susie Morton, 90 days	29.50	NR
1988	MISTRESS OF THE DARK, Susie Morton, 90 days	29.50	NR

Elvis Presley

1987	THE KING, Susie Morton, retrd	39.50	NR
1987	LOVING YOU, Susie Morton, retrd	39.50	NR
1987	EARLY YEARS, Susie Morton, retrd	39.50	NR
1987	TENDERLY, Susie Morton, retrd	39.50	NR
1988	FOREVER YOURS, Susie Morton, retrd	39.50	NR
1988	ROCKIN' IN THE MOONLIGHT, Susie Morton, retrd	39.50	NR
1988	MOODY BLUES, Susie Morton, retrd	39.50	NR
1988	ELVIS PRESLEY, Susie Morton, retrd	39.50	NR
1989	ELVIS PRESLEY—SPECIAL REQUEST, Susie Morton, retrd	150.00	NR

Fishing Boats

1983	SUNSET AT MONTEREY, Scott Kuhnly, <1 year	24.50	NR

Fogg and Steam

1986	PRIDE OF THE NORTHWEST, Howard Fogg, 7,500	39.50	NR
1986	AUTUMN IN NEW ENGLAND, Howard Fogg, 7,500	39.50	NR

Fondest Memories

1986	MOTHER'S PEARLS, Ann Marry-Kenyon, limited	60.00	NR
1986	A TOUCHING MOMENT, Ann Marry-Kenyon, limited	60.00	NR

Autumn in New England
Photo courtesy of *Collectors News*

John Wayne
Photo courtesy of *Collectors News*

		ISSUE	CURRENT
Go for the Gold			
1985	VALERIE, Susie Morton, 5,000	29.50	NR
Hollywood Greats			
1981	HENRY FONDA, Susie Morton, 27,500	29.95	55.00
1981	JOHN WAYNE, Susie Morton, 27,500	29.95	90.00
1981	GARY COOPER, Susie Morton, 27,500	29.95	40.00
1982	CLARK GABLE, Susie Morton, 27,500	29.95	65.00
1984	ALAN LADD, Susie Morton, 27,500	29.95	60.00
Hollywood Walk of Fame			
1989	JIMMY STEWART, Susie Morton, retrd	39.50	NR
1989	ELIZABETH TAYLOR, Susie Morton, retrd	39.50	NR
1989	TOM SELLECK, Susie Morton, retrd	39.50	NR
1989	JOAN COLLINS, Susie Morton, retrd	39.50	NR
1990	BURT REYNOLDS, Susie Morton, retrd	39.50	NR
1990	SYLVESTER STALLONE, Susie Morton, retrd	39.50	NR
Liebchen			
1983	AUTUMN LIEBCHEN, Von Ault, <1 year	19.50	NR
1983	SPRING LIEBCHEN, Von Ault, <1 year	19.50	NR
1983	SUMMER LIEBCHEN, Von Ault, <1 year	19.50	NR
1983	WINTER LIEBCHEN, Von Ault, <1 year	19.50	NR
Little Misses Young and Fair			
1983	HEART OF A CHILD, Alan Murray, 29,000	60.00	NR
1984	WHERE WILDFLOWERS GROW, Alan Murray, 29,000	60.00	NR
1986	FINAL TOUCH, Alan Murray, 29,000	60.00	NR
Love Story			
1982	CHAPTER I, Adam Shields, <1 year	24.50	NR

		ISSUE	CURRENT
1983	CHAPTER II, Adam Shields, <1 year	24.50	NR

Me and Mom

1986	BEACH BABY, Susie Morton, 5,000	29.50	NR
1986	WHAT'S THIS?, Susie Morton, 5,000	29.50	NR

Mommy and Me

1982	FIRST TEA, Rusty Money, <1 year	35.00	NR
1983	BABY'S SLEEPING, Rusty Money, <1 year	35.00	NR

My Fair Ladies

1982	LADY SABRINA, Rusty Money, 29,000	50.00	NR
1983	LADY VICTORIA, Rusty Money, 29,000	50.00	NR

Narrow Gauge

1983	HALFWAY TO ALAMOSA, Jack Hamilton, <1 year	29.50	NR
1984	DOWN FROM RICO, Jack Hamilton, limited	29.50	NR

Republic Pictures Library (Hamilton Collection)

1991	SHOWDOWN WITH LAREDO, Susie Morton, 28 days	37.50	NR
1991	THE RIDE HOME, Susie Morton, 28 days	37.50	NR
1991	ATTACK AT TARAWA, Susie Morton, 28 days	37.50	NR
1991	THOUGHTS OF ANGELIQUE, Susie Morton, 28 days	37.50	NR
1992	WAR OF THE WILDCATS, Susie Morton, 28 days	37.50	NR
1992	THE FIGHTING SEABEES, Susie Morton, 28 days	37.50	NR
1992	THE QUIET MAN, Susie Morton, 28 days	37.50	NR
1992	ANGEL AND THE BADMAN, Susie Morton, 28 days	37.50	NR
1993	SANDS OF IWO JIMA, Susie Morton, 28 days	37.50	NR
1993	FLYING TIGERS, Susie Morton, 28 days	37.50	NR
1993	THE TRIBUTE, Susie Morton, 28 days	37.50	NR
1994	THE TRIBUTE, Susie Morton, 28 days, artist proof, 8¼"	95.00	NR

Beach Baby
Photo courtesy of *Collectors News*

Mr. Spock
Photo courtesy of *Collectors News*

		ISSUE	CURRENT

Seems Like Yesterday

1981	STOP AND SMELL THE ROSES, Rusty Money, 10 days	24.50	30.00
1982	HOME BY LUNCH, Rusty Money,10 days	24.50	35.00
1982	LISA'S CREEK, Rusty Money, 10 days	24.50	NR
1983	IT'S GOT MY NAME ON IT, Rusty Money, 10 days	24.50	30.00
1983	MY MAGIC HAT, Rusty Money, 10 days	24.50	NR
1984	LITTLE PRINCE, Rusty Money, 10 days	24.50	NR

Shades of Time

1986	SCENT AND SATIN, Alan Murray, 5,000	45.00	NR

So Young, So Sweet

1982	GIRL WITH STRAW HAT, Susie Morton, 10 days	39.50	NR
1983	MY FAVORITE NECKLACE, Susie Morton, 10 days	39.50	NR
1983	BREAKFAST TIME, Susie Morton, 10 days	39.50	NR

Star Trek

1984	MR. SPOCK, Susie Morton, 90 days	29.50	125.00
1985	DR. MCCOY—MEDICAL OFFICER, Susie Morton, 90 days	29.50	75.00
1985	SULU, Susie Morton, 90 days	29.50	65.00
1985	SCOTTY, Susie Morton, 90 days	29.50	65.00
1985	UHURA, Susie Morton, 90 days	29.50	65.00
1985	CHEKOV, Susie Morton, 90 days	29.50	65.00
1985	CAPTAIN KIRK, Susie Morton, 90 days	29.50	65.00
1985	BEAM US DOWN, SCOTTY, Susie Morton, 90 days	29.50	80.00
1985	THE ENTERPRISE, Susie Morton, 90 days	39.50	150.00

Star Trek Commemorative

1987	THE TROUBLE WITH TRIBBLES, Susie Morton, limited	29.50	135.00
1987	MIRROR, MIRROR, Susie Morton, limited	29.50	150.00
1987	A PIECE OF THE ACTION, Susie Morton, limited	29.50	75.00
1987	THE DEVIL IN THE DARK, Susie Morton, limited	29.50	100.00
1987	AMOK TIME, Susie Morton, limited	29.50	100.00
1987	THE CITY ON THE EDGE OF FOREVER, Susie Morton, limited	29.50	100.00
1987	JOURNEY TO BABEL, Susie Morton, limited	29.50	80.00
1988	THE MENAGERIE, Susie Morton, limited	29.50	80.00

This Land Is Our Land

1986	SAND DUNES, Gage Taylor, 5,000	29.50	NR

Turn of the Century

1981	RIVERBOAT HONEYMOON, Rusty Money,10 days	35.00	BR
1982	CHILDREN'S CAROUSEL, Rusty Money, 10 days	35.00	BR
1984	FLOWER MARKET, Rusty Money, 10 days	35.00	BR
1985	BALLOON RACE, Rusty Money, 10 days	35.00	BR

Yesterday

1982	AMBER, Glenice,10 days	24.50	NR
1983	ELMER, Glenice,10 days	24.50	NR
1976	KATIE, Glenice, 10 days	24.50	NR

		ISSUE	CURRENT

Single Issues

1978	DEGRAZIA BY MARCO, J. Marco, 5,000	65.00	NR
1983	TRIBUTE TO HENRY FONDA, Susie Morton, 10 days	45.00	NR
1984	MARILYN MONROE, Susie Morton, 61 days	29.50	NR

ESCALERA PRODUCTION ART UNITED STATES

Olympiad Triumphs Collection

1984	TRACK, Rudy Escalera, 19,500	60.00	NR
1984	FIELD EVENTS, Rudy Escalera, 19,500	60.00	NR
1984	BASKETBALL, Rudy Escalera, 19,500	60.00	NR
1984	SWIMMING, Rudy Escalera, 19,500	60.00	NR
1984	SOCCER, Rudy Escalera, 19,500	60.00	NR
1984	BASEBALL AND TENNIS, Rudy Escalera, 19,500	60.00	NR
1984	BOXING, Rudy Escalera, 19,500	60.00	NR
1984	GYMNASTICS, Rudy Escalera, 19,500	60.00	NR

EVERGREEN PRESS UNITED STATES

Catalina Island

1986	AVALON BAY, Roger Upton, 5,000	39.95	NR
1986	PLEASURE PIER, Roger Upton, 5,000	39.95	NR
1987	CATALINA CALLS, Frank Loudin, 5,000	39.95	NR
1987	REFLECTIONS, Frank Loudin, 5,000	39.95	NR
1987	CASINO WAY, Frank Loudin, 5,000	39.95	NR

FAIRMONT CHINA UNITED STATES

(Armstrong's, Artists of the World, Hackett American)

America's Most Beloved

1980	JOHN WAYNE, Clarence Thorpe, 5,000	13.95	NR
1981	PORTRAIT OF ROCKWELL, Clarence Thorpe, 15,000	40.00	NR

Child of America

1979	ESKIMO GIRL, Laura Johnson, 3,000	48.00	NR

Children of the World

1976	LOS NIÑOS, Ted DeGrazia, 5,000	35.00	1,000.00
1976	LOS NIÑOS, Ted DeGrazia, sgd, 500	100.00	1,500.00
1977	WHITE DOVE, Ted DeGrazia, 5,000	40.00	150.00
1977	WHITE DOVE, Ted DeGrazia, sgd, 500	100.00	300.00
1978	FLOWER GIRL, Ted DeGrazia, 9,500	45.00	NR
1978	FLOWER GIRL, Ted DeGrazia, sgd, 500	100.00	300.00
1979	FLOWER BOY, Ted DeGrazia, 9,500	45.00	60.00
1979	FLOWER BOY, Ted DeGrazia, sgd, 500	100.00	300.00
1980	LITTLE COCOPAH INDIAN GIRL, Ted DeGrazia, 9,500	50.00	65.00
1980	LITTLE COCOPAH INDIAN GIRL, Ted DeGrazia, sgd, 500	100.00	300.00
1981	BEAUTIFUL BURDEN, Ted DeGrazia, 9,500	50.00	NR
1981	BEAUTIFUL BURDEN, Ted DeGrazia, sgd, 500	100.00	350.00

		ISSUE	CURRENT
1981	MERRY LITTLE INDIAN, Ted DeGrazia, 9,500	55.00	90.00
1981	MERRY LITTLE INDIAN, Ted DeGrazia, sgd, 500	100.00	350.00
1983	WONDERING, Ted DeGrazia, 10,000	60.00	NR
1984	PINK PAPOOSE, Ted DeGrazia, 10,000	65.00	BR
1985	SUNFLOWER BOY, Ted DeGrazia, 10,000	65.00	BR

Dreams Do Come True

1984	LITTLE BALLERINA, Anthony Sidoni, 5,000	29.95	NR
1984	ORGAN GRINDER, Anthony Sidoni, 5,000	29.95	NR

Little Ballerina
Photo courtesy of *Collectors News*

Early Works

1979	OLD MAN WINTER, Norman Rockwell, 15,000	19.95	50.00
1980	THE INVENTOR, Norman Rockwell, 15,000	19.95	NR
1980	READY FOR SCHOOL, Norman Rockwell, 15,000	19.95	NR
1980	MUSIC MAKER, Norman Rockwell, 15,000	19.95	NR
1981	THE TINKERER, Norman Rockwell, 15,000	19.95	NR

Famous Clowns (Armstrong's)

1976	FREDDIE THE FREELOADER, Red Skelton, 10,000	55.00	275.00
1977	W. C. FIELDS, Red Skelton, 10,000	55.00	BR
1978	HAPPY, Red Skelton, 10,000	55.00	75.00
1979	THE PLEDGE, Red Skelton, 10,000	55.00	65.00

Gnome Four Seasons

1980	LITTLE SWINGER, Rien Poortvliet, 15,000	29.50	NR
1980	GNOME DE BLOOM, Rien Poortvliet, 15,000	29.50	NR
1980	THE LOOKOUTS, Rien Poortvliet, 15,000	29.50	NR
1980	FIRST SKATER, Rien Poortvliet, 15,000	29.50	NR
1981	SPRING SHARING, Rien Poortvliet, 15,000	29.95	NR
1981	FUN AND GAMES, Rien Poortvliet, 15,000	29.95	NR
1981	UP, UP AND AWAY, Rien Poortvliet, 15,000	29.95	NR
1981	FIRST SKIER, Rien Poortvliet, 15,000	29.95	NR
1982	GNOME KNOWLEDGE, Rien Poortvliet, 15,000	29.95	NR
1982	THE BERRY PICKERS, Rien Poortvliet, 15,000	29.95	NR
1982	GNOME MADE, Rien Poortvliet, 15,000	29.95	NR
1982	KEEP THE GNOME FIRES BURNING, Rien Poortvliet, 15,000	29.95	NR

		ISSUE	CURRENT

Gnome Holiday

1980	GNOME BLUES, Rien Poortvliet, 5,000	24.50	NR
1981	GIFT OF LOVE, Rien Poortvliet, 5,000	29.95	NR

Hobo Joe

1982	DO NOT DISTURB, Ron Lee, 7,500	50.00	NR

Israeli Commemorative (Ghent Collection)

1978	THE PROMISED LAND, Alton S. Tobey, 5,738	79.00	85.00

Jansen's International Beauties

NA	LISA, Leo Jansen, 7,500	55.00	NR
NA	INGRID, Leo Jansen, 7,500	55.00	NR

Legend of the Gnomes

1984	BIRTHDAY PLANTING, Rien Poortvliet, 15,000	29.95	NR
1984	FOREST FIRST AID, Rien Poortvliet, 15,000	29.95	NR
1984	GNOME HOME, Rien Poortvliet, 15,000	29.95	NR
1984	GNOME KNOW HOW, Rien Poortvliet, 15,000	29.95	NR
1984	HAPPY PASTIME, Rien Poortvliet, 15,000	29.95	NR
1984	LABOR OF LOVE, Rien Poortvliet, 15,000	29.95	NR
1984	LITTLE COUNSELOR, Rien Poortvliet, 15,000	29.95	NR
1984	WINTER SHARING, Rien Poortvliet, 15,000	29.95	NR

Long Road West

1981	THE TRAILBLAZERS, Jim Henson, 20,000	40.00	NR
1981	PRAIRIE SCHOONER PIONEER, Jim Henson, 20,000	40.00	NR
1981	PONY EXPRESS, Jim Henson, 20,000	40.00	NR
1981	THE PEACE MAKERS, Jim Henson, 20,000	40.00	NR
1981	COWBOYS OF THE WEST, Jim Henson, 20,000	40.00	NR
1981	LAWMEN OF THE WEST, Jim Henson, 20,000	40.00	NR

Lords of the Plains

1979	SITTING BULL, Richard Nickerson, 5,000	60.00	NR

Memory Annual (Ghent Collection)

1977	MEMORY PLATE, 1,977	77.00	85.00
1978	MEMORY PLATE, 1,978	78.00	85.00
1979	MEMORY PLATE, 1,979	80.00	NR
1980	MEMORY PLATE, 1,980	80.00	NR

Passing of Plains Indians (Collector's Heirlooms)

1979	CHEYENNE CHIEFTAIN, Andre Bouche, 7,500	65.00	NR

Ruthven Birds Feathered Friends

1978	CHICKADEES, John Ruthven, 5,000	39.50	NR
1981	SCREECH OWLS, John Ruthven, 5,000	39.50	NR

Spencer Annual

1977	PATIENT ONES, Irene Spencer, 10,000	42.50	100.00

		ISSUE	CURRENT
1978	YESTERDAY, TODAY AND TOMORROW, Irene Spencer, 10,000	47.50	85.00

Spencer Special

1978	HUG ME, Irene Spencer, 10,000	55.00	95.00
1978	SLEEP LITTLE BABY, Irene Spencer, 10,000	65.00	NR

Timeless Moments

1978	TENDERNESS, Clarence Thorpe, 5,000	45.00	NR
1979	RENAISSANCE, Clarence Thorpe, 5,000	45.00	NR
1980	COMING IN GLORY, Clarence Thorpe, 5,000	39.95	NR

Vanishing Americana

1984	AMERICAN EAGLE, Clarence Thorpe, 15,000	13.50	NR
1984	THE COUNTRY DOCTOR, Clarence Thorpe, 15,000	13.50	NR

When I Grow Up

1981	I'LL BE LOVED, Ann Hershenburgh, 7,500	29.95	NR
1981	I'LL BE LIKE MOMMY, Ann Hershenburgh, 7,500	29.95	NR
1981	I'LL BE FIRST LADY, Ann Hershenburgh, 7,500	29.95	NR
1981	I'LL BE A STAR, Ann Hershenburgh, 7,500	29.95	NR

Single Issues

1978	THE FENCE, St. Clair, 5,000	45.00	NR
1978	SIOUX WARRIOR, Olaf Wieghorst, 5,000	65.00	95.00
1978	THE SCOUT, Olaf Wieghorst, 5,000	65.00	NR
1983	MY LITTLE SHELTIE, Clarence Thorpe, 5,000	39.95	NR

My Little Sheltie
Photo courtesy of *Collectors News*

FENTON ART GLASS UNITED STATES

Alliance

1975	LAFAYETTE AND WASHINGTON, blue satin glass, 1 year	15.00	30.00
1975	LAFAYETTE AND WASHINGTON, red satin glass, 1 year	17.50	30.00
1975	LAFAYETTE AND WASHINGTON, white satin glass, 1 year	15.00	30.00

		ISSUE	CURRENT
1976	LAFAYETTE AND WASHINGTON, blue satin glass, 1 year	15.00	30.00
1976	LAFAYETTE AND WASHINGTON, chocolate glass, 1 year	17.50	30.00
1976	LAFAYETTE AND WASHINGTON, white satin glass, 1 year	15.00	30.00

American Classic Series

1986	JUPITER TRAIN, M. Dickinson, opal satin, 5,000	75.00	NR
1986	STUDEBAKER-GARFORD CAR, M. Dickinson, opal satin, 5,000	75.00	NR

American Craftsman Carnival

1970	GLASSMAKER, 1 year	10.00	50.00
1970	GLASSMAKER, black, 600	10.00	125.00
1970	GLASSMAKER, 200	10.00	200.00
1971	PRINTER, 1 year	10.00	50.00
1972	BLACKSMITH, 1 year	10.00	50.00
1973	SHOEMAKER, 1 year	10.00	50.00
1974	PIONEER COOPER, 1 year	11.00	50.00
1975	PAUL REVERE, PATRIOT & SILVERSMITH, 1 year	12.50	50.00
1976	GUNSMITH, 1 year	13.50	50.00
1977	POTTER, 1 year	15.00	50.00
1978	WHEELWRIGHT, 1 year	15.00	50.00
1979	CABINETMAKER, 1 year	15.00	50.00
1980	TANNER, 1 year	16.50	50.00
1981	HOUSEWRIGHT, 1 year	17.50	50.00

Birds of Winter

1987	PLATE 7418BC, Diane Johnson, 4,500, with stand	39.50	NR
1988	PLATE 7418BD, Diane Johnson, 4,500, with stand	39.50	NR
1990	PLATE 7418BL, Diane Johnson, 4,500, with stand	39.50	NR

Childhood Treasure

1983	TEDDY BEAR, Diane Johnson, 15,000	45.00	NR

Christmas

1979	NATURE'S CHRISTMAS, K. Cunningham, 1 year	35.00	NR
1980	GOING HOME, Diane Johnson, 1 year	38.50	NR
1981	ALL IS CALM, Diane Johnson, 1 year	42.50	NR
1982	COUNTRY CHRISTMAS, R. Spindler, 1 year	42.50	NR
1983	ANTICIPATION, Diane Johnson, 7,500	45.00	NR
1984	EXPECTATION, Diane Johnson, 7,500	50.00	NR
1985	HEART'S DESIRE, Diane Johnson, 7,500	50.00	NR
1986	SHARING THE SPIRIT, Linda Everson, 1 year	50.00	NR
1987	CARDINAL IN THE CHURCHYARD, Diane Johnson, 4,500	39.50	NR
1988	A CHICKADEE BALLET, Diane Johnson, 4,500	39.50	NR
1989	DOWNY PECKER-CHISELED SONG, Diane Johnson, 4,500	39.50	NR
1990	A BLUEBIRD IN SNOWFALL, Diane Johnson, 4,500	39.50	NR
1990	SLEIGH RIDE, Frances Burton, 3,500	45.00	NR
1991	CHRISTMAS EVE, Frances Burton, 3,500	45.00	NR
1992	FAMILY TRADITION, Frances Burton, 3,500	49.00	NR
1993	FAMILY HOLIDAY, Frances Burton, 3,500	49.00	RI

Christmas at Home

1990	PLATE 7418HD, Frances Burton, 3,500, with stand	45.00	NR

		ISSUE	CURRENT
1990	PLATE 7418HJ, Frances Burton, 3,500, with stand	45.00	NR
1992	PLATE 7418HQ, Frances Burton, 3,500, with stand	45.00	NR
1993	PLATE 7418HT, Frances Burton, 3,500, with stand	45.00	NR

Christmas Classics

1979	PLATE 7418NC, K. Cunningham	35.00	NR
1980	PLATE 7418GH, Diane Johnson	38.50	NR
1981	PLATE 7418AC, Diane Johnson	42.50	NR
1982	PLATE 7418NA, R. Spindler	42.50	NR

Christmas Fantasy

1983	PLATE 7418AO, Diane Johnson, 7,500	45.00	NR
1984	PLATE 7418GE, Diane Johnson, 7,500	45.00	NR
1985	PLATE 7418WP, Diane Johnson, 7,500	45.00	NR
1987	PLATE 7418CV, Diane Johnson, 7,500	45.00	NR

Christmas in America

1970	LITTLE BROWN CHURCH IN VALE, carnival glass, 1 year	12.50	NR
1970	LITTLE BROWN CHURCH IN VALE, blue satin glass, 1 year	12.50	50.00
1971	LITTLE BROWN CHURCH IN VALE, white satin glass, 1 year	12.50	35.00
1971	OLD BRICK CHURCH, carnival glass, 1 year	12.50	NR
1971	OLD BRICK CHURCH, blue satin glass, 1 year	12.50	40.00
1971	OLD BRICK CHURCH, white satin glass, 1 year	12.50	30.00
1972	TWO-HORNED CHURCH, carnival glass, 1 year	12.50	NR
1972	TWO-HORNED CHURCH, blue satin glass, 1 year	12.50	40.00
1972	TWO-HORNED CHURCH, white satin glass, 1 year	12.50	25.00
1973	SAINT MARY'S/MOUNTAINS, carnival glass, 1 year	12.50	NR
1973	SAINT MARY'S/MOUNTAINS, blue satin glass, 1 year	12.50	35.00
1973	SAINT MARY'S/MOUNTAINS, white satin glass, 1 year	12.50	25.00
1974	NATION'S CHURCH, carnival glass, 1 year	13.50	NR
1974	NATION'S CHURCH, blue satin glass, 1 year	13.50	30.00
1974	NATION'S CHURCH, white satin glass, 1 year	13.50	25.00
1975	BIRTHPLACE OF LIBERTY, carnival glass, 1 year	13.50	NR
1975	BIRTHPLACE OF LIBERTY, blue satin glass, 1 year	13.50	30.00
1975	BIRTHPLACE OF LIBERTY, white satin glass, 1 year	13.50	25.00
1976	OLD NORTH CHURCH, carnival glass, 1 year	15.00	NR
1976	OLD NORTH CHURCH, blue satin glass, 1 year	15.00	25.00
1976	OLD NORTH CHURCH, white satin glass, 1 year	15.00	25.00
1977	SAN CARLOS BOROMEO DE CARMELO, carnival glass, 1 year	15.00	NR
1977	SAN CARLOS BOROMEO DE CARMELO, blue satin glass, 1 year	15.00	NR
1977	SAN CARLOS BOROMEO DE CARMELO, white satin glass, 1 year	15.00	NR
1978	CHURCH OF THE HOLY TRINITY, carnival glass, 1 year	15.00	NR
1978	CHURCH OF THE HOLY TRINITY, blue satin glass, 1 year	15.00	NR
1978	CHURCH OF THE HOLY TRINITY, white satin glass, 1 year	15.00	NR
1979	SAN JOSE Y MIGUEL DE AQUAYO, carnival glass, 1 year	15.00	NR
1979	SAN JOSE Y MIGUEL DE AQUAYO, blue satin glass, 1 year	15.00	NR
1979	SAN JOSE Y MIGUEL DE AQUAYO, white satin glass, 1 year	15.00	NR
1980	CHRIST CHURCH, ALEXANDRIA, VA, carnival glass, 1 year	16.50	NR
1980	CHRIST CHURCH, ALEXANDRIA, VA, blue satin glass, 1 year	16.50	NR
1980	CHRIST CHURCH, ALEXANDRIA, VA, white satin glass, 1 year	16.50	NR
1981	MISSION OF SAN XAVIER DEL BAC, carnival glass, 1 year	18.50	NR
1981	MISSION OF SAN XAVIER DEL BAC, blue satin glass, 1 year	18.50	NR

		ISSUE	CURRENT
1981	MISSION OF SAN XAVIER DEL BAC, white satin glass, 1 year	18.50	NR
1981	MISSION OF SAN XAVIER DEL BAC, florentine glass, 1 year	25.00	NR

Christmas Star

1994	SILENT NIGHT, Frances Burton, 1,500	65.00	RI
1995	OUR HOME IS BLESSED, Frances Burton, 1,500	65.00	RI
1996	STAR OF WONDER, Frances Burton, 1,750	65.00	RI
1997	THE WAY HOME, Frances Burton, 1,750	85.00	RI

Silent Night
Photo courtesy of *Collectors News*

Currier & Ives Limited Edition

1980	WINTER IN THE COUNTRY—THE OLD GRIST MILL, Anthony Rosena, 1 year	25.00	NR
1981	HARVEST, Anthony Rosena, 1 year	25.00	NR
1982	THE OLD HOMESTEAD IN WINTER, Anthony Rosena, 1 year	25.00	NR
1983	WINTER PASTIME, Anthony Rosena, 1 year	25.00	NR

Designer Series

1983	DOWN HOME, Gloria Fina, 1,000	65.00	NR
1983	LIGHTHOUSE POINT, Gloria Fina, 1,000	65.00	NR

Easter

1995	COVERED HEN & EGG, 5188YZ, Martha Reynolds, opal iridescent, 950	95.00	RI
1997	COVERED HEN & EGG, 5188YZ, R. Spindler, opal iridescent, 950	115.00	RI

Mary Gregory

1994	PLATE WITH STAND, Martha Reynolds, closed, 9"	65.00	RI
1995	PLATE WITH STAND, Martha Reynolds, closed, 9"	65.00	RI

Mother's Day I

1971	MADONNA WITH SLEEPING CHILD, carnival glass, 1 year	10.75	30.00
1971	MADONNA WITH SLEEPING CHILD, blue satin glass, 1 year	10.75	35.00
1972	MADONNA OF THE GOLDFINCH, carnival glass, 1 year	12.50	35.00
1972	MADONNA OF THE GOLDFINCH, blue satin glass, 1 year	12.50	30.00
1972	MADONNA OF THE GOLDFINCH, white satin glass, 1 year	12.50	25.00

		ISSUE	CURRENT
1973	SMALL COWPER MADONNA, carnival glass, 1 year	12.50	30.00
1973	SMALL COWPER MADONNA, blue satin glass, 1 year	12.50	30.00
1973	SMALL COWPER MADONNA, white satin glass, 1 year	12.50	20.00
1974	MADONNA OF THE GROTTO, carnival glass, 1 year	13.50	25.00
1974	MADONNA OF THE GROTTO, blue satin glass, 1 year	13.50	25.00
1974	MADONNA OF THE GROTTO, white satin glass, 1 year	13.50	20.00
1975	TADDEI MADONNA, carnival glass, 1 year	13.50	30.00
1975	TADDEI MADONNA, blue satin glass, 1 year	13.50	30.00
1975	TADDEI MADONNA, white satin glass, 1 year	13.50	25.00
1976	HOLY NIGHT, carnival glass, 1 year	13.50	25.00
1976	HOLY NIGHT, blue satin glass, 1 year	13.50	NR
1976	HOLY NIGHT, white satin glass, 1 year	13.50	NR
1977	MADONNA AND CHILD WITH POMEGRANATE, carnival glass, 1 year	15.00	NR
1977	MADONNA AND CHILD WITH POMEGRANATE, blue satin glass, 1 year	15.00	NR
1977	MADONNA AND CHILD WITH POMEGRANATE, white satin glass, 1 year	15.00	NR
1978	MADONNINA, carnival glass, 1 year	15.00	NR
1978	MADONNINA, blue satin glass, 1 year	15.00	NR
1978	MADONNINA, white satin glass, 1 year	15.00	NR
1979	MADONNA OF THE ROSE HEDGE, carnival glass, 1 year	15.00	NR
1979	MADONNA OF THE ROSE HEDGE, blue satin glass, 1 year	15.00	NR
1979	MADONNA OF THE ROSE HEDGE, white satin glass, 1 year	15.00	NR
1979	MADONNA OF THE ROSE HEDGE, ruby iridescent, 5,000	35.00	BR

Mother's Day II

1990	MOTHER SWAN, Linda Everson, opal satin glass	45.00	NR
1991	MOTHER'S WATCHFUL EYE, Martha Reynolds, opal satin glass	45.00	NR
1992	LET'S PLAY WITH MOM, Martha Reynolds, opal satin glass	49.50	NR
1993	MOTHER DEER, Martha Reynolds, opal satin glass	49.50	RI
1994	LOVING PUPPY, Martha Reynolds, opal satin glass	49.50	RI

Mother's Day, Hand Painted

1980	NEW BORN, Linda Everson, custard satin glass	28.50	NR
1981	GENTLE FAWN, Linda Everson, custard satin glass	32.50	NR
1982	NATURE'S AWAKENING, Linda Everson, custard satin glass	35.00	NR
1983	WHERE'S MOM, Linda Everson, custard satin glass	35.00	NR
1984	PRECIOUS PANDA, Linda Everson, custard satin glass	35.00	NR
1985	MOTHER'S LITTLE LAMB, Linda Everson, custard satin glass	45.00	NR

Valentine's Day

1972	ROMEO AND JULIET, carnival glass, 1 year	15.00	25.00
1972	ROMEO AND JULIET, blue satin glass, 1 year	15.00	25.00

THE FIELDS COLLECTION

Small World/Beautiful Children

1983	JENNIFER'S WORLD, Charlene Mitchell, limited	35.00	NR

Single Issues

1982	MICHAEL'S MIRACLE	NA	NA
1982	SUSAN'S WORLD	NA	NA

FINE ARTS MARKETING CANADA

Autumn Flights

		ISSUE	CURRENT
1986	CANADIAN GEESE, Jerold Bishop, 5,000	55.00	NR
1986	MALLARD DUCKS, Jerold Bishop, 5,000	55.00	NR

Turn, Turn, Turn

1986	AUTUMN BACK HOME, Jerold Bishop, 5,000	50.00	NR
1986	WINTER MEMORIES, Jerold Bishop, 5,000	50.00	NR

Single Issue

1993	AN AMERICAN LEGACY (ROSS PEROT), Sam Kalash, 150 days	29.95	RI

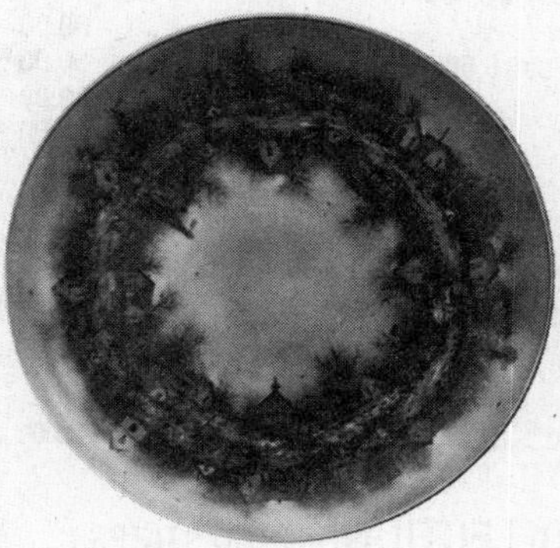

Autumn Back Home
Photo courtesy of *Collectors News*

FIREHOUSE COLLECTIBLES UNITED STATES

This Ole Bear

1984	BUSTER AND SAM, Janet Tuck, 5,000	39.50	NR
1984	MATILDA JANE, Janet Tuck, 5,000	39.50	NR

FITZ AND FLOYD, INC. UNITED STATES

Fitz and Floyd Annual Christmas Plate

1992	NUTCRACKER SUITE'S "THE MAGIC OF THE NUTCRACKER," R. Havins, closed	65.00	RI
1993	CHARLES DICKENS' "A CHRISTMAS CAROL," T. Kerr, 5,000	75.00	RI
1994	NIGHT BEFORE CHRISTMAS, T. Kerr, 7,500	75.00	RI

Myth of Santa Claus

1993	RUSSIAN SANTA, R. Havins, 5,000	70.00	RI
1993	FATHER FROST, R. Havins, 5,000	70.00	RI
1994	CANDYLAND SANTA, R. Havins, 5,000	75.00	RI

		ISSUE	CURRENT

Twelve Days of Christmas

1993	A PARTRIDGE IN A PEAR TREE, T. Kerr, 5,000	70.00	RI

Wonderland

1993	A MAD TEA PARTY, R. Havins, 5,000	70.00	RI

FLAMBRO IMPORTS UNITED STATES

Emmett Kelly, Jr.

1983	WHY ME?, Plate I, C. Kelly, 10,000	40.00	275.00
1984	BALLOONS FOR SALE, Plate II, C. Kelly, 10,000	40.00	275.00
1985	BIG BUSINESS, Plate III, C. Kelly, 10,000	40.00	250.00
1986	AND GOD BLESS AMERICA, Plate IV, C. Kelly, 10,000	40.00	200.00
1988	'TIS THE SEASON, D. L. Rust, 10,000	50.00	120.00
1989	LOOKING BACK—65TH BIRTHDAY, D. L. Rust, 6,500	50.00	150.00
1991	WINTER, D. L. Rust, 10,000	30.00	85.00
1992	SPRING, D. L. Rust, 10,000	30.00	85.00
1992	SUMMER, D. L. Rust, 10,000	30.00	85.00
1992	AUTUMN, D. L. Rust, 10,000	30.00	30.00
1993	SANTA'S STOWAWAY, D. L. Rust, 5,000	30.00	RI
1994	70TH BIRTHDAY COMMEMORATIVE, D. L. Rust, 5,000	30.00	RI
1995	ALL WRAPPED UP IN CHRISTMAS, D. L. Rust, 5,000	30.00	RI

Raggedy Ann and Andy

1988	70 YEARS YOUNG, C. Beylon, 10,000	35.00	45.00

THE FLEETWOOD COLLECTION UNITED STATES

Birds and Flowers of the Meadow and Garden

1980	BALTIMORE ORIOLE AND MORNING GLORY, Don Balke, limited	39.00	NR
1980	GOLDFINCH AND BULLTHISTLE, Don Balke, limited	39.00	NR
1980	CARDINAL AND LUPINE, Don Balke, limited	39.00	NR
1980	EASTERN BLUE BIRD AND BLACKEYED SUSAN, Don Balke, limited	39.00	NR
1980	CAPPED CHICKADEE AND NEW ENGLAND ASTER, Don Balke, limited	39.00	NR
1980	ROBIN AND CRABAPPLE, Don Balke, limited	39.00	NR
1980	PAINTED BUNTING AND BLACKBERRY, Don Balke, limited	39.00	NR
1980	GOLDEN CROWNED KINGLET AND DOWNY PHLOX, Don Balke, limited	39.00	NR
1980	REDBREASTED NUTHATCH AND JAPANESE HONEYSUCKLE, Don Balke, limited	39.00	NR
1980	MAGNOLIA WARBLER AND COMMON DAY LILY, Don Balke, limited	39.00	NR
1980	HUMMINGBIRD AND FIRE PINK, Don Balke, limited	39.00	NR
1980	SCARLET TANAGER AND BLUE COLUMBINE, Don Balke, limited	39.00	NR

Blossoms of China

1982	PEONY, Ren Yu, 7,500	49.50	NR
1982	HERBACEOUS PEONY, Ren Yu, 7,500	49.50	NR
1982	CHRYSANTHEMUM, Ren Yu, 7,500	49.50	NR
1982	MAGNOLIA, Ren Yu, 7,500	49.50	NR
1982	PLUM BLOSSOM, Ren Yu, 7,500	49.50	NR
1982	NARCISSUS, Ren Yu, 7,500	49.50	NR

Christmas

		ISSUE	CURRENT
1980	MAGI, Fritz Wegner, 5,000	45.00	55.00
1981	HOLY CHILD, Fritz Wegner, 7,500	49.50	NR
1982	THE SHEPHERDS, Fritz Wegner, 5,000	50.00	NR
1985	COMING HOME FOR CHRISTMAS, F. Jacques, 5,000	50.00	NR

Golden Age of Sail

1981	*FLYING CLOUD*, Charles Lundgren, 5,000	39.00	NR
1982	*NEW WORLD*, Charles Lundgren, 5,000	39.00	NR
1982	*YOUNG AMERICA*, Charles Lundgren, 5,000	39.00	NR
1982	*COURIER*, Charles Lundgren, 5,000	39.00	NR
1982	*SEA WITCH*, Charles Lundgren, 5,000	39.00	NR
1983	*GREAT REPUBLIC*, Charles Lundgren, 5,000	39.00	NR

Mother's Day

1980	COTTONTAILS, Don Balke, 5,000	45.00	60.00
1981	RACCOONS, Don Balke, 5,000	45.00	NR
1982	WHITETAIL DEER, Don Balke, 5,000	50.00	NR
1983	CANADA GEESE, Don Balke, 5,000	50.00	NR

Pandas of Wu Zuoren

1981	MOTHER AND BABY, Wu Zuoren, 5,000	39.00	NR
1981	SLEEPING PANDA, Wu Zuoren, 5,000	39.00	NR
1981	TWO PANDAS, Wu Zuoren, 5,000	39.00	NR
1981	MOTHER AND BABY PLAYING, Wu Zuoren, 5,000	39.00	NR
1981	MOTHER HOLDING BABY, Wu Zuoren, 5,000	39.00	NR
1981	PANDA ON A ROCK, Wu Zuoren, 5,000	39.00	NR

Royal Wedding

1981	PRINCE CHARLES/LADY DIANA, Jeffrey Mathews, 9,500	49.50	65.00
1986	PRINCE ANDREW/SARAH FERGUSON, Jeffrey Mathews, 10,000	50.00	NR

Statue of Liberty

1986	STATUE OF LIBERTY, Jeffrey Mathews, 10,000	50.00	NR

Tsarevich's Bride

1981	AN ARROW IN THE AIR, A. M. Kurkin, 7,500	50.00	60.00
1982	BOYER'S COURTYARD, A. M. Kurkin, 7,500	50.00	60.00
1982	RICH MERCHANT'S YARD, A. M. Kurkin, 7,500	50.00	60.00
1983	MOUTH OF A FROG, A. M. Kurkin, 7,500	50.00	60.00

Single Issue

1982	MOM'S APPLE PIE, Gene Boyer, <1 year	29.00	NR

FONTANA

Christmas

1972	18TH CENTURY COUPLE WITH DOG, 2,000	35.00	BR
1973	SLEIGHING, 1,000	35.00	BR

		ISSUE	CURRENT
Mother's Day			
1973	MOTHER AND CHILD, 2,000	35.00	BR

FORT U.S.A.

Holiday Collection, pewter			
1997	SANTA AND THE ELVES, Heidi Dion, 1 year	34.95	RI
Single Issue			
1997	MARY OF NAZARETH, open	34.95	RI

FOSTORIA GLASS UNITED STATES

American Milestones			
1971	BETSY ROSS FLAG, 5,000	12.50	25.00
1972	NATIONAL ANTHEM, 8,000	12.50	NR
1973	WASHINGTON CROSSING DELAWARE, 1 year	12.50	NR
1974	SPIRIT OF '76, 1 year	13.00	NR
1975	MOUNT RUSHMORE, 1 year	16.00	NR
State Plates			
1971	CALIFORNIA, 6,000	12.50	NR
1971	NEW YORK, 12,000	12.50	NR
1971	OHIO, 3,000	12.50	NR
1972	FLORIDA, 1 year	12.50	NR
1972	HAWAII, 1 year	12.50	NR
1972	PENNSYLVANIA, 1 year	12.50	NR
1972	MASSACHUSETTS, 1 year	13.00	NR
1972	TEXAS, 1 year	13.00	NR
1973	MICHIGAN, 1 year	13.50	NR

FOUNTAINHEAD UNITED STATES

(Pickard)

As Free as the Wind			
1988	AS FREE AS THE WIND, Mario Fernandez	295.00	300.00
Seasons			
1986	FALL CARDINALS, Mario Fernandez, 5,000	85.00	NR
1987	SPRING ROBINS, Mario Fernandez, 5,000	85.00	NR
1987	SUMMER GOLDFINCHES, Mario Fernandez, 5,000	85.00	NR
1987	WINTER CHICKADEES, Mario Fernandez, 5,000	85.00	NR
Twelve Days of Christmas			
1988	A PARTRIDGE IN A PEAR TREE, Mario Fernandez, 7,500	155.00	NR
1988	TWO TURTLEDOVES, Mario Fernandez, 7,500	155.00	NR
1989	FOUR CALLING BIRDS, Mario Fernandez, 7,500	155.00	NR
1989	THREE FRENCH HENS, Mario Fernandez, 7,500	155.00	NR

		ISSUE	CURRENT

Wings of Freedom

		ISSUE	CURRENT
1985	COURTSHIP FLIGHT, Mario Fernandez, 2,500	250.00	1,250.00
1986	WINGS OF FREEDOM, Mario Fernandez, 2,500	250.00	1,250.00

FRANKLIN MINT UNITED STATES

American Portrait

		ISSUE	CURRENT
1998	COWS IN WINTER, Lowell Herrero, 45 days	29.95	RI
1998	2nd RELEASE, Lowell Herrero, 45 days	29.95	RI
1998	3rd RELEASE, Lowell Herrero, 45 days	29.95	RI
1998	4th RELEASE, Lowell Herrero, 45 days	29.95	RI
1998	5th RELEASE, Lowell Herrero, 45 days	29.95	RI
1998	6th RELEASE, Lowell Herrero, 45 days	29.95	RI

American Revolution

		ISSUE	CURRENT
1976–77	BOSTON TEA PARTY, Steven Dohanos, 3,596	75.00	NR
1976–77	PATRICK HENRY URGES ARMED RESISTANCE, Paul Calle, 3,596	75.00	NR
1976–77	PAUL REVERE'S RIDE, John Falter, 3,596	75.00	NR
1976–77	THE BATTLE OF CONCORD BRIDGE, Paul Rickert, 3,596	75.00	NR
1976–77	THE CAPTURE OF FORT TICONDEROGA, Dean Fausett, 3,596	75.00	NR
1976–77	THE BATTLE OF BUNKER HILL, Alton S. Tobey, 3,596	75.00	NR
1976–77	THE SIGNING OF THE DECLARATION, Gordon Phillips, 3,596	75.00	NR
1976–77	WASHINGTON CROSSES THE DELAWARE, Alexander Farnham, 3,596	75.00	NR
1976–77	BURGOYNE DEFEATED AT SARATOGA, Don Stone, 3,596	75.00	NR
1976–77	WINTER AT VALLEY FORGE, Isa Barratt, 3,596	75.00	NR
1976–77	*BON HOMME RICHARD* DEFEATS *SERAPIS*, John Pike, 3,596	75.00	NR
1976–77	VICTORY AT YORKTOWN, John Chumley, 3,596	75.00	NR

Annual

		ISSUE	CURRENT
1977	TRIBUTE TO THE ARTS, 1,901	280.00	300.00
1978	TRIBUTE TO NATURE, 435	280.00	300.00

Arabian Nights

		ISSUE	CURRENT
1981–82	ALADDIN AND HIS WONDERFUL LAMP, Christopher McEwan, 690	27.50	NR
1981–82	ALI BABA AND FORTY THIEVES, Christopher McEwan, 690	27.50	NR
1981–82	THE CITY OF BRASS, Christopher McEwan, 690	27.50	NR
1981–82	THE FAIR PERSIAN, Christopher McEwan, 690	27.50	NR
1981–82	THE FISHERMAN, Christopher McEwan, 690	27.50	NR
1981–82	THE MAGIC HORSE, Christopher McEwan, 690	27.50	NR
1981–82	THE MERCHANT AND THE GENIE, Christopher McEwan, 690	27.50	NR
1981–82	PRINCE AGIB, Christopher McEwan, 690	27.50	NR
1981–82	PRINCE CAMARAIZAMAN AND THE PRINCESS BADOURA, Christopher McEwan, 690	27.50	NR
1981–82	SINBAD THE SAILOR, Christopher McEwan, 690	27.50	NR
1981–82	THE VIZIER WHO WAS PUNISHED, Christopher McEwan, 690	27.50	NR
1981–82	THE YOUNG KING OF THE EBONY ISLES, Christopher McEwan, 690	27.50	NR

Audubon Society

		ISSUE	CURRENT
1972	THE GOLDFINCH, James Fenwick Lansdowne, 10,193	125.00	BR
1972	THE WOOD DUCK, James Fenwick Lansdowne, 10,193	125.00	BR
1973	THE CARDINAL, James Fenwick Lansdowne, 10,193	125.00	BR

		ISSUE	CURRENT
1973	THE RUFFED GROUSE, James Fenwick Lansdowne, 10,193	125.00	BR
Bernard Buffet			
1973	GAZELLE, Bernard Buffet, 570	150.00	275.00
1974	PANDA, Bernard Buffet, 408	150.00	250.00
1975	GIRAFFE, Bernard Buffet, 333	150.00	250.00
1976	LION, Bernard Buffet, 263	150.00	250.00
1977	RHINOCEROS, Bernard Buffet, 200	150.00	250.00
Bicentennial			
1973	JEFFERSON DRAFTING DECLARATION OF INDEPENDENCE, 8556	175.00	210.00
1974	JOHN ADAMS CHAMPIONS CAUSE OF INDEPENDENCE, 8,442	175.00	210.00
1975	CAESAR RODNEY DECIDES VOTE ON INDEPENDENCE, 8,319	175.00	210.00
1976	JOHN HANCOCK SIGNS DECLARATION OF INDEPENDENCE, 10,166	175.00	210.00
Birds			
1972	CARDINAL, Richard Evans Younger, 13,939	125.00	135.00
1972	BOB WHITE, Richard Evans Younger, 13,939	125.00	135.00
1972	MALLARDS, Richard Evans Younger, 13,939	125.00	135.00
1973	AMERICAN BALD EAGLE, Richard Evans Younger, 13,939	125.00	145.00
Birds and Flowers of Beautiful Cathay			
1981–82	BEGINNING OF WINTER, Wei Tseng Yang	35.00	NR
1981–83	BIG SNOW, Wei Tseng Yang	35.00	NR
1981–83	CHING CHE (AWAKENING OF INSECTS), Wei Tseng Yang	35.00	NR
1981–83	CH'ING MING (PURE BRIGHTNESS), Wei Tseng Yang	35.00	NR
1981–83	CH'UN FEN (DIVISION OF SPRING), Wei Tseng Yang	35.00	NR
1981–83	COLD DEW, Wei Tseng Yang	35.00	NR
1981–83	HSIA CHIH (ARRIVAL OF SUMMER), Wei Tseng Yang	35.00	NR
1981–83	HSIAO HAN (SMALL COLD), Wei Tseng Yang	35.00	NR
1981–83	HSIAO MAN (RIPENING GRAIN), Wei Tseng Yang	35.00	NR
1981–83	HSIAO SHU (SMALL HEAT), Wei Tseng Yang	35.00	NR
1981–83	KU YU (CORN RAIN), Wei Tseng Yang	35.00	NR
1981–83	LI CH'IU (BEGINNING OF AUTUMN), Wei Tseng Yang	35.00	NR
1981–83	LI CH'UN (BEGINNING OF SPRING), Wei Tseng Yang	35.00	NR
1981–83	LI HSIA (BEGINNING OF SUMMER), Wei Tseng Yang	35.00	NR
1981–83	LIMIT OF HEAT, Wei Tseng Yang	35.00	NR
1981–83	MANG CHUNG (GRAIN IN THE EAR), Wei Tseng Yang	35.00	NR
1981–83	SCARLET FINCHES AND CHRYSANTHEMUMS, Wei Tseng Yang	35.00	NR
1981–83	SMALL SNOW, Wei Tseng Yang	35.00	NR
1981–83	TA HAN (GREAT COLD), Wei Tseng Yang	35.00	NR
1981–83	TA SHUS (GREAT HEAT), Wei Tseng Yang	35.00	NR
1981–83	WHITE DEW, Wei Tseng Yang	35.00	NR
1981–83	WINTER SOLSTICE, Wei Tseng Yang	35.00	NR
1981–83	YU SHUI (RAIN WATER), Wei Tseng Yang	35.00	NR
Birds and Flowers of the Orient			
1979–80	ROOSTER AND MORNING GLORY, Naoka Nobata, 32,373	55.00	NR
1979–80	LOTUS AND WATER FOWL, Naoka Nobata, 32,373	55.00	NR
1979–80	MAPLE TREE AND SHRIKE, Naoka Nobata, 32,373	55.00	NR
1979–80	WHITE CRANE AND THE PINE, Naoka Nobata, 32,373	55.00	NR
1979–80	WHITE EYE AND PEACH, Naoka Nobata, 32,373	55.00	NR
1979–80	MANDARIN DUCK AND IRIS, Naoka Nobata, 32,373	55.00	NR

		ISSUE	CURRENT
1979–80	EGRET AND WATER LILY, Naoka Nobata, 32,373	55.00	NR
1979–80	TREE SPARROW AND CHRYSANTHEMUM, Naoka Nobata, 32,373	55.00	NR
1979–80	WREN AND NARCISSUS, Naoka Nobata, 32,373	55.00	NR
1979–80	BUSH WARBLER AND APRICOT, Naoka Nobata, 32,373	55.00	NR
1979–80	CHINESE BLUE PIE AND CHERRY, Naoka Nobata, 32,373	55.00	NR
1979–80	PEONY AND PEACOCK, Naoka Nobata, 32,373	55.00	NR

Butterflies of the World

1977–79	SOUTH AMERICA, 481	240.00	275.00
1977–79	AUSTRALIA, 481	240.00	275.00
1977–79	NORTH AMERICA, 481	240.00	275.00
1977–79	EUROPE, 481	240.00	275.00
1977–79	AFRICA, 481	240.00	275.00
1977–79	ASIA, 481	240.00	275.00

Calendar

1981	TURN-OF-THE-CENTURY SCENE, Deborah Bell Jarratt, 5,634	55.00	NR
1982	TURN-OF-THE-CENTURY CHILDREN, Margaret Murphy, 5,634	58.00	NR
1983	CHILDREN CELEBRATING VICTORIAN MONTHS, Kate Lloyd Jones	55.00	NR
1984	CHILDREN WITH TEDDY BEARS, Margaret Murphy	55.00	NR

Carol Lawson Annual

1981	STORYTIME, Carol Lawson, 1 year	35.00	NR
1982	TEACHER'S PET, Carol Lawson, 1 year	35.00	NR
1983	TEATIME SURPRISE, Carol Lawson, 1 year	35.00	NR

Christmas

1976	SILENT NIGHT, 19,286	65.00	NR
1977	DECK THE HALLS, 9,185	75.00	NR
1978	WE THREE KINGS, 6,737	75.00	NR
1979	HARK THE HERALD ANGELS SING, 4,784	75.00	NR
1980	JOY TO THE WORLD	125.00	NR
1981	O HOLY NIGHT	125.00	NR

Christmas—International

1981	CHRISTMAS IN FRANCE, Yves Beaujard	35.00	NR
1982	CHRISTMAS IN ENGLAND, Peter D. Jackson	35.00	NR
1983	CHRISTMAS IN AMERICA, William Plummer	35.00	NR

Clipper Ships

1982–83	*ARIEL*, L. J. Pearce	55.00	NR
1982–83	*CHALLENGE*, L. J. Pearce	55.00	NR
1982–83	*CUTTY SARK*, L. J. Pearce	55.00	NR
1982–83	*FLYING CLOUD*, L. J. Pearce	55.00	NR
1982–83	*GREAT REPUBLIC*, L. J. Pearce	55.00	NR
1982–83	*MARCO POLO*, L. J. Pearce	55.00	NR
1982–83	*NIGHTINGALE*, L. J. Pearce	55.00	NR
1982–83	*ORIENTAL*, L. J. Pearce	55.00	NR
1982–83	*PATRIARCH*, L. J. Pearce	55.00	NR
1982–83	*RED JACKET*, L. J. Pearce	55.00	NR
1982–83	*SEA WITCH*, L. J. Pearce	55.00	NR
1982–83	*THERMOPYLAE*, L. J. Pearce	55.00	NR

		ISSUE	CURRENT

Cobblestone Kids

		ISSUE	CURRENT
1982	MAKING FRIENDS, Deborah Bell Jarratt	65.00	NR
1983	A STITCH IN TIME, Deborah Bell Jarratt	65.00	NR
1983	EXTRA! EXTRA!, Deborah Bell Jarratt	65.00	NR
1983	FEEDING THE RACCOON, Deborah Bell Jarratt	65.00	NR
1983	JUST DUCKY, Deborah Bell Jarratt	65.00	NR

Country Diary

		ISSUE	CURRENT
1984	JANUARY—DECEMBER, Geoff Mowery, limited, set of 12	660.00	NR

Country Year

		ISSUE	CURRENT
1980–82	COUNTRY PATH IN MAY, Peter Barratt, 89,173	55.00	NR
1980–82	JANUARY—LAMBING SEASON, Peter Barratt, 89,173	55.00	NR
1980–82	OCTOBER—COLOURS OF AUTUMN, Peter Barratt, 89,173	55.00	NR
1980–82	WHEAT FIELDS IN AUGUST, Peter Barratt, 89,173	55.00	NR
1980–82	SEPTEMBER ON THE MOORS, Peter Barratt, 89,173	55.00	NR
1980–82	JUNE IN A COTTAGE GARDEN, Peter Barratt, 89,173	55.00	NR
1980–82	COUNTRY CHURCH IN MARCH, Peter Barratt, 89,173	55.00	NR
1980–82	SECLUDED STREAM IN NOVEMBER, Peter Barratt, 89,173	55.00	NR
1980–82	WOODLANDS IN APRIL, Peter Barratt, 89,173	55.00	NR
1980–82	COUNTRY LANE IN DECEMBER, Peter Barratt, 89,173	55.00	NR
1980–82	JULY BESIDE THE RIVER, Peter Barratt, 89,173	55.00	NR
1980–82	FEBRUARY ON THE COAST, Peter Barratt, 89,173	55.00	NR

Currier & Ives

		ISSUE	CURRENT
1977–79	WINTER PASTIME, Currier & Ives, 1,836	39.50	45.00
1977–79	PREPARING FOR MARKET, Currier & Ives, 1,836	39.50	45.00
1977–79	WINTER IN THE COUNTRY, Currier & Ives, 1,836	39.50	45.00
1977–79	AMERICAN HOMESTEAD—WINTER, Currier & Ives, 1,836	39.50	45.00
1977–79	AMERICAN FOREST SCENE, Currier & Ives, 1,836	39.50	45.00
1977–79	AMERICAN HOMESTEAD—SUMMER, Currier & Ives, 1,836	39.50	45.00
1977–79	AMERICAN HOMESTEAD—AUTUMN, Currier & Ives, 1,836	39.50	45.00
1977–79	HAYING TIME—THE LAST LOAD, Currier & Ives, 1,836	39.50	45.00
1977–79	CATCHING A TROUT, Currier & Ives, 1,836	39.50	45.00
1977–79	YOSEMITE VALLEY, Currier & Ives, 1,836	39.50	45.00

Days of the Week

		ISSUE	CURRENT
1979–80	MONDAY'S CHILD IS FAIR OF FACE, Caroline Ebborn, 1,890	39.00	NR
1979–80	TUESDAY'S CHILD IS FULL OF GRACE, Caroline Ebborn, 1,890	39.00	NR
1979–80	WEDNESDAY'S CHILD IS FULL OF WOE, Caroline Ebborn, 1,890	39.00	NR
1979–80	THURSDAY'S CHILD HAS FAR TO GO, Caroline Ebborn, 1,890	39.00	NR
1979–80	FRIDAY'S CHILD IS LOVING AND GIVING, Caroline Ebborn, 1,890	39.00	NR
1979–80	SATURDAY'S CHILD WORKS HARD FOR A LIVING, Caroline Ebborn, 1,890	39.00	NR
1979–80	SUNDAY'S CHILD IS BORN ON THE SABBATH DAY, Caroline Ebborn, 1,890	39.00	NR

Easter

		ISSUE	CURRENT
1973	RESURRECTION, Evangelos Frudakis, 7,116	175.00	185.00
1974	HE IS RISEN, Abram Belski, 3,719	185.00	195.00
1975	THE LAST SUPPER, Oriol Sunyer, 2,004	200.00	225.00
1976	THE CRUCIFIXION, Marguerite Gaudin, 3,904	250.00	300.00
1977	RESURRECTION, 1,206	250.00	300.00

Fairy Tales Miniatures

		ISSUE	CURRENT
1979–84	THE THREE BEARS, Carol Lawson, 15,207	14.50	NR
1979–84	LITTLE RED RIDING HOOD, Carol Lawson, 15,207	14.50	NR
1979–84	THE LITTLE MERMAID, Carol Lawson, 15,207	14.50	NR
1979–84	SNOW WHITE AND THE SEVEN DWARFS, Carol Lawson, 15,207	14.50	NR
1979–84	ALADDIN AND THE WONDERFUL LAMP, Carol Lawson, 15,207	14.50	NR
1979–84	THE SNOW QUEEN, Carol Lawson, 15,207	14.50	NR
1979–84	TOM THUMB, Carol Lawson, 15,207	14.50	NR
1979–84	ALI BABA, Carol Lawson, 15,207	14.50	NR
1979–84	JACK AND THE BEANSTALK, Carol Lawson, 15,207	14.50	NR
1979–84	PUSS IN BOOTS, Carol Lawson, 15,207	14.50	NR
1979–84	THE FROG PRINCE, Carol Lawson, 15,207	14.50	NR
1979–84	CINDERELLA, Carol Lawson, 15,207	14.50	NR
1979–84	PRINCESS AND THE PEA, Carol Lawson, 15,207	14.50	NR
1979–84	THE PIED PIPER, Carol Lawson, 15,207	14.50	NR
1979–84	VALIANT LITTLE TAILOR, Carol Lawson, 15,207	14.50	NR
1979–84	THE UGLY DUCKLING, Carol Lawson, 15,207	14.50	NR
1979–84	THE THREE LITTLE PIGS, Carol Lawson, 15,207	14.50	NR
1979–84	RAPUNZEL, Carol Lawson, 15,207	14.50	NR
1979–84	THE LITTLE MATCH GIRL, Carol Lawson, 15,207	14.50	NR
1979–84	THUMBELINA, Carol Lawson, 15,207	14.50	NR
1979–84	THE NIGHTINGALE, Carol Lawson, 15,207	14.50	NR
1979–84	THE STEADFAST TIN SOLDIER, Carol Lawson, 15,207	14.50	NR
1979–84	THE GOOSE THAT LAID THE GOLDEN EGGS, Carol Lawson, 15,207	14.50	NR
1979–84	HENNY-PENNY, Carol Lawson, 15,207	14.50	NR
1979–84	EAST OF THE SUN AND WEST OF THE MOON, Carol Lawson, 15,207	14.50	NR
1979–84	BILLY GOAT'S GRUFF, Carol Lawson, 15,207	14.50	NR
1979–84	SINBAD THE SAILOR, Carol Lawson, 15,207	14.50	NR
1979–84	BEAUTY AND THE BEAST, Carol Lawson, 15,207	14.50	NR
1979–84	THE RED SHOES, Carol Lawson, 15,207	14.50	NR
1979–84	RUMPELSTILTSKIN, Carol Lawson, 15,207	14.50	NR
1979–84	SLEEPING BEAUTY, Carol Lawson, 15,207	14.50	NR
1979–84	THE TWELVE DANCING PRINCESSES, Carol Lawson, 15,207	14.50	NR
1979–84	HANSEL AND GRETEL, Carol Lawson, 15,207	14.50	NR
1979–84	SNOW WHITE AND ROSE RED, Carol Lawson, 15,207	14.50	NR
1979–84	THE BRONZE RING, Carol Lawson, 15,207	14.50	NR
1979–84	JORINDA AND JORINDEL, Carol Lawson, 15,207	14.50	NR
1979–84	PINOCCHIO, Carol Lawson, 15,207	14.50	NR
1979–84	THE GOLDEN GOOSE, Carol Lawson, 15,207	14.50	NR
1979–84	THE SORCERER'S APPRENTICE, Carol Lawson, 15,207	14.50	NR
1979–84	TOWN MOUSE AND COUNTRY MOUSE, Carol Lawson, 15,207	14.50	NR
1979–84	SIX SWANS, Carol Lawson, 15,207	14.50	NR
1979–84	MAID MALEEN, Carol Lawson, 15,207	14.50	NR
1979–84	THE GINGERBREAD BOY, Carol Lawson, 15,207	14.50	NR

Flowers of the American Wilderness

1978–80	NEW ENGLAND, Jeanne Holgate, 8,759	39.00	NR
1978–80	ALASKA, Jeanne Holgate, 8,759	39.00	NR
1978–80	EVERGLADES OF FLORIDA, Jeanne Holgate, 8,759	39.00	NR
1978–80	MISSISSIPPI DELTA, Jeanne Holgate, 8,759	39.00	NR
1978–80	CALIFORNIA, Jeanne Holgate, 8,759	39.00	NR
1978–80	ROCKY MOUNTAINS, Jeanne Holgate, 8,759	39.00	NR
1978–80	CAPE COD, Jeanne Holgate, 8,759	39.00	NR

		ISSUE	CURRENT
1978–80	NORTHWEST, Jeanne Holgate, 8,759	39.00	NR
1978–80	SOUTHWEST, Jeanne Holgate, 8,759	39.00	NR
1978–80	APPALACHIAN MOUNTAINS, Jeanne Holgate, 8,759	39.00	NR
1978–80	PRAIRIES, Jeanne Holgate, 8,759	39.00	NR
1978–80	GREAT LAKES, Jeanne Holgate, 8,759	39.00	NR

Flowers of the Year

1976	JANUARY, Leslie Greenwood, 27,394	50.00	NR
1976	FEBRUARY, Leslie Greenwood, 27,394	50.00	NR
1977	MARCH, Leslie Greenwood, 27,394	50.00	NR
1977	APRIL, Leslie Greenwood, 27,394	50.00	NR
1977	MAY, Leslie Greenwood, 27,394	50.00	NR
1978	JUNE, Leslie Greenwood, 27,394	50.00	NR
1978	JULY, Leslie Greenwood, 27,394	50.00	NR
1978	AUGUST, Leslie Greenwood, 27,394	50.00	NR
1978	SEPTEMBER, Leslie Greenwood, 27,394	50.00	NR
1978	OCTOBER, Leslie Greenwood, 27,394	50.00	NR
1978	NOVEMBER, Leslie Greenwood, 27,394	50.00	NR
1978	DECEMBER, Leslie Greenwood, 27,394	50.00	NR

Four Seasons Champleve

1975	SPRING BLOSSOMS, Rene Restoueux, 2,648	240.00	BR
1975	SUMMER BOUQUET, Rene Restoueux, 2,648	240.00	BR
1976	AUTUMN GARLAND, Rene Restoueux, 2,648	240.00	BR
1976	WINTER SPRAY, Rene Restoueux, 2,648	240.00	BR

Game Birds of the World

1978–80	CHINESE RING-NECKED PHEASANT, Basil Ede, 76,294	55.00	NR
1978–80	RED-LEGGED PARTRIDGE, Basil Ede, 76,294	55.00	NR
1978–80	COMMON SNIPE, Basil Ede, 76,294	55.00	NR
1978–80	COMMON PARTRIDGE, Basil Ede, 76,294	55.00	NR
1978–80	ROCK PTARMIGAN, Basil Ede, 76,294	55.00	NR
1978–80	WOODCOCK, Basil Ede, 76,294	55.00	NR
1978–80	COMMON PHEASANT, Basil Ede, 76,294	55.00	NR
1978–80	HAZEL GROUSE, Basil Ede, 76,294	55.00	NR
1978–80	RED GROUSE, Basil Ede, 76,294	55.00	NR
1978–80	BLACK GROUSE, Basil Ede, 76,294	55.00	NR
1978–80	CAPERCAILLIE, Basil Ede, 76,294	55.00	NR
1978–80	COMMON QUAIL, Basil Ede, 76,294	55.00	NR

Garden Birds of the World

1984	AMERICAN ROBIN, Basil Ede, sgd, limited	55.00	NR
1984	BLACKBIRD, Basil Ede, sgd, limited	55.00	NR
1984	BLACK-CAPPED CHICKADEE, Basil Ede, sgd, limited	55.00	NR
1984	CARDINAL, Basil Ede, sgd, limited	55.00	NR
1984	EASTERN BLUEBIRD, Basil Ede, sgd, limited	55.00	NR
1984	GOLDFINCH, Basil Ede, sgd, limited	55.00	NR
1984	GREAT TITMOUSE, Basil Ede, sgd, limited	55.00	NR
1984	KINGFISHER, Basil Ede, sgd, limited	55.00	NR
1984	MOCKINGBIRD, Basil Ede, sgd, limited	55.00	NR
1984	SONG THRUSH, Basil Ede, sgd, limited	55.00	NR
1984	SWALLOW, Basil Ede, sgd, limited	55.00	NR
1984	WHITE-BREASTED NUTHATCH, Basil Ede, sgd, limited	55.00	NR

Garden Year

		ISSUE	CURRENT
1984	JANUARY—DECEMBER, David Hurrell, sgd, limited, set of 12	330.00	NR

Grimm's Fairy Tales

1978	SLEEPING BEAUTY, Carol Lawson, 27,006	42.00	NR
1978	TWELVE DANCING PRINCESSES, Carol Lawson, 27,006	42.00	NR
1979	BREMEN TOWN MUSICIANS, Carol Lawson, 27,006	42.00	NR
1979	GOLDEN GOOSE, Carol Lawson, 27,006	42.00	NR
1979	HANSEL AND GRETEL, Carol Lawson, 27,006	42.00	NR
1979	RAPUNZEL, Carol Lawson, 27,006	42.00	NR
1979	SNOW WHITE AND THE SEVEN DWARFS, Carol Lawson, 27,006	42.00	NR
1979	FROG PRINCE, Carol Lawson, 27,006	42.00	NR
1979	RED RIDING HOOD, Carol Lawson, 27,006	42.00	NR
1979	RUMPELSTILTSKIN, Carol Lawson, 27,006	42.00	NR
1979	CINDERELLA, Carol Lawson, 27,006	42.00	NR
1979	SHOEMAKER AND THE ELVES, Carol Lawson, 27,006	42.00	NR

Hans Christian Andersen

1976	PRINCESS AND THE PEA, Pauline Ellison, 16,875	38.00	70.00
1976	UGLY DUCKLING, Pauline Ellison, 16,875	38.00	70.00
1976	LITTLE MERMAID, Pauline Ellison, 16,875	38.00	70.00
1976	EMPEROR'S NEW CLOTHES, Pauline Ellison, 16,875	38.00	70.00
1976	STEADFAST TIN SOLDIER, Pauline Ellison, 16,875	38.00	70.00
1976	LITTLE MATCH GIRL, Pauline Ellison, 16,875	38.00	70.00
1977	SNOW QUEEN, Pauline Ellison, 16,875	38.00	70.00
1977	RED SHOES, Pauline Ellison, 16,875	38.00	70.00
1977	TINDER BOX, Pauline Ellison, 16,875	38.00	70.00
1977	NIGHTINGALE, Pauline Ellison, 16,875	38.00	70.00
1977	THUMBELINA, Pauline Ellison, 16,875	38.00	70.00
1977	SHEPHERDESS AND CHIMNEY SWEEP, Pauline Ellison, 16,875	38.00	70.00

Hometown Memories

1979	COUNTRY FAIR, Jo Sickbert, 4,715	29.00	NR
1980	RED SCHOOLHOUSE, Jo Sickbert, 4,715	29.00	NR
1981	SUNDAY PICNIC, Jo Sickbert, 4,715	29.00	NR
1982	SKATING PARTY, Jo Sickbert, 4,715	29.00	NR

House of Capo di Monte

1995	THE ROSES OF CAPO DI MONTE, 45 days	55.00	RI

International Gallery of Flowers

1980–81	WHEAT, BLACK-EYED SUSAN, COLUMBINE, MAYFLOWER, CALIFORNIA POPPY, Jeanne Holgate, 4,294	55.00	NR
1980–81	ORCHID, Marion Ruff Sheehan, 4,294	55.00	NR
1980–81	IRISES, Claus Caspari, 4,294	55.00	NR
1980–81	CAMELIAS, Anne Marie Trechslin, 4,294	55.00	NR
1980–81	CHERRY BLOSSOMS, Yoai Ohta, 4,294	55.00	NR
1980–81	ENGLISH SPRING WILD FLOWERS, Mary Grierson, 4,294	55.00	NR
1980–81	FUCHSIAS, Raphael Henri/Charles Ghislain, 4,294	55.00	NR
1980–81	FLAME AZALEAS, Martha Prince, 4,294	55.00	NR
1980–81	ROSES, Gabriele Gossner, 4,294	55.00	NR
1980–81	ENGLISH GARDEN FLOWERS, Barbara Everard, 4,294	55.00	NR

		ISSUE	CURRENT
1980–81	TULIPS, Elizabeth Riemer-Gerbardt, 4,294	55.00	NR
1980–81	DESERT PEA, Paul Jones, 4,294	55.00	NR

James Wyeth

1972	ALONG THE BRANDYWINE, James Wyeth, 19,760	125.00	140.00
1973	WINTER FOX, James Wyeth, 10,394	125.00	NR
1974	RIDING TO THE HUNT, James Wyeth, 10,751	150.00	NR
1975	SKATING ON THE BRANDYWINE, James Wyeth, 8,058	175.00	BR
1976	BRANDYWINE BATTLEFIELD, James Wyeth, 6,968	180.00	NR

John James Audubon

1973	THE WOOD THRUSH, John James Audubon, 5,273	150.00	BR
1973	THE BALD EAGLE, John James Audubon, 3,040	150.00	BR
1974	THE NIGHT HERON, John James Audubon, 3,005	150.00	BR
1974	AUDUBON'S WARBLER, John James Audubon, 3,034	150.00	BR

Joys of the Victorian Year

1983	JANUARY—DECEMBER, Kate Lloyd Jones, limited, set of 12	660.00	NR

Mark Twain

1977	WHITEWASHING THE FENCE, Yves Beaujard, 2,645	38.00	55.00
1977	STEALING A KISS, Yves Beaujard, 2,645	38.00	45.00
1977	TRAVELING THE RIVER, Yves Beaujard, 2,645	38.00	45.00
1977	RAFTING DOWN THE RIVER, Yves Beaujard, 2,645	38.00	NR
1978	RIDING A BRONC, Yves Beaujard, 2,645	38.00	NR
1978	JUMPING FROG FENCE, Yves Beaujard, 2,645	38.00	NR
1978	FACING A CHARGING KNIGHT, Yves Beaujard, 2,645	38.00	NR
1978	DISGUISING HUCK, Yves Beaujard, 2,645	38.00	NR
1978	LIVING ALONG THE RIVER, Yves Beaujard, 2,645	38.00	NR
1978	LEARNING TO SMOKE, Yves Beaujard, 2,645	38.00	NR
1978	FINGER PRINTING PAYS OFF, Yves Beaujard, 2,645	38.00	NR

Mother's Day

1977	A MOTHER'S LOVE, Adelaid Sundin, 12,392	65.00	NR
1978	A MOTHER'S JOY, Deborah Bell	65.00	NR
1979	A MOTHER'S GIFT, Deborah Bell, 1 year	75.00	NR

Mother's Day by Spencer

1972	MOTHER AND CHILD, Irene Spencer, 21,987	125.00	175.00
1973	MOTHER AND CHILD, Irene Spencer, 6,154	125.00	140.00
1974	MOTHER AND CHILD, Irene Spencer, 5,116	150.00	160.00
1975	MOTHER AND CHILD, Irene Spencer, 2,704	175.00	NR
1976	MOTHER AND CHILD, Irene Spencer, 1,858	180.00	190.00

Owl Plates

1986	THE SNOWY OWL, Raymond Watson	NA	NA

Poor Richard

1979–81	HASTE MAKES WASTE, 13,133	12.50	NR
1979–81	WHEN THE WELL'S DRY, WE KNOW THE WORTH OF WATER, 13,133	12.50	NR
1979–81	LOVE THY NEIGHBOR, YET DON'T PULL DOWN YOUR HEDGE, 13,133	12.50	NR
1979–81	DILIGENCE IS THE MOTHER OF GOOD LUCK, 13,133	12.50	NR

		ISSUE	CURRENT
1979–81	WHO PLEASURE GIVES, SHALL JOY RECEIVE, 13,133	12.50	NR
1979–81	THE ROTTEN APPLE SPOILS HIS COMPANION, 13,133	12.50	NR
1979–81	A SPOONFUL OF HONEY WILL CATCH MORE FLIES THAN A GALLON OF VINEGAR, 13,133	12.50	NR
1979–81	THERE'S A TIME TO WINK AS WELL AS A TIME TO SEE, 13,133	12.50	NR
1979–81	A TRUE FRIEND SAVED IS A PENNY EARNED, 13,133	12.50	NR
1979–81	GREAT TALKERS, LITTLE DOERS, 13,133	12.50	NR
1979–81	EARLY TO BED, AND EARLY TO RISE, MAKES A MAN HEALTHY, WEALTHY AND WISE, 13,133	12.50	NR
1979–81	LOST TIME IS NEVER FOUND AGAIN, 13,133	12.50	NR
1979–81	THE WORST WHEEL OF THE CART MAKES THE MOST NOISE, 13,133	12.50	NR
1979–81	KEEP THY SHOP AND THY SHOP WILL KEEP THEE, 13,133	12.50	NR
1979–81	AN EMPTY BAG CANNOT STAND UPRIGHT, 13,133	12.50	NR
1979–81	'TIS EASIER TO PREVENT BAD HABITS THAN TO BREAK THEM, 13,133	12.50	NR
1979–81	THE GOLDEN AGE NEVER WAS THE PRESENT AGE, 13,133	12.50	NR
1979–81	NO GAINS WITHOUT PAINS, 13,133	12.50	NR
1979–81	YOU CANNOT PLUCK ROSES WITHOUT FEAR OF THORNS, 13,133	12.50	NR
1979–81	BEWARE OF LITTLE EXPENSES, A SMALL LEAK WILL SINK A GREAT SHIP, 13,133	12.50	NR
1979–81	NOW I'VE A SHEEP AND A COW, EVERY BODY BIDS ME GOOD MORNING, 13,133	12.50	NR
1979–81	A QUARRELSOME MAN HAS NO GOOD NEIGHBOURS, 13,133	12.50	NR
1979–81	LOVE AND BE LOVED, 13,133	12.50	NR
1979–81	LOOK BEFORE, OR YOU'LL FIND YOURSELF BEHIND, 13,133	12.50	NR

Presidential Inaugural

1973	NIXON/AGNEW, Gilroy Roberts, 10,483	150.00	160.00
1974	FORD, Mico Kaufman, 11	3,500.00	3,600.00
1974	FORD, Mico Kaufman, 1,141	200.00	225.00
1977	CARTER, Julian Harris, 928	225.00	NR

Roberts' Zodiac

1973–80	ARIES, Gilroy Roberts	150.00	165.00
1973–80	TAURUS, Gilroy Roberts	150.00	165.00
1973–80	GEMINI, Gilroy Roberts	150.00	165.00
1973–80	CANCER, Gilroy Roberts	150.00	165.00

The Snowy Owl

		ISSUE	CURRENT
1973–80	LEO, Gilroy Roberts	150.00	165.00
1973–80	VIRGO, Gilroy Roberts	150.00	165.00
1973–80	LIBRA, Gilroy Roberts	150.00	165.00
1973–80	SCORPIO, Gilroy Roberts	150.00	165.00
1973–80	SAGITTARIUS, Gilroy Roberts	150.00	165.00
1973–80	CAPRICORN, Gilroy Roberts	150.00	165.00
1973–80	AQUARIUS, Gilroy Roberts	150.00	165.00
1973–80	PISCES, Gilroy Roberts	150.00	165.00

Rockwell American Sweethearts

1977	YOUNGSTERS AT PLAY, Norman Rockwell, 1,004	120.00	160.00
1977	TEENAGERS TOGETHER, Norman Rockwell, 1,004	120.00	160.00
1978	BRIDE AND GROOM, Norman Rockwell, 1,004	120.00	160.00
1978	PROUD PARENTS, Norman Rockwell, 1,004	120.00	160.00
1978	GRADUATION DAY, Norman Rockwell, 1,004	120.00	160.00
1979	RETIREMENT KISS, Norman Rockwell, 1,004	120.00	160.00

Rockwell Christmas

1970	BRINGING HOME THE TREE, Norman Rockwell, 18,321	100.00	310.00
1971	UNDER THE MISTLETOE, Norman Rockwell, 24,792	100.00	175.00
1972	THE CAROLERS, Norman Rockwell, 29,074	125.00	165.00
1973	TRIMMING THE TREE, Norman Rockwell, 18,010	125.00	170.00
1974	HANGING THE WREATH, Norman Rockwell, 12,822	175.00	BR
1975	HOME FOR CHRISTMAS, Norman Rockwell, 11,059	180.00	190.00

Seven Seas

1976	ATLANTIC OCEAN, James Wyeth, 2,799	120.00	NR
1977	CARIBBEAN SEA, James Wyeth, 2,799	120.00	NR
1978	INDIAN OCEAN, James Wyeth, 2,799	120.00	NR
1979	PACIFIC OCEAN, James Wyeth, 2,799	120.00	NR
1980	ARCTIC OCEAN, James Wyeth, 2,799	120.00	NR
1981	MEDITERRANEAN SEA, James Wyeth, 2,799	120.00	NR
1982	SOUTH CHINA SEA, James Wyeth, 2,799	120.00	NR

Songbirds of the World

1977–81	BALTIMORE ORIOLE, Arthur Singer, 20,225	55.00	NR
1977–81	BOHEMIAN WAXWING, Arthur Singer, 20,225	55.00	NR
1977–81	MAGNOLIA WARBLER, Arthur Singer, 20,225	55.00	NR
1977–81	BOBOLINK, Arthur Singer, 20,225	55.00	NR
1977–81	WESTERN BLUEBIRD, Arthur Singer, 20,225	55.00	NR
1977–81	CARDINAL, Arthur Singer, 20,225	55.00	NR
1977–81	EUROPEAN GOLDFINCH, Arthur Singer, 20,225	55.00	NR
1977–81	WOOD THRUSH, Arthur Singer, 20,225	55.00	NR
1977–81	SCARLET TANAGER, Arthur Singer, 20,225	55.00	NR
1977–81	BARN SWALLOW, Arthur Singer, 20,225	55.00	NR
1977–81	BLUETHROAT, Arthur Singer, 20,225	55.00	NR
1977–81	TURQUOISE WREN, Arthur Singer, 20,225	55.00	NR

Songbirds of the World Miniatures

1980–83	GOLDFINCH, Colin Newman	14.50	NR
1980–83	PAINTED BUNTING, Colin Newman	14.50	NR
1980–83	BLUE TIT, Colin Newman	14.50	NR
1980–83	CHAFFINCH, Colin Newman	14.50	NR

		ISSUE	CURRENT
1980–83	YELLOWHAMMER, Colin Newman	14.50	NR
1980–83	EUROPEAN ROBIN, Colin Newman	14.50	NR
1980–83	CARDINAL, Colin Newman	14.50	NR
1980–83	GOLDEN-FRONTED LEAFBIRD, Colin Newman	14.50	NR
1980–83	REDSTART, Colin Newman	14.50	NR
1980–83	RUFOUS OVENBIRD, Colin Newman	14.50	NR
1980–83	GOLDEN ORIOLE, Colin Newman	14.50	NR
1980–83	DIAMOND FIRETAIL FINCH, Colin Newman	14.50	NR
1980–83	RUFOUS BELLIED NITAVA, Colin Newman	14.50	NR
1980–83	ASIAN FAIRY BLUEBIRD, Colin Newman	14.50	NR
1980–83	BARN SWALLOW, Colin Newman	14.50	NR
1980–83	WESTERN TANAGER, Colin Newman	14.50	NR
1980–83	BLUE JAY, Colin Newman	14.50	NR

Tales of Enchantment

1982	ALICE IN WONDERLAND, Carol Lawson, limited	55.00	NR
1982	PETER PAN, Carol Lawson, limited	55.00	NR
1982	THE WIND IN THE WILLOWS, Carol Lawson, limited	55.00	NR

Teddy Bear Museum

1994	JUST MARRIED, Brooks	NA	RI

Thanksgiving by Dohanos

1972	THE FIRST THANKSGIVING, Steven Dohanos, 10,142	125.00	150.00
1973	AMERICAN WILD TURKEY, Steven Dohanos, 3,547	125.00	150.00
1974	THANKSGIVING PRAYER, Steven Dohanos, 5,150	150.00	NR
1975	FAMILY THANKSGIVING, Steven Dohanos, 3,025	175.00	200.00
1976	HOME FROM THE HUNT, Steven Dohanos, 3,474	175.00	200.00

Three Stooges Lifetime of Laughter

1996	THE COOKING LESSON, Drew Struzan, 45 days	29.95	RI

Western Series

1972	HORIZONS WEST, Richard Baldwin, sterling silver, 5,860	150.00	160.00
1972	HORIZONS WEST, Richard Baldwin, 22KT gold, 67	2,200.00	2,350.00
1973	MOUNTAIN MAN, Gordon Phillips, sterling silver, 5,860	150.00	185.00
1973	MOUNTAIN MAN, Gordon Phillips, 22KT gold, 67	2,200.00	2,350.00
1973	PROSPECTOR, Gus Shaefer, sterling silver, 5,860	150.00	185.00
1973	PROSPECTOR, Gus Shaefer, 22KT gold, 69	2,200.00	2,350.00
1973	PLAINS HUNTER, John Weaver, sterling silver, 5,860	150.00	185.00
1973	PLAINS HUNTER, John Weaver, 22KT gold, 67	2,200.00	2,350.00

Woodland Birds of the World

1980–82	BLUE JAY, Arthur Singer, 5,507	65.00	NR
1980–82	WHITE-WINGED CROSSBILL, Arthur Singer, 5,507	65.00	NR
1980–82	PAINTED REDSTART, Arthur Singer, 5,507	65.00	NR
1980–82	RIVOLI'S HUMMINGBIRD, Arthur Singer, 5,507	65.00	NR
1980–82	CHAFFINCH, Arthur Singer, 5,507	65.00	NR
1980–82	COLLARED TROGON, Arthur Singer, 5,507	65.00	NR
1980–82	EVENING GROSBEAK, Arthur Singer, 5,507	65.00	NR
1980–82	GREAT SPOTTED WOODPECKER, Arthur Singer, 5,507	65.00	NR
1980–82	RAINBOW LORIKEET, Arthur Singer, 5,507	65.00	NR

		ISSUE	CURRENT
1980–82	TAWNY OWL, Arthur Singer, 5,507	65.00	NR
1980–82	WOODLAND KINGFISHER, Arthur Singer, 5,507	65.00	NR
1980–82	GOLDEN PHEASANT, Arthur Singer, 5,507	65.00	NR

Woodland Year

1980–83	FAWNS IN THE JUNE MEADOW, Peter Barratt	55.00	NR
1980–83	BUTTERFLY CHASE IN MAY, Peter Barratt	55.00	NR
1980–83	RABBITS IN A JULY FIELD, Peter Barratt	55.00	NR
1980–83	STRIPED SKUNKS AT A MARCH STREAM, Peter Barratt	55.00	NR
1980–83	SQUIRRELING FOR NUTS IN JANUARY, Peter Barratt	55.00	NR
1980–83	CURIOUS RACCOONS AT AN APRIL POND, Peter Barratt	55.00	NR
1980–83	AMERICAN MARTEN IN THE NOVEMBER PINES, Peter Barratt	55.00	NR
1980–83	THE PLAYFUL BADGERS IN OCTOBER, Peter Barratt	55.00	NR
1980–83	COZY DORMOUSE IN THE DECEMBER WOODS, Peter Barratt	55.00	NR
1980–83	WOODCHUCKS IN FEBRUARY THAW, Peter Barratt	55.00	NR
1980–83	OTTER AT SEPTEMBER WATERFALL, Peter Barratt	55.00	NR

World's Great Porcelain Houses

1981–83	CROWN STAFFORDSHIRE	19.50	NR
1981–83	MOSA	19.50	NR
1981–83	HUTSCHENREUTHER	19.50	NR
1981–83	HAVILAND	19.50	NR
1981–83	WEDGWOOD	19.50	NR
1981–83	LANGENTHAL	19.50	NR
1981–83	PORSGRUND	19.50	NR
1981–83	NORITAKE	19.50	NR
1981–83	ROSTRAND	19.50	NR
1981–83	FRANKLIN	19.50	NR
1981–83	AK KAISER	19.50	NR
1981–83	THE ROYAL COPENHAGEN	19.50	NR
1981–83	ROYAL DOULTON	19.50	NR
1981–83	ZSOLNAY	19.50	NR
1981–83	OKURA	19.50	NR
1981–83	VERBANO	19.50	NR
1981–83	LILIEN PORZELAN	19.50	NR
1981–83	ROYAL WORCESTER	19.50	NR
1981–83	GINORY	19.50	NR
1981–83	LLADRO	19.50	NR
1981–83	FRANCISCAN	19.50	NR
1981–83	RAYNAUD	19.50	NR

Single Issues

1976	LIBERTY TREE CRYSTAL, 10,927	120.00	130.00
1976	PARTRIDGE IN A PEAR TREE, 1,453	150.00	185.00
1977	INFANT, Abram Belski, 290	210.00	275.00
1977	LAFAYETTE AND WASHINGTON, 546	275.00	325.00
1977	OLD-FASHIONED THANKSGIVING, Norman Rockwell, 1,361	185.00	225.00
1977	THE SKATING PARTY, Vincent Miller, 908	55.00	BR
1978	AIR FORCE ASSOCIATION	95.00	105.00
1978	BEN FRANKLIN, PRINTER, 281	65.00	NR
1978	CINDERELLA, Pauline Ellison, 29,439	55.00	NR
1978	ORIENTAL	32.50	NR
1979	BUTTERFLY, set of 4	38.00	NR

		ISSUE	CURRENT
1979	PETER PAN, Carol Lawson, 5,391	39.00	NR
1979	PRINCE AND PRINCESS, T. Okamoto	85.00	NR
1979	UNIVERSITY OF PENNSYLVANIA, T. T. McKenzie, 226	125.00	140.00
1980	ANGEL WITH TRUMPET, Maureen Jensen, 8,696	17.50	NR
1980	GREAT EGRETS, James Fenwick Lansdowne, 2,384	65.00	NR
1980	LE JOUR DES AMOUREUS, Raymond Peynet, 5,332	50.00	NR
1981	ROYAL WEDDING BOUQUET, Mary Grierson	75.00	NR
1983	THE BARN OWL, Basil Ede, limited	95.00	NR
1995	KITTEN COMPANIONS, N. Matthes, 45 days	55.00	RI
1995	THE IMPERIAL HUMMINGBIRD, T. Politowica, 45 days	29.95	RI
1997	PRINCESS DIANA TRIBUTE PLATE	29.95	RI
1998	THE THREE STOOGES, Drew Struzan	58.00	RI
1998	THE DRAGON MASTER, Myles Pinkney (Royal Doulton)	29.95	RI

FRANKLIN PORCELAIN UNITED STATES

Birds of the Countryside (National Audubon Society)

1983	BUILDING THE NEST (NORTHERN ORIOLE), Anthony J. Rudisill, 1 year	55.00	NR
1983	EXPLORING THE WOODS (WOODPECKER), Anthony J. Rudisill, 1 year	55.00	NR
1983	EMBRACING CHICKS (BARN OWL), Anthony J. Rudisill, 1 year	55.00	NR
1983	PROTECTING THE NEST (BLUE JAY), Anthony J. Rudisill, 1 year	55.00	NR
1983	LEARNING TO FLY (SCARLET TANAGER), Anthony J. Rudisill, 1 year	55.00	NR
1983	BATHING IN POND (GOLDFINCH), Anthony J. Rudisill, 1 year	55.00	NR

Exploring the Woods
Photo courtesy of *Collectors News*

FRANKOMA POTTERY UNITED STATES

Bicentennial

1972	PROVOCATIONS, John Frank, 1 year	5.00	40.00
1973	PATRIOTS—LEADERS, John Frank, 1 year	5.00	40.00
1974	BATTLES FOR INDEPENDENCE, Joniece Frank, 1 year	5.00	40.00
1975	VICTORIES FOR INDEPENDENCE, Joniece Frank, 1 year	5.00	40.00
1976	SYMBOLS OF FREEDOM, Joniece Frank, 1 year	6.00	40.00

Christmas

		ISSUE	CURRENT
1965	GOODWILL TOWARD MEN, John Frank, 1 year	3.50	300.00
1966	JOY TO THE WORLD, John Frank, 1 year	3.50	90.00
1967	GIFTS FOR THE CHRIST CHILD, John Frank, 1 year	3.50	75.00
1968	FLIGHT INTO EGYPT, John Frank, 1 year	3.50	55.00
1969	LAID IN A MANGER, John Frank, 1 year	4.50	40.00
1970	KING OF KINGS, John Frank, 1 year	4.50	40.00
1971	NO ROOM IN THE INN, John Frank, 1 year	4.50	35.00
1972	SEEKING THE CHRIST CHILD, John Frank, 1 year	5.00	35.00
1973	THE ANNUNCIATION, John Frank, 1 year	5.00	35.00
1974	SHE LOVED AND CARED, Joniece Frank, 1 year	5.00	35.00
1975	PEACE ON EARTH, Joniece Frank, 1 year	5.00	35.00
1976	THE GIFT OF LOVE, Joniece Frank, 1 year	6.00	30.00
1977	BIRTH OF ETERNAL LIFE, Joniece Frank, 1 year	6.00	30.00
1978	ALL NATURE REJOICED, Joniece Frank, 1 year	7.50	30.00
1979	THE STAR OF HOPE, Joniece Frank, 1 year	7.50	30.00
1980	UNTO US A CHILD IS BORN, Joniece Frank, 1 year	10.00	30.00
1981	O COME LET US ADORE HIM, Joniece Frank, 1 year	12.00	25.00
1982	THE WISE MEN REJOICE, Joniece Frank, 1 year	12.00	25.00
1983	THE WISE MEN BRING GIFTS, Joniece Frank, 1 year	12.00	25.00
1984	FAITH, HOPE AND LOVE, Joniece Frank, 1 year	12.00	25.00
1985	THE ANGELS WATCHED, Joniece Frank, 1 year	12.00	25.00
1986	FOR THEE I PLAY MY DRUM, Joniece Frank, 1 year	12.00	25.00
1987	GOD'S CHOSEN FAMILY, Joniece Frank, 1 year	12.00	25.00
1988	THE GUIDING LIGHT	NA	25.00
1989	THE BLESSING OF CHRISTMAS	NA	25.00
1990	THE ANGELS REJOICE	NA	25.00
1991	LET THERE BE PEACE	NA	20.00
1992	AND HE CALLED HIS NAME JESUS	NA	20.00
1993	PROCLAIMING THE MIRACLE	NA	RI
1994	THE FIRST CHRISTMAS CAROL	NA	RI

Madonna Plates

1977	THE GRACE MADONNA, Grace Lee Frank, 1 year	12.50	25.00
1978	MADONNA OF LOVE, Grace Lee Frank, 1 year	12.50	25.00
1981	THE ROSE MADONNA, Grace Lee Frank, 1 year	15.00	NR
1986	THE YOUTHFUL MADONNA, Grace Lee Frank, 1 year	15.00	NR

Teenagers of the Bible

1972	JESUS THE CARPENTER, John Frank, 1 year	5.00	40.00
1974	DAVID THE MUSICIAN, John Frank, 1 year	5.00	40.00
1975	JONATHAN THE ARCHER, John Frank, 1 year	5.00	40.00
1976	DORCAS THE SEAMSTRESS, Joniece Frank, 1 year	6.00	45.00
1977	PETER THE FISHERMAN, Joniece Frank, 1 year	6.00	30.00
1978	MARTHA THE HOMEMAKER, Joniece Frank, 1 year	7.50	30.00
1979	DANIEL THE COURAGEOUS, Joniece Frank, 1 year	7.50	30.00
1980	RUTH THE DEVOTED, Joniece Frank, 1 year	10.00	30.00
1981	JOSEPH THE DREAMER, Joniece Frank, 1 year	12.00	30.00
1982	MARY THE MOTHER, Joniece Frank, 1 year	12.00	30.00

Wildlife

1972	BOBWHITE QUAIL, 1,000	NA	80.00
1973	WHITE-TAILED DEER, 1,000	NA	80.00

		ISSUE	CURRENT
1974	PRAIRIE CHICKEN, 1,000	NA	80.00
1975	LARGEMOUTH BASS, 1,000	NA	80.00
1977	GRAY SQUIRREL, 1,000	NA	70.00
1978	WILD TURKEY, 1,000	NA	70.00
1979	BUFFALO, 1,000	NA	70.00

Single Issues

1971	CONESTOGA WAGON, John Frank, 2,000, 8½"	NA	85.00
1977	THE BRAILLE SYSTEM, Joniece Frank, 500, 9"	NA	65.00
1989	OKLAHOMA LAND RUN	NA	15.00
1993	FRANKOMA 60TH ANNIVERSARY, Joniece Frank	NA	RI
NA	THE SOONER STATE, OKLAHOMA	NA	RI
NA	TEXAS STATE PLATE	NA	RI

FUKAGAWA JAPAN

Warabe No Haiku

1977	BENEATH PLUM BRANCH, Shunsuke Suetomi, 1 year	38.00	45.00
1978	CHILD OF STRAW, Shunsuke Suetomi, 1 year	42.00	NR
1979	DRAGON DANCE, Shunsuke Suetomi, 1 year	42.50	NR
1980	MASK DANCING, Shunsuke Suetomi, 1 year	42.00	90.00

FURSTENBERG GERMANY

(Reco International)

Christmas

1971	RABBITS, 7,000	15.00	30.00
1972	SNOWY VILLAGE, 6,000	15.00	NR
1973	CHRISTMAS EVE, 4,000	18.00	35.00
1974	SPARROWS, 4,000	20.00	30.00
1975	DEER FAMILY, 4,000	22.00	30.00
1976	WINTER BIRDS, 4,000	25.00	NR

Deluxe Christmas

1971	WISE MEN, E. Grossberg, 1,500	45.00	NR
1972	HOLY FAMILY, E. Grossberg, 2,000	45.00	NR
1973	CHRISTMAS EVE, E. Grossberg, 2,000	60.00	NR

Easter

1971	SHEEP, 3,500	15.00	150.00
1972	CHICKS, 6,000	15.00	60.00
1973	BUNNIES, 4,000	16.00	80.00
1974	PUSSYWILLOW, 4,000	20.00	35.00
1975	EASTER WINDOW, 4,000	22.00	30.00
1976	FLOWER COLLECTING, 4,000	25.00	NR

Mother's Day

1972	HUMMINGBIRDS, 6,000	15.00	45.00
1973	HEDGEHOGS, 5,000	16.00	40.00
1974	DOE AND FAWN, 4,000	20.00	30.00

		ISSUE	CURRENT
1975	SWANS, 4,000	22.00	NR
1976	KOALA BEARS, 4,000	25.00	30.00

Muninger's Romantic Winter Impressions

1987	ICE SKATERS/EVENING SUN, Muninger	34.50	NR
1987	ICE FISHERS/VILLAGE POND, Muninger	34.50	NR
1987	REFRESHMENTS/WINTER FEST, Muninger	37.50	NR
1987	VISIT OF THE PEDDLER, Muninger	37.50	NR
1988	ON THE WAY TO CHURCH, Muninger	37.50	NR
1988	A REST AFTER WORK, Muninger	37.50	NR
1988	RETURN OF THE WOODCUTTERS, Muninger	39.50	NR
1988	FIRST SIGNS OF SPRING, Muninger	39.50	NR

Olympic

1972	MUNICH, J. Poluszynski, 5,000	20.00	75.00
1976	MONTREAL, J. Poluszynski, 5,000	37.50	NR

Wild Beauties

1989	BY THE WAYSIDE	34.50	NR
1989	AT THE POND	34.50	NR
1989	ON THE WALL	37.50	NR
1990	BETWEEN THE ROCKS	37.50	NR
1991	IN THE GLADE	37.50	NR
1991	IN THE BOG	37.50	NR
1991	AT THE WATERFALL	39.50	NR
1991	IN THE UNDERGROWTH	39.50	60.00
1991	BY THE CORNFIELD	42.50	70.00
1992	BY THE CASTLE RUIN	42.50	RI
1992	AT THE FOUNTAIN	42.50	RI

GALWAY IRISH CRYSTAL UNITED STATES

Christmas Annual

1987	THE HOLY FAMILY, Raphael	75.00	NR

The Holy Family
Photo courtesy of *Collectors News*

GANZ

Cottage Collectibles

		ISSUE	CURRENT
1998	CELEBRATION, Carol E. Kirby, 2,400	24.00	RI

Watching Over You

		ISSUE	CURRENT
1996	WINGS OF THE WIND, C. Thammavongsa, open	40.00	RI

GARTLAN USA UNITED STATES

Al Barlick

		ISSUE	CURRENT
1991	PLATE, M. Taylor, open, 3¼"	16.00	NR

Bob Cousy

		ISSUE	CURRENT
1994	SIGNED PLATE, M. Taylor, 950, 10¼"	175.00	RI
1994	PLATE, M. Taylor, 10,000, 8½"	30.00	RI
1994	PLATE, M. Taylor, open, 3¼"	15.00	RI

Brett and Bobby Hull

		ISSUE	CURRENT
1992	HOCKEY'S GOLDEN BOYS, sgd, M. Taylor, 950, 10¼"	250.00	150.00
1992	HOCKEY'S GOLDEN BOYS, M. Taylor, 10,000, 8½"	30.00	NR
1992	HOCKEY'S GOLDEN BOYS, M. Taylor, open, 3¼"	15.00	NR
1992	HOCKEY'S GOLDEN BOYS, sgd, M. Taylor, artist proof, 300, 10¼"	350.00	BR

Carl Yastrzemski—The Impossible Dream

		ISSUE	CURRENT
1993	SIGNED PLATE, M. Taylor, 950, 10¼"	175.00	RI
1993	PLATE, M. Taylor, 10,000, 8½"	30.00	RI
1993	PLATE, M. Taylor, open, 3¼"	15.00	RI

Carlton Fisk

		ISSUE	CURRENT
1993	SIGNED PLATE, M. Taylor, 950, 10¼"	175.00	RI
1993	SIGNED PLATE, M. Taylor, artist proof, 300, 10¼"	175.00	RI
1993	PLATE, M. Taylor, 5,000, 8½"	30.00	RI
1993	PLATE, M. Taylor, open, 3¼"	15.00	RI

Club Gift

		ISSUE	CURRENT
1989	PETE ROSE, B. Forbes, 1 year, 8½"	gift	NA
1990	AL BARLICK, M. Taylor, 1 year, 8½"	gift	NA
1991	JOE MONTANA, M. Taylor, 1 year, 8½"	gift	NA
1992	KEN GRIFFEY JR., M. Taylor, 1 year, 8½"	gift	NA
1993	GORDIE HOWE, M. Taylor, 1 year, 8½"	gift	RI
1994	SHAQUILLE O'NEAL, M. Taylor, 1 year, 8½"	gift	RI
1996	RINGO STARR, M. Taylor, 1 year, 8½"	gift	RI
1997	JERRY GARCIA, M. Taylor, 1 year, 8⅛"	gift	RI

Coaching Classics—John Wooden

		ISSUE	CURRENT
1989	SIGNED PLATE, M. Taylor, 1,975, 10¼"	150.00	NR
1989	PLATE, M. Taylor, 10,000, 8½"	40.00	NR
1989	PLATE, M. Taylor, open, 3¼"	15.00	NR

		ISSUE	CURRENT

Dale Earnhardt

		ISSUE	CURRENT
1995	SIGNED PLATE, M. Taylor, 1,995, 10¼"	150.00	RI
1995	PLATE, M. Taylor, 10,000, 8½"	40.00	RI
1995	PLATE, M. Taylor, open, 3¼"	15.00	RI

Darryl Strawberry

		ISSUE	CURRENT
1991	SIGNED PLATE, M. Taylor, 2,500, 10¼"	150.00	BR
1991	PLATE, M. Taylor, 10,000, 8½"	40.00	BR
1991	PLATE, M. Taylor, open, 3¼"	15.00	NR

Frank Thomas

		ISSUE	CURRENT
1994	SIGNED PLATE, M. Taylor, 1,994, 10¼"	150.00	RI
1994	PLATE, M. Taylor, 10,000, 8½"	40.00	RI
1994	PLATE, M. Taylor, open, 3¼"	15.00	RI

George Brett Gold Crown Collection

		ISSUE	CURRENT
1986	GEORGE BRETT "BASEBALL'S ALL STAR," John Martin, sgd, 2,000, 10¼"	100.00	200.00
1986	GEORGE BRETT "BASEBALL'S ALL STAR," John Martin, open, 3¼"	15.00	NR
1986	GEORGE BRETT "BASEBALL'S ALL STAR," John Martin, artist proof, 24, 10¼"	225.00	BR

Gordie Howe

		ISSUE	CURRENT
1993	SIGNED PLATE, M. Taylor, 2,358, 10¼"	150.00	RI
1993	SIGNED PLATE, M. Taylor, artist proof, 250, 10¼"	195.00	RI
1993	PLATE, M. Taylor, 10,000, 8½"	30.00	RI
1993	PLATE, M. Taylor, open, 3¼"	15.00	RI

Jerry Garcia

		ISSUE	CURRENT
1997	JERRY GARCIA, M. Taylor, 1,995, 10¼"	125.00	RI
1997	JERRY GARCIA, M. Taylor, 300, artist proof, 10¼"	225.00	RI
1997	JERRY GARCIA, M. Taylor, open, 3¼"	15.00	RI
1997	JERRY GARCIA, M. Taylor, 10,000, 8¼"	30.00	RI

Joe Montana

		ISSUE	CURRENT
1991	SIGNED PLATE, M. Taylor, 2,250, 10¼"	125.00	275.00
1991	SIGNED PLATE, M. Taylor, artist proof, 250, 10¼"	195.00	375.00
1991	PLATE, M. Taylor, 10,000, 8½"	30.00	NR
1991	PLATE, M. Taylor, open, 3¼"	15.00	NR

John Lennon

		ISSUE	CURRENT
1997	JOHN LENNON CHRISTMAS, J. Lennon, 10,000, 8⅛"	30.00	RI
1997	JOHN LENNON CHRISTMAS, J. Lennon, open, plate/ornament, 3¼"	15.00	RI

John Lennon Artwork

		ISSUE	CURRENT
1998	PEACE BROTHER, J. Lennon, 10,000, 8⅛"	30.00	RI
1998	BORROWED TIME, J. Lennon, 10,000, 8⅛"	30.00	RI
1998	FAMILY TREE, J. Lennon, 10,000, 8⅛"	30.00	RI
1998	IMAGINE, J. Lennon, 10,000, 8⅛"	30.00	RI

Johnny Bench

		ISSUE	CURRENT
1989	SIGNED PLATE, M. Taylor, 1,989, 10¼"	100.00	NR

		ISSUE	CURRENT
1989	PLATE, M. Taylor, open, 3¼"	15.00	NR

Kareem Abdul-Jabbar Sky-Hook Collection

1989	KAREEM ABDUL-JABBAR "PATH OF GLORY," M. Taylor, sgd, 1,989, 10¼"	100.00	150.00
1989	PLATE, M. Taylor, closed, 3¼"	15.00	NR

Ken Griffey, Jr.

1992	SIGNED PLATE, M. Taylor, 1,989, 10¼"	150.00	BR
1992	SIGNED PLATE, M. Taylor, artist proof, 300, 10½"	195.00	NR
1992	PLATE, M. Taylor, 10,000, 8½"	30.00	NR
1992	PLATE, M. Taylor, open, 3¼"	15.00	NR

KISS Kollectibles

1997	KISS, M. Taylor, sgd, 1,000, 10¼"	275.00	RI
1997	KISS, M. Taylor, sgd, 250, artist proof, 10¼"	495.00	RI
1997	KISS, M. Taylor, open, 3¼"	15.00	RI
1997	KISS, M. Taylor, 10,000, 8¼"	30.00	RI

Kristi Yamaguchi

1993	SIGNED PLATE, M. Taylor, 950, 10¼"	150.00	RI
1993	PLATE, M. Taylor, 5,000, 8½"	30.00	RI
1993	PLATE, M. Taylor, open, 3¼"	15.00	RI

Leave It to Beaver

1995	JERRY MATHERS, M. Taylor, sgd, 1,963, 10¼"	125.00	RI
1995	JERRY MATHERS, M. Taylor, sgd, 234, artist proof, 10¼"	175.00	RI
1995	JERRY MATHERS, M. Taylor, 10,000, 8¼"	39.95	RI
1995	JERRY MATHERS, M. Taylor, open, 3¼"	14.95	RI

Luis Aparicio

1990	SIGNED PLATE, M. Taylor, 1,984, 10¼"	150.00	250.00
1990	SIGNED PLATE, M. Taylor, artist proof, 250, 10¼"	150.00	NR
1990	PLATE, M. Taylor, 10,000, 8½"	30.00	NR
1990	PLATE, M. Taylor, open, 3¼"	15.00	NR

Magic Johnson Gold Rim Collection

1987	MAGIC JOHNSON "THE MAGIC SHOW," R. Winslow, sgd, 1,987, 10¼"	100.00	350.00
1987	MAGIC JOHNSON "THE MAGIC SHOW," R. Winslow, closed, 3¼"	14.50	NR

Mike Schmidt "500th" Home Run Edition

1987	MIKE SCHMIDT "POWER AT THE PLATE," Christopher Paluso, sgd, 1,987, 10¼"	100.00	325.00
1987	MIKE SCHMIDT "POWER AT THE PLATE," Christopher Paluso, open, 3¼"	14.50	NR
1987	MIKE SCHMIDT, Christopher Paluso, artist proof, 56	150.00	NR

Patrick Ewing

1995	SIGNED PLATE, M. Taylor, 950, 10¼"	150.00	RI
1995	PLATE, M. Taylor, 10,000, 8½"	29.95	RI
1995	PLATE, M. Taylor, open, 3¼"	14.95	RI

Pete Rose Diamond Collection

		ISSUE	CURRENT
1988	PETE ROSE "THE REIGNING LEGEND," B. Forbes, sgd, 950, 10¼"	195.00	250.00
1988	PETE ROSE "THE REIGNING LEGEND," B. Forbes, sgd, artist proof, 50, 10¼"	300.00	350.00
1988	PETE ROSE "THE REIGNING LEGEND," B. Forbes, open, 3¼"	14.50	NR

Pete Rose Platinum Edition

1985	PETE ROSE "THE BEST OF BASEBALL," Ted Sizemore, sgd, 4,192, 10¼"	100.00	275.00
1985	PETE ROSE, "THE BEST OF BASEBALL," Ted Sizemore, open, 3¼"	12.95	NR

Phil Esposito

1992	SIGNED PLATE, M. Taylor, 1,984, 10¼"	150.00	NR
1992	SIGNED PLATE, M. Taylor, artist proof, 250, 10¼"	195.00	NR
1992	PLATE, M. Taylor, 10,000, 8½"	49.00	NR
1992	PLATE, M. Taylor, open, 3¼"	19.00	NR

Ringo All-Starr Collection

1996	RINGO STARR, M. Taylor, sgd, 1,000, 10¼"	225.00	RI
1996	RINGO STARR, M. Taylor, sgd, artist proof, 250, 10¼"	400.00	RI
1996	RINGO STARR, M. Taylor, 10,000, 8¼"	29.95	RI
1996	RINGO STARR, M. Taylor, open, 3¼"	14.95	RI

Rod Carew

1991	ROD CAREW "HITTING FOR THE HALL," M. Taylor, 950, 10¼"	150.00	NR
1991	ROD CAREW "HITTING FOR THE HALL," M. Taylor, 10,000, 8½"	30.00	NR
1991	ROD CAREW "HITTING FOR THE HALL," M. Taylor, open, 3¼"	15.00	NR

Roger Staubach Sterling Collection

1987	ROGER STAUBACH, Charles Soileau, sgd, 1,979, 10¼"	100.00	300.00
1987	ROGER STAUBACH, Charles Soileau, open, 3¼"	12.95	20.00

Round Tripper

1986	REGGIE JACKSON, John Martin, open, 3¼"	12.50	NR

Mike Schmidt "Power at the Plate"
Photo courtesy of *Collectors News*

Rod Carew "Hitting for the Hall"
Photo courtesy of *Collectors News*

		ISSUE	CURRENT

Sam Snead

		ISSUE	CURRENT
1994	SIGNED PLATE, M. Taylor, 950, 10¼"	100.00	RI
1994	PLATE, M. Taylor, 5,000, 8½"	30.00	RI
1994	PLATE, M. Taylor, open, 3¼"	15.00	RI

Shaquille O'Neal

		ISSUE	CURRENT
1994	SIGNED PLATE, M. Taylor, 1,993, 10¼"	195.00	RI
1994	PLATE, M. Taylor, 10,000, 8½"	30.00	RI
1994	PLATE, M. Taylor, open, 3¼"	14.95	RI

Shaquille O'Neal Club Plate

		ISSUE	CURRENT
1994	PLATE, M. Taylor	30.00	RI

Tom Seaver

		ISSUE	CURRENT
1993	SIGNED PLATE, M. Taylor, 1,992, 10¼"	150.00	RI
1993	SIGNED PLATE, M. Taylor, artist proof, 250, 10¼"	195.00	RI
1993	PLATE, M. Taylor, 10,000, 8½"	30.00	RI
1993	PLATE, M. Taylor, open, 3¼"	15.00	RI

Troy Aikman

		ISSUE	CURRENT
1994	SIGNED PLATE, M. Taylor, 1,993, 10¼"	225.00	RI
1994	PLATE, M. Taylor, 10,000, 8½"	30.00	RI
1994	PLATE, M. Taylor, open, 3¼"	14.95	RI

Wayne Gretzky

		ISSUE	CURRENT
1989	SIGNED PLATE, M. Taylor, sgd by Gretzky and Howe, 1,851, 10¼"	225.00	250.00
1989	SIGNED PLATE, M. Taylor, sgd by Gretzky and Howe, artist proof, 300, 10¼"	300.00	450.00
1989	PLATE, M. Taylor, 10,000, 8½"	30.00	NR
1989	PLATE, M. Taylor, open, 3¼"	15.00	NR

Whitey Ford

		ISSUE	CURRENT
1991	SIGNED PLATE, M. Taylor, 2,360, 10¼"	150.00	NR
1991	SIGNED PLATE, M. Taylor, artist proof, 250, 10¼"	175.00	NR
1991	PLATE, M. Taylor, 10,000, 8½"	30.00	NR
1991	PLATE, M. Taylor, open, 3¼"	15.00	NR

Yogi Berra

		ISSUE	CURRENT
1989	SIGNED PLATE, M. Taylor, sgd, 2,150, 10¼"	150.00	BR
1989	SIGNED PLATE, M. Taylor, sgd, artist proof, 250, 10¼"	175.00	NR
1989	PLATE, M. Taylor, 10,000, 8½"	45.00	NR
1989	PLATE, M. Taylor, open, 3¼"	16.00	NR

W. S. GEORGE UNITED STATES

Alaska: The Last Frontier

		ISSUE	CURRENT
1991	ICY MAJESTY, H. Lambson, 150 days	34.50	NR
1991	AUTUMN GRANDEUR, H. Lambson, 150 days	34.50	NR
1992	MOUNTAIN MONARCH, H. Lambson, 150 days	37.50	NR
1992	DOWN THE TRAIL, H. Lambson, 150 days	37.50	NR
1992	MOONLIGHT LOOKOUT, H. Lambson, 150 days	37.50	55.00

		ISSUE	CURRENT
1992	GRACEFUL PASSAGE, H. Lambson, 150 days	39.50	60.00
1992	ARCTIC JOURNEY, H. Lambson, 150 days	39.95	50.00
1992	SUMMIT DOMAIN, H. Lambson, 150 days	39.50	60.00

Along an English Lane

1993	SUMMER'S BRIGHT WELCOME, M. Harvey, 95 days	29.50	RI
1993	GREETING THE DAY, M. Harvey, 95 days	29.50	RI
1993	FRIENDS AND FLOWERS	29.50	RI
1993	COTTAGE AROUND THE BEND	29.50	RI

America's Pride

1992	MISTY FJORDS, R. Richert, 150 days	29.50	35.00
1992	RUGGED SHORES, R. Richert, 150 days	29.50	40.00
1992	MIGHTY SUMMIT, R. Richert, 150 days	32.50	45.00
1993	LOFTY REFLECTIONS, R. Richert, 150 days	32.50	RI
1993	TRANQUIL WATERS, R. Richert, 150 days	32.50	RI
1993	MOUNTAIN MAJESTY, R. Richert, 150 days	34.50	RI
1993	CANYON CLIMB, R. Richert, 150 days	34.50	RI
1993	GOLDEN VISTA, R. Richert, 150 days	34.50	RI

America the Beautiful

1988	YOSEMITE FALLS, H. Johnson, 150 days	34.50	BR
1988	THE GRAND CANYON, H. Johnson, 150 days	34.50	BR
1989	YELLOWSTONE RIVER, H. Johnson, 150 days	37.50	NR
1989	THE GREAT SMOKEY MOUNTAINS, H. Johnson, 150 days	37.50	BR
1990	THE EVERGLADES, H. Johnson, 150 days	37.50	NR
1990	ACADIA, H. Johnson, 150 days	37.50	NR
1990	THE GRAND TETONS, H. Johnson, 150 days	39.50	BR
1990	CRATER LAKE, H. Johnson, 150 days	39.50	BR

Art Deco

1989	A FLAPPER WITH GREYHOUNDS, M. McDonald, 150 days	39.50	NR
1990	TANGO DANCERS, M. McDonald, 150 days	39.50	55.00
1990	ARRIVING IN STYLE, M. McDonald, 150 days	39.50	55.00
1990	ON THE TOWN, M. McDonald, 150 days	39.50	60.00

Baby Cats of the Wild

1992	MORNING MISCHIEF, Charles Fracé, 95 days	29.50	45.00
1993	TOGETHERNESS, Charles Fracé, 95 days	29.50	RI
1993	THE BUDDY SYSTEM, Charles Fracé, 95 days	32.50	RI
1993	NAP TIME, Charles Fracé, 95 days	32.50	RI

Bear Tracks (Bradford Exchange)

1992	DENALI FAMILY, John Seerey-Lester, 150 days	29.50	NR
1993	THEIR FIRST SEASON, John Seerey-Lester, 150 days	29.50	RI
1993	HIGH COUNTRY CHAMPION, John Seerey-Lester, 150 days	29.50	RI
1993	HEAVY GOING, John Seerey-Lester, 150 days	29.50	RI
1993	BREAKING COVER, John Seerey-Lester, 150 days	29.50	RI
1993	ALONG THE ICE FLOW, John Seerey-Lester, 150 days	29.50	RI

Beloved Hymns of Childhood

1988	THE LORD'S MY SHEPHERD, Cicely Mary Barker, 150 days	29.50	NR

		ISSUE	CURRENT
1988	AWAY IN A MANGER, Cicely Mary Barker, 150 days	29.50	NR
1989	NOW THANK WE ALL OUR GOD, Cicely Mary Barker, 150 days	32.50	NR
1989	LOVE DIVINE, Cicely Mary Barker, 150 days	32.50	NR
1989	I LOVE TO HEAR THE STORY, Cicely Mary Barker, 150 days	32.50	NR
1989	ALL GLORY, LAUD AND HONOUR, Cicely Mary Barker, 150 days	32.50	NR
1990	ALL PEOPLE ON EARTH DO DWELL, Cicely Mary Barker, 150 days	34.50	NR
1990	LOVING SHEPHERD OF THY SHEEP, Cicely Mary Barker, 150 days	34.50	NR

Black Tie Affair: The Penguin (Bradford Exchange)

1992	LITTLE EXPLORER, Carolyn Jagodits, 150 days	29.50	40.00
1992	PENGUIN PARADE, Carolyn Jagodits, 150 days	29.50	35.00
1992	BABY-SITTERS, Carolyn Jagodits, 150 days	29.50	50.00
1993	BELLY FLOPPING, Carolyn Jagodits, 150 days	29.50	RI

Blessed Are the Children

1990	LET THE CHILDREN COME TO ME, Walter Rane, 150 days	29.50	40.00
1990	I AM THE GOOD SHEPHERD, Walter Rane, 150 days	29.50	NR
1991	WHOEVER WELCOMES/CHILD, Walter Rane, 150 days	32.50	NR
1991	HOSANNA IN THE HIGHEST, Walter Rane, 150 days	32.50	NR
1991	JESUS HAD COMPASSION ON THEM, Walter Rane, 150 days	32.50	45.00
1991	BLESSED ARE THE PEACEMAKERS, Walter Rane, 150 days	34.50	55.00
1991	I AM THE VINE, YOU ARE THE BRANCHES, Walter Rane, 150 days	34.50	50.00
1991	SEEK AND YOU WILL FIND, Walter Rane, 150 days	34.50	NR

Bonds of Love

1989	PRECIOUS EMBRACE, Brenda Burke, 150 days	29.50	NR
1990	CHERISHED MOMENT, Brenda Burke, 150 days	29.50	NR
1991	TENDER CARESS, Brenda Burke, 150 days	32.50	NR
1992	LOVING TOUCH, Brenda Burke, 150 days	32.50	NR
1993	TREASURED KISSES, Brenda Burke, 150 days	32.50	RI
1994	ENDEARING WHISPER, Brenda Burke, 150 days	32.50	RI

Christmas Story

1992	GIFTS OF THE MAGI, Hector Garrido, 150 days	29.50	40.00
1993	REST ON THE FLIGHT INTO EGYPT, Hector Garrido, 150 days	29.50	RI
1993	JOURNEY OF THE MAGI, Hector Garrido, 150 days	29.50	RI
1993	THE NATIVITY, Hector Garrido, 150 days	29.50	RI
1993	THE ANNUNCIATION, Hector Garrido, 150 days	29.50	RI
1993	ADORATION OF THE SHEPHERDS, Hector Garrido, 150 days	29.50	RI

Classic Waterfowl: Ducks Unlimited

1988	MALLARDS AT SUNRISE, Lynn Kaatz, 150 days	36.50	BR
1988	GEESE IN THE AUTUMN FIELDS, Lynn Kaatz, 150 days	36.50	BR
1989	GREEN WINGS/MORNING MARSH, Lynn Kaatz, 150 days	39.50	BR
1989	CANVASBACKS, BREAKING AWAY, Lynn Kaatz, 150 days	39.50	BR
1989	PINTAILS IN INDIAN SUMMER, Lynn Kaatz, 150 days	39.50	BR
1990	WOOD DUCKS TAKING FLIGHT, Lynn Kaatz, 150 days	39.50	BR
1990	SNOW GEESE AGAINST NOVEMBER SKIES, Lynn Kaatz, 150 days	41.50	BR
1990	BLUEBILLS COMING IN, Lynn Kaatz, 150 days	41.50	BR

Columbus Discovers America: The 500th Anniversary

1991	UNDER FULL SAIL, J. Penalva, 150 days	29.50	BR

		ISSUE	CURRENT
1992	ASHORE AT DAWN, J. Penalva, 150 days	29.50	NR
1992	COLUMBUS RAISES THE FLAG, J. Penalva, 150 days	32.50	NR
1992	BRINGING TOGETHER TWO CULTURES, J. Penalva, 150 days	32.50	40.00
1992	THE QUEEN'S APPROVAL, J. Penalva, 150 days	32.50	BR
1992	TREASURES FROM THE NEW WORLD, J. Penalva, 150 days	32.50	50.00

Country Bouquets

1991	MORNING SUNSHINE, Glenna Kurz, 150 days	29.50	40.00
1991	SUMMER PERFUME, Glenna Kurz, 150 days	29.50	NR
1992	WARM WELCOME, Glenna Kurz, 150 days	32.50	50.00
1992	GARDEN'S BOUNTY, Glenna Kurz, 150 days	32.50	45.00

Country Nostalgia

1989	THE SPRING BUGGY, M. Harvey, 150 days	29.50	BR
1989	THE APPLE CIDER PRESS, M. Harvey, 150 days	29.50	BR
1989	THE VINTAGE SEED PLANTER, M. Harvey, 150 days	29.50	NR
1989	THE OLD HAND PUMP, M. Harvey, 150 days	32.50	45.00
1990	THE WOODEN BUTTER CHURN, M. Harvey, 150 days	32.50	NR
1990	THE DAIRY CANS, M. Harvey, 150 days	32.50	NR
1990	THE FORGOTTEN PLOW, M. Harvey, 150 days	34.50	NR
1990	THE ANTIQUE SPINNING WHEEL, M. Harvey, 150 days	34.50	BR

Critic's Choice: *Gone with the Wind*

1991	MARRY ME, SCARLETT, P. Jennis, 150 days	27.50	35.00
1991	WAITING FOR RHETT, P. Jennis, 150 days	27.50	NR
1991	A DECLARATION OF LOVE, P. Jennis, 150 days	30.50	40.00
1991	THE PARIS HAT, P. Jennis, 150 days	30.50	50.00
1991	SCARLETT ASKS FOR A FAVOR, P. Jennis, 150 days	30.50	50.00
1992	SCARLETT GETS HER WAY, P. Jennis, 150 days	32.50	50.00
1992	THE SMITTEN SUITOR, P. Jennis, 150 days	32.50	45.00
1992	SCARLETT'S SHOPPING SPREE, P. Jennis, 150 days	32.50	50.00
1992	THE BUGGY RIDE, P. Jennis, 150 days	32.50	50.00
1992	SCARLETT GETS DOWN TO BUSINESS, P. Jennis, 150 days	34.50	NR
1993	SCARLETT'S HEART IS WITH TARA	34.50	RI
1993	AT CROSS PURPOSES	34.50	RI

Delicate Balance: Vanishing Wildlife (Bradford Exchange)

1992	TOMORROW'S HOPE, Greg Beecham, 95 days	29.50	40.00
1993	TODAY'S FUTURE, Greg Beecham, 95 days	29.50	RI
1993	PRESENT DREAMS, Greg Beecham, 95 days	32.50	RI
1993	EYES ON THE NEW DAY, Greg Beecham, 95 days	32.50	RI

Dr. Zhivago

1990	ZHIVAGO AND LARA, George Bush, 150 days	39.50	BR
1991	LOVE POEMS FOR LARA, George Bush, 150 days	39.50	BR
1991	ZHIVAGO SAYS FAREWELL, George Bush, 150 days	39.50	NR
1991	LARA'S LOVE, George Bush, 150 days	39.50	50.00

Elegant Birds

1988	THE SWAN, J. Faulkner, 150 days	32.50	BR
1988	GREAT BLUE HERON, J. Faulkner, 150 days	32.50	BR

		ISSUE	CURRENT
1989	SNOWY EGRET, J. Faulkner, 150 days	32.50	BR
1989	THE ANHINGA, J. Faulkner, 150 days	35.50	BR
1989	THE FLAMINGO, J. Faulkner, 150 days	35.50	BR
1990	SANDHILL AND WHOOPING CRANE, J. Faulkner, 150 days	35.50	BR

Enchanted Garden

1993	A PEACEFUL RETREAT, E. Antonaccio, 95 days	24.50	RI
1993	PLEASANT PATHWAYS, E. Antonaccio, 95 days	24.50	RI
1993	A PLACE TO DREAM, E. Antonaccio, 95 days	24.50	RI
1993	TRANQUIL HIDEAWAY, E. Antonaccio, 95 days	24.50	RI

Endangered Species

1989	THE RED WOLF	30.50	NR

Eyes of the Wild (Bradford Exchange)

1993	EYES IN THE MIST, Daniel Renn Pierce, 95 days	29.50	RI
1993	EYES IN THE PINES, Daniel Renn Pierce, 95 days	29.50	RI
1993	EYES ON THE SKY, Daniel Renn Pierce, 95 days	29.50	RI
1993	EYES OF GOLD, Daniel Renn Pierce, 95 days	29.50	RI
1993	EYES OF SILENCE, Daniel Renn Pierce, 95 days	29.50	RI
1993	EYES IN THE SNOW, Daniel Renn Pierce, 95 days	29.50	RI
1994	EYES OF WONDER, Daniel Renn Pierce, 95 days	29.50	RI
1994	EYES OF STRENGTH, Daniel Renn Pierce, 95 days	29.50	RI

Faces of Nature (Bradford Exchange0

1992	CANYON OF THE CAT, Julie Kramer Cole, 150 days	29.50	45.00
1992	WOLF RIDGE, Julie Kramer Cole, 150 days	29.50	45.00
1993	TRAIL OF THE TALISMAN, Julie Kramer Cole, 150 days	29.50	RI
1993	WOLFPACK OF THE ANCIENTS, Julie Kramer Cole, 150 days	29.50	RI
1993	TWO BEARS CAMP, Julie Kramer Cole, 150 days	29.50	RI
1993	WINTERING WITH THE WAPITI, Julie Kramer Cole, 150 days	29.50	RI
1993	WITHIN SUNRISE, Julie Kramer Cole, 150 days	29.50	RI
1993	WAMBLI, OKIYE, Julie Kramer Cole, 150 days	29.50	RI

Federal Duck Stamps

1990	THE LESSER SCAUP, 150 days	27.50	BR
1990	MALLARD, 150 days	27.50	35.00
1990	THE RUDDY DUCKS, 150 days	30.50	BR
1990	CANVASBACKS, 150 days	30.50	BR
1991	PINTAILS, 150 days	30.50	BR
1991	WIGEONS, 150 days	30.50	NR
1991	CINNAMON TEAL, 150 days	32.50	NR
1991	FULVOUS WHISTLING DUCK, Burton Moore, Jr., 150 days	32.50	45.00
1991	THE REDHEADS, Arthur Anderson	32.50	45.00
1991	SNOW GOOSE, 150 days	32.50	NR

Feline Fancy

1993	GLOBETROTTERS	34.50	RI
1993	LITTLE ATHLETES	34.50	RI
1993	YOUNG ADVENTURERS	34.50	RI
1993	THE GEOGRAPHERS	34.50	RI

ISSUE	CURRENT

Field Birds of North America

		ISSUE	CURRENT
1991	WINTER COLORS: RING-NECKED PHEASANT, Darrell Bush, 150 days	39.50	NR
1991	IN DISPLAY: RUFFED GOOSE, Darrell Bush, 150 days	39.50	NR
1991	MORNING LIGHT: BOBWHITE QUAIL, Darrell Bush, 150 days	42.50	NR
1991	MISTY CLEARING: WILD TURKEY, Darrell Bush, 150 days	42.50	70.00
1992	AUTUMN MOMENT: AMERICAN WOODCOCK, Darrell Bush, 150 days	42.50	50.00
1992	SEASON'S END: WILLOW PTARMIGAN, Darrell Bush, 150 days	42.50	60.00

Flash of Cats

1993	MOONLIGHT CHASE: COUGAR, John Seerey-Lester, 150 days	29.50	RI

Floral Fancies

1993	SITTING SOFTLY	34.50	RI
1993	SITTING PRETTY	34.50	RI
1993	SITTING SUNNY	34.50	RI
1993	SITTING PINK	34.50	RI

Flowers from Grandma's Garden

1990	COUNTRY CUTTINGS, Glenna Kurz, 150 days	24.50	40.00
1990	THE MORNING BOUQUET, Glenna Kurz, 150 days	24.50	35.00
1991	HOMESPUN BEAUTY, Glenna Kurz, 150 days	27.50	35.00
1991	HARVEST IN THE MEADOW, Glenna Kurz, 150 days	27.50	40.00
1991	GARDENER'S DELIGHT, Glenna Kurz, 150 days	27.50	40.00
1991	NATURE'S BOUNTY, Glenna Kurz, 150 days	27.50	45.00
1991	A COUNTRY WELCOME, Glenna Kurz, 150 days	29.50	50.00
1991	THE SPRINGTIME ARRANGEMENT, Glenna Kurz, 150 days	29.50	50.00

Flowers of Your Garden

1988	ROSES, Vieonne Morley, 150 days	24.50	NR
1988	LILACS, Vieonne Morley, 150 days	24.50	50.00
1988	DAISIES, Vieonne Morley, 150 days	27.50	BR
1988	PEONIES, Vieonne Morley, 150 days	27.50	BR
1988	CHRYSANTHEMUMS, Vieonne Morley, 150 days	27.50	BR
1989	DAFFODILS, Vieonne Morley, 150 days	27.50	BR
1989	TULIPS, Vieonne Morley, 150 days	29.50	BR
1989	IRISES, Vieonne Morley, 150 days	29.50	BR

Garden of the Lord

1992	LOVE ONE ANOTHER, Chuck Gillies, 150 days	29.50	40.00
1992	PERFECT PEACE, Chuck Gillies, 150 days	29.50	NR
1992	TRUST IN THE LORD, Chuck Gillies, 150 days	32.50	NR
1992	THE LORD'S LOVE, Chuck Gillies, 150 days	32.50	NR
1992	THE LORD BLESS YOU, Chuck Gillies, 150 days	32.50	NR
1992	ASK IN PRAYER, Chuck Gillies, 150 days	34.50	NR
1993	PEACE BE WITH YOU, Chuck Gillies, 150 days	34.50	RI
1993	GIVE THANKS TO THE LORD, Chuck Gillies, 150 days	34.50	RI

Gardens of Paradise

1992	TRANQUILITY, Lily Chang, 150 days	29.50	40.00
1992	SERENITY, Lily Chang, 150 days	29.50	35.00
1993	SPLENDOR, Lily Chang, 150 days	32.50	RI
1993	HARMONY, Lily Chang, 150 days	32.50	RI

Precious Embrace

Under Full Sail

Marry Me, Scarlet

Lilacs

Cardinals on a Snowy Branch

Family Outing

Photos courtesy of *Collectors News*

		ISSUE	CURRENT
1993	BEAUTY, Lily Chang, 150 days	32.50	RI
1993	ELEGANCE, Lily Chang, 150 days	32.50	RI
1993	GRANDEUR, Lily Chang, 150 days	32.50	RI
1993	MAJESTY, Lily Chang, 150 days	32.50	RI

Gentle Beginnings

1991	TENDER LOVING CARE, Will Nelson, 150 days	34.50	NR
1991	A TOUCH OF LOVE, Will Nelson, 150 days	34.50	45.00
1991	UNDER WATCHFUL EYES, Will Nelson, 150 days	37.50	70.00
1991	LAP OF LOVE, Will Nelson, 150 days	37.50	60.00
1991	HAPPY TOGETHER, Will Nelson, 150 days	37.50	80.00
1991	FIRST STEPS, Will Nelson, 150 days	37.50	80.00

Glorious Songbirds

1991	CARDINALS ON A SNOWY BRANCH, Russell Cobane, 150 days	29.50	BR
1991	INDIGO BUNTINGS AND BLOSSOMS, Russell Cobane, 150 days	29.50	BR
1991	CHICKADEES AMONG THE LILACS, Russell Cobane, 150 days	32.50	BR
1991	GOLDFINCHES IN THISTLE, Russell Cobane, 150 days	32.50	BR
1991	CEDAR WAXWING/WINTER BERRIES, Russell Cobane, 150 days	32.50	BR
1991	BLUEBIRDS IN A BLUEBERRY BUSH, Russell Cobane, 150 days	34.50	NR
1991	BALTIMORE ORIOLES/AUTUMN LEAVES, Russell Cobane, 150 days	34.50	45.00
1991	ROBINS WITH DOGWOOD IN BLOOM, Russell Cobane, 150 days	34.50	45.00

Golden Age of the Clipper Ships

1989	*THE TWILIGHT* UNDER FULL SAIL, Charles Vickery, 150 days	29.50	BR
1989	*THE BLUE JACKET* AT SUNSET, Charles Vickery, 150 days	29.50	BR
1989	*YOUNG AMERICA*, HOMEWARD, Charles Vickery, 150 days	32.50	BR
1990	*FLYING CLOUD*, Charles Vickery, 150 days	32.50	NR
1990	*DAVY CROCKETT* AT DAYBREAK, Charles Vickery, 150 days	32.50	BR
1990	*GOLDEN EAGLE* CONQUERS WIND, Charles Vickery, 150 days	32.50	NR
1990	*THE LIGHTNING* IN LIFTING FOG, Charles Vickery, 150 days	34.50	BR
1990	*SEA WITCH*, MISTRESS OF THE OCEANS, Charles Vickery, 150 days	34.50	NR

Gone with the Wind: Golden Anniversary

1988	SCARLETT AND HER SUITORS, H. Rogers, 150 days	24.50	85.00
1988	THE BURNING OF ATLANTA, H. Rogers, 150 days	24.50	35.00
1988	SCARLETT AND ASHLEY AFTER THE WAR, H. Rogers, 150 days	27.50	40.00
1988	THE PROPOSAL, H. Rogers, 150 days	27.50	50.00
1989	HOME TO TARA, H. Rogers, 150 days	27.50	35.00
1989	STROLLING IN ATLANTA, H. Rogers, 150 days,	27.50	NR
1989	A QUESTION OF HONOR, H. Rogers, 150 days,	29.50	NR
1989	SCARLETT'S RESOLVE, H. Rogers, 150 days,	29.50	40.00
1989	FRANKLY MY DEAR, H. Rogers, 150 days,	29.50	50.00
1989	MELANIE AND ASHLEY, H. Rogers, 150 days,	32.50	BR
1990	A TOAST TO BONNIE BLUE, H. Rogers, 150 days,	32.50	40.00
1990	SCARLETT AND RHETT'S HONEYMOON, H. Rogers, 150 days,	32.50	NR

Gone with the Wind: Passions of Scarlett O'Hara

1992	FIERY EMBRACE, P. Jennis, 150 days	29.50	NR
1992	PRIDE AND PASSION, P. Jennis, 150 days	29.50	NR
1992	DREAMS OF ASHLEY, P. Jennis, 150 days	32.50	NR
1992	AS GOD IS MY WITNESS, P. Jennis, 150 days	34.50	NR
1993	BRAVE SCARLETT	34.50	RI

		ISSUE	CURRENT
1992	THE FOND FAREWELL, P. Jennis, 150 days	32.50	RI
1992	THE WALTZ, P. Jennis, 150 days	32.50	RI
1993	NIGHTMARE	34.50	RI
1993	EVENING PRAYERS	34.50	RI
1993	NAP TIME	36.50	RI
1993	DANGEROUS ATTRACTION	36.50	RI
1993	THE END OF AN ERA	36.50	RI

Grand Safari: Images of Africa

1992	A MOMENT'S REST, Charles Fracé, 150 days	34.50	NR
1992	ELEPHANTS OF KILIMANJARO, Charles Fracé, 150 days	34.50	50.00
1992	UNDIVIDED ATTENTION, Charles Fracé, 150 days	37.50	45.00
1993	QUIET TIME IN SAMBURU, Charles Fracé, 150 days	37.50	RI
1993	LONE HUNTER, Charles Fracé, 150 days	37.50	RI
1993	THE GREATER KUDO, Charles Fracé, 150 days	37.50	RI

Heart of the Wild

1991	A GENTLE TOUCH, Greg Beecham, 150 days	29.50	NR
1992	MOTHER'S PRIDE, Greg Beecham, 150 days	29.50	35.00
1992	AN AFTERNOON TOGETHER, Greg Beecham, 150 days	32.50	45.00
1992	QUIET TIME, Greg Beecham, 150 days	32.50	50.00

Hollywood's Glamour Girls

1989	JEAN HARLOW—*DINNER AT EIGHT*, E. Dzenis, 150 days	24.50	BR
1990	LANA TURNER—*THE POSTMAN RINGS TWICE*, E. Dzenis, 150 days	29.50	NR
1990	CAROLE LOMBARD—*THE GAY BRIDE*, E. Dzenis, 150 days	29.50	NR
1990	GRETA GARBO—*GRAND HOTEL*, E. Dzenis, 150 days	29.50	BR

Hometown Memories

1993	MOONLIGHT SKATERS, H. T. Becker, 150 days	29.50	RI
1993	MOUNTAIN SLEIGH RIDE, H. T. Becker, 150 days	29.50	RI
1993	HEADING HOME, H. T. Becker, 150 days	29.50	RI
1993	A WINTER RIDE, H. T. Becker, 150 days	29.50	RI

Last of Their Kind: Endangered Species

1988	PANDA, Will Nelson, 150 days	27.50	BR
1988	SNOW LEOPARD, Will Nelson, 150 days	27.50	BR
1989	RED WOLF, Will Nelson, 150 days	30.50	BR
1989	ASIAN ELEPHANT, Will Nelson, 150 days	30.50	BR
1990	SLENDER-HORNED GAZELLE, Will Nelson, 150 days	30.50	BR
1990	BRIDLED WALLABY, Will Nelson, 150 days	30.50	BR
1990	BLACK-FOOTED FERRET, Will Nelson, 150 days	33.50	BR
1990	SIBERIAN TIGER, Will Nelson, 150 days	33.50	NR
1991	VICUNA, Will Nelson, 150 days	33.50	BR
1991	PRZEWALSKI'S HORSE, Will Nelson, 150 days	33.50	NR

Lena Liu's Basket Bouquets (Bradford Exchange)

1992	ROSES, Lena Liu, 150 days	29.50	NR
1992	PANSIES, Lena Liu, 150 days	29.50	NR
1992	TULIPS AND LILACS, Lena Liu, 150 days	32.50	50.00
1992	IRISES, Lena Liu, 150 days	32.50	45.00
1992	LILIES, Lena Liu, 150 days	32.50	NR

		ISSUE	CURRENT
1992	PARROT TULIPS, Lena Liu, 150 days	32.50	50.00
1992	PEONIES, Lena Liu, 150 days	32.50	45.00
1993	BEGONIAS, Lena Liu, 150 days	32.50	RI
1993	MAGNOLIAS, Lena Liu, 150 days	32.50	RI
1993	CALLA LILIES, Lena Liu, 150 days	32.50	RI
1993	ORCHIDS, Lena Liu, 150 days	32.50	RI
1993	HYDRANGEAS, Lena Liu, 150 days	32.50	RI

Lena Liu's Flower Fairies (Bradford Exchange)

1993	MAGIC MAKERS, Lena Liu, 95 days	29.50	RI
1993	PETAL PLAYMATES, Lena Liu, 95 days	29.50	RI
1993	DELICATE DANCERS, Lena Liu, 95 days	32.50	RI
1993	MISCHIEF MASTERS, Lena Liu, 95 days	32.50	RI
1993	AMOROUS ANGELS, Lena Liu, 95 days	32.50	RI
1993	WINGED WONDERS, Lena Liu, 95 days	34.50	RI
1993	MINIATURE MERMAIDS, Lena Liu, 95 days	34.50	RI
1993	FANCIFUL FAIRIES, Lena Liu, 95 days	34.50	RI

Lena Liu's Hummingbird Treasury (Bradford Exchange)

1992	RUBY-THROATED HUMMINGBIRD, Lena Liu, 150 days	29.50	RI
1992	ANNA'S HUMMINGBIRD, Lena Liu, 150 days	29.50	RI
1992	VIOLET-CROWNED HUMMINGBIRD, Lena Liu, 150 days	32.50	RI
1992	RUFOUS HUMMINGBIRD, Lena Liu, 150 days	32.50	RI
1993	WHITE-EARED HUMMINGBIRD, Lena Liu, 150 days	32.50	RI
1993	BROAD-BILLED HUMMINGBIRD	34.50	RI
1993	CALLIOPE HUMMINGBIRD	34.50	RI
1993	ALLEN'S HUMMINGBIRD	34.50	RI

Little Angels (Bradford Exchange)

1992	ANGELS WE HAVE HEARD ON HIGH, Brenda Burke, 150 days	29.50	NR
1992	O TANNENBAUM, Brenda Burke, 150 days	29.50	50.00
1993	JOY TO THE WORLD, Brenda Burke, 150 days	32.50	RI
1993	HARK THE HERALD ANGELS SING, Brenda Burke, 150 days	32.50	RI
1993	IT CAME UPON A MIDNIGHT CLEAR	32.50	RI
1993	FIRST NOEL	32.50	RI

Loving Look: Duck Families

1990	FAMILY OUTING, Bruce Langton, 150 days	34.50	BR
1991	SLEEPY START, Bruce Langton, 150 days	34.50	BR
1991	QUIET MOMENT, Bruce Langton, 150 days	37.50	NR
1991	SAFE AND SOUND, Bruce Langton, 150 days	37.50	NR
1991	SPRING ARRIVALS, Bruce Langton, 150 days	37.50	NR
1991	FAMILY TREE, Bruce Langton, 150 days	37.50	NR

Majestic Horse

1992	CLASSIC BEAUTY: THOROUGHBRED, P. Wildermuth, 150 days	34.50	NR
1992	AMERICAN GOLD: QUARTERHORSE, P. Wildermuth, 150 days	34.50	50.00
1992	REGAL SPIRIT: THE ARABIAN, P. Wildermuth, 150 days	34.50	75.00
1992	WESTERN FAVORITE: AMERICAN PAINT HORSE, P. Wildermuth, 150 days	34.50	50.00

Melodies in the Mist

1993	EARLY MORNING RAIN, A. Sakhavarz, closed	34.50	RI

		ISSUE	CURRENT
1993	AMONG THE DEWDROPS, A. Sakhavarz, closed	34.50	RI
1993	FEEDING TIME, A. Sakhavarz, closed	37.50	RI
1994	GARDEN PARTY, A. Sakhavarz, closed	37.50	RI
1994	UNPLEASANT SURPRISE, A. Sakhavarz, closed	37.50	RI
1994	SPRING RAIN, A. Sakhavarz, closed	37.50	RI

Memories of a Victorian Childhood

1992	YOU'D BETTER NOT POUT, 150 days	29.50	NR
1992	SWEET SLUMBER, 150 days	29.50	55.00
1992	THROUGH THICK AND THIN, 150 days	32.50	45.00
1992	AN ARMFUL OF TREASURES, 150 days	32.50	60.00
1993	A TRIO OF BOOKWORMS, 150 days	32.50	RI
1993	PUGNACIOUS PLAYMATE, 150 days	32.50	RI

Nature's Legacy

1990	BLUE SNOW AT HALF DOME, Jean Sias, 150 days	24.50	BR
1991	MISTY MORNING/MT. MCKINLEY, Jean Sias, 150 days	24.50	BR
1991	MOUNT RANIER, Jean Sias, 150 days	27.50	BR
1991	HAVASU CANYON, Jean Sias, 150 days	27.50	NR
1991	AUTUMN SPLENDOR IN THE SMOKEY MOUNTAINS, Jean Sias, 150 days	27.50	NR
1991	WINTER PEACE IN YELLOWSTONE PARK, Jean Sias, 150 days	29.50	NR
1991	GOLDEN MAJESTY/ROCKY MOUNTAINS, Jean Sias, 150 days	29.50	NR
1991	RADIANT SUNSET OVER THE EVERGLADES, Jean Sias, 150 days	29.50	NR

Nature's Lovables

1990	THE KOALA, Charles Fracé, 150 days	27.50	NR
1991	NEW ARRIVAL, Charles Fracé, 150 days	27.50	NR
1991	CHINESE TREASURE, Charles Fracé, 150 days	27.50	NR
1991	BABY HARP SEAL, Charles Fracé, 150 days	30.50	NR
1991	BOBCAT: NATURE'S DAWN, Charles Fracé, 150 days	30.50	BR
1991	CLOUDED LEOPARD, Charles Fracé, 150 days	32.50	BR
1991	ZEBRA FOAL, Charles Fracé, 150 days	32.50	NR
1991	BANDIT, Charles Fracé, 150 days	32.50	45.00

Nature's Playmates

1991	PARTNERS, Charles Fracé, 150 days	29.50	NR
1991	SECRET HEIGHTS, Charles Fracé, 150 days	29.50	NR
1991	RECESS, Charles Fracé, 150 days	32.50	NR
1991	DOUBLE TROUBLE, Charles Fracé, 150 days	32.50	NR
1991	PALS, Charles Fracé, 150 days	32.50	NR
1992	CURIOUS TRIO, Charles Fracé, 150 days	34.50	45.00
1992	PLAYMATES, Charles Fracé, 150 days	34.50	NR
1992	SURPRISE, Charles Fracé, 150 days	34.50	BR
1992	PEACE ON ICE, Charles Fracé, 150 days	36.50	45.00
1992	AMBASSADORS, Charles Fracé, 150 days	36.50	NR

Nature's Poetry

1989	MORNING SERENADE, Lena Liu, 150 days	24.50	NR
1989	SONG OF PROMISE, Lena Liu, 150 days	24.50	NR
1990	TENDER LULLABYE, Lena Liu, 150 days	27.50	NR
1990	NATURE'S HARMONY, Lena Liu, 150 days	27.50	NR
1990	GENTLE REFRAIN, Lena Liu, 150 days	27.50	NR
1990	MORNING CHORUS, Lena Liu, 150 days	27.50	NR

		ISSUE	CURRENT
1990	MELODY AT DAYBREAK, Lena Liu, 150 days	29.50	NR
1991	DELICATE ACCORD, Lena Liu, 150 days	29.50	NR
1991	LYRICAL BEGINNINGS, Lena Liu, 150 days	29.50	NR
1991	SONG OF SPRING, Lena Liu, 150 days	32.50	NR
1991	MOTHER'S MELODY, Lena Liu, 150 days	32.50	NR
1991	CHERUB CHORALE, Lena Liu, 150 days	32.50	NR

On Golden Wings (Bradford Exchange)

1993	MORNING LIGHT, Wilhelm Goebel	29.50	RI
1993	EARLY RISERS, Wilhelm Goebel	29.50	RI
1993	AS DAY BREAKS, Wilhelm Goebel	32.50	RI
1993	DAYLIGHT FLIGHT, Wilhelm Goebel	32.50	RI
1994	WINTER DAWN, Wilhelm Goebel	32.50	RI
1994	FIRST LIGHT, Wilhelm Goebel	32.50	RI

On Gossamer Wings

1988	MONARCH BUTTERFLIES, Lena Liu, 150 days	24.50	NR
1988	WESTERN TIGER SWALLOWTAILS, Lena Liu, 150 days	24.50	35.00
1988	RED-SPOTTED PURPLE, Lena Liu, 150 days	27.50	35.00
1988	MALACHITES, Lena Liu, 150 days	27.50	NR
1988	WHITE PEACOCKS, Lena Liu, 150 days	27.50	NR
1988	EASTERN TAILED BLUES, Lena Liu, 150 days	27.50	BR
1988	ZEBRA SWALLOWTAILS, Lena Liu, 150 days	29.50	BR
1988	RED ADMIRALS, Lena Liu, 150 days	29.50	BR

On the Wing

1992	WINGED SPLENDOR, T. Humphrey, 150 days	29.50	NR
1992	RISING MALLARD, T. Humphrey, 150 days	29.50	NR
1992	GLORIOUS ASCENT, T. Humphrey, 150 days	32.50	NR
1992	TAKING WING, T. Humphrey, 150 days	32.50	NR
1992	UPWARD BOUND, T. Humphrey, 150 days	32.50	NR
1993	WONDROUS MOTION, T. Humphrey, 150 days	34.50	RI
1993	SPRINGING FORTH, T. Humphrey, 150 days	34.50	RI
1993	ON THE WING, T. Humphrey, 150 days	34.50	RI

On Wings of Snow

1991	THE SWANS, Lena Liu, 150 days	34.50	NR
1991	THE DOVES, Lena Liu, 150 days	34.50	NR
1991	THE PEACOCKS, Lena Liu, 150 days	37.50	NR
1991	THE EGRETS, Lena Liu, 150 days	37.50	50.00
1991	THE COCKATOOS, Lena Liu, 150 days	37.50	45.00
1991	THE HERONS, Lena Liu, 150 days	37.50	NR

Our Woodland Friends

1990	FASCINATION, Carl Brenders, 150 days	29.50	BR
1990	BENEATH THE PINES, Carl Brenders, 150 days	29.50	BR
1990	HIGH ADVENTURE, Carl Brenders, 150 days	32.50	BR
1990	SHY EXPLORERS, Carl Brenders, 150 days	32.50	NR
1991	GOLDEN SEASON: GRAY SQUIRREL, Carl Brenders, 150 days	32.50	NR
1991	FULL HOUSE: FOX FAMILY, Carl Brenders, 150 days	32.50	NR
1991	A JUMP INTO LIFE: SPRING FAWN, Carl Brenders, 150 days	34.50	NR
1991	FOREST SENTINEL: BOBCAT, Carl Brenders, 150 days	34.50	NR

Fascination

The Appaloosa

Christmas Eve

Freedom

I'll Be Home for Christmas

Iris Quartet

Photos courtesy of *Collectors News*

		ISSUE	CURRENT

Petal Pals (Bradford Exchange)

1992	GARDEN DISCOVERY, Lily Chang, 150 days	24.50	NR
1992	FLOWERING FASCINATION, Lily Chang, 150 days	24.50	NR
1993	ALLURING LILIES, Lily Chang, 150 days	24.50	RI
1993	SPRINGTIME OASIS, Lily Chang, 150 days	24.50	RI
1993	BLOSSOMING ADVENTURE, Lily Chang, 150 days	24.50	RI
1993	DANCING DAFFODILS, Lily Chang, 150 days	24.50	RI
1993	SUMMER SURPRISE, Lily Chang, 150 days	24.50	RI
1993	MORNING MELODY, Lily Chang, 150 days	24.50	RI

Poetic Cottages

1992	GARDEN PATHS OF OXFORDSHIRE, C. Valente, 150 days	29.50	35.00
1992	TWILIGHT AT WOODGREEN POND, C. Valente, 150 days	29.50	70.00
1992	STONEWALL BROOK BLOSSOMS, C. Valente, 150 days	32.50	65.00
1992	BEDFORDSHIRE EVENING SKY, C. Valente, 150 days	32.50	50.00
1993	WISTERIA SUMMER, C. Valente, 150 days	32.50	50.00
1993	WILTSHIRE ROSE ARBOR, C. Valente, 150 days	32.50	50.00
1993	ALDERBURY GARDENS, C. Valente, 150 days	32.50	55.00
1993	HAMPSHIRE SPRING SPLENDOR, C. Valente, 150 days	32.50	NR

Portraits of Christ

1991	FATHER, FORGIVE THEM, Jose F. De Salamanca, 150 days	29.50	85.00
1991	THY WILL BE DONE, Jose F. De Salamanca, 150 days	29.50	50.00
1991	THIS IS MY BELOVED SON, Jose F. De Salamanca, 150 days	32.50	45.00
1991	LO, I AM WITH YOU, Jose F. De Salamanca, 150 days	32.50	50.00
1991	BECOME AS LITTLE CHILDREN, Jose F. De Salamanca, 150 days	32.50	55.00
1991	PEACE I LEAVE WITH YOU, Jose F. De Salamanca, 150 days	34.50	50.00
1992	FOR GOD SO LOVED THE WORLD, Jose F. De Salamanca, 150 days	34.50	50.00
1992	I AM THE WAY, THE TRUTH AND THE LIFE, Jose F. De Salamanca, 150 days	34.50	50.00
1992	WEEP NOT FOR ME, Jose F. De Salamanca, 150 days	34.50	55.00
1992	FOLLOW ME, Jose F. De Salamanca, 150 days	34.50	60.00

Portraits of Exquisite Birds

1990	BACKYARD TREASURE: CHICKADEE, Carl Brenders, 150 days	29.50	NR
1990	THE BEAUTIFUL BLUEBIRD, Carl Brenders, 150 days	29.50	BR
1991	SUMMER GOLD: THE ROBIN, Carl Brenders, 150 days	32.50	BR
1991	THE MEADOWLARK'S SONG, Carl Brenders, 150 days	32.50	BR
1991	IVORY-BILLED WOODPECKER, Carl Brenders, 150 days	32.50	NR
1991	RED-WINGED BLACKBIRD, Carl Brenders, 150 days	32.50	NR

Purebred Horses of the Americas

1989	THE APPALOOSA, D. Schwartz, 150 days	34.50	BR
1989	THE TENNESSEE WALKER, D. Schwartz, 150 days	34.50	NR
1990	THE QUARTERHORSE, D. Schwartz, 150 days	37.50	BR
1990	THE SADDLEBRED, D. Schwartz, 150 days	37.50	BR
1990	THE MUSTANG, D. Schwartz, 150 days	37.50	NR
1990	THE MORGAN, D. Schwartz, 150 days	37.50	NR

Rare Encounters (Bradford Exchange)

1993	SOFTLY, SOFTLY, John Seerey-Lester, 95 days	29.50	RI
1993	BLACK MAGIC, John Seerey-Lester, 95 days	29.50	RI
1993	FUTURE SONG, John Seerey-Lester, 95 days	32.50	RI

		ISSUE	CURRENT
1993	HIGH AND MIGHTY, John Seerey-Lester, 95 days	32.50	RI
1993	LAST SANCTUARY, John Seerey-Lester, 95 days	32.50	RI
1993	SOMETHING STIRRED, John Seerey-Lester, 95 days	34.50	RI

Romantic Gardens

1989	THE WOODLAND GARDEN, C. Smith, 150 days	29.50	NR
1989	THE PLANTATION GARDEN, C. Smith, 150 days	29.50	BR
1990	THE COTTAGE GARDEN, C. Smith, 150 days	32.50	BR
1990	THE COLONIAL GARDEN, C. Smith, 150 days	32.50	NR

Romantic Harbors

1993	ADVENT OF THE GOLDEN BOUGH, Charles Vickery, 95 days	34.50	RI
1993	CHRISTMAS TREE SCHOONER, Charles Vickery	34.50	RI
1993	PRELUDE TO THE JOURNEY, Charles Vickery	37.50	RI
1993	SHIMMERING LIGHT OF DUSK, Charles Vickery	37.50	RI

Romantic Roses (Bradford Exchange)

1993	VICTORIAN BEAUTY, Vieonne Morley, 95 days	29.50	RI
1993	OLD-FASHIONED GRACE, Vieonne Morley, 95 days	29.50	RI
1993	COUNTRY CHARM, Vieonne Morley, 95 days	32.50	RI
1993	SUMMER ROMANCE, Vieonne Morley, 95 days	32.50	RI
1993	PASTORAL DELIGHT, Vieonne Morley, 95 days	32.50	RI
1993	SPRINGTIME ELEGANCE, Vieonne Morley, 95 days	34.50	RI
1993	VINTAGE SPLENDOR, Vieonne Morley, 95 days	34.50	RI
1994	HEAVENLY PERFECTION, Vieonne Morley, 95 days	34.50	RI

Scenes of Christmas Past (Bradford Exchange)

1987	HOLIDAY SKATERS, Lloyd Garrison, 150 days	27.50	NR
1988	CHRISTMAS EVE, Lloyd Garrison, 150 days	27.50	NR
1989	THE HOMECOMING, Lloyd Garrison, 150 days	30.50	NR
1990	THE TOY STORE, Lloyd Garrison, 150 days	30.50	BR
1991	THE CAROLLERS, Lloyd Garrison, 150 days	30.50	NR
1992	FAMILY TRADITIONS, Lloyd Garrison, 150 days	30.50	NR
1993	HOLIDAY PAST, Lloyd Garrison, 150 days	30.50	RI
1994	A GATHERING OF FAITH, Lloyd Garrison, 150 days	32.50	RI

Secret World of the Panda

1990	A MOTHER'S CARE, Joyce Bridgett, 150 days	27.50	BR
1991	A FROLIC IN THE SNOW, Joyce Bridgett, 150 days	27.50	BR
1991	LAZY AFTERNOON, Joyce Bridgett, 150 days	30.50	BR
1991	A DAY OF EXPLORING, Joyce Bridgett, 150 days	30.50	NR
1991	A GENTLE HUG, Joyce Bridgett, 150 days	32.50	NR
1991	A BAMBOO FEAST, Joyce Bridgett, 150 days	32.50	65.00

Soaring Majesty

1990	FREEDOM, Charles Fracé, 150 days	29.50	BR
1991	THE NORTHERN GOSHAWK, Charles Fracé, 150 days	29.50	BR
1991	PEREGRINE FALCON, Charles Fracé, 150 days	32.50	BR
1991	RED-TAILED HAWK, Charles Fracé, 150 days	32.50	NR
1991	THE OSPREY, Charles Fracé, 150 days	32.50	BR
1991	THE GYRFALCON, Charles Fracé, 150 days	34.50	NR
1991	THE GOLDEN EAGLE, Charles Fracé, 150 days	34.50	NR

		ISSUE	CURRENT
1992	RED-SHOULDERED HAWK, Charles Fracé, 150 days	34.50	BR

Sonnets in Flowers

1992	SONNET OF BEAUTY, Glenna Kurz, 150 days	29.50	35.00
1992	SONNET OF HAPPINESS, Glenna Kurz, 150 days	34.50	40.00
1992	SONNET OF LOVE, Glenna Kurz, 150 days	34.50	35.00
1992	SONNET OF PEACE, Glenna Kurz, 150 days	34.50	50.00

Sound of Music: 25th Anniversary

1991	THE HILLS ARE ALIVE, Victor Gadino, 150 days	29.50	NR
1992	LET'S START AT THE VERY BEGINNING, Victor Gadino, 150 days	29.50	NR
1992	SOMETHING GOOD, Victor Gadino, 150 days	32.50	NR
1992	MARIA'S WEDDING DAY, Victor Gadino, 150 days	32.50	NR

Spirit of Christmas

1990	SILENT NIGHT, Jean Sias, 150 days	29.50	BR
1991	JINGLE BELLS, Jean Sias, 150 days	29.50	BR
1991	DECK THE HALLS, Jean Sias, 150 days	32.50	NR
1991	I'LL BE HOME FOR CHRISTMAS, Jean Sias, 150 days	32.50	NR
1991	WINTER WONDERLAND, Jean Sias, 150 days	32.50	NR
1991	O CHRISTMAS TREE, Jean Sias, 150 days	32.50	NR

Spirits of the Sky (Bradford Exchange)

1992	TWILIGHT GLOW, Cynthie Fisher, 150 days	29.50	35.00
1992	FIRST LIGHT, Cynthie Fisher, 150 days	29.50	60.00
1992	EVENING GLIMMER, Cynthie Fisher, 150 days	32.50	75.00
1992	GOLDEN DUSK, Cynthie Fisher, 150 days	32.50	NR
1993	SUNSET SPLENDOR, Cynthie Fisher, 150 days	32.50	RI
1993	AMBER FLIGHT, Cynthie Fisher, 150 days	34.50	RI
1993	WINGED RADIANCE, Cynthie Fisher, 150 days	34.50	RI
1993	DAYS END, Cynthie Fisher, 150 days	34.50	RI

Splash of Cats

1992	MOONLIGHT CHASE: COUGAR, J. Seerey-Lester, closed	29.50	NR

Symphony of Shimmering Beauties

1991	IRIS QUARTET, Lena Liu, 150 days	29.50	35.00
1991	TULIP ENSEMBLE, Lena Liu, 150 days	29.50	NR
1991	POPPY PASTORALE, Lena Liu, 150 days	32.50	NR
1991	LILY CONCERTO, Lena Liu, 150 days	32.50	40.00
1991	PEONY PRELUDE, Lena Liu, 150 days	32.50	NR
1991	ROSE FANTASY, Lena Liu, 150 days	34.50	40.00
1991	HIBISCUS MEDLEY, Lena Liu, 150 days	34.50	NR
1992	DAHLIA MELODY, Lena Liu, 150 days	34.50	45.00
1992	HOLLYHOCK MARCH, Lena Liu, 150 days	34.50	NR
1992	CARNATION SERENADE, Lena Liu, 150 days	36.50	NR
1992	GLADIOLUS ROMANCE, Lena Liu, 150 days	36.50	NR
1992	ZINNIA FINALE, Lena Liu, 150 days	36.50	NR

'Tis the Season

1993	A WORLD DRESSED IN SNOW	29.50	RI
1993	A TIME FOR TRADITION	29.50	RI

		ISSUE	CURRENT
1993	WE SHALL COME REJOICING	29.50	RI
1993	OUR FAMILY TREE	29.50	RI

Tomorrow's Promise

1992	CURIOSITY: ASIAN ELEPHANTS, Will Nelson, 150 days	29.50	NR
1992	PLAYTIME PANDAS, Will Nelson, 150 days	29.50	35.00
1992	INNOCENCE: RHINOS, Will Nelson, 150 days	32.50	60.00
1992	FRISKINESS: KIT FOXES, Will Nelson, 150 days	32.50	45.00

Touching the Spirit (Bradford Exchange)

1993	RUNNING WITH THE WIND, Julie Kramer Cole, 95 days	29.50	RI
1993	KINDRED SPIRITS, Julie Kramer Cole, 95 days	29.50	RI
1983	THE MARKING TREE, Julie Kramer Cole, 95 days	29.50	RI
1993	WAKAN TNAKA, Julie Kramer Cole, 95 days	29.50	RI
1993	HE WHO WATCHES, Julie Kramer Cole, 95 days	29.50	RI
1994	TWICE TRAVELLED TRAIL, Julie Kramer Cole, 95 days	29.50	RI
1994	KEEPER OF THE SECRET, Julie Kramer Cole, 95 days	29.50	RI
1994	CAMP OF THE SACRED DOGS, Julie Kramer Cole, 95 days	29.50	RI

Treasury of Songbirds

1992	SPRINGTIME SPLENDOR, R. Stine, 150 days	29.50	35.00
1992	MORNING'S GLORY, R. Stine, 150 days	29.50	35.00
1992	GOLDEN DAYBREAK, R. Stine, 150 days	32.50	45.00
1992	AFTERNOON CALM, R. Stine, 150 days	32.50	40.00
1992	DAWN'S RADIANCE, R. Stine, 150 days	32.50	40.00
1993	SCARLET SUNRISE, R. Stine, 150 days	34.50	RI
1993	SAPPHIRE DAWN, R. Stine, 150 days	34.50	RI
1993	ALLURING DAYLIGHT	34.50	RI

Vanishing Gentle Giants

1991	JUMPING FOR JOY, Anthony Casay, 150 days	32.50	BR
1991	SONG OF THE HUMPBACK, Anthony Casay, 150 days	32.50	NR
1991	MONARCH OF THE DEEP, Anthony Casay, 150 days	35.50	NR
1991	TRAVELERS OF THE SEA, Anthony Casay, 150 days	35.50	50.00
1991	WHITE WHALE OF THE NORTH, Anthony Casay, 150 days	35.50	45.00
1991	UNICORN OF THE SEA, Anthony Casay, 150 days	35.50	NR

Victorian Cat

1990	MISCHIEF WITH THE HATBOX, Henriette Bonner, 150 days	24.50	30.00
1991	STRING QUARTET, Henriette Bonner, 150 days	24.50	40.00
1991	DAYDREAMS, Henriette Bonner, 150 days	27.50	35.00
1991	FRISKY FELINES, Henriette Bonner, 150 days	27.50	35.00
1991	KITTENS AT PLAY, Henriette Bonner, 150 days	27.50	35.00
1991	PLAYING IN THE PARLOR, Henriette Bonner, 150 days	29.50	BR
1991	PERFECTLY POISED, Henriette Bonner, 150 days	29.50	40.00
1992	MIDDAY REPOSE, Henriette Bonner, 150 days	29.50	BR

Victorian Cat Capers

1992	WHO'S THE FAIREST OF THEM ALL?, F. Paton, 150 days	24.50	50.00
1992	PUSS IN BOOTS, 150 days	24.50	40.00
1992	MY BOWL IS EMPTY, W. Hepple, 150 days	27.50	35.00
1992	A CURIOUS KITTY, W. Hepple, 150 days	27.50	NR

		ISSUE	CURRENT
1992	VANITY FAIR, W. Hepple, 150 days	27.50	NR
1992	FORBIDDEN FRUIT, W. Hepple, 150 days	29.50	45.00
1993	THE PURR-FECT PEN PAL, W. Hepple, 150 days	29.50	RI
1993	THE KITTEN EXPRESS, W. Hepple, 150 days	29.50	RI

Wild Innocents

1993	REFLECTIONS, Charles Fracé, 95 days	29.50	RI
1993	SPIRITUAL HEIR, Charles Fracé, 95 days	29.50	RI
1993	LION CUB, Charles Fracé, 95 days	29.50	RI
1993	SUNNY SPOT, Charles Fracé, 95 days	29.50	RI

Wild Spirits (Bradford Exchange)

1992	SOLITARY WATCH, Thomas Hirata, 150 days	29.50	NR
1992	TIMBER GHOST, Thomas Hirata, 150 days	29.50	50.00
1992	MOUNTAIN MAGIC, Thomas Hirata, 150 days	32.50	NR
1993	SILENT GUARD, Thomas Hirata, 150 days	32.50	RI
1993	SLY EYES, Thomas Hirata, 150 days	32.50	RI
1993	MIGHTY PRESENCE, Thomas Hirata, 150 days	34.50	RI
1993	QUIET VIGIL, Thomas Hirata, 150 days	34.50	RI
1993	LONE VANGUARD, Thomas Hirata, 150 days	34.50	RI

Wings of Winter

1992	MOONLIGHT RETREAT, D. L. Rust, 150 days	29.50	35.00
1992	TWILIGHT SERENADE, D. L. Rust, 150 days	29.50	40.00
1992	SILENT SUNSET, D. L. Rust, 150 days	29.50	40.00
1993	NIGHT LIGHTS, D. L. Rust, 150 days	29.50	RI
1993	WINTER HAVEN, D. L. Rust, 150 days	29.50	RI
1993	FULL MOON COMPANIONS, D. L. Rust, 150 days	29.50	RI
1993	WHITE NIGHT, D. L. Rust, 150 days	29.50	RI
1993	WINTER REFLECTIONS, D. L. Rust, 150 days	29.50	RI

Winter's Majesty

1992	THE QUEST, Charles Fracé, 150 days	34.50	NR
1992	THE CHASE, Charles Fracé, 150 days	34.50	NR
1993	ALASKAN FRIEND, Charles Fracé, 150 days	34.50	RI
1993	AMERICAN COUGAR, Charles Fracé, 150 days	34.50	RI
1993	ON WATCH, Charles Fracé, 150 days	34.50	RI
1993	SOLITUDE, Charles Fracé, 150 days	34.50	RI

Wonders of the Sea

1991	STAND BY ME, Ray Harm, 150 days	34.50	NR
1991	HEART TO HEART, Ray Harm, 150 days	34.50	NR
1991	WARM EMBRACE, Ray Harm, 150 days	34.50	NR
1991	A FAMILY AFFAIR, Ray Harm, 150 days	34.50	NR

World's Most Magnificent Cats

1991	FLEETING ENCOUNTER, Charles Fracé, 150 days	24.50	NR
1991	COUGAR, Charles Fracé, 150 days	24.50	NR
1991	ROYAL BENGAL, Charles Fracé, 150 days	27.50	NR
1991	POWERFUL PRESENCE, Charles Fracé, 150 days	27.50	40.00
1991	JAGUAR, Charles Fracé, 150 days	27.50	NR
1991	THE CLOUDED LEOPARD, Charles Fracé, 150 days	29.50	NR

Fleeting Encounter
Photo courtesy of *Collectors News*

		ISSUE	CURRENT
1991	THE AFRICAN LEOPARD, Charles Fracé, 150 days	29.50	NR
1991	MIGHTY WARRIOR, Charles Fracé, 150 days	29.50	40.00
1992	THE CHEETAH, Charles Fracé, 150 days	31.50	40.00
1992	SIBERIAN TIGER, Charles Fracé, 150 days	31.50	50.00

GEORGE WASHINGTON MINT UNITED STATES

Indians

1972	CURLEY, Sawyer, gold, 100	2,000.00	2,250.00
1972	CURLEY, Sawyer, sterling silver, 7,300	150.00	BR
1973	TWO MOONS, Sawyer, gold, 100	2,000.00	2,250.00
1973	TWO MOONS, Sawyer, sterling silver, 7,300	150.00	BR

Mother's Day

1972	WHISTLER'S MOTHER, gold, 100	2,000.00	2,250.00
1972	WHISTLER'S MOTHER, sterling silver, 9,800	150.00	BR
1973	MOTHERHOOD, gold, 100	2,000.00	2,250.00
1973	MOTHERHOOD, sterling silver, 9,800	175.00	BR

N. C. Wyeth

1972	UNCLE SAM'S AMERICA, N. C. Wyeth, gold, 100	2,000.00	2,250.00
1972	UNCLE SAM'S AMERICA, N. C. Wyeth, sterling silver, 9,800	150.00	BR
1973	MASSED FLAGS, N. C. Wyeth, gold, 100	2,000.00	2,250.00
1973	MASSED FLAGS, N. C. Wyeth, sterling silver, 2,300	150.00	BR

Picasso

1972	DON QUIXOTE, gold, 100	2,000.00	2,300.00
1972	DON QUIXOTE, sterling silver, 9,800	125.00	155.00
1974	RITES OF SPRING, sterling silver, 9,800	150.00	185.00

Remington Series

1972	RATTLESNAKE, Frederic Remington, 100	2,000.00	2,200.00
1972	RATTLESNAKE, Frederic Remington, 800	250.00	390.00
1974	COMING THROUGH THE RYE, Frederic Remington, 2,500	300.00	365.00

		ISSUE	CURRENT

Single Issues

1972	LAST SUPPER, Leonardo da Vinci	125.00	140.00
1973	ISRAEL ANNIVERSARY, 10,000	300.00	335.00

GEORGETOWN COLLECTION UNITED STATES

Children of the Great Spirit

1993	BUFFALO CHILD, C. Theroux, 35 days	29.95	RI
1993	WINTER BABY, C. Theroux, 35 days	29.95	RI

Hearts in Song

1993	BUFFALO CHILD, C. Theroux, 35 days	29.95	RI

GHENT COLLECTION UNITED STATES

(Bing & Grøndahl, Fairmont, Gorham, Villetta)

American Bicentennial Wildlife

1976	AMERICAN BALD EAGLE, Harry J. Moeller, 2,500	95.00	NR
1976	AMERICAN WHITE-TAILED DEER, Edward J. Bierly, 2,500	95.00	NR
1976	AMERICAN BISON, Charles Fracé, 2,500	95.00	NR
1976	AMERICAN WILD TURKEY, Albert Earl Gilbert, 2,500	95.00	NR

Caverswall Christmas Carol

1979	GOOD KING WENCESLAS, Holmes Gray, 2,500	300.00	NR
1980	THE FIRST NOEL, Holmes Gray, 2,500	300.00	NR

Christmas Wildlife

1974	CARDINALS IN SNOW, Albert Earl Gilbert, 10,030	20.00	55.00
1975	WE THREE KINGS, Harry J. Moeller, 12,750	29.00	40.00
1976	PARTRIDGES AND PEAR TREE, Guy Tudor, 12,750	32.00	50.00
1977	FOXES AND EVERGREEN, Edward J. Bierly, 12,750	32.00	50.00
1978	SNOWY OWLS, Jay H. Matterness, 12,750	32.00	NR

Country Diary of an Edwardian Lady

1979	APRIL, Edith Holden, 10,000	80.00	NR
1979	JUNE, Edith Holden, 10,000	80.00	NR
1980	JANUARY, Edith Holden, 10,000	80.00	NR
1980	MAY, Edith Holden, 10,000	80.00	NR
1980	SEPTEMBER, Edith Holden, 10,000	80.00	NR
1980	DECEMBER, Edith Holden, 10,000	80.00	NR
1981	JULY, Edith Holden, 10,000	80.00	NR
1981	OCTOBER, Edith Holden, 10,000	80.00	NR

Fausett Mural Plates

1976	FROM SEA TO SHINING SEA, Dean Fausett, 1,976	76.00	230.00

Lands of Fable

1981	XANADU, F. F. Long, 17,500	55.00	NR

		ISSUE	CURRENT
1982	ATLANTIS, F. F. Long, 17,500	55.00	NR

Mother's Day

1975	COTTONTAIL, Harry J. Moeller, 12,750	22.00	40.00
1976	MALLARD FAMILY, Guy Tudor, 12,750	29.00	40.00
1977	CHIPMUNKS AND TRILLIUM, Albert Earl Gilbert, 12,750	32.00	40.00
1978	RACCOON FAMILY, Edward J. Bierly, 12,750	32.00	NR
1979	MAYTIME ROBINS, Jay H. Matterness, 12,750	32.00	NR

Single Issues

1979	PILGRIM OF PEACE, Alton S. Tobey, 15 days	29.50	NR
1980	1970s DECADE PLATE, Alton S. Tobey, 5,000	80.00	NR

GNOMES UNITED UNITED STATES

Gnome Patrol

1979	NUMBER ONE, Edith McLennan Choma, 5,000	45.00	60.00
1980	GREAT GOO ROO YU-HOO, Edith McLennan Choma, 5,000	48.00	NR
1981	FLEAFUT, Edith McLennan Choma, 5,000	50.00	NR

Single Issue

1982	GNOME ON THE RANGE, Rex T. Reed, 10,000	23.00	NR

GOEBEL / M. I. HUMMEL GERMANY

(House of Global Art)

American Heritage (House of Global Art)

1979	FREEDOM AND JUSTICE SOARING, Gunther Granget, 15,000	100.00	NR
1980	WILD AND FREE, Gunther Granget, 10,000	120.00	NR
1981	WHERE BUFFALO ROAM, Gunther Granget, 5,000	125.00	NR

Annual Crystal (House of Global Art)

1978	PRAYING GIRL, 1 year	45.00	NR
1979	PRAYING BOY, 1 year	50.00	NR
1980	PRAYING ANGEL, 15,000	50.00	NR
1981	GIRL WITH TEDDY BEARS, 10,000	50.00	NR

Bavarian Forest (House of Global Art)

1980	OWLS, 7,500	150.00	NR
1981	DEER, 7,500	150.00	NR

Berta Hummel Gift Collection

1997	SPECIAL DELIVERY, Berta Hummel	25.00	RI
1997	SPRING BLOSSOMS, Berta Hummel	25.00	RI
1997	FROM THIS DAY FORWARD, Berta Hummel	25.00	RI

Brastoff Series

1979	STAR STEED, Sascha Brastoff, 15,000	125.00	140.00

A Gift of Joy
Photo courtesy of *Collectors News*

		ISSUE	CURRENT
Charlot Byj Series			
1973	SANTA AT TREE, Charlot Byj, 1 year	16.50	NR
1974	SANTA AND GIRL, Charlot Byj, 1 year	22.00	NR
1975	UP AND AWAY, Charlot Byj, 1 year	25.00	NR
1976	BOY WITH TEDDY BEAR, Charlot Byj, 1 year	25.00	NR
1977	JOY TO THE WORLD, Charlot Byj, 1 year	25.00	NR
Christmas in Kinderland			
1982	A GIFT OF JOY, Lore, 10,000	49.50	60.00
1983	A MIDNIGHT CLEAR, Lore, 10,000	49.50	NR
Little Hugs			
NA	DOLLY DEAREST, Marian Flahavin, 7,500	NA	NA
NA	BEAR HUG, Marian Flahavin, 7,500	NA	NA
M. I. Hummel Anniversary Plates			
1975	STORMY WEATHER, HUM280, M. I. Hummel	100.00	NR
1980	RING AROUND THE ROSIE, HUM281, M. I. Hummel	225.00	NR
1985	AUF WIEDERSEHEN, HUM282, M. I. Hummel	225.00	NR
M. I. Hummel Annual Figural Christmas Plates			
1995	FESIVAL HARMONY WITH FLUTE, 693, M. I. Hummel, 1 year	125.00	RI
1996	CHRISTMAS SONG, 692, M. I. Hummel, 1 year	130.00	RI
1997	THANKSGIVING PRAYER, 694, M. I. Hummel, 1 year	140.00	RI
M. I. Hummel Club Exclusive—Celebration (Goebel Collectors Club)			
1986	VALENTINE GIFT, Hum738, M. I. Hummel, limited	90.00	150.00
1987	VALENTINE JOY, Hum737, M. I. Hummel, limited	98.00	150.00
1988	DAISIES DON'T TELL, Hum736, M. I. Hummel, limited	115.00	150.00
1989	IT'S COLD, Hum735, M. I. Hummel, limited	120.00	150.00
M. I. Hummel Collectibles Anniversary Plates			
1975	STORMY WEATHER, 280, M. I. Hummel, 1 year	100.00	BR

		ISSUE	CURRENT
1980	SPRING DANCE, 281, M. I. Hummel, 1 year	225.00	BR
1985	AUF WIEDERSEHEN, 282, M. I. Hummel, 1 year	225.00	200.00

M. I. Hummel Collectibles—Annual Plates

1971	HEAVENLY ANGEL, 264, M. I. Hummel, 1 year	25.00	500.00
1972	HEAR YE, HEAR YE, 265, M. I. Hummel, 1 year	30.00	40.00
1973	GLOBE TROTTER, 266, M. I. Hummel, 1 year	32.50	70.00
1974	GOOSE GIRL, 267, M. I. Hummel, 1 year	40.00	NR
1975	RIDE INTO CHRISTMAS, 268, M. I. Hummel, 1 year	50.00	BR
1976	APPLE TREE GIRL, 269, M. I. Hummel, 1 year	50.00	BR
1977	APPLE TREE BOY, 270, M. I. Hummel, 1 year	52.50	BR
1978	HAPPY PASTIME, 271, M. I. Hummel, 1 year	65.00	BR
1979	SINGING LESSON, 272, M. I. Hummel, 1 year	90.00	BR
1980	SCHOOL GIRL, 273, M. I. Hummel, 1 year	100.00	BR
1981	UMBRELLA BOY, 274, M. I. Hummel, 1 year	100.00	BR
1982	UMBRELLA GIRL, 275, M. I. Hummel, 1 year	100.00	BR
1983	THE POSTMAN, 276, M. I. Hummel, 1 year	108.00	150.00
1984	LITTLE HELPER, 277, M. I. Hummel, 1 year	108.00	BR
1985	CHICK GIRL, 278, M. I. Hummel, 1 year	110.00	BR
1986	PLAYMATES, 279, M. I. Hummel, 1 year	125.00	BR
1987	FEEDING TIME, 283, M. I. Hummel, 1 year	135.00	350.00
1988	LITTLE GOAT HERDER, 284, M. I. Hummel, 1 year	145.00	BR
1989	FARM BOY, 285, M. I. Hummel, 1 year	160.00	BR
1990	SHEPHERD'S BOY, 286, M. I. Hummel, 1 year	170.00	250.00
1991	JUST RESTING, 287, M. I. Hummel, 1 year	196.00	BR
1992	WAYSIDE HARMONY, 288, M. I. Hummel, 1 year	210.00	250.00
1993	DOLL BATH, 289, M. I. Hummel, 1 year	210.00	RI
1994	DOCTOR, 290, M. I. Hummel, 1 year	225.00	RI
1995	COME BACK SOON, 291, M. I. Hummel, 1 year	250.00	RI

M. I. Hummel—Four Seasons

1996	WINTER MELODY, 296, M. I. Hummel, 1 year	195.00	RI
1997	SPRINGTIME SERENADE, 197, M. I. Hummel, 1 year	195.00	RI

M. I. Hummel—Friends Forever

1992	MEDITATION, 292, M. I. Hummel, open	180.00	195.00
1993	FOR FATHER, 293, M. I. Hummel, open	195.00	RI
1994	SWEET GREETINGS, 297, M. I. Hummel, open	205.00	RI
1995	SURPRISE, 295, M. I. Hummel, open	210.00	RI

M. I. Hummel—Little Homemakers

1988	LITTLE SWEEPER, Hum745, M. I. Hummel, 1 year	45.00	50.00
1989	WASH DAY, Hum746, M. I. Hummel, closed	50.00	NR
1990	A STITCH IN TIME, Hum747, M. I. Hummel, closed	50.00	60.00
1991	CHICKEN LICKEN, Hum748, M. I. Hummel, closed	70.00	NR

M. I. Hummel—Little Music Maker

1984	LITTLE FIDDLER, 744, M. I. Hummel, 1 year	30.00	75.00
1985	SERENADE, 741, M. I. Hummel, 1 year	30.00	75.00
1986	SOLOIST, 743, M. I. Hummel, 1 year	35.00	75.00
1987	BAND LEADER, 742, M. I. Hummel, 1 year	40.00	75.00

		ISSUE	CURRENT

Mothers

1975	RABBITS, 1 year	45.00	NR
1976	CATS, 1 year	45.00	NR
1977	PANDAS, 1 year	45.00	NR
1978	DEER, 1 year	50.00	NR
1979	OWL, 1 year, 10,000	65.00	NR
1980	RACCOONS, 10,000	75.00	NR

Native Companions

1982	RACHEL, Eddie LePage, 10,000	49.50	NR
1983	HUMMINGBIRD, Eddie LePage, 10,000	49.50	NR
1983	RABBIT DANCER, Eddie LePage, 10,000	49.50	NR

North American Wildlife

1980	BEAVER, Lissa Calvert, 10,000	126.00	NR
1982	HARP SEALS, Lissa Calvert, 10,000	126.00	NR
1983	POLAR BEAR, Lissa Calvert, 10,000	126.00	NR

Old Testament

1978	TWELVE TRIBES OF ISRAEL, 10,000	125.00	NR
1979	TEN COMMANDMENTS, 10,000	175.00	NR
1980	TRADITION, 10,000	225.00	NR

Robson Christmas

1975	FLIGHT TO EGYPT, pewter, Robson, 1 year	45.00	NR
1975	FLIGHT TO EGYPT, porcelain, Robson, 1 year	50.00	NR

Wildlife

1974	ROBIN, 1 year	45.00	NR
1975	BLUE TITMOUSE, 1 year	50.00	NR
1976	BARN OWL, 1 year	50.00	NR
1977	BULLFINCH, 1 year	50.00	NR
1978	SEA GULL, 1 year	55.00	NR

Winged Fantasies

1982	STRAWBERRIES, Toller Cranston, 10,000	49.50	NR
1983	BACCHANALIA, Toller Cranston, 10,000	49.50	NR
1984	CERISES, Toller Cranston, 10,000	49.50	NR
1984	BRAMBLEBERRIES, Toller Cranston, 10,000	49.50	NR

Single Issues

1979	CHRISTMAS, 200	5,000.00	5,200.00
1982	THIS IS WHAT IT'S ALL ABOUT, Irene Spencer	49.50	NR

GOLDCROWN CERAMICS, LTD. CANADA

Famous Fighter Aircraft of World War II

NA	CHANCE-VOUGHT F41-1, Ross Tylor	49.95	NR

Chance-Vought F41-1
Photo courtesy of *Collectors News*

Ford 6-AT-AS Tri-Motor
Photo courtesy of *Collectors News*

Through the Years...The Bush Pilot Planes

		ISSUE	CURRENT
1983	FOKKER UNIVERSAL, Robert Banks, 10,000	NA	NA
1983	DE HAVILLAND DH80 PUSS MOTH, Robert Banks, 10,000	NA	NA
1983	FORD 6-AT-AS TRI-MOTOR, Robert Banks, 10,000	NA	NA
1983	FAIRCHILD 71B, Robert Banks, 10,000	NA	NA

GORHAM COLLECTION UNITED STATES

(Artists of the World, Ghent Collection, Kern Collectibles)

American Artists

1976	APACHE MOTHER AND CHILD, R. Donnelly, 9,800	25.00	55.00

American Landscapes

1980	SUMMER RESPITE, Norman Rockwell, 1 year	45.00	NR
1981	AUTUMN REFLECTION, Norman Rockwell, 1 year	45.00	NR
1982	WINTER DELIGHT, Norman Rockwell, 1 year	50.00	NR
1983	SPRING RECESS, Norman Rockwell, 1 year	60.00	NR

America's Cup

1975	COURAGEOUS, 5,000	50.00	NR

America's Cup Set

1975	*AMERICA* 1861, 1,000	200.00	NR
1975	*PURITAN*, 1,000	200.00	NR
1975	*RELIANCE*, 1,000	200.00	NR
1975	*RANGER*, 1,000	200.00	NR
1975	*COURAGEOUS*, 1,000	200.00	NR

April Fool Annual (Ghent Collection)

1978	APRIL FOOL'S DAY, Norman Rockwell, 10,000	35.00	50.00

		ISSUE	CURRENT
1979	APRIL FOOL'S DAY, Norman Rockwell, 10,000	35.00	NR
1980	APRIL FOOL'S DAY, Norman Rockwell, 10,000	37.50	NR

Audubon American Wildlife Heritage (Volair)

1977	HOUSE MOUSE, 2,500	90.00	NR
1977	ROYAL LOUISIANA HERON, 2,500	90.00	NR
1977	VIRGINIA DEER, 2,500	90.00	NR
1977	SNOWY OWL, 2,500	90.00	NR

Barrymore

1971	QUIET WATERS, Barrymore, 15,000	25.00	NR
1972	SAN PEDRO HARBOR, Barrymore, 15,000	25.00	NR
1972	NANTUCKET, sterling, Barrymore, 1,000	100.00	NR
1972	LITTLE BOATYARD, sterling, Barrymore, 1,000	100.00	145.00

Bas Relief

1981	SWEET SONG SO YOUNG, Norman Rockwell, 17,500	100.00	NR
1981	BEGUILING BUTTERCUP, Norman Rockwell, 17,500	62.50	70.00
1982	FLOWERS IN TENDER BLOOM, Norman Rockwell, 17,500	100.00	NR
1982	FLYING HIGH, Norman Rockwell, 17,500	62.50	NR

Bicentennial

1971	BURNING OF THE GASPEE, pewter, R. Pailthorpe, 5,000	35.00	NR
1972	BURNING OF THE GASPEE, silver, R. Pailthorpe, 750	500.00	NR
1972	THE 1776 PLATE, china, 18,500	17.50	35.00
1972	THE 1776 PLATE, silver, Gorham, 500	500.00	NR
1972	THE 1776 PLATE, vermeil, Gorham, 250	750.00	800.00
1972	BOSTON TEA PARTY, pewter, R. Pailthorpe, 5,000	35.00	NR
1973	BOSTON TEA PARTY, silver, R. Pailthorpe, 750	550.00	575.00
1976	1776 BICENTENNIAL, china, Gorham, 8,000	17.50	35.00

Boy Scout

1975	OUR HERITAGE, Norman Rockwell, 18,500	19.50	75.00
1976	A SCOUT IS LOYAL, Norman Rockwell, 18,500	19.50	50.00
1977	THE SCOUTMASTER, Norman Rockwell, 18,500	19.50	80.00
1977	A GOOD SIGN ALL OVER THE WORLD, Norman Rockwell, 18,500	19.50	50.00
1978	POINTING THE WAY, Norman Rockwell, 18,500	19.50	50.00
1978	CAMPFIRE STORY, Norman Rockwell, 18,500	19.50	NR
1980	BEYOND THE EASEL, Norman Rockwell, 18,500	45.00	NR

Charles Russell

1981	BRONC TO BREAKFAST, Charles Russell, 9,800	38.00	65.00
1981	IN WITHOUT KNOCKING, Charles Russell, 9,800	38.00	75.00
1982	WHEN IGNORANCE IS BLISS, Charles Russell, 9,800	45.00	85.00
1983	COWBOY LIFE, Charles Russell, 9,800	45.00	100.00

Children's Television Workshop Christmas

1981	*SESAME STREET* CHRISTMAS, 1 year	17.50	NR
1982	*SESAME STREET* CHRISTMAS, 1 year	17.50	NR
1983	*SESAME STREET* CHRISTMAS, 1 year	19.50	NR

Christmas

		ISSUE	CURRENT
1974	TINY TIM, Norman Rockwell, 1 year	12.50	25.00
1975	GOOD DEEDS, Norman Rockwell, 1 year	17.50	50.00
1976	CHRISTMAS TRIO, Norman Rockwell, 1 year	19.50	30.00
1977	YULETIDE RECKONING, Norman Rockwell, 18,500	19.50	45.00
1978	PLANNING CHRISTMAS VISIT, Norman Rockwell, 1 year	24.50	30.00
1979	SANTA'S HELPERS, Norman Rockwell, 1 year	24.50	30.00
1980	LETTER TO SANTA, Norman Rockwell, 1 year	27.50	NR
1981	SANTA PLANS HIS VISIT, Norman Rockwell, 1 year	29.50	NR
1982	THE JOLLY COACHMAN, Norman Rockwell, 1 year	29.50	NR
1983	CHRISTMAS DANCERS, Norman Rockwell, 1 year	29.50	NR
1984	CHRISTMAS MEDLEY, Norman Rockwell, 17,500	29.95	NR
1985	HOME FOR THE HOLIDAYS, Norman Rockwell, 17,500	29.95	NR
1986	MERRY CHRISTMAS GRANDMA, Norman Rockwell, 17,500	29.95	65.00
1987	THE HOMECOMING, Norman Rockwell, 17,500	35.00	NR
1988	DISCOVERY, Norman Rockwell, 17,500	37.50	NR

Clowns (Brown and Bigelow)

		ISSUE	CURRENT
1977	THE RUNAWAY, Norman Rockwell, 7,500	45.00	60.00
1978	IT'S YOUR MOVE, Norman Rockwell, 7,500	45.00	NR
1979	UNDERSTUDY, Norman Rockwell, 7,500	45.00	NR
1980	THE IDOL, Norman Rockwell, 7,500	45.00	NR

Cowboys (Brown and Bigelow)

		ISSUE	CURRENT
1980	SHARING AN APPLE, 5,000	35.00	NR
1980	SPLIT DECISION, 5,000	35.00	NR
1980	HIDING OUT, 5,000	35.00	NR

Encounters, Survival and Celebration

		ISSUE	CURRENT
1982	A FINE WELCOME, John Clymer, 7,500	50.00	80.00
1983	WINTER TRAIL, John Clymer, 7,500	50.00	80.00
1983	ALOUETTE, John Clymer, 7,500	62.50	80.00
1983	THE TRADER, John Clymer, 7,500	62.50	NR
1983	WINTER CAMP, John Clymer, 7,500	62.50	75.00
1983	THE TRAPPER TAKES A WIFE, John Clymer, 7,500	62.50	NR

First Ladies

		ISSUE	CURRENT
1988	AMY AND ROSALYNN, Thornton Utz	NA	45.00

Four Seasons—Sets

		ISSUE	CURRENT
1971	A BOY AND HIS DOG, Norman Rockwell, 1 year	50.00	175.00
1972	YOUNG LOVE, Norman Rockwell, 1 year	60.00	130.00
1973	FOUR AGES OF LOVE, Norman Rockwell, 1 year	60.00	135.00
1974	GRANDPA AND ME, Norman Rockwell, 1 year	60.00	90.00
1975	ME AND MY PAL, Norman Rockwell, 1 year	70.00	NR
1976	GRAND PALS, Norman Rockwell, 1 year	70.00	120.00
1977	GOING ON SIXTEEN, Norman Rockwell, 1 year	75.00	100.00
1978	TENDER YEARS, Norman Rockwell, 1 year	100.00	BR
1979	A HELPING HAND, Norman Rockwell, 1 year	100.00	BR
1980	DAD'S BOY, Norman Rockwell, 1 year	135.00	BR
1981	OLD TIMERS, Norman Rockwell, 1 year	100.00	NR

		ISSUE	CURRENT
1982	LIFE WITH FATHER, Norman Rockwell, 1 year	100.00	NR
1983	OLD BUDDIES, Norman Rockwell, 1 year	115.00	NR
1984	TRAVELING SALESMAN, Norman Rockwell, 1 year	115.00	NR

Four Seasons—A Boy and His Dog

1971	BOY MEETS HIS DOG, Norman Rockwell, 1 year	—	—
1971	ADVENTURERS BETWEEN ADVENTURES, Norman Rockwell, 1 year	—	—
1971	THE MYSTERIOUS MALADY, Norman Rockwell, 1 year	—	—
1971	PRIDE OF PARENTHOOD, Norman Rockwell, 1 year	—	—
	Set of 4	50.00	175.00

Four Seasons—Dad's Boy

1980	SKI SKILLS, Norman Rockwell, 1 year	—	—
1980	IN HIS SPIRITS, Norman Rockwell, 1 year	—	—
1980	TROUT DINNER, Norman Rockwell, 1 year	—	—
1980	CAREFUL AIM, Norman Rockwell, 1 year	—	—
	Set of 4	135.00	BR

Four Seasons—Four Ages of Love

1973	GAILY SHARING VINTAGE TIME, Norman Rockwell, 1 year	—	—
1973	FLOWERS IN TENDER BLOOM, Norman Rockwell, 1 year	—	—
1973	SWEET SONG SO YOUNG, Norman Rockwell, 1 year	—	—
1973	FONDLY WE DO REMEMBER, Norman Rockwell, 1 year	—	—
	Set of 4	60.00	135.00

Four Seasons—Going on Sixteen

1977	CHILLING CHORE, Norman Rockwell, 1 year	—	—
1977	SWEET SERENADE, Norman Rockwell, 1 year	—	—
1977	SHEAR AGONY, Norman Rockwell, 1 year	—	—
1977	PILGRIMAGE, Norman Rockwell, 1 year	—	—
	Set of 4	75.00	100.00

Four Seasons—Grandpa and Me

1974	GAY BLADES, Norman Rockwell, 1 year	—	—
1974	DAY DREAMERS, Norman Rockwell, 1 year	—	—
1974	GOIN' FISHING, Norman Rockwell, 1 year	—	—
1974	PENSIVE PALS, Norman Rockwell, 1 year	—	—
	Set of 4	60.00	90.00

Four Seasons—Grand Pals

1976	SNOW SCULPTURING, Norman Rockwell, 1 year	—	—
1976	SOARING SPIRITS, Norman Rockwell, 1 year	—	—
1976	FISH FINDERS, Norman Rockwell, 1 year	—	—
1976	GHOSTLY GOURDS, Norman Rockwell, 1 year	—	—
	Set of 4	70.00	120.00

Four Seasons—A Helping Hand

1979	YEAR END COURT, Norman Rockwell, 1 year	—	—
1979	CLOSED FOR BUSINESS, Norman Rockwell, 1 year	—	—
1979	SWATTER'S RIGHTS, Norman Rockwell, 1 year	—	—
1979	COAL SEASON'S COMING, Norman Rockwell, 1 year	—	—
	Set of 4	100.00	BR

ISSUE	CURRENT

Four Seasons—Life with Father

		ISSUE	CURRENT
1982	BIG DECISION, Norman Rockwell, 1 year	—	—
1982	BLASTING OUT, Norman Rockwell, 1 year	—	—
1982	CHEERING THE CHAMPS, Norman Rockwell, 1 year	—	—
1982	A TOUGH ONE, Norman Rockwell, 1 year	—	—
	Set of 4	100.00	NR

Four Seasons—Me and My Pal

1975	A LICKIN' GOOD BATH, Norman Rockwell, 1 year	—	—
1975	YOUNG MAN'S FANCY, Norman Rockwell, 1 year	—	—
1975	FISHERMAN'S PARADISE, Norman Rockwell, 1 year	—	—
1975	DISASTROUS DARING, Norman Rockwell, 1 year	—	—
	Set of 4	70.00	NR

Four Seasons—Old Buddies

1983	SHARED SUCCESS, Norman Rockwell, 1 year	—	—
1983	ENDLESS DEBATE, Norman Rockwell, 1 year	—	—
1983	HASTY RETREAT, Norman Rockwell, 1 year	—	—
1983	FINAL SPEECH, Norman Rockwell, 1 year	—	—
	Set of 4	115.00	NR

Four Seasons—Old Timers

1981	CANINE SOLO, Norman Rockwell, 1 year	—	—
1981	SWEET SURPRISE, Norman Rockwell, 1 year	—	—
1981	LAZY DAYS, Norman Rockwell, 1 year	—	—
1981	FANCY FOOTWORK, Norman Rockwell, 1 year	—	—
	Set of 4	100.00	NR

Four Seasons—Tender Years

1978	NEW YEAR LOOK, Norman Rockwell, 1 year	—	—
1978	SPRING TONIC, Norman Rockwell, 1 year	—	—
1978	COOL AID, Norman Rockwell, 1 year	—	—
1978	CHILLY RECEPTION, Norman Rockwell, 1 year	—	—
	Set of 4	100.00	BR

Four Seasons—Traveling Salesman

1984	TRAVELING SALESMAN, Norman Rockwell, 1 year	—	—
1984	COUNTRY PEDDLER, Norman Rockwell, 1 year	—	—
1984	EXPERT SALESMAN, Norman Rockwell, 1 year	—	—
1984	HORSE TRADER, Norman Rockwell, 1 year	—	—
	Set of 4	115.00	NR

Four Seasons—Young Love

1972	DOWNHILL DARING, Norman Rockwell, 1 year	—	—
1972	BEGUILING BUTTERCUP, Norman Rockwell, 1 year	—	—
1972	FLYING HIGH, Norman Rockwell, 1 year	—	—
1972	A SCHOLARLY PACE, Norman Rockwell, 1 year	—	—
	Set of 4	60.00	130.00

Gallery of Masters

1971	MAN WITH A GILT HELMET, Rembrandt, 10,000	50.00	NR
1972	SELF-PORTRAIT WITH SASKIA, Rembrandt, 10,000	50.00	NR

		ISSUE	CURRENT
1973	THE HONORABLE MRS. GRAHAM, Gainsborough, 7,500	50.00	NR

Grandpa and Me (Brown and Bigelow)

1977	GAY BLADES, 1 year	55.00	NR

Irene Spencer

1975	DEAR CHILD, Irene Spencer, 10,000	37.50	100.00
1976	PROMISES TO KEEP, Irene Spencer, 10,000	40.00	50.00

Julian Ritter

1977	CHRISTMAS VISIT, Julian Ritter, 9,800	24.50	NR
1978	VALENTINE FLUTTERING HEART, Julian Ritter 7,500	45.00	NR

Julian Ritter—Fall in Love

1977	ENCHANTMENT, Julian Ritter, 5,000	—	—
1977	FROLIC, Julian Ritter, 5,000	—	—
1977	GUTSY GAL, Julian Ritter, 5,000	—	—
1977	LONELY CHILL, Julian Ritter, 5,000	—	—
	Set of 4	100.00	NR

Julian Ritter—To Love a Clown

1978	AWAITED REUNION, Julian Ritter, 5,000	120.00	NR
1978	TWOSOME TIME, Julian Ritter, 5,000	120.00	NR
1978	SHOWTIME BECKONS, Julian Ritter, 5,000	120.00	NR
1978	TOGETHER IN MEMORIES, Julian Ritter, 5,000	120.00	NR

Landscapes

1980	SUMMER RESPITE, Norman Rockwell, 1 year	45.00	55.00
1981	AUTUMN REFLECTIONS, Norman Rockwell, 1 year	45.00	55.00
1982	WINTER DELIGHT, Norman Rockwell, 1 year	50.00	NR
1983	SPRING RECESS, Norman Rockwell, 1 year	60.00	NR

Lewis and Clark Expedition (Hamilton Collection)

1981	IN THE BITTERROOTS, John Clymer, 10 days	55.00	75.00
1981	SACAJAWEA AT THE BIG WATER, John Clymer, 10 days	55.00	65.00
1981	THE LEWIS CROSSING, John Clymer, 10 days	55.00	NR
1981	CAPTAIN CLARK AND THE BUFFALO GANG, John Clymer, 10 days	55.00	NR
1982	THE SALT MAKER, John Clymer, 10 days	55.00	NR
1982	UP THE JEFFERSON, John Clymer, 10 days	55.00	NR
1982	ARRIVAL OF SERGEANT PRYOR, John Clymer, 10 days	55.00	NR
1982	VISITORS AT FORT CLATSOP, John Clymer, 10 days	55.00	NR

Leyendecker Annual Christmas

1988	CHRISTMAS HUG, J. C. Leyendecker, 10,000	37.50	50.00

Moppets Anniversary

1976	ANNIVERSARY, 20,000	13.00	NR

Moppets Christmas

1973	CHRISTMAS MARCH, 20,000	10.00	35.00
1974	DECORATING THE TREE, 20,000	12.00	NR

		ISSUE	CURRENT
1975	BRINGING HOME THE TREE, 20,000	13.00	NR
1976	CHRISTMAS TREE, 10,000	13.00	NR
1977	PLACING THE STAR, 18,500	13.00	NR
1978	THE PRESENTS, 18,500	10.00	NR
1979	MOPPETS, 18,500	12.00	NR
1980	MOPPETS CHRISTMAS, 1 year	12.00	NR
1981	MOPPETS CHRISTMAS, 1 year	12.00	NR
1982	MOPPETS CHRISTMAS, 1 year	12.00	NR
1983	MOPPETS CHRISTMAS, 1 year	12.00	NR

Moppets Mother's Day

1973	MOTHER'S DAY, 20,000	10.00	30.00
1974	MOTHER'S DAY, 20,000	12.00	20.00
1975	MOTHER'S DAY, 20,000	13.00	NR
1976	MOTHER'S DAY, 20,000	13.00	NR
1977	MOTHER'S DAY, 18,500	13.00	NR
1978	MOTHER'S DAY, 18,500	10.00	NR

Mother's Day (Brown and Bigelow)

1980	FAMILY CIRCUS, 5,000	25.00	NR

Museum Doll

1984	LYDIA, Gorham, 5,000	29.00	125.00
1984	BELTON BEBE, Gorham, 5,000	29.00	NR
1984	CHRISTMAS LADY, Gorham, 7,500	32.50	NR
1985	LUCILLE, Gorham, 5,000	29.00	NR
1985	JUMEAU, Gorham, 5,000	29.00	NR

Omnibus Muralis

1976	200 YEARS WITH OLD GLORY, 15,000	60.00	NR
1977	LIFE OF CHRIST, 15,000	60.00	NR

Pastoral Symphony

1982	WHEN I WAS A CHILD, Bettie Felder, 7,500	42.50	50.00
1982	GATHER THE CHILDREN, Bettie Felder, 7,500	42.50	50.00
1984	SUGAR AND SPICE, Bettie Felder, 7,500	42.50	50.00
1985	HE LOVES ME, Bettie Felder, 7,500	42.50	50.00

Presidential Series

1976	KENNEDY, Norman Rockwell, 9,800	30.00	65.00
1976	EISENHOWER, Norman Rockwell, 9,800	30.00	35.00

Remington Western

1973	NEW YEAR ON THE CIMARRON, Frederic Remington, 1 year	25.00	35.00
1973	AIDING A COMRADE, Frederic Remington, 1 year	25.00	NR
1973	THE FLIGHT, Frederic Remington, 1 year	25.00	NR
1973	FIGHT FOR THE WATER HOLE, Frederic Remington, 1 year	25.00	NR
1975	OLD RAMOND, Frederic Remington, 1 year	30.00	NR
1975	A BREED, Frederic Remington, 1 year	30.00	NR
1976	CAVALRY OFFICER, Frederic Remington, 5,000	37.50	60.00
1976	A TRAPPER, Frederic Remington, 5,000	37.00	60.00

Christmas Dancers
Photo courtesy of *Collectors News*

Miss Emily, Bearing Up
Photo courtesy of *Collectors News*

Time Machine Teddies

		ISSUE	CURRENT
1986	MISS EMILY, BEARING UP, Beverly Port, 5,000	32.50	45.00
1987	BIG BEAR, THE TOY COLLECTOR, Beverly Port, 5,000	32.50	45.00
1988	HUNNY MUNNY, Beverly Port, 5,000	37.50	NR

Traveling Salesman (Brown and Bigelow)

1977	TRAVELING SALESMAN, 7,500	35.00	NR
1978	COUNTRY PEDDLER, 7,500	40.00	NR
1979	HORSE TRADER, 7,500	40.00	NR

Single Issues

1970	AMERICAN FAMILY TREE, Norman Rockwell, 5,000	17.00	100.00
1974	BIG THREE, Norman Rockwell, 10,000	17.50	NR
1974	THE GOLDEN RULE, Norman Rockwell, 1 year	12.50	30.00
1974	WEIGHING IN, Norman Rockwell, 10,000	12.50	80.00
1975	BENJAMIN FRANKLIN, Norman Rockwell, 18,500	19.50	35.00
1976	THE MARRIAGE LICENSE, Norman Rockwell, 1 year	37.50	50.00
1976	BLACK REGIMENT 1778, F. Quagon, 7,500	25.00	55.00
1976	WAGON TRAIN, <1 year	19.50	NR
1976	MEMORIAL PLATE, Norman Rockwell, 1 year	37.50	NR
1978	TRIPLE SELF-PORTRAIT, Norman Rockwell, 1 year	37.50	50.00
1980	THE ANNUAL VISIT, Norman Rockwell, 1 year	32.50	70.00
1981	A DAY IN THE LIFE OF A BOY, Norman Rockwell, 1 year	50.00	80.00
1981	A DAY IN THE LIFE OF A GIRL, Norman Rockwell, 1 year	50.00	80.00

GRANDE COPENHAGEN DENMARK

Christmas

1975	ALONE TOGETHER, 1 year	24.50	NR
1976	CHRISTMAS WREATH, 1 year	24.50	NR
1977	FISHWIVES AT GAMMELSTRAND, 1 year	26.50	NR

		ISSUE	CURRENT
1978	HANS CHRISTIAN ANDERSEN, 1 year	32.50	NR
1979	PHEASANTS, 1 year	34.50	NR
1980	SNOW QUEEN IN THE TIVOLI, Frode Bahnsen, <1 year	39.50	NR
1981	LITTLE MATCH GIRL IN NYHAVN, Frode Bahnsen, 1 year	42.50	NR
1982	SHEPHERDESS/CHIMNEY SWEEP, Frode Bahnsen, 1 year	45.00	NR
1983	LITTLE MERMAID NEAR KRONBORG, Frode Bahnsen, 1 year	45.00	100.00
1984	SANDMAN AT AMALIENBORG, Frode Bahnsen, 1 year	45.00	NR

Ugly Duckling

1985	NOT LIKE THE OTHERS	29.00	BR
1985	HE WILL GROW UP STRONG	29.00	NR
1986	COME WITH US	32.00	NR
1986	YOU DON'T UNDERSTAND ME	32.00	NR
1986	WHAT BEAUTIFUL BIRDS	32.00	NR
1986	MOST BEAUTIFUL OF ALL	32.00	NR

Single Issue

1976	BICENTENNIAL—GREAT SEAL, 1 year	35.00	NR

GRANDE DANICA DENMARK

Mother's Day

1977	DOG WITH PUPPIES, 10,000	25.00	NR
1978	STORKS, 10,000	25.00	NR
1979	BADGERS, 10,000	25.00	NR

Mother's Day—Kate Greenaway

1971	KATE GREENAWAY	14.95	NR
1972	KATE GREENAWAY	14.95	NR
1973	KATE GREENAWAY	16.95	NR
1974	KATE GREENAWAY	16.95	NR

GREENTREE POTTERIES UNITED STATES

American Landmarks

1970	MT. RUSHMORE, 2,000	10.00	NR
1971	NIAGARA FALLS, 2,000	10.00	NR

Grant Wood

1971	STUDIO, Grant Wood, 2,000	10.00	NR
1972	ANTIOCH SCHOOL, Grant Wood, 2,000	10.00	NR
1973	AT STONE CITY, Grant Wood, 2,000	10.00	NR
1974	ADOLESCENCE, Grant Wood, 2,000	10.00	NR
1975	BIRTHPLACE, Grant Wood, 2,000	10.00	NR
1976	AMERICAN GOTHIC, Grant Wood, 2,000	10.00	NR

Kennedy

1972	CENTER FOR PERFORMING ARTS, 2,000	20.00	NR
1973	BIRTHPLACE, BROOKLINE, MASS., 2,000	12.00	NR

		ISSUE	CURRENT
Mississippi River			
1973	DELTA QUEEN, 2,000	20.00	NR
1973	TRI-CENTENNIAL, 2,000	20.00	NR
Motorcar			
1972	1929 PACKARD DIETRICH CONVERTIBLE, 2,000	20.00	NR
1973	MODEL "A" FORD, 2,000	20.00	NR

GROLIER UNITED STATES

Snow White and the Seven Dwarfs

1984	AT THE WISHING WELL, Disney Studios, 15,000	24.95	NR

Three Little Pigs 50th Anniversary

1984	FIFER PIG, Disney Studios, 15,000	14.95	NR

DAVE GROSSMAN CREATIONS UNITED STATES

Children of the Week

1978	MONDAY'S CHILD, Barbard, 5,000	30.00	NR
1979	TUESDAY'S CHILD, Barbard, 5,000	30.00	NR
1979	WEDNESDAY'S CHILD, Barbard, 5,000	30.00	NR
1980	THURSDAY'S CHILD, Barbard, 5,000	30.00	NR
1980	FRIDAY'S CHILD, Barbard, 5,000	30.00	NR
1981	SATURDAY'S CHILD, Barbard, 5,000	30.00	NR
1981	SUNDAY'S CHILD, Barbard, 5,000	30.00	NR

Christmas

1978	PEACE, Barbard, 5,000	55.00	BR
1979	SANTA, Barbard, 5,000	55.00	BR

Emmett Kelly Christmas

1986	CHRISTMAS CAROL, Barry Leighton-Jones, 1 year	20.00	350.00
1987	CHRISTMAS WREATH, Barry Leighton-Jones, 1 year	20.00	200.00
1988	CHRISTMAS DINNER, Barry Leighton-Jones, 1 year	20.00	50.00
1989	CHRISTMAS FEAST, Barry Leighton-Jones, 1 year	22.00	40.00
1990	JUST WHAT I NEEDED, Barry Leighton-Jones, 1 year	24.00	40.00
1991	EMMETT THE SNOWMAN, Barry Leighton-Jones, 1 year	25.00	45.00
1992	CHRISTMAS TUNES, Barry Leighton-Jones, 1 year	25.00	35.00
1993	DOWNHILL—CHRISTMAS PLATE, Barry Leighton-Jones, 2 years	30.00	RI
1994	HOLIDAY SKATER, Barry Leighton-Jones, 2 years	30.00	RI
1995	MERRY CHRISTMAS MR. SCROOGE, Barry Leighton-Jones, 2 years	30.00	RI
1995	CHRISTMAS TUNES, Barry Leighton-Jones	30.00	RI

Magic People

1982	MUSIC FOR A QUEEN, Lynn Lupetti, 10,000	65.00	NR
1983	FANTASY FESTIVAL, Lynn Lupetti, 10,000	65.00	NR
1983	BUBBLE CHARIOT, Lynn Lupetti, 10,000	65.00	NR
NA	KITE CARRIAGE, Lynn Lupetti, 10,000	65.00	NR

Music for a Queen
Photo courtesy of *Collectors News*

Margaret Keane

		ISSUE	CURRENT
1976	BALLOON GIRL, Margaret Keane, 1 year	25.00	40.00
1977	MY KITTY, Margaret Keane, 1 year	25.00	NR
1978	BEDTIME, Margaret Keane, 1 year	25.00	NR

Native American

1991	LONE WOLF, E. Roberts, 10,000	45.00	NR
1992	TORTOISE LADY, E. Roberts, 10,000	45.00	RI
1994	BUFFALO CHIEF, E. Roberts, 10,000	45.00	RI
1994	CORN PRINCESS, E. Roberts, 10,000	45.00	RI

Norman Rockwell Bas Relief

1979	LEAPFROG, NRP-79, Rockwell-inspired, 1 year, 7½"	50.00	NR
1980	LOVERS, NRP-80, Rockwell-inspired, 1 year, 7½"	60.00	NR
1981	DREAMS OF LONG AGO, NRP-81, Rockwell-inspired, 1 year, 7½"	60.00	NR
1982	DOCTOR & DOLL, NRP-82, Rockwell-inspired, 1 year, 7½"	65.00	95.00

Norman Rockwell Bas Relief II

1983	CIRCUS, NRP-83, Rockwell-inspired, 9,500, 8½"	65.00	NR
1984	VISIT WITH NORMAN ROCKWELL, NRP-84, Rockwell-inspired, 9,500, 8½"	65.00	NR

Norman Rockwell Bas Relief Christmas

1980	CHRISTMAS TRIO, RXP-80, Rockwell-inspired, 1 year, 7½"	75.00	NR
1981	SANTA'S GOOD BOYS, RXP-81, Rockwell-inspired, 1 year, 7½"	75.00	NR
1982	FACES OF CHRISTMAS, RXP-82, Rockwell-inspired, 1 year, 7½"	75.00	NR

Norman Rockwell Bas Relief Christmas II

1983	CHRISTMAS CHORES, RXP-83, Rockwell-inspired, 9,500, 8½"	75.00	NR
1984	TINY TIM, RXP-84, Rockwell-inspired, 9,500, 8½"	75.00	NR

Norman Rockwell Bas Relief—Miniature

1980	BACK TO SCHOOL, RMP-80, Rockwell-inspired, 10,000, 4½"	24.00	NR
1981	NO SWIMMING, RMP-81, Rockwell-inspired, 10,000, 4½"	25.00	NR
1982	LOVE LETTER, RMP-82, Rockwell-inspired, 10,000, 4½"	27.00	NR

		ISSUE	CURRENT
1983	DOCTOR AND DOLL, RMP-83, Rockwell-inspired, 10,000, 4½"	27.00	NR
1984	BIG MOMENT, RMP-84, Rockwell-inspired, 10,000, 4½"	27.00	NR

Norman Rockwell Boy Scout

1981	CAN'T WAIT, BSP-01, Rockwell-inspired, 10,000	30.00	45.00
1982	A GUIDING HAND, BSP-02, Rockwell-inspired, 10,000	30.00	NR
1983	TOMORROW'S LEADER, BSP-03, Rockwell-inspired, 10,000	30.00	40.00

Norman Rockwell Collection

1978	YOUNG DOCTOR, RDP-26, Rockwell-inspired, 5,000	50.00	65.00
1979	BUTTERBOY, RP-01, Rockwell-inspired	40.00	NR
1982	AMERICAN MOTHER, RGP-42, Rockwell-inspired, 17,500	45.00	NR

Norman Rockwell Collection—Milk Glass

1983	DREAMBOATS, RGP-83, Rockwell-inspired, 15,000, 8½"	24.00	30.00

Norman Rockwell—Huckleberry Finn

1979	THE SECRET, HFP-01, Rockwell-inspired	40.00	NR
1980	LISTENING, HFP-02, Rockwell-inspired	40.00	NR
1980	NO KINGS NOR DUKES, HFP-03, Rockwell-inspired	40.00	NR
1981	THE SNAKE ESCAPES, HFP-04, Rockwell-inspired	40.00	NR

Norman Rockwell—Tom Sawyer

1975	WHITEWASHING FENCE, TSP-01, Rockwell-inspired	26.00	35.00
1976	FIRST SMOKE, TSP-02, Rockwell-inspired	26.00	35.00
1977	TAKE YOUR MEDICINE, TSP-03, Rockwell-inspired	26.00	40.00
1978	LOST IN CAVE, TSP-04, Rockwell-inspired	26.00	40.00

Saturday Evening Post

1991	DOWNHILL DARING, BRP-91, Rockwell-inspired, 1 year	25.00	NR
1991	MISSED, BRP-101, Rockwell-inspired, 1 year	25.00	NR
1992	CHOOSIN' UP, BRP-102, Rockwell-inspired, 1 year	25.00	NR

Single Issue

1990	EMMETT KELLY COMMEMORATIVE	25.00	NR

Circus
Photo courtesy of *Collectors News*

H & G STUDIOS UNITED STATES

Bearly Hiding

		ISSUE	CURRENT
1991	BEAR COTTAGE, Dennis Patrick Lewan, 7,500	35.00	NR

Mother's Day Annual

		ISSUE	CURRENT
1996	A MOTHER'S JOY, Brenda Burke, 7,500	39.00	NR

HACKETT AMERICAN UNITED STATES

(Fairmont China)

Classical American Beauties (Fairmont China)

		ISSUE	CURRENT
1978	COLLEEN, Michael Vincent, 7,500	60.00	NR
1979	HEATHER, Michael Vincent, 7,500	60.00	NR
1980	DAWN, Michael Vincent, 7,500	60.00	NR
1982	EVE, Michael Vincent, 7,500	60.00	NR

Corita Kent Annual

		ISSUE	CURRENT
1983	BELINDA, Chuck Oberstein, 7,500	39.50	NR

Crazy Cats

		ISSUE	CURRENT
1982	DAISY KITTEN, Sadako Mano, 7,500	42.50	NR
1982	DAISY CAT, Sadako Mano, 7,500	42.50	NR

Days Remembered

		ISSUE	CURRENT
1982	FIRST BIRTHDAY, David Smith, 19,500	29.50	NR
1983	FIRST HAIRCUT, David Smith, 19,500	35.00	NR

Early Discoveries

		ISSUE	CURRENT
1982	LET'S PLAY, Rudy Escalera, 7,500	42.50	NR

Endangered Species

		ISSUE	CURRENT
1980	CALIFORNIA SEA OTTERS, Sadako Mano, 7,500	35.00	75.00
1981	ASIAN PANDAS, Sadako Mano, 7,500	37.50	65.00
1982	AUSTRALIAN KOALAS, Sadako Mano, 7,500	37.50	NR
1982	RIVER OTTERS, Sadako Mano, 7,500	39.50	NR

Escalera's Father's Day

		ISSUE	CURRENT
1982	DADDY'S ROSE, Rudy Escalera, 7,500	42.50	NR
1983	DADDY'S WISH, Rudy Escalera, 7,500	42.50	NR

Everyone's Friends

		ISSUE	CURRENT
1982	SPRINGTIME, Sadako Mano, 7,500	42.50	NR
1982	AUTUMN BANDIT, Sadako Mano, 7,500	42.50	NR
1983	SNOW BUNNIES, Sadako Mano, 10,000	42.50	NR
1984	SUMMER'S BANDIT, Sadako Mano, 10,000	42.50	NR

Famous Planes of Yesterday

		ISSUE	CURRENT
1983	SPIRIT OF ST. LOUIS, Robert Banks, 5,000	39.50	NR

		ISSUE	CURRENT
1984	BYRD ANTARCTIC, Robert Banks, 5,000	39.50	NR
1984	WINNIE MAE, Robert Banks, 5,000	39.50	NR

Fashions by Irene

1983	ELEGANT LADY, Virginia Fisher, 15,000	45.00	NR

Favorite Dreams

1983	DADDY'S SAILOR, Christopher Paluso, 7,500	39.50	NR
1984	DADDY'S ENGINEER, Christopher Paluso, 7,500	39.50	NR

Daddy's Engineer
Photo courtesy of *Collectors News*

'53 Corvette
Photo courtesy of *Collectors News*

Friends of the Forest

1981	FOREST ALERT, David Smith, 7,500	50.00	NR
1982	BROOKSIDE PROTECTION, David Smith, 7,500	50.00	NR
1982	MOUNTAIN GUARDIAN, David Smith, 7,500	50.00	NR
1983	FRIENDS OF THE FOREST, David Smith, 7,500	50.00	NR

Golfing Greats

1983	ARNOLD PALMER, Cassidy J. Alexander, autographed, 100 days	125.00	NR
1984	GARY PLAYER GRAND SLAM EDITION, Cassidy J. Alexander, 3,000	125.00	NR
1984	GARY PLAYER CHAMPION EDITION, Cassidy J. Alexander, <1 year	45.00	NR

Grandparents

1984	GRANDPA'S DELIGHT, Greensmith, 10,000	27.50	NR

Horses in Action

1981	THE CHALLENGE, Violet Parkhurst, 7,500	50.00	NR
1982	COUNTRY DAYS, Violet Parkhurst, 7,500	50.00	NR
1982	FAMILY PORTRAIT, Violet Parkhurst, 7,500	50.00	NR
1983	ALL GROWN UP, Violet Parkhurst, 7,500	50.00	NR

		ISSUE	CURRENT
Huggable Moments			
1983	NAPTIME, Irish McCalla, 10,000	39.50	NR
1983	PLAYTIME, Irish McCalla, 10,000	39.50	NR
Impressions			
1982	WINDY DAY, Jo Anne Mix, 7,500	42.50	NR
1982	SUNNY DAY, Jo Anne Mix, 7,500	42.50	NR
1983	SUMMER'S DAY, Jo Anne Mix, 7,500	42.50	NR
Kelly's Stable			
1982	MY CHAMPION, C. Kelly, 15,000	42.50	NR
1983	GLORY BOUND, C. Kelly, 15,000	42.50	NR
1983	ARABIAN SPRING, C. Kelly, 15,000	42.50	NR
Landfalls			
1982	SAN FRANCISCO BAY, Bob Russell, 7,500	39.50	NR
1983	NEWPORT HARBOR, Bob Russell, 7,500	39.50	NR
1984	MIAMI BEACH, Bob Russell, 7,500	39.50	NR
Little Friends			
1984	TINY CREATURES, David Smith, 5,000	35.00	NR
1984	FOREST FRIENDS, David Smith, 5,000	35.00	NR
Little Orphans			
1982	SURPRISE PACKAGE, Ozz Franca, 19,500	29.50	NR
1983	CASTAWAY, Ozz Franca, 19,500	32.50	NR
1984	FURRY SURPRISE, Ozz Franca, 19,500	35.00	NR
Memorable Impressions			
1983	BEACHCOMBER, Ivan Anderson, 7,500	39.50	NR
1983	BEACH GIRL, Ivan Anderson, 7,500	39.50	NR
Milestone Automobiles			
1983	'57 CHEVY, Carl Pope, 5,000	39.50	NR
1984	'57 THUNDERBIRD, Carl Pope, 5,000	39.50	NR
1984	'53 CORVETTE, Carl Pope, 5,000	39.50	NR
Mix Annual Christmas			
1982	CHRISTMAS LOVE, Jo Anne Mix, 7,500	39.50	NR
Mother and Child			
1981	MOTHER'S LOVE, Ozz Franca, 7,500	42.50	NR
1982	TENDERNESS, Ozz Franca, 7,500	42.50	NR
1983	SERENITY, Ozz Franca, 7,500	42.50	NR
1984	NAVAJO MADONNA, Ozz Franca, 7,500	42.50	NR
Ocean Moods			
1981	SUNSET TIDES, Violet Parkhurst, 5,000	50.00	NR
1981	MOONLIGHT FLIGHT, Violet Parkhurst, 5,000	50.00	NR
1982	MORNING SURF, Violet Parkhurst, 5,000	50.00	NR

		ISSUE	CURRENT
1982	AFTERNOON SURF, Violet Parkhurst, 5,000	50.00	NR

Ocean Stars

1982	SEA HORSE, Carl Pope, 7,500	42.50	NR
1982	DOLPHINS, Carl Pope, 7,500	42.50	NR
1983	WHALES, Carl Pope, 10,000	42.50	NR

Sea Horse
Photo courtesy of *Collectors News*

Owl and the Pussycat

1983	THE OWL, Lenore Béran, 5,000	40.00	NR
1983	THE PUSSYCAT, Lenore Béran, 5,000	40.00	NR

Parkhurst Annual Christmas

1981	CHRISTMAS TEAR, Violet Parkhurst, 7,500	39.50	NR
1982	CHRISTMAS MORNING, Violet Parkhurst, 7,500	39.50	NR
1983	NIGHT BEFORE CHRISTMAS, Violet Parkhurst, 7,500	39.50	NR

Parkhurst Annual Mother's Day

1981	DAISIES FOR MOTHER, Violet Parkhurst, 7,500	39.50	NR

Parkhurst Diamond Collection

1982	CHANCE ENCOUNTER, Violet Parkhurst, 1,500	300.00	NR

Peaceful Retreat

1982	REFUGE, Joan Horton, 19,500	29.50	NR
1983	SOLITUDE, Joan Horton, 19,500	29.50	NR
1983	TRANQUILITY, Joan Horton, 19,500	35.00	NR
1984	SECLUSION, Joan Horton, 19,500	35.00	NR

Playful Memories (Fairmont China)

1981	RENEE, Sue Etem, 10,000	39.50	BR
1982	JEREMY, Sue Etem, 10,000	42.50	BR
1983	JAMIE, Sue Etem, 10,000	42.50	BR
1983	RANDY, Sue Etem, 10,000	45.00	BR

Prairie Children

		ISSUE	CURRENT
1982	YOUNG PIONEER, Louise Sigle, 19,500	32.50	NR
1983	ADAM, Louise Sigle, 19,500	35.00	NR

Puzzling Moments

		ISSUE	CURRENT
1983	THE PROBLEM SOLVER, William Selden, 7,500	39.50	NR
1983	PRACTICE MAKES PERFECT, Louise Sigle, 19,500	39.50	NR

Reflections of the Sea

		ISSUE	CURRENT
1983	GOLDEN SHORES, Violet Parkhurst, 5,000	42.50	NR
1984	SUMMER SANDS, Violet Parkhurst, 5,000	39.50	NR
1984	BIG SUR, Violet Parkhurst, 5,000	39.50	NR

Sadako's Helpers

		ISSUE	CURRENT
1983	ARTIST'S PAL, Sadako Mano, 7,500	39.50	NR
1983	ARTIST'S HELPER, Sadako Mano, 7,500	39.50	NR

Sadako Mano's Christmas

		ISSUE	CURRENT
1983	SANTA'S SPECIAL GIFT, Sadako Mano, 5,000	39.50	NR
1984	A GIFT FROM SANTA, Sadako Mano, 5,000	39.50	NR

Save the Whales

		ISSUE	CURRENT
1980	TRUST AND LOVE, 10,000	30.00	NR

Sensitive Moments

		ISSUE	CURRENT
1983	SHARING THE BEAUTY, Rudy Escalera, 5,000	39.50	NR

Side by Side

		ISSUE	CURRENT
1982	MY HERO, Jo Anne Mix, 19,500	32.50	45.00
1983	SIPPIN' SODA, Jo Anne Mix, 19,500	35.00	NR

Snow Babies

		ISSUE	CURRENT
1981	CANADIAN HARP SEALS, Violet Parkhurst, 5,000	39.50	65.00
1981	POLAR BEAR CUBS, Violet Parkhurst, 5,000	39.50	NR
1982	SNOW LEOPARDS, Violet Parkhurst, 5,000	42.50	NR
1982	ARCTIC FOXES, Violet Parkhurst, 5,000	42.50	NR

Special Moments

		ISSUE	CURRENT
1982	APRIL, Rudy Escalera, 7,500	42.50	NR
1983	RACHAEL, Rudy Escalera, 7,500	42.50	NR

Sports

		ISSUE	CURRENT
1981	REGGIE JACKSON, MR. OCTOBER, Christopher Paluso, 464	100.00	600.00
1983	NOLAN RYAN/INNINGS PITCHED, Christopher Paluso, 1,598	100.00	500.00
1983	REGGIE JACKSON 500 HOME RUNS, Cassidy J. Alexander, retrd	125.00	NR
1983	REGGIE JACKSON 500 HOME RUNS, Cassidy J. Alexander, artist proof, retrd	250.00	NR
1983	STEVE GARVEY, Christopher Paluso, 1,269	100.00	150.00
1983	TOM SEAVER/STRIKE OUT, Christopher Paluso, 3,272	100.00	200.00
1984	STEVE CARLTON, Christopher Paluso, retrd	100.00	NR
1985	E. MATHEWS, Christopher Paluso, retrd	125.00	NR

Artist's Helper

Monday—Wash

Returning Home

Henry Fonda

Laurel and Hardy

Reggie Jackson

Photos courtesy of *Collectors News*

		ISSUE	CURRENT
1985	H. KILLEBREW, Christopher Paluso, retrd	125.00	NR
1985	HANK AARON, Christopher Paluso, retrd	125.00	NR
1985	SANDY KOUFAX, Christopher Paluso, 1,000	125.00	NR
1985	WHITEY FORD, Christopher Paluso, retrd	125.00	NR
1985	WILLIE MAYS, Christopher Paluso, retrd	125.00	NR
1986	DON SUTTON GREAT EVENTS, Christopher Paluso, 300	125.00	NR
1986	JOE MONTANA, Cassidy J. Alexander, retrd	125.00	NR
1986	REGGIE JACKSON GREAT EVENTS, Christopher Paluso, retrd	125.00	NR
1986	ROGER CLEMENS GREAT EVENTS, Christopher Paluso, retrd	125.00	NR
1986	T. SEAVER, Christopher Paluso, 1,200	125.00	NR
1986	WALLY JOYNER GREAT EVENTS, Christopher Paluso, retrd	125.00	NR
NA	GARY CARTER, Simon, retrd	125.00	NR

Summer Fun

1983	FISHING TOGETHER, Gina Conche, 7,500	39.50	NR
1984	SWINGING TOGETHER, Gina Conche, 7,500	39.50	NR

Sun Bonnet Babies

1984	SUNDAY—SATURDAY, Charlotte Gutshall, limited, set of 7	136.50	NR

Sunday Best

1981	STACEY, Jo Anne Mix, 7,500	42.50	NR
1982	LAURIE, Jo Anne Mix, 7,500	42.50	NR

True Love

1982	HOG HEAVEN, Sadako Mano, 15,000	42.50	NR
1983	FROG HEAVEN, Sadako Mano, 15,000	39.50	NR
1983	OTTER HEAVEN, Sadako Mano, 15,000	39.50	NR
1984	OWL HEAVEN, Sadako Mano, 15,000	39.50	NR

Waterbird Families

1981	MARSH VENTURE, Dave Chapple, 7,500	42.50	NR
1982	AFTERNOON SWIM, Dave Chapple, 7,500	42.50	NR
1983	NESTING WOOD DUCKS, Dave Chapple, 10,000	42.50	NR
1983	RETURNING HOME, Dave Chapple, 10,000	42.50	NR

Wonderful World of Clowns

1981	KISS FOR A CLOWN, Chuck Oberstein, 5,000	39.50	NR
1981	RAINBOW'S END, Chuck Oberstein, 5,000	39.50	NR
1982	HAPPY DAYS, Chuck Oberstein, 5,000	39.50	NR
1982	FILLING POP'S SHOES, Chuck Oberstein, 5,000	42.50	NR

Wondrous Years

1981	AFTER THE RAINS, Rudy Escalera, 5,000	39.50	NR
1982	I GOT ONE, Rudy Escalera, 5,000	42.50	NR

World of Ozz Franca

1982	IMAGES, Ozz Franca, 7,500	42.50	NR
1982	LOST AND FOUND, Ozz Franca, 7,500	42.50	NR
1983	BEST FRIENDS, Ozz Franca, 7,500	42.50	NR

		ISSUE	CURRENT

Yesterday's Impressions

		ISSUE	CURRENT
1983	GLORIA, Kalan, 5,000	39.50	NR

Single Issues

		ISSUE	CURRENT
1982	JOHN LENNON TRIBUTE, Cassidy J. Alexander, 10,000	45.00	NR
1982	JOHN WAYNE, Cassidy J. Alexander, 10,000	39.50	BR
1983	BILL ROGERS, 7,991	42.50	NR
1983	BILL ROGERS/KING OF THE ROAD, 2,009	95.00	NR
1983	HENRY FONDA, Cassidy J. Alexander, 10,000	39.50	NR
1983	JOHN WAYNE—MILITARY, Cassidy J. Alexander, 10,000	42.50	NR
1983	LAUREL AND HARDY, Cassidy J. Alexander, 15,000	42.50	NR
1983	NOLAN RYAN, 8,402	42.50	NR
1983	REGGIE JACKSON, Christopher Paluso, 10,000	60.00	NR
1983	STEVE GARVEY, Christopher Paluso, 10,000	60.00	NR
1983	TOM SEAVER, 6,728	42.50	NR
1984	AMERICAN FRONTIER, Cassidy J. Alexander, 5,000	39.50	NR
1984	FOREVER YOURS, Cassidy J. Alexander, 15,000	42.50	NR
1984	KING REMEMBERED (ELVIS PRESLEY), Cassidy J. Alexander, 10,000	50.00	NR
1984	SALVATION ARMY, William Selden, 5,000	32.50	NR
1985	DWIGHT GOODEN, unsgd, Cassidy J. Alexander, retrd, 8½"	55.00	NR

HADLEY HOUSE UNITED STATES

American Memories

		ISSUE	CURRENT
1987	COMING HOME, Terry Redlin, 9,500, 10½"	85.00	NR
1988	LIGHTS OF HOME, Terry Redlin, 9,500, 10½"	85.00	150.00
1989	HOMEWARD BOUND, Terry Redlin, 9,500, 10½"	85.00	NR
1991	FAMILY TRADITIONS, Terry Redlin, 9,500, 10½"	85.00	NR

Annual Christmas Edition

		ISSUE	CURRENT
1996	THE PERFECT TREE, Dave Barnhouse, 45 days	29.95	RI
1996	WINTER VISITORS, Darrell Bush, 45 days	29.95	RI

Annual Christmas Series

		ISSUE	CURRENT
1991	HEADING HOME, Terry Redlin, 9,500, 9¼"	65.00	225.00
1992	PLEASURES OF WINTER, Terry Redlin, 19,500, 9¼"	65.00	125.00
1993	WINTER WONDERLAND, Terry Redlin, 19,500, 9¼"	65.00	RI
1994	ALMOST HOME, Terry Redlin, 19,500, 9¼"	65.00	RI
1995	SHARING THE EVENING, Terry Redlin, 19,500, 9¼"	29.95	RI
1996	NIGHT ON THE TOWN, Terry Redlin, 4,500, 9¼", master's edition	65.00	RI
1996	NIGHT ON THE TOWN, Terry Redlin, 45 days, 8¼"	29.95	RI
1997	TRIMMING THE TREE, Terry Redlin, 9,500	69.95	RI

Birds of Prey

		ISSUE	CURRENT
1990	FALCON, M. Dumas, 5,000	75.00	NR
1990	EAGLE, M. Dumas, 5,000	75.00	NR
1990	OWL, M. Dumas, 5,000	75.00	NR
1990	HAWK, M. Dumas, 5,000	75.00	NR

Cherished Moments

		ISSUE	CURRENT
1993	THINGS WORTH KEEPING, Steve Hanks, 15,000, 9¼"	39.95	RI

		ISSUE	CURRENT
1993	AN INNOCENT VIEW, Steve Hanks, 15,000, 9¼"	39.95	RI
1993	THE NEW ARRIVAL, Steve Hanks, 15,000, 9¼"	42.95	RI
1993	PEEKING OUT, Steve Hanks, 15,000, 9¼"	42.95	RI

Country Doctor

1995	WEDNESDAY AFTERNOON, Terry Redlin, 45 days, 8¼"	29.95	RI
1995	HOUSE CALL, Terry Redlin, 45 days, 8¼"	29.95	RI
1995	OFFICE HOURS, Terry Redlin, 45 days, 8¼"	29.95	RI
1995	MORNING ROUNDS, Terry Redlin, 45 days, 8¼"	29.95	RI

Country Life

1995	REPAIRS, Dave Barnhouse, 45 days, 8¼"	29.95	RI
1996	STARTING THEM YOUNG, Dave Barnhouse, 45 days	29.95	RI
1997	BRAGGING RIGHTS, Dave Barnhouse, 45 days	29.95	RI

Country Spirit

1996	SUNDAY MORNING, Terry Redlin, 45 days, 8¼"	29.95	RI
1996	CELEBRATION OF FAITH, Terry Redlin, 45 days, 8¼"	29.95	RI
1996	HARVEST BLESSINGS, Terry Redlin, 45 days, 8¼"	29.95	RI
1996	EVENING PRAYER, Terry Redlin, 45 days, 8¼"	29.95	RI

Days of Innocence

1995	DUET, Steve Hanks, 45 days, 8¼"	29.95	RI
1995	A WORLD FOR OUR CHILDREN, Steve Hanks, 45 days, 8¼"	29.95	RI
1995	STEPPING STONES, Steve Hanks, 45 days, 8¼"	29.95	RI

Desperadoes

NA	JAMES YOUNGER GANG, Bryan Moon, 15,000, 8½"	29.95	RI
NA	BUTCH CASSIDY AND THE SUNDANCE KID, Bryan Moon, 15,000, 8½"	29.95	RI

Glow Series

1985	EVENING GLOW, Terry Redlin, 5,000	55.00	325.00
1985	MORNING GLOW, Terry Redlin, 5,000	55.00	125.00
1985	TWILIGHT GLOW, Terry Redlin, 5,000	55.00	125.00
1988	AFTERNOON GLOW, Terry Redlin, 5,000	55.00	85.00

Heartland Collection

1995	PICKETS AND VINES, Mike Capser, 45 days	29.95	RI
1995	BIRD'S EYE VIEW, Stephen Hamrick, 45 days	29.95	RI

Hunters Paradise

1996	TOTAL COMFORT, Terry Redlin, 4,500, 9¼"	65.00	RI
1996	LIFETIME COMPANIONS, Terry Redlin, 4,500, 9¼"	65.00	RI
1997	HUNTER'S HAVEN, Terry Redlin, 4,500, 9¼"	65.00	RI
1997	CAMPFIRE TALES, Terry Redlin, 4,500, 9¼"	65.00	RI

Lovers Collection

1992	THE LOVERS, Ozz Franca, 9,500, 9¼"	50.00	NR

Midnight Magic

1996	MOONDANCE, Darrell Bush, 45 days, 8½"	29.95	RI

		ISSUE	CURRENT
1997	CRESCENT MOON BAY, Darrell Bush, 45 days, 8½"	29.95	RI

Mountain Majesty

1990	AMERICAN BALD EAGLE, T. Blaylock, 5,000	50.00	NR
1991	TRUMPETER PASS, T. Blaylock, 5,000	50.00	NR
1992	DAYBREAK ON CINNAMON CREEK, T. Blaylock, 5,000	50.00	NR
1993	BRING UP A GRANDCHILD, T. Blaylock, 5,000	50.00	RI

Nature Collection

1989	ALGONQUIN SUMMER, M. Dumas, 5,000	50.00	NR

Navajo Visions Suite

1993	NAVAJO FANTASY, Ozz Franca, 9,500, 9¼"	50.00	NR
1993	YOUNG WARRIOR, Ozz Franca, 9,500, 9¼"	50.00	NR

Navajo Woman

1990	FEATHERED HAIR TIES, Ozz Franca, 5,000, 9¼"	50.00	NR
1991	NAVAJO SUMMER, Ozz Franca, 5,000, 9¼"	50.00	NR
1992	TURQUOISE NECKLACE, Ozz Franca, 5,000, 9¼"	50.00	NR
1993	PINK NAVAJO, Ozz Franca, 5,000, 9¼"	50.00	NR

North American Legacy

1990	LEGACY LOON, James Meger, 7,500, 9¼"	60.00	NR
1991	LEGACY TIMBERWOLVES, James Meger, 7,500, 9¼"	60.00	NR
1992	LEGACY EAGLE, James Meger, 7,500, 9¼"	60.00	NR
1992	LEGACY MOOSE, James Meger, 7,500, 9¼"	60.00	NR

Retreat Series

1987	MORNING RETREAT, Terry Redlin, 9,500	65.00	100.00
1987	EVENING RETREAT, Terry Redlin, 9,500	65.00	100.00
1988	GOLDEN RETREAT, Terry Redlin, 9,500	65.00	120.00
1989	MOONLIGHT RETREAT, Terry Redlin, 9,500	65.00	85.00

Evening Glow
Photo courtesy of *Collectors News*

Morning Retreat
Photo courtesy of *Collectors News*

		ISSUE	CURRENT

Seasons

		ISSUE	CURRENT
1994	AUTUMN EVENING, Terry Redlin, 45 days, 8¼"	29.95	RI
1995	SPRING FEVER, Terry Redlin, 45 days, 8¼"	29.95	RI
1995	SUMMERTIME, Terry Redlin, 45 days, 8¼"	29.95	RI
1995	WINTERTIME, Terry Redlin, 45 days, 8¼"	29.95	RI

Special Edition

		ISSUE	CURRENT
NA	MOTHER & CHILD BOND, Steve Hanks, 45 days, 8¼"	29.95	RI
NA	THE DALTON GANG, Bryan Moon, 45 days, 8¼"	29.95	RI

Special Selections

		ISSUE	CURRENT
1989	QUIET WATER, Les Didier, 9,500, 8½"	45.00	NR
1992	THE QUEST, Les Didier, 5,000, 9¼"	50.00	NR

That Special Time

		ISSUE	CURRENT
1991	EVENING SOLITUDE, Terry Redlin, 9,500	65.00	95.00
1991	THAT SPECIAL TIME, Terry Redlin, 9,500	65.00	95.00
1992	AROMA OF FALL, Terry Redlin, 9,500	65.00	NR
1993	WELCOME TO PARADISE, Terry Redlin, 9,500	65.00	RI

Tranquility Suite

		ISSUE	CURRENT
1994	BLUE TRANQUILITY, Ozz Franca, 9,500, 9¼"	50.00	RI
1994	NAVAJO MEDITATING, Ozz Franca, 9,500, 9¼"	50.00	RI
1994	BLUE NAVAJO, Ozz Franca, 9,500, 9¼"	50.00	RI
1995	NAVAJO REFLECTION, Ozz Franca, 9,500, 9¼"	50.00	RI

Tranquil Retreats

		ISSUE	CURRENT
1998	BOWOOD COTTAGE, Marty Bell, 45 days	29.95	RI
1998	COTTONTAIL LODGE, Marty Bell, 45 days	29.95	RI
1998	IRIS COTTAGE, Marty Bell, 45 days	29.95	RI

Whitetail Deer

		ISSUE	CURRENT
1997	THE BIRCH LINE, Terry Redlin, 45 days	29.95	RI

Wildlife Memories

		ISSUE	CURRENT
1994	SHARING THE SOLITUDE, Terry Redlin, 19,500, 9¼"	65.00	RI
1994	COMFORTS OF HOME, Terry Redlin, 19,500, 9¼"	65.00	RI
1994	BEST FRIENDS, Terry Redlin, 19,500, 9¼"	65.00	RI
1994	PURE CONTENTMENT, Terry Redlin, 19,500, 9¼"	65.00	RI

Windows to the Wild

		ISSUE	CURRENT
1990	THE MASTER'S DOMAIN, Terry Redlin, 9,500, 9¼"	65.00	NR
1991	WINTER WINDBREAK, Terry Redlin, 9,500, 9¼"	65.00	NR
1992	EVENING COMPANY, Terry Redlin, 9,500, 9¼"	65.00	NR
1994	NIGHT MAPLING, Terry Redlin, 9,500, 9¼"	65.00	RI

Winner's Circle

		ISSUE	CURRENT
1991	FRIENDS, Judi Kent Pyrah, 5,000, 9¼"	50.00	NR
1993	ROSIE, Judi Kent Pyrah, 5,000, 9¼"	50.00	RI

		ISSUE	CURRENT

Winter Grotto Collection

1990	WINTER GROTTO—CARDINAL, Les Didier, 5,000	55.00	NR

JAN HAGARA COLLECTABLES

Fall in Love Again

1995	TAMMY, Jan Hagara, 7,500	39.00	RI

Victorian Children

1984	CHRIS, Jan Hagara, 15,000	45.00	NR
1985	NOEL, Jan Hagara, 15,000	45.00	NR
1986	LESLEY, Jan Hagara, 15,000	45.00	NR
1987	NIKKI, Jan Hagara, 15,000	45.00	NR
1988	HANNAH, Jan Hagara, 15,000	50.00	NR

HALLMARK GALLERIES UNITED STATES

Days to Remember—Norman Rockwell

1992	SWEET SONG SO YOUNG, pewter medallion, D. Unruh, 9,500	45.00	NR
1992	SLEEPING CHILDREN, pewter medallion, D. Unruh, 9,500	45.00	NR
1992	A BOY MEETS HIS DOG, pewter medallion, D. Unruh, 9,500	45.00	NR
1992	FISHERMAN'S PARADISE, pewter medallion, D. Unruh, 9,500	45.00	NR
1993	BREAKING HOME TIES, D. Unruh, 9,500	35.00	RI

Easter

1995	EASTER, QE0821-9, L. Votruba, 1 year	7.95	RI
1996	KEEPING A SECRET, QE0822-1, L. Votruba, 1 year	7.95	RI

Enchanted Garden

1992	SWAN LAKE (tile), E. Richardson, 9,500	35.00	NR
1992	FAIRY BUNNY TALE: BEGINNING (tile), E. Richardson, 14,500	25.00	NR
1992	FAIRY BUNNY TALE: BEGINNING II (tile), E. Richardson, 14,500	35.00	NR
1992	NEIGHBORHOOD DREAMER, E. Richardson, 9,500	45.00	NR

Family and Friends

1996	BABY'S FIRST CHRISTMAS, QX575-1, Bessie Pease Gutmann	10.95	RI
1996	OUR FIRST CHRISTMAS TOGETHER, QX580-1, L. Votruba	10.95	RI

Innocent Wonders

1992	DINKY TOOT, Thomas Blackshear, 9,500	35.00	NR
1992	PINKY POO, Thomas Blackshear, 9,500	35.00	NR
1993	POCKETS, Thomas Blackshear, 9,500	35.00	RI

L. Votruba Collector Plates

1987	LIGHT SHINES AT CHRISTMAS, 800QX481-7, L. Votruba, 1 year	8.00	NR
1988	WAITING FOR SANTA, 800QX406-1, L. Votruba, 1 year	8.00	NR
1989	MORNING OF WONDER, 825QX461-2, L. Votruba, 1 year	8.25	NR
1990	COOKIES FOR SANTA, 875QX443-6, L. Votruba, 1 year	8.75	NR
1991	LET IT SNOW!, 875QX436-9, L. Votruba, 1 year	8.75	NR

		ISSUE	CURRENT
1992	SWEET HOLIDAY HARMONY, 875QX446-1, L. Votruba, 1 year	8.75	NR

Majestic Wilderness

1992	VIXEN AND KITS, M. Newman, 9,500	35.00	NR
1992	TIMBER WOLVES, porcelain, M. Newman, 9,500	35.00	NR

Marjolein Bastin's Colors of Nature

1996	BLUE, Marjolein Bastin, 14 days	38.00	RI
1996	RED, Marjolein Bastin, 14 days	38.00	RI
1996	YELLOW, Marjolein Bastin, 14 days	38.00	RI
1996	BROWN, Marjolein Bastin, 14 days	38.00	RI

Marjolein Bastin's Seasons of Nature

1996	SPRING, Marjolein Bastin, 14 days	38.00	RI
1996	SUMMER, Marjolein Bastin, 14 days	38.00	RI
1996	AUTUMN, Marjolein Bastin, 14 days	38.00	RI
1996	WINTER CARDINAL, Marjolein Bastin, 14 days	38.00	RI

Olympic Games

1996	PARADE OF NATIONS, QHC819-4, open	NA	RI

Tobin Fraley Carousels

1992	PHILADELPHIA TOBOGGAN CO. 1920, pewter medallion, Tobin Fraley, 9,500	45.00	NR
1993	MAGICAL RIDE, Tobin Fraley, 9,500	35.00	RI

Victorian Christmas Collection

1997	VICTORIAN ELEGANCE, 24,500	30.00	RI

THE HAMILTON COLLECTION UNITED STATES

(Boehm Studios, R. J. Ernst, Gorham, Heinrich Porzellan, Metal Arts Co., Pickard China, Porcelaine Ariel, Reco International, River Shore, Royal Devon, Royal Worcester, Sports Impressions, Viletta China, Woodmere China)

All in a Day's Work

1994	WHERE'S THE FIRE?, Jim Lamb, 28 days	29.50	RI
1994	LUNCH BREAK, Jim Lamb, 28 days	29.50	RI
1994	PUPPY PATROL, Jim Lamb, 28 days	29.50	RI
1994	DECOY DELIVERY, Jim Lamb, 28 days	29.50	RI
1994	BUDDING ARTIST, Jim Lamb, 28 days	29.50	RI
1994	GARDEN GUARDS, Jim Lamb, 28 days	29.50	RI
1994	SADDLING UP, Jim Lamb, 28 days	29.50	RI
1995	TAKING THE LEAD, Jim Lamb, 28 days	29.50	RI

All Star Memories

1995	THE MANTLE STORY, D. Spindel, 28 days	35.00	RI
1996	MEMENTOS OF THE MICK, D. Spindel, 28 days	35.00	RI
1996	MANTLE APPRECIATION DAY, D. Spindel, 28 days	35.00	RI
1996	LIFE OF A LEGEND, D. Spindel, 28 days	35.00	RI
1996	YANKEE PRIDE, D. Spindel, 28 days	35.00	RI

		ISSUE	CURRENT
1996	A WORLD SERIES TRIBUTE, D. Spindel, 28 days	35.00	RI
1996	THE ULTIMATE ALL STAR, D. Spindel, 28 days	35.00	RI
1997	TRIPLE CROWN, D. Spindel, 28 days	35.00	RI

American Civil War

1990	GENERAL ROBERT E. LEE, D. Prechtel, 14 days	37.50	75.00
1990	GENERALS GRANT AND LEE AT APPOMATTOX, D. Prechtel, 14 days	37.50	65.00
1990	GENERAL THOMAS "STONEWALL" JACKSON, D. Prechtel, 14 days	37.50	55.00
1990	ABRAHAM LINCOLN, D. Prechtel, 14 days	37.50	65.00
1991	GENERAL J.E.B. STUART, D. Prechtel, 14 days	37.50	45.00
1991	GENERAL PHILIP SHERIDAN, D. Prechtel, 14 days	37.50	65.00
1991	A LETTER FROM HOME, D. Prechtel, 14 days	37.50	65.00
1991	GOING HOME, D. Prechtel, 14 days	37.50	65.00
1992	ASSEMBLING THE TROOPS, D. Prechtel, 14 days	37.50	75.00
1992	STANDING WATCH, D. Prechtel, 14 days	37.50	75.00

American Rose Garden

1988	AMERICAN SPIRIT, P. J. Sweany, 14 days	29.50	NR
1988	PEACE ROSE, P. J. Sweany, 14 days	29.50	NR
1989	WHITE KNIGHT, P. J. Sweany, 14 days	29.50	NR
1989	AMERICAN HERITAGE, P. J. Sweany, 14 days	29.50	NR
1989	ECLIPSE, P. J. Sweany, 14 days	29.50	NR
1989	BLUE MOON, P. J. Sweany, 14 days	29.50	NR
1989	CORAL CLUSTER, P. J. Sweany, 14 days	29.50	NR
1989	PRESIDENT HERBERT HOOVER, P. J. Sweany, 14 days	29.50	NR

American Water Birds

1988	WOOD DUCK, Rod Lawrence, 14 days	37.50	NR
1988	HOODED MERGANSERS, Rod Lawrence, 14 days	37.50	NR
1988	PINTAIL, Rod Lawrence, 14 days	37.50	NR
1988	CANADA GEESE, Rod Lawrence, 14 days	37.50	NR
1988	AMERICAN WIDGEONS, Rod Lawrence, 14 days	37.50	NR
1988	CANVASBACKS, Rod Lawrence, 14 days	37.50	NR
1988	MALLARD PAIR, Rod Lawrence, 14 days	37.50	NR
1988	SNOW GEESE, Rod Lawrence, 14 days	37.50	NR

American Wilderness

1995	GRAY WOLF, M. Richter, 28 days	29.95	RI
1995	SILENT WATCH, M. Richter, 28 days	29.95	RI
1995	MOON SONG, M. Richter, 28 days	29.95	RI
1995	SILENT PURSUIT, M. Richter, 28 days	29.95	RI
1996	STILL OF THE NIGHT, M. Richter, 28 days	29.95	RI
1996	NIGHTTIME SERENITY, M. Richter, 28 days	29.95	RI
1996	AUTUMN SOLITUDE, M. Richter, 28 days	29.95	RI
1996	ARCTIC WOLF, M. Richter, 28 days	29.95	RI

America's Greatest Sailing Ships

1988	U.S.S. *CONSTITUTION*, T. Freeman, 14 days	29.50	50.00
1988	*GREAT REPUBLIC*, T. Freeman, 14 days	29.50	50.00
1988	*AMERICA*, T. Freeman, 14 days	29.50	50.00
1988	*CHARLES W. MORGAN*, T. Freeman, 14 days	29.50	50.00
1988	*EAGLE*, T. Freeman, 14 days	29.50	45.00
1988	*BONHOMME RICHARD*, T. Freeman, 14 days	29.50	40.00

		ISSUE	CURRENT
1988	*GERTRUDE L. THEBAUD*, T. Freeman, 14 days	29.50	45.00
1988	*ENTERPRISE*, T. Freeman, 14 days	29.50	40.00

Andy Griffith

1992	SHERIFF ANDY TAYLOR, Robert Tanenbaum, 28 days	29.50	75.00
1992	A STARTLING CONCLUSION, Robert Tanenbaum, 28 days	29.50	75.00
1993	MAYBERRY SING-ALONG, Robert Tanenbaum, 28 days	29.50	RI
1993	AUNT BEE'S KITCHEN, Robert Tanenbaum, 28 days	29.50	RI
1993	SURPRISE! SURPRISE!, Robert Tanenbaum, 28 days	29.50	RI
1993	AN EXPLOSIVE SITUATION, Robert Tanenbaum, 28 days	29.50	RI
1993	MEETING AUNT BEE, Robert Tanenbaum, 28 days	29.50	RI
1993	OPIE'S BIG CATCH, Robert Tanenbaum, 28 days	29.50	RI

Angler's Prize

1991	TROPHY BASS, M. Susinno, 14 days	29.50	35.00
1991	BLUE RIBBON TROUT, M. Susinno, 14 days	29.50	NR
1991	SUN DANCERS, M. Susinno, 14 days	29.50	NR
1991	FRESHWATER BARRACUDA, M. Susinno, 14 days	29.50	35.00
1991	BRONZEBACK FIGHTER, M. Susinno, 14 days	29.50	35.00
1991	AUTUMN BEAUTY, M. Susinno, 14 days	29.50	35.00
1992	OLD MOONEYES, M. Susinno, 14 days	29.50	35.00
1992	SILVER KING, M. Susinno, 14 days	29.50	NR

Beauty of Winter

1992	SILENT NIGHT, 28 days	29.50	NR
1992	MOONLIGHT SLEIGH RIDE, 28 days	29.50	NR

Bialosky® and Friends

1992	FAMILY ADDITION, P. & A. Bialosky, 28 days	29.50	NR
1993	SWEETHEART, P. & A. Bialosky, 28 days	29.50	RI
1993	LET'S GO FISHING, P. & A. Bialosky, 28 days	29.50	RI
1993	U.S. MAIL, P & A. Bialosky, 28 days	29.50	RI
1993	SLEIGH RIDE, P. & A. Bialosky, 28 days	29.50	RI
1993	HONEY FOR SALE, P. & A. Bialosky, 28 days	29.50	RI
1993	BREAKFAST IN BED, P. & A. Bialosky, 28 days	29.50	RI
1993	MY FIRST TWO-WHEELER, P. & A. Bialosky, 28 days	29.50	RI

Big Cats of the World

1989	AFRICAN SHADE, Douglas Manning, 14 days	29.50	35.00
1989	VIEW FROM ABOVE, Douglas Manning, 14 days	29.50	NR
1990	ON THE PROWL, Douglas Manning, 14 days	29.50	NR
1990	DEEP IN THE JUNGLE, Douglas Manning, 14 days	29.50	NR
1990	SPIRIT OF THE MOUNTAIN, Douglas Manning, 14 days	29.50	NR
1990	SPOTTED SENTINEL, Douglas Manning, 14 days	29.50	NR
1990	ABOVE THE TREETOPS, Douglas Manning, 14 days	29.50	NR
1990	MOUNTAIN SWELLER, Douglas Manning, 14 days	29.50	NR
1992	JUNGLE HABITAT, Douglas Manning, 14 days	29.50	NR
1992	SOLITARY SENTRY, Douglas Manning, 14 days	29.50	NR

Birds of the Temple Gardens

1989	DOVES OF FIDELITY, J. Cheng, 14 days	29.50	NR
1989	CRANES OF ETERNAL LIFE, J. Cheng, 14 days	29.50	NR

		ISSUE	CURRENT
1989	HONORABLE SWALLOWS, J. Cheng, 14 days	29.50	NR
1989	ORIENTAL WHITE EYES OF BEAUTY, J. Cheng, 14 days	29.50	NR
1989	PHEASANTS OF GOOD FORTUNE, J. Cheng, 14 days	29.50	NR
1989	IMPERIAL GOLDCREST, J. Cheng, 14 days	29.50	NR
1989	GOLDFINCHES OF VIRTUE, J. Cheng, 14 days	29.50	NR
1989	MAGPIES: BIRDS OF GOOD OMEN, J. Cheng, 14 days	29.50	NR

Bundles of Joy

1988	AWAKENING, Bessie Pease Gutmann, 14 days	24.50	100.00
1988	HAPPY DREAMS, Bessie Pease Gutmann, 14 days	24.50	65.00
1988	TASTING, Bessie Pease Gutmann, 14 days	24.50	50.00
1988	SWEET INNOCENCE, Bessie Pease Gutmann, 14 days	24.50	50.00
1988	TOMMY, Bessie Pease Gutmann, 14 days	24.50	30.00
1988	A LITTLE BIT OF HEAVEN, Bessie Pease Gutmann, 14 days	24.50	90.00
1988	BILLY, Bessie Pease Gutmann, 14 days	24.50	35.00
1988	SUN KISSED, Bessie Pease Gutmann, 14 days	24.50	30.00

Butterfly Garden

1987	SPICEBUSH SWALLOWTAIL, P. J. Sweany, 14 days	29.50	45.00
1987	COMMON BLUE, P. J. Sweany, 14 days	29.50	40.00
1987	ORANGE SULPHUR, P. J. Sweany, 14 days	29.50	35.00
1987	MONARCH, P. J. Sweany, 14 days	29.50	45.00
1987	TIGER SWALLOWTAIL, P. J. Sweany, 14 days	29.50	NR
1987	CRIMSON-PATCHED LONGWING, P. J. Sweany, 14 days	29.50	40.00
1988	MORNING CLOAK, P. J. Sweany, 14 days	29.50	NR
1988	RED ADMIRAL, P. J. Sweany, 14 days	29.50	40.00

Call of the North

1993	WINTER'S DAWN, J. Tift, 28 days	29.50	RI
1994	EVENING SILENCE, J. Tift, 28 days	29.50	RI
1994	MOONLIT WILDERNESS, J. Tift, 28 days	29.50	RI
1994	SILENT SNOWFALL, J. Tift, 28 days	29.50	RI
1994	SNOWY WATCH, J. Tift, 28 days	29.50	RI
1994	SENTINELS OF THE SUMMIT, J. Tift, 28 days	29.50	RI
1994	ARCTIC SECLUSION, J. Tift, 28 days	29.50	RI
1994	FOREST TWILIGHT, J. Tift, 28 days	29.50	RI
1994	MOUNTAIN EXPLORER, J. Tift, 28 days	29.50	RI
1994	THE CRY OF WINTER, J. Tift, 28 days	29.50	RI

Call to Adventure

1993	USS *CONSTITUTION*, R. Cross, 28 days	29.50	RI
1993	THE BOUNTY, R. Cross, 28 days	29.50	RI
1994	*BONHOMME RICHARD*, R. Cross, 28 days	29.50	RI
1994	OLD NANTUCKET, R. Cross, 28 days	29.50	RI
1994	GOLDEN WEST, R. Cross, 28 days	29.50	RI
1994	BOSTON, R. Cross, 28 days	29.50	RI
1994	HANNAH, R. Cross, 28 days	29.50	RI
1994	IMPROVEMENT, R. Cross, 28 days	29.50	RI
1995	ANGLO-AMERICAN, R. Cross, 28 days	29.50	RI
1995	CHALLENGE, R. Cross, 28 days	29.50	RI

Cameo Kittens

1993	GINGER SNAP, Q. Lemonds, 28 days	29.50	RI

		ISSUE	CURRENT
1993	CAT TAILS, Q. Lemonds, 28 days	29.50	RI
1993	LADY BLUE, Q. Lemonds, 28 days	29.50	RI
1993	TINY HEART STEALER, Q. Lemonds, 28 days	29.50	RI
1993	BLOSSOM, Q. Lemonds, 28 days	29.50	RI
1994	WHISKER ANTICS, Q. Lemonds, 28 days	29.50	RI
1994	TIGER'S TEMPTATION, Q. Lemonds, 28 days	29.50	RI
1994	SCOUT, Q. Lemonds, 28 days	29.50	RI
1995	TIMID TABBY, Q. Lemonds, 28 days	29.50	RI
1995	ALL WRAPPED UP, Q. Lemonds, 28 days	29.50	RI

Childhood Reflections

1991	HARMONY, Bessie Pease Gutmann, 14 days	29.50	65.00
1991	KITTY'S BREAKFAST, Bessie Pease Gutmann, 14 days	29.50	40.00
1991	FRIENDLY ENEMIES, Bessie Pease Gutmann, 14 days	29.50	40.00
1991	SMILE, SMILE, SMILE, Bessie Pease Gutmann, 14 days	29.50	40.00
1991	LULLABY, Bessie Pease Gutmann, 14 days	29.50	40.00
1991	OH! OH! A BUNNY, Bessie Pease Gutmann, 14 days	29.50	NR
1991	LITTLE MOTHER, Bessie Pease Gutmann, 14 days	29.50	35.00
1991	THANK YOU, GOD, Bessie Pease Gutmann, 14 days	29.50	40.00

Child's Best Friend

1985	IN DISGRACE, Bessie Pease Gutmann, 14 days	24.50	125.00
1985	THE REWARD, Bessie Pease Gutmann, 14 days	24.50	100.00
1985	WHO'S SLEEPY, Bessie Pease Gutmann, 14 days	24.50	80.00
1985	GOOD MORNING, Bessie Pease Gutmann, 14 days	24.50	80.00
1985	SYMPATHY, Bessie Pease Gutmann, 14 days	24.50	55.00
1985	ON THE UP AND UP, Bessie Pease Gutmann, 14 days	24.50	60.00
1985	MINE, Bessie Pease Gutmann, 14 days	24.50	95.00
1985	GOING TO TOWN, Bessie Pease Gutmann, 14 days	24.50	125.00

Child's Christmas

1995	ASLEEP IN THE HAY, Juan Ferràndiz, 28 days	29.95	RI
1995	MERRY LITTLE FRIENDS, Juan Ferràndiz, 28 days	29.95	RI
1995	LOVE IS WARM ALL OVER, Juan Ferràndiz, 28 days	29.95	RI
1995	LITTLE SHEPHERD FAMILY, Juan Ferràndiz, 28 days	29.95	RI
1995	LIFE'S LITTLE BLESSINGS, Juan Ferràndiz, 28 days	29.95	RI
1995	HAPPINESS IS BEING LOVED, Juan Ferràndiz, 28 days	29.95	RI
1995	MY HEART BELONGS TO YOU, Juan Ferràndiz, 28 days	29.95	RI
1996	LIL' DREAMERS, Juan Ferràndiz, 28 days	29.95	RI

Chinese Blossoms of the Four Seasons

1985	SPRING PEONY BLOSSOM, 9,800	95.00	NR
1985	SUMMER LOTUS BLOSSOM, 9,800	95.00	NR
1985	AUTUMN CHRYSANTHEMUM, 9,800	95.00	NR
1985	WINTER PLUM BLOSSOM, 9,800	95.00	NR

Chinese Symbols of the Universe

1984	THE DRAGON, Mou-Sien Tseng, 7,500	90.00	NR
1984	THE PHOENIX, Mou-Sien Tseng, 7,500	90.00	NR
1984	THE TIGER, Mou-Sien Tseng, 7,500	90.00	NR
1984	THE TORTOISE, Mou-Sien Tseng, 7,500	90.00	NR
1984	MAN, Mou-Sien Tseng, 7,500	90.00	NR

Civil War Generals

		ISSUE	CURRENT
1994	ROBERT E. LEE, M. Gnatek, 28 days	29.50	RI
1994	J.E.B. STEWART, M. Gnatek, 28 days	29.50	RI
1994	JOSHUA L. CHAMBERLAIN, M. Gnatek, 28 days	29.50	RI
1994	GEORGE ARMSTRONG CUSTER, M. Gnatek, 28 days	29.50	RI
1994	NATHAN BEDFORD FORREST, M. Gnatek, 28 days	29.50	RI
1994	JAMES LONGSTREET, M. Gnatek, 28 days	29.50	RI
1995	THOMAS "STONEWALL" JACKSON, M. Gnatek, 28 days	29.50	RI
1995	CONFEDERATE HEROES, M. Gnatek, 28 days	29.50	RI

Classic American Santas

1993	A CHRISTMAS EVE VISITOR, G. Hinke, 28 days	29.50	RI
1994	UP ON THE ROOFTOP, G. Hinke, 28 days	29.50	RI
1994	SANTA'S CANDY KITCHEN, G. Hinke, 28 days	29.50	RI
1994	A CHRISTMAS CHORUS, G. Hinke, 28 days	29.50	RI
1994	AN EXCITING CHRISTMAS EVE, G. Hinke, 28 days	29.50	RI
1994	REST YE MERRY GENTLEMEN, G. Hinke, 28 days	29.50	RI
1994	PREPARING THE SLEIGH, G. Hinke, 28 days	29.50	RI
1994	THE REINDEER'S STABLE, G. Hinke, 28 days	29.50	RI
1994	HE'S CHECKING HIS LIST, G. Hinke, 28 days	29.50	RI

Classic Corvettes

1994	1957 CORVETTE, Mark Lacourciere, 28 days	29.50	RI
1994	1963 CORVETTE, Mark Lacourciere, 28 days	29.50	RI
1994	1968 CORVETTE, Mark Lacourciere, 28 days	29.50	RI
1994	1966 CORVETTE, Mark Lacourciere, 28 days	29.50	RI
1995	1967 CORVETTE, Mark Lacourciere, 28 days	29.50	RI
1995	1953 CORVETTE, Mark Lacourciere, 28 days	29.50	RI
1995	1962 CORVETTE, Mark Lacourciere, 28 days	29.50	RI
1995	1990 CORVETTE, Mark Lacourciere, 28 days	29.50	RI

Classic Sporting Dogs

1989	GOLDEN RETRIEVERS, Bob Christie, 14 days	24.50	50.00
1989	LABRADOR RETRIEVERS, Bob Christie, 14 days	24.50	50.00
1989	BEAGLES, Bob Christie, 14 days	24.50	35.00
1989	POINTERS, Bob Christie, 14 days	24.50	35.00
1989	SPRINGER SPANIELS, Bob Christie, 14 days	24.50	35.00
1990	GERMAN SHORT-HAIRED POINTERS, Bob Christie, 14 days	24.50	55.00
1990	IRISH SETTERS, Bob Christie, 14 days	24.50	35.00
1990	BRITTANY SPANIELS, Bob Christie, 14 days	24.50	50.00

Classic TV Westerns

1990	THE LONE RANGER AND TONTO, K. Milnazik, 14 days	29.50	95.00
1990	*BONANZA*™, K. Milnazik, 14 days	29.50	60.00
1990	ROY ROGERS AND DALE EVANS, K. Milnazik, 14 days	29.50	45.00
1991	*RAWHIDE*, K. Milnazik, 14 days	29.50	50.00
1991	*WILD WILD WEST*, K. Milnazik, 14 days	29.50	50.00
1991	*HAVE GUN, WILL TRAVEL*, K. Milnazik, 14 days	29.50	60.00
1991	*THE VIRGINIAN*, K. Milnazik, 14 days	29.50	50.00
1991	HOPALONG CASSIDY, K. Milnazik, 14 days	29.50	60.00

Cloak of Visions

		ISSUE	CURRENT
1994	VISIONS IN A FULL MOON, A. Farley, 28 days	29.50	RI
1994	PROTECTOR OF THE CHILD, A. Farley, 28 days	29.50	RI
1995	SPIRITS OF THE CANYON, A. Farley, 28 days	29.50	RI
1995	FREEDOM SOARS, A. Farley, 28 days	29.50	RI
1995	MYSTIC REFLECTIONS, A. Farley, 28 days	29.50	RI
1995	STAFF OF LIFE, A. Farley, 28 days	29.50	RI
1995	SPRINGTIME HUNTERS, A. Farley, 28 days	29.50	RI
1996	MOONLIT SOLACE, A. Farley, 28 days	29.50	RI

Comical Dalmatians

1996	I WILL NOT BARK IN CLASS, Landmark, 28 days	29.95	RI
1996	THE MASTER, Landmark, 28 days	29.95	RI
1996	SPOT AT PLAY, Landmark, 28 days	29.95	RI
1996	A DALMATIAN'S DREAM, Landmark, 28 days	29.95	RI
1996	TO THE RESCUE, Landmark, 28 days	29.95	RI
1996	MAID FOR A DAY, Landmark, 28 days	29.95	RI
1996	DALMATIAN CELEBRATION, Landmark, 28 days	29.95	RI
1996	CONCERT IN D-MINOR, Landmark, 28 days	29.95	RI

Coral Paradise

1989	THE LIVING OASIS, B. Higgins Bond, 14 days	29.50	40.00
1990	RICHES OF THE CORAL SEA, B. Higgins Bond, 14 days	29.50	40.00
1990	TROPICAL PAGEANTRY, B. Higgins Bond, 14 days	29.50	40.00
1990	CARIBBEAN SPECTACLE, B. Higgins Bond, 14 days	29.50	40.00
1990	UNDERSEA VILLAGE, B. Higgins Bond, 14 days	29.50	40.00
1990	SHIMMERING REEF DWELLERS, B. Higgins Bond, 14 days	29.50	40.00
1990	MYSTERIES OF THE GALAPAGOS, B. Higgins Bond, 14 days	29.50	40.00
1990	FOREST BENEATH THE SEA, B. Higgins Bond, 14 days	29.50	40.00

Cottage Puppies

1993	LITTLE GARDENERS, K. George, 28 days	29.50	RI
1993	SPRINGTIME FANCY, K. George, 28 days	29.50	RI
1993	ENDEARING INNOCENCE, K. George, 28 days	29.50	RI
1994	PICNIC PLAYTIME, K. George, 28 days	29.50	RI
1994	LAZY AFTERNOON, K. George, 28 days	29.50	RI
1994	SUMMERTIME PALS, K. George, 28 days	29.50	RI
1994	A GARDENING TRIO, K. George, 28 days	29.50	RI
1994	TAKING A BREAK, K. George, 28 days	29.50	RI

Country Garden Calendar Collection (Bing & Grøndahl)

1984	SEPTEMBER, Linda Thompson, 12,500	55.00	NR
1984	OCTOBER, Linda Thompson, 12,500	55.00	NR
1984	NOVEMBER, Linda Thompson, 12,500	55.00	NR
1984	DECEMBER, Linda Thompson, 12,500	55.00	NR
1984	JANUARY, Linda Thompson, 12,500	55.00	NR
1984	FEBRUARY, Linda Thompson, 12,500	55.00	NR
1984	MARCH, Linda Thompson, 12,500	55.00	NR
1984	APRIL, Linda Thompson, 12,500	55.00	NR
1984	MAY, Linda Thompson, 12,500	55.00	NR
1984	JUNE, Linda Thompson, 12,500	55.00	NR
1984	JULY, Linda Thompson, 12,500	55.00	NR
1984	AUGUST, Linda Thompson, 12,500	55.00	NR

June
Photo courtesy of *Collectors News*

Rock and Rollers

Country Garden Cottages

		ISSUE	CURRENT
1992	RIVERBANK COTTAGE, E. Dertner, 28 days	29.50	35.00
1992	SUNDAY OUTING, E. Dertner, 28 days	29.50	NR
1992	SHEPHERD'S COTTAGE, E. Dertner, 28 days	29.50	NR
1993	DAYDREAM COTTAGE, E. Dertner, 28 days	29.50	RI
1993	GARDEN GLORIOUS, E. Dertner, 28 days	29.50	RI
1993	THIS SIDE OF HEAVEN, E. Dertner, 28 days	29.50	RI
1993	SUMMER SYMPHONY, E. Dertner, 28 days	29.50	RI
1993	APRIL COTTAGE, E. Dertner, 28 days	29.50	RI

Country Kitties

		ISSUE	CURRENT
1989	MISCHIEF MAKERS, Gré Gerardi, 14 days	24.50	45.00
1989	TABLE MANNERS, Gré Gerardi, 14 days	24.50	45.00
1989	ATTIC ATTACK, Gré Gerardi, 14 days	24.50	45.00
1989	ROCK AND ROLLERS, Gré Gerardi, 14 days	24.50	45.00
1989	JUST FOR THE FERN OF IT, Gré Gerardi, 14 days	24.50	45.00
1989	ALL WASHED UP, Gré Gerardi, 14 days	24.50	45.00
1989	STROLLER DERBY, Gré Gerardi, 14 days	24.50	45.00
1989	CAPTIVE AUDIENCE, Gré Gerardi, 14 days	24.50	45.00

Country Season of Horses

		ISSUE	CURRENT
1990	FIRST DAY OF SPRING, J. M. Vass, 14 days	29.50	40.00
1990	SUMMER SPLENDOR, J. M. Vass, 14 days	29.50	35.00
1990	A WINTER'S WALK, J. M. Vass, 14 days	29.50	35.00
1990	AUTUMN GRANDEUR, J. M. Vass, 14 days	29.50	NR
1990	CLIFFSIDE BEAUTY, J. M. Vass, 14 days	29.50	NR
1990	FROSTY MORNING, J. M. Vass, 14 days	29.50	NR
1990	CRISP COUNTRY MORNING, J. M. Vass, 14 days	29.50	NR
1990	RIVER RETREAT, J. M. Vass, 14 days	29.50	NR

Country Summer

		ISSUE	CURRENT
1985	BUTTERFLY BEAUTY, Nancy A. Noël, 10 days	29.50	35.00

		ISSUE	CURRENT
1985	THE GOLDEN PUPPY, Nancy A. Noël, 10 days	29.50	NR
1985	THE ROCKING CHAIR, Nancy A. Noël, 10 days	29.50	35.00
1985	THE BRAHMA CALF, Nancy A. Noël, 10 days	29.50	NR
1988	THE PIGLET, Nancy A. Noël, 10 days	29.50	NR
1988	TEAMMATES, Nancy A. Noël, 10 days	29.50	NR
1985	MY BUNNY, Nancy A. Noël, 10 days	29.50	35.00
1985	THE TRICYCLE, Nancy A. Noël, 10 days	29.50	NR

Curious Kittens

1990	RAINY DAY FRIENDS, Bob Harrison, 14 days	29.50	35.00
1990	KEEPING IN STEP, Bob Harrison, 14 days	29.50	35.00
1991	DELIGHTFUL DISCOVERY, Bob Harrison, 14 days	29.50	35.00
1991	CHANCE MEETING, Bob Harrison, 14 days	29.50	35.00
1991	ALL WOUND UP, Bob Harrison, 14 days	29.50	35.00
1991	MAKING TRACKS, Bob Harrison, 14 days	29.50	35.00
1991	PLAYING CAT AND MOUSE, Bob Harrison, 14 days	29.50	35.00
1991	A PAW'S IN THE ACTION, Bob Harrison, 14 days	29.50	35.00
1992	LITTLE SCHOLAR, Bob Harrison, 14 days	29.50	35.00
1992	CAT BURGLAR, Bob Harrison, 14 days	29.50	35.00

Dale Earnhardt

1996	THE INTIMIDATOR, Sam Bass, 28 days	35.00	RI
1996	THE MAN IN BLACK, Robert Tanenbaum, 28 days	35.00	RI
1996	SILVER SELECT, Sam Bass, 28 days	35.00	RI
1996	BACK IN BLACK, Robert Tanenbaum, 28 days	35.00	RI
1996	READY TO RUMBLE, Robert Tanenbaum,28 days	35.00	RI

Daughters of the Sun

1993	SUN DANCER, K. Thayer, 28 days	29.50	RI
1993	SHINING FEATHER, K. Thayer, 28 days	29.50	RI
1993	DELIGHTED DANCER, K. Thayer, 28 days	29.50	RI
1993	EVENING DANCER, K. Thayer, 28 days	29.50	RI
1993	A SECRET GLANCE, K. Thayer, 28 days	29.50	RI
1993	CHIPPEWA CHARMER, K. Thayer, 28 days	29.50	RI
1994	PRIDE OF THE YAKIMA, K. Thayer, 28 days	29.50	RI
1994	RADIANT BEAUTY, K. Thayer, 28 days	29.50	RI

Dear to My Heart

1990	CATHY, Jan Hagara, 14 days	29.50	NR
1990	ADDIE, Jan Hagara, 14 days	29.50	NR
1990	JIMMY, Jan Hagara, 14 days	29.50	NR
1990	DACY, Jan Hagara, 14 days	29.50	NR
1990	PAUL, Jan Hagara, 14 days	29.50	NR
1991	SHELLY, Jan Hagara, 14 days	29.50	NR
1991	JENNY, Jan Hagara, 14 days	29.50	NR
1991	JOY, Jan Hagara, 14 days	29.50	NR

Delights of Childhood

1989	CRAYON CREATIONS, Jim Lamb, 14 days	29.50	NR
1989	LITTLE MOTHER, Jim Lamb, 14 days	29.50	NR
1990	BATHING BEAUTY, Jim Lamb, 14 days	29.50	NR
1990	IS THAT YOU, GRANNY?, Jim Lamb, 14 days	29.50	NR

		ISSUE	CURRENT
1990	NATURE'S LITTLE HELPER, Jim Lamb, 14 days	29.50	NR
1990	SO SORRY, Jim Lamb, 14 days	29.50	NR
1990	SHOWER TIME, Jim Lamb, 14 days	29.50	NR
1990	STORYTIME FRIENDS, Jim Lamb, 14 days	29.50	NR

Dolphin Discovery

1995	SUNRISE REVERIE, D. Queen, 28 days	29.50	RI
1995	DOLPHIN'S PARADISE, D. Queen, 28 days	29.50	RI
1995	CORAL COVE, D. Queen, 28 days	29.50	RI
1995	UNDERSEA JOURNEY, D. Queen, 28 days	29.50	RI
1995	DOLPHIN CANYON, D. Queen, 28 days	29.50	RI
1995	CORAL GARDEN, D. Queen, 28 days	29.50	RI
1996	DOLPHIN DUO, D. Queen, 28 days	29.50	RI
1996	UNDERWATER TRANQUILITY, D. Queen, 28 days	29.50	RI

Dreamsicles Christmas Annual Sculptural

1996	THE FINISHING TOUCHES, Kristin Haynes, open	39.95	RI

Dreamsicles Classics

1994	THE FLYING LESSON, Kristin Haynes, 28 days	19.50	RI
1995	BY THE LIGHT OF THE MOON, Kristin Haynes, 28 days	19.50	RI
1995	THE RECITAL, Kristin Haynes, 28 days	19.50	RI
1995	HEAVENLY PIROUETTES, Kristin Haynes, 28 days	19.50	RI
1995	BLOSSOMS AND BUTTERFLIES, Kristin Haynes, 28 days	19.50	RI
1995	LOVE'S SHY GLANCE, Kristin Haynes, 28 days	19.50	RI
1996	WISHING UPON A STAR, Kristin Haynes, 28 days	19.50	RI
1996	RAINY DAY FRIENDS, Kristin Haynes, 28 days	19.50	RI
1996	STARBOATS AHOY!, Kristin Haynes, 28 days	19.50	RI
1996	TEETER TOTS, Kristin Haynes, 28 days	19.50	RI
1996	STAR MAGIC, Kristin Haynes, 28 days	19.50	RI
1996	HEAVENLY TEA PARTY, Kristin Haynes, 28 days	19.50	RI

Dreamsicles Heaven Sent

1996	QUIET BLESSINGS, 28 days	29.95	RI
1996	A HEARFELT EMBRACE, 28 days	29.95	RI
1996	EARTH'S BLESSINGS, 28 days	29.95	RI
1996	A MOMENT IN DREAMLAND, 28 days	29.95	RI
1996	SEW CUDDLY, 28 days	29.95	RI
1996	HOMEMADE WITH LOVE, 28 days	29.95	RI
1996	A SWEET TREAT, 28 days	29.95	RI
1996	PAMPERED AND PRETTY, 28 days	29.95	RI

Dreamsicles Life's Little Blessings

1995	HAPPINESS, Kristin Haynes, 28 days	29.95	RI
1996	PEACE, Kristin Haynes, 28 days	29.95	RI
1996	LOVE, Kristin Haynes, 28 days	29.95	RI
1996	CREATIVITY, Kristin Haynes, 28 days	29.95	RI
1996	FRIENDSHIP, Kristin Haynes, 28 days	29.95	RI
1996	KNOWLEDGE, Kristin Haynes, 28 days	29.95	RI
1996	HOPE, Kristin Haynes, 28 days	29.95	RI
1996	FAITH, Kristin Haynes, 28 days	29.95	RI

Dreamsicles Sculptural

		ISSUE	CURRENT
1995	THE FLYING LESSON, open	37.50	RI
1996	BY THE LIGHT OF THE MOON, open	37.50	RI
1996	THE RECITAL, open	37.50	RI
1996	TEETER TOTS, open	37.50	RI
1996	POETRY IN MOTION, open	37.50	RI
1996	ROCK-A-BYE DREAMSICLES, open	37.50	RI
1996	THE BIRTH CERTIFICATE, open	37.50	RI
1996	SHARING HEARTS, open	37.50	RI

Dreamsicles Special Friends

1995	A HUG FROM THE HEART, Kristin Haynes, 28 days	29.95	RI
1995	HEAVEN'S LITTLE HELPER, Kristin Haynes, 28 days	29.95	RI
1995	BLESS US ALL, Kristin Haynes, 28 days	29.95	RI
1996	LOVE'S GENTLE TOUCH, Kristin Haynes, 28 days	29.95	RI
1996	THE BEST GIFT OF ALL, Kristin Haynes, 28 days	29.95	RI
1996	A HEAVENLY HOORAH!, Kristin Haynes, 28 days	29.95	RI
1996	A LOVE LIKE NO OTHER, Kristin Haynes, 28 days	29.95	RI
1996	CUDDLE UP, Kristin Haynes, 28 days	29.95	RI

Dreamsicles Special Friends Sculptural

1995	HEAVEN'S LITTLE HELPER, open	37.50	RI
1996	A HUG FROM THE HEART, open	37.50	RI
1996	BLESS US ALL, open	37.50	RI
1996	THE BEST GIFT OF ALL, open	37.50	RI
1996	A HEAVENLY HOORAH!, open	37.50	RI
1996	A LOVE LIKE NO OTHER, open	37.50	RI

Dreamsicles Sweethearts

1996	STOLEN KISS, Kristin Haynes, 28 days	35.00	RI
1996	SHARING HEARTS, Kristin Haynes, 28 days	35.00	RI
1996	LOVE LETTERS, Kristin Haynes, 28 days	35.00	RI
1996	I LOVE YOU, Kristin Haynes, 28 days	35.00	RI
1996	DAISIES & DREAMSICLES, Kristin Haynes, 28 days	35.00	RI

Drivers of Victory Lane

1994	BILL ELLIOTT #11, Robert Tannenbaum, 28 days	29.50	RI
1994	JEFF GORDON #24, Robert Tannenbaum, 28 days	29.50	RI
1994	RUSTY WALLACE #2, Robert Tannenbaum, 28 days	29.50	RI
1995	GEOFF BODINE #7, Robert Tannenbaum, 28 days	29.50	RI
1995	DALE EARNHARDT #3, Robert Tannenbaum, 28 days	29.50	RI
1996	STERLING MARLIN #4, Robert Tannenbaum, 28 days	29.50	RI
1996	TERRY LABONTE #5, Robert Tannenbaum, 28 days	29.50	RI
1996	KEN SCHARDER #25, Robert Tannenbaum, 28 days	29.50	RI
1996	JEFF GORDON #24, Robert Tannenbaum, 28 days	29.50	RI
1996	BILL ELLIOTT #94, Robert Tannenbaum, 28 days	29.50	RI
1996	RUSTY WALLACE, Robert Tannenbaum, 28 days	29.50	RI
1996	MARK MARTIN #6, Robert Tannenbaum, 28 days	29.50	RI
1996	DALE EARNHARDT #3, Robert Tannenbaum, 28 days	29.50	RI

Easyriders

1995	AMERICAN CLASSIC, Mark Lacourciere, 28 days	29.95	RI

		ISSUE	CURRENT
1995	SYMBOLS OF FREEDOM, Mark Lacourciere, 28 days	29.95	RI
1996	PATRIOT'S PRIDE, Mark Lacourciere, 28 days	29.95	RI
1996	THE WAY OF THE WEST, Mark Lacourciere, 28 days	29.95	RI
1996	REVIVAL OF AN ERA, Mark Lacourciere, 28 days	29.95	RI
1996	HOLLYWOOD STYLE, Mark Lacourciere, 28 days	29.95	RI
1996	VIETNAM EXPRESS, Mark Lacourciere, 28 days	29.95	RI
1998	LAS VEGAS, Mark Lacourciere, 28 days	29.95	RI
1996	BEACH CRUISING, Mark Lacourciere, 28 days	29.95	RI
1996	NEW ORLEANS SCENE, Mark Lacourciere, 28 days	29.95	RI

Elvis Remembered

1989	LOVING YOU, Susie Morton, 90 days	37.50	75.00
1989	EARLY YEARS, Susie Morton, 90 days	37.50	65.00
1989	TENDERLY, Susie Morton, 90 days	37.50	75.00
1989	THE KING, Susie Morton, 90 days	37.50	75.00
1989	FOREVER YOURS, Susie Morton, 90 days	37.50	75.00
1989	ROCKIN' IN THE MOONLIGHT, Susie Morton, 90 days	37.50	75.00
1989	MOODY BLUES, Susie Morton, 90 days	37.50	75.00
1989	ELVIS PRESLEY, Susie Morton, 90 days	37.50	100.00

Early Years
Photo courtesy of *Collectors News*

Ikebana
Photo courtesy of *Collectors News*

Enchanted Seascapes

1993	SANCTUARY OF THE DOLPHIN, J. Enright, 28 days	29.50	RI
1994	RHAPSODY OF HOPE, J. Enright, 28 days	29.50	RI
1994	OASIS OF THE GODS, J. Enright, 28 days	29.50	RI
1994	SPHERE OF LIFE, J. Enright, 28 days	29.50	RI
1994	EDGE OF TIME, J. Enright, 28 days	29.50	RI
1994	SEA OF LIGHT, J. Enright, 28 days	29.50	RI
1994	LOST BENEATH THE BLUE, J. Enright, 28 days	29.50	RI
1994	BLUE PARADISE, J. Enright, 28 days	29.50	RI
1995	MORNING ODYSSEY, J. Enright, 28 days	29.50	RI
1995	PARADISE COVE, J. Enright, 28 days	29.50	RI

English Country Cottages

		ISSUE	CURRENT
1990	PERIWINKLE TEA ROOM, Marty Bell, 14 days	29.50	45.00
1991	GAMEKEEPER'S COTTAGE, Marty Bell, 14 days	29.50	75.00
1991	GINGER COTTAGE, Marty Bell, 14 days	29.50	60.00
1991	LARKSPUR COTTAGE, Marty Bell, 14 days	29.50	45.00
1991	THE CHAPLAIN'S COTTAGE, Marty Bell, 14 days	29.50	35.00
1991	LORNA DOONE COTTAGE, Marty Bell, 14 days	29.50	45.00
1991	MURRIE COTTAGE, Marty Bell, 14 days	29.50	35.00
1991	LULLABYE COTTAGE, Marty Bell, 14 days	29.50	NR

Eternal Wishes of Good Fortune

1983	FRIENDSHIP, Shuho and Senkin Kage, limited	34.95	70.00
1983	PURITY AND PERFECTION, Shuho and Senkin Kage, limited	34.95	70.00
1983	ILLUSTRIOUS OFFSPRING, Shuho and Senkin Kage, limited	34.95	70.00
1983	LONGEVITY, Shuho and Senkin Kage, limited	34.95	NR
1983	YOUTH, Shuho and Senkin Kage, limited	34.95	70.00
1983	IMMORTALITY, Shuho and Senkin Kage, limited	34.95	70.00
1983	MARITAL BLISS, Shuho and Senkin Kage, limited	34.95	70.00
1983	LOVE, Shuho and Senkin Kage, limited	34.95	70.00
1983	PEACE, Shuho and Senkin Kage, limited	34.95	70.00
1983	BEAUTY, Shuho and Senkin Kage, limited	34.95	70.00
1983	FERTILITY, Shuho and Senkin Kage, limited	34.95	NR
1983	FORTITUDE, Shuho and Senkin Kage, limited	34.95	70.00

Exotic Tigers of Asia

1995	LORD OF THE RAINFOREST, K. Ottinger, 28 days	29.50	RI
1995	SNOW KING, K. Ottinger, 28 days	29.50	RI
1995	RULER OF THE WETLANDS, K. Ottinger, 28 days	29.50	RI
1996	MAJESTIC VIGIL, K. Ottinger, 28 days	29.50	RI
1996	KEEPER OF THE JUNGLE, K. Ottinger, 28 days	29.50	RI
1996	EYES OF THE JUNGLE, K. Ottinger, 28 days	29.50	RI
1996	SOVEREIGN RULER, K. Ottinger, 28 days	29.50	RI
1996	LORD OF THE LOWLANDS, K. Ottinger, 28 days	29.50	RI

Fairy Tales of Old Japan

1984	THE OLD MAN WHO MADE CHERRY TREES BLOSSOM, Shigekasu Hotta, 10 days	39.50	NR
1984	LITTLE ONE INCH, Shigekasu Hotta, 10 days	39.50	NR
1984	MY LORD BAG OF RICE, Shigekasu Hotta, 10 days	39.50	NR
1984	THE TONGUE-CUT SPARROW, Shigekasu Hotta, 10 days	39.50	NR
1984	THE BAMBOO CUTTER AND THE MOON CHILD, Shigekasu Hotta, 10 days	39.50	NR
1984	THE FISHER LAD, Shigekasu Hotta, 10 days	39.50	NR
1984	THE MAGIC TEA KETTLE, Shigekasu Hotta, 10 days	39.50	NR

Familiar Spirits

1996	FAITHFUL GUARDIANS, David Wright, 28 days	29.95	RI
1996	SHARING NATURE'S INNOCENCE, David Wright, 28 days	29.95	RI
1996	TRUSTED FRIEND, David Wright, 28 days	29.95	RI
1996	A FRIENDSHIP BEGINS, David Wright, 28 days	29.95	RI
1996	WINTER HOMAGE, David Wright, 28 days	29.95	RI
1996	THE BLESSING, David Wright, 28 days	29.95	RI
1996	HEALING POWERS, David Wright, 28 days	29.95	RI

Farmyard Friends

		ISSUE	CURRENT
1992	MISTAKEN IDENTITY, Jim Lamb, 28 days	29.50	NR
1992	LITTLE COWHANDS, Jim Lamb, 28 days	29.50	NR
1993	SHREDDING THE EVIDENCE, Jim Lamb, 28 days	29.50	RI
1993	PARTNERS IN CRIME, Jim Lamb, 28 days	29.50	RI
1993	FOWL PLAY, Jim Lamb, 28 days	29.50	RI
1993	FOLLOW THE LEADER, Jim Lamb, 28 days	29.50	RI
1993	PONY TALES, Jim Lamb, 28 days	29.50	RI
1993	AN APPLE A DAY, Jim Lamb, 28 days	29.50	RI

Favorite American Songbirds

1989	BLUE JAYS OF SPRING, D. O'Driscoll, 14 days	29.50	35.00
1989	RED CARDINALS OF WINTER, D. O'Driscoll, 14 days	29.50	35.00
1989	ROBINS AND APPLE BLOSSOMS, D. O'Driscoll, 14 days	29.50	35.00
1989	GOLDFINCHES OF SUMMER, D. O'Driscoll, 14 days	29.50	35.00
1990	AUTUMN CHICKADEES, D. O'Driscoll, 14 days	29.50	35.00
1990	BLUEBIRDS AND MORNING GLORIES, D. O'Driscoll, 14 days	29.50	35.00
1990	TUFTED TITMOUSE AND HOLLY, D. O'Driscoll, 14 days	29.50	NR
1991	CAROLINA WRENS OF SPRING, D. O'Driscoll, 14 days	29.50	NR

Favorite Old Testament Stories

1994	JACOB'S DREAM, Samuel Butcher, 28 days	35.00	RI
1995	THE BABY MOSES, Samuel Butcher, 28 days	35.00	RI
1995	ESTHER'S GIFT TO HER PEOPLE, Samuel Butcher, 28 days	35.00	RI
1995	A PRAYER FOR VICTORY, Samuel Butcher, 28 days	35.00	RI
1995	WHERE YOU GO, I WILL GO, Samuel Butcher, 28 days	35.00	RI
1995	A PRAYER ANSWERED, A PROMISE KEPT, Samuel Butcher, 28 days	35.00	RI
1996	JOSEPH SOLD INTO SLAVERY, Samuel Butcher, 28 days	35.00	RI
1996	DANIEL IN THE LION'S DEN, Samuel Butcher, 28 days	35.00	RI
1996	NOAH AND THE ARK, Samuel Butcher, 28 days	35.00	RI

Fierce and the Free

1992	BIG MEDICINE, Frank McCarthy, 28 days	29.50	NR
1993	LAND OF THE WINTER HAWK, Frank McCarthy, 28 days	29.50	RI
1993	WARRIOR OF SAVAGE SPLENDOR, Frank McCarthy, 28 days	29.50	RI
1994	WAR PARTY, Frank McCarthy, 28 days	29.50	RI
1994	THE CHALLENGE, Frank McCarthy, 28 days	29.50	RI
1994	OUT OF THE RISING MIST, Frank McCarthy, 28 days	29.50	RI
1994	THE AMBUSH, Frank McCarthy, 28 days	29.50	RI
1994	DANGEROUS CROSSING, Frank McCarthy, 28 days	29.50	RI

Flower Festivals of Japan

1985	CHRYSANTHEMUM, Norio Hara, 10 days	45.00	NR
1985	HOLLYHOCK, Norio Hara, 10 days	45.00	NR
1985	PLUM BLOSSOM, Norio Hara, 10 days	45.00	NR
1985	MORNING GLORY, Norio Hara, 10 days	45.00	NR
1985	CHERRY BLOSSOM, Norio Hara, 10 days	45.00	NR
1985	IRIS, Norio Hara, 10 days	45.00	NR
1985	LILY, Norio Hara, 10 days	45.00	NR
1985	PEACH BLOSSOM, Norio Hara, 10 days	45.00	NR

Forging New Frontiers

		ISSUE	CURRENT
1994	THE RACE IS ON, Jim Deneen, 28 days	29.50	RI
1994	BIG BOY, Jim Deneen, 28 days	29.50	RI
1994	CRESTING THE SUMMIT, Jim Deneen, 28 days	29.50	RI
1994	SPRING ROUNDUP, Jim Deneen, 28 days	29.50	RI
1994	WINTER IN THE ROCKIES, Jim Deneen, 28 days	29.50	RI
1994	HIGH COUNTRY LOGGING, Jim Deneen, 28 days	29.50	RI
1994	CONFRONTATION, Jim Deneen, 28 days	29.50	RI
1994	A WELCOME SIGHT, Jim Deneen, 28 days	29.50	RI

Garden of Verses

1983	PICTURE BOOKS IN WINTER, Jessie Wilcox Smith, 10 days	24.50	NR
1983	LITTLE DROPS OF WATER, Jessie Wilcox Smith, 10 days	24.50	NR
1983	A CHILD'S QUESTION, Jessie Wilcox Smith, 10 days	24.50	NR
1983	LOOKING GLASS RIVER, Jessie Wilcox Smith, 10 days	24.50	NR
1983	THE LITTLE BUSY BEE, Jessie Wilcox Smith, 10 days	24.50	NR
1983	AT THE SEASIDE, Jessie Wilcox Smith, 10 days	24.50	NR
1983	THE TEA PARTY, Jessie Wilcox Smith, 10 days	24.50	NR
1983	FOREIGN LANDS, Jessie Wilcox Smith, 10 days	24.50	NR
1983	THE HAYLOFT, Jessie Wilcox Smith, 10 days	24.50	NR
1983	AMONG THE POPPIES, Jessie Wilcox Smith, 10 days	24.50	NR
1983	FIVE O'CLOCK TEA, Jessie Wilcox Smith, 10 days	24.50	NR
1983	I LOVE LITTLE KITTY, Jessie Wilcox Smith, 10 days	24.50	NR

Gardens of the Orient

1983	FLOWERING OF SPRING, Shunsuke Suetomi, 10 days	19.50	NR
1983	FESTIVAL OF MAY, Shunsuke Suetomi, 10 days	19.50	NR
1983	CHERRY BLOSSOM BROCADE, Shunsuke Suetomi, 10 days	19.50	NR
1983	A WINTER'S REPOSE, Shunsuke Suetomi, 10 days	19.50	NR
1983	THE GARDEN SANCTUARY, Shunsuke Suetomi, 10 days	19.50	NR
1983	SUMMER'S GLORY, Shunsuke Suetomi, 10 days	19.50	NR
1983	JUNE'S CREATION, Shunsuke Suetomi, 10 days	19.50	NR
1983	NEW YEAR'S DAWN, Shunsuke Suetomi, 10 days	19.50	NR
1983	AUTUMN SERENITY, Shunsuke Suetomi, 10 days	19.50	NR
1983	HARVEST MORNING, Shunsuke Suetomi, 10 days	19.50	NR
1983	TRANQUIL POND, Shunsuke Suetomi, 10 days	19.50	NR
1983	MORNING SONG, Shunsuke Suetomi, 10 days	19.50	NR

Garden Song

1994	WINTER'S SPLENDOR, M. Hanson, 28 days	29.50	RI
1994	IN FULL BLOOM, M. Hanson, 28 days	29.50	RI
1994	GOLDEN GLORIES, M. Hanson, 28 days	29.50	RI
1995	AUTUMN'S ELEGANCE, M. Hanson, 28 days	29.50	RI
1995	FIRST SNOWFALL, M. Hanson, 28 days	29.50	RI
1995	ROBINS IN SPRING, M. Hanson, 28 days	29.50	RI
1995	FALL'S SERENADE, M. Hanson, 28 days	29.50	RI
1996	SOUNDS OF WINTER, M. Hanson, 28 days	29.50	RI
1996	SPRINGTIME HAVEN, M. Hanson, 28 days	29.50	RI

Gentle Arts of the Geisha

1983	IKEBANA, Yasuhiko Adachi, limited	21.50	NR

		ISSUE	CURRENT

Glory of the Game

1994	B. THOMPSON'S SHOT HEARD ROUND THE WORLD, T. Fogarty	29.50	RI
1994	HANK AARON'S RECORD-BREAKING HOME RUN, T. Fogarty	29.50	RI

Golden Age of American Railroads

1991	THE BLUE COMET, Theodore A. Xaras, 14 days	29.50	45.00
1991	THE MORNING LOCAL, Theodore A. Xaras, 14 days	29.50	55.00
1991	THE PENNSYLVANIA K-4, Theodore A. Xaras, 14 days	29.50	55.00
1991	ABOVE THE CANYON, Theodore A. Xaras, 14 days	29.50	60.00
1991	PORTRAIT IN STEAM, Theodore A. Xaras, 14 days	29.50	70.00
1991	THE SANTA FE SUPER CHIEF, Theodore A. Xaras, 14 days	29.50	90.00
1991	BIG BOY, Theodore A. Xaras, 14 days	29.50	60.00
1991	THE EMPIRE BUILDER, Theodore A. Xaras, 14 days	29.50	75.00
1992	AN AMERICAN CLASSIC, Theodore A. Xaras, 14 days	29.50	60.00
1992	FINAL DESTINATION, Theodore A. Xaras, 14 days	29.50	60.00

Golden Classics

1987	SLEEPING BEAUTY, Carol Lawson, 14 days	37.50	NR
1987	RUMPELSTILTSKIN, Carol Lawson, 14 days	37.50	NR
1987	JACK AND THE BEANSTALK, Carol Lawson, 14 days	37.50	NR
1987	SNOW WHITE AND ROSE RED, Carol Lawson, 14 days	37.50	NR
1987	HANSEL AND GRETEL, Carol Lawson, 14 days	37.50	NR
1987	CINDERELLA, Carol Lawson, 14 days	37.50	NR
1987	THE GOLDEN GOOSE, Carol Lawson, 14 days	37.50	NR
1987	THE SNOW QUEEN, Carol Lawson, 14 days	37.50	NR

Golden Discoveries

1995	BOOT BANDITS, L. Budge, 28 days	29.95	RI
1995	HIDING THE EVIDENCE, L. Budge, 28 days	29.95	RI
1995	DECOY DILEMMA, L. Budge, 28 days	29.95	RI
1995	FISHING FOR DINNER, L. Budge, 28 days	29.95	RI
1996	LUNCHTIME COMPANIONS, L. Budge, 28 days	29.95	RI
1996	FRIEND OR FOE?, L. Budge, 28 days	29.95	RI

Golden Puppy Portraits

1994	DO NOT DISTURB!, P. Braun, 28 days	29.50	RI
1995	TEETHING TIME, P. Braun, 28 days	29.50	RI
1995	TABLE MANNERS, P. Braun, 28 days	29.50	RI
1995	A GOLDEN BOUQUET, P. Braun, 28 days	29.50	RI
1995	TIME FOR BED, P. Braun, 28 days	29.50	RI
1995	BATHTIME BLUES, P. Braun, 28 days	29.50	RI
1996	SPINNING A YARN, P. Braun, 28 days	29.50	RI
1996	PARTYTIME PUPPY, P. Braun, 28 days	29.50	RI

Good Sports

1990	WIDE RETRIEVER, Jim Lamb, 14 days	29.50	45.00
1990	DOUBLE PLAY, Jim Lamb, 14 days	29.50	50.00
1990	HOLE IN ONE, Jim Lamb, 14 days	29.50	35.00
1990	THE BASS MASTERS, Jim Lamb, 14 days	29.50	40.00
1990	SPOTTED ON THE SIDELINE, Jim Lamb, 14 days	29.50	35.00
1990	SLAP SHOT, Jim Lamb, 14 days	29.50	45.00
1991	NET PLAY, Jim Lamb, 14 days	29.50	NR

		ISSUE	CURRENT
1991	BASSETBALL, Jim Lamb, 14 days	29.50	40.00
1992	BOXER REBELLION, Jim Lamb, 14 days	29.50	35.00
1992	GREAT TRY, Jim Lamb, 14 days	29.50	40.00

Great Fighter Planes of World War II

1992	OLD CROW, R. Waddey, 14 days	29.50	35.00
1992	BIG HOG, R. Waddey, 14 days	29.50	35.00
1992	P-47 THUNDERBOLT, R. Waddey, 14 days	29.50	35.00
1992	P-40 FLYING TIGER, R. Waddey, 14 days	29.50	35.00
1992	F4F WILDCAT, R. Waddey, 14 days	29.50	35.00
1992	P-38F LIGHTNING, R. Waddey, 14 days	29.50	NR
1993	F6F HELLCAT, R. Waddey, 14 days	29.50	RI
1993	P-39M AIRACOBRA, R. Waddey, 14 days	29.50	RI
1995	MEMPHIS BELLE, R. Waddey, 14 days	29.50	RI
1995	THE DRAGON AND HIS TAIL, R. Waddey, 14 days	29.50	RI
1995	BIG BEAUTIFUL DOLL, R. Waddey, 14 days	29.50	RI
1995	BATS OUT OF HELL, R. Waddey, 14 days	29.50	RI

Great Mammals of the Sea

1991	ORCA TRIO, Wyland, 14 days	35.00	45.00
1991	HAWAII DOLPHINS, Wyland, 14 days	35.00	45.00
1991	ORCA JOURNEY, Wyland, 14 days	35.00	40.00
1991	DOLPHIN PARADISE, Wyland, 14 days	35.00	45.00
1991	CHILDREN OF THE SEA, Wyland, 14 days	35.00	60.00
1991	KISSING DOLPHINS, Wyland, 14 days	35.00	40.00
1991	ISLANDS, Wyland, 14 days	35.00	60.00
1991	ORCAS, Wyland, 14 days	35.00	45.00

Greatest Show on Earth (Porcelaine Ariel)

1981	CLOWNS, Franklin Moody, 10 days	30.00	65.00
1981	ELEPHANTS, Franklin Moody, 10 days	30.00	50.00
1981	AERIALISTS, Franklin Moody, 10 days	30.00	40.00
1981	GREAT PARADE, Franklin Moody, 10 days	30.00	40.00
1981	MIDWAY, Franklin Moody, 10 days	30.00	40.00
1981	EQUESTRIANS, Franklin Moody, 10 days	30.00	40.00
1981	LION TAMER, Franklin Moody, 10 days	30.00	40.00
1981	GRANDE FINALE, Franklin Moody, 10 days	30.00	40.00

Growing Up Together

1990	MY VERY BEST FRIENDS, P. Brooks, 14 days	29.50	35.00
1990	TEA FOR TWO, P. Brooks, 14 days	29.50	NR
1990	TENDER LOVING CARE, P. Brooks, 14 days	29.50	NR
1990	PICNIC PALS, P. Brooks, 14 days	29.50	NR
1991	NEWFOUND FRIENDS, P. Brooks, 14 days	29.50	NR
1991	KITTEN CABOODLE, P. Brooks, 14 days	29.50	NR
1991	FISHING BUDDIES, P. Brooks, 14 days	29.50	NR
1991	BEDTIME BLESSINGS, P. Brooks, 14 days	29.50	NR

Historic Railways

1995	HARPER'S FERRY, Theodore A. Xaras, 28 days	29.95	RI
1995	HORSESHOE CURVE, Theodore A. Xaras, 28 days	29.95	RI
1995	KENTUCKY'S RED RIVER, Theodore A. Xaras, 28 days	29.95	RI
1995	SHERMAN HILL CHALLENGER, Theodore A. Xaras, 28 days	29.95	RI

		ISSUE	CURRENT
1996	NEW YORK CENTRAL'S 4-6-4 HUDSON, Theodore A. Xaras, 28 days	29.95	RI
1996	RAILS BY THE SEASHORE, Theodore A. Xaras, 28 days	29.95	RI
1996	STEAM IN THE HIGH SIERRAS, Theodore A. Xaras, 28 days	29.95	RI
1996	EVENING DEPARTURE, Theodore A. Xaras, 28 days	29.95	RI

I Love Lucy Plate Collection

1989	CALIFORNIA, HERE WE COME, J. Kritz, 14 days	29.50	100.00
1989	IT'S JUST LIKE CANDY, J. Kritz, 14 days	29.50	125.00
1990	THE BIG SQUEEZE, J. Kritz, 14 days	29.50	125.00
1990	EATING THE EVIDENCE, J. Kritz, 14 days	29.50	225.00
1990	TWO OF A KIND, J. Kritz, 14 days	29.50	125.00
1991	QUEEN OF THE GYPSIES, J. Kritz, 14 days	29.50	125.00
1992	NIGHT AT THE COPA, J. Kritz, 14 days	29.50	125.00
1992	A RISING PROBLEM, J. Kritz, 14 days	29.50	125.00

James Dean Commemorative Issue

1991	JAMES DEAN, Thomas Blackshear, 14 days	29.50	NR

James Dean the Legend

1992	UNFORGOTTEN REBEL, Morgan Weistling, 28 days	29.50	NR

Japanese Blossoms of Autumn

1985	BELLFLOWER, Koseki and Ebihara, 10 days	45.00	NR
1985	ARROWROOT, Koseki and Ebihara, 10 days	45.00	NR
1985	WILD CARNATION, Koseki and Ebihara, 10 days	45.00	NR
1985	MAIDEN FLOWER, Koseki and Ebihara, 10 days	45.00	NR
1985	PAMPAS GRASS, Koseki and Ebihara, 10 days	45.00	NR
1985	BUSH CLOVER, Koseki and Ebihara, 10 days	45.00	NR
1985	PURPLE TROUSERS, Koseki and Ebihara, 10 days	45.00	NR

Japanese Floral Calendar

1981	NEW YEAR'S DAY, Shuho and Senkin Kage, 10 days	32.50	40.00
1982	EARLY SPRING, Shuho and Senkin Kage, 10 days	32.50	40.00
1982	SPRING, Shuho and Senkin Kage, 10 days	32.50	40.00
1982	GIRL'S DOLL DAY FESTIVAL, Shuho and Senkin Kage, 10 days	32.50	40.00
1982	BUDDHA'S BIRTHDAY, Shuho and Senkin Kage, 10 days	32.50	40.00
1982	EARLY SUMMER, Shuho and Senkin Kage, 10 days	32.50	40.00
1982	BOY'S DOLL DAY FESTIVAL, Shuho and Senkin Kage, 10 days	32.50	40.00
1982	SUMMER, Shuho and Senkin Kage, 10 days	32.50	NR
1982	AUTUMN, Shuho and Senkin Kage, 10 days	32.50	NR
1983	FESTIVAL OF THE FULL MOON, Shuho and Senkin Kage, 10 days	32.50	NR
1983	LATE AUTUMN, Shuho and Senkin Kage, 10 days	32.50	NR
1983	WINTER, Shuho and Senkin Kage, 10 days	32.50	NR

Jeweled Hummingbirds

1989	RUBY-THROATED HUMMINGBIRDS, James Landenberger, 14 days	37.50	45.00
1989	GREAT SAPPHIRE WING HUMMINGBIRDS, James Landenberger, 14 days	37.50	45.00
1989	RUBY-TOPAZ HUMMINGBIRDS, James Landenberger, 14 days	37.50	45.00
1989	ANDEAN EMERALD HUMMINGBIRDS, James Landenberger, 14 days	37.50	45.00
1989	GARNET-THROATED HUMMINGBIRDS, James Landenberger, 14 days	37.50	45.00
1989	BLUE-HEADED SAPPHIRE HUMMINGBIRDS, James Landenberger, 14 days	37.50	45.00
1989	PEARL CORONET HUMMINGBIRDS, James Landenberger, 14 days	37.50	45.00

		ISSUE	CURRENT
1989	AMETHYST-THROATED SUNANGETS, James Landenberger, 14 days	37.50	45.00

Joe Montana

1996	40,000 YARDS, Robert Tanenbaum, 28 days	35.00	RI
1996	FINDING A WAY TO WIN, Joseph Catalano, 28 days	35.00	RI
1996	COMEBACK KID, Joseph Catalano, 28 days	35.00	RI
1996	CHIEF ON THE FIELD, Petronella, 28 days	35.00	RI

Knick Knack Kitty Cat Sculptural

1996	KITTENS IN THE CUPBOARD, L. Yencho, open	39.95	RI
1996	KITTENS IN THE CUSHION, L. Yencho, open	39.95	RI
1996	KITTENS IN THE PLANT, L. Yencho, open	39.95	RI
1996	KITTENS IN THE YARN, L. Yencho, open	39.95	RI

Last Warriors

1993	WINTER OF '41, Chuck Ren, 28 days	29.50	RI
1993	MORNING OF RECKONING, Chuck Ren, 28 days	29.50	RI
1993	TWILIGHT'S LAST GLEAMING, Chuck Ren, 28 days	29.50	RI
1993	LONE WINTER JOURNEY, Chuck Ren, 28 days	29.50	RI
1994	VICTORY'S REWARD, Chuck Ren, 28 days	29.50	RI
1994	SOLITARY HUNTER, Chuck Ren, 28 days	29.50	RI
1994	SOLEMN REFLECTION, Chuck Ren, 28 days	29.50	RI
1994	CONFRONTING DANGER, Chuck Ren, 28 days	29.50	RI
1995	MOMENT OF CONTEMPLATION, Chuck Ren, 28 days	29.50	RI
1995	THE LAST SUNSET, Chuck Ren, 28 days	29.50	RI

Legend of Father Christmas

1994	THE RETURN OF FATHER CHRISTMAS, V. Dezerin, 28 days	29.50	RI
1994	GIFTS FROM FATHER CHRISTMAS, V. Dezerin, 28 days	29.50	RI
1994	THE FEAST OF THE HOLIDAY, V. Dezerin, 28 days	29.50	RI
1995	CHRISTMAS DAY VISITORS, V. Dezerin, 28 days	29.50	RI
1995	DECORATING THE TREE, V. Dezerin, 28 days	29.50	RI
1995	THE SNOW SCULPTURE, V. Dezerin, 28 days	29.50	RI
1995	SKATING ON THE POND, V. Dezerin, 28 days	29.50	RI
1995	HOLY NIGHT, V. Dezerin, 28 days	29.50	RI

Legendary Warriors

1995	WHITE QUIVER AND SCOUT, M. Gentry, 28 days	29.95	RI
1995	LAKOTA RENDEZVOUS, M. Gentry, 28 days	29.95	RI
1995	CRAZY HORSE, M. Gentry, 28 days	29.95	RI
1995	SITTING BULL'S VISION, M. Gentry, 28 days	29.95	RI
1996	NOBLE SURRENDER, M. Gentry, 28 days	29.95	RI
1996	SIOUX THUNDER, M. Gentry, 28 days	29.95	RI
1996	EAGLE DANCER, M. Gentry, 28 days	29.95	RI
1996	THE TRAP, M. Gentry, 28 days	29.95	RI

Lisi Martin Christmas

1992	SANTA'S LITTLEST REINDEER, Lisi Martin, 28 days	29.50	NR
1993	NOT A CREATURE WAS STIRRING, Lisi Martin, 28 days	29.50	RI
1993	CHRISTMAS DREAMS, Lisi Martin, 28 days	29.50	RI
1993	THE CHRISTMAS STORY, Lisi Martin, 28 days	29.50	RI
1993	TRIMMING THE TREE, Lisi Martin, 28 days	29.50	RI

		ISSUE	CURRENT
1993	A TASTE OF THE HOLIDAYS, Lisi Martin, 28 days	29.50	RI
1993	THE NIGHT BEFORE CHRISTMAS, Lisi Martin, 28 days	29.50	RI
1993	CHRISTMAS WATCH, Lisi Martin, 28 days	29.50	RI
1995	CHRISTMAS PRESENCE, Lisi Martin, 28 days	29.50	RI
1995	NOSE TO NOSE, Lisi Martin, 28 days	29.50	RI

Little Fawns of the Forest

1995	IN THE MORNING LIGHT, Ruanne Manning, 28 days	29.95	RI
1995	COOL REFLECTIONS, Ruanne Manning, 28 days	29.95	RI
1995	NATURE'S LESSON, Ruanne Manning, 28 days	29.95	RI
1996	A FRIENDSHIP BLOSSOMS, Ruanne Manning, 28 days	29.95	RI
1996	INNOCENT COMPANIONS, Ruanne Manning, 28 days	29.95	RI
1996	NEW LIFE, NEW DAY, Ruanne Manning, 28 days	29.95	RI

Little Ladies

1989	PLAYING BRIDESMAID, Maud Humphrey Bogart, 14 days	29.50	100.00
1990	THE SEAMSTRESS, Maud Humphrey Bogart, 14 days	29.50	80.00
1990	LITTLE CAPTIVE, Maud Humphrey Bogart, 14 days	29.50	50.00
1990	PLAYING MAMA, Maud Humphrey Bogart, 14 days	29.50	60.00
1990	SUSANNA, Maud Humphrey Bogart, 14 days	29.50	50.00
1990	KITTY'S BATH, Maud Humphrey Bogart, 14 days	29.50	50.00
1990	A DAY IN THE COUNTRY, Maud Humphrey Bogart, 14 days	29.50	50.00
1991	SARAH, Maud Humphrey Bogart, 14 days	29.50	50.00
1991	FIRST PARTY, Maud Humphrey Bogart, 14 days	29.50	50.00
1991	THE MAGIC KITTEN, Maud Humphrey Bogart, 14 days	29.50	60.00

Little Rascals

1985	THREE FOR THE SHOW, 10 days	24.50	40.00
1985	MY GAL, 10 days	24.50	NR
1985	SKELETON CREW, 10 days	24.50	NR
1985	ROUGHIN' IT, 10 days	24.50	NR
1985	SPANKY'S PRANKS, 10 days	24.50	NR
1985	BUTCH'S CHALLENGE, 10 days	24.50	NR
1985	DARLA'S DEBUT, 10 days	24.50	NR
1985	PETE'S PAL, 10 days	24.50	NR

Little Shopkeepers

1990	SEW TIRED, Gré Gerardi, 14 days	29.50	NR
1991	BREAK TIME, Gré Gerardi, 14 days	29.50	NR
1991	PURRFECT FIT, Gré Gerardi, 14 days	29.50	NR
1991	TOYING AROUND, Gré Gerardi, 14 days	29.50	35.00
1991	CHAIN REACTION, Gré Gerardi, 14 days	29.50	45.00
1991	INFERIOR DECORATORS, Gré Gerardi, 14 days	29.50	35.00
1991	TULIP TAG, Gré Gerardi, 14 days	29.50	35.00
1991	CANDY CAPERS, Gré Gerardi, 14 days	29.50	35.00

Lore of the West

1993	A MILE IN HIS MOCASSINS, L. Danielle, 28 days	29.50	RI
1993	PATH OF HONOR, L. Danielle, 28 days	29.50	RI
1993	A CHIEF'S PRIDE, L. Danielle, 28 days	29.50	RI
1994	PATHWAYS OF THE PUEBLO, L. Danielle, 28 days	29.50	RI
1994	IN HER STEPS, L. Danielle, 28 days	29.50	RI
1994	GROWING UP BRAVE, L. Danielle, 28 days	29.50	RI

		ISSUE	CURRENT
1994	NOMADS OF THE SOUTHWEST, L. Danielle, 28 days	29.50	RI
1994	SACRED SPIRIT OF THE PLAINS, L. Danielle, 28 days	29.50	RI
1994	WE'LL FIGHT NO MORE, L. Danielle, 28 days	29.50	RI
1994	THE END OF THE TRAIL, L. Danielle, 28 days	29.50	RI

Love's Messengers

1995	TO MY LOVE, John Grossman, 28 days	29.50	RI
1995	CUPID'S ARROW, John Grossman, 28 days	29.50	RI
1995	LOVE'S MELDOY, John Grossman, 28 days	29.50	RI
1995	A TOKEN OF LOVE, John Grossman, 28 days	29.50	RI
1995	HARMONY OF LOVE, John Grossman, 28 days	29.50	RI
1996	TRUE LOVE'S OFFERING, John Grossman, 28 days	29.50	RI
1996	LOVE'S IN BLOOM, John Grossman, 28 days	29.50	RI
1996	TO MY SWEETHEART, John Grossman, 28 days	29.50	RI

Lucille Ball Official Commemorative Plate

1993	LUCY, Morgan Weistling, 28 days	37.50	RI

Madonna and Child

1992	MADONNA DELLA SEIDA, R. Sanzio, 28 days	37.50	NR
1992	VIRGIN OF THE ROCKS, Leonardo da Vinci, 28 days	37.50	NR
1993	MADONNA OF ROSARY, Bartolomé Esteban Murillo, 28 days	37.50	RI
1993	SISTINE MADONNA, R. Sanzio, 28 days	37.50	RI
1993	VIRGIN ADORING CHRIST CHILD, A. Correggio, 28 days	37.50	RI
1993	VIRGIN OF THE GRAPE, P. Mignard, 28 days	37.50	RI
1993	MADONNA DEL MAGNIFICAT, Sandro Botticelli, 28 days	37.50	RI
1993	MADONNA COL BAMBINO, Sandro Botticelli, 28 days	37.50	RI

Magical World of Legends and Myths

1993	A MOTHER'S LOVE, J. Shalatain, 28 days	35.00	RI
1993	DREAMS OF PEGASUS, J. Shalatain, 28 days	35.00	RI
1994	FLIGHT OF THE PEGASUS, J. Shalatain, 28 days	35.00	RI
1994	THE AWAKENING, J. Shalatain, 28 days	35.00	RI
1994	ONCE UPON A DREAM, J. Shalatain, 28 days	35.00	RI
1994	THE DAWN OF ROMANCE, J. Shalatain, 28 days	35.00	RI
1994	THE ASTRAL UNICORN, J. Shalatain, 28 days	35.00	RI
1994	FLIGHT INTO PARADISE, J. Shalatain, 28 days	35.00	RI
1995	PEGASUS IN THE STARS, J. Shalatain, 28 days	35.00	RI
1995	UNICORN OF THE SEA, J. Shalatain, 28 days	35.00	RI

Majestic Birds of Prey

1983	GOLDEN EAGLE, C. Ford Riley, 12,500	55.00	65.00
1983	COOPER'S HAWK, C. Ford Riley, 12,500	55.00	60.00
1983	GREAT HORNED OWL, C. Ford Riley, 12,500	55.00	60.00
1983	BALD EAGLE, C. Ford Riley, 12,500	55.00	60.00
1983	BARRED OWL, C. Ford Riley, 12,500	55.00	60.00
1983	SPARROW HAWK, C. Ford Riley, 12,500	55.00	60.00
1983	PEREGRINE FALCON, C. Ford Riley, 12,500	55.00	60.00
1983	OSPREY, C. Ford Riley, 12,500	55.00	60.00

Majesty of Flight

1989	THE EAGLE SOARS, Thomas Hirata, 14 days	37.50	50.00

		ISSUE	CURRENT
1989	REALM OF THE RED-TAIL, Thomas Hirata, 14 days	37.50	NR
1989	COASTAL JOURNEY, Thomas Hirata, 14 days	37.50	45.00
1989	SENTRY OF THE NORTH, Thomas Hirata, 14 days	37.50	BR
1989	COMMANDING THE MARSH, Thomas Hirata, 14 days	37.50	NR
1990	THE VANTAGE POINT, Thomas Hirata, 14 days	29.50	45.00
1990	SILENT WATCH, Thomas Hirata, 14 days	29.50	50.00
1990	FIERCE AND FREE, Thomas Hirata, 14 days	29.50	45.00

Man's Best Friend

1992	SPECIAL DELIVERY, L. Picken, 28 days	29.50	NR
1992	MAKING WAVES, L. Picken, 28 days	29.50	NR
1992	GOOD CATCH, L. Picken, 28 days	29.50	NR
1993	TIME FOR A WALK, L. Picken, 28 days	29.50	RI
1993	FAITHFUL FRIEND, L. Picken, 28 days	29.50	RI
1993	LET'S PLAY BALL, L. Picken, 28 days	29.50	RI
1993	SITTING PRETTY, L. Picken, 28 days	29.50	RI
1993	BEDTIME STORY, L. Picken, 28 days	29.50	RI
1993	TRUSTED COMPANION, L. Picken, 28 days	29.50	RI

Mickey Mantle

1996	THE MICK, Robert Tanenbaum, 28 days	35.00	RI
1996	536 HOME RUNS, Robert Tanenbaum, 28 days	35.00	RI
1996	2,401 GAMES, Robert Tanenbaum, 28 days	35.00	RI
1996	SWITCH HITTER, Robert Tanenbaum, 28 days	35.00	RI
1996	16 TIME ALL STAR, Robert Tanenbaum, 28 days	35.00	RI
1996	18 WORLD SERIES HOME RUNS, Robert Tanenbaum, 28 days	35.00	RI
1997	1956—A CROWNING YEAR, Robert Tanenbaum, 28 days	35.00	RI
1997	REMEMBERING A LEGENDARY YANKEE, Robert Tanenbaum, 28 days	35.00	RI

Mike Schmidt

1994	THE ULTIMATE COMPETITOR: MIKE SCHMIDT, Robert Tanenbaum, 28 days	29.50	RI
1995	A HOMERUN KING, Robert Tanenbaum, 28 days	29.50	RI
1995	AN ALL TIME, ALL STAR, Robert Tanenbaum, 28 days	29.50	RI
1995	A CAREER RETROSPECTIVE, Robert Tanenbaum, 28 days	29.50	RI

Milestones in Space

1994	MOON LANDING, D. Dixon, 28 days	29.50	RI
1995	SPACE LAB, D. Dixon, 28 days	29.50	RI
1995	MAIDEN FLIGHT OF COLUMBIA, D. Dixon, 28 days	29.50	RI
1995	FREE WALK IN SPACE, D. Dixon, 28 days	29.50	RI
1995	LUNAR ROVER, D. Dixon, 28 days	29.50	RI
1995	HANDSHAKE IN SPACE, D. Dixon, 28 days	29.50	RI
1995	FIRST LANDING ON MARS, D. Dixon, 28 days	29.50	RI
1995	VOYAGER'S EXPLORATION, D. Dixon, 28 days	29.50	RI

Mixed Company

1990	TWO AGAINST ONE, Pam Cooper, 14 days	29.50	NR
1990	A STICKY SITUATION, Pam Cooper, 14 days	29.50	NR
1990	WHAT'S UP?, Pam Cooper, 14 days	29.50	NR
1990	ALL WRAPPED UP, Pam Cooper, 14 days	29.50	NR
1990	PICTURE PERFECT, Pam Cooper, 14 days	29.50	NR
1991	A MOMENT TO UNWIND, Pam Cooper, 14 days	29.50	NR
1991	OLÉ, Pam Cooper, 14 days	29.50	NR

		ISSUE	CURRENT
1991	PICNIC PROWLERS, Pam Cooper, 14 days	29.50	NR

Murals from the Precious Moments Chapel

1995	THE PEARL OF GREAT PRICE, Samuel Butcher, 28 days	35.00	RI
1995	THE GOOD SAMARITAN, Samuel Butcher, 28 days	35.00	RI
1996	THE PRODIGAL SON, Samuel Butcher, 28 days	35.00	RI
1996	THE GOOD SHEPHERD, Samuel Butcher, 28 days	35.00	RI

Mystic Warriors

1992	DELIVERANCE, Chuck Ren, 28 days	29.50	NR
1992	MYSTIC WARRIOR, Chuck Ren, 28 days	29.50	NR
1992	SUN SEEKER, Chuck Ren, 28 days	29.50	NR
1992	TOP GUN, Chuck Ren, 28 days	29.50	NR
1992	MAN WHO WALKS ALONE, Chuck Ren, 28 days	29.50	NR
1992	WINDRIDER, Chuck Ren, 28 days	29.50	NR
1992	SPIRIT OF THE PLAINS, Chuck Ren, 28 days	29.50	NR
1993	BLUE THUNDER, Chuck Ren, 28 days	29.50	RI
1993	SUN GLOW, Chuck Ren, 28 days	29.50	RI
1993	PEACE MAKER, Chuck Ren, 28 days	29.50	RI

Native American Legends

1996	PEACE PIPE, A. Biffignandi, 28 days	29.95	RI
1996	FEATHER-WOMAN, A. Biffignandi, 28 days	29.95	RI
1996	SPIRIT OF SERENITY, A. Biffignandi, 28 days	29.95	RI
1996	ENCHANTED WARRIOR, A. Biffignandi, 28 days	29.95	RI
1996	MYSTICAL SERENADE, A. Biffignandi, 28 days	29.95	RI
1996	LEGEND OF BRIDAL VEIL, A. Biffignandi, 28 days	29.95	RI
1996	SEASONS OF LOVE, A. Biffignandi, 28 days	29.95	RI
1996	A BASHFUL COURTSHIP, A. Biffignandi, 28 days	29.95	RI

Nature's Majestic Cats

1993	SIBERIAN TIGER, M. Richter, 28 days	29.50	RI
1993	HIMALAYAN SNOW LEOPARD, M. Richter, 28 days	29.50	RI
1993	AFRICAN LION, M. Richter, 28 days	29.50	RI
1994	ASIAN CLOUDED LEOPARD, M. Richter, 28 days	29.50	RI
1994	AMERICAN COUGAR, M. Richter, 28 days	29.50	RI
1994	EAST AFRICAN LEOPARD, M. Richter, 28 days	29.50	RI
1994	AFRICAN CHEETAH, M. Richter, 28 days	29.50	RI
1994	CANADIAN LYNX, M. Richter, 28 days	29.50	RI

Nature's Nighttime Realm

1992	BOBCAT, G. Murray, 28 days	29.50	NR
1992	COUGAR, G. Murray, 28 days	29.50	NR
1993	JAGUAR, G. Murray, 28 days	29.50	RI
1993	WHITE TIGER, G. Murray, 28 days	29.50	RI
1993	LYNX, G. Murray, 28 days	29.50	RI
1993	LION, G. Murray, 28 days	29.50	RI
1993	SNOW LEOPARDS, G. Murray, 28 days	29.50	RI
1993	CHEETAH, G. Murray, 28 days	29.50	RI

Nature's Quiet Moments

1988	A CURIOUS PAIR, Ron Parker, 14 days	37.50	75.00

		ISSUE	CURRENT
1988	NORTHERN MORNING, Ron Parker, 14 days	37.50	55.00
1988	JUST RESTING, Ron Parker, 14 days	37.50	50.00
1989	WAITING OUT THE STORM, Ron Parker, 14 days	37.50	40.00
1989	CREEKSIDE, Ron Parker, 14 days	37.50	40.00
1989	AUTUMN FORAGING, Ron Parker, 14 days	37.50	40.00
1989	OLD MAN OF THE MOUNTAIN, Ron Parker, 14 days	37.50	40.00
1989	MOUNTAIN BLOOMS, Ron Parker, 14 days	37.50	40.00

Noble American Indian Women

1989	SACAJAWEA, David Wright, 14 days	29.50	60.00
1990	POCAHONTAS, David Wright, 14 days	29.50	50.00
1990	MINNEHAHA, David Wright, 14 days	29.50	50.00
1990	PINE LEAF, David Wright, 14 days	29.50	45.00
1990	LILY OF THE MOHAWK, David Wright, 14 days	29.50	45.00
1990	WHITE ROSE, David Wright, 14 days	29.50	50.00
1991	LOZEN, David Wright, 14 days	29.50	45.00
1991	FALLING STAR, David Wright, 14 days	29.50	40.00

Noble Owls of America

1986	MORNING MIST, John Seerey-Lester, 15,000	55.00	BR
1987	PRAIRIE SUNDOWN, John Seerey-Lester, 15,000	55.00	NR
1987	WINTER VIGIL, John Seerey-Lester, 15,000	55.00	BR
1987	AUTUMN MIST, John Seerey-Lester, 15,000	55.00	BR
1987	DAWN IN THE WILLOWS, John Seerey-Lester, 15,000	55.00	NR
1987	SNOWY WATCH, John Seerey-Lester, 15,000	55.00	NR
1988	HIDING PLACE, John Seerey-Lester, 15,000	55.00	NR
1988	WAITING FOR DUSK, John Seerey-Lester, 15,000	55.00	NR

Nolan Ryan

1994	THE STRIKEOUT EXPRESS, Robert Tanenbaum, 28 days	29.50	RI
1994	BIRTH OF A LEGEND, Robert Tanenbaum, 28 days	29.50	RI
1994	MR. FASTBALL, Robert Tanenbaum, 28 days	29.50	RI
1994	MILLION-DOLLAR PLAYER, Robert Tanenbaum, 28 days	29.50	RI
1994	27 SEASONS, Robert Tanenbaum, 28 days	29.50	RI
1994	FAREWELL, Robert Tanenbaum, 28 days	29.50	RI
1994	THE RYAN EXPRESS, Robert Tanenbaum, 28 days	29.50	RI

North American Ducks

1991	AUTUMN FLIGHT, Rod Lawrence, 14 days	29.50	35.00
1991	THE RESTING PLACE, Rod Lawrence, 14 days	29.50	NR
1991	TWIN FLIGHT, Rod Lawrence, 14 days	29.50	NR
1991	MISTY MORNING, Rod Lawrence, 14 days	29.50	NR
1992	SPRINGTIME THAW, Rod Lawrence, 14 days	29.50	NR
1992	SUMMER RETREAT, Rod Lawrence, 14 days	29.50	NR
1992	OVERCAST, Rod Lawrence, 14 days	29.50	NR
1992	PERFECT PINTAILS, Rod Lawrence, 14 days	29.50	NR

North American Gamebirds

1990	RING-NECKED PHEASANT, Jim Killen, 14 days	37.50	NR
1990	BOBWHITE QUAIL, Jim Killen, 14 days	37.50	45.00
1990	RUFFED GROUSE, Jim Killen, 14 days	37.50	NR
1990	GAMBEL QUAIL, Jim Killen, 14 days	37.50	NR
1990	MOURNING DOVE, Jim Killen, 14 days	37.50	45.00

		ISSUE	CURRENT
1990	WOODCOCK, Jim Killen, 14 days	37.50	45.00
1991	CHUKAR PARTRIDGE, Jim Killen, 14 days	37.50	45.00
1991	WILD TURKEY, Jim Killen, 14 days	37.50	45.00

North American Waterbirds

1988	WOOD DUCKS, Rod Lawrence, 14 days	37.50	45.00
1988	HOODED MERGANSERS, Rod Lawrence, 14 days	37.50	50.00
1988	PINTAILS, Rod Lawrence, 14 days	37.50	NR
1988	CANADA GEESE, Rod Lawrence, 14 days	37.50	NR
1989	AMERICAN WIDGEONS, Rod Lawrence, 14 days	37.50	55.00
1989	CANVASBACKS, Rod Lawrence, 14 days	37.50	55.00
1989	MALLARD PAIR, Rod Lawrence, 14 days	37.50	60.00
1989	SNOW GEESE, Rod Lawrence, 14 days	37.50	45.00

Official Honeymooners Plate Collection

1987	THE HONEYMOONERS, D. Kilmer, 14 days	24.50	115.00
1987	THE HUCKLEBUCK, D. Kilmer, 14 days	24.50	115.00
1987	BABY, YOU'RE THE GREATEST, D. Kilmer, 14 days	24.50	115.00
1988	THE GOLFER, D. Kilmer, 14 days	24.50	100.00
1988	THE TV CHEFS, D. Kilmer, 14 days	24.50	100.00
1988	BANG! ZOOM!, D. Kilmer, 14 days	24.50	125.00
1988	THE ONLY WAY TO TRAVEL, D. Kilmer, 14 days	24.50	100.00
1988	THE HONEYMOON EXPRESS, D. Kilmer, 14 days	24.50	140.00
1993	THE OFFICIAL HONEYMOONER'S COMMEMORATIVE PLATE, D. Bobnick, 28 days	37.50	RI

The Hucklebuck

Passage to China

1983	EMPRESS OF CHINA, R. Massey, 15,000	55.00	NR
1983	ALLIANCE, R. Massey, 15,000	55.00	NR
1985	GRAND TURK, R. Massey, 15,000	55.00	NR
1985	SEA WITCH, R. Massey, 15,000	55.00	NR
1985	FLYING CLOUD, R. Massey, 15;000	55.00	NR
1985	ROMANCE OF THE SEAS, R. Massey, 15,000	55.00	NR
1985	SEA SERPENT, R. Massey, 15,000	55.00	NR
1985	CHALLENGE, R. Massey, 15,000	55.00	NR

		ISSUE	CURRENT

Petals and Purrs

		ISSUE	CURRENT
1988	BLUSHING BEAUTIES, Bob Harrison, 14 days	24.50	55.00
1988	SPRING FEVER, Bob Harrison, 14 days	24.50	40.00
1988	MORNING GLORIES, Bob Harrison, 14 days	24.50	45.00
1988	FORGET-ME-NOT, Bob Harrison, 14 days	24.50	35.00
1989	GOLDEN FANCY, Bob Harrison, 14 days	24.50	30.00
1989	PINK LILIES, Bob Harrison, 14 days	24.50	30.00
1989	SUMMER SUNSHINE, Bob Harrison, 14 days	24.50	55.00
1989	SIAMESE SUMMER, Bob Harrison, 14 days	24.50	55.00

Portraits of Childhood

1981	BUTTERFLY MAGIC, Thornton Utz, 28 days	24.95	NR
1981	SWEET DREAMS, Thornton Utz, 28 days	24.95	NR
1981	TURTLE TALK, Thornton Utz, 28 days	24.95	35.00
1981	FRIENDS FOREVER, Thornton Utz, 28 days	24.95	NR

Portraits of Jesus

1994	JESUS, THE GOOD SHEPHERD, W. Sallman, 28 days	29.50	RI
1994	JESUS IN THE GARDEN, W. Sallman, 28 days	29.50	RI
1994	JESUS, CHILDREN'S FRIEND, W. Sallman, 28 days	29.50	RI
1994	THE LORD'S SUPPER, W. Sallman, 28 days	29.50	RI
1994	CHRIST AT DAWN, W. Sallman, 28 days	29.50	RI
1994	CHRIST AT HEART'S DOOR, W. Sallman, 28 days	29.50	RI
1994	PORTRAIT OF CHRIST, W. Sallman, 28 days	29.50	RI
1994	MADONNA AND CHRIST CHILD, W. Sallman, 28 days	29.50	RI

Portraits of the Bald Eagle

1993	RULER OF THE SKY, J. Pitcher, 28 days	37.50	RI
1993	IN BOLD DEFIANCE, J. Pitcher, 28 days	37.50	RI
1993	MASTER OF THE SUMMER SKIES, J. Pitcher, 28 days	37.50	RI
1993	SPRING'S SENTINEL, J. Pitcher, 28 days	37.50	RI

Precious Moments Bible Story

1990	COME LET US ADORE HIM, Samuel Butcher, 28 days	29.50	NR
1992	THEY FOLLOWED THE STAR, Samuel Butcher, 28 days	29.50	NR
1992	THE FLIGHT INTO EGYPT, Samuel Butcher, 28 days	29.50	NR
1992	THE CARPENTER SHOP, Samuel Butcher, 28 days	29.50	NR
1992	JESUS IN THE TEMPLE, Samuel Butcher, 28 days	29.50	NR
1992	THE CRUCIFIXION, Samuel Butcher, 28 days	29.50	NR
1993	HE IS NOT HERE, Samuel Butcher, 28 days	29.50	RI

Precious Moments Classics

1993	GOD LOVETH A CHEERFUL GIVER, Samuel Butcher, 28 days	35.00	RI
1993	A JOYFUL NOISE, Samuel Butcher, 28 days	35.00	RI
1994	LOVE ONE ANOTHER, Samuel Butcher, 28 days	35.00	RI
1994	YOU HAVE TOUCHED SO MANY HEARTS, Samuel Butcher, 28 days	35.00	RI
1994	PRAISE THE LORD ANYHOW, Samuel Butcher, 28 days	35.00	RI
1994	I BELIEVE IN MIRACLES, Samuel Butcher, 28 days	35.00	RI
1994	GOOD FRIENDS ARE FOREVER, Samuel Butcher, 28 days	35.00	RI
1994	JESUS LOVES ME, Samuel Butcher, 28 days	35.00	RI
1995	FRIENDSHIP HITS THE SPOT, Samuel Butcher, 28 days	35.00	RI
1995	TO MY DEER FRIEND, Samuel Butcher, 28 days	35.00	RI

Precious Moments of Childhood

		ISSUE	CURRENT
1979	FRIEND IN THE SKY, Thornton Utz, 28 days	21.50	50.00
1980	SAND IN HER SHOE, Thornton Utz, 28 days	21.50	40.00
1980	SNOW BUNNY, Thornton Utz, 28 days	21.50	40.00
1980	SEASHELLS, Thornton Utz, 28 days	21.50	35.00
1981	DAWN, Thornton Utz, 28 days	21.50	NR
1982	MY KITTY, Thornton Utz, 28 days	21.50	35.00

Precious Portraits

1987	SUNBEAM, Bessie Pease Gutmann, 14 days	24.50	45.00
1987	MISCHIEF, Bessie Pease Gutmann, 14 days	24.50	30.00
1987	PEACH BLOSSOM, Bessie Pease Gutmann, 14 days	24.50	30.00
1987	GOLDILOCKS, Bessie Pease Gutmann, 14 days	24.50	40.00
1987	FAIRY GOLD, Bessie Pease Gutmann, 14 days	24.50	45.00
1987	BUNNY, Bessie Pease Gutmann, 14 days	24.50	30.00

Prideful Ones

1994	VILLAGE MARKERS, Chuck DeHaan, 28 days	29.50	RI
1994	HIS PRIDE, Chuck DeHaan, 28 days	29.50	RI
1994	APPEASING THE WATER PEOPLE, Chuck DeHaan, 28 days	29.50	RI
1994	TRIBAL GUARDIAN, Chuck DeHaan, 28 days	29.50	RI
1994	AUTUMN PASSAGE, Chuck DeHaan, 28 days	29.50	RI
1994	WINTER HUNTER, Chuck DeHaan, 28 days	29.50	RI
1994	SILENT TRAIL BREAK, Chuck DeHaan, 28 days	29.50	RI
1994	WATER BREAKING, Chuck DeHaan, 28 days	29.50	RI
1994	CROSSING AT THE BIG TREES, Chuck DeHaan, 28 days	29.50	RI
1995	WINTER SONGSINGER, Chuck DeHaan, 28 days	29.50	RI

Princesses of the Plains

1993	PRAIRIE FLOWER, David Wright, 28 days	29.50	RI
1993	SNOW PRINCESS, David Wright, 28 days	29.50	RI
1993	WILD FLOWER, David Wright, 28 days	29.50	RI
1993	NOBLE BEAUTY, David Wright, 28 days	29.50	RI
1993	WINTER'S ROSE, David Wright, 28 days	29.50	RI
1993	GENTLE BEAUTY, David Wright, 28 days	29.50	RI
1994	NATURE'S GUARDIAN, David Wright, 28 days	29.50	RI
1994	MOUNTAIN PRINCESS, David Wright, 28 days	29.50	RI
1995	PROUD DREAMER, David Wright, 28 days	29.50	RI
1995	SPRING MAIDEN, David Wright, 28 days	29.50	RI

Protector of the Wolf Shield Collection (Bradford Exchange)

1996	WINTER MAJESTY, limited	39.95	RI

Proud Indian Families

1991	THE STORYTELLER, K. Freeman, 14 days	29.50	50.00
1991	THE POWER OF THE BASKET, K. Freeman, 14 days	29.50	35.00
1991	THE NAMING CEREMONY, K. Freeman, 14 days	29.50	NR
1992	PLAYING WITH TRADITION, K. Freeman, 14 days	29.50	NR
1992	PREPARING THE BERRY HARVEST, K. Freeman, 14 days	29.50	NR
1992	CEREMONIAL DRESS, K. Freeman, 14 days	29.50	NR
1992	SOUNDS OF THE FOREST, K. Freeman, 14 days	29.50	NR
1992	THE MARRIAGE CEREMONY, K. Freeman, 14 days	29.50	NR

		ISSUE	CURRENT
1993	THE JEWELRY MAKER, K. Freeman, 14 days	29.50	RI
1993	BEAUTIFUL CREATIONS, K. Freeman, 14 days	29.50	RI

Proud Innocence

1994	DESERT BLOOM, Jay Schmidt, 28 days	29.50	RI
1994	LITTLE DRUMMER, Jay Schmidt, 28 days	29.50	RI
1995	YOUNG ARCHER, Jay Schmidt, 28 days	29.50	RI
1995	MORNING CHILD, Jay Schmidt, 28 days	29.50	RI
1995	WISE ONE, Jay Schmidt, 28 days	29.50	RI
1995	SUN BLOSSOM, Jay Schmidt, 28 days	29.50	RI
1995	LAUGHING HEART, Jay Schmidt, 28 days	29.50	RI
1995	GENTLE FLOWER, Jay Schmidt, 28 days	29.50	RI

Proud Nation

1989	NAVAJO LITTLE ONE, R. Swanson, 14 days	24.50	50.00
1989	IN A BIG LAND, R. Swanson, 14 days	24.50	NR
1989	OUT WITH MAMA'S FLOCK, R. Swanson, 14 days	24.50	NR
1989	NEWEST LITTLE SHEEPHERDER, R. Swanson, 14 days	24.50	35.00
1989	DRESSED UP FOR THE POWWOW, R. Swanson, 14 days	24.50	35.00
1989	JUST A FEW DAYS OLD, R. Swanson, 14 days	24.50	30.00
1989	AUTUMN TREAT, R. Swanson, 14 days	24.50	30.00
1989	UP IN THE RED ROCKS, R. Swanson, 14 days	24.50	NR

Quiet Moments of Childhood

1991	ELIZABETH'S AFTERNOON TEA, D. Green, 14 days	29.50	45.00
1991	CHRISTINA'S SECRET GARDEN, D. Green, 14 days	29.50	35.00
1991	ERIC AND ERIN'S STORYTIME, D. Green, 14 days	29.50	NR
1992	JESSICA'S TEA PARTY, D. Green, 14 days	29.50	NR
1992	MEGAN AND MONIQUE'S BAKERY, D. Green, 14 days	29.50	35.00
1992	CHILDREN'S DAY BY THE SEA, D. Green, 14 days	29.50	NR
1992	JORDAN'S PLAYFUL PUPS, D. Green, 14 days	29.50	NR
1992	DANIEL'S MORNING PLAYTIME, D. Green, 14 days	29.50	NR

Quilted Countryside: Mel Steele Signature Collection

1991	THE OLD COUNTRY STORE, M. Steele, 14 days	29.50	NR
1991	WINTER'S END, M. Steele, 14 days	29.50	NR
1991	THE QUILTER'S CABIN, M. Steele, 14 days	29.50	45.00
1991	SPRING CLEANING, M. Steele, 14 days	29.50	NR
1991	SUMMER HARVEST, M. Steele, 14 days	29.50	NR
1991	THE COUNTRY MERCHANT, M. Steele, 14 days	29.50	NR
1992	WASH DAY, M. Steele, 14 days	29.50	NR
1992	THE ANTIQUES STORE, M. Steele, 15 days	29.50	NR

Remembering Norma Jeane

1994	THE GIRL NEXT DOOR, F. Accornero, 28 days	29.50	RI
1994	HER DAY IN THE SUN, F. Accornero, 28 days	29.50	RI
1994	A STAR IS BORN, F. Accornero, 28 days	29.50	RI
1994	BEAUTY SECRETS, F. Accornero, 28 days	29.50	RI
1995	IN THE SPOTLIGHT, F. Accornero, 28 days	29.50	RI
1995	BATHING BEAUTY, F. Accornero, 28 days	29.50	RI
1995	YOUNG & CAREFREE, F. Accornero, 28 days	29.50	RI
1995	FREE SPIRIT, F. Accornero, 28 days	29.50	RI
1995	A COUNTRY GIRL AT HEART, F. Accornero, 28 days	29.50	RI

		ISSUE	CURRENT
1996	HOMETOWN GIRL, F. Accornero, 28 days	29.50	RI

Renaissance Angels

1994	DOVES OF PEACE, L. Bywaters, 28 days	29.50	RI
1994	ANGELIC INNOCENCE, L. Bywaters, 28 days	29.50	RI
1994	JOY TO THE WORLD, L. Bywaters, 28 days	29.50	RI
1995	ANGEL OF FAITH, L. Bywaters, 28 days	29.50	RI
1995	THE CHRISTMAS STAR, L. Bywaters, 28 days	29.50	RI
1995	TRUMPETER'S CALL, L. Bywaters, 28 days	29.50	RI
1995	HARMONIOUS HEAVENS, L. Bywaters, 28 days	29.50	RI
1995	THE ANGELS SING, L. Bywaters, 28 days	29.50	RI

Rockwell Home of the Brave (Royal Devon)

1981	REMINISCING, Norman Rockwell, 18,000	35.00	50.00
1981	HERO'S WELCOME, Norman Rockwell, 18,000	35.00	50.00
1981	BACK TO HIS OLD JOB, Norman Rockwell, 18,000	35.00	50.00
1981	WAR HERO, Norman Rockwell, 18,000	35.00	35.00
1982	WILLIE GILLIS IN CHURCH, Norman Rockwell, 18,000	35.00	50.00
1982	WAR BOND, Norman Rockwell, 18,000	35.00	35.00
1982	UNCLE SAM TAKES WINGS, Norman Rockwell, 18,000	35.00	75.00
1982	TAKING MOTHER OVER THE TOP, Norman Rockwell, 18,000	35.00	35.00

Rockwell's Mother's Day (Royal Devon)

1975	DOCTOR AND DOLL, Norman Rockwell, 1 year	23.50	50.00
1976	PUPPY LOVE, Norman Rockwell, 1 year	24.50	75.00
1977	THE FAMILY, Norman Rockwell, 1 year	24.50	85.00
1978	MOTHER'S DAY OFF, Norman Rockwell, 1 year	27.00	35.00
1979	MOTHER'S EVENING OUT, Norman Rockwell, 1 year	30.00	NR
1980	MOTHER'S TREAT, Norman Rockwell, 1 year	32.50	NR

Rockwell's *Saturday Evening Post* Baseball Plates

1992	100TH YEAR OF BASEBALL, Norman Rockwell, open	19.50	NR
1993	THE ROOKIE, Norman Rockwell, open	19.50	RI
1993	THE DUGOUT, Norman Rockwell, open	19.50	RI
1993	BOTTOM OF THE SIXTH, Norman Rockwell, open	19.50	RI

Romance of the Rails

1994	STARLIGHT LIMITED, D. Tutwiler, 28 days	29.50	RI
1994	PORTLAND ROSE, D. Tutwiler, 28 days	29.50	RI
1994	ORANGE BLOSSOM SPECIAL, D. Tutwiler, 28 days	29.50	RI
1994	MORNING STAR, D. Tutwiler, 28 days	29.50	RI
1994	CRESCENT LIMITED, D. Tutwiler, 28 days	29.50	RI
1994	SUNSET LIMITED, D. Tutwiler, 28 days	29.50	RI
1994	WESTERN STAR, D. Tutwiler, 28 days	29.50	RI
1994	SUNRISE LIMITED, D. Tutwiler, 28 days	29.50	RI
1995	THE BLUE BONNET, D. Tutwiler, 28 days	29.50	RI
1995	THE PINE TREE LIMITED, D. Tutwiler, 28 days	29.50	RI

Romantic Flights of Fancy

1994	SUNLIT WALTZ, Q. Lemonds, 28 days	29.50	RI
1994	MORNING MINUET, Q. Lemonds, 28 days	29.50	RI
1994	EVENING SOLO, Q. Lemonds, 28 days	29.50	RI

		ISSUE	CURRENT
1994	SUMMER SONATA, Q. Lemonds, 28 days	29.50	RI
1995	TWILIGHT TANGO, Q. Lemonds, 28 days	29.50	RI
1995	SUNSET BALLET, Q. Lemonds, 28 days	29.50	RI
1995	EXOTIC INTERLUDE, Q. Lemonds, 28 days	29.50	RI
1995	SUNRISE SAMBA, Q. Lemonds, 28 days	29.50	RI

Romantic Victorian Keepsake

1992	DEAREST KISS, John Grossman, 28 days	35.00	NR
1992	FIRST LOVE, John Grossman, 28 days	35.00	NR
1992	AS FAIR AS A ROSE, John Grossman, 28 days	35.00	NR
1992	SPRINGTIME BEAUTY, John Grossman, 28 days	35.00	NR
1992	SUMMERTIME FANCY, John Grossman, 28 days	35.00	NR
1992	BONNIE BLUE EYES, John Grossman, 28 days	35.00	NR
1992	PRECIOUS FRIENDS, John Grossman, 28 days	35.00	NR
1994	BONNETS AND BOUQUETS, John Grossman, 28 days	35.00	RI
1994	MY BELOVED TEDDY, John Grossman, 28 days	35.00	RI
1994	A SWEET ROMANCE, John Grossman, 28 days	35.00	RI

Salute to Mickey Mantle

1996	1961 HOME RUN DUEL, T. Fogarty, 28 days	35.00	RI
1996	POWER AT THE PLATE, T. Fogarty, 28 days	35.00	RI
1996	SALUTING A MAGNIFICENT YANKEE, T. Fogarty, 28 days	35.00	RI
1996	TRIPLE CROWN ACHIEVEMENT, T. Fogarty, 28 days	35.00	RI
1996	1953 GRAND SLAM, T. Fogarty, 28 days	35.00	RI
1997	1963'S FAMOUS FACADE HOME, T. Fogarty, 28 days	35.00	RI
1997	MICKEY AS A ROOKIE, T. Fogarty, 28 days	35.00	RI
1997	A LOOK BACK, T. Fogarty, 28 days	35.00	RI

Santa Takes a Break

1995	SANTA'S LAST STOP, Tom Newsom, 28 days	29.95	RI
1995	SANTA'S RAILROAD, Tom Newsom, 28 days	29.95	RI
1995	A JOLLY GOOD CATCH, Tom Newsom, 28 days	29.95	RI
1995	SIMPLE PLEASURES, Tom Newsom, 28 days	29.95	RI
1996	SKATING ON PENGUIN POND, Tom Newsom, 28 days	29.95	RI
1996	SANTA'S SING ALONG, Tom Newsom, 28 days	29.95	RI
1996	SLEDDING ADVENTURES, Tom Newsom, 28 days	29.95	RI
1996	SANTA'S SWEET TREATS, Tom Newsom, 28 days	29.95	RI

Saturday Evening Post

1989	THE WONDERS OF RADIO, Norman Rockwell, 14 days	35.00	45.00
1989	EASTER MORNING, Norman Rockwell, 14 days	35.00	60.00
1989	THE FACTS OF LIFE, Norman Rockwell, 14 days	35.00	45.00
1990	THE WINDOW WASHER, Norman Rockwell, 14 days	35.00	45.00
1990	FIRST FLIGHT, Norman Rockwell, 14 days	35.00	55.00
1990	TRAVELING COMPANION, Norman Rockwell, 14 days	35.00	NR
1990	JURY ROOM, Norman Rockwell, 14 days	35.00	NR
1990	FURLOUGH, Norman Rockwell, 14 days	35.00	NR

Scenes of an American Christmas

1994	I'LL BE HOME FOR CHRISTMAS, B. Perry, 28 days	29.50	RI
1994	CHRISTMAS EVE WORSHIP, B. Perry, 28 days	29.50	RI
1994	A HOLDIAY HAPPENING, B. Perry, 28 days	29.50	RI
1994	A LONG WINTER'S NIGHT, B. Perry, 28 days	29.50	RI

		ISSUE	CURRENT
1994	THE SOUNDS OF CHRISTMAS, B. Perry, 28 days	29.50	RI
1994	DEAR SANTA, B. Perry, 28 days	29.50	RI
1995	AN AFTERNOON OUTING, B. Perry, 28 days	29.50	RI
1995	WINTER WORSHIP, B. Perry, 28 days	29.50	RI

Seasons of the Bald Eagle

1991	AUTUMN IN THE MOUNTAINS, J. Pitcher, 14 days	37.50	75.00
1991	WINTER IN THE VALLEY, J. Pitcher, 14 days	37.50	65.00
1991	SPRING ON THE RIVER, J. Pitcher, 14 days	37.50	60.00
1991	SUMMER ON THE SEACOAST, J. Pitcher, 14 days	37.50	50.00

Sharing Life's Most Precious Memories

1995	THEE IN LOVE, Samuel Butcher, 28 days	35.00	RI
1995	THE JOY OF THE LORD IS MY STRENGTH, Samuel Butcher, 28 days	35.00	RI
1995	MAY YOUR EVERY WISH COME TRUE, Samuel Butcher, 28 days	35.00	RI
1996	I'M SO GLAD THAT GOD, Samuel Butcher, 28 days	35.00	RI
1996	HEAVEN BLESS YOU, Samuel Butcher, 28 days	35.00	RI

Sharing the Moments

1995	YOU HAVE TOUCHED SO MANY HEARTS, Samuel Butcher, 28 days	35.00	RI
1996	FRIENDSHIP HITS THE SPOT, Samuel Butcher, 28 days	35.00	RI
1996	JESUS LOVES ME, Samuel Butcher, 28 days	35.00	RI

Small Wonders of the Wild

1989	HIDEAWAY, Charles Fracé, 14 days	29.50	45.00
1990	YOUNG EXPLORERS, Charles Fracé, 14 days	29.50	40.00
1990	THREE OF A KIND, Charles Fracé, 14 days	29.50	60.00
1990	QUIET MORNING, Charles Fracé, 14 days	29.50	35.00
1990	EYES OF WONDER, Charles Fracé, 14 days	29.50	45.00
1990	READY FOR ADVENTURE, Charles Fracé, 14 days	29.50	35.00
1990	UNO, Charles Fracé, 14 days	29.50	45.00
1990	EXPLORING A NEW WORLD, Charles Fracé, 14 days	29.50	NR

Space, The Final Frontier

1996	TO BOLDLY GO…, D. Ward, 28 days	37.50	RI
1996	SECOND STAR FROM THE RIGHT, D. Ward, 28 days	37.50	RI
1996	SIGNS OF INTELLIGENCE, D. Ward, 28 days	37.50	RI
1996	PREPARING TO CLOAK, D. Ward, 28 days	37.50	RI

Spanning America's Railways

1996	ROYAL YORK, D. Tutwiler, 28 days	29.95	RI

Spirit of the Mustang

1995	WINTER'S THUNDER, Chuck DeHaan, 28 days	29.95	RI
1995	MOONLIT RUN, Chuck DeHaan, 28 days	29.95	RI
1995	MORNING REVERIE, Chuck DeHaan, 28 days	29.95	RI
1995	AUTUMN RESPITE, Chuck DeHaan, 28 days	29.95	RI
1996	SPRING FROLIC, Chuck DeHaan, 28 days	29.95	RI
1996	DUELING MUSTANGS, Chuck DeHaan, 28 days	29.95	RI
1996	TRANQUIL WATERS, Chuck DeHaan, 28 days	29.95	RI
1996	SUMMER SQUALL, Chuck DeHaan, 28 days	29.95	RI

Furlough
Photo courtesy of *Collectors News*

Gunther Gebel-Williams
Photo courtesy of *Collectors News*

		ISSUE	CURRENT

Spock® Commemorative Wall Plaque

1993	SPOCK® COMMEMORATIVE WALL PLAQUE, 2,500	195.00	RI

Sporting Generation

1991	LIKE FATHER, LIKE SON, Jim Lamb, 14 days	29.50	45.00
1991	GOLDEN MOMENTS, Jim Lamb, 14 days	29.50	35.00
1991	THE LOOKOUT, Jim Lamb, 14 days	29.50	NR
1992	PICKING UP THE SCENT, Jim Lamb, 14 days	29.50	NR
1992	FIRST TIME OUT, Jim Lamb, 14 days	29.50	40.00
1992	WHO'S TRACKING WHO?, Jim Lamb, 14 days	29.50	NR
1992	SPRINGING INTO ACTION, Jim Lamb, 14 days	29.50	NR
1992	POINT OF INTEREST, Jim Lamb, 14 days	29.50	NR

Stained Glass Gardens

1989	PEACOCK AND WISTERIA, 15,000	55.00	NR
1989	GARDEN SUNSET, 15,000	55.00	NR
1989	THE COCKATOO'S GARDEN, 15,000	55.00	NR
1989	WATERFALL AND IRIS, 15,000	55.00	NR
1990	ROSES AND MAGNOLIAS, 15,000	55.00	NR
1990	A HOLLYHOCK SUNRISE, 15,000	55.00	NR
1990	PEACEFUL WATERS, 15,000	55.00	NR
1990	SPRINGTIME IN THE VALLEY, 15,000	55.00	NR

Stars of the Circus

1983	GUNTHER GEBEL-WILLIAMS, Franklin Moody, limited	29.50	NR

Star Trek®: Deep Space 9

1994	COMMANDER BENJAMIN SISKO, Morgan Weistling, 28 days	35.00	RI
1994	SECURITY CHIEF ODO, Morgan Weistling, 28 days	35.00	RI
1994	MAJOR KIRA NERYS, Morgan Weistling, 28 days	35.00	RI
1994	SPACE STATION, Morgan Weistling, 28 days	35.00	RI
1994	PROPRIETOR QUARK, Morgan Weistling, 28 days	35.00	RI

		ISSUE	CURRENT
1995	DOCTOR JULIAN BASHIR, Morgan Weistling, 28 days	35.00	RI
1995	LIEUTENANT JADZIA DAX, Morgan Weistling, 28 days	35.00	RI
1995	CHIEF MILES O'BRIEN, Morgan Weistling, 28 days	35.00	RI

Star Trek®: Generations

1996	THE ULTIMATE CONFRONTATION, K. Birdsong, 28 days	35.00	RI
1996	KIRK'S FINAL VOYAGE, K. Birdsong, 28 days	35.00	RI
1996	MEETING IN THE NEXUS, K. Birdsong, 28 days	35.00	RI
1996	PICARD'S CHRISTMAS IN THE NEXUS, K. Birdsong, 28 days	35.00	RI
1996	WORF'S CEREMONY, K. Birdsong, 28 days	35.00	RI
1996	THE FINAL PLOT/SURAS SISTERS, K. Birdsong, 28 days	35.00	RI

Star Trek®: The Movies

1994	*STAR TREK IV: THE VOYAGE HOME*, Morgan Weistling, 28 days	35.00	RI
1994	*STAR TREK II: THE WRATH OF KHAN*, Morgan Weistling, 28 days	35.00	RI
1994	*STAR TREK VI: THE UNDISCOVERED COUNTRY*, Morgan Weistling, 28 days	35.00	RI
1995	*STAR TREK III: THE SEARCH FOR SPOCK*, Morgan Weistling, 28 days	35.00	RI
1995	*STAR TREK V: THE FINAL FRONTIER*, Morgan Weistling, 28 days	35.00	RI
1996	TRIUMPHANT RETURN, Morgan Weistling, 28 days	35.00	RI
1996	DESTRUCTION OF THE RELIANT, Morgan Weistling, 28 days	35.00	RI
1996	*STAR TREK: THE MOTION PICTURE*, Morgan Weistling, 28 days	35.00	RI

Star Trek®: The Next Generation

1993	CAPTAIN JEAN-LUC PICARD, Thomas Blackshear, 28 days	35.00	RI
1993	COMMANDER WILLIAM RIKER, Thomas Blackshear, 28 days	35.00	RI
1994	LIEUTENANT COMMANDER DATA, Thomas Blackshear, 28 days	35.00	RI
1994	LIEUTENANT WORF, Thomas Blackshear, 28 days	35.00	RI
1994	COUNSELOR DEANNA TROI, Thomas Blackshear, 28 days	35.00	RI
1995	DR. BEVERLY CRUSHER, Thomas Blackshear, 28 days	35.00	RI
1995	LIEUTENANT COMMANDER LAFORGE, Thomas Blackshear, 28 days	35.00	RI
1996	ENSIGN W. CRUSHER, Thomas Blackshear, 28 days	35.00	RI

Star Trek®: The Next Generation, The Episodes

1994	THE BEST OF BOTH WORLDS, K. Birdsong, 28 days	35.00	RI
1994	ENCOUNTER AT FAR POINT, K. Birdsong, 28 days	35.00	RI
1995	UNIFICATION, K. Birdsong, 28 days	35.00	RI
1995	YESTERDAY'S ENTERPRISE, K. Birdsong, 28 days	35.00	RI
1995	ALL GOOD THINGS, K. Birdsong, 28 days	35.00	RI
1995	DESCENT, K. Birdsong, 28 days	35.00	RI
1996	RELICS, K. Birdsong, 28 days	35.00	RI
1996	REDEMPTION, K. Birdsong, 28 days	35.00	RI
1996	THE BIG GOODBYE, K. Birdsong, 28 days	35.00	RI
1996	THE INNER LIGHT, K. Birdsong, 28 days	35.00	RI

Star Trek®: The Original Episodes

1996	THE THOLIAN WEB, John Martin, 28 days	35.00	RI
1996	SPACE SEED, John Martin, 28 days	35.00	RI
1996	THE MENAGERIE, John Martin, 28 days	35.00	RI
1996	CITY ON THE EDGE, John Martin, 28 days	35.00	RI
1996	JOURNEY TO BABEL, John Martin, 28 days	35.00	RI
1996	TROUBLE WITH TRIBBLES, John Martin, 28 days	35.00	RI
1996	WHERE NO MAN HAS GONE, John Martin, 28 days	35.00	RI
1996	DEVIL IN THE DARK, John Martin, 28 days	35.00	RI

		ISSUE	CURRENT

Star Trek®: The Power of Command

1996	CAPTAIN PICARD, K. Birdsong, 28 days	35.00	RI
1996	ADMIRAL KIRK, K. Birdsong, 28 days	35.00	RI
1996	CAPTAIN SISKO, K. Birdsong, 28 days	35.00	RI
1996	CAPTAIN SULU, K. Birdsong, 28 days	35.00	RI
1996	JANEWAY, K. Birdsong, 28 days	35.00	RI
1996	KHAN, K. Birdsong, 28 days	35.00	RI
1996	GENERAL CHANG, K. Birdsong, 28 days	35.00	RI
1996	DUKAT, K. Birdsong, 28 days	35.00	RI

Star Trek®: The Voyagers

1994	U.S.S. *ENTERPRISE* NCC-1701, K. Birdsong, 28 days	35.00	RI
1994	U.S.S. *ENTERPRISE* NCC1701-D, K. Birdsong, 28 days	35.00	RI
1994	KLINGON BATTLECRUISER, K. Birdsong, 28 days	35.00	RI
1994	ROMULAN WARBIRD, K. Birdsong, 28 days	35.00	RI
1994	U.S.S. *ENTERPRISE* NCC-1701-A, K. Birdsong, 28 days	35.00	RI
1995	FERENGI MARAUDER, K. Birdsong, 28 days	35.00	RI
1995	KLINGON BIRD OF PREY, K. Birdsong, 28 days	35.00	RI
1995	TRIPLE NACELLED U.S.S. *ENTERPRISE*, K. Birdsong, 28 days	35.00	RI
1995	CARDASSIAN GALOR WARSHIP, K. Birdsong, 28 days	35.00	RI
1995	U.S.S. *EXCELSIOR*, K. Birdsong, 28 days	35.00	RI

Star Trek® 25th Anniversary Commemorative Collection

1991	STAR TREK 25TH ANNIVERSARY, Thomas Blackshear, 14 days	37.50	150.00
1991	SPOCK, Thomas Blackshear, 14 days	35.00	100.00
1991	KIRK, Thomas Blackshear, 14 days	35.00	75.00
1992	MCCOY, Thomas Blackshear, 14 days	35.00	60.00
1992	UHURA, Thomas Blackshear, 14 days	35.00	60.00
1992	SCOTTY, Thomas Blackshear, 14 days	35.00	60.00
1993	SULU, Thomas Blackshear, 14 days	35.00	RI
1993	CHEKOV, Thomas Blackshear, 14 days	35.00	RI
1994	U.S.S. ENTERPRISE NCC-1701, Thomas Blackshear, 14 days	35.00	RI

Star Trek®: Voyager

1996	THE VOYAGE BEGINS, D. Curry, 28 days	35.00	RI
1996	BONDS OF FRIENDSHIP, D. Curry, 28 days	35.00	RI
1996	LIFE SIGNS, D. Curry, 28 days	35.00	RI
1996	THE VIDIANS, D. Curry, 28 days	35.00	RI

Star Wars

1987	HAN SOLO, Thomas Blackshear, 14 days	29.50	150.00
1987	R2-D2 AND WICKET, Thomas Blackshear, 14 days	29.50	150.00
1987	LUKE SKYWALKER AND DARTH VADER, Thomas Blackshear, 14 days	29.50	150.00
1987	PRINCESS LEIA, Thomas Blackshear, 14 days	29.50	150.00
1987	THE IMPERIAL WALKERS, Thomas Blackshear, 14 days	29.50	150.00
1987	LUKE AND YODA, Thomas Blackshear, 14 days	29.50	150.00
1988	SPACE BATTLE, Thomas Blackshear, 14 days	29.50	200.00
1988	CREW IN COCKPIT, Thomas Blackshear, 14 days	29.50	200.00

Star Wars Space Vehicles

1995	MILLENNIUM FALCON, S. Hillios, 28 days	35.00	RI
1995	TIE FIGHTERS, S. Hillios, 28 days	35.00	RI

		ISSUE	CURRENT
1995	RED FIVE X-WING FIGHTERS, S. Hillios, 28 days	35.00	RI
1995	IMPERIAL SHUTTLE, S. Hillios, 28 days	35.00	RI
1995	STAR DESTROYER, S. Hillios, 28 days	35.00	RI
1996	SNOW SPEEDERS, S. Hillios, 28 days	35.00	RI
1996	B-WING FIGHTER, S. Hillios, 28 days	35.00	RI
1996	THE SLAVE I, S. Hillios, 28 days	35.00	RI
1996	MEDICAL FRIGATE, S. Hillios, 28 days	35.00	RI
1996	JABBA'S SAIL BARGE, S. Hillios, 28 days	35.00	RI

Star Wars 10th Anniversary Commemorative

1990	STAR WARS 10TH ANNIVERSARy, Thomas Blackshear, 15 days	39.50	150.00

Star Wars Trilogy

1993	*STAR WARS*, Morgan Weistling, 28 days	37.50	RI
1993	*THE EMPIRE STRIKES BACK*, Morgan Weistling, 28 days	37.50	RI
1993	*RETURN OF THE JEDI*, Morgan Weistling, 28 days	37.50	RI

Story of Heidi

1981	HEIDI, 14,750	45.00	NR
1981	GRANDFATHER, 14,750	45.00	NR
1981	GRANDMOTHER, 14,750	45.00	NR
1981	HEIDI AND PETER, 14,750	45.00	NR
1982	KITTENS, 14,750	45.00	NR
1982	MOUNTAIN CURE, 14,750	45.00	NR

Story of Noah's Ark

1981	TWO BY TWO...EVERY LIVING CREATURE, Laetitia, 12,500	45.00	NR
1982	IN DIVINE HARMONY, Laetitia, 12,500	45.00	NR
1982	FINALLY A RAINBOW, Laetitia, 12,500	45.00	NR
1982	THE ARK BECKONS, Laetitia, 12,500	45.00	NR

Summer Days of Childhood

1983	MOUNTAIN FRIENDS, Thornton Utz, 10 days	29.50	NR
1983	GARDEN MAGIC, Thornton Utz, 10 days	29.50	NR
1983	LITTLE BEACHCOMBER, Thornton Utz, 10 days	29.50	NR
1983	BLOWING BUBBLES, Thornton Utz, 10 days	29.50	NR
1983	THE BIRTHDAY PARTY, Thornton Utz, 10 days	29.50	NR
1983	PLAYING DOCTOR, Thornton Utz, 10 days	29.50	NR
1983	A STOLEN KISS, Thornton Utz, 10 days	29.50	NR
1983	KITTY'S BATHTIME, Thornton Utz, 10 days	29.50	NR
1983	COOLING OFF, Thornton Utz, 10 days	29.50	NR
1983	FIRST CUSTOMER, Thornton Utz, 10 days	29.50	NR
1983	A JUMPING CONTEST, Thornton Utz, 10 days	29.50	NR
1983	BALLOON CARNIVAL, Thornton Utz, 10 days	29.50	NR

Symphony of the Sea

1995	FLUID GRACE, R. Koni, 28 days	29.95	RI
1995	DOLPHIN'S DANCE, R. Koni, 28 days	29.95	RI
1995	ORCA BALLET, R. Koni, 28 days	29.95	RI
1995	MOONLIT MINUET, R. Koni, 28 days	29.95	RI
1995	SAILFISH SERENADE, R. Koni, 28 days	29.95	RI
1995	STARLIT WALTZ, R. Koni, 28 days	29.95	RI

		ISSUE	CURRENT
1995	SUNSET SPLENDOR, R. Koni, 28 days	29.95	RI
1995	CORAL CHORUS, R. Koni, 28 days	29.95	RI

Tale of Genji

1985	SERENE AUTUMN MOON, Shigekasu Hotta, 10 days	45.00	NR
1985	DRAGON AND PHOENIX BOATS, Shigekasu Hotta, 10 days	45.00	NR
1985	ROMANTIC DUET, Shigekasu Hotta, 10 days	45.00	NR
1985	WAVES OF THE BLUE OCEAN DANCE, Shigekasu Hotta, 10 days	45.00	NR
1985	EVENING FACES, Shigekasu Hotta, 10 days	45.00	NR
1985	THE ARCHERY MEET, Shigekasu Hotta, 10 days	45.00	NR
1985	MOON VIEWING, Shigekasu Hotta, 10 days	45.00	NR
1985	THE TABLE GAME, Shigekasu Hotta, 10 days	45.00	NR

Thornton Utz 10th Anniversary Commemorative

1989	DAWN, Thornton Utz, 14 days	29.50	NR
1989	JUST LIKE MOMMY, Thornton Utz, 14 days	29.50	NR
1989	PLAYING DOCTOR, Thornton Utz, 14 days	29.50	NR
1989	MY KITTY, Thornton Utz, 14 days	29.50	NR
1989	TURTLE TALK, Thornton Utz, 14 days	29.50	NR
1989	BEST FRIENDS, Thornton Utz, 14 days	29.50	NR
1989	AMONG THE DAFFODILS, Thornton Utz, 14 days	29.50	NR
1989	FRIENDS IN THE SKY, Thornton Utz, 14 days	29.50	NR
1989	TEDDY'S BATHTIME, Thornton Utz, 14 days	29.50	NR
1989	LITTLE EMILY, Thornton Utz, 14 days	29.50	NR

Those Delightful Dalmatians

1995	YOU MISSED A SPOT, 28 days	29.95	RI
1995	HERE'S A GOOD SPOT, 28 days	29.95	RI
1996	THE BEST SPOT, 28 days	29.95	RI
1996	SPOTTED IN THE HEADLINES, 28 days	29.95	RI
1996	A SPOT IN MY HEART, 28 days	29.95	RI
1996	SWEET SPOTS, 28 days	29.95	RI
1996	NAPTIME ALREADY?, 28 days	29.95	RI
1996	HE'S IN MY SPOT, 28 days	29.95	RI
1996	THE SERIOUS STUDYING SPOT, 28 days	29.95	RI
1996	CHECK OUT MY SPOTS, 28 days	29.95	RI

Timeless Expressions of the Orient

1990	FIDELITY, M. Tseng, 15,000	75.00	90.00
1991	FEMININITY, M. Tseng, 15,000	75.00	NR
1991	LONGEVITY, M. Tseng, 15,000	75.00	NR
1991	BEAUTY, M. Tseng, 15,000	55.00	NR
1992	COURAGE, M. Tseng, 15,000	55.00	NR

Treasured Days

1987	ASHLEY, B. Higgins Bond, 14 days	24.50	150.00
1987	CHRISTOPHER, B. Higgins Bond, 14 days	24.50	30.00
1987	SARA, B. Higgins Bond, 14 days	24.50	30.00
1987	JEREMY, B. Higgins Bond, 14 days	24.50	30.00
1987	AMANDA, B. Higgins Bond, 14 days	24.50	30.00
1988	NICHOLAS, B. Higgins Bond, 14 days	24.50	30.00

		ISSUE	CURRENT
1988	LINDSAY, B. Higgins Bond, 14 days	24.50	30.00
1988	JUSTIN, B. Higgins Bond, 14 days	24.50	30.00

Treasures of the Chinese Mandarins

1981	THE BIRD OF PARADISE, 2,500	75.00	125.00
1982	THE GUARDIANS OF HEAVEN, 2,500	75.00	100.00
1982	THE TREE OF IMMORTALITY, 2,500	75.00	90.00
1982	THE DRAGON OF ETERNITY, 2,500	75.00	80.00

Treasury of Cherished Teddies

1994	HAPPY HOLIDAYS, FRIEND, Priscilla Hillman, 28 days	29.50	RI
1995	A NEW YEAR WITH OLD FRIENDS, Priscilla Hillman, 28 days	29.50	RI
1995	VALENTINES FOR YOU, Priscilla Hillman, 28 days	29.50	RI
1995	FRIENDSHIP IS IN THE AIR, Priscilla Hillman, 28 days	29.50	RI
1995	SHOWERS OF FRIENDSHIP, Priscilla Hillman, 28 days	29.50	RI
1996	FRIENDSHIP IS IN BLOOM, Priscilla Hillman, 28 days	29.50	RI
1996	PLANTING THE SEEDS OF FRIENDSHIP, Priscilla Hillman, 28 days	29.50	RI
1996	A DAY IN THE PARK, Priscilla Hillman, 28 days	29.50	RI
1996	SMOOTH SAILING, Priscilla Hillman, 28 days	29.50	RI
1996	SCHOOL DAYS, Priscilla Hillman, 28 days	29.50	RI

Unbridled Mystery

1995	MIDNIGHT MAJESTY, Kim McElroy	29.95	RI
1995	SHADOW DANCER, Kim McElroy	29.95	RI
1996	DARK SPLENDOR, Kim McElroy	29.95	RI
1996	WILD SPIRIT, Kim McElroy	29.95	RI

Unbridled Spirit

1992	SURF DANCER, Chuck DeHaan, 28 days	29.50	NR
1992	WINTER RENEGADE, Chuck DeHaan, 28 days	29.50	NR
1992	DESERT SHADOWS, Chuck DeHaan, 28 days	29.50	NR
1993	PAINTED SUNRISE, Chuck DeHaan, 28 days	29.50	RI
1993	DESERT DUEL, Chuck DeHaan, 28 days	29.50	RI
1993	MIDNIGHT RUN, Chuck DeHaan, 28 days	29.50	RI
1993	MOONLIGHT MAJESTY, Chuck DeHaan, 28 days	29.50	RI
1993	AUTUMN REVERIE, Chuck DeHaan, 28 days	29.50	RI
1993	BLIZZARD'S PERIL, Chuck DeHaan, 28 days	29.50	RI
1993	SUNRISE SURPRISE, Chuck DeHaan, 28 days	29.50	RI

Under the Sea

1993	TALES OF TAVARUA, C. L. Bragg, 28 days	29.50	RI
1993	WATER'S EDGE, C. L. Bragg, 28 days	29.50	RI
1994	BEAUTY OF THE REEF, C. L. Bragg, 28 days	29.50	RI
1994	RAINBOW REEL, C. L. Bragg, 28 days	29.50	RI
1994	ORCA ODYSSEY, C. L. Bragg, 28 days	29.50	RI
1994	RESCUE THE REEF, C. L. Bragg, 28 days	29.50	RI
1994	UNDERWATER DANCE, C. L. Bragg, 28 days	29.50	RI
1994	GENTLE GIANTS, C. L. Bragg, 28 days	29.50	RI
1995	UNDERSEA ENCHANTMENT, C. L. Bragg, 28 days	29.50	RI
1995	PENGUIN PARADISE, C. L. Bragg, 28 days	29.50	RI

		ISSUE	CURRENT

Utz Mother's Day

1983	A GIFT OF LOVE, Thorton Utz, 1 year	27.50	40.00
1983	MOTHER'S HELPING HAND, Thorton Utz, 1 year	27.50	NR
1983	MOTHER'S ANGEL, Thorton Utz, 1 year	27.50	NR

Vanishing Rural America

1991	QUIET REFLECTIONS, J. Harrison, 14 days	29.50	45.00
1991	AUTUMN'S PASSAGE, J. Harrison, 14 days	29.50	45.00
1991	STOREFRONT MEMORIES, J. Harrison, 14 days	29.50	NR
1991	COUNTRY PATH, J. Harrison, 14 days	29.50	NR
1991	WHEN THE CIRCUS CAME TO TOWN, J. Harrison, 14 days	29.50	NR
1991	COVERED IN FALL, J. Harrison, 14 days	29.50	40.00
1991	AMERICA'S HEARTLAND, J. Harrison, 14 days	29.50	NR
1991	RURAL DELIVERY, J. Harrison, 14 days	29.50	NR

Victorian Christmas Memories

1992	A VISIT FROM ST. NICHOLAS, John Grossman, 28 days	29.50	NR
1993	CHRISTMAS DELIVERY, John Grossman, 28 days	29.50	RI
1993	CHRISTMAS ANGELS, John Grossman, 28 days	29.50	RI
1993	WITH VISIONS OF SUGAR PLUMS, John Grossman, 28 days	29.50	RI
1993	MERRY OLDE KRIS KRINGLE, John Grossman, 28 days	29.50	RI
1993	GRANDFATHER FROST, John Grossman, 28 days	29.50	RI
1993	JOYOUS NOEL, John Grossman, 28 days	29.50	RI
1993	CHRISTMAS INNOCENCE, John Grossman, 28 days	29.50	RI
1993	DREAMING OF SANTA, John Grossman, 28 days	29.50	RI
1993	MISTLETOE & HOLLY, John Grossman, 28 days	29.50	RI

Victorian Playtime

1991	A BUSY DAY, Maud Humphrey Bogart, 14 days	29.50	NR
1992	LITTLE MASTERPIECE, Maud Humphrey Bogart, 14 days	29.50	NR
1992	PLAYING BRIDE, Maud Humphrey Bogart, 14 days	29.50	60.00
1992	WAITING FOR A NIBBLE, Maud Humphrey Bogart, 14 days	29.50	NR
1992	TEA AND GOSSIP, Maud Humphrey Bogart, 14 days	29.50	NR
1992	CLEANING HOUSE, Maud Humphrey Bogart, 14 days	29.50	NR
1992	A LITTLE PERSUASION, Maud Humphrey Bogart, 14 days	29.50	NR
1992	PEEK-A-BOO, Maud Humphrey Bogart, 14 days	29.50	NR

Warrior's Pride

1994	CROW WAR PONY, Chuck DeHaan, 28 days	29.50	RI
1994	RUNNING FREE, Chuck DeHaan, 28 days	29.50	RI
1994	BLACKFOOT WAR PONY, Chuck DeHaan, 28 days	29.50	RI
1994	SOUTHERN CHEYENNE, Chuck DeHaan, 28 days	29.50	RI
1995	SHOSHONI WAR PONIES, Chuck DeHaan, 28 days	29.50	RI
1995	A CHAMPION'S REVELRY, Chuck DeHaan, 28 days	29.50	RI
1995	BATTLE COLORS, Chuck DeHaan, 28 days	29.50	RI
1995	CALL OF THE DRUMS, Chuck DeHaan, 28 days	29.50	RI

West of Frank McCarthy

1991	ATTACKING THE IRON HORSE, Frank McCarthy, 14 days	37.50	60.00
1991	ATTEMPT ON THE STAGE, Frank McCarthy, 14 days	37.50	45.00
1991	THE PRAYER, Frank McCarthy, 14 days	37.50	55.00
1991	ON THE OLD NORTH TRAIL, Frank McCarthy, 14 days	37.50	50.00

		ISSUE	CURRENT
1991	THE HOSTILE THREAT, Frank McCarthy, 14 days	37.50	45.00
1991	BRINGING OUT THE FURS, Frank McCarthy, 14 days	37.50	45.00
1991	KIOWA RAIDER, Frank McCarthy, 14 days	37.50	45.00
1991	HEADED NORTH, Frank McCarthy, 14 days	37.50	NR

White House China

1986	ABRAHAM LINCOLN	NA	NA
1986	GEORGE WASHINGTON	NA	NA
1986	JAMES K. POLK	NA	NA
1986	FRANKLIN PIERCE	NA	NA
1988	BENJAMIN HARRISON	NA	NA
1988	JOHN QUINCY ADAMS	NA	NA

Franklin Pierce

Wilderness Spirits

1994	EYES OF THE NIGHT, P. Koni, 28 days	29.95	RI
1995	HOWL OF INNOCENCE, P. Koni, 28 days	29.95	RI
1995	MIDNIGHT CALL, P. Koni, 28 days	29.95	RI
1995	BREAKING THE SILENCE, P. Koni, 28 days	29.95	RI
1995	MOONLIGHT RUN, P. Koni, 28 days	29.95	RI
1995	SUNSET VIGIL, P. Koni, 28 days	29.95	RI
1995	SUNRISE SPIRIT, P. Koni, 28 days	29.95	RI
1996	VALLEY OF THE WOLF, P. Koni, 28 days	29.95	RI

Winged Reflections

1989	FOLLOWING MAMA, Ron Parker, 14 days	37.50	NR
1989	ABOVE THE BREAKERS, Ron Parker, 14 days	37.50	NR
1989	AMONG THE REEDS, Ron Parker, 14 days	37.50	NR
1989	FREEZE UP, Ron Parker, 14 days	37.50	NR
1989	WINGS ABOVE THE WATER, Ron Parker, 14 days	37.50	NR
1990	SUMMER LOON, Ron Parker, 14 days	29.50	NR
1990	EARLY SPRING, Ron Parker, 14 days	29.50	NR
1990	AT THE WATER'S EDGE, Ron Parker, 14 days	29.50	NR

Winter Rails

		ISSUE	CURRENT
1992	WINTER CROSSING, Theodore A. Xaras, 28 days	29.50	NR
1993	COAL COUNTRY, Theodore A. Xaras, 28 days	29.50	RI
1993	DAYLIGHT RUN, Theodore A. Xaras, 28 days	29.50	RI
1993	BY SEA OR RAIL, Theodore A. Xaras, 28 days	29.50	RI
1993	COUNTRY CROSSROADS, Theodore A. Xaras, 28 days	29.50	RI
1993	TIMBER LINE, Theodore A. Xaras, 28 days	29.50	RI
1993	THE LONG HAUL, Theodore A. Xaras, 28 days	29.50	RI
1993	DARBY CROSSING, Theodore A. Xaras, 28 days	29.50	RI
1995	EAST BROAD TOP, Theodore A. Xaras, 28 days	29.50	RI
1995	LANDSDOWNE STATION, Theodore A. Xaras, 28 days	29.50	RI

Winter Wildlife

1989	CLOSE ENCOUNTERS, John Seerey-Lester, 15,000	55.00	NR
1989	AMONG THE CATTAILS, John Seerey-Lester, 15,000	55.00	NR
1989	THE REFUGE, John Seerey-Lester, 15,000	55.00	NR
1989	OUT OF THE BLIZZARD, John Seerey-Lester, 15,000	55.00	NR
1989	FIRST SNOW, John Seerey-Lester, 15,000	55.00	NR
1989	LYING IN WAIT, John Seerey-Lester, 15,000	55.00	NR
1989	WINTER HIDING, John Seerey-Lester, 15,000	55.00	NR
1989	EARLY SNOW, John Seerey-Lester, 15,000	55.00	NR

Wizard of Oz Commemorative

1988	WE'RE OFF TO SEE THE WIZARD, Thomas Blackshear, 14 days	24.50	100.00
1988	DOROTHY MEETS THE SCARECROW, Thomas Blackshear, 14 days	24.50	100.00
1989	THE TIN MAN SPEAKS, Thomas Blackshear, 14 days	24.50	100.00
1989	A GLIMPSE OF THE MUNCHKINS, Thomas Blackshear, 14 days	24.50	100.00
1989	THE WITCH CASTS A SPELL, Thomas Blackshear, 14 days	24.50	100.00
1989	IF I WERE KING OF THE FOREST, Thomas Blackshear, 14 days	24.50	100.00
1989	THE GREAT AND POWERFUL OZ, Thomas Blackshear, 14 days	24.50	100.00
1989	THERE'S NO PLACE LIKE HOME, Thomas Blackshear, 14 days	24.50	100.00

Wizard of Oz—Fifty Years of Oz

1989	FIFTY YEARS OF OZ, Thomas Blackshear, 14 days	37.50	150.00

Wizard of Oz—Portraits from Oz

1989	DOROTHY, Thomas Blackshear, 14 days	29.50	200.00
1989	SCARECROW, Thomas Blackshear, 14 days	29.50	200.00
1989	TIN MAN, Thomas Blackshear, 14 days	29.50	200.00
1990	COWARDLY LION, Thomas Blackshear, 14 days	29.50	200.00
1990	GLINDA, Thomas Blackshear, 14 days	29.50	200.00
1990	WIZARD, Thomas Blackshear, 14 days	29.50	200.00
1990	WICKED WITCH, Thomas Blackshear, 14 days	29.50	200.00
1990	TOTO, Thomas Blackshear, 14 days	29.50	300.00

Woodland Babies

1995	HOLLOW HIDEAWAY, Ruanne Manning, 28 days	29.95	RI
1995	A SPRINGTIME ADVENTURE, Ruanne Manning, 28 days	29.95	RI
1995	AMBER EYES, Ruanne Manning, 28 days	29.95	RI
1996	PEACEFUL DREAMS, Ruanne Manning, 28 days	29.95	RI
1996	COZY NEST, Ruanne Manning, 28 days	29.95	RI
1996	TREE HOUSE TRIO, Ruanne Manning, 28 days	29.95	RI

		ISSUE	CURRENT

Woodland Encounters

		ISSUE	CURRENT
1991	WANT TO PLAY?, G. Giordano, 14 days	29.50	NR
1991	PEEK-A-BOO!, G. Giordano, 14 days	29.50	NR
1991	LUNCHTIME VISITOR, G. Giordano, 14 days	29.50	NR
1991	ANYONE FOR A SWIM?, G. Giordano, 14 days	29.50	NR
1991	NATURE SCOUTS, G. Giordano, 14 days	29.50	NR
1991	MEADOW MEETING, G. Giordano, 14 days	29.50	NR
1991	HI NEIGHBOR, G. Giordano, 14 days	29.50	NR
1992	FIELD DAY, G. Giordano, 14 days	29.50	NR

World of Puppy Adventures

		ISSUE	CURRENT
1995	THE WATER'S FIRE, J. Ren, 28 days	29.95	RI
1996	SWIMMING LESSON, J. Ren, 28 days	29.95	RI
1996	BREAKFAST IS SERVED, J. Ren, 28 days	29.95	RI
1996	LAUNDRY TUG O' WAR, J. Ren, 28 days	29.95	RI
1996	DID I DO THAT?, J. Ren, 28 days	29.95	RI
1996	DECOY DISMAY, J. Ren, 28 days	29.95	RI
1996	PUPPY PICNIC, J. Ren, 28 days	29.95	RI
1996	SWEET TERRORS, J. Ren, 28 days	29.95	RI

World of Zolan

		ISSUE	CURRENT
1992	FIRST KISS, Donald Zolan, 28 days	29.50	75.00
1992	MORNING DISCOVERY, Donald Zolan, 28 days	29.50	NR
1993	LITTLE FISHERMAN, Donald Zolan, 28 days	29.50	RI
1993	LETTER TO GRANDMA, Donald Zolan, 28 days	29.50	RI
1993	TWILIGHT PRAYER, Donald Zolan, 28 days	29.50	RI
1993	FLOWERS FOR MOTHER, Donald Zolan, 28 days	29.50	RI

Year of the Wolf

		ISSUE	CURRENT
1993	BROKEN SILENCE, A. Agnew, 28 days	29.50	RI
1993	LEADER OF THE PACK, A. Agnew, 28 days	29.50	RI
1993	SOLITUDE, A. Agnew, 28 days	29.50	RI
1994	TUNDRA LIGHT, A. Agnew, 28 days	29.50	RI
1994	GUARDIANS OF THE HIGH COUNTRY, A. Agnew, 28 days	29.50	RI
1994	A SECOND GLANCE, A. Agnew, 28 days	29.50	RI
1994	FREE AS THE WIND, A. Agnew, 28 days	29.50	RI
1994	SONG OF THE WOLF, A. Agnew, 28 days	29.50	RI
1995	LORDS OF THE TUNDRA, A. Agnew, 28 days	29.50	RI
1995	WILDERNESS COMPANIONS, A. Agnew, 28 days	29.50	RI

Young Lords of the Wild

		ISSUE	CURRENT
1994	SIBERIAN TIGER CUB, M. Richter, 28 days	29.95	RI
1995	SNOW LEOPARD CUB, M. Richter, 28 days	29.95	RI
1995	LION CUB, M. Richter, 28 days	29.95	RI
1995	CLOUDED LEOPARD CUB, M. Richter, 28 days	29.95	RI
1995	COUGAR CUB, M. Richter, 28 days	29.95	RI
1995	LEOPARD CUB, M. Richter, 28 days	29.95	RI
1995	CHEETAH CUB, M. Richter, 28 days	29.95	RI
1996	CANADIAN LYNX CUB, M. Richter, 28 days	29.95	RI

Single Issues

		ISSUE	CURRENT
1983	PRINCESS GRACE, Thornton Utz, 21 days	39.50	50.00

HAMILTON MINT UNITED STATES

Kennedy

		ISSUE	CURRENT
1974	Gold on pewter, 1 year	40.00	NR
1974	Pewter, 1 year	25.00	40.00

Picasso

		ISSUE	CURRENT
1972	LE GOURMET, Alan Brunettin, sterling silver, 5,000	125.00	NR
1972	LE GOURMET, Alan Brunettin, 18K gold, 51	NA	NA
1972	THE TRAGEDY, Alan Brunettin, sterling silver, 5,000	125.00	NR
1972	THE TRAGEDY, Alan Brunettin, 18K gold, 51	NA	NA
1973	THE LOVERS, Alan Brunettin, sterling silver, 5,000	125.00	NR
1973	THE LOVERS, Alan Brunettin, 18K gold, 51	NA	NA

Single Issue

		ISSUE	CURRENT
1971	ST. PATRICK, H. Alvin Sharpe	75.00	NR

HAMPTON HOUSE STUDIOS

Single Issue

		ISSUE	CURRENT
1977	NANCY WARD/CHEROKEE NATION, B. Hampton, 3,000	48.00	300.00

HANTAN PORCELAIN WORKS CHINA

Chinese and American Historical (China Trade Corporation)

		ISSUE	CURRENT
1982	THE EAGLE AND THE PANDA, Zhu Bohua, 10,000	195.00	215.00

HAVILAND FRANCE

1001 Arabian Nights

		ISSUE	CURRENT
1979	MAGIC HORSE, Liliane Tellier, 5,000	54.50	NR
1980	ALADDIN AND HIS LAMP, Liliane Tellier, 5,000	54.50	NR
1981	SCHEHERAZADE, Liliane Tellier, 5,000	54.50	NR
1982	SINBAD THE SAILOR, Liliane Tellier, 5,000	54.50	NR

Bicentennial

		ISSUE	CURRENT
1972	BURNING OF THE GASPEE, Remy Hetreau, 10,000	39.95	45.00
1973	BOSTON TEA PARTY, Remy Hetreau, 10,000	39.95	NR
1974	CONTINENTAL CONGRESS, Remy Hetreau, 10,000	39.95	NR
1975	PAUL REVERE, Remy Hetreau, 10,000	39.95	50.00
1976	THE DECLARATION, Remy Hetreau, 10,000	39.95	45.00

Fleurs et Rubans

		ISSUE	CURRENT
1981	ORCHIDEE, 5,000	120.00	NR
1981	LYS, 7,500	120.00	NR
1981	PIVOINE, 7,500	120.00	NR

		ISSUE	CURRENT
1981	PAVOT (POPPY), 7,500	120.00	NR
1981	AIL SAUVAGE (WILD GARLIC), 7,500	120.00	NR
1982	HIBISCUS, 7,500	120.00	NR

French Collection Mother's Day

1973	BREAKFAST, Remy Hetreau, 10,000	29.95	BR
1974	THE WASH, Remy Hetreau, 10,000	29.95	BR
1975	IN THE PARK, Remy Hetreau, 10,000	30.00	NR
1976	TO MARKET, Remy Hetreau, 10,000	38.00	NR
1977	WASH BEFORE DINNER, Remy Hetreau, 10,000	38.00	NR
1978	AN EVENING AT HOME, Remy Hetreau, 10,000	40.00	NR
1979	HAPPY MOTHER'S DAY, Remy Hetreau, 10,000	30.00	45.00
1980	A CHILD AND HIS ANIMALS, Remy Hetreau, 10,000	55.00	NR

Historical

1968	MARTHA WASHINGTON, 2,500	35.00	80.00
1969	LINCOLN, 2,500	100.00	BR
1970	GRANT, 3,000	100.00	BR
1971	HAYES, 2,500	100.00	BR

Théâtre des Saisons

1978	SPRING, 5,000	120.00	140.00
1978	SUMMER, 5,000	120.00	140.00
1978	AUTUMN, 5,000	120.00	140.00
1978	WINTER, 5,000	120.00	140.00

Traditional Christmas Cards

1986	DECK THE HALLS, Elisa Stone, 2,000	75.00	NR

Twelve Days of Christmas

1970	PARTRIDGE, Remy Hetreau, 30,000	25.00	80.00
1971	TWO TURTLE DOVES, Remy Hetreau, 30,000	25.00	NR
1972	THREE FRENCH HENS, Remy Hetreau, 30,000	27.50	NR
1973	FOUR CALLING BIRDS, Remy Hetreau, 30,000	28.50	NR
1974	FIVE GOLDEN RINGS, Remy Hetreau, 30,000	30.00	NR
1975	SIX GEESE A-LAYING, Remy Hetreau, 30,000	32.50	NR
1976	SEVEN SWANS, Remy Hetreau, 30,000	38.00	NR
1977	EIGHT MAIDS, Remy Hetreau, 30,000	40.00	NR
1978	NINE LADIES DANCING, Remy Hetreau, 30,000	45.00	NR
1979	TEN LORDS A-LEAPING, Remy Hetreau, 30,000	50.00	NR
1980	ELEVEN PIPERS PIPING, Remy Hetreau, 30,000	55.00	NR
1981	TWELVE DRUMMERS, Remy Hetreau, 30,000	60.00	NR

Visit from Saint Nicholas

1980	NIGHT BEFORE CHRISTMAS, 1 year	55.00	NR
1981	CHILDREN WERE NESTLED, 5,000	60.00	NR
1982	FOR YOU, SANTA, 5,000	60.00	NR
1982	WHEN WHAT TO MY WONDERING EYES..., 1,500	60.00	NR
1985	HAPPY CHRISTMAS TO ALL, Loretta Jones	60.00	NR

HAVILAND AND PARLON FRANCE

Christmas Madonnas

		ISSUE	CURRENT
1972	MADONNA AND CHILD, Raphael, 5,000	35.00	40.00
1973	MADONNA, Robert Feruzzi, 5,000	40.00	75.00
1974	COWPER MADONNA AND CHILD, Raphael, 5,000	42.50	NR
1975	MADONNA AND CHILD, Bartolomé Esteban Murillo, 7,500	42.50	NR
1976	MADONNA AND CHILD, Sandro Botticelli, 7,500	45.00	NR
1977	MADONNA AND CHILD, Bellini, 7,500	48.00	NR
1978	MADONNA AND CHILD, Fra Filippo Lippi, 7,500	48.00	55.00
1979	MADONNA OF THE EUCHARIST, Sandro Botticelli, 7,500	49.50	110.00

Lady and the Unicorn

		ISSUE	CURRENT
1977	TO MY ONLY DESIRE, 20,000	45.00	NR
1978	SIGHT, 20,000	45.00	NR
1979	SOUND, 20,000	47.50	NR
1980	TOUCH, 15,000	52.50	100.00
1981	SCENT, 10,000	59.00	NR
1982	TASTE, 10,000	59.00	NR

Mother's Day

		ISSUE	CURRENT
1975	MOTHER AND CHILD, 15,000	37.50	80.00
1976	PINKY AND BABY, 15,000	42.50	BR
1977	AMY AND SNOOPY, 15,000	45.00	BR

Songbirds

		ISSUE	CURRENT
1980	CARDINALS, Patti Canaris, 5,000	65.00	90.00
1981	BLUE BIRDS, Patti Canaris, 5,000	70.00	NR
1982	ORIOLES, Patti Canaris, 5,000	70.00	NR
1982	GOLDFINCHES, Patti Canaris, 5,000	70.00	NR

Tapestry I

		ISSUE	CURRENT
1971	UNICORN IN CAPTIVITY, 10,000	35.00	65.00
1972	START OF THE HUNT, 10,000	35.00	NR
1973	CHASE OF THE UNICORN, 10,000	35.00	80.00
1974	END OF THE HUNT, 10,000	37.50	50.00
1975	UNICORN SURROUNDED, 10,000	40.00	50.00
1976	BROUGHT TO THE CASTLE, 10,000	42.50	50.00

Single Issues

		ISSUE	CURRENT
1971	CHINA TRADE PLATE	30.00	BR
1971	EMPRESS	60.00	NR
1972	MEISSEN PLATE	30.00	BR
1973	PEACEABLE KINGDOM, Nan Lee, 5,000	30.00	65.00
1977	ASTROLOGICAL MAN, 5,000	50.00	NR
1978	SCARAB, 2,500	100.00	NR

HEARTLAND COLLECTION UNITED STATES

Single Issue

		ISSUE	CURRENT
1996	NIGHT ON THE TOWN, Terry Redlin, 45 days	29.95	RI

HEINRICH PORZELLAN GERMANY

(Reco International, Villeroy & Boch)

Fairies of the Fields and Flowers

		ISSUE	CURRENT
1982	RAGGED ROBIN, Cicely Mary Barker, 21 days	49.00	125.00
1983	WILLOW, Cicely Mary Barker, 21 days	49.00	125.00
1983	ELDERBERRY FAIRY, Cicely Mary Barker, 21 days	49.00	90.00
1983	VETCH FAIRY, Cicely Mary Barker, 21 days	49.00	75.00
1984	NARCISSUS, Cicely Mary Barker, 21 days	49.00	75.00
1984	NASTURTIUM, Cicely Mary Barker, 21 days	49.00	95.00

Flower Fairy (Reco International, Villeroy & Boch)

1979	LAVENDER, Cicely Mary Barker, 21 days	35.00	50.00
1980	SWEET PEA, Cicely Mary Barker, 21 days	35.00	NR
1980	CANDYTUFT, Cicely Mary Barker, 21 days	35.00	NR
1981	HELIOTROPE, Cicely Mary Barker, 21 days	35.00	NR
1981	THE BLACKTHORN FAIRY, Cicely Mary Barker, 21 days	35.00	NR
1981	APPLEBLOSSOM, Cicely Mary Barker, 21 days	35.00	NR

Flower Fairy II (Reco International, Villeroy & Boch)

1985	COLUMBINE, Cicely Mary Barker, 21 days	39.00	NR
1985	CORNFLOWER, Cicely Mary Barker, 21 days	39.00	NR
1985	MALLOW, Cicely Mary Barker, 21 days	39.00	NR
1985	BLACK MEDICK, Cicely Mary Barker, 21 days	39.00	NR
1985	CANTERBURY BELL, Cicely Mary Barker, 21 days	39.00	NR
1985	FUCHSIA, Cicely Mary Barker, 21 days	39.00	NR

Russian Fairy Tales—The Firebird (Villeroy & Boch)

1982	IN SEARCH OF THE FIREBIRD, Boris Zvorykin, 27,500	70.00	BR
1982	IVAN AND TSAREVNA ON THE GREY WOLF, Boris Zvorykin, 27,500	70.00	BR
1982	THE WEDDING OF TSAREVNA ELENA THE FAIR, Boris Zvorykin, 27,500	70.00	BR

Nasturtium
Photo courtesy of *Collectors News*

Cornflower
Photo courtesy of *Collectors News*

		ISSUE	CURRENT

Russian Fairy Tales—Maria Morevna (Villeroy & Boch)

1983	MARIA MOREVNA AND TSAREVICH IVAN, Boris Zvorykin, 27,500	70.00	BR
1983	KOSHCHEY CARRIES OFF MARIA MOREVNA, Boris Zvorykin, 27,500	70.00	BR
1983	TSAREVICH IVAN AND THE BEAUTIFUL CASTLE, Boris Zvorykin, 27,500	70.00	BR

Russian Fairy Tales—The Red Knight (Villeroy & Boch)

1981	THE RED KNIGHT, Boris Zvorykin, 27,500	70.00	BR
1981	VASSILISSA AND HER STEPSISTERS, Boris Zvorykin, 27,500	70.00	BR
1981	VASSILISSA IS PRESENTED TO THE TSAR, Boris Zvorykin, 27,500	70.00	BR

Russian Fairy Tales—Snow Maiden (Villeroy & Boch)

1980	THE SNOW MAIDEN AND HER PARENTS, Boris Zvorykin, 27,500	70.00	80.00
1980	THE SNOWMAIDEN AT THE COURT OF TSAR BERENDEI, Boris Zvorykin, 27,500	70.00	BR
1980	THE SNOWMAIDEN AND LEL THE SHEPHERD BOY, Boris Zvorykin, 27,500	70.00	BR

HEIRLOOMS OF THE HEART UNITED STATES

African-American Family Collection

1993	PRECIOUS GIFTS, Ron Hicks, 25,000	32.50	RI

HEIRLOOM TRADITION UNITED STATES

Cinema Classics

1985	HIGH NOON, Susan Edison, 10,000	35.00	NR
1986	YOUNG AT HEART, Susan Edison, 10,000	35.00	NR
1986	RIO GRANDE, Susan Edison, 10,000	35.00	NR
1986	INDISCREET, Susan Edison, 10,000	35.00	NR

Hollywood's View of Christmas

1986	CHARLES DICKENS' CHRISTMAS CAROL, Susan Edison, 10,000	35.00	NR

It's a Wonderful Life
Photo courtesy of *Collectors News*

Single Issues

		ISSUE	CURRENT
1985	IT'S A WONDERFUL LIFE, Susan Edison	35.00	NR
1986	VARGA, Alberto Vargas, 10,000	45.00	NR
1986	BARRY MANILOW, 20,000	35.00	NR
1986	MISS AMERICA, 1927, Louis Icart, 7,500	50.00	65.00

EDNA HIBEL STUDIOS GERMANY

(Anthony Arts, Edwin M. Knowles, Hutschenreuther, March of Dimes, Rosenthal, Royal Doulton)

Allegro (Hutschenreuther)

1978	PLATE AND BOOK, Edna Hibel, 7,500	120.00	150.00

Arte Ovale (Rosenthal)

1980	TAKARA, Edna Hibel, cobalt blue, 1,000	595.00	2,350.00
1980	TAKARA, Edna Hibel, gold, 300	1,000.00	4,200.00
1980	TAKARA, Edna Hibel, blanco, 700	450.00	1,200.00
1984	TARO-KUN, Edna Hibel, cobalt blue, 1,000	595.00	1,050.00
1984	TARO-KUN, Edna Hibel, gold, 300	1,000.00	2,700.00
1984	TARO-KUN, Edna Hibel, blanco, 700	450.00	825.00

Christmas Annual

1985	ANGELS' MESSAGE, Edna Hibel, 1 year	45.00	NR
1986	GIFT OF THE MAGI, Edna Hibel, 1 year	45.00	NR
1987	FLIGHT INTO EGYPT, Edna Hibel, 1 year	49.00	NR
1988	ADORATION OF THE SHEPHERDS, Edna Hibel, 1 year	49.00	NR
1989	PEACEFUL KINGDOM, Edna Hibel, 1 year	49.00	NR
1990	THE NATIVITY, Edna Hibel, 1 year	49.00	80.00

David Series

1979	THE WEDDING OF DAVID AND BATHSHEBA, Edna Hibel, 5,000	250.00	650.00
1980	DAVID, BATHSHEBA AND SOLOMON, Edna Hibel, 5,000	275.00	425.00
1982	DAVID THE KING, Edna Hibel, 5,000	275.00	300.00
1982	DAVID THE KING, Edna Hibel, cobalt A/P, 25	275.00	1,200.00
1984	BATHSHEBA, Edna Hibel, 5,000	275.00	300.00
1984	BATHSHEBA, Edna Hibel, cobalt A/P, 100	275.00	1,200.00

Edna Hibel Holiday

1991	THE FIRST HOLIDAY, Edna Hibel, 1 year	49.00	85.00
1991	THE FIRST HOLIDAY, Edna Hibel, gold, 1,000	99.00	150.00
1992	THE CHRISTMAS ROSE, Edna Hibel, 1 year	49.00	70.00
1992	THE CHRISTMAS ROSE, Edna Hibel, gold, 1,000	99.00	125.00
1993	HOLIDAY JOY, Edna Hibel, 1 year	49.00	RI
1993	HOLIDAY JOY, Edna Hibel, gold, 1,000	99.00	RI

Eroica

1990	COMPASSION, Edna Hibel, 10,000	49.50	65.00
1992	DARYA, Edna Hibel, 10,000	49.50	NR

Erté Collection (Anthony Arts International)

		ISSUE	CURRENT
1982	APPLAUSE, Erté, 7,500	79.00	85.00

Famous Women and Children (Rosenthal)

		ISSUE	CURRENT
1980	PHARAOH'S DAUGHTER AND MOSES, Edna Hibel, gold, 2,500	350.00	625.00
1980	PHARAOH'S DAUGHTER AND MOSES, Edna Hibel, cobalt blue, 500	350.00	1,350.00
1982	CORNELIA AND HER JEWELS, Edna Hibel, gold, 2,500	350.00	500.00
1982	CORNELIA AND HER JEWELS, Edna Hibel, cobalt blue, 500	350.00	1,350.00
1982	ANNA AND THE CHILDREN OF THE KING OF SIAM, Edna Hibel, gold, 2,500	350.00	500.00
1982	ANNA AND THE CHILDREN OF THE KING OF SIAM, Edna Hibel, cobalt blue, 500	350.00	1,350.00
1984	MOZART AND THE EMPRESS MARIA THERESA, Edna Hibel, gold, 2,500	350.00	400.00
1984	MOZART AND THE EMPRESS MARIA THERESA, Edna Hibel, cobalt blue, 500	350.00	975.00

Flower Girl Annual

		ISSUE	CURRENT
1985	LILY, Edna Hibel, 15,000	79.00	200.00
1986	IRIS, Edna Hibel, 15,000	79.00	200.00
1987	ROSE, Edna Hibel, 15,00 0	79.00	200.00
1988	CAMELLIA, Edna Hibel, 15,000	79.00	200.00
1989	PEONY, Edna Hibel, 15,000	79.00	200.00
1992	WISTERIA, Edna Hibel, 15,000	79.00	225.00

International Mother Love French

		ISSUE	CURRENT
1985	YVETTE AVEC SES INFANTS, Edna Hibel, 5,000	125.00	225.00
1991	LIBERTÉ, ÉGALITÉ, FRATERNITÉ, Edna Hibel, 5,000	95.00	NR

International Mother Love German

		ISSUE	CURRENT
1982	GESA UND KINDER, Edna Hibel, 5,000	195.00	NR
1983	ALEXANDRA UND KINDER, Edna Hibel, 5,000	195.00	NR

Mother and Child

		ISSUE	CURRENT
1973	COLETTE AND CHILD, Edna Hibel, 15,000	40.00	500.00
1974	SAYURI AND CHILD, Edna Hibel, 15,000	40.00	175.00
1975	KRISTINA AND CHILD, Edna Hibel, 15,000	50.00	125.00
1976	MARILYN AND CHILD, Edna Hibel, 15,000	55.00	110.00
1977	LUCIA AND CHILD, Edna Hibel, 15,000	60.00	90.00
1978	KATHLEEN AND CHILD, Edna Hibel, 15,000	85.00	125.00

Mother's Day

		ISSUE	CURRENT
1992	MOLLY AND ANNIE, Edna Hibel, <1 year	39.00	75.00
1992	MOLLY AND ANNIE, Edna Hibel, gold, 2,500	95.00	150.00
1992	MOLLY AND ANNIE,Edna Hibel, platinum, 500	275.00	275.00
1993	OLIVIA AND HILDY, Edna Hibel, <1 year	39.00	RI
1993	OLIVIA AND HILDY, Edna Hibel, gold, 2,500	95.00	RI
1993	OLIVIA AND HILDY, Edna Hibel, platinum, 500	275.00	RI
1994	JACLYN AND RENE, Edna Hibel, <1 year	39.00	RI
1994	JACLYN AND RENE, Edna Hibel, gold, 2,500	95.00	RI
1994	JACLYN AND RENE, Edna Hibel, platinum, 500	275.00	RI
1995	TAMMY AND KALI JO, Edna Hibel, <1 year	39.00	RI
1995	TAMMY AND KALI JO, Edna Hibel, gold, 2,500	95.00	RI
1995	TAMMY AND KALI JO, Edna Hibel, platinum, 500	275.00	RI

Mother's Day Annual

		ISSUE	CURRENT
1984	ABBY & LISA, Edna Hibel, <1 year	29.50	300.00
1985	ERICA & JAMIE, Edna Hibel, <1 year	29.50	300.00
1986	EMILY & JENNIFER, Edna Hibel, <1 year	29.50	300.00
1987	CATHERINE & HEATHER, Edna Hibel, <1 year	34.50	300.00
1988	SARAH & TESS, Edna Hibel, <1 year	34.90	300.00
1989	JESSICA & KATE, Edna Hibel, <1 year	34.90	300.00
1990	ELIZABETH, JORDAN & JANIE, Edna Hibel, <1 year	36.90	300.00
1991	MICHELE & ANNA, Edna Hibel, <1 year	36.90	300.00
1992	OLIVIA & HILDY, Edna Hibel, <1 year	29.90	300.00

Museum Commemorative (Hutschenreuther)

1977	FLOWER GIRL OF PROVENCE, Edna Hibel, 12,750	175.00	425.00
1980	DIANA, Edna Hibel, 3,000	350.00	400.00

David, Bathsheba and Solomon

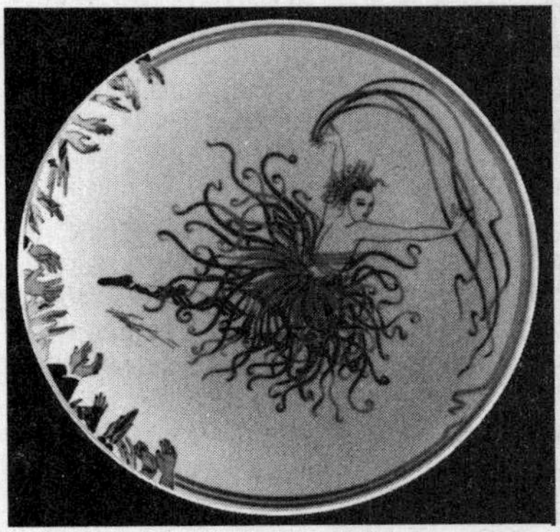

Applause

Cornelia and Her Jewels (cobalt blue)

O'Hana

Photos courtesy of *Collectors News*

		ISSUE	CURRENT
Nobility of Children (Rosenthal)			
1976	LA CONTESSA ISABELLA, Edna Hibel, 12,750	120.00	NR
1977	LE MARQUIS MAURICE PIERRE, Edna Hibel, 12,750	120.00	NR
1978	BARONESSE JOHANNA-MARYKE VAN VOLLENDAM TOT MARKEN, Edna Hibel, 12,750	130.00	140.00
1979	CHIEF RED FEATHER, Edna Hibel, 12,750	140.00	180.00
Nordic Families			
1987	A TENDER MOMENT, Edna Hibel, 7,500	79.00	95.00
Oriental Gold (Rosenthal)			
1975	YASUKO, Edna Hibel, 2,000	275.00	650.00
1976	MR. OBATA, Edna Hibel, 2,000	275.00	500.00
1978	SAKURA, Edna Hibel, 2,000	295.00	400.00
1979	MICHIO, Edna Hibel, 2,000	325.00	375.00
Scandinavian Mother and Child			
1987	PEARL AND FLOWERS, Edna Hibel, 7,500	55.00	225.00
1989	ANEMONE AND VIOLET, Edna Hibel, 7,500	75.00	95.00
1990	HOLLY AND TALIA, Edna Hibel, 7,500	75.00	85.00
To Life Annual			
1986	GOLDEN'S CHILD, Edna Hibel, 5,000	99.00	200.00
1987	TRIUMPH! EVERONE A WINNER!, Edna Hibel, 19,500	55.00	NR
1988	THE WHOLE EARTH BLOOMED AS A SACRED PLACE, Edna Hibel, 15,000	85.00	NR
1989	LOVERS OF THE SUMMER PALACE, Edna Hibel, 5,000	65.00	75.00
1992	PEOPLE OF THE FIELDS, Edna Hibel, 5,000	49.00	NR
Tribute to All Children			
1984	GISELLE, Edna Hibel, 19,500	55.00	90.00
1984	GERARD, Edna Hibel, 19,500	55.00	90.00
1985	WENDY, Edna Hibel, 19,500	55.00	70.00
1986	TODD, Edna Hibel, 19,500	55.00	125.00
World I Love			
1981	LEAH'S FAMILY, Edna Hibel, 17,500	85.00	175.00
1982	KAYLIN, Edna Hibel, 17,500	85.00	300.00
1983	EDNA'S MUSIC, Edna Hibel, 17,500	85.00	200.00
1983	O'HANA, Edna Hibel, 17,500	85.00	200.00

JOHN HINE, LTD.

(Enesco, Viletta China)

David Winter Plate Collection (Viletta China)			
1991	A CHRISTMAS CAROL, Michael Fisher, 10,000	30.00	NR
1991	COTSWOLD VILLAGE, Michael Fisher, 10,000	30.00	NR
1992	CHICHESTER CROSS, Michael Fisher, 10,000	30.00	NR
1992	LITTLE MILL, Michael Fisher, 10,000	30.00	NR
1992	OLD CURIOSITY SHOP, Michael Fisher, 10,000	30.00	NR
1992	EBENEZER SCROOGE'S COUNTING HOUSE, Michael Fisher, 10,000	30.00	NR
1993	DOVE COTTAGE, Michael Fisher, 10,000	30.00	RI

Old Curiosity Shop
Photo courtesy of *Collectors News*

		ISSUE	CURRENT
1993	THE FORGE, Michael Fisher, 10,000	30.00	RI
NA	HOUSE ON TOP	NA	NA
NA	TYTHE BARN	NA	NA

David Winter Guild Membership

1993	ON THE RIVERBANK, Michael Fisher	gift	RI

HISTORIC PROVIDENCE MINT UNITED STATES

(Royal Wickford Porcelain)

Alice in Wonderland

1986	THE TEA PARTY, George Terp, 45 days	29.50	NR
1986	THE CATERPILLAR, George Terp, 45 days	29.50	NR
1986	THE WHITE KNIGHT, George Terp, 45 days	29.50	NR
1986	THE DUCHESS AND COOK, George Terp, 45 days	29.50	NR
1986	OFF WITH THEIR HEADS!, George Terp, 45 days	29.50	NR
1986	RED AND WHITE QUEENS, George Terp, 45 days	29.50	NR
1986	THE WHITE RABBIT, George Terp, 45 days	29.50	NR
1986	TALKING FLOWERS, George Terp, 45 days	29.50	NR
1986	TWEEDLEDEE—TWEEDLEDUM, George Terp, 45 days	29.50	NR
1986	WALRUS AND CARPENTER, George Terp, 45 days	29.50	NR
1986	LION AND UNICORN, George Terp, 45 days	29.50	NR
1986	HUMPTY DUMPTY, George Terp, 45 days	29.50	NR

America the Beautiful

1981	SPACIOUS SKIES, Ben Essenburg, 17,500	37.50	NR
1981	AMBER WAVES OF GRAIN, Ben Essenburg, 17,500	37.50	NR
1981	PURPLE MOUNTAINS MAJESTY, Ben Essenburg, 17,500	37.50	NR
1981	GOD SHED HIS GRACE, Ben Essenburg, 17,500	37.50	NR
1981	CROWN THY GOOD WITH BROTHERHOOD, Ben Essenburg, 17,500	37.50	NR
1981	FROM SEA TO SHINING SEA, Ben Essenburg, 17,500	37.50	NR

Children of the Seasons

1980	CHILDREN OF SPRING, 3,000	107.50	NR

Lancaster Barn

		ISSUE	CURRENT

Lil' Peddlers

1986	FORGET ME NOTS, Lee Dubin	29.50	NR
1986	POPPIN' CORN, Lee Dubin	29.50	NR
1986	BALLOONS 'N THINGS, Lee Dubin	29.50	NR
1986	PENNY CANDY, Lee Dubin	29.50	NR
1986	TODAY'S CATCH, Lee Dubin	29.50	NR
1986	JUST PICKED, Lee Dubin	29.50	NR
1986	COBBLESTONE DELI, Lee Dubin	29.50	NR
1986	CHIMNEY SWEEP, Lee Dubin	29.50	NR
1986	APPLE A DAY, Lee Dubin	29.50	NR
1986	EXTRA, EXTRA, Lee Dubin	29.50	NR
1986	OPEN FRESH, Lee Dubin	29.50	NR
1986	COOLIN' OFF, Lee Dubin	29.50	NR

Vanishing American Barn

1983	LOG BARN, Harris Hien, 14,500	39.50	NR
1983	APPALACHIAN BARN, Harris Hien, 14,500	39.50	NR
1983	BUCKS COUNTY BARN, Harris Hien, 14,500	39.50	NR
1983	ROUND BARN, Harris Hien, 14,500	39.50	NR
1983	LANCASTER BARN, Harris Hien, 14,500	39.50	NR
1983	VICTORIAN BARN, Harris Hien, 14,500	39.50	NR
1983	NEW ENGLAND BARN, Harris Hien, 14,500	39.50	NR
1983	THATCHED BARN, Harris Hien, 14,500	39.50	NR
1983	HUDSON RIVER BARN, Harris Hien, 14,500	39.50	NR
1983	SOUTHERN TOBACCO FARM, Harris Hien, 14,500	39.50	NR
1983	FOREBAY BARN, Harris Hien, 14,500	39.50	NR
1983	CONNECTED BARN, Harris Hien, 14,500	39.50	NR

Single Issue

1979	THE CHILDREN'S YEAR, 3,000	95.00	NR

HOLIDAY GALLERY

The Dreamin'

1997	SNEAKERS, R. J. McDonald, open	60.00	RI

HORNE'S STUDIO & GALLERY UNITED STATES

Lovely Lady

		ISSUE	CURRENT
1996	CAMILLE, Lois Horne, 75 days	65.95	RI

HORNSEA GREAT BRITAIN

Christmas

1979	C—NATIVITY, 10,000	24.00	50.00
1980	H—MARY AND CHILD, 10,000	28.00	50.00
1981	R—THREE WISEMEN, 10,000	28.00	50.00

HOUSE OF GLOBAL ART UNITED STATES

(Goebel / M. I. Hummel)

Blue-Button Trains Christmas

1983	BY THE FIREPLACE, Helen Nyce, 10,000	30.00	NR
1983	DOWN THE STAIRS, Helen Nyce, 10,000	30.00	NR

Christmas Morning in Dingle Dell

1983	BILLIE BUMP'S CHRISTMAS, Grace Drayton, 19,000	30.00	NR
1983	DOLLY CELEBRATES CHRISTMAS, Grace Drayton, 10,000	30.00	NR

Dolly Dingle World Traveler

1982	DOLLY DINGLE VISITS GERMANY, Grace G. Drayton, 10,000	30.00	NR
1982	DOLLY DINGLE VISITS ITALY, Grace G. Drayton, 10,000	30.00	NR
1982	DOLLY DINGLE VISITS HOLLAND, Grace G. Drayton, 10,000	30.00	NR
1982	DOLLY DINGLE VISITS SPAIN, Grace G. Drayton, 10,000	30.00	NR
1982	DOLLY DINGLE VISITS SCOTLAND, Grace G. Drayton, 10,000	30.00	NR
1982	DOLLY DINGLE VISITS FRANCE, Grace G. Drayton, 10,000	30.00	NR

English Countryside Cats Collection

1983	JAMES, Sharon Jervis, 10,000	35.00	NR
1983	HENRY, Sharon Jervis, 10,000	35.00	NR

Dolly Dingle Visits Holland
Photo courtesy of *Collectors News*

		ISSUE	CURRENT
1983	LILY, Sharon Jervis, 10,000	35.00	NR
1983	LUCY, Sharon Jervis, 10,000	35.00	NR

HOYLE PRODUCTS UNITED STATES

(Royal Orleans)

Bygone Days

1983	BREAKFAST WITH TEDDY, Jessie Wilcox Smith, 12,500	35.00	NR
1983	A FLOWER BASKET, Jessie Wilcox Smith, 12,500	35.00	NR

Family Circus Christmas

1980	CHRISTMAS, Bil Keane, 5,000	25.00	NR
1981	CHRISTMAS, Bil Keane, 5,000	30.00	NR

Gothic Romance

1982	MOONLIGHT ROMANCE, Jondar, 5,000	30.00	NR

Hilda

1982	TOASTING MARSHMALLOWS, 5,000	25.00	NR

Mother's Day

1980	MOTHER'S DAY, Bil Keane, 5,000	25.00	NR

Norman Rockwell Clowns

1977	THE RUNAWAY, Norman Rockwell, 7,500	45.00	75.00
1978	IT'S YOUR MOVE, Norman Rockwell, 7,500	45.00	65.00
1979	THE UNDERSTUDY, Norman Rockwell, 7,500	45.00	NR
1980	THE IDOL, Norman Rockwell, 7,500	45.00	NR

Norman Rockwell Salesman

1977	THE TRAVELING SALESMAN, Norman Rockwell, 7,500	35.00	NR
1978	THE COUNTRY PEDDLER, Norman Rockwell, 7,500	40.00	NR
1979	THE HORSE TRADER, Norman Rockwell, 7,500	40.00	NR
1980	THE EXPERT SALESMAN, Norman Rockwell, 7,500	45.00	NR

Nostalgia

1981	PEPSI COLA GIRL, 5,000	25.00	65.00
1982	OLYMPIA GIRL, 5,000	30.00	NR
1982	SAVANNAH BEER GIRL, 5,000	30.00	NR
1982	DR. PEPPER GIRL, 5,000	30.00	NR

Nostalgia—Children

1983	PEAR'S SOAP AD, 12,500	35.00	NR

Nostalgic Magazine Covers (Royal Orleans)

1983	*LADIES' HOME JOURNAL*, Hayden, 12,500	35.00	NR

Rare Rockwell

1980	MRS. O'LEARY'S COW, Norman Rockwell, 7,500	30.00	NR

		ISSUE	CURRENT
1981	COME AND GET IT, Norman Rockwell, 7,500	30.00	NR

Remember When

1982	A SURPRISE FOR KITTY, Maud Humphrey, 10,000	30.00	NR
1982	WASHDAY, Maud Humphrey, 10,000	30.00	NR
1983	PLAYING GRANDMOTHER, Maud Humphrey, 10,000	30.00	NR
1983	THE PHYSICIAN, Maud Humphrey, 10,000	30.00	NR

Western Series

1977	SHARING AN APPLE, 5,000	35.00	NR
1978	SPLIT DECISION, 5,000	35.00	NR
1979	HIDING OUT, 5,000	35.00	NR
1980	IN TROUBLE, 5,000	35.00	NR

Wilderness Wings

1978	GLIDING IN, David Maass, 5,000	35.00	NR
1979	TAKEOFF, 5,000	40.00	NR
1980	JOINING UP, 5,000	45.00	NR
1981	CANVASBACKS, 5,000	47.50	NR

Wilderness Wings (Brown and Bigelow / Gorham)

1978	GLIDING IN, David Maass, 5,000	35.00	NR
1979	TAKING OFF, David Maass, 5,000	40.00	NR
1980	JOINING UP, David Maass, 5,000	45.00	NR
1981	CANVASBACKS, David Maass, 5,000	47.50	NR
1982	MOMENT OF REST, David Maass, 5,000	30.00	NR
1983	MOURNING DOVES, David Maass, 5,000	30.00	NR

Wings of the Wild

1982	CINNAMON TEAL, David Maass, 5,000	30.00	NR
1982	MOMENT OF REST, David Maass, 5,000	30.00	NR
1983	MOURNING DOVES, David Maass, 5,000	30.00	NR

Olympia Girl
Photo courtesy of *Collectors News*

Cinnamon Teal
Photo courtesy of *Collectors News*

HUDSON PEWTER UNITED STATES

(Lance Corporation)

Single Issue

		ISSUE	CURRENT
1976	BICENTENNIAL	42.00	NR

HUTSCHENREUTHER GERMANY

(Hibel Studios)

Allegro Ensemble

1978	ALLEGRO, Edna Hibel, 7,500	—	—
1978	FLUTIST, Edna Hibel, 7,500	—	—
	Set of 2	120.00	140.00

Arzberg

1986	BODO AND THE BOAT, Kathia Berger, limited	47.50	NR

Birds of Paradise

1981	BLUE BIRD OF PARADISE, Ole Winther, 10,000	175.00	NR
1981	RAGGIS GREAT BIRD OF PARADISE, Ole Winther, 10,000	175.00	NR

Birth Plates

1978	BIRTH PLATE, Ole Winther, 10,000	165.00	NR

Bouquets of the Seasons

1987	SPRING MORNING	24.50	BR
1987	EASTER BOUQUET	24.50	BR
1987	SUMMER PROMISE	27.50	BR
1987	SUMMER GLORY	27.50	BR
1988	AUTUMN TINTS	27.50	BR
1988	AUTUMN MEMORIES	27.50	BR
1988	WINTER TWILIGHT	29.50	NR
1988	FROSTY BEAUTY	29.50	NR

Christmas

1978	CHRISTMAS, Ole Winther, 2,000	260.00	NR
1979	CHRISTMAS, Ole Winther, 2,500	295.00	NR
1980	CHRISTMAS, Ole Winther, 1 year	360.00	NR
1981	CHRISTMAS, Ole Winther, 1 year	400.00	NR
1982	CHRISTMAS CONCERTO, Ole Winther, 1 year	400.00	NR
1983	THE ANNUNCIATION, Ole Winther, 1 year	135.00	NR
1984	HOLY NIGHT, Ole Winther, 1 year	135.00	NR

Country Birds of the Year

1983	LESSER SPOTTED WOODPECKER, Martin Camm, 15 days	29.95	NR
1983	LONG TAILED TIT, Martin Camm, 15 days	29.95	NR
1986	JANUARY, Martin Camm, open	29.50	NR
1986	FEBRUARY, Martin Camm, open	29.50	NR
1986	MARCH, Martin Camm, open	29.50	NR

		ISSUE	CURRENT
1986	APRIL, Martin Camm, open	29.50	NR
1986	MAY, Martin Camm, open	29.50	NR
1986	JUNE, Martin Camm, open	29.50	NR
1986	JULY, Martin Camm, open	29.50	NR
1986	AUGUST, Martin Camm, open	29.50	NR
1986	SEPTEMBER, Martin Camm, open	29.50	NR
1986	OCTOBER, Martin Camm, open	29.50	NR
1986	NOVEMBER, Martin Camm, open	29.50	NR
1986	DECEMBER, Martin Camm, open	29.50	NR

Der Ring des Nibelungen

1986	MOTIF I—DAS RHEINGOLD, Charlotte and William Hallett, 5,000	125.00	NR
1986	MOTIF II—DIE WALKUERE, Charlotte and William Hallett, 5,000	125.00	NR
1986	MOTIF III—SIEGFRIED, Charlotte and William Hallett, 5,000	125.00	NR
1986	MOTIF IV—GOETTERDAEMMERUNG, Charlotte and William Hallett, 5,000	125.00	NR

Early Memories

1983	DO THEY BITE?, James Keirstead, 7,500	72.50	NR
1983	TUG OF WAR, James Keirstead, 7,500	72.50	NR
1983	THE EXPLORERS, James Keirstead, 7,500	72.50	NR
1983	MY TURN, James Keirstead, 7,500	72.50	NR

Enchanted Seasons of a Unicorn

1985	JOYOUS SPRING, Charlotte and William Hallett, 12,500	39.50	NR
1985	PEACEFUL SUMMER, Charlotte and William Hallett, 12,500	39.50	NR
1985	GLORIOUS AUTUMN, Charlotte and William Hallett, 12,500	39.50	NR
1985	WINTER'S TRANQUILITY, Charlotte and William Hallett, 12,500	39.50	NR

Enchantment

1979	PRINCESS SNOWFLAKE, Dolores Valenza, 5,000	50.00	60.00
1979	BLOSSOM QUEEN, Dolores Valenza, 5,000	62.50	NR
1980	PRINCESS MARINA, Dolores Valenza, 5,000	87.50	NR
1981	PRINCESS STARBRIGHT, Dolores Valenza, 2,500	87.50	NR
1981	HARVEST QUEEN, Dolores Valenza, 5,000	87.50	NR
1982	PRINCESS AURA, Dolores Valenza, 5,000	87.50	NR

Flowers That Never Fade

1982	ANNUAL, Ole Winther, 1 year	27.50	NR
1983	ANNUAL, Ole Winther, 1 year	27.50	NR
1984	ANNUAL, Ole Winther, 1 year	27.50	NR

Friendship Annual

1978	FRIENDSHIP, Ole Winther, 1 year	80.00	NR

Glory of Christmas

1982	THE NATIVITY, Charlotte and William Hallett, 25,000	80.00	125.00
1983	THE ANGELS, Charlotte and William Hallett, 25,000	80.00	115.00
1984	THE SHEPHERDS, Charlotte and William Hallett, 25,000	80.00	100.00
1985	THE WISEMEN, Charlotte and William Hallett, 25,000	80.00	100.00

Gunther Granget

1972	AMERICAN SPARROWS, Gunther Granget, 5,000	50.00	75.00

		ISSUE	CURRENT
1972	EUROPEAN SPARROWS, Gunther Granget, 5,000	30.00	65.00
1973	AMERICAN KILDEER, Gunther Granget, 2,500	75.00	NR
1973	AMERICAN SQUIRREL, Gunther Granget, 2,500	75.00	NR
1973	EUROPEAN SQUIRREL, Gunther Granget, 2,500	35.00	50.00
1974	AMERICAN PARTRIDGE, Gunther Granget, 2,500	75.00	90.00
1976	AMERICAN RABBITS, Gunther Granget, 2,500	90.00	NR
1976	FREEDOM IN FLIGHT, Gunther Granget, 5,000	100.00	NR
1976	FREEDOM IN FLIGHT, gold, Gunther Granget, 200	200.00	NR
1976	WRENS, Gunther Granget, 2,500	100.00	NR
1977	BEARS, Gunther Granget, 2,500	100.00	NR
1978	FOXES' JOURNEY, Gunther Granget, 1,000	125.00	200.00

Hans Achtziger

1979	HEADING SOUTH, Hans Achtziger, 5,000	150.00	NR
1980	PLAYFUL FLIGHT, Hans Achtziger, 5,000	187.50	NR
1981	TROPICAL SKIES, Hans Achtziger, 5,000	245.00	NR
1982	CARRIED BY THE WIND, Hans Achtziger, 5,000	250.00	NR
1983	TOWARD THE SUN, Hans Achtziger, 5,000	250.00	NR
1985	OVER LAND AND SEA, Hans Achtziger, 5,000	250.00	NR

Hummingbirds

1982	SWORD-BILLED HUMMINGBIRD, Ole Winther	—	—
1982	TRAIN-BEARER, Ole Winther	—	—
1982	RUFOUS HUMMINGBIRD, Ole Winther	—	—
1982	HELIOTHRIX, Ole Winther	—	—
1982	HORNED SUNGEM, Ole Winther	—	—
1982	VERVIAN HUMMINGBIRD, Ole Winther		
	Set of 6	200.00	NR

Kathia's Cats

1983	IN A FLOWER BASKET, Kathia Berger	18.50	NR
1983	IN THE PASTURE, Kathia Berger	18.50	NR
1983	CONVERSATION WITH A SEAGULL, Kathia Berger	18.50	NR

Do They Bite?
Photo courtesy of *Collectors News*

The Smell of Roses
Photo courtesy of *Collectors News*

		ISSUE	CURRENT
1983	MY FAVORITE PLACE, Kathia Berger	18.50	NR
1983	PLAY IN THE SNOW, Kathia Berger	18.50	NR
1983	BODO AND THE BOAT, Kathia Berger	47.50	NR

Legend of St. George

1985	THE KNIGHT, Charlotte and William Hallett, 5,000	100.00	NR
1985	THE LADY KNIGHT, Charlotte and William Hallett, 5,000	100.00	NR
1985	THE CONTEST, Charlotte and William Hallett, 5,000	100.00	NR
1985	THE WEDDING, Charlotte and William Hallett, 5,000	100.00	NR

Love for All Seasons

1981	THE RIDE OUT, Charlotte and William Hallett, 10,000	125.00	NR
1982	THE MINSTREL SONG, Charlotte and William Hallett, 10,000	125.00	NR
1982	AFFECTION, Charlotte and William Hallett, 10,000	125.00	NR
1982	THE TOURNAMENT, Charlotte and William Hallett, 10,000	125.00	NR
1983	THE FALCON HUNT, Charlotte and William Hallett, 10,000	125.00	NR
1983	WINTER ROMANCE, Charlotte and William Hallett, 10,000	125.00	NR

Mother and Child Annual

1978	MOTHER AND CHILD, Ole Winther, 2,500	65.00	NR
1979	MOTHER AND CHILD, Ole Winther, 2,500	65.00	NR
1980	MOTHER AND CHILD, Ole Winther, 2,500	87.50	NR
1981	MOTHER AND CHILD, Ole Winther, 2,500	87.50	NR
1982	MOTHER AND CHILD, Ole Winther, 2,500	87.50	NR
1983	MOTHER AND CHILD, Ole Winther, 2,500	87.50	NR

Mother and Child II

1983	MOTHER AND CHILD, Ole Winther, 1 year	47.50	NR
1984	MOTHER AND CHILD, Ole Winther, 1 year	47.50	NR

Plate of the Month

1978	JANUARY—WREN, Ole Winther	—	—
1978	FEBRUARY—GREAT TITMOUSE, Ole Winther	—	—
1978	MARCH—PEEWEE, Ole Winther	—	—
1978	APRIL—STARLING, Ole Winther	—	—
1978	MAY—CUCKOO, Ole Winther	—	—
1978	JUNE—NIGHTINGALE, Ole Winther	—	—
1978	JULY—LARK, Ole Winther	—	—
1978	AUGUST—SWALLOW, Ole Winther	—	—
1978	SEPTEMBER—BLACKBIRD, Ole Winther	—	—
1978	OCTOBER—PIGEON, Ole Winther	—	—
1978	NOVEMBER—WOODCOCK, Ole Winther	—	—
1978	DECEMBER—BULLFINCH, Ole Winther	—	—
	Set of 12	324.00	NR

Richard Wagner

1986	TANNHAEUSER, Charlotte and William Hallett, 5,000	125.00	NR
1986	PARSIFAL, Charlotte and William Hallett, 5,000	125.00	NR

Ruthven Songbirds

1972	BLUEBIRD AND GOLDFINCH, John Ruthven, 5,000	100.00	BR
1973	MOCKINGBIRD AND ROBIN, John Ruthven, 5,000	100.00	BR

		ISSUE	CURRENT

Songbirds of North America

		ISSUE	CURRENT
1981	ROSE-BREASTED GROSBEAK, Ole Winther, 12,500	60.00	NR
1981	EASTERN BLUEBIRD, Ole Winther, 12,500	60.00	NR
1981	AMERICAN GOLDFINCH, Ole Winther, 12,500	60.00	NR
1981	MOCKINGBIRD, Ole Winther, 12,500	60.00	NR

Spring in the World of Birds

		ISSUE	CURRENT
1985	THE PHEASANTS, Hans Achtziger, 2,500	325.00	NR
1986	HERON, Hans Achtziger, 2,500	350.00	NR

Unicorns in Dreamer's Garden

		ISSUE	CURRENT
1986	THE SIGHT OF WONDERS, Charlotte and William Hallett, 12,500	—	—
1986	THE SMELL OF ROSES, Charlotte and William Hallett, 12,500	—	—
1986	THE SOUND OF MELODIES, Charlotte and William Hallett,12,500	—	—
1986	THE TASTE OF SWEETNESS, Charlotte and William Hallett, 12,500	—	—
1986	THE TOUCH OF A DREAM, Charlotte and William Hallett, 12,500	—	—
	Set of 5	197.50	NR

Waterbabies

		ISSUE	CURRENT
1983	TOM AND THE DRAGON FLY (#1), Sandy Nightingale, limited	45.00	NR
1983	THE FAIRIES TAKE CARE OF TOM (#2), Sandy Nightingale, limited	45.00	NR
1983	TOM AND MRS. DO AS YOU WOULD BE DONE BY (#3), Sandy Nightingale, limited	45.00	NR
1984	TOM AND THE SWEET-CHEST, Sandy Nightingale, 15 days	45.00	NR
1984	ELLIE TEACHES TOM, Sandy Nightingale, 15 days	45.00	NR
1984	TOM TAKES CARE OF THE BABY, Sandy Nightingale, 15 days	45.00	NR
1984	TOM MEETS ELLIE AGAIN, Sandy Nightingale, 15 days	45.00	NR

Wedding

		ISSUE	CURRENT
1979	WEDDING PLATE, Ole Winther, 10,000	210.00	235.00

World of Legends

		ISSUE	CURRENT
1982	GRIFFIN, Charlotte and William Hallett, 12,500	—	—
1982	UNICORN, Charlotte and William Hallett, 12,500	—	—
1982	PEGASUS, Charlotte and William Hallett, 12,500	—	—
1982	DRAGON, Charlotte and William Hallett, 12,500	—	—
	Set of 4	175.00	NR

Zodiac

		ISSUE	CURRENT
1978	AQUARIUS, Ole Winther, 2,000	125.00	135.00
1978	ARIES, Ole Winther, 2,000	125.00	135.00
1978	CANCER, Ole Winther, 2,000	125.00	135.00
1978	CAPRICORN, Ole Winther, 2,000	125.00	135.00
1978	GEMINI, Ole Winther, 2,000	125.00	135.00
1978	LEO, Ole Winther, 2,000	125.00	135.00
1978	LIBRA, Ole Winther, 2,000	125.00	135.00
1978	PISCES, Ole Winther, 2,000	125.00	135.00
1978	SAGITTARIUS, Ole Winther, 2,000	125.00	135.00
1978	SCORPIO, Ole Winther, 2,000	125.00	135.00
1978	TAURUS, Ole Winther, 2,000	125.00	135.00
1978	VIRGO, Ole Winther, 2,000	125.00	135.00

Single Issues

		ISSUE	CURRENT
1970	UN COMMEMORATIVE	8.00	15.00
1973	CHRISTMAS	37.00	45.00

IMPERIAL UNITED STATES

America the Beautiful

1969	U.S. CAPITOL, 500	17.50	NR
1970	MOUNT RUSHMORE, 500	17.50	NR
1971	STATUE OF LIBERTY, 500	17.50	NR
1972	MONUMENT VALLEY, ARIZONA, 500	17.50	NR
1973	LIBERTY BELL, 500	17.50	NR
1974	GOLDEN GATE, 500	19.95	NR
1975	MT. VERNON, 500	19.95	NR

Christmas

1970	PARTRIDGE, carnival glass, 1 year	12.00	30.00
1970	PARTRIDGE, crystal, 1 year	15.00	25.00
1971	TURTLEDOVES, carnival glass, 1 year	12.00	35.00
1971	TURTLEDOVES, crystal, 1 year	16.50	30.00
1972	HENS, carnival glass, 1 year	12.00	30.00
1972	HENS, crystal, 1 year	16.50	25.00
1973	COLLY BIRDS, carnival glass, 1 year	12.00	35.00
1973	COLLY BIRDS, crystal, 1 year	16.50	25.00
1974	GOLDEN RINGS, carnival glass, 1 year	12.00	20.00
1974	GOLDEN RINGS, crystal, 1 year	16.50	25.00
1975	GEESE, carnival glass, 1 year	14.00	35.00
1975	GEESE, crystal, 1 year	19.00	25.00
1976	SWANS, carnival glass, 1 year	16.00	NR
1976	SWANS, crystal, 1 year	21.00	NR
1977	MAIDS, carnival glass, 1 year	18.00	NR
1977	MAIDS, crystal, 1 year	23.00	NR
1978	DRUMMERS, carnival glass, 1 year	20.00	30.00
1978	DRUMMERS, crystal, 1 year	25.00	NR
1979	PIPERS, carnival glass, 1 year	22.00	NR
1979	PIPERS, crystal, 1 year	27.00	NR
1980	LADIES, carnival glass, 1 year	24.00	NR
1980	LADIES, crystal, 1 year	29.00	NR
1981	LORDS, carnival glass, 1 year	28.00	NR
1981	LORDS, crystal, 1 year	34.00	NR

Coin Plates

1971	KENNEDY COIN	15.00	NR
1972	IKE COIN	15.00	NR
1976	BICENTENNIAL COIN	20.00	NR

IMPERIAL CHING-TE CHEN PEOPLES REPUBLIC OF CHINA

Beauties of the Red Mansion

1986	PAO-CHAI, Zhao Huimin, 115 days	27.92	BR
1986	YUAN-CHUN, Zhao Huimin, 115 days	27.92	BR

		ISSUE	CURRENT
1987	HSI-FENG, Zhao Huimin, 115 days	30.92	BR
1987	HSI-CHUN, Zhao Huimin, 115 days	30.92	BR
1988	MIAO-YU, Zhao Huimin, 115 days	30.92	BR
1988	YING-CHUN, Zhao Huimin, 115 days	30.92	BR
1988	TAI-YU, Zhao Huimin, 115 days	32.92	NR
1988	LI-WAN, Zhao Huimin, 115 days	32.92	NR
1988	KO-CHING, Zhao Huimin, 115 days	32.92	NR
1988	HSIANG-YUN, Zhao Huimin, 115 days	34.92	NR
1989	TAN-CHUN, Zhao Huimin, 115 days	34.92	BR
1989	CHIAO-CHIEH, Zhao Huimin, 115 days	34.92	BR

Blessings from a Chinese Garden

1988	THE GIFT OF PURITY, Z. Song Mao, 175 days	39.92	BR
1989	THE GIFT OF GRACE, Z. Song Mao, 175 days	39.92	BR
1989	THE GIFT OF BEAUTY, Z. Song Mao, 175 days	42.92	BR
1989	THE GIFT OF HAPPINESS, Z. Song Mao, 175 days	42.92	BR
1990	THE GIFT OF TRUTH, Z. Song Mao, 175 days	42.92	BR
1990	THE GIFT OF JOY, Z. Song Mao, 175 days	42.92	BR

China's Imperial Palace: The Forbidden City

1990	PAVILION OF 10,000 SPRINGS, Sheng Fu, 150 days	39.92	BR
1990	FLYING KITES ON A SPRING DAY, Sheng Fu, 150 days	39.92	BR
1990	PAVILION/FLOATING JADE GREEN, Sheng Fu, 150 days	42.92	BR
1991	THE LANTERN FESTIVAL, Sheng Fu, 150 days	42.92	BR
1991	NINE DRAGON SCREEN, Sheng Fu, 150 days	42.92	BR
1991	THE HALL OF THE CULTIVATING MIND, Sheng Fu, 150 days	42.92	BR
1991	DRESSING THE EMPRESS, Sheng Fu, 150 days	45.92	BR
1991	PAVILION OF FLOATING CUPS, Sheng Fu, 150 days	45.92	BR

Flower Goddesses of China

1991	THE LOTUS GODDESS, Zhao Huimin, 175 days	34.92	BR
1991	THE CHRYSANTHEMUM GODDESS, Zhao Huimin, 175 days	34.92	BR
1991	THE PLUM BLOSSOM GODDESS, Zhao Huimin, 175 days	37.92	BR
1991	THE PEONY BLOSSOM GODDESS, Zhao Huimin, 175 days	37.92	BR
1991	THE NARCISSUS BLOSSOM GODDESS, Zhao Huimin, 175 days	37.92	50.00
1991	THE CAMELIA BLOSSOM GODDESS, Zhao Huimin, 175 days	37.92	BR

Garden of Satin Wings

1992	A MORNING DREAM, Jiang Xue-bing, 115 days	29.92	NR
1993	AN EVENING MIST, Jiang Xue-bing, 115 days	29.92	RI
1993	A GARDEN WHISPER, Jiang Xue-bing, 115 days	29.92	RI
1993	AN ENCHANTING INTERLUDE, Jiang Xue-bing, 115 days	29.92	RI

Legends of West Lake

1989	LADY WHITE, Jiang Xue-bing, 175 days	29.92	BR
1990	LADY SILKWORM, Jiang Xue-bing, 175 days	29.92	BR
1990	LAUREL PEAK, Jiang Xue-bing, 175 days	29.92	BR
1990	RISING SUN TERRACE, Jiang Xue-bing, 175 days	32.92	BR
1990	THE APRICOT FAIRY, Jiang Xue-bing, 175 days	32.92	BR
1990	BRIGHT PEARL, Jiang Xue-bing, 175 days	32.92	BR
1990	THREAD OF SKY, Jiang Xue-bing, 175 days	34.92	BR
1991	PHOENIX MOUNTAIN, Jiang Xue-bing, 175 days	34.92	BR

Pavilion of 10,000 Springs
Photo courtesy of *Collectors News*

Lady White
Photo courtesy of *Collectors News*

		ISSUE	CURRENT
1991	ANCESTORS OF TEA, Jiang Xue-bing, 175 days	34.92	BR
1991	THREE POOLS MIRRORING/MOON, Jiang Xue-bing, 175 days	36.92	BR
1991	FLY-IN PEAK, Jiang Xue-bing, 175 days	36.92	BR
1991	THE CASE OF THE FOLDING FANS, Jiang Xue-bing, 175 days	36.92	NR

Maidens of the Folding Sky

1992	LADY LU, Jiang Xue-bing, 175 days	29.92	40.00
1992	MISTRESS YANG, Jiang Xue-bing, 175 days	29.92	50.00
1992	BRIDE YEN CHUN, Jiang Xue-bing, 175 days	32.92	50.00
1993	PARROT MAIDEN, Jiang Xue-bing, 175 days	32.92	RI

Scenes from the Summer Palace

1988	THE MARBLE BOAT, Z. Song Mao, 175 days	29.92	BR
1988	JADE BELT BRIDGE, Z. Song Mao, 175 days	29.92	BR
1989	HALL THAT DISPELS THE CLOUDS, Z. Song Mao, 175 days	32.92	NR
1989	THE LONG PROMENADE, Z. Song Mao, 175 days	32.92	NR
1989	GARDEN/HARMONIOUS PLEASURE, Z. Song Mao, 175 days	32.92	BR
1989	THE GREAT STAGE, Z. Song Mao, 175 days	32.92	NR
1989	SEVENTEEN ARCH BRIDGE, Z. Song Mao, 175 days	34.92	BR
1990	BOATERS ON KUMMING LAKE, Z. Song Mao, 175 days	34.92	BR

INCOLAY STUDIOS UNITED STATES

Christmas Cameos

1990	HOME WITH THE TREE, Roger Akers	60.00	NR
1991	SKATERS AT TWILIGHT, Roger Akers	60.00	NR
1992	EVENING CAROLERS, Roger Akers	65.00	NR
1993	SLEDDING BY STARLIGHT, Roger Akers	65.00	NR
1994	PROPOSAL UNDER THE STARS, Roger Akers	65.00	NR
1995	CHRISTMAS VIGIL, Roger Akers	65.00	NR

Home with the Tree

Jennifer's World

Flying Cloud

Happy Christmas

In the Pond's Shallow (Moose)

432 Fairview Lane

Photos courtesy of *Collectors News*

		ISSUE	CURRENT
Enchanted Moments			
1984	TIFFANY'S WORLD, Rosemary Calder, 7,500	95.00	NR
1985	JENNIFER'S WORLD, Rosemary Calder, 7,500	95.00	NR
Fall of Troy			
1988	JUDGMENT OF PARIS, Alan Brunettin	55.00	NR
1988	PARIS AND HELEN, Alan Brunettin	55.00	NR
1989	HECTOR AND ANDROMACHE, Alan Brunettin	60.00	NR
1989	THE TROJAN HORSE, Alan Brunettin	60.00	NR
Four Elements			
1983	AIR, Artisans of Incolay Studios	25.00	NR
1983	FIRE, Artisans of Incolay Studios	25.00	NR
1983	WATER, Artisans of Incolay Studios	25.00	NR
1983	EARTH, Artisans of Incolay Studios	25.00	NR
	Set of 4	95.00	NR
Great Romances of History			
1979	ANTONY AND CLEOPATRA, Carl Romanelli	65.00	NR
1980	TAJ MAHAL LOVERS, Carl Romanelli	65.00	NR
1981	LANCELOT AND GUINEVERE, Carl Romanelli	65.00	NR
1982	LORD NELSON AND LADY HAMILTON, Carl Romanelli	70.00	NR
Life's Interludes			
1979	UNCERTAIN BEGINNING, James W. Roberts	95.00	NR
1980	FINALLY FRIENDS, James W. Roberts	95.00	NR
Love Themes from the Grand Opera			
1991	CARMEN, Roger Akers	65.00	NR
1991	MADAME BUTTERFLY, Roger Akers	65.00	NR
1992	THE MARRIAGE OF FIGARO, Roger Akers	70.00	NR
1992	AIDA, Roger Akers	70.00	NR
1992	TRISTAN AND ISOLDE, Roger Akers	70.00	NR
1992	LA TRAVIATA, Roger Akers	70.00	NR
Majestic Sailing Ships			
1992	*FLYING CLOUD*, Daniel Stapleford	65.00	NR
1992	*CHARLES W. MORGAN*, Daniel Stapleford	65.00	NR
1992	*SEA WITCH*, Daniel Stapleford	65.00	NR
1992	*DREADNOUGHT*, Daniel Stapleford	65.00	NR
Night Before Christmas			
1992	HAPPY CHRISTMAS, Roger Akers	69.00	NR
1992	UP ON THE ROOFTOP, Roger Akers	69.00	NR
1992	IT MUST BE ST. NICK, Roger Akers	74.00	NR
1992	VISIONS OF SUGARPLUMS, Roger Akers	74.00	NR
1993	I SPRANG FROM MY BED, Roger Akers	74.00	RI
1993	UP THE CHIMNEY, Roger Akers	74.00	RI
North American Wildlife Heritage			
1991	AT STREAM'S EDGE (DEER), Don Cliff	65.00	NR

		ISSUE	CURRENT
1991	IN THE POND'S SHALLOW (MOOSE), Don Cliff	65.00	NR
1992	ON THE RIVERBANK (BEAR), Don Cliff	70.00	NR
1992	UPON THE ROCKY LEDGE (MOUNTAIN LION), Don Cliff	70.00	NR
1992	BENEATH THE OPEN SKY (RAM), Don Cliff	70.00	NR
1992	BESIDE THE SHELTERING KNOLL (WOLF), Don Cliff	75.00	NR
1992	THE GRASSY CLEARING (ELK), Don Cliff	75.00	NR
1993	NEAR THE RUNNING BROOK (BISON), Don Cliff	75.00	RI

Romantic Poets

1977	SHE WALKS IN BEAUTY, Gayle Bright Appleby	60.00	80.00
1978	A THING OF BEAUTY, Gayle Bright Appleby	60.00	NR
1979	ODE TO A SKYLARK, Gayle Bright Appleby	65.00	NR
1980	PHANTOM OF DELIGHT, Gayle Bright Appleby	65.00	NR
1981	THE KISS, Roger Akers	65.00	NR
1982	MY HEART LEAPS UP, Roger Akers	70.00	NR
1983	I STOOD TIPTOE, Roger Akers	70.00	NR
1984	THE DREAM, Roger Akers	70.00	NR
1985	THE RECOLLECTION, Roger Akers	70.00	NR

Shakespearean Lovers

1990	ROMEO AND JULIET, Roger Akers	65.00	NR
1990	HAMLET AND OPHELIA, Roger Akers	65.00	NR
1991	PETRUCHIO AND KATHARINA, Roger Akers	70.00	NR
1991	MACBETH AND LADY MACBETH, Roger Akers	70.00	NR
1991	BENEDICK AND BEATRICE, Roger Akers	70.00	NR
1992	LYSANDER AND HERMIA, Roger Akers	70.00	NR
1992	OTHELLO AND DESDEMONA, Roger Akers	75.00	NR
1992	FERDINAND AND MIRANDA, Roger Akers	75.00	NR

Sonnets of Shakespeare

1987	SHALL I COMPARE THEE TO A SUMMER'S DAY, Roger Akers	55.00	NR
1987	THOU ART TOO DEAR, Roger Akers	55.00	NR
1988	LOVE ALTERS NOT, Roger Akers	60.00	NR
1988	SINCE FIRST I SAW YOU, Roger Akers	60.00	NR
1989	YOUR FAIR EYES, Roger Akers	60.00	NR
1989	YOU SHALL SHINE MORE BRIGHT, Roger Akers	60.00	NR

Victorian Dream Homes

1993	125 MAIN STREET, Corrine Workmaster	55.00	RI
1993	212 THIRD AVENUE, Corrine Workmaster	55.00	RI
1993	367 RIVERSIDE DRIVE, Corrine Workmaster	60.00	RI
1993	432 FAIRVIEW LANE, Corrine Workmaster	60.00	RI

Voyages of Ulysses

1984	ISLE OF CIRCE, Alan Brunettin	50.00	60.00
1985	THE SIRENS, Alan Brunettin	50.00	NR
1986	ISLE OF CALYPSO, Alan Brunettin	55.00	NR
1986	LAND OF THE PHAECIANS, Alan Brunettin	55.00	NR
1986	RETURN OF ULYSSES, Alan Brunettin	55.00	NR
1987	THE REUNION, Alan Brunettin	55.00	NR

INTERNATIONAL SILVER UNITED STATES

Bicentennial

		ISSUE	CURRENT
1972	SIGNING DECLARATION, Manuel de Oliveira, 7,500	40.00	310.00
1973	PAUL REVERE, Manuel de Oliveira, 7,500	40.00	160.00
1974	CONCORD BRIDGE, Manuel de Oliveira, 7,500	40.00	115.00
1975	CROSSING DELAWARE, Manuel de Oliveira, 7,500	50.00	80.00
1976	VALLEY FORGE, Manuel de Oliveira, 7,500	50.00	65.00
1977	SURRENDER AT YORKTOWN, Manuel de Oliveira, 7,500	50.00	60.00

Christmas

1974	TINY TIM, Carl Sundberg, 7,500	75.00	NR
1975	CAUGHT, Beverly Chase, 7,500	75.00	NR
1976	BRINGING HOME THE TREE, Albert Petitto, 7,500	75.00	NR
1977	CHRISTMAS BALL, Albert Petitto, 7,500	75.00	NR
1978	ALLELUIA, Albert Petitto, 7,500	75.00	NR
1979	REJOICE, Albert Petitto, 7,500	100.00	NR

INTERNATIONAL MUSEUM UNITED STATES

Letter Writer's

1982	PORTRAIT OF MICHELANGELO, 15,000	37.50	NR
1982	MRS. JOHN DOUGLAS, 15,000	37.50	NR
1983	DON ANTONIO, 15,000	37.50	NR
1983	LOVELY READER, 15,000	37.50	NR
1984	LADY WRITING LETTER, 15,000	37.50	NR

Stamp Art

1979	GINGERBREAD SANTA, 9,900	29.00	90.00
1980	MADONNA AND CHILD, 9,900	37.50	75.00
1981	BOTTICELLI'S MADONNA AND CHILD, 9,900	45.00	60.00
1982	MADONNA OF THE GOLDFINCH, 9,900	45.00	NR
1983	RAPHAEL'S MADONNA, 9,900	39.50	NR

Superheroes

1983	SUPERMAN, limited	29.50	NR

INTERPACE UNITED STATES

Architects of Democracy

1974	GEORGE WASHINGTON, 1,776	—	—
1974	JOHN ADAMS, 1,776	—	—
1974	THOMAS JEFFERSON, 1,776	—	—
1974	ALEXANDER HAMILTON, 1,776	—	—
	Set of 4	225.00	280.00

Modigliani Series

1972	CARYATID, 10,000	60.00	70.00

ISLANDIA INTERNATIONAL UNITED STATES

Coming Home

		ISSUE	CURRENT
1998	THE AMERICAN ARMY, Cliff Hayes, open	29.95	RI

People of Africa

1998	PEUL WOMAN AND ZEBRAS, Wayne Anthony Still, open	34.95	RI

ISRAEL CREATIONS

(Naaman Ltd.)

Commemorative

1967	WAILING WALL, 5,000	7.50	30.00
1967	TOWER OF DAVID, 5,000	7.50	30.00
1968	MASADA, 5,000	17.50	25.00
1969	RACHEL'S TOMB, 5,000	17.50	25.00
1970	TIBERIAS, 5,000	8.00	25.00
1971	NAZARETH, 5,000	9.00	25.00
1972	BETHSHEBA, 5,000	9.00	25.00
1973	ACRE, 5,000	9.00	25.00

ANTHONY JACKSON UNITED STATES

Single Issue

1982	PRESIDENTIAL PLATE, Anthony C. Jackson, 5,000	195.00	NR

GEORG JENSEN DENMARK

Chagall Series

1972	THE LOVERS, 12,500	50.00	120.00

Doves

		ISSUE	CURRENT
Christmas			
1972	DOVES, 1 year	15.00	55.00
1973	CHRISTMAS EVE, 1 year	15.00	40.00
1974	CHRISTMAS STORY, 1 year	17.50	25.00
1975	WINTER SCENE, 1 year	22.50	50.00
1976	CHRISTMAS IN THE COUNTRY, 1 year	27.00	35.00
Mother's Day			
1973	MOTHER AND CHILD, 1 year	15.00	40.00
1974	SWEET DREAMS, 1 year	17.50	30.00
1975	A MOTHER'S WORLD, 1 year	22.50	30.00

SVEND JENSEN DENMARK

Anniversary

1980	HANS CHRISTIAN ANDERSEN'S HOME	60.00	75.00

Christmas/Andersen Fairy Tales

1970	HANS CHRISTIAN ANDERSEN HOUSE, Gerhard Sausmark, 20,136	14.50	85.00
1971	LITTLE MATCH GIRL, Mads Stage, 20,000	15.00	40.00
1972	MAID OF COPENHAGEN, Edvard Eriksen, 22,122	16.50	45.00
1973	THE FIR TREE, Svend Otto, 11,000	22.00	40.00
1974	CHIMNEY SWEEP, Svend Otto, 11,000	25.00	NR
1975	THE UGLY DUCKLING, Svend Otto, 1 year	27.50	NR
1976	THE SNOW QUEEN, Mads Stage, 1 year	27.50	40.00
1977	THE SNOWMAN, Svend Otto, 1 year	29.50	40.00
1978	LAST DREAM OF THE OLD OAK TREE, Svend Otto, 1 year	32.00	45.00
1979	OLD STREET LAMP, Svend Otto, 1 year	36.50	NR
1980	WILLIE WINKIE, Svend Otto, 1 year	42.50	NR
1981	UTTERMOST PART OF THE SEA, Svend Otto, 1 year	49.50	NR
1982	TWELVE BY THE MAILCOACH, Svend Otto, 1 year	54.50	NR
1983	THE STORY OF THE YEAR, Svend Otto, 1 year	54.50	NR
1984	THE NIGHTINGALE, Svend Otto, 1 year	54.50	NR

Mother's Day

1970	BOUQUET FOR MOTHER, Maggi Baaring, 13,740	14.50	75.00
1971	MOTHER'S LOVE, Nulle Oigaard, 14,310	15.00	40.00
1972	GOOD NIGHT, Mads Stage, 11,018	16.50	35.00
1973	FLOWERS FOR MOTHER, Mads Stage, 11,000	20.00	35.00
1974	DAISIES FOR MOTHER, Mads Stage, 11,000	25.00	35.00
1975	SURPRISE FOR MOTHER, Mads Stage, 15,000	27.50	NR
1976	COMPLETE GARDENER, Mads Stage, 1 year	27.50	NR
1977	LITTLE FRIENDS, Mads Stage, 1 year	29.50	NR
1978	DREAMS, Mads Stage, 1 year	32.00	NR
1979	PROMENADE, Mads Stage, 1 year	36.50	NR
1980	NURSERY SCENE, Mads Stage, 1 year	42.50	NR
1981	DAILY DUTIES, Mads Stage, 1 year	49.50	NR
1982	MY BEST FRIEND, Mads Stage, 1 year	54.50	NR
1983	AN UNEXPECTED MEETING, Mads Stage, 1 year	54.50	NR
1984	WHO ARE YOU?, Mads Stage, 1 year	54.50	NR

JM COMPANY UNITED STATES

			ISSUE	CURRENT
Competitive Sports				
1979	DOWNHILL RACING SLALOM, Hal Reed, 5,000		30.00	NR
Love				
1980	LOVE'S SERENADE, Hal Reed, 5,000		50.00	NR
Oriental Birds				
1976	WINDOW AT TIGER SPRING TEMPLE, Hal Reed, 10,000		39.00	NR

JOSAIR FRANCE

Bicentennial

1972	AMERICAN EAGLE, 400	250.00	NR
1973	AMERICAN FLAG, 400	250.00	NR
1974	ABRAHAM LINCOLN, 400	250.00	NR
1975	GEORGE WASHINGTON, 400	250.00	NR
1976	DECLARATION OF INDEPENDENCE, 400	250.00	NR

JUDAIC HERITAGE SOCIETY UNITED STATES

(Avondale, Villeta)

Great Jewish Women

1976	GOLDA MEIR, 4,000	35.00	NR
1976	HENRIETTA SZOLD, 4,000	35.00	NR
1976	EMMA LAZARUS, 4,000	35.00	NR

Heritage

1976	RABBI, 4,000	35.00	NR
1976	HASIDIM, 4,000	35.00	NR
1976	SHTETL, 4,000	35.00	NR

Israel's 30th Anniversary Commemorative (Viletta)

1979	L'CHAYIM TO ISRAEL, 10,000	59.50	NR
1979	PROPHECY OF ISAIAH, 10,000	59.50	NR

Jerusalem Wedding

1979	BRIDE OF JERUSALEM, 6,000	65.00	BR
1979	HASIDIC DANCERS, 6,000	65.00	BR

Jewish Holidays

1972	PESACH, gold, 25	1,900.00	NR
1972	PESACH, silver, 2,000	150.00	NR
1972	PURIM, silver, 2,000	150.00	NR
1973	CHANUKAH, gold, 100	1,900.00	NR
1973	CHANUKAH, silver, 2,000	150.00	NR
1974	PURIM, silver, 1,000	150.00	NR

		ISSUE	CURRENT
1979	CHANUKAH, 2,500	50.00	NR
1979	PURIM, 2,500	50.00	NR
1979	SHAVOUTH, 2,500	50.00	NR
1979	ROSH HASHANA, 2,500	50.00	NR
1979	SIMCHAT TORAH, 2,500	50.00	NR
1979	PESACH, 2,500	50.00	NR

Single Issues

1977	JACOB AND ANGEL, 5,000	45.00	NR
1977	HATIKVAH, copper, 5,000	55.00	NR
1977	HATIKVAH, gold plate, 1,000	75.00	NR
1977	HATIKVAH, sterling silver, 500	180.00	NR
1980	SHALOM—PEACE, 6,000	95.00	NR

KAISER GERMANY

America the Beautiful

1988	CALIFORNIA QUAIL, Gerda Neubacher, 9,500	49.50	NR
1988	SNOWY EGRET, Gerda Neubacher, 9,500	49.50	NR
1990	BROWSING FOR DELICACIES, Gerda Neubacher, 9,500	49.50	NR
1990	SCANNING THE TERRITORY, Gerda Neubacher, 9,500	49.50	NR

American Cats

1991	KITS IN A CRADLE, SIAMESE, G. Williams, 7,500	49.50	NR
1991	LAZY RIVER DAYS, SHORTHAIRS, G. Williams, 7,500	49.50	NR
1991	TAKING IT EASY, PERSIANS, G. Williams, 7,500	49.50	NR
1991	TREE VIEW, SHORTHAIRS, G. Williams, 7,500	49.50	NR

Anniversary

1972	LOVE BIRDS, Toni Schoener, 12,000	16.50	30.00
1973	IN THE PARK, Toni Schoener, 7,000	16.50	25.00
1974	CANOEING, Toni Schoener, 7,000	20.00	30.00
1975	TENDER MOMENT, Kurt Bauer, 7,000	25.00	NR
1976	SERENADE, Toni Schoener, 7,000	25.00	NR
1977	SIMPLE GIFT, Toni Schoener, 1 year	25.00	NR
1978	VIKING TOAST, Toni Schoener, 1 year	30.00	NR
1979	ROMANTIC INTERLUDE, Hannelore Blum, 1 year	32.00	NR
1980	LOVE AT PLAY, Hannelore Blum, 1 year	40.00	NR
1981	RENDEZVOUS, Hannelore Blum, 1 year	40.00	NR
1982	BETROTHAL, Kurt Bauer, 1 year	40.00	NR
1983	SUNDAY AFTERNOON, Toni Schoener, 1 year	40.00	NR

Arabian Nights

1989	SCHEHERAZADE, R. Hersey, 9,500	75.00	NR

Bicentennial

1976	SIGNING DECLARATION, J. Trumball, 1,000	75.00	150.00

Bird Dogs

NA	COCKER SPANIEL, J. Francis, 19,500	39.50	NR
NA	BEAGLE, J. Francis, 19,500	39.50	NR

		ISSUE	CURRENT
NA	ENGLISH SETTER, J. Francis, 19,500	39.50	NR
NA	BLACK LABRADOR, J. Francis, 19,500	39.50	NR
NA	GERMAN SHORT-HAIR POINTER, J. Francis, 19,500	39.50	NR
NA	GOLDEN LABRADOR, J. Francis, 19,500	39.50	NR
NA	ENGLISH POINTER, J. Francis, 19,500	39.50	NR
NA	IRISH SETTER, J. Francis, 19,500	39.50	NR

Childhood Memories

1985	WAIT A LITTLE, A. Schlesinger, 9,800	29.00	NR

Children's Prayer

1982	NOW I LAY ME DOWN TO SLEEP, Willy Freuner, 5,000	29.50	NR
1982	SAYING GRACE, Willy Freuner, 5,000	29.50	NR

Christmas

1970	WAITING FOR SANTA CLAUS, Toni Schoener, 1 year	12.50	25.00
1971	SILENT NIGHT, Kurt Bauer, 10,000	13.50	20.00
1972	COMING HOME FOR CHRISTMAS, Kurt Bauer, 10,000	16.50	25.00
1973	HOLY NIGHT, Toni Schoener, 8,000	18.00	40.00
1974	CHRISTMAS CAROLERS, Kurt Bauer, 8,000	25.00	NR
1975	BRINGING HOME THE TREE, Joann Northcott, 1 year	25.00	NR
1976	CHRIST THE SAVIOUR IS BORN, Carlo Maratti, 1 year	25.00	35.00
1977	THE THREE KINGS, Toni Schoener, 1 year	25.00	NR
1978	SHEPHERDS IN THE FIELD, Toni Schoener, 1 year	30.00	NR
1979	CHRISTMAS EVE, Hannelore Blum, 1 year	32.00	40.00
1980	JOYS OF WINTER, Hannelore Blum, 1 year	40.00	NR
1981	ADORATION OF THREE KINGS, Kurt Bauer, 1 year	40.00	NR
1982	BRINGING HOME THE TREE, Kurt Bauer, 1 year	40.00	NR

Classic Fairy Tales

1982	THE FROG KING, Gerda Neubacher, 50 days	39.50	50.00
1983	PUSS IN BOOTS, Gerda Neubacher, 50 days	39.50	NR
1983	LITTLE RED RIDING HOOD, Gerda Neubacher, 50 days	39.50	NR
1984	HANSEL AND GRETEL, Gerda Neubacher, 50 days	39.50	NR
1984	CINDERELLA, Gerda Neubacher, 50 days	39.50	NR
1984	SLEEPING BEAUTY, Gerda Neubacher, 50 days	39.50	NR

Classic Lullabies of the World

1985	SLEEP BABY SLEEP, Gerda Neubacher	39.50	NR
1986	ROCKABYE BABY, Gerda Neubacher	39.50	NR
1986	A MOCKINGBIRD, Gerda Neubacher	39.50	NR
1986	AU CLAIR DE LUNE, Gerda Neubacher	39.50	NR
1987	WELSH LULLABYE, Gerda Neubacher	39.50	NR
1988	BRAHMS' LULLABYE, Gerda Neubacher	39.50	NR

Dance, Ballerina, Dance

1982	FIRST SLIPPERS, Robert Clarke, 14,500	47.50	NR
1983	AT THE BARRE, Robert Clarke, 14,500	47.50	NR
NA	THE RECITAL, Robert Clarke, 14,500	47.50	NR
NA	PIROUETTE, Robert Clarke, 14,500	47.50	NR
NA	SWAN LAKE, Robert Clarke, 14,500	47.50	NR
NA	OPENING NIGHT, Robert Clarke, 14,500	47.50	NR

Au Clair de Lune
Photo courtesy of *Collectors News*

First Slippers
Photo courtesy of *Collectors News*

Egyptian

		ISSUE	CURRENT
1978	KING TUT, 15,000	65.00	80.00
1980	NEFERTITI, 10,000	275.00	350.00
1980	TUTANKHAMEN, 10,000	275.00	350.00

Faithful Companion

1990	BEAGLE, R. J. May, 9,500	49.50	NR
1990	BOXER, R. J. May, 9,500	49.50	NR
1990	COCKER SPANIEL, R. J. May, 9,500	49.50	NR
1990	DASHCHUND, R. J. May, 9,500	49.50	NR
1990	DOBERMAN, R. J. May, 9,500	49.50	NR
1990	ENGLISH SPRINGER SPANIEL, R. J. May, 9,500	49.50	NR
1990	GERMAN SHEPHERD, R. J. May, 9,500	49.50	NR
1990	GOLDEN RETRIEVER, R. J. May, 9,500	49.50	NR
1990	POODLE, R. J. May, 9,500	49.50	NR
1990	ROTTWEILER, R. J. May, 9,500	49.50	NR
1990	ROUGH COLLIE (MAY), R. J. May, 9,500	49.50	NR
1991	LABRADOR RETRIEVER, R. J. May, 9,500	49.50	NR
1991	YORKSHIRE TERRIERS, R. J. May, 9,500	49.50	NR

Famous Horses

1983	SNOW KNIGHT, Adolf Lohmann, 3,000	95.00	NR
1984	NORTHERN DANCER, Adolf Lohmann, 3,000	95.00	NR

Forest Surprises

1989	DEERHEAD ORCHID, Gerda Neubacher, 9,500	49.50	NR
1989	MARSH MARIGOLD, Gerda Neubacher, 9,500	49.50	NR
1990	VIOLETS, Gerda Neubacher, 9,500	49.50	NR
1990	WILD IRIS, Gerda Neubacher, 9,500	49.50	NR

Four Seasons

1981	SPRING, Ivo Cenkovcan, 1 year	50.00	NR

		ISSUE	CURRENT
1981	SUMMER, Ivo Cenkovcan, 1 year	50.00	NR
1981	AUTUMN, Ivo Cenkovcan, 1 year	50.00	NR
1981	WINTER, Ivo Cenkovcan, 1 year	50.00	NR

Garden and Songbirds

1973	CARDINAL, Wolfgang Gawantka, 2,000	200.00	250.00
1973	BLUE TITMOUSE, Wolfgang Gawantka, 2,000	200.00	250.00

Glen Loates' Feathered Friends

1978	BLUE JAYS, Glen Loates, 10,000	70.00	100.00
1979	CARDINALS, Glen Loates, 10,000	80.00	90.00
1980	CEDAR WAXWINGS, Glen Loates, 10,000	80.00	NR
1981	GOLDFINCH, Glen Loates, 10,000	80.00	NR

Graduate

1986	BOY, K. McKernan, 7,500	39.50	NR
1986	GIRL, K. McKernan, 7,500	39.50	NR

Happy Days

1981	THE AEROPLANE, Gerda Neubacher, 5,000	75.00	NR
1982	JULIE, Gerda Neubacher, 5,000	75.00	NR
1982	WINTER FUN, Gerda Neubacher, 5,000	75.00	NR
1983	THE LOOKOUT, Gerda Neubacher, 5,000	75.00	NR

Harmony and Nature

1985	SPRING ENCORE, John Littlejohn, 9,800	39.50	NR

Little Clowns

1981	THE RED MASK, Lorraine Trester, 9,500	35.00	NR
1982	PIGTAILS AND PUPPIES, Lorraine Trester, 9,500	35.00	NR
1983	CONCERTINA, Lorraine Trester, 9,500	35.00	NR

King Tut

1978	KING TUT	65.00	NR

Little Men (Gorham)

1977	COME RIDE WITH ME, Lorraine Trester, 9,500	60.00	NR
1980	A MAGICAL MOMENT, Lorraine Trester, 9,500	60.00	NR
1983	DAY TO REMEMBER, Lorraine Trester, 9,500	60.00	NR

Memories of Christmas

1983	THE WONDER OF CHRISTMAS, Gerda Neubacher, closed	42.50	NR
1984	A CHRISTMAS DREAM, Gerda Neubacher, closed	39.50	NR
1985	CHRISTMAS EVE, Gerda Neubacher, closed	39.50	NR
1986	A VISIT WITH SANTA, Gerda Neubacher, closed	39.50	NR

Mother's Day

1971	MARE AND FOAL, Toni Schoener, 1 year	13.00	25.00
1972	FLOWERS FOR MOTHER, Toni Schoener, 8,000	16.50	NR
1973	CAT AND KITTENS, Toni Schoener, 7,000	17.00	40.00
1974	FOX AND YOUNG, Toni Schoener, 7,000	20.00	40.00

		ISSUE	CURRENT
1975	GERMAN SHEPHERD WITH PUPS, Toni Schoener, 7,000	25.00	85.00
1976	SWAN AND CYGNETS, Toni Schoener, 7,000	25.00	NR
1977	MOTHER RABBIT WITH YOUNG, Joann Northcott, 1 year	25.00	NR
1978	HEN AND CHICKS, Toni Schoener, 1 year	30.00	50.00
1979	MOTHER'S DEVOTION, Nori Peter, 1 year	32.00	40.00
1980	RACCOON FAMILY, Joann Northcott, 1 year	40.00	NR
1981	SAFE NEAR MOTHER, Hannelore Blum	40.00	NR
1982	PHEASANT FAMILY, Kurt Bauer	40.00	NR
1983	TENDER CARD, Kurt Bauer	40.00	65.00

Noble Horse

1988	ARABIAN, L. Turner	49.50	NR
1988	GELDERLANDER, L. Turner	49.50	NR
1988	HOLSTEIN, L. Turner	49.50	NR
1988	QUARTER HORSE, L. Turner	49.50	NR
1988	THOROUGHBRED, L. Turner	49.50	NR
1988	TRAKEHNER, L. Turner	49.50	NR

Oberammergau Passion Play

1970	OBERAMMERGAU, Toni Schoener, 1 year	25.00	NR
1970	OBERAMMERGAU, Kurt Bauer, 1 year	40.00	NR
1991	OBERAMMERGAU, sepia, 700	38.00	NR
1991	OBERAMMERGAU, cobalt, 400	64.00	NR

On the Farm

1981	THE DUCK, Adolf Lohmann, 1 year	50.00	75.00
1982	THE ROOSTER, Adolf Lohmann, 1 year	50.00	75.00
1983	THE POND, Adolf Lohmann, 1 year	50.00	75.00
1983	THE HORSES, Adolf Lohmann, 1 year	50.00	75.00
NA	WHITE HORSE, Adolf Lohmann, 1 year	50.00	75.00
NA	DUCKS ON THE POND, Adolf Lohmann, 1 year	50.00	75.00
NA	GIRL WITH GOATS, Adolf Lohmann, 1 year	50.00	75.00
NA	GIRL FEEDING ANIMALS, Adolf Lohmann, 1 year	50.00	75.00

Passion Play

1970	THE LAST SUPPER, Toni Schoener, 1 year	25.00	NR
1980	THE CRUCIFIXION, Kurt Bauer, 1 year	40.00	NR

People of the Midnight Sun

1978	NORTHERN LULLABY, Nori Peter, 15,000	65.00	NR
1979	ILAGA, MY FRIEND, Nori Peter, 15,000	75.00	NR
1980	MOTHERHOOD, Nori Peter, 15,000	85.00	NR
1981	ODARK AND SON SAMIK, Nori Peter, 15,000	90.00	NR
1982	ANANA WITH LITTLE MUTAK, Nori Peter, 15,000	90.00	NR
1983	THE HUNTER'S REWARD, Nori Peter, 15,000	90.00	NR

Racing for Pride and Profit

1984	THE AGING VICTOR, Roger Horton, 9,500	50.00	NR
1985	SECOND GOES HUNGRY, Roger Horton, 9,500	50.00	NR
1986	NO TIME TO BOAST, Roger Horton, 9,500	50.00	NR
1987	FIRST FISH TO MARKET, Roger Horton, 9,500	50.00	NR
1988	GYPSY TRADERS, Roger Horton, 9,500	50.00	NR

First Fish to Market
Photo courtesy of *Collectors News*

Cinderella
Photo courtesy of *Collectors News*

		ISSUE	CURRENT
Romantic Portraits			
1981	LILIE, Gerda Neubacher, 5,000	200.00	225.00
1982	CAMELIA, Gerda Neubacher, 5,000	175.00	200.00
1983	ROSE, Gerda Neubacher, 5,000	175.00	185.00
1984	DAISY, Gerda Neubacher, 5,000	175.00	NR
Stable Door Collection			
1988	FIRST STEPS, D. Twinney	29.50	NR
1988	IMPUDENCE, D. Twinney	29.50	NR
1988	PRIDE, D. Twinney	29.50	NR
1988	THE VISITOR, D. Twinney	29.50	NR
Traditional Fairy Tales			
1983	CINDERELLA, Dorothea King, limited	39.50	NR
1983	JACK AND THE BEANSTALK, Dorothea King, limited	39.50	NR
1984	THREE LITTLE PIGS, Dorothea King, limited	39.50	NR
1985	GOLDILOCKS, Dorothea King, limited	39.50	NR
1985	DICK WITTINGTON, Dorothea King, limited	39.50	NR
Treasures of Tutankhamen			
1978	THE GOLDEN MASK, 3,247	90.00	120.00
1978	THE GOLDEN THRONE, 3,247	90.00	120.00
1978	THE HORUS FALCON, 3,247	90.00	120.00
1978	THE IVORY CHEST, 3,247	90.00	120.00
Water Fowl			
1985	MALLARD DUCKS, Edward J. Bierly, 19,500	55.00	75.00
1985	CANVASBACK DUCKS, Edward J. Bierly, 19,500	55.00	75.00
1985	WOOD DUCKS, Edward J. Bierly, 19,500	55.00	75.00
1985	PINTAIL DUCKS, Edward J. Bierly, 19,500	55.00	75.00
1989	CAROLINA WOOD DUCKS, T. Boyer, 15,000	49.50	NR
1989	GREENWINGED TEALS, T. Boyer, 15,000	49.50	NR

		ISSUE	CURRENT
1989	REDHEADS, T. Boyer, 15,000	49.50	NR
1989	PAIR OF CANVASBACKS, T. Boyer, 15,000	49.50	NR
1989	PAIR OF CAROLINA WOOD DUCKS, T. Boyer, 15,000	49.50	NR
1989	PAIR OF GREENWINGED TEALS, T. Boyer, 15,000	49.50	NR
1989	PAIR OF MALLARDS, T. Boyer, 15,000	49.50	NR
1989	PAIR OF PINTAILS, T. Boyer, 15,000	49.50	NR
1989	PAIR OF REDHEADS, T. Boyer, 15,000	49.50	NR

Wildflowers

1986	TRILLIUM, Gerda Neubacher, 9,500	39.50	55.00
1987	SPRING BEAUTY, Gerda Neubacher, 9,500	45.00	55.00
1987	WILD ASTERS, Gerda Neubacher, 9,500	45.00	55.00
1987	WILD ROSES, Gerda Neubacher, 9,500	49.50	55.00

Wildlife

1973	LITTLE CRITTERS, 5,000, set of 6	100.00	125.00

Woodland Creatures (Hamilton Collection)

1985	SPRINGTIME FROLIC, R. Orr, 10 days	37.50	NR
1985	FISHING TRIP, R. Orr, 10 days	37.50	NR
1985	RESTING IN THE GLEN, R. Orr, 10 days	37.50	NR
1985	MEADOWLAND VIGIL, R. Orr, 10 days	37.50	NR
1985	MORNING LESSON, R. Orr, 10 days	37.50	NR
1985	FIRST ADVENTURE, R. Orr, 10 days	37.50	NR
1985	THE HIDING PLACE, R. Orr, 10 days	37.50	NR
1985	STARTLED SENTRY, R. Orr, 10 days	37.50	NR

Yachts

1972	CETONIA, Kurt Bauer, 1,000	50.00	NR
1972	WESTWARD, Kurt Bauer, 1,000	50.00	NR

Yesterday's World

1978	A TIME FOR DREAMING, Lorraine Trester, 5,000	70.00	NR
1979	SUMMER IS FOREVER, Lorraine Trester, 5,000	75.00	NR
1980	SUNDAY AFTERNOON, Lorraine Trester, 5,000	80.00	NR
1984	BREATH OF SPRING, Lorraine Trester, 5,000	80.00	NR

Single Issue

1973	TORONTO HORSE SHOW, 1,000	29.00	40.00

DAVID KAPLAN STUDIOS UNITED STATES

Fiddler's People

1978	FIDDLER ON THE ROOF, Rik Vig, 7,500	60.00	NR
1979	TEVYA, Rik Vig, 7,500	60.00	NR
1980	MIRACLE OF LOVE, Rik Vig, 7,500	60.00	NR
1981	THE WEDDING, Rik Vig, 7,500	60.00	NR

Loveables

1982	LITTLE ANGEL, Sol Dember, 10,000	40.00	NR

KEIRSTEAD GALLERY CANADA

Sisters

		ISSUE	CURRENT
1987	BRENDA'S MILL, James Keirstead, 4,000	55.00	NR

Single Issue

1985	DAWN, PEGGY'S COVE, James Keirstead, 7,500	98.00	NR

Brenda's Mill
Photo courtesy of *Collectors News*

KERA DENMARK

Christmas

1967	KOBENHAVN, 1 year	6.00	25.00
1968	FORSTE, 1 year	6.00	20.00
1969	ANDERSEN'S HOUSE, 1 year	6.00	20.00
1970	LANGELINIE, 1 year	6.00	15.00
1971	LITTLE PETER, 1 year	6.00	15.00

Moon

1969	APOLLO II, 1 year	6.00	NR
1970	APOLLO 13, 1 year	6.00	NR

Mother's Day

1970	MOTHER'S DAY, 1 year	6.00	NR
1971	MOTHER'S DAY, 1 year	6.00	NR

KERN COLLECTIBLES UNITED STATES

(Gorham, Haviland & Parlon and Pickard, Royal Bayreuth)

Adventures of the Old West

1981	GRIZZLY AMBUSH, Harland Young, 7,500	65.00	NR
1982	THE TRIAN ROBBERS, Harland Young, 7,500	65.00	NR

		ISSUE	CURRENT
1983	BANK HOLDUP, Harland Young, 7,500	65.00	NR
1985	NATURE STRIKES, Harland Young, 7,500	75.00	NR

Butterflies

1983	MONARCHS, Patti Canaris, 7,500	75.00	NR

Children of the Southwest

1984	NAVAJO PIXIE, Jay Schmidt, 7,500	36.00	NR
1984	MORNING SUN, Jay Schmidt, 7,500	36.00	NR

Child's World

1983	KATHIE, Leo Jansen, 9,800	45.00	NR
1983	MEREDITH, Leo Jansen, 9,800	45.00	NR
1984	FREDDIE, Leo Jansen, 9,800	45.00	NR
1984	JAMIE, Leo Jansen, 9,800	45.00	NR

Christmas of Yesterday

1978	CHRISTMAS CALL, Marvin Nye, 5,000	45.00	NR
1979	WOODCUTTER'S CHRISTMAS, Marvin Nye, 5,000	50.00	NR
1980	BAKING CHRISTMAS GOODIES, Marvin Nye, 5,000	65.00	NR
1981	SINGING CHRISTMAS CAROLS, Marvin Nye, 5,000	55.00	NR

Companions

1978	CUBS, Gregory Perillo, 5,000	40.00	90.00
1978	MIGHTY SIOUX, Gregory Perillo, 5,000	40.00	70.00
1979	NATURE GIRL, Gregory Perillo, 5,000	50.00	NR
1980	BUFFALO BOY, Gregory Perillo, 5,000	50.00	65.00
1981	SHEPHERDS, Gregory Perillo, 5,000	55.00	NR

Country Friends

1984	ELIZABETH, Leesa Hoffman, 7,500	35.00	NR

Favorite Pets

1981	SCHNAUZERS, Leo Jansen, 7,500	39.95	85.00
1982	COCKER SPANIELS, Leo Jansen, 7,500	39.95	NR
1983	POINTERS, Leo Jansen, 7,500	39.95	NR

Great Achievements in Art

1980	THE ARABIAN, Harland Young, 3,000	65.00	170.00
1981	THE LONGHORNS, Harland Young, 3,000	60.00	NR

Horses of Harland Young

1982	QUARTERHORSES, Harland Young, 10,000	55.00	NR
1983	ARABIANS, Harland Young, 10,000	55.00	NR
1984	MUSTANGS, Harland Young, 10,000	55.00	NR

Kitty Cats

1983	MORRIE, Leo Jansen, 7,500	39.00	NR
1984	TATTOO, Leo Jansen, 7,500	39.00	NR

Jamie

Tattoo

Canadian Geese

Swinging

Elephants

Champ

Photos courtesy of *Collectors News*

		ISSUE	CURRENT

Leaders of Tomorrow (Gorham)

1980	FUTURE PHYSICIAN, Leo Jansen, 9,800	50.00	65.00
1981	FUTURE FARMER, Leo Jansen, 9,800	50.00	NR
1982	FUTURE FLORIST, Leo Jansen, 9,800	50.00	NR
1983	FUTURE TEACHER, Leo Jansen, 9,800	50.00	NR

Linda's Little Loveables

1978	THE BLESSING, Linda Avey, 7,500	30.00	40.00
1978	APPRECIATION, Linda Avey, 7,500	37.50	NR
1979	ADOPTED BURRO, Linda Avey, 7,500	42.50	NR

Mother's Day

1976	MOTHER AND CHILDREN, Leslie De Mille, 7,500	40.00	NR
1977	DARCY, Edward Runci, 7,500	50.00	NR
1978	MOMENT TO REFLECT, Edward Runci, 5,000	55.00	NR
1979	FULFILLMENT, Edward Runci, 5,000	45.00	NR
1980	A RENEWAL OF FAITH, Edward Runci, 5,000	45.00	NR

North American Game Birds

1983	CANADIAN GEESE, Derk Hansen, 7,500	60.00	NR
1984	MALLARDS, Derk Hansen, 7,500	60.00	NR
1984	PHEASANTS, Derk Hansen, 7,500	60.00	NR

Portrait of Innocence

1977	JOHNNIE AND DUKE, Leo Jansen, 7,500	40.00	55.00
1978	RANDY AND REX, Leo Jansen, 7,500	42.50	65.00
1979	FURRY FRIENDS, Leo Jansen, 7,500	47.50	NR
1980	BENJI'S BURRO, Leo Jansen, 7,500	50.00	115.00

Prince Tatters

1979	FURRY FRIENDS, Leo Jansen, 7,500	47.50	NR

School Days

1982	APPLE FOR MY TEACHER, Marvin Nye, 7,500	65.00	BR
1983	THE ARITHMETIC LESSON, Marvin Nye, 7,500	65.00	BR

Sugar and Spice

1976	DANA AND DEBBIE, Leo Jansen, 7,500	40.00	130.00
1977	BECKY AND BABY, Leo Jansen, 7,500	42.50	75.00
1978	JEANNETTE AND JULIE, Leo Jansen, 7,500	47.50	60.00
1980	RAMONA AND RACHEL, Leo Jansen, 7,500	50.00	100.00

Sun Bonnet Babies Playtime (Royal Bayreuth)

1981	SWINGING, 5,000	55.00	NR
1981	ROUND DANCE, 5,000	60.00	NR
1982	MARBLES, 5,000	60.00	NR
1982	PLAYING CATCH, 5,000	60.00	NR

This Little Pig Went to Market

1982	THIS LITTLE PIG WENT TO MARKET, Linda Nye, 9,800	39.95	NR
1983	THIS LITTLE PIG STAYED HOME, Linda Nye, 9,800	42.50	NR

		ISSUE	CURRENT
1984	THIS LITTLE PIG HAD ROAST BEEF, Linda Nye, 9,800	45.00	NR
1985	THIS LITTLE PIG HAD NONE, Linda Nye, 9,800	45.00	NR

Tribal Companions

1984	MY BEST FRIEND, Derk Hansen, 6,000	35.00	NR

Zoological Garden

1983	ELEPHANTS, Mike Carroll, 5,000	55.00	NR
1984	TIGERS, Mike Carroll, 5,000	55.00	NR

Single Issue

1984	CHAMP, Leo Jansen, 7,500	39.50	NR

KETSUZAN—KILN JAPAN

Poetic Visions of Japan

1988	PLUM BLOSSOMS	39.93	BR
1989	A BUTTERFLY	39.93	BR
1989	SNOWY HERON	42.93	BR
1989	ORPHAN SPARROW	42.93	BR
1990	CHERRY FLOWERS	42.93	BR
1990	LEAVES	42.93	BR
1990	HARVEST MOON	44.93	BR
1990	CRYSTAL SPRING	44.93	BR

A Butterfly
Photo courtesy of *Collectors News*

KHOLUI ART STUDIOS RUSSIA

Legend of the Snowmaiden

1989	SNOWMAIDEN, SNEGUROCHKA	35.87	BR
1990	SNOWMAIDEN AND HER PARENTS	35.87	BR
1990	JUDGMENT OF TSAR BERENDEY	38.87	BR

		ISSUE	CURRENT
1990	A SONG OF LOVE	38.87	BR
1990	A DANCE OF FRIENDSHIP	38.87	BR
1990	LET'S SERENADE	38.87	BR
1991	LOVE'S FINALE	40.87	BR
1991	THE SNOWMAIDEN WITH SPRING AND WINTER	40.87	BR

Light of Christ

1993	JESUS WALKS ON WATER	29.87	RI
1993	THE ASCENSION	29.87	RI
1993	THE BAPTISM OF CHRIST	29.87	RI
1993	THE ACT OF BLESSING	29.87	RI

KING'S ITALY

Christmas

1973	ADORATION, Merli, 1,500	100.00	220.00
1974	MADONNA, Merli, 1,500	150.00	200.00
1975	HEAVENLY CHOIR, Merli, 1,500	160.00	215.00
1976	SIBLINGS, Merli, 1,500	200.00	230.00

Flowers

1973	CARNATION, Aldo Falchi, 1,000	85.00	130.00
1974	RED ROSE, Aldo Falchi, 1,000	100.00	145.00
1975	YELLOW DAHLIA, Aldo Falchi, 1,000	110.00	160.00
1976	BLUEBELLS, Aldo Falchi, 1,000	130.00	165.00
1977	ANEMONES, Aldo Falchi, 1,000	130.00	175.00

Mother's Day

1973	DANCING GIRL, Merli, 1,500	100.00	185.00
1974	DANCING BOY, Merli, 1,500	115.00	185.00
1975	MOTHERLY LOVE, Merli, 1,500	140.00	200.00
1976	MAIDEN, Merli, 1,500	180.00	200.00

KIRK UNITED STATES

Bicentennial

1972	WASHINGTON, 5,000	75.00	NR
1972	CONSTELLATION, 825	75.00	NR

Christmas

1972	FLIGHT INTO EGYPT, 3,500	150.00	NR

Mother's Day

1972	MOTHER AND CHILD, 3,500	75.00	NR
1973	MOTHER AND CHILD, 2,500	80.00	NR

Thanksgiving

1972	THANKSGIVING WAYS AND MEANS, 3,500	150.00	NR

JODI KIRK UNITED STATES

DeGrazia Series

		ISSUE	CURRENT
1972	HEAVENLY BLESSING, Ted DeGrazia, 200	75.00	85.00

L. L. KNICKERBOCKER COMPANY, INC.

Single Issue

1994	VARSITY BEAR PHOTO, C15001, R. T. Gordon, 2,500	31.25	RI

EDWIN M. KNOWLES UNITED STATES

(Bradford Exchange, Dominion, Rockwell Society, Roman, Inc., Tirschenreuth)

101 Dalmatians (Bradford Exchange)

1993	WATCH DOGS, Disney Studios, 95 days	29.90	RI
1994	A HAPPY REUNION, Disney Studios, 95 days	29.90	RI
1994	HELLO DARLINGS, Disney Studios, 95 days	32.90	RI
1994	SERGEANT TIBS SAVES THE DAY, Disney Studios, 95 days	32.90	RI
1994	HALFWAY HOME, Disney Studios, 95 days	32.90	RI
1994	TRUE LOVE, Disney Studios, 95 days	32.90	RI
1995	BEDTIME, Disney Studios, 95 days	34.90	RI
1995	A MESSY GOOD TIME, Disney Studios, 95 days	34.90	RI

Aesop's Fables

1988	THE GOOSE THAT LAID THE GOLDEN EGG, Michael Hampshire, 150 days	27.90	BR
1988	THE HARE AND THE TORTOISE, Michael Hampshire, 150 days	27.90	BR
1988	THE FOX AND THE GRAPES, Michael Hampshire, 150 days	30.90	NR
1989	THE LION AND THE MOUSE, Michael Hampshire, 150 days	30.90	NR
1989	THE MILK MAID AND HER PAIL, Michael Hampshire, 150 days	30.90	NR
1989	THE JAY AND THE PEACOCK, Michael Hampshire, 150 days	30.90	NR

Americana Holidays

1978	THE FOURTH OF JULY, Don Spaulding, 1 year	26.00	BR
1979	THANKSGIVING, Don Spaulding, 1 year	26.00	BR
1980	EASTER, Don Spaulding, 1 year	26.00	BR
1981	VALENTINE'S DAY, Don Spaulding, 1 year	26.00	BR
1982	FATHER'S DAY, Don Spaulding, 1 year	26.00	BR
1983	CHRISTMAS, Don Spaulding, 1 year	26.00	BR
1984	MOTHER'S DAY, Don Spaulding, 1 year	26.00	BR

American Innocents

1986	ABIGAIL IN THE ROSE GARDEN, Barbara Marsten and Valentin Mandrajji, 150 days	19.50	NR
1986	ANN BY THE TERRACE, Barbara Marsten and Valentin Mandrajji, 150 days	19.50	NR
1986	ELLEN AND JOHN IN THE PARLOR, Barbara Marsten and Valentin Mandrajji, 150 days	19.50	BR
1986	WILLIAM ON THE ROCKING HORSE, Barbara Marsten and Valentin Mandrajji, 150 days	19.50	25.00

American Journey

		ISSUE	CURRENT
1987	WESTWARD HO, Mort Künstler, 150 days	29.90	BR
1988	KITCHEN WITH A VIEW, Mort Künstler, 150 days	29.90	BR
1988	CROSSING THE RIVER, Mort Künstler, 150 days	29.90	BR
1988	CHRISTMAS AT THE NEW CABIN, Mort Künstler, 150 days	29.90	BR

Amy Brackenberry's Cat Tales

1987	A CHANCE MEETING: WHITE AMERICAN SHORTHAIRS, Amy Brackenbury, 150 days	21.50	NR
1987	GONE FISHING: MAINE COONS, Amy Brackenbury, 150 days	21.50	35.00
1988	STRAWBERRIES AND CREAM: CREAM PERSIANS, Amy Brackenbury, 150 days	24.90	45.00
1988	FLOWER BED: BRITISH SHORTHAIRS, Amy Brackenbury, 150 days	24.90	BR
1988	KITTENS AND MITTENS: SILVER TABBIES, Amy Brackenbury, 150 days	24.90	NR
1988	ALL WRAPPED UP: HIMALAYANS, Amy Brackenbury, 150 days	24.90	40.00

Annie

1983	ANNIE AND SANDY, William Chambers, 100 days	19.00	BR
1983	DADDY WARBUCKS, William Chambers, 100 days	19.00	BR
1983	ANNIE AND GRACE, William Chambers, 100 days	19.00	BR
1984	ANNIE AND THE ORPHANS, William Chambers, 100 days	21.00	BR
1985	TOMORROW, William Chambers, 100 days	21.00	BR
1985	ANNIE AND MISS HANNIGAN, William Chambers, 100 days	21.00	BR
1986	ANNIE, LILY AND ROOSTER, William Chambers, 100 days	24.00	BR
1986	GRAND FINALE, William Chambers, 100 days	24.00	BR

Baby Owls of North America

1991	PEEK-A-WHOO: SCREECH OWLS, Joe Thornbrugh, 150 days	27.90	NR
1991	FORTY WINKS: SAW-WHET OWLS, Joe Thornbrugh, 150 days	27.90	35.00
1991	THE TREE HOUSE: NORTHERN PYGMY OWLS, Joe Thornbrugh, 150 days	30.90	40.00
1991	THREE OF A KIND: GREAT HORNED OWLS, Joe Thornbrugh, 150 days	30.90	35.00
1991	OUT ON A LIMB: GREAT GRAY OWLS, Joe Thornbrugh, 150 days	30.90	NR
1991	BEGINNING TO EXPLORE: BOREAL OWLS, Joe Thornbrugh, 150 days	32.90	50.00
1992	THREE'S COMPANY: LONG-EARED OWLS, Joe Thornbrugh, 150 days	32.90	40.00
1992	WHOO'S THERE?: BARRED OWL, Joe Thornbrugh, 150 days	32.90	50.00

Backyard Harmony

1991	THE SINGING LESSON, Joe Thornbrugh, 150 days	27.90	NR
1991	WELCOMING A NEW DAY, Joe Thornbrugh, 150 days	27.90	NR
1991	ANNOUNCING SPRING, Joe Thornbrugh, 150 days	30.90	50.00
1992	THE MORNING HARVEST, Joe Thornbrugh, 150 days	30.90	45.00
1992	SPRINGTIME PRIDE, Joe Thornbrugh, 150 days	30.90	55.00
1992	TREETOP SERENADE, Joe Thornbrugh, 150 days	32.90	60.00
1992	AT THE PEEP OF DAY, Joe Thornbrugh, 150 days	32.90	45.00
1992	TODAY'S DISCOVERIES, Joe Thornbrugh, 150 days	32.90	45.00

Bambi

1992	BASHFUL BAMBI, Disney Studios, 150 days	34.90	NR
1992	BAMBI'S NEW FRIENDS, Disney Studios, 150 days	34.90	60.00
1992	HELLO LITTLE PRINCE, Disney Studios, 150 days	37.90	45.00

		ISSUE	CURRENT
1992	BAMBI'S MORNING GREETINGS, Disney Studios, 150 days	37.90	45.00
1992	BAMBI'S SKATING LESSON, Disney Studios, 150 days	37.90	70.00
1993	WHAT'S UP POSSUMS?, Disney Studios, 150 days	37.90	RI

Beauty and the Beast (Bradford Exchange)

1993	LOVE'S FIRST DANCE, Disney Studios, 150 days	29.90	RI
1993	A BLOSSOMING ROMANCE, Disney Studios, 150 days	29.90	RI
1993	PAPA'S WORKSHOP, Disney Studios, 150 days	29.90	RI
1993	LEARNING TO LOVE, Disney Studios, 150 days	32.90	RI
1993	WARMING UP, Disney Studios, 150 days	32.90	RI
1994	A GIFT FOR BELLE, Disney Studios, 150 days	32.90	RI
1993	A MISMATCH, Disney Studios, 150 days	34.90	RI
1993	BE OUR GUEST, Disney Studios, 150 days	34.90	RI
1993	BELLE'S FAVORITE STORY, Disney Studios, 150 days	34.90	RI
1994	ENCHANTE'S CHERIE, Disney Studios, 150 days	34.90	RI
1994	A SPOT OF TEA, Disney Studios, 150 days	36.90	RI
1994	SPELL IS BROKEN, Disney Studios, 150 days	36.90	RI

Biblical Mothers

1983	BATHSHEBA AND SOLOMON, Eve Licea, 1 year	39.50	BR
1984	JUDGMENT OF SOLOMON, Eve Licea, 1 year	39.50	BR
1984	PHARAOH'S DAUGHTER AND MOSES, Eve Licea, 1 year	39.50	BR
1985	MARY AND JESUS, Eve Licea, 1 year	39.50	BR
1985	SARAH AND ISAAC, Eve Licea, 1 year	44.50	BR
1985	REBEKAH, JACOB AND ESAU, Eve Licea, 1 year	44.50	BR

Birds of the Seasons

1990	CARDINALS IN WINTER, Sam Timm, 150 days	24.90	35.00
1990	BLUEBIRDS IN SPRING, Sam Timm, 150 days	24.90	40.00
1991	NUTHATCHES IN FALL, Sam Timm, 150 days	27.90	BR
1991	BALTIMORE ORIOLES IN SUMMER, Sam Timm, 150 days	27.90	BR
1991	BLUE JAYS IN EARLY FALL, Sam Timm, 150 days	27.90	35.00
1991	ROBINS IN EARLY SPRING, Sam Timm, 150 days	27.90	BR
1991	CEDAR WAXWINGS IN FALL, Sam Timm, 150 days	29.90	35.00
1991	CHICKADEES IN WINTER, Sam Timm, 150 days	29.90	55.00

Call of the Wilderness

1991	FIRST OUTING, Keven Daniel, 150 days	29.90	NR
1991	HOWLING LESSON, Kevin Daniel, 150 days	29.90	200.00
1991	SILENT WATCH, Kevin Daniel, 150 days	32.90	50.00
1991	WINTER TRAVELERS, Kevin Daniel, 150 days	32.90	45.00
1992	AHEAD OF THE PACK, Kevin Daniel, 150 days	32.90	45.00
1992	NORTHERN SPIRITS, Kevin Daniel, 150 days	34.90	50.00
1992	TWILIGHT FRIENDS, Kevin Daniel, 150 days	34.90	50.00
1992	A NEW FUTURE, Kevin Daniel, 150 days	34.90	50.00
1992	MORNING MIST, Kevin Daniel, 150 days	36.90	60.00
1992	THE SILENT ONE, Kevin Daniel, 150 days	36.90	55.00

Carousel

1987	IF I LOVED YOU, D. Brown, 150 days	24.90	BR
1988	MR. SNOW, D. Brown, 150 days	24.90	NR
1988	THE CAROUSEL WALTZ, D. Brown, 150 days	24.90	NR
1988	YOU'LL NEVER WALK ALONE, D. Brown, 150 days	24.90	BR

Christmas

Annie and the Orphans

Peek-A-Whoo: Screech Owls

A Dream Is a Wish

Lazy Morning

Cardinal

Photos courtesy of *Collectors News*

ISSUE	CURRENT

Casablanca

1990	HERE'S LOOKING AT YOU, KID, James Griffin, 150 days	34.90	NR
1990	WE'LL ALWAYS HAVE PARIS, James Griffin, 150 days	34.90	NR
1991	WE LOVED EACH OTHER ONCE, James Griffin, 150 days	37.90	NR
1991	RICK'S CAFE AMERICAIN, James Griffin, 150 days	37.90	NR
1991	A FRANC FOR YOUR THOUGHTS, James Griffin, 150 days	37.90	45.00
1991	PLAY IT SAM, James Griffin, 150 days	37.90	45.00

China's Natural Treasures

1992	SIBERIAN TIGER, T. C. Chiu, 150 days	29.90	40.00
1992	SNOW LEOPARD, T. C. Chiu, 150 days	29.90	35.00
1992	GIANT PANDA, T. C. Chiu, 150 days	32.90	45.00
1992	TIBETAN BROWN BEAR, T. C. Chiu, 150 days	32.90	40.00
1992	ASIAN ELEPHANT, T. C. Chiu, 150 days	32.90	50.00
1992	GOLDEN MONKEY, T. C. Chiu, 150 days	34.90	45.00

Christmas in the City

1992	A CHRISTMAS SNOWFALL, A. Leimanis, 150 days	34.90	NR
1992	YULETIDE CELEBRATION, A. Leimanis, 150 days	34.90	50.00
1993	HOLIDAY CHEER, A. Leimanis, 150 days	34.90	RI
1993	THE MAGIC OF CHRISTMAS, A. Leimanis, 150 days	34.90	RI

Cinderella (Bradford Exchange)

1988	BIBBIDI-BOBBIDI-BOO, Disney Studios, 150 days	29.90	40.00
1988	A DREAM IS A WISH, Disney Studios, 150 days	29.90	50.00
1989	OH SING SWEET NIGHTINGALE, Disney Studios, 150 days	32.90	55.00
1989	A DRESS FOR CINDERELLA, Disney Studios, 150 days	32.90	70.00
1989	SO THIS IS LOVE, Disney Studios, 150 days	32.90	50.00
1990	AT THE STROKE OF MIDNIGHT, Disney Studios, 150 days	32.90	50.00
1990	IF THE SHOE FITS, Disney Studios, 150 days	34.90	45.00
1990	HAPPILY EVER AFTER, Disney Studios, 150 days	34.90	NR

Classic Fairy Tales

1991	GOLDILOCKS AND THE THREE BEARS, Scott Gustafson, 150 days	29.90	40.00
1991	LITTLE RED RIDING HOOD, Scott Gustafson, 150 days	29.90	45.00
1991	THE THREE LITTLE PIGS, Scott Gustafson, 150 days	32.90	NR
1991	THE FROG PRINCE, Scott Gustafson, 150 days	32.90	50.00
1992	JACK AND THE BEANSTALK, Scott Gustafson, 150 days	32.90	NR
1992	HANSEL AND GRETEL, Scott Gustafson, 150 days	34.90	NR
1992	PUSS IN BOOTS, Scott Gustafson, 150 days	34.90	NR
1992	TOM THUMB, Scott Gustafson, 150 days	34.90	NR

Classic Mother Goose

1992	LITTLE MISS MUFFET, Scott Gustafson, 150 days	29.90	BR
1992	MARY HAD A LITTLE LAMB, Scott Gustafson, 150 days	29.90	40.00
1992	MARY, MARY, QUITE CONTRARY, Scott Gustafson, 150 days	29.90	45.00
1992	LITTLE BO PEEP, Scott Gustafson, 150 days	29.90	35.00

Comforts of Home

1992	SLEEPYHEADS, Hannah Hollister Ingmire, 150 days	24.90	NR
1992	CURIOUS PAIR, Hannah Hollister Ingmire, 150 days	24.90	NR
1993	MOTHER'S RETREAT, Hannah Hollister Ingmire, 150 days	27.90	RI

		ISSUE	CURRENT
1993	WELCOME FRIENDS, Hannah Hollister Ingmire, 150 days	27.90	RI
1993	PLAYTIME, Hannah Hollister Ingmire, 150 days	27.90	RI
1993	FELINE FROLIC, Hannah Hollister Ingmire, 150 days	29.90	RI
1993	WASHDAY HELPERS, Hannah Hollister Ingmire, 150 days	29.90	RI
1993	A COZY FIRESIDE, Hannah Hollister Ingmire, 150 days	29.90	RI

Cozy Country Corners

1990	LAZY MORNING, Hannah Hollister Ingmire, 150 days	24.90	35.00
1990	WARM RETREAT, Hannah Hollister Ingmire, 150 days	24.90	35.00
1991	A SUNNY SPOT, Hannah Hollister Ingmire, 150 days	27.90	NR
1991	ATTIC AFTERNOON, Hannah Hollister Ingmire, 150 days	27.90	40.00
1991	MIRROR MISCHIEF, Hannah Hollister Ingmire, 150 days	27.90	45.00
1991	HIDE AND SEEK, Hannah Hollister Ingmire, 150 days	29.90	40.00
1991	APPLE ANTICS, Hannah Hollister Ingmire, 150 days	29.90	60.00
1991	TABLE TROUBLE, Hannah Hollister Ingmire, 150 days	29.90	50.00

Csatari Grandparent

1980	BEDTIME STORY, Joseph Csatari, 1 year	18.00	NR
1981	SKATING LESSON, Joseph Csatari, 1 year	20.00	NR
1982	COOKIE TASTING, Joseph Csatari, 1 year	20.00	NR
1983	THE SWINGER, Joseph Csatari, 1 year	20.00	NR
1984	THE SKATING QUEEN, Joseph Csatari, 1 year	22.00	NR
1985	PATRIOT'S PARADE, Joseph Csatari, 1 year	22.00	NR
1986	THE HOME RUN, Joseph Csatari, 1 year	22.00	NR
1987	THE SNEAK PREVIEW, Joseph Csatari, 1 year	22.00	NR

Disney Treasured Moments Collection

1992	CINDERELLA, Disney Studios, 150 days	29.90	NR
1992	SNOW WHITE AND THE SEVEN DWARFS, Disney Studios, 150 days	29.90	NR
1993	ALICE IN WONDERLAND, Disney Studios, 150 days	32.90	RI
1993	SLEEPING BEAUTY, Disney Studios, 150 days	32.90	RI
1993	PETER PAN, Disney Studios, 150 days	32.90	RI
1993	PINOCCHIO, Disney Studios, 150 days	34.90	RI
1994	JUNGLE BOOK, Disney Studios, 150 days	34.90	RI
1994	BEAUTY AND THE BEAST, Disney Studios, 150 days	34.90	RI

Encyclopaedia Britannica Birds of Your Garden

1984	CARDINAL, Kevin Daniel, 100 days	19.50	NR
1985	BLUEJAY, Kevin Daniel, 100 days	19.50	NR
1985	ORIOLE, Kevin Daniel, 100 days	22.50	NR
1986	CHICKADEES, Kevin Daniel, 100 days	22.50	NR
1986	BLUEBIRD, Kevin Daniel, 100 days	22.50	NR
1986	ROBIN, Kevin Daniel, 100 days	22.50	NR
1986	HUMMINGBIRD, Kevin Daniel, 100 days	24.50	NR
1987	GOLDFINCH, Kevin Daniel, 100 days	24.50	NR
1987	DOWNY WOODPECKER, Kevin Daniel, 100 days	24.50	NR
1987	CEDAR WAXWING, Kevin Daniel, 100 days	24.90	NR

Eve Licea Christmas

1987	THE ANNUNCIATION, Eve Licea, 1 year	44.90	NR
1988	THE NATIVITY, Eve Licea, 1 year	44.90	NR
1989	ADORATION OF THE SHEPHERDS, Eve Licea, 1 year	49.90	55.00
1990	JOURNEY OF THE MAGI, Eve Licea, 1 year	49.90	60.00

		ISSUE	CURRENT
1991	GIFTS OF THE MAGI, Eve Licea, 1 year	49.90	65.00
1992	REST ON THE FLIGHT INTO EGYPT, Eve Licea, 1 year	49.90	65.00

Fantasia (The Sorcerer's Apprentice) Golden Anniversary

1990	THE APPRENTICE'S DREAM, Disney Studios, 150 days	29.90	55.00
1990	MISCHIEVOUS APPRENTICE, Disney Studios, 150 days	29.90	75.00
1991	DREAMS OF POWER, Disney Studios, 150 days	32.90	45.00
1991	MICKEY'S MAGICAL WHIRLPOOL, Disney Studios, 150 days	32.90	40.00
1991	WIZARDRY GONE WILD, Disney Studios, 150 days	32.90	NR
1991	MICKEY MAKES MAGIC, Disney Studios, 150 days	34.90	45.00
1991	THE PENITENT APPRENTICE, Disney Studios, 150 days	34.90	NR
1992	AN APPRENTICE AGAIN, Disney Studios, 150 days	34.90	NR

Father's Love

1984	OPEN WIDE, Barbara Bradley, 100 days	19.50	NR
1984	BATTER UP, Barbara Bradley, 100 days	19.50	NR
1985	LITTLE SHAVER, Barbara Bradley, 100 days	19.50	NR
1985	SWING TIME, Barbara Bradley, 100 days	22.50	NR

Field Puppies

1987	DOG TIRED—THE SPRINGER SPANIEL, Lynn Kaatz, 150 days	24.90	40.00
1987	CAUGHT IN THE ACT—THE GOLDEN RETRIEVER, Lynn Kaatz, 150 days	24.90	35.00
1988	MISSING / POINT—IRISH SETTER, Lynn Kaatz, 150 days	27.90	35.00
1988	A PERFECT SET—LABRADOR, Lynn Kaatz, 150 days	27.90	40.00
1988	FRITZ'S FOLLY—GERMAN SHORTHAIRED POINTER, Lynn Kaatz, 150 days	27.90	NR
1988	SHIRT TALES—COCKER SPANIEL, Lynn Kaatz, 150 days	27.90	NR
1989	FINE FEATHERED FRIENDS—ENGLISH SETTER, Lynn Kaatz, 150 days	29.90	BR
1989	COMMAND PERFORMANCE—WEIMARANER, Lynn Kaatz, 150 days	29.90	BR

Field Trips

1990	GONE FISHING, Lynn Kaatz, 150 days	24.90	NR
1991	DUCKING DUTY, Lynn Kaatz, 150 days	24.90	NR
1991	BOXED IN, Lynn Kaatz, 150 days	27.90	BR
1991	PUPS 'N BOOTS, Lynn Kaatz, 150 days	27.90	BR
1991	PUPPY TALES, Lynn Kaatz, 150 days	27.90	BR
1991	PAIL PALS, Lynn Kaatz, 150 days	29.90	NR
1992	CHESAPEAKE BAY RETRIEVERS, Lynn Kaatz, 150 days	29.90	NR
1992	HAT TRICK, Lynn Kaatz, 150 days	29.90	BR

First Impressions

1991	TAKING A GANDER, Joseph Giordano, 150 days	29.90	40.00
1991	TWO'S COMPANY, Joseph Giordano, 150 days	29.90	35.00
1991	FINE FEATHERED FRIENDS, Joseph Giordano, 150 days	32.90	40.00
1991	WHAT'S UP?, Joseph Giordano, 150 days	32.90	45.00
1991	ALL EARS, Joseph Giordano, 150 days	32.90	50.00
1992	BETWEEN FRIENDS, Joseph Giordano, 150 days	32.90	35.00

Four Ancient Elements

1984	EARTH, Georgia Lambert, limited	27.50	BR
1984	WATER, Georgia Lambert, limited	27.50	BR
1985	AIR, Georgia Lambert, limited	29.50	BR
1985	FIRE, Georgia Lambert, limited	29.50	35.00

Adoration of the Shepherds

Little Shaver

The Chipmunk

Melanie

Fringe Benefits

Shall We Dance?

Photos courtesy of *Collectors News*

Frances Hook's Words of Love

		ISSUE	CURRENT
1986	I LOVE YOU, Frances Hook	NA	NA
1987	THAT'S MY BOY, Frances Hook	NA	NA
1991	DON'T BE SCARED, Frances Hook	NA	NA
1991	HAPPILY EVER AFTER, Frances Hook	NA	NA
1991	LET'S SEE YOU SMILE, Frances Hook	NA	NA
1991	YOU'RE DOING FINE, Frances Hook	NA	NA

Free as the Wind

1992	SKYWARD, M. Budden, 150 days	29.90	55.00
1992	ALOFT, M. Budden, 150 days	29.90	55.00
1992	AIRBORNE, M. Budden, 150 days	32.90	NR
1993	FLIGHT, M. Budden, 150 days	32.90	RI
1993	ASCENT, M. Budden, 150 days	32.90	RI
1993	HEAVENWARD, B. Budden, 150 days	32.90	RI

Friends of the Forest

1987	THE RABBIT, Kevin Daniel, 150 days	24.50	BR
1987	THE RACCOON, Kevin Daniel, 150 days	24.50	BR
1987	THE SQUIRREL, Kevin Daniel, 150 days	27.90	BR
1988	THE CHIPMUNK, Kevin Daniel, 150 days	27.90	BR
1988	THE FOX, Kevin Daniel, 150 days	27.90	BR
1988	THE OTTER, Kevin Daniel, 150 days	27.90	BR

Garden Secrets

1993	NINE LIVES, B. Higgins Bond, 150 days	24.90	RI
1993	FLORAL PURR-FUME, B. Higgins Bond, 150 days	24.90	RI
1993	BLOOMIN' KITTIES, B. Higgins Bond, 150 days	24.90	RI
1993	KITTY CORNER, B. Higgins Bond, 150 days	24.90	RI
1993	FLOWER FANCIERS, B. Higgins Bond, 150 days	24.90	RI
1993	MEADOW MISCHIEF, B. Higgins Bond, 150 days	24.90	RI
1993	PUSSYCAT POTPOURRI, B. Higgins Bond, 150 days	24.90	RI
1993	FRISKY BUSINESS, B. Higgins Bond, 150 days	24.90	RI

Gone with the Wind

1978	SCARLETT, Raymond Kursar, 1 year	21.50	100.00
1979	ASHLEY, Raymond Kursar, 1 year	21.50	60.00
1980	MELANIE, Raymond Kursar, 1 year	21.50	30.00
1981	RHETT, Raymond Kursar, 1 year	23.50	30.00
1982	MAMMY LACING SCARLETT, Raymond Kursar, 1 year	23.50	40.00
1983	MELANIE GIVES BIRTH, Raymond Kursar, 1 year	23.50	45.00
1984	SCARLETT'S GREEN DRESS, Raymond Kursar, 1 year	25.50	40.00
1985	RHETT AND BONNIE, Raymond Kursar, 1 year	25.50	50.00
1985	SCARLETT AND RHETT: THE FINALE, Raymond Kursar, 1 year	29.50	40.00

Great Cats of the Americas

1989	JAGUAR, Lee Cable, 150 days	29.90	40.00
1989	COUGAR, Lee Cable, 150 days	29.90	40.00
1989	LYNX, Lee Cable, 150 days	32.90	40.00
1990	OCELOT, Lee Cable, 150 days	32.90	BR
1990	BOBCAT, Lee Cable, 150 days	32.90	BR
1990	JAGUARUNDI, Lee Cable, 150 days	32.90	BR

		ISSUE	CURRENT
1990	MARGAY, Lee Cable, 150 days	34.90	BR
1991	PAMPAS CAT, Lee Cable, 150 days	34.90	BR

Heirlooms and Lace

1990	ANNA, Corinne Layton, 150 days	34.90	NR
1990	VICTORIA, Corinne Layton, 150 days	34.90	50.00
1990	TESS, Corinne Layton, 150 days	37.90	65.00
1990	OLIVIA, Corinne Layton, 150 days	37.90	95.00
1991	BRIDGET, Corinne Layton, 150 days	37.90	75.00
1991	REBECCA, Corinne Layton, 150 days	37.90	70.00

Home Sweet Home

1988	THE VICTORIAN, Renee McGinnis, 150 days	39.90	BR
1989	THE GREEK REVIVAL, Renee McGinnis, 150 days	39.90	BR
1989	THE GEORGIAN, Renee McGinnis, 150 days	39.90	NR
1990	THE MISSION, Renee McGinnis, 150 days	39.90	NR

It's a Dog's Life

1992	WE'VE BEEN SPOTTED, Lynn Kaatz, 150 days	29.90	NR
1992	LITERARY LABS, Lynn Kaatz, 150 days	29.90	NR
1993	RETRIEVING OUR DIGNITY, Lynn Kaatz, 150 days	32.90	RI
1993	LODGING A COMPLAINT, Lynn Kaatz, 150 days	32.90	RI
1993	BARRELING ALONG, Lynn Kaatz, 150 days	32.90	RI
1993	PLAY BALL, Lynn Kaatz, 150 days	34.90	RI
1993	DOGS AND SUDS, Lynn Kaatz, 150 days	34.90	RI
1993	PAWS FOR A PICNIC, Lynn Kaatz, 150 days	34.90	RI

Jeanne Down's Friends I Remember

1983	FISH STORY, Jeanne Down, limited	17.50	NR
1984	OFFICE HOURS, Jeanne Down, limited	17.50	NR
1985	A COAT OF PAINT, Jeanne Down, limited	17.50	NR
1985	HERE COMES THE BRIDE, Jeanne Down, limited	19.50	NR
1985	FRINGE BENEFITS, Jeanne Down, limited	19.50	NR
1986	HIGH SOCIETY, Jeanne Down, limited	19.50	NR
1986	FLOWER ARRANGEMENT, Jeanne Down, limited	21.50	NR
1986	TASTE TEST, Jeanne Down, limited	21.50	NR

Jerner's Less Traveled Road

1988	THE WEATHERED BARN, Bart Jerner, 150 days	29.90	BR
1988	THE MURMURING STREAM, Bart Jerner, 150 days	29.90	BR
1988	THE COVERED BRIDGE, Bart Jerner, 150 days	32.90	NR
1989	WINTER'S PEACE, Bart Jerner, 150 days	32.90	NR
1989	THE FLOWERING MEADOW, Bart Jerner, 150 days	32.90	NR
1989	THE HIDDEN WATERFALL, Bart Jerner, 150 days	32.90	NR

Jessie Wilcox Smith Childhood Holidays

1986	EASTER, Jessie Wilcox Smith	19.50	BR
1986	THANKSGIVING, Jessie Wilcox Smith	19.50	BR
1986	CHRISTMAS, Jessie Wilcox Smith	19.50	BR
1986	VALENTINE'S DAY, Jessie Wilcox Smith	22.50	BR
1987	MOTHER'S DAY, Jessie Wilcox Smith	22.50	BR
1987	FOURTH OF JULY, Jessie Wilcox Smith	22.50	BR

		ISSUE	CURRENT
Jessie Wilcox Smith's Not So Long Ago			
1988	STORY TIME, Jessie Wilcox Smith, 150 days	24.90	BR
1988	WASH DAY FOR DOLLY, Jessie Wilcox Smith, 150 days	24.90	BR
1988	SUPPERTIME FOR KITTY, Jessie Wilcox Smith, 150 days	24.90	BR
1988	MOTHER'S LITTLE HELPER, Jessie Wilcox Smith, 150 days	24.90	BR
Jewels of the Flowers			
1991	SAPPHIRE WINGS, T. C. Chiu, 150 days	29.90	BR
1991	TOPAZ BEAUTIES, T. C. Chiu, 150 days	29.90	NR
1991	AMETHYST FLIGHT, T. C. Chiu, 150 days	32.90	BR
1991	RUBY ELEGANCE, T. C. Chiu, 150 days	32.90	NR
1991	EMERALD PAIR, T. C. Chiu, 150 days	32.90	50.00
1991	OPAL SPLENDOR, T. C. Chiu, 150 days	34.90	NR
1992	PEARL LUSTER, T. C. Chiu, 150 days	34.90	50.00
1992	AQUAMARINE GLIMMER, T. C. Chiu, 150 days	34.90	40.00
Keepsake Rhymes			
1992	HUMPTY DUMPTY, Scott Gustafson, 150 days	29.90	NR
1993	PETER PUMPKIN EATER, Scott Gustafson, 150 days	29.90	RI
1993	PAT-A-CAKE, Scott Gustafson, 150 days	29.90	RI
1993	OLD KING COLE	29.90	RI
The King and I			
1984	A PUZZLEMENT, William Chambers, 1 year	19.50	NR
1984	SHALL WE DANCE?, William Chambers, 1 year	19.50	NR
1985	GETTING TO KNOW YOU, William Chambers, 1 year	19.50	NR
1985	WE KISS IN A SHADOW, William Chambers, 1 year	19.50	NR
***Lady and the Tramp* (Bradford Exchange)**			
1992	FIRST DATE, Disney Studios, 150 days	34.90	60.00
1992	PUPPY LOVE, Disney Studios, 150 days	34.90	55.00
1992	DOG POUND BLUES, Disney Studios, 150 days	37.90	40
1993	MERRY CHRISTMAS TO ALL, Disney Studios, 150 days	37.90	RI
1993	DOUBLE SIAMESE TROUBLE, Disney Studios, 150 days	37.90	RI
1993	RUFF HOUSE, Disney Studios, 150 days	39.90	RI
1993	TELLIING TALES, Disney Studios, 150 days	39.90	RI
1993	MOONLIGHT ROMANCE, Disney Studios, 150 days	39.90	RI
Lincoln, Man of America			
1986	THE GETTYSBURG ADDRESS, Mort Künstler, 150 days	24.50	BR
1987	THE INAUGURATION, Mort Künstler, 150 days	24.50	BR
1987	THE LINCOLN-DOUGLAS DEBATES, Mort Künstler, 150 days	27.50	BR
1987	BEGINNINGS IN NEW SALEM, Mort Künstler, 150 days	27.90	BR
1988	THE FAMILY MAN, Mort Künstler, 150 days	27.90	BR
1988	EMANCIPATION PROCLAMATION, Mort Künstler, 150 days	27.90	BR
***Little Mermaid* (Bradford Exchange)**			
1993	A SONG FROM THE SEA, Disney Studios, 95 days	29.90	RI
1993	A VISIT TO THE SURFACE, Disney Studios, 95 days	32.90	RI
1993	DADDY'S GIRL, Disney Studios, 95 days	32.90	RI
1993	UNDERWATER BUDDIES, Disney Studios, 95 days	32.90	RI

		ISSUE	CURRENT
1994	ARIEL'S TREASURED COLLECTION, Disney Studios, 95 days	32.90	RI
1994	KISS THE GIRL, Disney Studios, 95 days	32.90	RI
1994	FIREWORKS AT FIRST SIGHT, Disney Studios, 95 days	34.90	RI
1994	FOREVER LOVE, Disney Studios, 95 days	34.90	RI

Living with Nature—Jerner's Ducks

1986	THE PINTAIL, Bart Jerner, 150 days	19.50	35.00
1986	THE MALLARD, Bart Jerner, 150 days	19.50	35.00
1987	THE WOOD DUCK, Bart Jerner, 150 days	22.50	35.00
1987	THE GREEN-WINGED TEAL, Bart Jerner, 150 days	22.50	30.00
1987	THE NORTHERN SHOVELER, Bart Jerner, 150 days	22.90	30.00
1987	THE AMERICAN WIDGEON, Bart Jerner, 150 days	22.90	NR
1987	THE GADWALL, Bart Jerner, 150 days	24.90	35.00
1988	THE BLUE-WINGED TEAL, Bart Jerner, 150 days	24.90	45.00

Majestic Birds of North America

1988	THE BALD EAGLE, David Smith, 150 days	29.90	BR
1988	PEREGRINE FALCON, David Smith, 150 days	29.90	BR
1988	THE GREAT HORNED OWL, David Smith, 150 days	32.90	BR
1989	THE RED-TAILED HAWK, David Smith, 150 days	32.90	BR
1989	THE WHITE GYRFALCON, David Smith, 150 days	32.90	BR
1989	THE AMERICAN KESTREL, David Smith, 150 days	32.90	BR
1990	THE OSPREY, David Smith, 150 days	34.90	BR
1990	THE GOLDEN EAGLE, David Smith, 150 days	34.90	BR

Mary Poppins

1989	MARY POPPINS, Michael Hampshire, 150 days	29.90	40.00
1989	A SPOONFUL OF SUGAR, Michael Hampshire, 150 days	29.90	NR
1990	A JOLLY HOLIDAY WITH MARY, Michael Hampshire, 150 days	32.90	NR
1990	WE LOVE TO LAUGH, Michael Hampshire, 150 days	32.90	NR
1991	CHIM CHIM CHER-EE, Michael Hampshire, 150 days	32.90	NR
1991	TUPPENCE A BAG, Michael Hampshire, 150 days	32.90	40.00

Mickey's Christmas Carol

1992	BAH HUMBUG!, Disney Studios, 150 days	29.90	NR
1992	WHAT'S SO MERRY ABOUT CHRISTMAS?, Disney Studios, 150 days	29.90	NR
1993	GOD BLESS US EVERY ONE, Disney Studios, 150 days	32.90	RI
1993	A CHRISTMAS SURPRISE, Disney Studios, 150 days	32.90	RI
1993	YULETIDE GREETINGS, Disney Studios, 150 days	32.90	RI
1993	MARLEY'S WARNING, Disney Studios, 150 days	34.90	RI
1993	A COZY CHRISTMAS, Disney Studios, 150 days	34.90	RI
1993	A CHRISTMAS FEAST, Disney Studios, 150 days	34.90	RI

Musical Moments from *The Wizard of Oz* (Bradford Exchange)

1993	OVER THE RAINBOW, Kimmerle Milnazik, 95 days	29.90	RI
1993	WE'RE OFF TO SEE THE WIZARD, Kimmerle Milnazik, 95 days	29.90	RI
1993	MUNCHKIN LAND, Kimmerle Milnazik, 95 days	29.90	RI
1994	IF I ONLY HAD A BRAIN, Kimmerle Milnazik, 95 days	29.90	RI
1994	DING DONG THE WITCH IS DEAD, Kimmerle Milnazik, 95 days	29.90	RI
1993	THE LULLABYE LEAGUE, Kimmerle Milnazik, 95 days	29.90	RI
1994	IF I WERE KING OF THE FOREST, Kimmerle Milnazik, 95 days	29.90	RI
1994	MERRY OLD LAND OF OZ, Kimmerle Milnazik, 95 days	29.90	RI

Mary Poppins

The Surrey with the Fringe on Top

Apple Crisp

New London Grist Mill

Little Red Riding Hood

First Touch

Photos courtesy of *Collectors News*

		ISSUE	CURRENT

My Fair Lady

		ISSUE	CURRENT
1989	OPENING DAY AT ASCOT, William Chambers, 150 days	24.90	BR
1989	I COULD HAVE DANCED ALL NIGHT, William Chambers, 150 days	24.90	BR
1989	THE RAIN IN SPAIN, William Chambers, 150 days	27.90	BR
1989	SHOW ME, William Chambers, 150 days	27.90	BR
1990	GET ME TO THE CHURCH ON TIME, William Chambers, 150 days	27.90	BR
1990	I'VE GROWN ACCUSTOMED TO HER FACE, William Chambers, 150 days	27.90	BR

Nature's Child

		ISSUE	CURRENT
1990	SHARING, Mimi Jobe, 150 days	29.90	BR
1990	THE LOST LAMB, Mimi Jobe, 150 days	29.90	NR
1990	SEEMS LIKE YESTERDAY, Mimi Jobe, 150 days	32.90	NR
1990	FAITHFUL FRIENDS, Mimi Jobe, 150 days	32.90	50.00
1990	TRUSTED COMPANION, Mimi Jobe, 150 days	32.90	50.00
1991	HAND IN HAND, Mimi Jobe, 150 days	32.90	45.00

Nature's Garden

		ISSUE	CURRENT
1993	SPRINGTIME FRIENDS, C. Decker, 95 days	29.90	RI
1993	A MORNING SPLASH, C. Decker, 95 days	29.90	RI
1993	FLURRY OF ACTIVITY, C. Decker, 95 days	29.90	RI
1993	HANGING AROUND, C. Decker, 95 days	29.90	RI
1993	TINY TWIRLING TREASURES, C. Decker, 95 days	29.90	RI

Nature's Nursery

		ISSUE	CURRENT
1992	TESTING THE WATERS, Joe Thornbrugh, 150 days	29.90	RI
1993	TAKING THE PLUNGE, Joe Thornbrugh, 150 days	29.90	RI
1993	RACE YA MOM, Joe Thornbrugh, 150 days	29.90	RI
1993	TIME TO WAKE UP, Joe Thornbrugh, 150 days	29.90	RI
1993	HIDE AND SEEK, Joe Thornbrugh, 150 days	29.90	RI
1993	PIGGYBACK RIDE, Joe Thornbrugh, 150 days	29.90	RI

North Woods Heritage

		ISSUE	CURRENT
1992	BRINGING HOME THE TREE, Persis Clayton Weir	NA	NA
1992	CROSSING THE BRIDGE, Persis Clayton Weir	NA	NA
1992	MAPLE SUGAR SEASON, Persis Clayton Weir	NA	NA
1992	WINTER'S WORK, Persis Clayton Weir	NA	NA
1993	END OF DAY, Persis Clayton Weir	NA	RI
1993	NORTHERN HAYRIDE, Persis Clayton Weir	NA	RI

Notorious Disney Villains (Bradford Exchange)

		ISSUE	CURRENT
1993	THE EVIL QUEEN, Disney Studios	29.90	RI
1994	MALEFICENT, Disney Studios	29.90	RI
1994	URSELLA, Disney Studios	29.90	RI
1994	CRUELLA DE VIL, Disney Studios	29.90	RI

Oklahoma!

		ISSUE	CURRENT
1985	OH, WHAT A BEAUTIFUL MORNIN', Mort Künstler	19.50	BR
1986	OKLAHOMA!, Mort Künstler	19.50	BR
1986	I CAIN'T SAY NO, Mort Künstler	19.50	BR
1986	THE SURREY WITH THE FRINGE ON TOP, Mort Künstler	19.50	BR

		ISSUE	CURRENT

Old-Fashioned Favorites

1991	APPLE CRISP, M. Weber, 150 days	29.90	65.00
1991	BLUEBERRY MUFFINS, M. Weber, 150 days	29.90	60.00
1991	PEACH COBBLER, M. Weber, 150 days	29.90	95.00
1991	CHOCOLATE CHIP OATMEAL COOKIES, M. Weber, 150 days	29.90	145.00

Old Mill Stream

1991	NEW LONDON GRIST MILL, Craig Tennant, 150 days	39.90	BR
1991	WAYSIDE INN GRIST MILL, Craig Tennant, 150 days	39.90	NR
1991	OLD RED MILL, Craig Tennant, 150 days	39.90	BR
1991	GLADE CREEK GRIST MILL, Craig Tennant, 150 days	39.90	NR

Once Upon a Time

1988	LITTLE RED RIDING HOOD, K. Pritchett, 150 days	24.90	NR
1988	RAPUNZEL, K. Pritchett, 150 days	24.90	BR
1988	THREE LITTLE PIGS, K. Pritchett, 150 days	27.90	BR
1989	THE PRINCESS AND THE PEA, K. Pritchett, 150 days	27.90	BR
1989	GOLDILOCKS AND THE THREE BEARS, K. Pritchett, 150 days	27.90	NR
1989	BEAUTY AND THE BEAST, K. Pritchett, 150 days	27.90	35.00

Pinocchio

1989	GEPPETTO CREATES PINOCCHIO, Disney Studios, 150 days	29.90	55.00
1990	PINOCCHIO AND THE BLUE FAIRY, Disney Studios, 150 days	29.90	50.00
1990	IT'S AN ACTOR'S LIFE FOR ME, Disney Studios, 150 days	32.90	40.00
1990	I'VE GOT NO STRINGS ON ME, Disney Studios, 150 days	32.90	NR
1991	PLEASURE ISLAND, Disney Studios, 150 days	32.90	NR
1991	A REAL BOY, Disney Studios, 150 days	32.90	40.00

Portraits of Motherhood

1987	MOTHER'S HERE, William Chambers, 150 days	29.50	BR
1988	FIRST TOUCH, William Chambers, 150 days	29.50	NR

Precious Little Ones

1988	LITTLE RED ROBINS, Maude T. Fangel, 150 days	29.90	BR
1988	LITTLE FLEDGLINGS, Maude T. Fangel, 150 days	29.90	BR
1988	SATURDAY NIGHT BATH, Maude T. Fangel, 150 days	29.90	NR
1988	PEEK-A-BOO, Maude T. Fangel, 150 days	29.90	NR

Proud Sentinels of the American West

1993	YOUNGBLOOD, Nancy Glazier, 150 days	29.90	RI
1993	CAT NAP, Nancy Glazier, 150 days	29.90	RI
1993	DESERT BIGHORN—MORMON RIDGE, Nancy Glazier, 150 days	32.90	RI
1993	CROWN PRINCE	32.90	RI

Purrfect Point of View

1991	UNEXPECTED VISITORS, Joseph Giordano, 150 days	29.90	NR
1992	WISTFUL MORNING, Joseph Giordano, 150 days	29.90	45.00
1992	AFTERNOON CATNAP, Joseph Giordano, 150 days	29.90	50.00
1992	COZY COMPANY, Joseph Giordano, 150 days	29.90	NR

		ISSUE	CURRENT

Pussyfooting Around

1991	FISH TALES, Christine Wilson, 150 days	24.90	BR
1991	TEATIME TABBIES, Christine Wilson, 150 days	24.90	BR
1991	YARN SPINNERS, Christine Wilson, 150 days	24.90	BR
1991	TWO MAESTROS, Christine Wilson, 150 days	24.90	BR

Romantic Age of Steam (Bradford Exchange)

1992	THE EMPIRE BUILDER, R. E. Pierce, 150 days	29.90	NR
1992	THE BROADWAY LIMITED, R. E. Pierce, 150 days	29.90	35.00
1992	TWENTIETH CENTURY LIMITED, R. E. Pierce, 150 days	32.90	45.00
1992	THE CHIEF, R. E. Pierce, 150 days	32.90	50.00
1992	THE CRESCENT LIMITED, R. E. Pierce, 150 days	32.90	80.00
1993	THE OVERLAND LIMITED, R. E. Pierce, 150 days	34.90	RI
1993	THE JUPITER, R. E. Pierce, 150 days	34.90	RI
1993	THE DAYLIGHT, R. E. Pierce, 150 days	34.90	RI

Santa's Christmas

1991	SANTA'S LOVE, Thomas Browning, 150 days	29.90	35.00
1991	SANTA'S CHEER, Thomas Browning, 150 days	29.90	40.00
1991	SANTA'S PROMISE, Thomas Browning, 150 days	32.90	60.00
1991	SANTA'S GIFT, Thomas Browning, 150 days	32.90	75.00
1992	SANTA'S SURPRISE, Thomas Browning, 150 days	32.90	55.00
1992	SANTA'S MAGIC, Thomas Browning, 150 days	32.90	55.00

Season for Song

1991	WINTER CONCERT, Mimi Jobe, 150 days	34.90	40.00
1991	SNOWY SYMPHONY, Mimi Jobe, 150 days	34.90	40.00
1991	FROSTY CHORUS, Mimi Jobe, 150 days	34.90	55.00
1991	SILVER SERENADE, Mimi Jobe, 150 days	34.90	65.00

Season of Splendor

1992	AUTUMN'S GRANDEUR, Kirk Randle, 150 days	29.90	40.00
1992	SCHOOL DAYS, Kirk Randle, 150 days	29.90	35.00
1992	WOODLAND MILL STREAM, Kirk Randle, 150 days	32.90	65.00
1992	HARVEST MEMORIES, Kirk Randle, 150 days	32.90	50.00
1992	A COUNTRY WEEKEND, Kirk Randle, 150 days	32.90	60.00
1993	INDIAN SUMMER, Kirk Randle, 150 days	32.90	55.00

Shadows and Light: Winter's Wildlife

1993	WINTER'S CHILDREN, Nancy Glazier, 150 days	29.90	RI
1993	CUB SCOUTS, Nancy Glazier, 150 days	29.90	RI
1993	LITTLE SNOWMAN, Nancy Glazier, 150 days	29.90	RI
1993	THE SNOW CAVE, Nancy Glazier, 150 days	29.90	RI

Singin' in the Rain

1990	SINGIN' IN THE RAIN, M. Skolsky, 150 days	32.90	BR
1990	GOOD MORNING, M. Skolsky, 150 days	32.90	BR
1991	BROADWAY MELODY, M. Skolsky, 150 days	32.90	NR
1991	WE'RE HAPPY AGAIN, M. Skolsky, 150 days	32.90	45.00

ISSUE	CURRENT

Sleeping Beauty

1991	ONCE UPON A DREAM, Disney Studios, 150 days	39.90	45.00
1991	AWAKENED BY A KISS, Disney Studios, 150 days	39.90	80.00
1991	HAPPY BIRTHDAY BRIAR ROSE, Disney Studios, 150 days	42.90	NR
1992	TOGETHER AT LAST, Disney Studios, 150 days	42.90	NR

Small Blessings

1992	NOW I LAY ME DOWN TO SLEEP, Corinne Layton, 150 days	29.90	NR
1992	BLESS US O LORD FOR THESE, THY GIFTS, Corinne Layton, 150 days	29.90	NR
1992	JESUS LOVES ME, THIS I KNOW, Corinne Layton, 150 days	32.90	NR
1992	THIS LITTLE LIGHT OF MINE, Corinne Layton, 150 days	32.90	NR
1992	BLESSED ARE THE PURE IN HEART, Corinne Layton, 150 days	32.90	NR
1993	BLESS OUR HOME, Corinne Layton, 150 days	32.90	40.00

Snow White and the Seven Dwarfs

1991	THE DANCE OF SNOW WHITE AND THE SEVEN DWARFS, Disney Studios, 150 days	29.90	45.00
1991	WITH A SMILE AND A SONG, Disney Studios, 150 days	29.90	NR
1991	A SPECIAL TREAT, Disney Studios, 150 days	32.90	45.00
1992	A KISS FOR DOPEY, Disney Studios, 150 days	32.90	40.00
1992	THE POISON APPLE, Disney Studios, 150 days	32.90	45.00
1992	FIRESIDE LOVE STORY, Disney Studios, 150 days	34.90	45.00
1992	STUBBORN GRUMPY, Disney Studios, 150 days	34.90	NR
1992	A WISH COME TRUE, Disney Studios, 150 days	34.90	NR
1993	TIME TO TIDY UP, Disney Studios, 150 days	34.90	RI
1993	MAY I HAVE THIS DANCE?, Disney Studios, 150 days	36.90	RI
1993	A SURPRISE IN THE CLEANING, Disney Studios, 150 days	36.90	RI
1993	HAPPY ENDING, Disney Studios, 150 days	36.90	RI

Songs of the American Spirit

1991	THE STAR SPANGLED BANNER, B. Higgins Bond, 150 days	29.90	BR
1991	BATTLE HYMN OF THE REPUBLIC, B. Higgins Bond, 150 days	29.90	45.00
1991	AMERICA THE BEAUTIFUL, B. Higgins Bond, 150 days	29.90	NR
1991	MY COUNTRY 'TIS OF THEE, B. Higgins Bond, 150 days	29.90	65.00

Sound of Music

1986	SOUND OF MUSIC, Tony Crnkovich, 150 days	19.50	NR
1986	DO-RE-MI, Tony Crnkovich, 150 days	19.50	NR
1986	MY FAVORITE THINGS, Tony Crnkovich, 150 days	22.50	NR
1986	LAENDLER WALTZ, Tony Crnkovich, 150 days	22.50	NR
1987	EDELWEISS, Tony Crnkovich, 150 days	22.50	NR
1987	I HAVE CONFIDENCE, Tony Crnkovich, 150 days	22.50	NR
1987	MARIA, Tony Crnkovich, 150 days	24.90	NR
1987	CLIMB EV'RY MOUNTAIN, Tony Crnkovich, 150 days	24.90	NR

South Pacific

1987	SOME ENCHANTED EVENING, Elaine Gignilliat, 150 days	24.50	BR
1987	HAPPY TALK, Elaine Gignilliat, 150 days	24.50	BR
1987	DITES MOI, Elaine Gignilliat, 150 days	24.90	BR
1988	HONEY BUN, Elaine Gignilliat, 150 days	24.90	BR

Stately Owls

		ISSUE	CURRENT
1989	THE SNOWY OWL, J. Beaudoin, 150 days	29.90	NR
1989	THE GREAT HORNED OWL, J. Beaudoin, 150 days	29.90	40.00
1990	THE BARN OWL, J. Beaudoin, 150 days	32.90	BR
1990	THE SCREECH OWL, J. Beaudoin, 150 days	32.90	NR
1990	THE SHORT-EARED OWL, J. Beaudoin, 150 days	32.90	BR
1990	THE BARRED OWL, J. Beaudoin, 150 days	32.90	NR
1990	THE GREAT GREY OWL, J. Beaudoin, 150 days	34.90	NR
1991	THE SAW-WHET OWL, J. Beaudoin, 150 days	34.90	NR

Storybook Treasury

		ISSUE	CURRENT
1992	GOLDILOCKS AND THE THREE BEARS, Carol Lawson	NA	NA
1992	LITTLE RED RIDING HOOD, Carol Lawson	NA	NA

Sundblom Santas

		ISSUE	CURRENT
1989	SANTA BY THE FIRE, Haddon Sundblom, closed	27.90	BR
1990	CHRISTMAS VIGIL, Haddon Sundblom, closed	27.90	NR
1991	TO ALL A GOOD NIGHT, Haddon Sundblom, closed	32.90	55.00
1992	SANTA'S ON HIS WAY, Haddon Sundblom, closed	32.90	55.00

A Swan Is Born

		ISSUE	CURRENT
1987	HOPES AND DREAMS, L. Roberts, 150 days	24.50	NR
1987	AT THE BARRE, L. Roberts, 150 days	24.50	NR
1987	IN POSITION, L. Roberts, 150 days	24.50	30.00
1988	JUST FOR SIZE, L. Roberts, 150 days	24.50	40.00

Sweetness and Grace

		ISSUE	CURRENT
1992	GOD BLESS TEDDY, Jennifer R. Welty, 130 days	34.90	NR
1992	SUNSHINE AND SMILES, Jennifer R. Welty, 130 days	34.90	45.00
1992	FAVORITE BUDDY, Jennifer R. Welty, 130 days	34.90	45.00
1992	SWEET DREAMS, Jennifer R. Welty, 130 days	34.90	60.00

Thomas Kinkade's Enchanted Cottages (Bradford Exchange)

		ISSUE	CURRENT
1993	FALLBROOKE COTTAGE, Thomas Kinkade, 95 days	29.90	RI
1993	JULIANNE'S COTTAGE, Thomas Kinkade, 95 days	29.90	RI
1993	SEASIDE COTTAGE, Thomas Kinkade, 95 days	29.90	RI
1993	SWEETHEART COTTAGE, Thomas Kinkade, 95 days	29.90	RI
1993	WEATHERVANE COTTAGE, Thomas Kinkade, 95 days	29.90	RI
1993	ROSE GARDEN COTTAGE, Thomas Kinkade, 95 days	29.90	RI

Thomas Kinkade's Garden Cottages of England

		ISSUE	CURRENT
1991	CHANDLER'S COTTAGE, Thomas Kinkade, 150 days	27.90	45.00
1991	CEDAR NOOK COTTAGE, Thomas Kinkade, 150 days	27.90	45.00
1991	CANDLELIT COTTAGE, Thomas Kinkade, 150 days	30.90	NR
1991	OPEN GATE COTTAGE, Thomas Kinkade, 150 days	30.90	40.00
1991	MCKENNA'S COTTAGE, Thomas Kinkade, 150 days	30.90	45.00
1992	WOODSMAN'S THATCH COTTAGE, Thomas Kinkade, 150 days	32.90	45.00
1992	MERRITT'S COTTAGE, Thomas Kinkade, 150 days	32.90	50.00
1992	STONEGATE COTTAGE, Thomas Kinkade, 150 days	32.90	65.00

Fish Tales

Chandler's Cottage

Olde Porterfield Tea Room

The Quail

King of Kings

Wicked Witch of the West

Photos courtesy of *Collectors News*

		ISSUE	CURRENT

Thomas Kinkade's Home for the Holidays

		ISSUE	CURRENT
1991	SLEIGH RIDE HOME, Thomas Kinkade, closed	29.90	NR
1991	HOME TO GRANDMA'S, Thomas Kinkade, closed	29.90	NR
1991	HOME BEFORE CHRISTMAS, Thomas Kinkade, closed	32.90	NR
1992	THE WARMTH OF HOME, Thomas Kinkade, closed	32.90	NR
1992	HOMESPUN HOLIDAY, Thomas Kinkade, closed	32.90	NR
1992	HOMETIME YULETIDE, Thomas Kinkade, closed	34.90	NR
1992	HOME AWAY FROM HOME, Thomas Kinkade, closed	34.90	NR
1992	THE JOURNEY HOME, Thomas Kinkade, closed	34.90	NR

Thomas Kinkade's Home Is Where the Heart Is

		ISSUE	CURRENT
1992	HOME SWEET HOME, Thomas Kinkade, closed	29.90	NR
1992	A WARM WELCOME HOME, Thomas Kinkade, closed	29.90	NR
1992	A CARRIAGE RIDE HOME, Thomas Kinkade, closed	32.90	NR
1993	AMBER AFTERNOON, Thomas Kinkade, closed	32.90	RI
1993	COUNTRY MEMORIES, Thomas Kinkade, closed	32.90	RI
1993	THE TWILIGHT CAFE, Thomas Kinkade, closed	34.90	RI
1993	OUR SUMMER HOME, Thomas Kinkade, closed	34.90	RI
1993	HOMETOWN HOSPITALITY, Thomas Kinkade, closed	34.90	RI

Thomas Kinkade's Thomashire

		ISSUE	CURRENT
1992	OLDE PORTERFIELD TEA ROOM, Thomas Kinkade, 150 days	29.90	40.00
1992	OLDE THOMASHIRE MILL, Thomas Kinkade, 150 days	29.90	50.00
1992	SWANBROOK COTTAGE, Thomas Kinkade, 150 days	32.90	100.00
1992	PYE CORNER COTTAGE, Thomas Kinkade, 150 days	32.90	55.00
1993	BLOSSOM HILL CHURCH, Thomas Kinkade, 150 days	32.90	50.00
1993	OLDE GARDEN COTTAGE, Thomas Kinkade, 150 days	32.90	70.00

Thomas Kinkade's Yuletide Memories

		ISSUE	CURRENT
1992	THE MAGIC OF CHRISTMAS, Thomas Kinkade, 150 days	29.90	70.00
1992	A BEACON OF FAITH, Thomas Kinkade, 150 days	29.90	50.00
1993	MOONLIT SLEIGH RIDE, Thomas Kinkade, 150 days	29.90	RI
1993	SILENT NIGHT, Thomas Kinkade, 150 days	29.90	RI
1993	OLDE PORTERFIELD GIFT SHOPPE, Thomas Kinkade, 150 days	29.90	RI
1993	THE WONDER OF THE SEASON, Thomas Kinkade, 150 days	29.90	RI
1993	A WINTER'S WALK, Thomas Kinkade, 150 days	29.90	RI
1993	SKATER'S DELIGHT, Thomas Kinkade, 150 days	32.90	RI

Tom Sawyer

		ISSUE	CURRENT
1987	WHITEWASHING THE FENCE, William Chambers, 150 days	27.90	NR
1987	TOM AND BECKY, William Chambers, 150 days	27.90	NR
1987	TOM SAWYER THE PIRATE, William Chambers, 150 days	27.90	NR
1988	FIRST PIPES, William Chambers, 150 days	27.90	BR

Under Mother's Wing

		ISSUE	CURRENT
1992	ARCTIC SPRING: SNOWY OWLS, J. Beaudoin, 150 days	29.90	45.00
1992	FOREST'S EDGE: GREAT GRAY OWLS, J. Beaudoin, 150 days	29.90	35.00
1992	TREETOP TRIO: LONG-EARED OWLS, J. Beaudoin, 150 days	32.90	45.00
1992	WOODLAND WATCH: SPOTTED OWLS, J. Beaudoin, 150 days	32.90	55.00
1992	VAST VIEW: SAWWHET OWLS, J. Beaudoin, 150 days	32.90	50.00
1992	LOFTY LIMB: GREAT HORNED OWL, J. Beaudoin, 150 days	34.90	50.00

		ISSUE	CURRENT
1993	PERFECT PERCH: BARRED OWLS, J. Beaudoin, 150 days	34.90	RI
1993	HAPPY HOME: SHORT-EARED OWL, J. Beaudoin, 150 days	34.90	RI

Upland Birds of North America

1986	THE PHEASANT, W. Anderson, 150 days	24.50	BR
1986	THE GROUSE, W. Anderson, 150 days	24.50	BR
1987	THE QUAIL, W. Anderson, 150 days	27.50	BR
1987	THE WILD TURKEY, W. Anderson, 150 days	27.50	BR
1987	THE GRAY PARTRIDGE, W. Anderson, 150 days	27.50	BR
1987	THE WOODCOCK, W. Anderson, 150 days	27.50	BR

Windows of Glory

1993	KING OF KINGS, Jennifer R. Welty, 95 days	29.90	RI
1993	PRINCE OF PEACE, Jennifer R. Welty, 95 days	29.90	RI
1993	THE MESSIAH, Jennifer R. Welty, 95 days	32.90	RI
1993	THE GOOD SHEPHERD, Jennifer R. Welty, 95 days	32.90	RI
1994	THE LIGHT, Jennifer R. Welty, 95 days	32.90	RI

Wizard of Oz

1977	OVER THE RAINBOW, J. Auckland, 100 days	19.00	50.00
1978	IF I ONLY HAD A BRAIN, J. Auckland, 100 days	19.00	50.00
1978	IF I ONLY HAD A HEART, J. Auckland, 100 days	19.00	45.00
1978	IF I WERE KING OF THE FOREST, J. Auckland, 100 days	19.00	50.00
1979	WICKED WITCH OF THE WEST, J. Auckland, 100 days	19.00	50.00
1979	FOLLOW THE YELLOW BRICK ROAD, J. Auckland, 100 days	19.00	50.00
1979	WONDERFUL WIZARD OF OZ, J. Auckland, 100 days	19.00	50.00
1980	THE GRAND FINALE, J. Auckland, 100 days	24.00	50.00

***Wizard of Oz*: A National Treasure**

1991	YELLOW BRICK ROAD, R. Laslo, 150 days	29.90	NR
1992	I HAVEN'T GOT A BRAIN, R. Laslo, 150 days	29.90	NR
1992	I'M A LITTLE RUSTY YET, R. Laslo, 150 days	32.90	40.00
1992	I EVEN SCARE MYSELF, R. Laslo, 150 days	32.90	50.00
1992	WE'RE OFF TO SEE THE WIZARD, R. Laslo, 150 days	32.90	NR
1992	I'LL NEVER GET HOME, R. Laslo, 150 days	34.90	50.00
1992	I'M MELTING, R. Laslo, 150 days	34.90	50.00
1992	THERE'S NO PLACE LIKE HOME, R. Laslo, 150 days	34.90	50.00

Yesterday's Innocents

1992	MY FIRST BOOK, Jessie Wilcox Smith, 150 days	29.90	45.00
1992	TIME TO SMELL THE ROSES, Jessie Wilcox Smith, 150 days	29.90	55.00
1993	HUSH, BABY'S SLEEPING, Jessie Wilcox Smith, 150 days	32.90	RI
1993	READY AND WAITING, Jessie Wilcox Smith, 150 days	32.90	RI

KÖNIGSZELT BAYERN GERMANY

Deutches Fachwerk

1984	BAUERNHAUS, Karl Bedal	24.00	BR
1984	NIEDERSACHSENHAUS, Karl Bedal	24.00	BR
1985	MOSELHAUS, Karl Bedal	27.00	BR
1985	WESTFALENHAUS, Karl Bedal	27.00	BR

		ISSUE	CURRENT
1986	MITTELFRANKENHAUS, Karl Bedal	27.00	BR
1986	BODENSEEHAUS, Karl Bedal	27.00	BR

Grimm's Fairy Tales

1981	RUMPELSTILZCHEN, Charles Gehm, 1 year	23.00	BR
1982	RAPUNZEL, Charles Gehm, 1 year	25.00	BR
1983	HANSEL AND GRETEL, Charles Gehm, 1 year	25.00	BR
1984	THE SHOEMAKER AND THE ELVES, Charles Gehm, 1 year	25.00	BR
1985	THE GOLDEN GOOSE, Charles Gehm, 1 year	29.00	BR
1986	SHOES THAT WERE DANCED, Charles Gehm, 1 year	29.00	BR
1987	SLEEPING BEAUTY, Charles Gehm, 1 year	29.00	BR
1988	SNOW WHITE, Charles Gehm, 1 year	29.00	BR

Hedi Keller Christmas

1979	THE ADORATION, Hedi Keller, 90 days	29.50	NR
1980	FLIGHT INTO EGYPT, Hedi Keller, 90 days	29.50	BR
1981	RETURN INTO GALILEE, Hedi Keller, 90 days	29.50	BR
1982	FOLLOWING THE STAR, Hedi Keller, 90 days	29.50	BR
1983	REST ON THE FLIGHT, Hedi Keller, 90 days	29.50	BR
1984	THE NATIVITY, Hedi Keller, 90 days	29.50	BR
1985	GIFT OF THE MAGI, Hedi Keller, 90 days	34.50	BR
1986	ANNUNCIATION, Hedi Keller, 90 days	34.50	BR

Love and Life

1986	SINCE I FIRST SAW HIM, Sulamith Wülfing, limited	29.85	NR
1986	HE, NOBLEST OF ALL, Sulamith Wülfing, limited	29.85	NR
1987	I CAN'T UNDERSTAND IT, Sulamith Wülfing, limited	29.85	NR

Sulamith's Christmas

1985	THE ANGELS' VIGIL, Sulamith Wülfing	35.00	BR
1986	CHRISTMAS CHILD, Sulamith Wülfing	35.00	BR
1987	THE CHRISTMAS ANGELS	39.00	BR
1988	THE ANGELS' ADORATION	39.00	BR
1989	HEAVEN'S GIFT	44.00	BR
1990	THE LIGHT OF THE HOLY NIGHT	44.00	NR

Following the Star
Photo courtesy of *Collectors News*

		ISSUE	CURRENT
1991	MARIA AND JOSEPH	49.00	120.00
1992	SENT FROM HEAVEN	49.00	90.00

Sulamith's Love Song

1982	THE MUSIC, Sulamith Wülfing, limited	29.00	BR
1983	THE PLEDGE, Sulamith Wülfing, limited	29.00	BR
1983	THE VISION, Sulamith Wülfing, limited	29.00	BR
1983	THE GIFT, Sulamith Wülfing, limited	29.00	BR
1984	THE CIRCLE, Sulamith Wülfing, limited	29.00	BR
1984	THE CENTRE	29.00	BR
1984	THE JOURNEY	29.00	BR
1984	THE COMPLETION	29.00	BR

KOSCHERAK BROTHERS CZECHOSLOVAKIA

Christmas

1973	CHRISTMAS, Mary Gregory, 1,000	55.00	NR
1974	CHRISTMAS, Mary Gregory, 1,000	60.00	NR
1975	CHRISTMAS, Mary Gregory, 1,000	60.00	NR
1976	CHRISTMAS, Mary Gregory, 1,000	60.00	NR

Mother's Day

1973	MOTHER'S DAY, Mary Gregory, 500	55.00	NR
1974	MOTHER'S DAY, Mary Gregory, 300	60.00	NR
1975	MOTHER'S DAY, Mary Gregory, 300	60.00	NR
1976	MOTHER'S DAY, Mary Gregory, 500	65.00	NR

KPM—ROYAL BERLIN GERMANY

Christmas

1969	CHRISTMAS STAR, 5,000	28.00	380.00
1970	THREE KINGS, 5,000	28.00	300.00
1971	CHRISTMAS TREE, 5,000	28.00	290.00
1972	CHRISTMAS ANGEL, 5,000	31.00	300.00
1973	CHRIST CHILD ON SLED, 5,000	33.00	280.00
1974	ANGEL AND HORN, 5,000	35.00	180.00
1975	SHEPHERDS, 5,000	40.00	165.00
1976	STAR OF BETHLEHEM, 5,000	43.00	140.00
1977	MARY AT CRIB, 5,000	46.00	100.00
1978	THREE WISEMEN, 5,000	49.00	NR
1979	THE MANGER, 5,000	55.00	NR
1980	SHEPHERDS IN FIELDS, 5,000	55.00	NR

LAKE SHORE PRINTS UNITED STATES

Rockwell Series

1973	BUTTER GIRLS, Norman Rockwell, 9,433	14.95	140.00
1974	TRUTH ABOUT SANTA, Norman Rockwell, 15,141	19.50	75.00
1975	HOME FROM FIELDS, Norman Rockwell, 8,500	24.50	60.00
1976	A PRESIDENT'S WIFE, Norman Rockwell, 2,500	70.00	80.00

LALIQUE SOCIETY OF AMERICA

Annual

		ISSUE	CURRENT
1965	DEUX OISEAUX (TWO BIRDS), Marie-Claude Lalique, 2,000	25.00	1,250.00
1966	ROSE DE SONGERIE (DREAMROSE), Marie-Claude Lalique, 5,000	25.00	75.00
1967	BALLET DE POISSON (FISH BALLET), Marie-Claude Lalique, 5,000	25.00	95.00
1968	GAZELLER FANTASIE (GAZELLE FANTASY), Marie-Claude Lalique, 5,000	25.00	70.00
1969	PAPILLON (BUTTERFLY), Marie-Claude Lalique, 5,000	30.00	50.00
1970	PAON (PEACOCK), Marie-Claude Lalique, 5,000	30.00	70.00
1971	HIBOU (OWL), Marie-Claude Lalique, 5,000	35.00	50.00
1972	COQUILLAGE (SHELL), Marie-Claude Lalique, 5,000	40.00	75.00
1973	PETIT GEAI (JAYLING), Marie-Claude Lalique, 5,000	42.50	100.00
1974	SOUS D'ARGENT (SILVER PENNIES), Marie-Claude Lalique, 5,000	47.50	95.00
1975	DUO DE POISSON (FISH DUET), Marie-Claude Lalique, 5,000	50.00	140.00
1976	AIGLE (EAGLE), Marie-Claude Lalique, 5,000	60.00	85.00

LANCE CORPORATION UNITED STATES

(Chilmark Pewter, Hudson Pewter)

12 Days of Christmas (Chilmark Pewter)

1979	PARTRIDGE IN A PEAR TREE, retrd	99.50	NR
1980	TWO TURTLEDOVES, retrd	99.50	NR

American Commemorative

1975	HYDE PARK, R. Lamb, retrd	NA	NA
1975	LOG CABIN, R. Lamb, retrd	NA	NA
1975	MONTICELLO, R. Lamb, retrd	NA	NA
1975	MT. VERNON, R. Lamb, retrd	NA	NA
1975	SPIRIT OF '76, R. Lamb, retrd	NA	NA

American Expansion (Hudson Pewter)

1975	SPIRIT OF '76, Prescott W. Baston, 4,812, 6"	27.50	100.00
1975	AMERICAN INDEPENDENCE, Prescott W. Baston, 18,462	NA	100.00
1975	AMERICAN EXPANSION, Prescott W. Baston, 2,250	NA	50.00
1975	THE AMERICAN WAR BETWEEN THE STATES, Prescott W. Baston, 825	NA	150.00

America's Favorite Birds (Hudson Pewter)

1978	CRYSTAL WREN, C. Terris, retrd	79.50	NR

America's Sailing Ships (Hudson Pewter)

1978	U.S.S. *CONSTITUTION*, Albert Petitto, 5,000	35.00	NR
1978	*AMERICA*, Albert Petitto, 5,000	35.00	NR
1978	*FLYING CLOUD*, Albert Petitto, 5,000	35.00	NR
1978	*MORGAN*, Albert Petitto, 5,000	35.00	NR

Child's Christmas (Hudson Pewter)

1978	BEDTIME STORY, Albert Petitto, 10,000	35.00	NR
1979	LITTLEST ANGELS, Albert Petitto, 10,000	35.00	NR
1980	HEAVEN'S CHRISTMAS TREE, Albert Petitto, 10,000	42.50	NR
1981	FILLING THE SKY, Albert Petitto, 10,000	47.50	NR

		ISSUE	CURRENT
Christmas (Chilmark Pewter)			
1977	CURRIER & IVES CHRISTMAS, retrd	60.00	NR
1978	TRIMMING THE TREE, retrd	65.00	NR
1979	THREE WISEMEN, retrd	65.00	NR
Christmas (Hudson Pewter)			
1986	BRINGING HOME THE TREE, J. Wanat, suspd	47.50	NR
1987	THE CAROLING ANGELS, Albert Petitto, suspd	47.50	NR
1993	CRACK THE WHIP, A. McGrory, 950	55.00	NR
1994	HOME FOR CHRISTMAS, A. McGrory, 950	50.00	NR
Mickey's Christmas (Hudson Pewter)			
1986	GOD BLESS US, EVERY ONE, D. Everhart, suspd	47.50	NR
1987	THE CAROLING ANGELS, Albert Petitto, suspd	47.50	NR
1987	JOLLY OLD SAINT NICK, D. Everhart, suspd	55.00	NR
1988	HE'S CHECKING IT TWICE, D. Everhart, suspd	50.00	NR
Mother's Day (Chilmark Pewter)			
1974	FLOWERS OF THE FIELD, retrd	60.00	NR
1980	1980 MOTHER'S DAY, retrd	90.00	NR
Mother's Day (Hudson Pewter)			
1979	CHERISHED, 10,000	42.50	35.00
1980	1980 MOTHER'S DAY, retrd	42.50	NR
Sebastian Plates			
1974	SPIRIT OF '76, Prescott W. Baston, retrd	27.50	NR
1976	DECLARATION OF INDEPENDENCE, Prescott W. Baston, retrd	25.00	NR
1978	MOTIF NO. 1, Prescott W. Baston, 4,878	75.00	BR
1978	ZODIAC, Prescott W. Baston, retrd	60.00	NR
1979	GRAND CANYON, Prescott W. Baston, 2,492	75.00	BR
1980	LONE CYPRESS, Prescott W. Baston, 718	75.00	160.00
1980	IN THE CANDY STORE, Prescott W. Baston, 9,098	39.50	NR
1981	THE DOCTOR, Prescott W. Baston, 7,547	39.50	NR
1983	LITTLE MOTHER, Prescott W. Baston, 2,710	39.50	NR
1984	SWITCHING THE FREIGHT, Prescott W. Baston, 706	42.50	90
Songbirds of the Four Seasons (Hudson Pewter)			
1979	HUMMINGBIRD (SUMMER), Andrea Hollis/Yourdon, 7,500	35.00	NR
1979	CARDINAL (WINTER), Andrea Hollis/Yourdon, 7,500	35.00	NR
1979	WOOD THRUSH (SPRING), Andrea Hollis/Yourdon, 7,500	35.00	NR
1979	SPARROW (AUTUMN), Andrea Hollis/Yourdon, 7,500	35.00	NR
Songs of Christmas (Hudson Pewter)			
1988	SILENT NIGHT, A. McGrory, susp	55.00	NR
1989	HARK! THE HERALD ANGELS SING, A. McGrory, suspd	60.00	NR
1990	THE FIRST NOEL, A. McGrory, suspd	60.00	NR
1991	WE THREE KINGS, A. McGrory, suspd	60.00	NR
'Twas the Night Before Christmas (Hudson Pewter)			
1982	NOT A CREATURE WAS STIRRING, Andrea Hollis, 10,000	47.50	NR

		ISSUE	CURRENT
1983	VISIONS OF SUGARPLUMS, Andrea Hollis, 10,000	47.50	NR
1984	HIS EYES HOW THEY TWINKLED, Andrea Hollis, 10,000	47.50	NR
1985	HAPPY CHRISTMAS TO ALL, Andrea Hollis, 10,000	47.50	NR

LANGENTHAL CHINA WORKS SWITZERLAND

Anker's Heritage

1986	THE FIRST SMILE, Albert Anker	34.86	NR
1986	GRANDFATHER TELLS A STORY, Albert Anker	34.86	NR
1987	GIRL FEEDING THE CHICKENS, Albert Anker	34.86	NR
1987	SCHOOL PROMENADE	34.86	NR
1987	THE CHEMIST	37.86	NR
1987	THE DAY NURSERY	37.86	NR
1987	THE SNOW BEAR	37.86	NR
1988	AT THE GRANDPARENTS	37.86	NR

LAPSYS UNITED STATES

Crystal Series

1977	SNOWFLAKE, crystal, 5,000	47.50	75.00
1978	PEACE ON EARTH, crystal, 5,000	47.50	NR

GEORGE ZOLTAN LEFTON UNITED STATES

Historic American Lighthouse Collection

1998	PIGEON POINT, CA, Mary Lingle, 150 days	30.00	RI
1998	ADMIRALTY HEAD, WA, Mary Lingle, 150 days	30.00	RI
1998	SPLIT ROCK, MN, Mary Lingle, 150 days	30.00	RI
1998	WEST QUODDY HEAD, ME, Mary Lingle, 150 days	30.00	RI
1998	MONTAUK POINT, NY, Mary Lingle, 150 days	30.00	RI
1998	CAPE MAY, NJ, Mary Lingle, 150 days	30.00	RI
1998	CAPE NEDDICK, ME, Mary Lingle, 150 days	30.00	RI
1998	THOMAS POINT SHOAL, MD, Mary Lingle, 150 days	30.00	RI

Cape Neddick, ME
Photo courtesy of *Collectors News*

		ISSUE	CURRENT
1998	PORTLAND HEAD, ME, Mary Lingle, 150 days	30.00	RI
1998	BARNEGAT, NJ, Mary Lingle, 150 days	30.00	RI
1998	BOSTON HARBOR, MA, Mary Lingle, 150 days	30.00	RI
1998	CAPE HATTERAS, NC, Mary Lingle, 150 days	30.00	RI
1998	FIRE ISLAND, NY, Mary Lingle, 150 days	30.00	RI
1998	WHITE SHOAL, MI, Mary Lingle, 150 days	30.00	RI
1998	ST. AUGUSTINE, FL, Mary Lingle, 150 days	30.00	RI
1998	ST. SIMONS, GA, Mary Lingle, 150 days	30.00	RI

LEGACY LIMITED UNITED STATES

Christmas

1986	CHRISTMAS 1986, Les Kouba, 5,000	39.50	NR

LENINGRAD PORCELAIN FACTORY RUSSIA

Firebird

1990	THE TSAREVICH AND THE FIREBIRD	29.87	BR
1990	PRINCESS ELENA AND IVAN	29.87	BR
1990	THE WEDDING FEAST	32.87	BR
1990	ELENA THE FAIR	32.87	BR
1990	THE GOLDEN BRIDLE	32.87	BR
1990	THE GOLDEN CAGE	32.87	BR
1991	AWAITING THE FIREBIRD	34.87	BR
1991	IVAN'S CONQUEST	34.87	NR
1991	THE MAGNIFICENT FIREBIRD	34.87	50.00
1991	JOURNEY OF TSAREVICH EVAN/ELENA	36.87	NR
1991	IN SEARCH OF THE FIREBIRD	36.87	50.00
1991	TSAREVICH IVAN AND THE GRAY WOLF	36.87	80.00

LENOX UNITED STATES

(American Express, Princeton Gallery)

American Wildlife

1982	BLACK BEARS, N. Adams, 9,500	65.00	NR
1982	MOUNTAIN LIONS, N. Adams, 9,500	65.00	NR
1982	POLAR BEARS, N. Adams, 9,500	65.00	NR
1982	OTTERS, N. Adams, 9,500	65.00	NR
1982	WHITE-TAILED DEER, N. Adams, 9,500	65.00	NR
1982	BUFFALO, N. Adams, 9,500	65.00	NR
1982	JACK RABBITS, N. Adams, 9,500	65.00	NR
1983	RED FOXES, N. Adams, 9,500	65.00	NR
1983	OCELOTS, N. Adams, 9,500	65.00	NR
1983	SEA LIONS, N. Adams, 9,500	65.00	NR
1983	RACCOONS, N. Adams, 9,500	65.00	NR
1983	DALL SHEEP, N. Adams, 9,500	65.00	NR

America's Almanac

NA	WINDSWEPT	39.95	NR
NA	WONDERLAND	39.95	NR

		ISSUE	CURRENT

Annual Christmas

		ISSUE	CURRENT
1991	SLEIGH, 1 year	75.00	NR
1993	MIDNIGHT SLEIGH RIDE, L. Bywaters, 1 year	119.00	RI
1997	CHRISTMAS LIST, 1 year	75.00	RI

Arctic Wolves (Princeton Gallery)

		ISSUE	CURRENT
1993	CRY OF THE WILD, J. Van Zyle, closed	29.90	RI
1993	FAR COUNTRY CROSSING, J. Van Zyle, closed	29.90	RI
1993	MIDNIGHT RENEGADE, J. Van Zyle, closed	29.90	RI
1993	NIGHTWATCH, J. Van Zyle, closed	29.90	RI
1993	ON THE EDGE, J. Van Zyle, closed	29.90	RI
1993	PICKING UP THE TRAIL, J. Van Zyle, closed	29.90	RI

Big Cats of the World

		ISSUE	CURRENT
1993	BLACK PANTHER, Q. Lemonds, open	39.50	RI
1993	BOBCAT, Q. Lemonds, open	39.50	RI
1993	CHINESE LEOPARD, Q. Lemonds, open	39.50	RI
1993	COUGAR, Q. Lemonds, open	39.50	RI
1993	LION, Q. Lemonds, open	39.50	RI
1993	SNOW LEOPARD, Q. Lemonds, open	39.50	RI
1993	TIGER, Q. Lemonds, open	39.50	RI
1993	WHITE TIGER, Q. Lemonds, open	39.50	RI

Birds of the Garden

		ISSUE	CURRENT
1992	SPRING GLORY, CARDINALS, W. Mumm, open	39.50	NR
1993	BLOSSOMING BOUGH, CHICKADEES, W. Mumm, open	39.50	RI
1993	BLUEBIRDS HAVEN, BLUEBIRDS, W. Mumm, open	39.50	RI
1993	INDIGO MEADOW, INDIGO BUNTINGS, W. Mumm, open	39.50	RI
1993	JEWELS OF THE GARDEN, HUMMINGBIRDS, W. Mumm, open	39.50	RI
1993	SCARLET TANAGERS, W. Mumm, open	39.50	RI
1993	SUNBRIGHT SONGBIRDS, GOLDFINCH, W. Mumm, open	39.50	RI

Boehm Birds

		ISSUE	CURRENT
1970	WOOD THRUSH, Edward Marshall Boehm, 1 year	35.00	90.00
1971	GOLDFINCH, Edward Marshall Boehm, 1 year	35.00	50.00
1972	MOUNTAIN BLUEBIRD, Edward Marshall Boehm, 1 year	37.50	50.00
1973	MEADOWLARK, Edward Marshall Boehm, 1 year	41.00	BR
1974	RUFOUS HUMMINGBIRD, Edward Marshall Boehm, 1 year	45.00	50.00
1975	AMERICAN REDSTART, Edward Marshall Boehm, 1 year	50.00	BR
1976	CARDINAL, Edward Marshall Boehm, 1 year	53.00	BR
1977	ROBINS, Edward Marshall Boehm, 1 year	55.00	BR
1978	MOCKINGBIRDS, Edward Marshall Boehm, 1 year	58.00	BR
1979	GOLDEN-CROWNED KINGLETS, Edward Marshall Boehm, 1 year	65.00	80.00
1980	BLACK-THROATED BLUE WARBLERS, Edward Marshall Boehm, 1 year	80.00	75.00
1981	EASTERN PHOEBES, Edward Marshall Boehm, 1 year	90.00	80.00

Boehm Birds/Young America

		ISSUE	CURRENT
1972	EAGLET, Edward Marshall Boehm, 5,000	175.00	NR
1973	EAGLET, Edward Marshall Boehm, 6,000	175.00	NR
1975	EAGLET, Edward Marshall Boehm, 6,000	175.00	NR

Boehm Woodland Wildlife

		ISSUE	CURRENT
1973	RACCOONS, Edward Marshall Boehm, 1 year	50.00	75.00
1974	RED FOXES, Edward Marshall Boehm, 1 year	52.50	75.00
1975	COTTONTAIL RABBITS, Edward Marshall Boehm, 1 year	58.50	75.00
1976	EASTERN CHIPMUNKS, Edward Marshall Boehm, 1 year	62.50	75.00
1977	BEAVER, Edward Marshall Boehm, 1 year	67.50	75.00
1978	WHITETAIL DEER, Edward Marshall Boehm, 1 year	70.00	75.00
1979	SQUIRRELS, Edward Marshall Boehm, 1 year	76.00	75.00
1980	BOBCATS, Edward Marshall Boehm, 1 year	92.50	80.00
1981	MARTENS, Edward Marshall Boehm, 1 year	100.00	100.00
1982	OTTERS, Edward Marshall Boehm, 1 year	100.00	100.00

Butterflies and Flowers

1982	QUESTION MARK BUTTERFLY AND NEW ENGLAND ASTER, Val Roy Gerischer, 25,000	60.00	NR
1983	SONORAN BLUE BUTTERFLY AND MARIPOSA LILY, Val Roy Gerischer, 25,000	65.00	NR
1983	MALACHITE BUTTERFLY AND ORCHID, Val Roy Gerischer, 25,000	65.00	NR
1984	AMERICAN PAINTED LADY AND VIRGINIA ROSE, Val Roy Gerischer, 25,000	70.00	NR
1984	RUDDY DAGGERWING AND LANTANA, Val Roy Gerischer, 25,000	70.00	NR
1985	BUCKEYE BUTTERFLY AND BLUEBELLS, Val Roy Gerischer, 25,000	75.00	NR

Children of the Sun & Moon

1993	DESERT BLOSSOM, D. Crowley, open	39.50	RI
1993	FEATHERS & FURS, D. Crowley, open	39.50	RI
1993	SHY ONE, D. Crowley, open	39.50	RI
1994	DAUGHTER OF THE SUN, D. Crowley, open	39.50	RI
1994	INDIGO GIRL, D. Crowley, open	39.50	RI
1994	LITTLE FLOWER, D. Crowley, open	39.50	RI
1994	RED FEATHERS, D. Crowley, open	39.50	RI
1994	STARS IN HER EYES, D. Crowley, open	39.50	RI

Children's Hour

NA	PLAYTIME	59.95	NR
NA	BEDTIME STORY	59.95	NR

Christmas Trees Around the World

1991	GERMANY, 1 year	75.00	NR
1992	FRANCE, 1 year	75.00	NR

Colonial Christmas Wreath

1981	COLONIAL VIRGINIA, 1 year	65.00	75.00
1982	MASSACHUSETTS, 1 year	70.00	95.00
1983	MARYLAND, 1 year	70.00	185.00
1984	RHODE ISLAND, 1 year	70.00	80.00
1985	CONNECTICUT, 1 year	70.00	NR
1986	NEW HAMPSHIRE, 1 year	70.00	NR
1987	PENNSYLVANIA, 1 year	70.00	NR
1988	DELAWARE, 1 year	70.00	155.00
1989	NEW YORK, 1 year	75.00	155.00
1990	NEW JERSEY, 1 year	75.00	NR
1991	SOUTH CAROLINA, 1 year	75.00	NR

		ISSUE	CURRENT
1992	NORTH CAROLINA, 1 year	75.00	155.00
1993	GEORGIA, 1 year	75.00	RI

Confederacy Collection

1971	THE WHITE HOUSE OF THE CONFEDERACY, W. Schiener, 1,201	—	—
1971	THE GREAT SEAL OF THE CONFEDERACY, W. Schiener, 1,201	—	—
1971	A CALL TO ARMS, W. Schiener, 1,201	—	—
1971	THE GENERAL, W. Schiener, 1,201	—	—
1971	LEE AND JACKSON, W. Schiener, 1,201	—	—
1971	THE MERRIMAC, W. Schiener, 1,201	—	—
1971	J.E.B. STUART, W. Schiener, 1,201	—	—
1971	CONFEDERATE CAMP, W. Schiener, 1,201	—	—
1971	BLOCKADE RUNNER, W. Schiener, 1,201	—	—
1971	FORT SUMTER, W. Schiener, 1,201	—	—
	Set of 10	900.00	NR

Cubs of the Big Cats (Princeton Gallery)

1993	JAGUAR CUB, Q. Lemonds, closed	29.90	RI

Darling Dalmatians (Princeton Gallery)

1993	ALL FIRED UP, L. Picken, closed	29.90	RI
1993	CAUGHT IN THE ACT, L. Picken, closed	29.90	RI
1993	FIRE BRIGADE, L. Picken, closed	29.90	RI
1993	PLEASE DON'T PICK THE FLOWERS, L. Picken, closed	29.90	RI
1993	PUPS IN BOOTS, L. Picken, closed	29.90	RI
1993	THREE ALARM FIRE, L. Picken, closed	29.90	RI

Dolphins of the Seven Seas

1993	BOTTLENOSE DOLPHINS, J. Holderby, open	39.50	RI

Eagle Conservation

1993	DAYBREAK ON RIVER'S EDGE, R. Kelly, open	39.50	RI
1993	EAGLES ON MT. MCKINLEY, R. Kelly, open	39.50	RI
1993	LONE SENTINEL, R. Kelly, open	39.50	RI
1993	NORTHERN HERITAGE, R. Kelly, open	39.50	RI
1993	NORTHWOOD'S LEGEND, R. Kelly, open	39.50	RI
1993	RIVER SCOUT, R. Kelly, open	39.50	RI
1993	SOARING THE PEAKS, R. Kelly, open	39.50	RI
1993	SOLO FLIGHT, R. Kelly, open	39.50	RI

Garden Birds

1988	CHICKADEE, limited	48.00	NR
1988	BLUEJAY, limited	48.00	NR
1989	HUMMINGBIRD, limited	48.00	NR
1991	DOVE, limited	48.00	NR
1991	CARDINAL, limited	48.00	NR
1992	GOLDFINCH, limited	48.00	NR

Great Cats of the World

1993	CHINESE LEOPARD, Guy Coheleach, open	39.50	RI

		ISSUE	CURRENT
1993	COUGAR, Guy Coheleach, open	39.50	RI
1993	JAGUAR, Guy Coheleach, open	39.50	RI
1993	LION, Guy Coheleach, open	39.50	RI
1993	LIONESS, Guy Coheleach, open	39.50	RI
1993	SIBERIAN TIGER, Guy Coheleach, open	39.50	RI
1993	SNOW LEOPARD, Guy Coheleach, open	39.50	RI
1993	WHITE TIGER, Guy Coheleach, open	39.50	RI

International Victorian Santas

1992	KRIS KRINGLE, R. Hoover, closed	39.50	NR
1993	FATHER CHRISTMAS, R. Hoover, closed	39.50	RI
1994	GRANDFATHER FROST, R. Hoover, closed	39.50	RI
1995	AMERICAN SANTA CLAUS, R. Hoover, closed	39.50	RI

King of the Plains

1994	AFRICAN ANCIENTS, S. Combes, open	39.90	RI
1994	END OF THE LINE, S. Combes, open	39.90	RI
1994	GUARDIAN, S. Combes, open	39.90	RI
1994	THE LAST ELEPHANT, S. Combes, open	39.90	RI
1994	PROTECTING THE FLANKS, S. Combes, open	39.90	RI
1994	RAINBOW TRAIL, S. Combes, open	39.90	RI
1994	SPARRING BULLS, S. Combes, open	39.90	RI
1994	TSAVA ELEPHANT, S. Combes, open	39.90	RI

Lenox Christmas Trees

1976	DOUGLAS FIR, 1 year	50.00	NR
1977	SCOTCH PINE, 1 year	55.00	NR
1978	BLUE SPRUCE, 1 year	65.00	NR
1979	BALSAM FIR, 1 year	65.00	NR
1980	BREWER'S SPRUCE, 1 year	75.00	NR
1981	CHINA FIR, 1 year	75.00	NR
1982	ALEPPO PINE, 1 year	80.00	NR

Magic of Christmas

1993	GIFTS FOR ALL, L. Bywaters, open	39.50	RI
1993	SANTA OF THE NORHTERN FOREST, L. Bywaters, open	39.50	RI
1993	SANTA'S GIFT OF PEACE, L. Bywaters, open	39.50	RI
1994	A BERRY MERRY CHRISTMAS, L. Bywaters, open	39.50	RI
1994	COMING HOME, L. Bywaters, open	39.50	RI
1994	SANTA'S SENTINELS, L. Bywaters, open	39.50	RI
1994	WONDER OF WONDERS, L. Bywaters, open	39.50	RI

Metropolitan Opera

1983	MADAME BUTTERFLY	95.00	NR
1986	LA TRAVIATA	95.00	NR
1987	ROMEO & JULIET	95.00	NR

Nature's Collage

1992	CEDAR WAXWING, AMONG THE BERRIES, C. McClung, open	34.50	NR
1992	GOLDFINCHES, GOLDEN SPLENDOR, C. McClung, open	34.50	NR

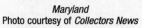

Maryland
Photo courtesy of *Collectors News*

Koalas
Photo courtesy of *Collectors News*

Nature's Nursery

		ISSUE	CURRENT
1982	SNOW LEOPARDS, Lynn Chase, 15,000	65.00	NR
1983	KOALAS, Lynn Chase, 15,000	65.00	NR
1983	LLAMAS, Lynn Chase, 15,000	70.00	NR
1984	BENGAL TIGERS, Lynn Chase, 15,000	70.00	NR
1985	EMPEROR PENGUINS, Lynn Chase, 15,000	75.00	NR
1985	POLAR BEARS, Lynn Chase, 15,000	75.00	NR
1986	ZEBRAS, Lynn Chase, 15,000	80.00	NR

Owls of North America

1993	SPIRIT OF THE ARCTIC, SNOWY OWL, L. Laffin, open	45.00	RI

Pierced Nativity

1993	HOLY FAMILY, open	45.00	RI
1994	HERALDING ANGELS, open	45.00	RI
1994	SHEPHERDS, open	45.00	RI
1994	THREE KINGS, open	45.00	RI

Royal Cats of Guy Coheleach

1994	AFTERNOON SHADE, Guy Coheleach, open	39.50	RI
1994	AMBUSH IN THE SNOW, Guy Coheleach, open	39.50	RI
1994	CAT NAP, Guy Coheleach, open	39.50	RI
1994	JUNGLE JAGUAR, Guy Coheleach, open	39.50	RI
1994	LION IN WAIT, Guy Coheleach, open	39.50	RI
1994	ROCKY MOUNTAIN PUMA, Guy Coheleach, open	39.50	RI
1994	ROCKY REFUGE, Guy Coheleach, open	39.50	RI
1994	SIESTA, Guy Coheleach, open	39.50	RI

Whale Conservation

1993	ORCA, J. Holderby, open	39.50	RI

LIGHTPOST PUBLISHING UNITED STATES

Thomas Kinkade Signature Collection

		ISSUE	CURRENT
1991	CHANDLER'S COTTAGE, Thomas Kinkade, 2,500	49.95	NR
1991	CEDAR NOOK, Thomas Kinkade, 2,500	49.95	BR
1991	SLEIGH RIDE HOME, Thomas Kinkade, 2,500	49.95	55.00
1991	HOME TO GRANDMA'S, Thomas Kinkade, 2,500	49.95	NR

LIHS LINDER GERMANY

America the Beautiful

1975	INDEPENDENCE HALL, 1,500	42.00	NR
1975	STATUE OF LIBERTY, 1,500	42.00	NR
1975	NIAGARA FALLS, 1,500	42.00	NR
1975	GRAND CANYON, 1,500	42.00	NR
1975	GOLDEN GATE, 1,500	42.00	NR
1975	CAPITOL, 1,500	42.00	NR

Child's Christmas

1978	HOLY NIGHT, Ferner, 5,000	40.00	NR
1979	SHEPHERDS IN THE FIELD, Ferner, 5,000	40.00	NR

Christmas

1972	LITTLE DRUMMER BOY, Josef Neubauer, 6,000	25.00	35.00
1973	CAROLERS, Josef Neubauer, 6,000	25.00	NR
1974	PEACE, Josef Neubauer, 6,000	25.00	NR
1975	CHRISTMAS CHEER, Josef Neubauer, 6,000	30.00	NR
1976	JOY OF CHRISTMAS, Josef Neubauer, 6,000	30.00	NR
1977	HOLLY JOLLY CHRISTMAS, Josef Neubauer, 6,000	30.00	NR
1978	HOLY NIGHT, Josef Neubauer, 5,000	40.00	NR

Easter

1973	HAPPY EASTER, 1,500	22.00	45.00
1974	SPRINGTIME, 1,500	25.00	NR
1975	WITH LOVE, 1,500	28.00	NR

Golden Spike Centennial

1977	CENTRAL PACIFIC JUPITER, 1,500	25.00	NR
1977	UNION PACIFIC 119, 1,500	25.00	NR

History

1973	TRIBUTE TO FLAG, 3,000	60.00	120.00
1974	GOLDEN SPIKE CENTENNIAL, 1,500	40.00	NR

Mother's Day

1972	MOTHER AND CHILD, 1,000	20.00	90.00
1973	MOTHER AND CHILD, 2,000	24.00	BR
1974	BOUQUET, 2,000	25.00	NR
1975	HAPPINESS, 2,000	28.00	NR

Holy Night

		ISSUE	CURRENT
Playmates			
1976	TIMMY AND FRIEND	45.00	55.00
1977	HEIDI AND FRIEND	45.00	NR

Single Issues

1972	UNION PACIFIC RAILROAD, 1,500	22.00	NR
1973	UNIION PACIFIC BIG BOY, 1,500	25.00	NR
1973	FLAG, 3,000	60.00	140.00
1976	DRUMMER BOY, 1,500	45.00	55.00
1976	FREEDOM TRAIN, 1,500	45.00	60.00
1978	UNION PACIFIC 8444, 1,500	27.50	NR
1979	UNION PACIFIC CHALLENGER, 1,500	30.00	NR

LILLIPUT LANE, LTD.

(Bradford Exchange, Enesco, Franklin Mint, Gift Link, Inc., Hamilton Gallery, Hamilton Mint)

3-D Plates

1996	COTMAN COTTAGE, <1 year	200.00	RI
1996	PARADISE LODGE, <1 year	250.00	RI
1996	ROSE COTTAGE, <1 year	300.00	RI

American Landmarks

1990	COUNTRY CHURCH, Ray Day, 5,000	35.00	NR
1990	MAIL BARN, Ray Day, 5,000	35.00	NR
1990	RIVERSIDE CHAPEL, Ray Day, 5,000	35.00	NR

Calendar Cottages of England

1996	WELFORD-ON-AVON, open	60.00	RI
1996	WHERWELL GREEN, open	60.00	RI

Coca-Cola Country Four Seasons

1998	SUMMER / CATCH OF THE DAY, Ray Day, open	40.00	RI
1998	WINTER / ICE COLD COKE, Ray Day, open	40.00	RI
1998	SPRING / SPRING HAS SPRUNG, Ray Day, open	40.00	RI

		ISSUE	CURRENT
1998	AUTUMN / WHEN I WAS YOUR AGE..., Ray Day, open	40.00	RI

Wishing Well Cottage

1994	WISHING WELL COTTAGE, 45 days	60.00	RI
1996	CONVENT IN THE WOODS, 45 days	35.00	RI
1996	THE GABLES, 45 days	35.00	RI
1996	GRANNY SMITHS, 45 days	35.00	RI
1996	PARADISE LODGE, 45 days	35.00	RI
1996	TITMOUSE COTTAGE, 45 days	35.00	RI

LIMOGES-TURGOT FRANCE

Durand's Children

1978	MARIE-ANGE, Paul Durand, 1 year	36.50	NR
1979	EMILIE ET PHILIPPE, Paul Durand, 1 year	36.50	NR
1980	CHRISTIANE ET FIFI, Paul Durand, 1 year	36.50	NR
1980	CECILE ET RAOUL, Paul Durand, 1 year	36.50	NR

Marie-Ange

Cinderella
Photo courtesy of *Collectors News*

Les Enfants de la Fin du Siècle

1984	PAINTINGS AU TROCADERO, Bernard Peltriauz, limited	24.82	NR
1985	PETITS VOILIERS AU BASSIN DES TUILERIES, Bernard Peltriauz, limited	29.82	40.00
1985	GUIGNOL AU LUXEMBOURG, Bernard Peltriauz, limited	29.82	40.00
1986	MANAGE AUX CHAMPS-ELYSEES, Bernard Peltriauz, limited	29.82	NR

Quellier's Morals of Perrault

1983	CINDERELLA, Andre Quellier, limited	28.67	NR
1984	LITTLE TOM THUMB, Andre Quellier, limited	28.67	NR
1984	LITTLE RED RIDING HOOD, Andre Quellier, limited	28.67	NR
1985	SLEEPING BEAUTY, Andre Quellier, limited	28.67	NR

LINCOLN MINT UNITED STATES

		ISSUE	CURRENT

Artists

1971	DALI UNICORN, gold, 100	1,500.00	1,600.00
1971	DALI UNICORN, silver, 5,000	100.00	NR
1972	DALI ATHENA, gold, 300	2,000.00	NR
1972	DALI ATHENA, vermeil, 2,500	1,150.00	NR
1972	DALI ATHENA, silver, 7,500	125.00	NR

Christmas

1978	SANTA BELONGS TO ALL CHILDREN, 7,500	29.50	NR

Easter

1972	DALI, gold, 10,000	200.00	215.00
1972	DALI, silver, 20,000	150.00	BR
1974	DALI, pewter	45.00	NR

Madonnas

1972	MADONNA DELLA SEGGIOLA, 3,000	125.00	BR

Mother's Day

1972	COLLIES, gold on silver	90.00	100.00
1972	COLLIES, silver	125.00	BR

LIONSHEAD MINT

Iditarod Race Champs

1984	RICK MACKEY, George Rodgers, 5,000	35.00	NR

LITT UNITED STATES

Annual

1979	APACHE SUNSET, enamel, 1,250	275.00	NR

Christmas

1978	MADONNA AND CHILD, enamel, 1,000	200.00	NR
1979	O HOLY NIGHT, 1,000	200.00	NR

LLADRÓ SPAIN

Christmas

1971	CAROLING, 1 year	27.50	NR
1972	CAROLERS, 1 year	35.00	NR
1973	BOY AND GIRL, 1 year	45.00	NR
1974	CAROLERS, 1 year	55.00	75.00
1975	CHERUBS, 1 year	60.00	NR
1976	CHRIST CHILD, 1 year	60.00	BR
1977	NATIVITY, 1 year	80.00	BR

		ISSUE	CURRENT
1978	CAROLING CHILD, 1 year	80.00	BR
1979	SNOW DANCE, 1 year	90.00	BR

Lladró Plate Collection

1993	THE GREAT VOYAGE L5964G, Lladró, limited	50.00	RI
1993	LOOKING OUT L5998G, Lladró, limited	38.00	RI
1993	SWINGING L5999G, Lladró, limited	38.00	RI
1993	DUCK PLATE L6000G, Lladró, limited	38.00	RI
1994	FRIENDS L6158, Lladró, open	32.00	RI
1994	APPLE PICKING L6159M, Lladró, open	32.00	RI
1994	TURTLEDOVE L6160, Lladró, open	32.00	RI
1994	FLAMINGO L6161M, Lladró, open	32.00	RI

Mother's Day

1971	KISS OF THE CHILD, 800	27.50	75.00
1972	BIRDS AND CHICKS, 3,500	27.50	NR
1973	MOTHER AND CHILDREN, 2,000	35.00	NR
1974	NURSING MOTHER, 1 year	45.00	125.00
1975	MOTHER AND CHILDREN, 1 year	60.00	NR
1976	VIGIL, 1 year	60.00	BR
1977	MOTHER AND DAUGHTER, 1 year	67.50	BR
1978	NEW ARRIVAL, 1 year	80.00	BR
1979	OFF TO SCHOOL, 1 year	90.00	NR

LONGTON CROWN POTTERY GREAT BRITAIN

Canterbury Tales

1980	MAN OF LAW'S TALE, G. A. Hoover	29.80	NR
1982	FRANKLIN'S TALE, G. A. Hoover	31.80	NR
1982	KNIGHT'S TALE, G. A. Hoover	31.80	NR
1982	WIFE OF BATH'S TALE, G. A. Hoover	31.80	NR

LOUISIANA HERITAGE ART GALLERIES UNITED STATES

Southern Backroads

1985	MORNING MYSTIQUE, Barrie Van Osdell	39.50	NR

JEAN-PAUL LOUP

Christmas

1971	NOEL, 300	125.00	1,000.00
1972	NOEL, 300	150.00	700.00
1973	NOEL, 300	175.00	500.00
1974	NOEL, 400	200.00	500.00
1975	NOEL, 250	250.00	500.00
1976	NOEL, 150	300.00	600.00

Mother's Day

1974	MOTHER AND CHILD, champleve, 500	250.00	1,100.00

		ISSUE	CURRENT
1975	MOTHER AND CHILD, enamel, 400	285.00	550.00
1976	MOTHER AND CHILD, enamel, 150	300.00	600.00

LUND AND CLAUSEN DENMARK

Christmas

1971	DEER, 1 year	13.50	NR
1972	STAVE CHURCH, 1 year	13.50	NR
1973	CHRISTMAS SCENE, 1 year	13.50	NR

Moon Series

1969	MOON LANDING, 1 year	10.00	NR
1971	APOLLO 13, 1 year	15.00	NR

Mother's Day

1969	ROSE, 1 year	10.00	20.00
1971	FORGET-ME-NOTS, 1 year	10.00	NR
1972	BLUEBELL, 1 year	15.00	NR
1973	LILY OF THE VALLEY, 1 year	16.00	NR

LYNELL UNITED STATES

American Adventures

1979	THE WHALER, Endre Szabo, 7,500	50.00	60.00
1980	THE TRAPPER, Endre Szabo, 7,500	50.00	NR
1980	THE FORTY-NINER, 7,500	50.00	NR
1981	THE PIONEER WOMAN, 7,500	50.00	NR
1981	THE WAGON MASTER, 7,500	50.00	NR
1982	WAGON HO!, 7,500	50.00	NR

Betsy Bates Annual

1979	OLDE COUNTRY INN, 7,500	38.50	45.00
1980	VILLAGE SCHOOLHOUSE, 7,500	38.50	NR
1981	VILLAGE BLACKSMITH, 7,500	38.50	NR
1982	CHRISTMAS VILLAGE, Betsy Bates, 15,000	24.50	NR

Children's Hour

1981	OFFICIAL BABYSITTER, Mike Hagel, 15,000	24.50	NR
1981	COWBOY CAPERS, Mike Hagel, 15,000	24.50	NR
1982	NURSE NANCY, Mike Hagel, 15,000	24.50	NR

Circus Dreams

1982	TWO FOR THE SHOW, Susan Neelon, 19,500	24.50	NR

Great Chiefs of Canada

1980	CHIEF JOSEPH BRANT, Murray Killman, 7,500	65.00	NR
1981	CHIEF CROWFOOT, Murray Killman, 7,500	65.00	NR
1982	TECUMSEH, Murray Killman, 7,500	65.00	NR

Emmett Kelly
Photo courtesy of *Collectors News*

Greatest Clowns of the Circus

		ISSUE	CURRENT
1982	EMMETT KELLY, Robert Weaver, 1 year	38.50	NR
1982	LOU JACOBS, Robert Weaver, 1 year	38.50	NR
1982	FELIX ADLER, Robert Weaver, 1 year	38.50	NR
1982	OTTO GRIEBLING, Robert Weaver, 1 year	38.50	NR

Hagel Christmas

1981	SH-H-H!, Mike Hagel, 17,500	25.90	NR
1982	A KISS FOR SANTA, Mike Hagel, 17,500	25.90	NR

Hagel Mother's Day

1982	ONCE UPON A TIME, Mike Hagel, 60 days	29.50	NR

Hobo Joe

1982	HOLD THE ONIONS, Ron Lee, 10,000	50.00	NR
1982	TRAVELING IN STYLE, Ron Lee, 10,000	50.00	NR

How the West Was Won

1981	PONY EXPRESS, Gayle Gibson, 19,500	38.50	NR
1981	THE OREGON TRAIL, Gayle Gibson, 19,500	38.50	NR
1982	CALIFORNIA GOLD RUSH, Gayle Gibson, 19,500	38.50	NR
1982	DRIVING THE GOLDEN SPIKE, Gayle Gibson, 19,500	38.50	NR
1982	CATTLE DRIVE, Gayle Gibson, 19,500	38.50	NR
1982	PEACE PIPE, Gayle Gibson, 19,500	38.50	NR

Little House on the Prairie

1982	WELCOME TO WALNUT CREEK, Eugene Christopherson, 1 year	45.00	NR
1982	COUNTRY GIRLS, Eugene Christopherson, 1 year	45.00	NR

Little Traveler

1978	ON HIS WAY, George Malik, 4,000	45.00	BR
1979	ON HER WAY, George Malik, 4,000	45.00	BR

Norman Rockwell Christmas

1979	SNOW QUEEN, Norman Rockwell, 60 days	29.50	NR

		ISSUE	CURRENT
1980	SURPRISES FOR ALL, Norman Rockwell, 60 days	29.50	NR
1981	GRANDPOP AND ME, Norman Rockwell, 60 days	29.50	NR
1982	SANTA'S SECRET, Norman Rockwell, 60 days	29.50	NR
1983	LOOKING FOR SANTA, Norman Rockwell, 15,000	35.00	NR

Norman Rockwell Collection of Legendary Art

1980	THE ARTIST'S DAUGHTER, Norman Rockwell, 15,000	65.00	NR
1980	POOR RICHARD'S ALMANAC, Norman Rockwell, 17,500	45.00	NR
1981	DAILY PRAYERS, Norman Rockwell, <1 year	29.50	NR

Norman Rockwell Mother's Day

1980	CRADLE OF LOVE, Norman Rockwell, 60 days	29.50	40.00
1981	A MOTHER'S BLESSING, Norman Rockwell, 30 days	29.50	NR
1982	MEMORIES, Norman Rockwell, 60 days	29.50	NR

North American Wildlife

1982	SNUGGLING COUGARS, Murray Killman, 7,500	65.00	NR

Popeye's 50th Anniversary

1980	HAPPY BIRTHDAY POPEYE, 1 year	22.50	NR

Rockwell's Scotty

1981	SCOTTY'S STOWAWAY, Norman Rockwell, 17,500	45.00	NR
1982	SCOTTY STRIKES A BARGAIN, Norman Rockwell, 17,500	35.00	NR

Soap Box Derby

1979	LAST MINUTE CHANGES, Norman Rockwell, 1 year	24.50	NR
1980	AT THE GATE, Norman Rockwell, 1 year	24.50	NR
1982	IN THE STRETCH, Norman Rockwell, 1 year	24.50	NR

Special Celebrities

1981	REAGAN/BUSH, Mike Hagel, 17,500	45.00	NR
1982	HOPE/THANKS FOR THE MEMORIES, Mike Hagel, limited	45.00	NR
1982	BURNS/YOUNG AT HEART, Mike Hagel, limited	45.00	NR
1982	I LOVE LUCY, Mike Hagel, limited	45.00	NR

Single Issues

1979	JOHN WAYNE TRIBUTE, Endre Szabo, 7,500	45.00	NR
1980	HIS MASTER'S VOICE, <1 year	24.50	NR
1981	EYES OF THE SEASONS, 19,500, set of 4	154.00	NR
1982	NORMAN ROCKWELL TRIBUTE, George Malik, 5,000	55.00	NR
1982	BETTY BOOP, 15,000	24.50	NR
1982	WHITE HOUSE PANDA, Bogdan Grom, 15,000	38.50	NR
1984	GO FOR IT, ROCKY, Mike Hagel, 1 year	25.00	NR

MAFEKING COLLECTION

Forever Friends

1993	THE HIDEAWAY, M. Green, 500	85.00	RI
1994	RUFOUS HUMMINGBIRD, M. Green, 500	34.75	RI

		ISSUE	CURRENT

Lord's Children

1993	A FRAGRANCE IN TIME, M. Green, 500	85.00	RI
1993	HEAR MY PRAYERS, M. Green, 500	75.00	RI
1994	TRADITIONS, M. Green, 500	39.95	RI

Man's Best Friend

1993	DEREK, LABRADOR RETRIEVER, M. Green, 500	65.00	RI
1993	DIVOT, GERMAN SHEPHERD, M. Green, 500	85.00	RI
1994	MICKEY, SPANIEL CROSS, M. Green, 500	39.95	RI
1994	PEPPER, AIREDALE, M. Green, 500	39.95	RI

My Little Bear

1993	BEAR WITH ME, M. Green, 500	85.00	RI
1993	SHIZAM THE MAGICIAN, M. Green, 500	85.00	RI

MANJUNDO JAPAN

Chinese Lunar Calendar

1972	YEAR OF THE RAT, 5,000	15.00	NR
1973	YEAR OF THE OX, 5,000	15.00	NR
1974	YEAR OF THE MONKEY, 5,000	15.00	NR

MARCH OF DIMES

(Artaffects, Edna Hibel Studios, Pemberton & Oakes, Reco International, Roman, Inc.)

Our Children, Our Future

1989	A TIME FOR PEACE, Donald Zolan, 150 days	29.00	40.00
1989	A TIME FOR LOVE, Sandra Kuck, 150 days	29.00	35.00
1989	A TIME TO PLANT, John McClelland, 150 days	29.00	NR

A Time for Love
Photo courtesy of *Collectors News*

A Time to Plant
Photo courtesy of *Collectors News*

		ISSUE	CURRENT
1989	A TIME TO BE BORN, Gregory Perillo, 150 days	29.00	NR
1990	A TIME TO EMBRACE, Edna Hibel, 150 days	29.00	NR
1990	A TIME TO LAUGH, Abbie Williams, 150 days	29.00	NR

MARIGOLD

Picasso

1984	TETE APPUYEE SUR LES MAINS, 7,777	50.00	NR

Sport

1989	MICKEY MANTLE, Pablo Carreno, 10,000	60.00	195.00
1989	MICKEY MANTLE, Pablo Carreno, sgd, 1,000	100.00	700.00
1989	JOE DIMAGGIO, Pablo Carreno, sgd, 10,000	100.00	NR
1989	JOE DIMAGGIO, Pablo Carreno, blue signature	60.00	NR
1989	JOE DIMAGGIO, Pablo Carreno, sgd, artist proof	NA	NA

MARMOT GERMANY

Christmas

1970	POLAR BEAR, 5,000	13.00	60.00
1971	AMERICAN BUFFALO, 6,000	14.50	50.00
1971	BUFFALO BILL, 6,000	16.00	35.00
1972	BOY AND GRANDFATHER, 5,000	20.00	55.00
1973	SNOWMAN, 3,000	22.00	45.00
1974	DANCING, 2,000	24.00	30.00
1975	QUAIL, 2,000	30.00	40.00
1976	WINDMILL, 2,000	40.00	NR

Father's Day

1970	STAG, 3,500	12.00	100.00
1971	HORSE, 3,500	12.50	40.00

Mother's Day

1972	SEAL, 6,000	16.00	60.00
1973	BEAR WITH CUB, 3,000	20.00	140.00
1974	PENGUINS, 2,000	24.00	50.00
1975	RACCOONS, 2,000	30.00	45.00
1976	DUCKS, 2,000	40.00	NR

Presidents

1971	WASHINGTON, 1,500	25.00	NR
1972	JEFFERSON, 1,500	25.00	NR
1973	JOHN ADAMS, 1,500	25.00	NR

MARTY BELL FINE ART UNITED STATES

In a Cottage Garden

1992	UPPER CHUTE, Marty Bell, 14 days	38.50	RI
1997	HOLLYBUSH, Marty Bell, 14 days	38.50	RI

MARURI UNITED STATES

Eagle Plate

		ISSUE	CURRENT
1984	FREE FLIGHT, W. Gaither, 995	150.00	NR

Treasures of the Sky

		ISSUE	CURRENT
1998	ANNA'S WITH LILY, open	39.95	RI

MARY ENGELBREIT SOCIETY UNITED STATES

Believe Series

		ISSUE	CURRENT
1986	SANTA'S TREASURE, Mary Engelbreit, 10,000	29.95	NR

MASON GREAT BRITAIN

Christmas

		ISSUE	CURRENT
1975	WINDSOR CASTLE, 1 year	75.00	NR
1976	HOLYROOD HOUSE, 1 year	75.00	NR
1977	BUCKINGHAM PALACE, 1 year	75.00	NR
1978	BALMORAL CASTLE, 1 year	75.00	NR
1979	HAMPTON COURT, 1 year	75.00	NR
1980	SANDRINGHAM HOUSE, 1 year	75.00	NR

MASTERS OF PALEKH

Gifts of the Seasons

		ISSUE	CURRENT
1993	THE TWELVE MONTHS	35.87	RI
1993	WOODLAND MAJESTY	35.87	RI
1993	A BASKET OF SNOWDROPS	35.87	RI
1993	THE WARMTH OF FRIENDSHIP	35.87	RI

MEISSEN GERMANY

Annual

		ISSUE	CURRENT
1973	WINTER COUNTRYSIDE BY SLEIGH, 5,000	71.00	NR
1974	SLEEPING BEAUTY, 5,000	75.00	NR
1975	ARCHWAY TO ALBRECHT'S CASTLE, 5,500	92.00	NR
1976	DOGE'S PALACE IN VENICE, 5,000	92.00	NR
1977	FRA HOLLE, 5,000	114.00	NR
1978	ICE CRYSTAL WITH CHILDREN, 7,000	123.00	NR
1979	WINTER FAIRY TALE, 7,000	151.00	NR
1980	BOOTED CAT	155.00	NR

METAL ARTS COMPANY UNITED STATES

Children of Norman Rockwell (Hamilton Collection)

		ISSUE	CURRENT
1979	DOCTOR AND DOLL, Norman Rockwell, 19,750	21.00	NR

		ISSUE	CURRENT
1979	KNUCKLES DOWN, Norman Rockwell, 19,750	21.00	NR
1979	GRANDPA'S GIRL, Norman Rockwell, 19,750	21.00	NR
1979	LEAPFROG, Norman Rockwell, 19,750	21.00	NR
1980	DOG GONE IT, Norman Rockwell, 19,750	21.00	NR
1980	LOOK OUT BELOW, Norman Rockwell, 19,750	21.00	NR
1980	BATTER UP, Norman Rockwell, 19,750	21.00	NR
1980	NO PEEKING, Norman Rockwell, 19,750	21.00	NR

Norman Rockwell Christmas (Hamilton Collection)

1978	THE CHRISTMAS GIFT, Norman Rockwell, 1 year	48.00	NR
1979	THE BIG MOMENT, Norman Rockwell, 1 year	48.00	NR
1980	SANTA'S HELPERS, Norman Rockwell, 1 year	48.00	NR
1981	SANTA, Norman Rockwell, 1 year	48.00	NR

Norman Rockwell Man's Best Friend (Hamilton Collection)

1979	THE HOBO, Norman Rockwell, 9,500	40.00	60.00
1979	THE DOCTOR, Norman Rockwell, 9,500	40.00	NR
1979	MAKING FRIENDS, Norman Rockwell, 9,500	40.00	NR
1979	GONE FISHING, Norman Rockwell, 9,500	40.00	NR
1980	THE THIEF, Norman Rockwell, 9,500	40.00	NR
1980	PUPPY LOVE, Norman Rockwell, 9,500	40.00	NR

Winslow Homer's The Sea

1977	BREEZING UP, 9,500	29.95	NR

Single Issues

1977	AMERICA'S FIRST FAMILY—CARTERS, 9,500	40.00	NR
1977	WASHINGTON AT VALLEY FORGE, pewter, 9,500	95.00	NR
1977	WASHINGTON AT VALLEY FORGE, sterling silver, 500	225.00	NR

METAWA NETHERLANDS

Christmas

1972	ICE SKATERS, 3,000	30.00	NR
1973	ONE-HORSE SLEIGH, 1,500	30.00	NR
1974	SAILBOAT, 1 year	35.00	NR

METROPOLITAN MUSEUM OF ART UNITED STATES

Metropolitan Cat

1986	TWO CATS, Felix Vallotton	12.00	NR

Treasures of Tutankhamen

1977	KING TUT, 2,500	150.00	170.00

METTLACH GERMANY

Christmas

1978	CHRISTMAS, 20,000	175.00	BR

		ISSUE	CURRENT
1979	MOTHER WITH CHILD, 10,000	298.00	BR
1980	MADONNA IN GLORY, 10,000	210.00	NR

Collectors Society

1980	SNOW WHITE AND SEVEN DWARFS, 1 year	60.00	NR

Mother's Day Plaque

1978	MOTHER'S DAY, 15,000	100.00	NR

MICHELON ENTERPRISES

Quiet Places

1981	DAY DREAMING, Tom Heflin, 5,000	75.00	NR
1981	TRY TO REMEMBER, Tom Heflin, 5,000	75.00	NR
1981	EMMETT'S GATE, Tom Heflin, 5,000	75.00	NR

Day Dreaming
Photo courtesy of *Collectors News*

MICHIGAN NATURAL RESOURCES UNITED STATES

Nature's Heritage

1982	WHITE-TAILED FAWN, Richard Timm, 14,500	37.50	NR

MINGOLLA / HOME PLATES UNITED STATES

Christmas

1973	CHRISTMAS, enamel on copper, 1,000	95.00	165.00
1974	CHRISTMAS, enamel on copper, 1,000	100.00	145.00
1974	CHRISTMAS, porcelain, 5,000	35.00	65.00
1975	CHRISTMAS, enamel on copper, 1,000	125.00	145.00
1975	CHRISTMAS, porcelain, 5,000	35.00	45.00
1976	CHRISTMAS, enamel on copper, 1,000	125.00	NR
1976	CHRISTMAS, porcelain, 5,000	35.00	NR
1977	WINTER WONDERLAND, enamel on copper, 2,000	200.00	NR

Four Seasons

		ISSUE	CURRENT
1978	DASHING THROUGH THE SNOW, 2,000	150.00	NR
1978	SPRING FLOWERS, 2,000	150.00	NR
1978	BEACH FUN, 2,000	150.00	NR
1978	BALLOON BREEZES, 2,000	150.00	NR

MISTWOOD DESIGNS UNITED STATES

American Wildlife

1981	DESPERADO AT THE WATERHOLE, Skipper Kendricks, 5,000	45.00	NR
1982	BAYOU BUNNIES, Skipper Kendricks, 5,000	45.00	NR

Desperado at the Waterhole
Photo courtesy of *Collectors News*

Enough for Two
Photo courtesy of *Collectors News*

MODERN CONCEPTS LIMITED UNITED STATES

Magic of the Sea

1983	FUTURE MISS, Lucelle Raad, limited	25.00	NR
1984	ONE, TWO, THREE!, Lucelle Raad, limited	26.50	NR

Nursery Rhyme Favorites

1984	SUGAR AND SPICE, Lucelle Raad, 7,500	38.50	NR
1984	SNIPS AND SNAILS, Lucelle Raad, 7,500	38.50	NR

Signs of Love

1983	WHEN HEARTS TOUCH, Lucelle Raad, 19,500	39.50	NR
1984	MY VERY OWN, Lucelle Raad, 19,500	39.50	NR

Special Moments

1982	DAVID'S DILEMMA, Lucelle Raad, 12,500	35.00	50.00

		ISSUE	CURRENT
1983	SECRETS, Lucelle Raad, 12,500	35.00	NR
1983	ENOUGH FOR TWO, Lucelle Raad,12,500	38.50	NR
1984	CHATTERBOX, Lucelle Raad, 12,500	38.50	NR

MODERN MASTERS UNITED STATES

Babes in the Woods

1982	NEWBORN FAWN, Sally Miller, 9,500	45.00	NR
1983	FIRST OUTING, Sally Miller, 9,500	45.00	NR
1983	BANDY BANDIT, Sally Miller, 9,500	50.00	NR
1984	MOMENT'S REST, Sally Miller, 9,500	50.00	BR

Child's Best Friend

1982	CHRISTI'S KITTY, Richard Zolan, 15 days	29.50	NR
1982	PATRICK'S PUPPY, Richard Zolan, 15 days	29.50	NR

Floral Felines

1983	THE BARON, Julie Shearer, 9,500	55.00	NR
1984	HER MAJESTY, Julie Shearer, 9,500	55.00	NR
1984	DUCHESS, Julie Shearer, 9,500	55.00	NR
1984	HIS LORDSHIP, Julie Shearer, 9,500	55.00	NR

Litter Baskets Collection

1983	LAST OF THE LITTER, Sally Miller, 15 days	35.00	NR
1984	DOUBLE DELIGHT, Sally Miller, 15 days	35.00	NR
1984	TENDER TRIO, Sally Miller, 15 days	35.00	NR
1985	LITTER BUG, Sally Miller, 15 days	35.00	NR
1985	HIDE 'N SEEK, Sally Miller, 15 days	35.00	NR
1985	POODLE PICNIC, Sally Miller, 15 days	35.00	NR

Little Ladies

1983	WHEN MOMMY'S AWAY, Claire Freedman, limited	29.50	NR
1984	BEFORE THE SHOW BEGINS, Claire Freedman, limited	29.50	NR

Sally Miller Christmas

1985	THEY CAME TO ADORE HIM, Sally Miller, 5,000	39.50	NR

Through the Eyes of Love

1981	ENCHANTED EYES, Karin Schaefers, 9,500	55.00	NR
1982	SUMMER SECRETS, Karin Schaefers, 9,500	55.00	NR
1983	GARDEN GATHERING, Karin Schaefers, 9,500	55.00	NR

Will Moses' America

1982	SEPTEMBER FAIR, Will Moses, 7,500	45.00	NR
1983	SPRING RECESS, Will Moses, 7,500	45.00	NR

Wings of Nobility

1984	AMERICAN BALD EAGLE, Sally Miller, 7,500	42.50	NR
1984	PEREGRINE FALCON, Sally Miller, 7,500	49.50	NR
1984	RED-SHOULDERED HAWK, Sally Miller, 7,500	49.50	NR

Christi's Kitty
Photo courtesy of *Collectors News*

American Bald Eagle
Photo courtesy of *Collectors News*

Single Issue

		ISSUE	CURRENT
1983	TWELVE DAYS OF CHRISTMAS, Will Moses, 12 days	45.00	NR

MONACO PORCELAIN FACTORY MONACO

Day and Night

		ISSUE	CURRENT
1983	LE NUIT, Erich Rozewica, 600	—	—
1983	LE JOUR, Erich Rozewica, 600	—	—
	Set of 2	200.00	NR

MOORCROFT

Annual

		ISSUE	CURRENT
1983	PLATE	NA	NA

MORGANTOWN CRYSTAL UNITED STATES

Heavens Above

		ISSUE	CURRENT
1989	CASSIOPEIA, Michael Yates, open	64.50	NR
1990	ORION, Michael Yates, open	64.50	NR
1990	PEGASUS, Michael Yates, open	64.50	NR
1991	CYGNUS, Michael Yates, open	64.50	NR

Star of Bethlehem

		ISSUE	CURRENT
1988	THE HOLY FAMILY, Merri Roderick, open	34.50	NR
1989	SHEPHERDS IN THE FIELD, Merri Roderick, open	34.50	NR
1990	LED BY THE STAR, Merri Roderick, open	37.50	NR
1991	TIDINGS OF GREAT JOY, Merri Roderick, open	37.50	NR

Tidings of Great Joy
Photo courtesy of *Collectors News*

Laurel
Photo courtesy of *Collectors News*

Yate's Country Ladies

		ISSUE	CURRENT
1981	ANGELICA, Michael Yates, open	75.00	NR
1982	VIOLET, Michael Yates, open	75.00	NR
1983	HEATHER, Michael Yates, open	75.00	NR
1984	LAUREL, Michael Yates, open	75.00	90.00

MOSER CZECHOSLOVAKIA

Christmas

1970	HRADCANY CASTLE, 400	75.00	170.00
1971	KARLSTEIN CASTLE, 1,365	75.00	85.00
1972	OLD TOWN HALL, 1,000	85.00	NR
1973	KARLOVY VARY CASTLE, 500	90.00	100.00

Mother's Day

1971	PEACOCKS, 350	75.00	100.00
1972	BUTTERFLIES, 750	85.00	NR
1973	SQUIRRELS, 500	90.00	NR

MOUSSALLI UNITED STATES

Birds of Four Seasons

1977	CEDAR WAXWING, 1,000	375.00	450.00
1978	CARDINAL, 1,000	375.00	425.00
1978	WREN, 1,000	375.00	NR
1979	HUMMINGBIRD, 1,000	375.00	NR
1979	INDIGO BUNTING, 1,000	375.00	NR

Mother's Day

1979	CHICKADEE, 500	450.00	NR

MUNRO COLLECTIBLES UNITED STATES

A World of Wonder

		ISSUE	CURRENT
1993	MY CAT PRINCESS, Frances Hook, 150 days	29.50	RI

NABISCO

Cream of Wheat Plates

		ISSUE	CURRENT
1996	ALREADY DREAMING, Haddon Sundblom, 1,500	29.95	RI
1996	AHEAD OF HIM, Haddon Sundblom, 1,500	29.95	RI

NASSAU ART GALLERY BAHAMAS

Collector Plates of the Bahamas

		ISSUE	CURRENT
1982	BAHAMAS 1982, Elyse Wasile, 5,000	35.00	NR
1982	GREGORY'S ARCH, Elyse Wasile, 5,000	35.00	NR

NEWELL POTTERY UNITED STATES

Calendar Series

		ISSUE	CURRENT
1984	JUNE, Sarah Stilwell Weber, limited	19.00	NR
1985	JULY, Sarah Stilwell Weber, limited	19.00	NR
1985	AUGUST, Sarah Stilwell Weber, limited	19.00	NR
1985	SEPTEMBER, Sarah Stilwell Weber, limited	19.00	NR
1985	OCTOBER, Sarah Stilwell Weber, limited	19.00	NR
1985	NOVEMBER, Sarah Stilwell Weber, limited	19.00	NR
1986	DECEMBER, Sarah Stilwell Weber, limited	19.00	NR
1986	JANUARY, Sarah Stilwell Weber, limited	19.00	NR
1986	FEBRUARY, Sarah Stilwell Weber, limited	19.00	NR
1986	MARCH, Sarah Stilwell Weber, limited	19.00	NR
1986	APRIL, Sarah Stilwell Weber, limited	19.00	25.00
1986	MAY, Sarah Stilwell Weber, limited	19.00	50.00

NORITAKE JAPAN

Annual

		ISSUE	CURRENT
1977	PARADISE BIRDS, 3,000	380.00	NR
1978	CHRYSANTHEMUMS, 3,000	494.00	NR
1979	CRANES, 3,000	556.00	NR
1980	WATER LILIES AND BUTTERFLIES, 3,000	575.00	NR

Christmas

		ISSUE	CURRENT
1975	MADONNA WITH CHILD, 3,000	42.00	NR
1975	GRATIA HOSO KAWA, 3,000	54.00	NR
1977	JULIA OTAA, 3,000	83.00	NR
1978	AMAKUSA SHIRO, 3,000	109.00	NR
1979	MUNZIO ITO, 3,000	124.00	NR
1980	FURST TAKAYANA, 3,000	125.00	NR

NORMAN ROCKWELL GALLERY UNITED STATES

(Rockwell Society)

Rockwell Centennial

		ISSUE	CURRENT
1993	THE TOY MAKER, Norman Rockwell	39.90	RI
1993	THE COBBLER, Norman Rockwell	39.90	RI
1994	THE LIGHTHOUSE KEEPER'S DAUGHTER, Norman Rockwell	44.90	RI
1994	THE SHIP BUILDER, Norman Rockwell	44.90	RI
1994	THE MUSIC MASTER, Norman Rockwell	44.90	RI
1994	THE TYCOON, Norman Rockwell	49.90	RI
1994	THE PAINTER, Norman Rockwell	49.90	RI
1994	THE STORYTELLER, Norman Rockwell	49.90	RI

Rockwell's Main Street

1994	THE STUDIO, Norman Rockwell	44.90	RI
1994	THE ANTIQUE SHOP, Norman Rockwell	44.90	RI
1994	THE COUNTRY STORE, Norman Rockwell	44.90	RI
1994	THE TOWN OFFICES, Norman Rockwell	44.90	RI

NOSTALGIA COLLECTIBLES UNITED STATES

Hispanic Collectors

1995	LA GARITA, E. Diuz, 9,000	30.00	RI
1995	RINCONCITO CRIOLLO, L. Casiga, 12,000	30.00	RI
1995	A LA LUZ DE MI BALCON, J. Fellin, 12,000	30.00	RI

O.K. COLLECTIBLES

Fantasy Farm

1984	LOWENA, Louise Sigle, 3,000	39.95	NR

Single Issues

1984	CHESTER, Ralph Waterhouse, 5,000	55.00	NR

Chester
Photo courtesy of *Collectors News*

		ISSUE	CURRENT
1984	MIDWESTERN SUMMER, Jeanne Horak, 4,500	50.00	NR
1984	MORNING IN THE MARSHLAND, Evel Knievel, 15,000	50.00	NR

ON BASE ORIGINALS UNITED STATES

Dr. K (Dwight Gooden)

1986	SIGNED PLATE, Joseph Catalano, 1,000	NA	NA
1986	UNSIGNED PLATE, Joseph Catalano, 2,000	NA	NA

OPA'S HAUS GERMANY

Annual German Christmas (Weihnachten)

1978	ANNUAL CHRISTMAS PLATE, 2,500	58.00	NR
1979	ANNUAL CHRISTMAS PLATE, 2,500	58.00	NR
1980	ANNUAL CHRISTMAS PLATE, 2,500	58.00	NR
1981	ANNUAL CHRISTMAS PLATE, 2,500	58.00	NR
1982	ANNUAL CHRISTMAS PLATE, 2,500	58.00	NR
1983	ANNUAL CHRISTMAS PLATE, 2,500	58.00	NR
1984	ANNUAL CHRISTMAS PLATE, 2,500	58.00	NR

ORREFORS SWEDEN

Annual Cathedral

1970	NOTRE DAME, 5,000	50.00	65.00
1971	WESTMINSTER ABBEY, 5,000	45.00	NR
1972	BASILICA DE SAN MARCO, 5,000	50.00	60.00
1973	COLOGNE CATHEDRAL, 5,000	50.00	65.00
1974	RUE DE LA VICTOIRE, 5,000	60.00	70.00
1975	BASILICA DE SAN PIETRO, 5,000	85.00	110.00
1976	CHRIST CHURCH, 3,000	85.00	NR
1977	MASJID-I-SHAH, 3,000	90.00	100.00
1978	SANTIAGO DE COMPOSTELA, 3,000	95.00	NR

Mother's Day

1971	FLOWERS FOR MOTHER, 1 year	45.00	60.00
1972	MOTHER AND CHILDREN, 1 year	45.00	NR
1973	MOTHER AND CHILD, 1 year	50.00	NR
1974	MOTHER AND CHILD, 1 year	50.00	NR
1975	MOTHER AND CHILD, 1 year	60.00	NR
1976	CHILDREN AND PUPPY, 1 year	75.00	BR
1977	CHILD AND DOVE, 1,500	85.00	NR
1978	MOTHER AND CHILD, 1,500	90.00	NR

OSIRIS PORCELAIN EGYPT

Cleopatra: Queen of Ancient Egypt

1991	CLEOPATRA MEETS ANTONY, Charles Grayson	39.84	60.00
1992	CLEOPATRA AND THE ASP, Charles Grayson	39.84	85.00

		ISSUE	CURRENT
1992	ADORNING THE QUEEN, Charles Grayson	39.84	70.00
1992	ENTERTAINING CLEOPATRA, Charles Grayson	39.84	95.00

Egypt: Splendors of an Ancient World

1993	GOLDEN MASK OF TUTANKHAMEN	79.00	RI
1993	NEFERTITI: THE ETERNAL BEAUTY	79.00	RI
1993	CLEOPATRA: EMPRESS AND ENCHANTRESS	84.00	RI
1993	RAMSES II—THE WARRIOR OF PHARAOH	84.00	RI
1993	THE REFORMER KING, AKHENATEN	84.00	RI
1993	HATSHEPSUT—THE PHARAOH QUEEN	84.00	RI

Legend of Tutankhamen

1991	TUTANKHAMEN AND HIS PRINCESS, Nageh Nassif Pichay	39.84	BR
1991	THE MARRIAGE OF TUTANKHAMEN, Nageh Nassif Pichay	39.84	NR
1991	BANQUET IN THE ROYAL GARDENS, Nageh Nassif Pichay	42.84	NR
1991	GAME OF SENET, Nageh Nassif Pichay	42.84	NR
1991	ADORNMENTS FOR THE KING, Nageh Nassif Pichay	42.84	NR
1992	FISHING ON THE NILE, Nageh Nassif Pichay	44.84	55.00
1992	GIFTS FROM FARAWAY PLACES, Nageh Nassif Pichay	44.84	70.00
1992	TRUE LOVES OF THE NEW KINGDOM, Nageh Nassif Pichay	44.84	75.00

Cleopatra Meets Antony
Photo courtesy of *Collectors News*

Banquet in the Royal Gardens
Photo courtesy of *Collectors News*

PACIFIC ART LIMITED UNITED STATES

Just Like Daddy's Hats

1983	JESSICA, Franklin Moody, 10,000	29.00	NR

Victoria and Jason

1983	VICTORIA, Lee Dubin, 7,500	—	—
1983	JASON, Lee Dubin, 7,500	—	—
	Set of 2	65.00	NR

		ISSUE	CURRENT

Single Issues

1983	MAE WEST, Bob Harman, 5,000	42.50	NR
1983	GUARDIAN ANGEL, Lily Cavell, 7,500	29.50	NR

PALISANDER DENMARK

Christmas

1971	RED ROBIN, 1,200	50.00	65.00
1972	FLYING GEESE, 1,200	50.00	60.00
1973	CHRISTMAS, 1,200	50.00	NR

Presidential

1971	WASHINGTON, 1,000	50.00	NR
1972	JEFFERSON, 1,000	50.00	NR
1973	JOHN ADAMS, 1,000	50.00	NR

Single Issue

1973	BICENTENNIAL, 250	50.00	NR

PALLADIUM PRESS UNITED STATES

America's Wars and Its Firearms

1997	GENERAL PATTON AT THE BATTLE OF THE BULGE, Jim Dietz	42.95	RI
1997	PICKETT'S CHARGE AT THE BATTLE OF GETTYSBURG, Jim Dietz	42.95	RI
1997	GEORGE WASHINGTON AT THE BATTLE OF TRENTON, Jim Dietz	42.95	RI
1997	ALVIN YORK AT THE BATTLE OF THE ARGONNE, Jim Dietz	42.95	RI
1997	ULYSSES S GRANT AT THE BATTLE OF VICKSBURG, Jim Dietz	42.95	RI
1997	BUFFALO BILL CODY IN THE SIOUX INDIAN WARS, Jim Dietz	42.95	RI
1997	THEODORE ROOSEVELT AT SAN JUAN HILL, Jim Dietz	42.95	RI
1997	THE BATTLE FOR HAMBURGER HILL, Jim Dietz	42.95	RI
1997	GENERAL OLIVER SMITH AT CHOSIN RESERVOIR, Jim Dietz	42.95	RI
1997	GENERAL WINFIELD SCOTT AT THE HALLS OF MONTEZUMA, Jim Dietz	42.95	RI
1997	GENERAL ANDY JACKSON AT THE BATTLE OF NEW ORLEANS, Jim Dietz	42.95	RI
1997	DAVY CROCKETT AT THE ALAMO, Jim Dietz	42.95	RI

PAPEL

Olympics

1984	SPORTS PLATE, 1 year	30.00	NR
1984	STAR IN MOTION, 25,000	17.00	NR
1984	SAM THE OLYMPIC EAGLE, 25,000	17.00	NR

PARKHURST & BOWER UNITED STATES

Single Issue

1984	I LOVE TEDDY BEARS, Violet Parkhurst	39.50	NR

PARKHURST ENTERPRISES UNITED STATES

International Wildlife Foundation

		ISSUE	CURRENT
1984	PANDAS, Violet Parkhurst, 1,000	60.00	NR
1984	GRIZZLIES, Violet Parkhurst, 1,000	60.00	NR
1984	ELEPHANTS, Violet Parkhurst, 1,000	60.00	NR
1984	BENGAL TIGERS, Violet Parkhurst, 1,000	60.00	NR
1984	POLAR BEARS, Violet Parkhurst, 1,000	60.00	NR
1984	SNOW LEOPARDS, Violet Parkhurst, 1,000	60.00	NR
1984	HARP SEALS, Violet Parkhurst, 1,000	60.00	NR
1984	GIRAFFES, Violet Parkhurst, 1,000	60.00	NR
1984	BACTRIAN CAMEL, Violet Parkhurst, 1,000	60.00	NR
1984	HIPPOS, Violet Parkhurst, 1,000	60.00	NR
1984	LIONS, Violet Parkhurst, 1,000	60.00	NR
1984	CHEETAHS, Violet Parkhurst, 1,000	60.00	NR

Lions
Photo courtesy of *Collectors News*

Cardinals and Mistletoe
Photo courtesy of *Collectors News*

PAVILION OF T'SANG YING-HAUAN TAIWAN

Chinese Children's Games

1986	CHINESE CHESS	29.00	BR
1986	KITE FLYING	29.00	BR
1986	SPINNING TOPS	32.00	BR
1987	ROLLING HOOPS	32.00	BR
1987	BLIND MAN BLUFF	32.00	NR
1988	KICKING GAMES	32.00	NR

PAWNEE CREEK PRESS

Christmas Classics

1984	CARDINALS AND MISTLETOE, James Landenberger, 2,000	50.00	NR

PEMBERTON & OAKES UNITED STATES

(March of Dimes, Viletta)

Adventures of Childhood

		ISSUE	CURRENT
1989	ALMOST HOME, Donald Zolan, 44 days	19.60	60.00
1989	CRYSTAL'S CREEK, Donald Zolan, 44 days	19.60	45.00
1989	SUMMER SUDS, Donald Zolan, 44 days	22.00	40.00
1990	SNOWY ADVENTURE, Donald Zolan, 44 days	22.00	40.00
1991	FORESTS AND FAIRY TALES, Donald Zolan, 44 days	24.40	40.00

The Best of Zolan in Miniature

1985	SABINA IN THE GRASS, Donald Zolan, 22 days	12.50	110.00
1986	ERIK AND THE DANDELION, Donald Zolan, 22 days	12.50	100.00
1986	TENDER MOMENT, Donald Zolan, 22 days	12.50	65.00
1986	TOUCHING THE SKY, Donald Zolan, 22 days	12.50	35.00
1987	A GIFT FOR LAURIE, Donald Zolan, 22 days	12.50	60.00
1987	SMALL WONDER, Donald Zolan, 22 days	12.50	40.00

Childhood Discoveries—Miniature

1990	COLORS OF SPRING, Donald Zolan, 19 days	14.40	35.00
1990	AUTUMN LEAVES, Donald Zolan, 19 days	14.40	40.00
1990	FIRST KISS, Donald Zolan, 19 days	14.40	45.00
1991	ENCHANTED FOREST, Donald Zolan, 19 days	16.60	30.00
1991	JUST DUCKY, Donald Zolan, 19 days	16.60	35.00
1991	RAINY DAY PALS, Donald Zolan, 19 days	16.60	30.00
1992	DOUBLE TROUBLE, Donald Zolan, 19 days	16.60	40.00
1993	PEPPERMINT KISS, Donald Zolan, 19 days	16.60	RI
1995	TENDER HEARTS, Donald Zolan, 19 days	16.60	RI

Childhood Friendship

1986	BEACH BREAK, Donald Zolan, 17 days	19.00	55.00
1987	LITTLE ENGINEERS, Donald Zolan, 17 days	19.00	60.00
1988	TINY TREASURES, Donald Zolan, 17 days	19.00	40.00
1988	SHARING SECRETS, Donald Zolan, 17 days	19.00	50.00
1988	DOZENS OF DAISIES, Donald Zolan, 17 days	19.00	45.00
1990	COUNTRY WALK, Donald Zolan, 17 days	19.00	35.00

Children and Pets

1984	TENDER MOMENT, Donald Zolan, 28 days	19.00	45.00
1984	GOLDEN MOMENT, Donald Zolan, 28 days	19.00	70.00
1985	MAKING FRIENDS, Donald Zolan, 28 days	19.00	50.00
1985	TENDER BEGINNING, Donald Zolan, 28 days	19.00	35.00
1986	BACKYARD DISCOVERY, Donald Zolan, 28 days	19.00	45.00
1986	WAITING TO PLAY, Donald Zolan, 28 days	19.00	35.00

Children at Christmas

1981	A GIFT FOR LAURIE, Donald Zolan, 15,000	48.00	60.00
1982	A CHRISTMAS PRAYER, Donald Zolan, 15,000	48.00	100.00
1983	ERIK'S DELIGHT, Donald Zolan, 15,000	48.00	70.00
1984	CHRISTMAS SECRET, Donald Zolan, 15,000	48.00	65.00
1985	CHRISTMAS KITTEN, Donald Zolan, 15,000	48.00	65.00
1986	LAURIE AND THE CRÈCHE, Donald Zolan, 15,000	48.00	80.00

Christmas

		ISSUE	CURRENT
1991	CANDLELIGHT MAGIC, Donald Zolan, open	24.80	40.00

Christmas—Miniature

		ISSUE	CURRENT
1993	SNOWY ADVENTURE, Donald Zolan, 19 days	16.60	RI
1994	CANDELIGHT MAGIC, Donald Zolan, 19 days	16.60	RI
1995	LAURIE'S CRÈCHE, Donald Zolan, 19 days	16.60	RI

Companion to Brotherly Love

		ISSUE	CURRENT
1989	SISTERLY LOVE, Donald Zolan, 15,000	22.00	35.00

Easter—Miniature

		ISSUE	CURRENT
1991	EASTER MORNING, Donald Zolan, 19 days	16.60	40.00

Father's Day

		ISSUE	CURRENT
1986	DADDY'S HOME, Donald Zolan, 19 days	19.00	65.00

Father's Day—Miniature

		ISSUE	CURRENT
1986	TWO OF A KIND, Donald Zolan	16.60	40.00

Grandparent's Day

		ISSUE	CURRENT
1990	IT'S GRANDMA AND GRANDPA, Donald Zolan, 19 days	24.40	40.00
1993	GRANDPA'S FENCE, Donald Zolan, 13 days	24.40	RI

Heirloom Ovals

		ISSUE	CURRENT
1992	MY KITTY, Donald Zolan, 1 year	18.80	45.00

Little Girls

		ISSUE	CURRENT
1985	CURIOUS KITTEN, Robert Anderson	29.00	85.00
1986	MAKING MAGIC, Robert Anderson	29.00	55.00
1986	SUNNY UMBRELLA, Robert Anderson	29.00	NR
1987	APPLE BLOSSOM TIME, Robert Anderson	29.00	NR

Membership—Miniature

		ISSUE	CURRENT
1987	FOR YOU, Donald Zolan, 19 days	12.50	100.00
1988	MAKING FRIENDS, Donald Zolan, 19 days	12.50	75.00
1989	GRANDMA'S GARDEN, Donald Zolan, 19 days	12.50	65.00
1990	A CHRISTMAS PRAYER, Donald Zolan, 19 days	14.40	55.00
1991	GOLDEN MOMENT, Donald Zolan, 19 days	16.60	45.00
1992	BROTHERLY LOVE, Donald Zolan, 19 days	16.60	75.00
1993	NEW SHOES, Donald Zolan, 19 days	16.60	RI
1994	MY KITTY, Donald Zolan, 19 days	NA	RI

Members Only Single Issues—Miniature

		ISSUE	CURRENT
1990	BY MYSELF, Donald Zolan, 19 days	14.40	45.00
1993	SUMMER'S CHILD, Donald Zolan, 19 days	16.60	RI
1994	LITTLE SLUGGER, Donald Zolan, 19 days	16.60	RI

Moments Alone

		ISSUE	CURRENT
1980	THE DREAMER, Robert Bentley, <1 year	28.80	45.00

		ISSUE	CURRENT
1981	REVERIE, Robert Bentley, <1 year	28.80	NR
1982	GENTLE THOUGHTS, Robert Bentley, <1 year	28.80	35.00
1983	WHEAT FIELDS, Robert Bentley, <1 year	28.80	NR

Moments to Remember—Miniature

1992	JUST WE TWO, Donald Zolan, 19 days	16.60	55.00
1992	ALMOST HOME, Donald Zolan, 19 days	16.60	40.00
1993	TINY TREASURES, Donald Zolan, 19 days	16.60	RI
1993	FOREST FRIENDS, Donald Zolan, 19 days	16.60	RI

Mother's Day

1988	MOTHER'S ANGELS, Donald Zolan, 19 days	19.00	75.00

Mother's Day—Miniature

1990	FLOWERS FOR MOTHER, Donald Zolan, 19 days	14.40	40.00
1992	TWILIGHT PRAYER, Donald Zolan, 19 days	16.60	35.00
1993	JESSICA'S FIELD, Donald Zolan, 19 days	16.60	RI
1994	ONE SUMMER DAY, Donald Zolan, 19 days	16.60	RI
1995	LITTLE BALLERINA, Donald Zolan, 19 days	16.60	RI

Nutcracker II

1981	GRANDE FINALE, Shell Fisher, <1 year	24.40	35.00
1982	THE ARABIAN DANCERS, Shell Fisher, <1 year	24.40	70.00
1983	DEW DROP FAIRY, Shell Fisher, limited	24.40	35.00
1984	CLARA'S DELIGHT, Shell Fisher, limited	24.40	40.00
1985	BEDTIME FOR NUTCRACKER, Shell Fisher, limited	24.40	45.00
1986	CROWNING OF CLARA, Shell Fisher, limited	24.40	35.00
1987	DANCE OF THE SNOWFLAKES, Donald Zolan, limited	24.40	50.00
1988	THE ROYAL WELCOME, Robert Anderson	24.40	35.00
1989	THE SPANISH DANCER, Mary Vickers	24.40	45.00

Paintings by Donald Zolan

1995	GOLDEN HARVEST, Donald Zolan, 1 year	16.60	RI
1995	MY NEW KITTEN, Donald Zolan, 1 year	16.60	RI
1995	REFLECTIONS, Donald Zolan, 1 year	16.60	RI
1995	SECRET FRIENDS, Donald Zolan, 1 year	16.60	RI

Plaques

1991	NEW SHOES, Donald Zolan, 1 year	18.80	35.00
1991	FLOWERS FOR MOTHER, Donald Zolan, 1 year	18.80	40.00
1992	GRANDMA'S GARDEN, Donald Zolan, 1 year	18.80	40.00
1992	SMALL WONDER, Donald Zolan, 1 year	18.80	40.00
1992	EASTER MORNING, Donald Zolan, 1 year	18.80	40.00

Special Moments of Childhood

1988	BROTHERLY LOVE, Donald Zolan, 19 days	19.00	95.00
1988	SUNNY SURPRISE, Donald Zolan, 19 days	19.00	45.00
1989	SUMMER'S CHILD, Donald Zolan, 19 days	22.00	45.00
1990	MEADOW MAGIC, Donald Zolan, 19 days	22.00	30.00
1990	CONE FOR TWO, Donald Zolan, 19 days	24.60	30.00
1990	RODEO GIRL, Donald Zolan, 19 days	24.60	30.00

Enchanted Forest

Little Engineers

Erik's Delight

Candlelight Magic

Easter Morning

Daddy's Home

Photos courtesy of *Collectors News*

Making Magic

Making Friends

Almost Home

Jessica's Field

I'm Thankful Too

Little Traveler

Photos courtesy of *Collectors News*

Swan Lake

		ISSUE	CURRENT
1983	SWAN QUEEN, Shell Fisher, 15,000	35.00	65.00
1984	SWAN MAIDENS, Shell Fisher, 15,000	35.00	45.00
1984	SWAN LAKE ADAGIO, Shell Fisher, 15,000	35.00	45.00
1984	THE BLACK SWAN, Shell Fisher, 15,000	35.00	45.00
1985	THE DYING SWAN, Shell Fisher, 15,000	35.00	65.00

Tenth Anniversary

1988	RIBBONS AND ROSES, Donald Zolan, 19 days	24.40	40.00

Thanksgiving Day

1981	I'M THANKFUL TOO, Donald Zolan, 19 days	19.00	100.00

Thanksgiving—Miniature

1993	I'M THANKFUL TOO, Donald Zolan, 19 days	16.60	40.00

Times to Treasure, Bone China—Miniature

1993	LITTLE TRAVELER, Donald Zolan, 19 days	16.60	RI
1993	GARDEN SWING, Donald Zolan, 19 days	16.60	RI
1994	SUMMER GARDEN, Donald Zolan, 19 days	16.60	RI
1994	SEPTEMBER GIRL, Donald Zolan, 19 days	16.60	RI

Wonder of Childhood

1982	TOUCHING THE SKY, Donald Zolan, 22 days	19.00	35.00
1983	SPRING INNOCENCE, Donald Zolan, 22 days	19.00	NR
1984	WINTER ANGEL, Donald Zolan, 22 days	22.00	30.00
1985	SMALL WONDER, Donald Zolan, 22 days	22.00	35.00
1986	GRANDMA'S GARDEN, Donald Zolan, 22 days	22.00	NR
1987	DAY DREAMER, Donald Zolan, 22 days	22.00	35.00

Yesterday's Children—Miniature

1994	LITTLE FRIENDS, Donald Zolan, retrd	16.60	RI
1994	SEASIDE TREASURE, Donald Zolan, retrd	16.60	RI

Zolan's Children (Viletta)

1978	ERIK AND THE DANDELION, Donald Zolan, 1 year	19.00	90.00
1979	SABINA IN THE GRASS, Donald Zolan, 1 year	22.00	70.00
1980	BY MYSELF, Donald Zolan, 1 year	24.00	60.00
1981	FOR YOU, Donald Zolan, 1 year	24.00	35.00

Single Issue

1993	WINTER FRIENDS, Donald Zolan, retrd	18.80	RI
1993	WINDOW OF DREAMS, Donald Zolan, 19 days	18.80	RI

Single Issue, Bone China—Miniature

1992	WINDOW OF DREAMS, Donald Zolan, 19 days	18.80	35.00
1995	LITTLE SPLASHER, Donald Zolan, 19 days	16.60	RI

Single Issue, Day to Day—Spode

		ISSUE	CURRENT
1991	DAISY DAYS, Donald Zolan, 15,000	48.00	55.00

Single Issues—Miniature

		ISSUE	CURRENT
1986	BACKYARD DISCOVERY, Donald Zolan, 22 days	12.50	105.00
1986	DADDY'S HOME, Donald Zolan, 19 days	12.50	80.00
1989	SUNNY SURPRISE, Donald Zolan, 19 days	12.50	55.00
1989	MY PUMPKIN, Donald Zolan, 19 days	14.40	65.00
1991	BACKYARD BUDDIES, Donald Zolan, 19 days	16.60	50.00
1991	THE THINKER, Donald Zolan, 19 days	16.60	45.00
1993	QUIET TIME, Donald Zolan, 19 days	16.60	RI
1994	LITTLE FISHERMAN, Donald Zolan, 19 days	16.60	RI

Single Issue—Plaque

		ISSUE	CURRENT
1991	FLOWERS FOR MOTHER, Donald Zolan, 1 year	16.80	25.00

PENDELFIN

Plate Series

		ISSUE	CURRENT
NA	MOTHER WITH BABY, J. Heap, retrd	40.00	150.00
NA	FATHER, J. Heap, 7,500	40.00	NR
NA	WHOPPER, D. Roberts, 7,500	50.00	NR
NA	GINGERBREAD DAY, J. Heap, 7,500	55.00	NR
NA	CARAVAN, D. Roberts, 7,500	60.00	NR
NA	OLD SCHOOLHOUSE, J. Heap, 7,500	60.00	NR

PFAFF

Heritage

		ISSUE	CURRENT
1977	GERMANY, 2,500	40.00	55.00
1978	HOLLAND, 2,500	40.00	NR
1979	SWITZERLAND, 2,500	40.00	NR
1980	NORWAY, 2,500	40.00	NR

PFALTZGRAFF UNITED STATES

Single Issues

		ISSUE	CURRENT
1993	LITTLEST ANGEL, B. B. Richards, 5,000	18.50	RI
1994	CHRISTMAS TRADITION, B. B. Richards, 10,000	15.00	RI
1994	HARVEST MEMORIES, B. B. Richards, 10,000	15.00	RI

PHILADELPHIA DECAL UNITED STATES

Single Issue

		ISSUE	CURRENT
1996	VANISHING PARADISE, Pete Moustakos, 3,744	29.98	RI

PICKARD UNITED STATES
(Fairmont China)

Christmas

		ISSUE	CURRENT
1976	ALBA MADONNA, Raphael, 7,500	60.00	90.00
1977	THE NATIVITY, L. Lotto, 7,500	65.00	NR
1978	REST ON THE FLIGHT INTO EGYPT, G. David, 10,000	65.00	NR
1979	ADORATION OF THE MAGI, Sandro Botticelli, 10,000	70.00	NR
1980	MADONNA AND CHILD/INFANT ST. JOHN, Sodoma, 10,000	80.00	NR
1981	MADONNA AND CHILD WITH ANGELS, Memling, 10,000	90.00	NR

Children of Christmas Past

1983	SLEDDING ON CHRISTMAS DAY, 7,500	60.00	NR

Children of Mary Cassatt

1983	SIMONE IN WHITE BONNET, Mary Cassatt, 7,500	60.00	NR
1983	CHILDREN PLAYING ON BEACH, Mary Cassatt, 7,500	60.00	NR
1984	GIRL IN A STRAW HAT, Mary Cassatt, 7,500	60.00	NR
1984	YOUNG GIRLS, Mary Cassatt, 7,500	60.00	NR

Children of Mexico

1981	MARIA, J. Sanchez, 5,000	85.00	NR
1981	MIGUEL, J. Sanchez, 5,000	85.00	NR
1982	REGINA, J. Sanchez, 5,000	90.00	NR
1983	RAPHAEL, J. Sanchez, 5,000	90.00	NR

Children of Renoir

1978	GIRL WITH WATERING CAN, Auguste Renoir, 5,000	50.00	125.00
1978	CHILD IN WHITE, Auguste Renoir, 5,000	50.00	125.00
1979	GIRL WITH HOOP, Auguste Renoir, 5,000	55.00	75.00
1979	AT THE PIANO, Auguste Renoir, 5,000	55.00	75.00
1980	TWO LITTLE CIRCUS GIRLS, Auguste Renoir, 5,000	60.00	70.00
1980	ARTIST'S SON JEAN, Auguste Renoir, 5,000	60.00	65.00

Gardens of Monet

1986	SUMMER SPLENDOR, 3,500	85.00	NR
1987	A TIME GONE BY, 3,500	85.00	NR

Gems of Nature (Bradford Exchange)

1990	RUBY-THROATED WITH LILIES, Cyndi Nelson, 150 days	29.00	NR
1990	RUFOUS WITH APPLE BLOSSOMS, Cyndi Nelson, 150 days	29.00	NR
1990	BROAD-BILLED WITH PENSTEMON, Cyndi Nelson, 150 days	32.00	NR
1990	CALLIOPE WITH GLADIOLI, Cyndi Nelson, 150 days	32.00	45.00
1991	BLACK-CHINNED WITH FUCHSIA, Cyndi Nelson, 150 days	32.00	NR
1991	WHITE-EARED WITH PEONIES, Cyndi Nelson, 150 days	32.00	45.00
1991	ANNAS WITH PETUNIAS, Cyndi Nelson, 150 days	34.00	45.00
1991	COSTA'S HUMMINGBIRD WITH HOLLYHOCKS, Cyndi Nelson, 150 days	34.00	60.00

Hawaiian Splendor (Bradford Exchange)

1992	TROPICAL ENCHANTMENT, 150 days	34.00	NR
1993	COASTAL HARMONY, 150 days	34.00	RI

		ISSUE	CURRENT
1993	EVENING IN THE ISLANDS, 150 days	34.00	RI
1993	TWILIGHT PARADISE, 150 days	34.00	RI

Holiday Traditions

1992	CHRISTMAS HOMECOMING, 150 days	29.00	NR
1993	QUIET UNDER THE EAVES, 150 days	29.00	RI
1993	SNOWS OF YESTERYEAR, 150 days	29.00	RI
1993	HEART OF CHRISTMAS, 150 days	29.00	RI

Innocent Encounters (Bradford Exchange)

1988	MAKING FRIENDS, 150 days	34.00	NR
1988	JUST PASSING BY, 150 days	34.00	NR
1989	EYE TO EYE, 150 days	34.00	BR
1989	LET'S PLAY, 150 days	34.00	NR

Legends of Camelot

1982	MERLIN THE MAGICIAN, David Palladini, 12,500	62.50	NR
1982	THE SECRET ROMANCE, David Palladini, 12,500	62.50	NR
1982	I KNIGHT THEE SIR LANCELOT, David Palladini, 12,500	62.50	NR
1982	KING ARTHUR AND HIS QUEEN, David Palladini, 12,500	62.50	NR

Costa's Hummingbird with Hollyhocks
Photo courtesy of *Collectors News*

Cleopatra
Photo courtesy of *Collectors News*

Let's Pretend

1984	CLEOPATRA, Irene Spencer, 5,000	80.00	NR
1984	MARK ANTONY, Irene Spencer, 5,000	80.00	NR
1985	ROBIN HOOD, Irene Spencer, 5,000	80.00	NR
1985	MAID MARIAN, Irene Spencer, 5,000	80.00	NR

Lockhart Wildlife

1970	WOODCOCK and RUFFED GROUSE, James Lockhart, 2,000, pair	150.00	210.00
1971	GREEN-WINGED TEAL and MALLARD, James Lockhart, 2,000, pair	150.00	170.00

		ISSUE	CURRENT
1972	CARDINAL and MOCKINGBIRD, James Lockhart, 2,000, pair	162.50	BR
1973	PHEASANT and WILD TURKEY, James Lockhart, 2,000, pair	162.50	200.00
1974	AMERICAN BALD EAGLE, James Lockhart, 2,000, 13"	150.00	675.00
1975	WHITE-TAILED DEER, James Lockhart, 2,500, 11"	100.00	110.00
1976	AMERICAN BUFFALO, James Lockhart, 2,500, 13"	165.00	BR
1977	GREAT HORNED OWL, James Lockhart, 2,500, 11"	100.00	BR
1978	AMERICAN PANTHER, James Lockhart, 2,500, 13"	175.00	BR
1979	RED FOX, James Lockhart, 2,500, 11"	120.00	BR
1980	TRUMPETER SWAN, James Lockhart, 2,500, 13"	200.00	BR

Most Beautiful Women of All Time

1981	HELEN OF TROY, Oleg Cassini, 1 year	75.00	NR
1982	MARIE ANTOINETTE, Oleg Cassini, 1 year	75.00	NR
1983	LILLIE LANGTRY, Oleg Cassini, 1 year	75.00	NR
1984	SALOME, Oleg Cassini, 1 year	75.00	NR

Mother's Love

1980	MIRACLE, Irene Spencer, 7,500	95.00	NR
1981	STORY TIME, Irene Spencer, 7,500	110.00	NR
1982	FIRST EDITION, Irene Spencer, 7,500	115.00	NR
1983	PRECIOUS MOMENT, Irene Spencer, 7,500	120.00	140.00

Nativity Triptych

1986	UNTO US A CHILD IS BORN, John Lawson, 3,500	95.00	NR

Pickard Commemorative

1982	GREAT SEAL OF THE UNITED STATES, 10,000	95.00	NR
1984	STATUE OF LIBERTY, 10,000	150.00	NR
1990	STAR SPANGLED BANNER, 10,000	150.00	NR

Presidential

1972	TRUMAN, 3,000	35.00	NR
1973	LINCOLN, 5,000	35.00	NR

Unto Us a Child Is Born
Photo courtesy of *Collectors News*

From High Above
Photo courtesy of *Collectors News*

		ISSUE	CURRENT

Romantic Castles of Europe (Hamilton Collection)

1990	LUDWIG'S CASTLE, 19,500	55.00	NR
1990	PALACE OF THE MOORS, 19,500	55.00	NR
1991	SWISS ISLE FORTRESS, 19,500	55.00	NR
1991	LEGENDARY CASTLE OF LEEDS, 19,500	55.00	NR
1991	LEONARDO DA VINCI'S CHAMBORD, 19,500	55.00	NR
1992	EILEAN DONAN, 19,500	55.00	NR
1992	ELTZ CASTLE, 19,500	55.00	NR
1992	KYLEMORE ABBY, 19,500	55.00	NR

Sanchez Miniatures

1985	CARMEN, J. Sanchez, 3,500	50.00	NR
1985	FELIPE, J. Sanchez, 3,500	50.00	NR

Symphony of Roses

1982	WILD IRISH ROSE, Irene Spencer, 10,000	85.00	95.00
1983	YELLOW ROSE OF TEXAS, Irene Spencer, 10,000	90.00	100.00
1984	HONEYSUCKLE ROSE, Irene Spencer, 10,000	95.00	115.00
1985	ROSE OF WASHINGTON SQUARE, Irene Spencer, 10,000	100.00	135.00

We the People

1987	FROM HIGH ABOVE, Adriano Manocchia, 1 year	59.95	NR

Single Issues (Paramount Classics)

1977	CORONATION PLATE, 5,000	95.00	NR
1977	KING GEORGE III, 5,000	95.00	NR
1977	QUEEN ELIZABETH, 5,000	375.00	400.00
1977	QUEEN VICTORIA, 5,000	95.00	NR
1977	QUEEN OF ENGLAND, 5,000	95.00	NR

POILLERAT FRANCE

Calendar

1972	JANUARY, 1,000	100.00	115.00
1972	FEBRUARY, 1,000	100.00	115.00
1973	MARCH, 1,000	125.00	145.00
1973	APRIL, 1,000	125.00	145.00

Christmas

1972	THREE KINGS, 500	350.00	375.00
1973	ROSE, 500	350.00	375.00

POOLE POTTERY GREAT BRITAIN

Birds of North America

1979	GREAT HORNED OWL, 11,000	37.50	NR

Cathedrals

1973	CHRIST ON CROSS, 11,000	125.00	NR

Christmas

		ISSUE	CURRENT
1973	ADORATION OF MAGI, 10,000	37.50	NR
1979	THREE WISE MEN, 10,000	37.50	NR

Medieval Calendar

		ISSUE	CURRENT
1972	JANUARY—DRINKING WINE BY FIRE, 1,000	100.00	NR
1972	FEBRUARY—CHOPPING WOOD, 1,000	100.00	NR
1973	MARCH—DIGGING IN FIELDS AND SETTING SEEDS, 1,000	125.00	NR
1973	APRIL—CARRYING FLOWERING BRANCH, 1,000	125.00	NR
1974	MAY—HAWKING, 1,000	125.00	NR
1974	JUNE—MOWING HAY, 1,000	125.00	NR
1975	JULY—CUTTING CORN WITH SICKLE, 1,000	125.00	NR
1975	AUGUST—THRESHING WITH FLAIL, 1,000	125.00	NR
1976	SEPTEMBER—PICKING GRAPES, 1,000	125.00	NR
1976	OCTOBER—SOWING WINTER CORN, 1,000	125.00	NR
1977	NOVEMBER—GATHERING ACORNS TO FEED PIGS, 1,000	125.00	NR
1977	DECEMBER—PIG KILLING, 1,000	125.00	NR

Mother's Day

		ISSUE	CURRENT
1979	TENDERNESS, 10,000	37.50	NR

PORCELAINE ARIEL UNITED STATES

(Hamilton Collection)

Tribute to Love—The Rubaiyat of Omar Khayyam

		ISSUE	CURRENT
1980	A SHAFT OF LIGHT, Mossan Eskandar, 17,500	45.00	NR
1981	A JUG OF WINE, Mossan Eskandar, 17,500	45.00	NR
1981	SULTAN AFTER SULTAN, Mossan Eskandar, 17,500	45.00	NR
1982	THE BIRD IS ON THE WING, Mossan Eskandar, 17,500	45.00	NR
1982	IF TODAY BE SWEET, Mossan Eskandar, 17,500	45.00	NR
1982	FLOWER THAT ONCE HAS BLOWN, Mossan Eskandar, 17,500	45.00	NR
1982	DOOR TO WHICH WE HAVE NO KEY, Mossan Eskandar, 17,500	45.00	NR
1982	AH, MY BELOVED FILL THE CUP, Mossan Eskandar, 17,500	45.00	NR
1982	THE MOVING FINGER WRITES, Mossan Eskandar, 17,500	45.00	NR

Waltzes of Johann Strauss (The Hamilton Collection)

		ISSUE	CURRENT
1981	THE EMPEROR'S WALTZ, Marca America, 10 days	25.00	NR
1981	THE BLUE DANUBE, Marca America, 10 days	25.00	NR
1981	VOICES OF SPRING, Marca America, 10 days	25.00	NR
1981	VIENNA LIFE, Marca America, 10 days	25.00	NR
1981	ROSES OF THE SOUTH, Marca America, 10 days	25.00	NR
1982	WINE, WOMEN AND SONG, Marca America, 10 days	25.00	NR
1982	ARTIST'S LIFE, Marca America, 10 days	25.00	NR
1982	TALES OF THE VIENNA WOODS, Marca America, 10 days	25.00	NR

PORCELANA GRANADA ARGENTINA

Christmas

		ISSUE	CURRENT
1971	THE ANNUNCIATION, Tom Fennell Jr., 5,000	12.00	NR
1972	MARY AND ELIZABETH, Tom Fennell Jr., 5,000	12.00	NR

		ISSUE	CURRENT
1973	ROAD TO BETHLEHEM, Tom Fennell Jr., 5,000	14.00	NR
1974	NO ROOM, Tom Fennell Jr., 5,000	16.00	NR
1975	SHEPHERDS IN THE FIELDS, Tom Fennell Jr., 5,000	16.50	NR
1976	NATIVITY, Tom Fennell Jr., 5,000	17.50	NR
1977	THREE KINGS, Tom Fennell Jr., 5,000	18.00	NR
1978	YOUNG CARPENTER, Tom Fennell Jr., 5,000	18.00	NR
1979	CALLING OF THE DISCIPLES, Tom Fennell Jr., 5,000	19.50	NR
1980	LOAVES AND FISHES, Tom Fennell Jr., 5,000	20.00	NR
1981	SUFFER THE LITTLE CHILDREN, Tom Fennell Jr., 5,000	20.00	NR
1982	TRIUMPHAL ENTRY, Tom Fennell Jr., 5,000	20.00	NR

PORSGRUND NORWAY

Castles

1970	HAMLET	13.00	NR
1971	ROSENBORG	13.00	NR

Christmas

1968	CHURCH SCENE, Gunnar Bratlie, 1 year	12.00	120.00
1969	THREE KINGS, Gunnar Bratlie, 1 year	12.00	NR
1970	ROAD TO BETHLEHEM, Gunnar Bratlie, 1 year	12.00	NR
1971	A CHILD IS BORN IN BETHLEHEM, Gunnar Bratlie, 1 year	12.00	NR
1972	HARK, THE HERALD ANGELS SING, Gunnar Bratlie, 1 year	12.00	NR
1973	PROMISE OF THE SAVIOR, Gunnar Bratlie, 1 year	15.00	NR
1974	THE SHEPHERDS, Gunnar Bratlie, 1 year	15.00	35.00
1975	JESUS ON THE ROAD TO THE TEMPLE, Gunnar Bratlie, 1 year	19.50	NR
1976	JESUS AND THE ELDERS, Gunnar Bratlie, 1 year	22.00	NR
1977	THE DROUGHT OF FISH, Gunnar Bratlie, 1 year	24.00	45.00

Christmas Deluxe

1970	ROAD TO BETHLEHEM, 3,000	50.00	NR
1971	A CHILD IS BORN, 3,000	50.00	NR
1972	HARK, THE HERALD ANGELS SING, 3,000	50.00	NR
1973	PROMISE OF THE SAVIOR, 3,000	50.00	NR

Easter

1972	DUCKS, 1 year	12.00	NR
1973	BIRDS, 1 year	12.00	NR
1974	BUNNIES, 1 year	15.00	NR
1975	CHICKS, 1 year	19.50	NR
1976	SHEEP, 1 year	22.00	NR
1977	BUTTERFLIES, 1 year	24.00	NR

Father's Day

1971	FISHING, 1 year	7.50	15.00
1972	COOKOUT, 1 year	8.00	15.00
1973	SLEDDING, 1 year	8.00	NR
1974	FATHER AND SON, 1 year	10.00	NR
1975	SKATING, 1 year	12.50	NR
1976	SKIING, 1 year	15.00	NR
1977	SOCCER, 1 year	16.50	NR
1978	CANOEING, 1 year	17.50	NR

		ISSUE	CURRENT
1979	FATHER AND DAUGHTER, 1 year	19.50	NR
1980	SAILING, 1 year	21.50	NR

Jubilee

1970	FEMBORINGER, 1 year	25.00	NR

Mother's Day

1970	MARE AND FOAL, Gunnar Bratlie, 1 year	7.50	15.00
1971	BOY AND GEESE, Gunnar Bratlie, 1 year	7.50	NR
1972	DOE AND FAWN, Gunnar Bratlie, 1 year	10.00	NR
1973	CAT AND KITTENS, Gunnar Bratlie, 1 year	10.00	NR
1974	BOY AND GOATS, Gunnar Bratlie, 1 year	10.00	NR
1975	DOG AND PUPPIES, Gunnar Bratlie, 1 year	12.50	NR
1976	GIRL AND CALF, Gunnar Bratlie, 1 year	15.00	NR
1977	BOY AND CHICKENS, Gunnar Bratlie, 1 year	16.50	NR
1978	GIRLS AND PIGS, Gunnar Bratlie, 1 year	17.50	NR
1979	BOY AND REINDEER, Gunnar Bratlie, 1 year	19.50	NR
1980	GIRL AND LAMBS, Gunnar Bratlie, 1 year	21.50	NR
1981	BOY AND BIRDS, Gunnar Bratlie, 1 year	24.00	NR
1982	GIRL AND RABBIT, Gunnar Bratlie, 1 year	26.00	NR
1983	MOTHER AND KITTENS, Gunnar Bratlie, 1 year	26.00	NR
1984	BY THE POND, Gunnar Bratlie, 1 year	26.00	NR

Traditional Norwegian Christmas

1978	GUESTS ARE COMING FOR CHRISTMAS EVE, Gunnar Bratlie, 1 year	27.00	NR
1979	HOME FOR CHRISTMAS, Gunnar Bratlie, 1 year	30.00	NR
1980	PREPARING FOR CHRISTMAS, Gunnar Bratlie, 1 year	34.00	NR
1981	CHRISTMAS SKATING, Gunnar Bratlie, 1 year	38.00	NR
1982	WHITE CHRISTMAS, Gunnar Bratlie, 1 year	42.00	NR
1983	CHRISTMAS NIGHT, Thorstein Rittun	42.00	BR

Single Issue

1909	CHRISTMAS FLOWERS	NA	1,150.00

PORTERFIELD'S UNITED STATES

Inspurrations

1996	MOONGLOW, Jamie Perry, 44 days	29.90	RI

Membership—Rob Anders Collectors' Society

1997	SHORT STORIES, Rob Anders	19.00	RI
1998	CUDDLING UP, Rob Anders	19.00	RI
1999	FIRST LOOK, Rob Anders	19.00	RI

Moments of Wonder—Miniature

1996	FIRST LOVE, Rob Anders, 19 days	16.60	RI
1996	TIME OUT, Rob Anders, 19 days	16.60	RI
1996	SAFE HARBOR, Rob Anders, 19 days	16.60	RI
1997	DIGGING IN, Rob Anders, 19 days	16.60	RI
1997	TWO BITES TO GO, Rob Anders, 19 days	16.60	RI
1997	SWEET DREAMS, Rob Anders, 19 days	16.60	RI

		ISSUE	CURRENT

Special Issue—Father's Day—Miniature

1997	COOKIES FOR DADDY, Rob Anders, 19 days	16.60	RI

Special Issue—Halloween—Miniature

1997	SPOOKY STORIES, Rob Anders, 10 days	16.60	RI

Special Issue—Mother's Day—Miniature

1998	TUCKED IN, Rob Anders, 10 days	16.60	RI

Treasures of the Heart—Miniature

1997	IN GOOD HANDS, Rob Anders, 10 days	16.60	RI
1997	BUBBLES AWAY, Rob Anders, 10 days	16.60	RI
1997	MR. MUSCLES, Rob Anders, 10 days	16.60	RI
1998	LAZY DAYS, Rob Anders, 10 days	16.60	RI

Single Issue

1995	CATTAILS, Jamie Perry, 44 days	29.20	RI

First Look
Photo courtesy of Porterfield's

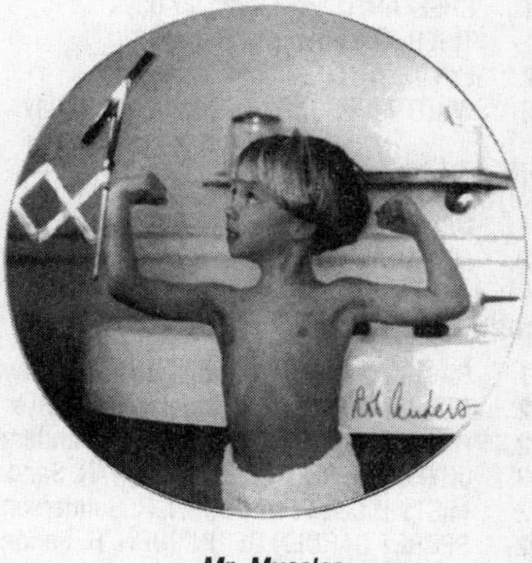

Mr. Muscles
Photo courtesy of *Collectors News*

PORZELLAN

The Nicest Places

1993	AT THE TILED STOVE	29.90	RI
1994	AT THE WINDOW	29.90	RI
1994	ON THE SOFA	32.90	RI
1994	IN THE LINEN PRESS	32.90	RI
1994	ON THE ROCKING CHAIR	32.90	RI
1994	IN THE BED	34.90	RI
1994	AT THE FEEDING DISH	34.90	RI
1994	AT THE EASEL	34.90	RI

POVERTY BAY PORCELAIN

		ISSUE	CURRENT

Henry's Loveable Model T

		ISSUE	CURRENT
1984	PAPA'S NEW FORD, Randy Giovenale, 5,000	29.95	NR

PRINCETON GALLERY

(Lenox)

Circus Friends

		ISSUE	CURRENT
1989	DON'T BE SHY, R. Sanderson	29.50	NR
1990	MAKE ME A CLOWN, R. Sanderson	29.50	NR
1990	LOOKS LIKE RAIN, R. Sanderson	29.50	NR
1990	CHEER UP MR. CLOWN, R. Sanderson	29.50	NR

Cubs of the Big Cats (Lenox)

		ISSUE	CURRENT
1990	COUGAR CUB, Q. Lemonds	29.50	NR
1991	LION CUB, Q. Lemonds, 90 days	29.50	NR
1991	SNOW LEOPARD, Q. Lemonds, 90 days	29.50	NR
1991	CHEETAH, Q. Lemonds, 90 days	29.50	NR
1991	TIGER, Q. Lemonds, 90 days	29.50	NR
1992	LYNX CUB, Q. Lemonds, 90 days	29.50	NR
1992	WHITE TIGER CUB, Q. Lemonds, 90 days	29.50	NR

Darling Dalmatians (Lenox)

		ISSUE	CURRENT
1991	DALMATIAN, L. Picken, 90 days	29.50	NR
1992	FIREHOUSE FROLIC, L. Picken, 90 days	29.50	NR

Enchanted World of the Unicorn

		ISSUE	CURRENT
1991	RAINBOW VALLEY, R. Sanderson, 90 days	29.50	NR
1992	GOLDEN SHORE, R. Sanderson, 90 days	29.50	NR
1992	HIDDEN GLADE OF UNICORN, R. Sanderson, 90 days	29.50	NR
1992	JOYFUL MEADOW OF UNICORN, R. Sanderson, 90 days	29.50	NR
1992	MISTY HILLS OF UNICORN, R. Sanderson, 90 days	29.50	NR
1992	SECRET GARDEN OF UNICORN, R. Sanderson, 90 days	29.50	NR
1992	SPRINGTIME PASTURE OF UNICORN, R. Sanderson, 90 days	29.50	NR
1992	TROPICAL PARADISE OF UNICORN, R. Sanderson, 90 days	29.50	NR

Single Issue

		ISSUE	CURRENT
1997	THE UNICORN OF THE SEA, Kim McElroy, 95 days	29.90	RI

CHRISTOPHER RADKO UNITED STATES

Home for the Holidays

		ISSUE	CURRENT
1997	KALEIDOSCOPE, Christopher Radko, 7,500	70.00	RI
1997	OLD ST. NICHOLAS, Christopher Radko, 1 year	30.00	RI

Marbles
Photo courtesy of *Collectors News*

RAINBOW TREASURY

Games We Used to Play

		ISSUE	CURRENT
1984	TEA PARTY, John Sloane	29.50	NR
1984	MARBLES, John Sloane	29.50	NR
1984	JACKS, John Sloane	29.50	NR

RAM UNITED STATES

Boston 500

1973	EASTER, 500	30.00	NR
1973	MOTHER'S DAY, 500	30.00	NR
1973	FATHER'S DAY, 500	30.00	NR
1973	CHRISTMAS, 500	30.00	NR

Great Bird Heroes

1973	CHER AMI, 1,000	7.95	NR
1973	MOCKER, 1,000	7.95	NR

RARE BIRD CANADA

Canadian Dream

1983	GOING TO THE RINK, Joan Healey, 7,500	45.00	NR
1984	LACING UP, Joan Healey, 7,500	45.00	NR
NA	FACE OFF, Joan Healey, 7,500	45.00	NR

Christmas in Canada

1986	THE WINDMILL, Joan Healey, 5,000	45.00	NR

RAYMON TROUP STUDIO UNITED STATES

American Landmarks

1995	THE OLD MILL, Wm. Raymon Troup, 1,500	39.95	RI
1995	IVY GREEN, Wm. Raymon Troup, 1,500	39.95	RI

		ISSUE	CURRENT

Single Issue

1998	STAR LIGHT, STAR BRIGHT, Wm. Raymon Troup, open	69.95	RI

RAYNAUD-LIMOGES FRANCE

Castle

1979	BODIAM CASTLE, 5,000	48.00	NR
1979	GLAMIS CASTLE, 5,000	48.00	NR
1979	TOWER OF LONDON, 5,000	48.00	NR

Children of the Season

1985	THE HIKER, Michael Vincent, 7,500	40.00	NR

Wildlife

1978	TIGER BOUQUET, Cowles, 1 year	50.00	NR

RECO INTERNATIONAL UNITED STATES

(Dresden, Hamilton Collection, Heinrich Porzellan, March of Dimes, Marmot, Moser)

Alan Maley's Past Impressions

1997	FESTIVE OCCASION, Alan Maley, 95 days	35.00	RI
1997	SLEIGH BELLS, Alan Maley, 95 days	35.00	RI
1997	SUMMER ELEGANCE, Alan Maley, 95 days	35.00	RI
1997	THE RECITAL, Alan Maley, 95 days	35.00	RI

Americana

1972	GASPEE INCIDENT, Stuart Devlin, 1,500	200.00	325.00

Amish Traditions

1994	GOLDEN HARVEST, Bill Farnsworth, 95 days	29.50	RI
1994	FAMILY OUTING, Bill Farnsworth, 95 days	29.50	RI
1994	THE QUILTING BEE, Bill Farnsworth, 95 days	29.50	RI
1995	LAST DAY OF SCHOOL, Bill Farnsworth, 95 days	29.50	RI

Arabelle and Friends

1982	ICE DELIGHT, Carol Greunke, 15,000	35.00	NR
1983	FIRST LOVE, Carol Greunke, 15,000	35.00	NR

Arta Christmas

1973	NATIVITY, 1,500	50.00	70.00

Arta Mother's Day

1973	FAMILY WITH PUPPY, 1,500	50.00	70.00

Barefoot Children

1987	NIGHT-TIME STORY, Sandra Kuck, 14 days	29.50	45.00
1987	GOLDEN AFTERNOON, Sandra Kuck, 14 days	29.50	NR
1988	LITTLE SWEETHEARTS, Sandra Kuck, 14 days	29.50	40.00

		ISSUE	CURRENT
1988	CAROUSEL MAGIC, Sandra Kuck, 14 days	29.50	NR
1988	UNDER THE APPLE TREE, Sandra Kuck, 14 days	29.50	40.00
1988	THE REHEARSAL, Sandra Kuck, 14 days	29.50	60.00
1988	PRETTY AS A PICTURE, Sandra Kuck, 14 days	29.50	45.00
1988	GRANDMA'S TRUNK, Sandra Kuck, 14 days	29.50	45.00

Becky's Day

1985	AWAKENING, John McClelland, 90 days	24.50	NR
1985	GETTING DRESSED, John McClelland, 90 days	24.50	NR
1986	BREAKFAST, John McClelland, 90 days	27.50	35.00
1986	LEARNING IS FUN, John McClelland, 90 days	27.50	NR
1986	MUFFIN MAKING, John McClelland, 90 days	27.50	NR
1986	TUB TIME, John McClelland, 90 days	27.50	35.00
1986	EVENING PRAYER, John McClelland, 90 days	27.50	NR

Birds of the Hidden Forest

1994	MACAW WATERFALL, Gamini Ratnavira, 96 days	29.50	RI
1994	PARADISE VALLEY, Gamini Ratnavira, 96 days	29.50	RI
1995	TOUCAN TREASURE, Gamini Ratnavira, 96 days	29.50	RI

Bohemian Annual

1974	1974, 500	130.00	155.00
1975	1975, 500	140.00	160.00
1976	1976, 500	150.00	160.00

Castles and Dreams

1992	THE BIRTH OF A DREAM, Jody Bergsma, 48 days	29.50	NR
1992	DREAMS COME TRUE, Jody Bergsma, 48 days	29.50	NR
1993	BELIEVE IN YOUR DREAMS, Jody Bergsma, 48 days	29.50	RI
1994	FOLLOW YOUR DREAMS, Jody Bergsma, 48 days	29.50	RI

Celebration of Love

1992	HAPPY ANNIVERSARY, J. Hall, 9¼"	35.00	NR
1992	10TH, J. Hall, 9¼"	35.00	NR
1992	25TH, J. Hall, 9¼"	35.00	NR
1992	50TH, J. Hall, 9¼"	35.00	NR
1992	HAPPY ANNIVERSARY, J. Hall, 6½"	25.00	NR
1992	10TH, J. Hall, 6½"	25.00	NR
1992	25TH, J. Hall, 6½"	25.00	NR
1992	50TH, J. Hall, 6½"	25.00	NR

Childhood Almanac

1985	FIRESIDE DREAMS—JANUARY, Sandra Kuck, 14 days	29.50	35.00
1985	BE MINE—FEBRUARY, Sandra Kuck, 14 days	29.50	35.00
1985	WINDS OF MARCH—MARCH, Sandra Kuck, 14 days	29.50	35.00
1985	EASTER MORNING—APRIL, Sandra Kuck, 14 days	29.50	35.00
1985	FOR MOM—MAY, Sandra Kuck, 14 days	29.50	35.00
1985	JUST DREAMING—JUNE, Sandra Kuck, 14 days	29.50	35.00
1985	STAR SPANGLED SKY—JULY, Sandra Kuck, 14 days	29.50	35.00
1985	SUMMER SECRETS—AUGUST, Sandra Kuck, 14 days	29.50	35.00
1985	SCHOOL DAYS—SEPTEMBER, Sandra Kuck, 14 days	29.50	35.00
1985	INDIAN SUMMER—OCTOBER, Sandra Kuck, 14 days	29.50	35.00

		ISSUE	CURRENT
1985	GIVING THANKS—NOVEMBER, Sandra Kuck, 14 days	29.50	35.00
1985	CHRISTMAS MAGIC—DECEMBER, Sandra Kuck, 14 days	35.00	NR

Children's Christmas Pageant

1986	SILENT NIGHT, Sandra Kuck, 1 year	32.50	80.00
1987	HARK THE HERALD ANGELS SING, Sandra Kuck, 1 year	32.50	45.00
1988	WHILE SHEPHERDS WATCHED..., Sandra Kuck, 1 year	32.50	NR
1989	WE THREE KINGS, Sandra Kuck, 1 year	32.50	NR

Children's Garden

1993	GARDEN FRIENDS, John McClelland, 150 days	29.50	RI
1993	TEA FOR THREE, John McClelland, 150 days	29.50	RI
1993	PUPPY LOVE, John McClelland, 150 days	29.50	RI

Christening Gifts

1995	GOD'S GIFT, Sandra Kuck, open	29.90	RI

Christmas Series

1990	DOWN THE GLISTENING LANE, Jody Bergsma, 14 days	35.00	NR
1991	A CHILD IS BORN, Jody Bergsma, retrd 1996	35.00	NR
1992	CHRISTMAS DAY, Jody Bergsma, retrd 1996	35.00	NR
1993	I WISH YOU AN ANGEL, Jody Bergsma, retrd 1996	35.00	NR

Christmas Wishes

1994	I WISH YOU LOVE, Jody Bergsma, 75 days	29.50	RI
1995	I WISH YOU JOY, Jody Bergsma, 75 days	29.50	RI
1996	I WISH YOU PEACE, Jody Bergsma, 75 days	29.50	RI

Days Gone By

1983	AMY'S MAGIC HORSE, Sandra Kuck, 14 days	29.50	NR
1983	SUNDAY BEST, Sandra Kuck, 14 days	29.50	NR
1984	LITTLE ANGLERS, Sandra Kuck, 14 days	29.50	NR
1984	AFTERNOON RECITAL, Sandra Kuck, 14 days	29.50	50.00
1984	LITTLE TUTOR, Sandra Kuck, 14 days	29.50	NR
1985	EASTER AT GRANDMA'S, Sandra Kuck, 14 days	29.50	NR
1985	THE MORNING SONG, Sandra Kuck, 14 days	29.50	NR
1985	THE SURREY RIDE, Sandra Kuck, 14 days	29.50	NR

Eagle of America

1996	LAND OF THE FREE, Sy Barlowe, 95 days	29.90	RI

Enchanted Gardens (Bradford Exchange)

1998	TEA FOR THREE, Sandra Kuck, 95 days	32.95	RI
1998	SWEETEST DELIGHTS, Sandra Kuck, 95 days	32.95	RI

Enchanted Norfin Trolls

1993	TROLL MAIDEN, C. Hopkins, 75 days	19.50	RI
1993	WIZARD TROLL, C. Hopkins, 75 days	19.50	RI
1993	THE TROLL AND HIS DRAGON, C. Hopkins, retrd 1996	19.50	RI
1994	TROLL IN SHINING ARMOR, C. Hopkins, retrd 1996	19.50	RI
1994	MINSTREL TROLL, C. Hopkins, retrd 1996	19.50	RI

		ISSUE	CURRENT
1994	IF TROLLS COULD FLY, C. Hopkins, retrd 1996	19.50	RI
1994	CHEF LE TROLL, C. Hopkins, retrd 1996	19.50	RI
1994	QUEEN OF TROLLS, C. Hopkins, retrd 1996	19.50	RI

Everlasting Friends

1996	SHARING SECRETS, Sandra Kuck, 95 days	29.95	RI
1996	SHARING BEAUTY, Sandra Kuck, 95 days	29.95	RI
1997	SHARING DREAMS, Sandra Kuck, 95 days	29.95	RI
1997	SHARING LOVE, Sandra Kuck, 95 days	29.95	RI
1998	SHARING HARMONY, Sandra Kuck, 95 days	29.95	RI

Everyday Heroes

1998	OUT OF THE BLAZE, Bradford Brown, 95 days	29.90	RI

Fishtales

1997	RAINBOW RIVER, Ruanne Manning, 76 days	29.90	RI

Flower Fairy Plate Collection

1990	THE RED CLOVER FAIRY, Cicely Mary Barker, retrd 1996	29.50	NR
1990	THE WILD CHERRY BLOSSOM FAIRY, Cicely Mary Barker, retrd 1996	29.50	NR
1990	THE PINE TREE FAIRY, Cicely Mary Barker, retrd 1996	29.50	NR
1990	THE ROSE HIP FAIRY, Cicely Mary Barker, retrd 1996	29.50	NR

Four Seasons

1973	SPRING, J. Poluszynksi, 2,500	50.00	75.00
1973	SUMMER, J. Poluszynksi, 2,500	50.00	75.00
1973	FALL, J. Poluszynksi, 2,500	50.00	75.00
1973	WINTER, J. Poluszynksi, 2,500	50.00	75.00

Friends for Keeps

1996	PUPPY LOVE, Sandra Kuck, 95 days	29.95	RI
1996	GONE FISHING, Sandra Kuck, 95 days	29.95	RI
1997	GOLDEN DAYS, Sandra Kuck, 95 days	29.95	RI
1997	TAKE ME HOME, Sandra Kuck, 95 days	29.95	RI

Games Children Play

1979	ME FIRST, Sandra Kuck, 10,000	45.00	NR
1980	FOREVER BUBBLES, Sandra Kuck, 10,000	45.00	NR
1981	SKATING PALS, Sandra Kuck, 10,000	45.00	NR
1982	JOIN ME, Sandra Kuck, 10,000	45.00	NR

Gardens of America

1992	COLONIAL SPLENDOR, Dorothea Barlowe, 48 days	29.50	NR

Gardens of Beauty

1988	ENGLISH COUNTRY GARDEN, Dorothea Barlowe, 14 days	29.50	NR
1988	DUTCH COUNTRY GARDEN, Dorothea Barlowe, 14 days	29.50	NR
1988	NEW ENGLAND GARDEN, Dorothea Barlowe, 14 days	29.50	NR
1988	JAPANESE GARDEN, Dorothea Barlowe, 14 days	29.50	NR
1989	ITALIAN GARDEN, Dorothea Barlowe, 14 days	29.50	NR
1989	HAWAIIAN GARDEN, Dorothea Barlowe, 14 days	29.50	NR

Tea for Three

Sharing Secrets

Out of the Blaze

Rainbow River

Sweetly Swinging

Guiding the Way

Photos courtesy of Reco International

		ISSUE	CURRENT
1989	GERMAN COUNTRY GARDEN, Dorothea Barlowe, 14 days	29.50	NR
1989	MEXICAN GARDEN, Dorothea Barlowe, 14 days	29.50	NR

Gardens of Innocence

1997	HEAVENLY HIDEAWAY, Sandra Kuck, 95 days	32.95	RI
1997	SWEETLY SWINGING, Sandra Kuck, 95 days	32.95	RI
1998	GENTLY GIVING, Sandra Kuck, 95 days	32.95	RI
1998	PRECIOUS PARTY, Sandra Kuck, 95 days	32.95	RI

Generations

1997	PASSING ON THE FAITH, Bradford Brown, 95 days	29.90	RI
1998	GUIDING THE WAY, Bradford Brown, 95 days	29.90	RI
1998	LEARNING TO IMAGINE, Bradford Brown, 95 days	29.90	RI
1998	4TH RELEASE, Bradford Brown, 95 days	29.90	RI

Gift of Love Mother's Day Collection

1993	MORNING GLORY, Sandra Kuck, 10,000	65.00	RI
1994	MEMORIES FROM THE HEART, Sandra Kuck, 10,000	65.00	RI

Glory of Christ (Hamilton Collection)

1992	THE ASCENSION, Clemente Micarelli, 48 days	29.50	NR
1993	JESUS TEACHING, Clemente Micarelli, 48 days	29.50	RI
1993	THE LAST SUPPER, Clemente Micarelli, 48 days	29.50	RI
1993	THE NATIVITY, Clemente Micarelli, 48 days	29.50	RI
1993	THE BAPTISM OF CHRIST, Clemente Micarelli, 48 days	29.50	RI
1993	JESUS HEALS THE SICK, Clemente Micarelli, 48 days	29.50	RI
1994	JESUS WALKS ON WATER, Clemente Micarelli, 48 days	29.50	RI
1994	DESCENT FROM THE CROSS, Clemente Micarelli, 48 days	29.50	RI

God's Own Country

1990	DAYBREAK, I. Drechsler, 14 days	30.00	NR
1990	COMING HOME, I. Drechsler, 14 days	30.00	NR
1990	PEACEFUL GATHERING, I. Drechsler, 14 days	30.00	NR
1990	QUIET WATERS, I. Drechsler, 14 days	30.00	NR

Golf

1992	PAR EXCELLENCE, John McClelland, 180 days	35.00	NR

Grafburg Christmas

1975	BLACK-CAPPED CHICKADEE, 5,000	20.00	60.00
1976	SQUIRRELS, 5,000	22.00	NR

Grandparent Collector's Plate

1981	GRANDMA'S COOKIE JAR, Sandra Kuck, 1 year	37.50	NR
1981	GRANDPA AND THE DOLLHOUSE, Sandra Kuck, 1 year	37.50	NR

Great Stories from the Bible

1987	MOSES IN THE BULRUSHES, Garri Katz, 14 days	29.50	NR
1987	KING DAVID AND SAUL, Garri Katz, 14 days	29.50	NR
1987	MOSES AND THE TEN COMMANDMENTS, Garri Katz, 14 days	29.50	NR
1987	JOSEPH'S COAT OF MANY COLORS, Garri Katz, 14 days	29.50	NR

		ISSUE	CURRENT
1988	REBEKAH AT THE WELL, Garri Katz, 14 days	29.50	NR
1988	DANIEL READS THE WRITING ON THE WALL, Garri Katz, 14 days	29.50	NR
1988	THE STORY OF RUTH, Garri Katz, 14 days	29.50	NR
1988	KING SOLOMON, Garri Katz, 14 days	29.50	NR

Guardians of the Kingdom

1990	RAINBOW TO RIDE ON, Jody Bergsma, 17,500	35.00	NR
1990	SPECIAL FRIENDS ARE FEW, Jody Bergsma, 17,500	35.00	NR
1990	GUARDIANS OF THE INNOCENT CHILDREN, Jody Bergsma, 17,500	35.00	NR
1990	THE MIRACLE OF LOVE, Jody Bergsma, 17,500	35.00	NR
1991	THE MAGIC OF LOVE, Jody Bergsma, 17,500	35.00	NR
1991	ONLY WITH THE HEART, Jody Bergsma, 17,500	35.00	NR
1991	TO FLY WITHOUT WINGS, Jody Bergsma, 17,500	35.00	NR
1991	IN FAITH I AM FREE, Jody Bergsma, 17,500	35.00	NR

Guiding Lights

1996	ROBBINS REEF LIGHTHOUSE, Danny Hahlbohm, 96 days	29.90	RI
1996	CAPE HATTERAS LIGHTHOUSE, Danny Hahlbohm, 96 days	29.90	RI
1997	CAPE NEDDICK LIGHTHOUSE, Danny Hahlbohm, 96 days	29.90	RI
1998	SPLIT ROCK LIGHTHOUSE, Danny Hahlbohm, 96 days	29.90	

Haven of the Hunters

1994	EAGLE'S CASTLE, Harold Roe, retrd 1996	29.50	RI
1994	SANCTUARY OF THE HAWK, Harold Roe, retrd 1996	29.50	RI

Heart of the Family

1992	SHARING SECRETS, Judy York, 48 days	29.50	NR
1993	SPINNING DREAMS, Judy York, 48 days	29.50	RI

Hearts and Flowers

1991	PATIENCE, Sandra Kuck, 120 days	29.50	45.00
1991	TEA PARTY, Sandra Kuck, 120 days	29.50	55.00
1992	CATS IN THE CRADLE, Sandra Kuck, 120 days	32.50	45.00
1992	CAROUSEL OF DREAMS, Sandra Kuck, 120 days	32.50	NR
1992	STORYBOOK MEMORIES, Sandra Kuck, 120 days	32.50	NR
1993	DELIGHTFUL BUNDLE, Sandra Kuck, 120 days	34.50	RI
1993	EASTER MORNING VISITOR, Sandra Kuck, 120 days	34.50	RI
1993	ME AND MY PONY, Sandra Kuck, 120 days	34.50	RI

Heavenly Kingdom

1997	THE BLESSED CHILD, Clemente Micarelli, 95 days	29.90	RI

Imaginary Gardens

1996	PUSSYWILLOWS, Sheila Somerville, 76 days	29.90	RI
1996	DOGWOOD, Sheila Somerville, 76 days	29.90	RI
1997	COW SLIP, Sheila Somerville, 76 days	29.90	RI

In the Eye of the Storm

1991	FIRST STRIKE, W. Lowe, 120 days	29.50	NR
1992	NIGHT FORCE, W. Lowe, 120 days	29.50	NR
1992	TRACKS ACROSS THE SAND, W. Lowe, 120 days	29.50	NR
1992	THE STORM HAS LANDED, W. Lowe, 120 days	29.50	NR

Jody Bergsma Mother's Day

		ISSUE	CURRENT
1990	THE BEAUTY OF LIFE, Jody Bergsma, 14 days	35.00	NR
1992	LIFE'S BLESSING, Jody Bergsma, 14 days	35.00	NR
1993	MY GREATEST TREASURES, Jody Bergsma, 14 days	35.00	RI
1994	FOREVER IN MY HEART, Jody Bergsma, 14 days	35.00	RI

Kingdom of the Great Cats

1995	OUT OF THE MIST, Peter Jepson, 36 days	29.50	RI
1995	SUMMIT SANCTUARY, Peter Jepson, 36 days	29.50	RI

King's Christmas

1973	ADORATION, Merli, 1,500	100.00	265.00
1974	MADONNA, Merli, 1,500	150.00	250.00
1975	HEAVENLY CHOIR, Merli, 1,500	160.00	235.00
1976	SIBLINGS, Merli, 1,500	200.00	225.00

King's Flowers

1973	CARNATION, Aldo Falchi, 1,000	85.00	130.00
1974	RED ROSE, Aldo Falchi, 1,000	100.00	145.00
1975	YELLOW DAHLIA, Aldo Falchi, 1,000	110.00	160.00
1976	BLUEBELLS, Aldo Falchi, 1,000	130.00	165.00
1977	ANEMONES, Aldo Falchi, 1,000	130.00	175.00

King's Mother's Day

1973	DANCING GIRL, Merli, 1,500	100.00	225.00
1974	DANCING BOY, Merli, 1,500	115.00	250.00
1975	MOTHERLY LOVE, Merli, 1,500	140.00	225.00
1976	MAIDEN, Merli, 1,500	180.00	200.00

Kittens 'n Hats

1994	OPENING NIGHT, Sheila Somerville, 48 days	35.00	RI
1994	SITTING PRETTY, Sheila Somerville, 48 days	35.00	RI
1995	LITTLE LEAGUE, Sheila Somerville, 48 days	35.00	RI

Land of Our Dreams

1989	LAND OF NOD, Jody Bergsma, 19,000	35.00	NR
1989	THE SECRET DOOR, Jody Bergsma, 19,000	35.00	NR
1989	THE STARS, Jody Bergsma, 19,000	35.00	NR
1989	THE SWING, Jody Bergsma, 19,000	35.00	NR

Life's Little Celebrations

1997	THE NEW BABY, Catherine Tait/Deborah Sargentson-inspired, 96 days	29.90	RI
1997	AN APPLE FOR THE TEACHER, Catherine Tait/Deborah Sargentson-inspired, 96 days	29.90	RI
1997	SCHOOL BELL, Catherine Tait/Deborah Sargentson-inspired, 96 days	29.90	RI
1997	GRADUATION SMILE, Catherine Tait/Deborah Sargentson-inspired, 96 days	29.90	RI
1997	GRADUATION SURPRISE, Catherine Tait/Deborah Sargentson-inspired, 96 days	29.90	RI
1997	CELEBRATION OF LOVE, Catherine Tait/Deborah Sargentson-inspired, 96 days	29.90	RI
1997	I LOVE YOU, Catherine Tait/Deborah Sargentson-inspired, 96 days	29.90	RI

Little Angel Plate Collection

		ISSUE	CURRENT
1994	ANGEL OF CHARITY, Sandra Kuck, 96 days	29.50	RI
1994	ANGEL OF JOY, Sandra Kuck, 96 days	29.50	RI

Little Professionals

1982	ALL IS WELL, Sandra Kuck, 10,000	39.50	95.00
1983	TENDER LOVING CARE, Sandra Kuck, 10,000	39.50	50.00
1984	LOST AND FOUND, Sandra Kuck, 10,000	39.50	45.00
1985	READING, WRITING, AND..., Sandra Kuck, 10,000	39.50	45.00

Magic Companions

1994	BELIEVE IN LOVE, Jody Bergsma, 48 days	29.90	RI
1994	IMAGINE PEACE, Jody Bergsma, 48 days	29.90	RI
1995	LIVE IN HARMONY, Jody Bergsma, 48 days	29.90	RI
1995	TRUST IN MAGIC, Jody Bergsma, 48 days	29.90	RI

McClelland Children's Circus

1981	TOMMY THE CLOWN, John McClelland, 100 days	29.50	50.00
1982	KATIE THE TIGHTROPE WALKER, John McClelland, 100 days	29.50	50.00
1983	JOHNNY THE STRONGMAN, John McClelland, 100 days	29.50	40.00
1984	MAGGIE THE ANIMAL TRAINER, John McClelland, 100 days	29.50	NR

McClelland's Mother Goose

1979	MARY, MARY, John McClelland, <1 year	22.50	65.00
1980	LITTLE BOY BLUE, John McClelland, <1 year	22.50	NR
1981	LITTLE MISS MUFFET, John McClelland, <1 year	24.50	NR
1982	LITTLE JACK HORNER, John McClelland, <1 year	24.50	30.00
1983	LITTLE BO PEEP, John McClelland, <1 year	24.50	NR
1984	DIDDLE DIDDLE DUMPLING, John McClelland, <1 year	24.50	NR
1985	MARY HAD A LITTLE LAMB, John McClelland, <1 year	27.50	NR
1986	JACK AND JILL, John McClelland, <1 year	27.50	40.00

Memories of Yesterday

1993	HUSH, Mabel Lucie Attwell, retrd 1996	29.50	RI
1993	TIME FOR BED, Mabel Lucie Attwell, retrd 1996	29.50	RI
1993	I'VE BEEN PAINTING, Mabel Lucie Attwell, retrd 1996	29.50	RI
1993	JUST LOOKING PRETTY, Mabel Lucie Attwell, retrd 1996	29.50	RI
1994	GIVE IT YOUR BEST SHOT, Mabel Lucie Attwell, retrd 1996	29.50	RI
1994	I PRAY THE LORD MY SOUL TO KEEP, Mabel Lucie Attwell, retrd 1996	29.50	RI
1994	JUST THINKING ABOUT YOU, Mabel Lucie Attwell, retrd 1996	29.50	RI
1994	WHAT WILL I GROW UP TO BE, Mabel Lucie Attwell, retrd 1996	29.50	RI

Moments at Home (Bradford Exchange)

1995	MOMENTS OF CARING, Sandra Kuck, 95 days	29.90	RI
1995	MOMENTS OF TENDERNESS, Sandra Kuck, 95 days	29.90	RI
1995	MOMENTS OF FRIENDSHIP, Sandra Kuck, 95 days	29.90	RI
1995	MOMENTS OF SHARING, Sandra Kuck, 95 days	29.90	RI
1995	MOMENTS OF LOVE, Sandra Kuck, 95 days	29.90	RI
1996	MOMENTS OF REFLECTION, Sandra Kuck, 95 days	29.90	RI

Cape Neddick Lighthouse

Cow Slip

School Bell

Lakeside Drive

The Recital

Photos courtesy of Reco International

Mother's Day

		ISSUE	CURRENT
1985	ONCE UPON A TIME, Sandra Kuck, <1 year	29.50	40.00
1986	TIMES REMEMBERED, Sandra Kuck, <1 year	29.50	NR
1987	A CHERISHED TIME, Sandra Kuck, <1 year	29.50	NR
1988	A TIME TOGETHER, Sandra Kuck, <1 year	29.50	NR

Noble and Free

		ISSUE	CURRENT
1993	GATHERING STORM, Kelly Stevens, 95 days	29.50	RI
1994	PROTECTED JOURNEY, Kelly Stevens, 95 days	29.50	RI
1994	MOONLIGHT RUN, Kelly Stevens, 95 days	29.50	RI

Nutcracker Ballet

		ISSUE	CURRENT
1989	CHRISTMAS EVE PARTY, Clemente Micarelli, 14 days	35.00	NR
1990	CLARA AND HER PRINCE, Clemente Micarelli, 14 days	35.00	NR
1990	THE DREAM BEGINS, Clemente Micarelli, 14 days	35.00	NR
1991	DANCE OF THE SNOW FAIRIES, Clemente Micarelli, 14 days	35.00	NR
1992	THE LAND OF THE SWEETS, Clemente Micarelli, 14 days	35.00	NR
1992	THE SUGAR PLUM FAIRY, Clemente Micarelli, 14 days	35.00	NR

On Wings of Eagles (Hamilton Collection)

		ISSUE	CURRENT
1994	BY DAWN'S EARLY LIGHT, J. Pitcher, 28 days	29.50	RI
1994	WINTER'S MAJESTIC FLIGHT, J. Pitcher, 28 days	29.50	RI
1994	OVER THE LAND OF THE FREE, J. Pitcher, 28 days	29.50	RI
1994	CHANGING OF THE GUARD, J. Pitcher, 28 days	29.50	RI
1995	FREE FLIGHT, J. Pitcher, 28 days	29.50	RI
1995	MORNING MAJESTY, J. Pitcher, 28 days	29.50	RI
1995	SOARING FREE, J. Pitcher, 28 days	29.50	RI
1995	MAJESTIC HEIGHTS, J. Pitcher, 28 days	29.50	RI

Open Road

		ISSUE	CURRENT
1997	LAKESIDE DRIVE, Bill Farnsworth, 76 days	29.90	RI

Oscar and Bertie's Edwardian Holiday

		ISSUE	CURRENT
1991	SNAPSHOT, Peter D. Jackson, 48 days	29.50	NR
1992	EARLY RISE, Peter D. Jackson, 48 days	29.50	NR
1992	ALL ABOARD, Peter D. Jackson, 48 days	29.50	NR
1992	LEARING TO SWIM, Peter D. Jackson, 48 days	29.50	NR

Our Cherished Seas (Hamilton Collection)

		ISSUE	CURRENT
1992	WHALE SONG, Sy Barlowe, 48 days	37.50	NR
1992	LIONS OF THE SEA, Sy Barlowe, 48 days	37.50	NR
1992	FLIGHT OF THE DOLPHINS, Sy Barlowe, 48 days	37.50	NR
1992	PALACE OF THE SEALS, Sy Barlowe, 48 days	37.50	NR
1993	ORCA BALLET, Sy Barlowe, 48 days	37.50	NR
1993	EMPERORS OF THE ICE, Sy Barlowe, 48 days	37.50	NR
1993	TURTLE TREASURE, Sy Barlowe, 48 days	37.50	NR
1993	SPLENDOR OF THE SEA, Sy Barlowe, 48 days	37.50	NR

Out of the Wild

		ISSUE	CURRENT
1996	THE PRIDE, Sy Barlowe, 76 days	29.90	RI
1997	GRACEFUL GIANTS, Sy Barlowe, 76 days	29.90	RI

Plate of the Month Collection

		ISSUE	CURRENT
1990	JANUARY, Sandra Kuck, 28 days	25.00	NR
1990	FEBRUARY, Sandra Kuck, 28 days	25.00	NR
1990	MARCH, Sandra Kuck, 28 days	25.00	NR
1990	APRIL, Sandra Kuck, 28 days	25.00	NR
1990	MAY, Sandra Kuck, 28 days	25.00	NR
1990	JUNE, Sandra Kuck, 28 days	25.00	NR
1990	JULY, Sandra Kuck, 28 days	25.00	NR
1990	AUGUST, Sandra Kuck, 28 days	25.00	NR
1990	SEPTEMBER, Sandra Kuck, 28 days	25.00	NR
1990	OCTOBER, Sandra Kuck, 28 days	25.00	NR
1990	NOVEMBER, Sandra Kuck, 28 days	25.00	NR
1990	DECEMBER, Sandra Kuck, 28 days	25.00	NR

Portraits of the Wild (Hamilton Collection)

1994	INTERLUDE, James Meger, 28 days	29.50	RI
1994	WINTER SOLITUDE, James Meger, 28 days	29.50	RI
1994	DEVOTED PROTECTOR, James Meger, 28 days	29.50	RI
1994	CALL OF AUTUMN, James Meger, 28 days	29.50	RI
1994	WATCHFUL EYES, James Meger, 28 days	29.50	RI
1994	BABIES OF SPRING, James Meger, 28 days	29.50	RI
1994	ROCKY MOUNTAIN GRANDEUR, James Meger, 28 days	29.50	RI
1995	UNBRIDLED POWER, James Meger, 28 days	29.50	RI
1995	MOONLIT VIGIL, James Meger, 28 days	29.50	RI
1995	MONARCH OF THE PLAINS, James Meger, 28 days	29.50	RI
1995	TENDER COURTSHIP, James Meger, 28 days	29.50	RI

Precious Angels

1995	ANGEL OF SHARING, Sandra Kuck, 95 days	29.90	RI
1995	ANGEL OF SUNSHINE, Sandra Kuck, 95 days	29.90	RI
1995	ANGEL OF LAUGHTER, Sandra Kuck, 95 days	29.90	RI
1995	ANGEL OF HOPE, Sandra Kuck, 95 days	29.90	RI
1995	ANGEL OF GRACE, Sandra Kuck, 95 days	29.90	RI
1995	ANGEL OF LOVE, Sandra Kuck, 95 days	29.90	RI
1995	ANGEL OF PEACE, Sandra Kuck, 95 days	29.90	RI
1995	ANGEL OF HAPPINESS, Sandra Kuck, 95 days	29.90	RI

Premier Collection I

1991	PUPPY, Sandra Kuck, 7,500	95.00	125.00
1991	KITTEN, Sandra Kuck, 7,500	95.00	NR
1992	LA BELLE, Sandra Kuck, 7,500	95.00	NR
1992	LE BEAU, Sandra Kuck, 7,500	95.00	NR

Premier Collection II

1991	LOVE, John McClelland, 7,500	75.00	NR

Protectors of the Wild

1998	GENESIS, Rusty Frentner, 95 days	29.90	RI

Romantic Cafes of Paris

1997	BY THE HEARTH, Viktor Shvaiko, 76 days	29.90	RI

Romantic Gardens

		ISSUE	CURRENT
1997	EMMA, Sandra Kuck, 95 days	35.00	RI
1997	ALEXANDRA, Sandra Kuck, 95 days	35.00	RI

Sandra Kuck's Mother's Day

		ISSUE	CURRENT
1995	HOME IS WHERE THE HEART IS, Sandra Kuck, 48 days	35.00	RI
1996	DEAR TO THE HEART, Sandra Kuck, 48 days	35.00	RI
1997	WELCOME HOME, Sandra Kuck, 48 days	35.00	RI
1998	WINGS OF LOVE, Sandra Kuck, 48 days	35.00	RI

Sculpted Heirlooms (Bradford Exchange)

		ISSUE	CURRENT
1996	BEST FRIENDS, Sandra Kuck, 2 years	29.90	RI
1996	TEA PARTY, Sandra Kuck, 2 years	29.90	RI
1996	PATIENCE, Sandra Kuck, 2 years	29.90	RI
1996	STORYBOOK MEMORIES, Sandra Kuck, 2 years	29.90	RI

Songs From the Garden

		ISSUE	CURRENT
1996	LOVE SONG, Gamini Ratnavira, 76 days	29.90	RI
1996	RHAPSODY IN BLUE, Gamini Ratnavira, 76 days	29.90	RI
1997	HUMMINGBIRDS IN HARMONY, Gamini Ratnavira, 76 days	29.90	RI
1997	GOLDEN MELODY, Gamini Ratnavira, 76 days	29.90	RI
1997	SPRING SERENADE, Gamini Ratnavira, 76 days	29.90	RI
1998	ODE TO THE ORIOLE, Gamini Ratnavira, 76 days	29.90	RI

Sophisticated Ladies

		ISSUE	CURRENT
1985	FELICIA, Aldo Fazio, 21 days	29.50	NR
1985	SAMANTHA, Aldo Fazio, 21 days	29.50	NR
1985	PHOEBE, Aldo Fazio, 21 days	29.50	NR
1985	CLEO, Aldo Fazio, 21 days	29.50	NR
1986	CERISSA, Aldo Fazio, 21 days	29.50	NR
1986	NATASHA, Aldo Fazio, 21 days	29.50	NR
1986	BIANKA, Aldo Fazio, 21 days	29.50	NR
1986	CHELSEA, Aldo Fazio, 21 days	29.50	NR

Special Occasions by Reco

		ISSUE	CURRENT
1988	THE WEDDING, Sandra Kuck, open	35.00	NR
1989	WEDDING DAY, Sandra Kuck, retrd, 6½"	25.00	NR
1990	THE SPECIAL DAY, Sandra Kuck, retrd	25.00	NR

Special Occasions—Wedding

		ISSUE	CURRENT
1991	FROM THIS DAY FORWARD, Clemente Micarelli, open, 9½"	35.00	NR
1991	FROM THIS DAY FORWARD, Clemente Micarelli, retrd, 6½"	25.00	NR
1991	TO HAVE AND TO HOLD, Clemente Micarelli, open, 9½"	35.00	NR
1991	TO HAVE AND TO HOLD, Clemente Micarelli, retrd, 6½"	25.00	NR

Springtime of Life (Hamilton Collection)

		ISSUE	CURRENT
1985	TEDDY'S BATHTIME, Thornton Utz, 14 days	29.50	NR
1986	JUST LIKE MOMMY, Thornton Utz, 14 days	29.50	NR
1986	AMONG THE DAFFODILS, Thornton Utz, 14 days	29.50	NR
1986	MY FAVORITE DOLLS, Thornton Utz, 14 days	29.50	NR
1986	AUNT TILLIE'S HATS, Thornton Utz, 14 days	29.50	NR

Genesis

By the Hearth

Emma

Photos courtesy of Reco International

Ode to the Oriole

Boston Balloon Party

		ISSUE	CURRENT
1986	LITTLE EMILY, Thornton Utz, 14 days	29.50	NR
1986	GRANNY'S BOOTS, Thornton Utz, 14 days	29.50	NR
1986	MY MASTERPIECE, Thornton Utz, 14 days	29.50	NR

Sugar and Spice

1993	BEST FRIENDS, Sandra Kuck, 95 days	29.90	RI
1993	SISTERS, Sandra Kuck, 95 days	29.90	RI
1994	LITTLE ONE, Sandra Kuck, 95 days	32.90	RI
1994	TEDDY BEAR TALES, Sandra Kuck, 95 days	32.90	RI
1994	MORNING PRAYERS, Sandra Kuck, 95 days	32.90	RI
1994	GARDEN OF SUNSHINE, Sandra Kuck, 95 days	34.90	RI
1994	FIRST SNOW, Sandra Kuck, 95 days	34.90	RI
1995	A SPECIAL DAY, Sandra Kuck, 95 days	34.90	RI

Tidings of Joy

1992	PEACE ON EARTH, Sandra Kuck, 75 days	35.00	RI
1993	REJOICE, Sandra Kuck, 75 days	35.00	RI
1994	NOEL, Sandra Kuck, 75 days	38.00	RI

Totems of the West

1994	THE WATCHMAN, Jody Bergsma, 96 days	29.50	RI
1995	PEACE AT LAST, Jody Bergsma, 96 days	29.50	RI
1995	NEVER ALONE, Jody Bergsma, 96 days	35.00	RI

Town and Country Dogs

1990	FOX HUNT (FOX HOUND), Sy Barlowe, 36 days	35.00	NR
1991	THE RETRIEVAL (LABRADOR RETRIEVER), Sy Barlowe, 36 days	35.00	NR
1991	GOLDEN FIELDS (GOLDEN RETRIEVER), Sy Barlowe, 36 days	35.00	NR
1993	FAITHFUL COMPANIONS (COCKER SPANIEL), Sy Barlowe, 36 days	35.00	RI

Trains of the Orient Express

1993	THE GOLDEN ARROW—ENGLAND, Robert Johnson, retrd 1996	29.50	RI
1994	AUSTRIA, Robert Johnson, retrd 1996	29.50	RI
1994	BAVARIA, Robert Johnson, retrd 1996	29.50	RI
1994	RUMANIA, Robert Johnson, retrd 1996	29.50	RI
1994	GREECE, Robert Johnson, retrd 1996	29.50	RI
1994	FRANKONIA, Robert Johnson, retrd 1996	29.50	RI
1994	TURKEY, Robert Johnson, retrd 1996	29.50	RI
1994	FRANCE, Robert Johnson, retrd 1996	29.50	RI

Treasured Songs of Childhood

1987	TWINKLE, TWINKLE, LITTLE STAR, John McClelland, 150 days	29.50	NR
1988	A TISKET, A TASKET, John McClelland, 150 days	29.50	NR
1988	BAA, BAA, BLACK SHEEP, John McClelland, 150 days	32.90	NR
1989	ROUND THE MULBERRY BUSH, John McClelland, 150 days	32.90	NR
1989	RAIN, RAIN GO AWAY, John McClelland, 150 days	32.90	NR
1989	I'M A LITTLE TEAPOT, John McClelland, 150 days	32.90	NR
1989	PAT-A-CAKE, John McClelland, 150 days	34.90	NR
1990	HUSH LITTLE BABY, John McClelland, 150 days	34.90	NR

Up, Up and Away

		ISSUE	CURRENT
1996	RALLY AT THE GRAND CANYON, Paul Alexander, 76 days	29.90	RI
1996	GATEWAY TO HEAVEN, Paul Alexander, 76 days	29.90	RI
1997	BOSTON BALLOON PARTY, Paul Alexander, 76 days	29.90	RI
1998	THROUGH GOLDEN GATES, Paul Alexander, 76 days	29.90	RI

Vanishing Animal Kingdoms

1986	RAMA THE TIGER, Dorothea and Sy Barlowe, 21,500	35.00	NR
1986	OLEPI THE BUFFALO, Dorothea and Sy Barlowe, 21,500	35.00	NR
1987	COOLIBAH THE KOALA, Dorothea and Sy Barlowe, 21,500	35.00	NR
1987	ORTWIN THE DEER, Dorothea and Sy Barlowe, 21,500	35.00	NR
1987	YEN-POH THE PANDA, Dorothea and Sy Barlowe, 21,500	35.00	NR
1988	MAMAKUU THE ELEPHANT, Dorothea and Sy Barlowe, 21,500	35.00	NR

Victorian Christmas

1995	DEAR SANTA, Sandra Kuck, 72 days	35.00	RI
1996	NIGHT BEFORE CHRISTMAS, Sandra Kuck, 72 days	35.00	RI
1997	WRAPPED WITH LOVE, Sandra Kuck, 72 days	35.00	RI
1998	CHRISTMAS DAY JOY, Sandra Kuck, 72 days	35.00	RI

Victorian Mother's Day

1989	MOTHER'S SUNSHINE, Sandra Kuck, 1 year	35.00	45.00
1990	REFLECTION OF LOVE, Sandra Kuck, 1 year	35.00	50.00
1991	A PRECIOUS TIME, Sandra Kuck, 1 year	35.00	45.00
1992	LOVING TOUCH, Sandra Kuck, 1 year	35.00	45.00

Western Series

1974	MOUNTAIN MAN, E. Berke, 1,000	165.00	NR

Women of the Plains

1994	PRIDE OF A MAIDEN, Cat Corcilious, 36 days	29.50	RI
1995	NO BOUNDARIES, Cat Corcilious, 36 days	29.50	RI
1995	SILENT COMPANIONS, Cat Corcilious, 36 days	35.00	RI

Wonder of Christmas (Hamilton Collection)

1991	SANTA'S SECRET, John McClelland, 28 days	29.50	NR
1992	MY FAVORTIE ORNAMENT, John McClelland, 28 days	29.50	NR
1992	WAITING FOR SANTA, John McClelland, 28 days	29.50	NR
1993	CANDLELIGHT CHRISTMAS, John McClelland, 28 days	29.50	RI

World of Children

1977	RAINY DAY FUN, John McClelland, 10,000	50.00	NR
1978	WHEN I GROW UP, John McClelland, 15,000	50.00	NR
1979	YOU'RE INVITED, John McClelland, 15,000	50.00	NR
1980	KITTENS FOR SALE, John McClelland, 15,000	50.00	NR

Single Issue

1997	HAPPINESS IN HEAVEN, Theude Gronland, 95 days	29.90	RI

MAYNARD REECE

Waterfowl

		ISSUE	CURRENT
1973	MALLARDS and WOOD DUCKS, 900, set of 2	250.00	375.00
1974	CANVASBACK and CANDIAN GEESE, 900, set of 2	250.00	375.00
1975	PINTAILS and TEAL, 900, set of 2	250.00	425.00

REED AND BARTON UNITED STATES

Annual

1972	FREE TRAPPER, 2,500	65.00	NR
1973	OUTPOST, 2,500	65.00	NR
1974	TOLL COLLECTOR, 2,500	65.00	NR
1975	INDIANS DISCOVERING LEWIS AND CLARK, 2,500	65.00	NR

Audubon

1970	PINE SISKIN, 5,000	60.00	175.00
1971	RED-SHOULDERED HAWK, 5,000	60.00	75.00
1972	STILT SANDPIPER, 5,000	60.00	70.00
1973	RED CARDINAL, 5,000	60.00	65.00
1974	BOREAL CHICKADEE, 5,000	65.00	NR
1975	YELLOW-BREASTED CHAT, 5,000	65.00	NR
1976	BAY-BREASTED WARBLER, 5,000	65.00	NR
1977	PURPLE FINCH, 5,000	65.00	NR

Bicentennial

1972	MONTICELLO, damascene, silver, 1,000	75.00	80.00
1972	MONTICELLO, silver plate, 200	200.00	225.00
1973	MT. VERNON, 1 year	75.00	80.00

Christmas

1970	A PARTRIDGE IN A PEAR TREE, Robert Johnson, 2,500	55.00	210.00
1971	WE THREE KINGS OF ORIENT ARE, Robert Johnson, 7,500	60.00	75.00
1972	HARK! THE HERALD ANGELS SING, Robert Johnson, 7,500	60.00	65.00
1973	ADORATION OF THE KINGS, Rogier van der Weyden, 7,500	60.00	65.00
1974	THE ADORATION OF THE MAGI, Fra Angelico and Fra Filippo Lippi, 7,500	65.00	NR
1975	ADORATION OF THE KINGS, Steven Lochner, 7,500	65.00	NR
1976	MORNING TRAIN, Maxwell Mays, 7,500	65.00	NR
1977	DECORATING THE CHURCH, Maxwell Mays, 7,500	65.00	NR
1978	THE GENERAL STORE AT CHRISTMAS TIME, Maxwell Mays, 7,500	65.00	BR
1979	MERRY OLD SANTA CLAUS, Thomas Nast, 2,500	55.00	NR
1980	GATHERING CHRISTMAS GREENS, 2,500	65.00	NR
1981	THE SHOPKEEPER AT CHRISTMAS, W. L. Sheppard, 2,500	75.00	BR

Currier & Ives

1972	VILLAGE BLACKSMITH, 1,500	85.00	NR
1972	WESTERN MIGRATION, 1,500	85.00	NR
1973	OAKEN BUCKET, 1,500	85.00	NR
1973	WINTER IN COUNTRY, 1,500	85.00	NR
1974	PREPARING FOR MARKET, 1,500	85.00	NR

Founding Fathers

		ISSUE	CURRENT
1974	GEORGE WASHINGTON, 2,500	65.00	NR
1975	THOMAS JEFFERSON, 2,500	65.00	NR
1976	BEN FRANKLIN, 2,500	65.00	NR
1976	PATRICK HENRY, 2,500	65.00	NR
1976	JOHN HANCOCK, 2,500	65.00	NR
1976	JOHN ADAMS, 2,500	65.00	NR

Kentucky Derby

1972	NEARING FINISH, 1,000	75.00	85.00
1973	RIVA RIDGE, 1,500	75.00	85.00
1974	100TH RUNNING, 1,500	75.00	85.00

Missions of California

1971	SAN DIEGO, 1,500	75.00	NR
1972	CARMEL, 1,500	75.00	NR
1973	SANTA BARBARA, 1,500	60.00	NR
1974	SANTA CLARA, 1,500	60.00	NR
1976	SAN GABRIEL, 1,500	65.00	NR

Thomas Nast Christmas (Collector Creations)

1973	CHRISTMAS, Thomas Nast, 750	100.00	110.00

'Twas the Night Before Christmas

1989	'TWAS THE NIGHT BEFORE CHRISTMAS, J. Downing, 4,000	75.00	NR
1990	VISIONS OF SUGARPLUMS, J. Downing, 3,500	75.00	NR
1991	AWAY TO THE WINDOW, J. Downing, 3,500	75.00	NR

Single Issues

1970	ZODIAC, 1,500	75.00	NR
1972	ROAD RUNNER, 1,500	65.00	NR
1972	DELTA QUEEN, 2,500	75.00	NR
1973	ALICE IN WONDERLAND, 750	100.00	110.00
1973	CHICAGO FIRE, 1 year	60.00	NR
1975	MISSISSIPPI QUEEN, 2,500	75.00	NR

REEFTON MEADOWS CANADA

Great Moments in Sports, Series I Hockey

1989	HE SHOOTS, Glen Green, 29,500	35.00	NR
1989	HE SCORES, Glen Green, 29,500	35.00	NR
1989	Price for pair	25.00	NR

Great Moments in Sports, Series II Soccer

1989	BREAKAWAY, Glen Green, 29,500, 8½" d	35.00	NR
1989	THE SAVE, Glen Green, 29,500, 8½" d	35.00	NR
1989	Price for pair of 4" mini plates	25.00	NR

RHEA SILVA PORCELAIN COLLECTION UNITED STATES

		ISSUE	CURRENT
Child's Garden of Verse			
1983	LAND OF COUNTERPANE, Tom Bharnson, 17,500	39.00	NR
Endangered Birds			
1983	WHOOPING CRANES, Frank DeMatteis, 5,000	60.00	NR
Feline Favorites			
1982	LONG-HAIRED LADIES, Patrick Oxenham, 10,000	47.00	NR
1983	SIAMESE AND APPLE BLOSSOMS, Patrick Oxenham, 10,000	47.00	NR

RHODES UNITED STATES

Bountiful Harvest			
1992	BASKET FULL OF APPLES	39.00	NR
1992	BUSHEL OF PEACHES	39.00	NR
1993	PEARS FROM THE GROVE	39.00	RI
1993	FRESH OFF THE PLUM TREE	39.00	RI
Legendary Steam Trains			
1989	AMERICAN STANDARD 4-4-0	64.00	75.00
1990	HUDSON J3 STREAMLINER 4-6-4	65.00	85.00
1990	BEST FRIEND CHARLESTON 0-4-0T	70.00	BR
1990	THE CHALLENGER CLASS 4-6-6-4	70.00	85.00
1991	THE K-28-8-2	70.00	80.00
1991	THE K4 CLASS 4-6-2	70.00	NR
Miracles of Light			
1992	NATIVITY OF LOVE	85.00	NR
1992	NATIVITY OF PEACE	85.00	NR
1992	NATIVITY OF HOPE	90.00	NR
1992	NATIVITY OF JOY	90.00	NR
1993	NATIVITY OF FAITH	90.00	RI
1993	NATIVITY OF PRAISE	90.00	RI
Sculptured Songbirds			
1993	TENDING THE NEST	49.00	RI
1993	CHORUS OF HAPPINESS	49.00	RI
1993	MORNING FEEDING	54.00	RI
1984	BREAKFAST BLOSSOMS	54.00	RI
1994	SYMPHONY IN THE AZALEAS	54.00	RI
Treasures of the Dore Bible			
1986	MOSES/TEN COMMANDMENTS	59.00	BR
1987	JACOB AND THE ANGEL	59.00	BR
1987	REBEKAH AT THE WELL	64.00	BR
1988	DANIEL IN THE LION'S DEN	64.00	BR

		ISSUE	CURRENT
1988	JUDGMENT OF SOLOMON	64.00	BR
1988	ELIJAH AND CHARIOT OF FIRE	64.00	75.00

Village Lights

1993	HOLLY STREET BAKERY	49.00	RI
1993	MISTLETOE TOY SHOP	49.00	RI
1993	MRS. SUGARPLUM'S CHOCOLATES	54.00	RI
1993	CHURCH AT THE BEND	54.00	RI
1993	EVERGREEN BOOKS	54.00	RI
1994	KRINGLE'S GENERAL STORE	54.00	RI

Waterfowl Legacy

1991	MALLARD'S DESCENT	69.00	110.00
1992	IN FLIGHT	69.00	NR
1992	TAKING OFF	74.00	NR
1992	WIND RIDERS	74.00	NR
1993	FLYING IN	74.00	RI
1993	RISING UP	74.00	RI

RICKER-BARTLETT CASTING STUDIOS UNITED STATES

America's Children

1981	DEL, Anthony Ricker, 5,000	20.00	NR

Single Issue

1982	MOTHER'S DAY, Michael Ricker, 5,250	65.00	NR

RIDGEWOOD UNITED STATES

Bicentennial

1974	FIRST IN WAR, 12,500	40.00	NR

Christmas

1975	CHRISTMAS MORNING, J. C. Leyendecker, 10,000	24.50	40.00
1976	CHRISTMAS SURPRISE, 10,000	26.50	40.00

Little Women

1976	SWEET LONG AGO, Lorraine Trester, 5,000	45.00	65.00
1976	SONG OF SPRING, Lorraine Trester, 5,000	45.00	75.00
1977	JOY IN THE MORNING, Lorraine Trester, 5,000	45.00	50.00

Mother's Day

1976	GRANDMA'S APPLE PIE, J. C. Leyendecker, 5,000	24.50	NR
1977	TENDERNESS, J. C. Leyendecker, 10,000	35.00	NR

Tom Sawyer

1974	TRYING A PIPE, Norman Rockwell, 3,000	9.98	NR
1974	LOST IN CAVE, Norman Rockwell, 3,000	9.98	NR

		ISSUE	CURRENT
1974	PAINTING FENCE, Norman Rockwell, 3,000	9.98	NR
1974	TAKING MEDICINE, Norman Rockwell, 3,000	9.98	NR

Vasils Series

1976	ALL HALLOWS EVE, 5,000	38.50	NR

Wild West

1975	DISCOVERY OF LAST CHANCE GULCH, 15,000	16.25	NR
1975	DOUBTFUL VISITOR, 15,000	16.25	NR
1975	BAD ONE, 15,000	16.25	NR
1975	CATTLEMAN, 15,000	16.25	NR

RIVER SHORE UNITED STATES

(Bradford Exchange, Hamilton Collection, Ohio Arts, Woodmere China)

America at Work (Hamilton Collection)

1984	THE SCHOOL TEACHER, Norman Rockwell, 10 days	29.50	NR
1984	THE PIANO TUNER, Norman Rockwell, 10 days	29.50	NR
1984	THE ZOO KEEPER, Norman Rockwell, 10 days	29.50	NR
1984	THE CLEANING LADIES, Norman Rockwell, 10 days	29.50	NR
1984	THE HATCHECK GIRL, Norman Rockwell, 10 days	29.50	NR
1984	THE ARTIST, Norman Rockwell, 10 days	29.50	NR
1984	THE CENSUS TAKER, Norman Rockwell, 10 days	29.50	NR

Baby Animals Collection

1979	AKIKU, Roger Brown, 20,000	50.00	80.00
1980	ROOSEVELT, Roger Brown, 20,000	50.00	90.00
1981	CLOVER, Roger Brown, 20,000	50.00	65.00
1982	ZUELA, Roger Brown, 20,000	50.00	65.00

Children of the American Frontier (Hamilton Collection)

1986	IN TROUBLE AGAIN, Don Crook, 10 days	24.50	35.00
1986	TUBS AND SUDS, Don Crook, 10 days	24.50	NR
1986	A LADY NEEDS A LITTLE PRIVACY, Don Crook, 10 days	24.50	NR
1986	THE DESPERADOES, Don Crook, 10 days	24.50	NR
1986	RIDERS WANTED, Don Crook, 10 days	24.50	30.00
1987	A COWBOY'S DOWNFALL, Don Crook	24.50	NR
1987	RUNAWAY BLUES, Don Crook, 10 days	24.50	NR
1987	A SPECIAL PATIENT, Don Crook, 10 days	24.50	40.00

Della Robbia Annual

1979	ADORATION, Roger Brown, 5,000	550.00	NR
1980	VIRGIN AND CHILD, Roger Brown, 5,000	450.00	NR

Famous Americans

1976	BROWN'S LINCOLN, Rockwell—Brown, 9,500	40.00	NR
1977	ROCKWELL'S TRIPLE SELF-PORTRAIT, Rockwell—Brown, 9,500	45.00	NR
1978	PEACE CORPS, Rockwell—Brown, 9,500	45.00	NR
1979	SPIRIT OF LINDBERGH, Rockwell—Brown, 9,500	50.00	NR

Famous American Songbirds

		ISSUE	CURRENT
1985	WESTERN TANGER, Linda Thompson, 14 days	19.50	NR
1985	PURPLE FINCHES, Linda Thompson, 14 days	19.50	NR
1985	MOUNTAIN BLUEBIRDS, Linda Thompson, 14 days	19.50	NR
1985	CARDINAL, Linda Thompson, 14 days	19.50	NR
1985	BARN SWALLOW, Linda Thompson, 14 days	19.50	NR
1985	CANYON WREN, Linda Thompson, 14 days	19.50	NR
1985	MOCKINGBIRD, Linda Thompson, 14 days	19.50	NR
1985	WOOD THRUSH, Linda Thompson, 14 days	19.50	NR

Grant Wood Single Issue

1982	AMERICAN GOTHIC, Grant Wood, 17,500	80.00	NR

The School Teacher

Founder's Day Picnic

Little House on the Prairie (Hamilton Collection)

1982	FOUNDER'S DAY PICNIC, Eugene Christopherson, 10 days	29.50	45.00
1982	WOMEN'S HARVEST, Eugene Christopherson, 10 days	29.50	45.00
1985	MEDICINE SHOW, Eugene Christopherson, 10 days	29.50	45.00
1985	CAROLINE'S EGGS, Eugene Christopherson, 10 days	29.50	45.00
1985	MARY'S GIFT, Eugene Christopherson, 10 days	29.50	45.00
1985	A BELL FOR WALNUT GROVE, Eugene Christopherson, 10 days	29.50	45.00
1985	INGALLS FAMILY, Eugene Christopherson, 10 days	29.50	45.00
1985	THE SWEETHEART TREE, Eugene Christopherson, 10 days	29.50	45.00

Lovable Teddies

1985	BEDTIME BLUES, M. Hague, 10 days	21.50	NR
1985	BEARLY FRIGHTFUL, M. Hague, 10 days	21.50	NR
1985	CAUGHT IN THE ACT, M. Hague, 10 days	21.50	NR
1985	FIRESIDE FRIENDS, M. Hague, 10 days	21.50	NR
1985	HARVEST TIME, M. Hague, 10 days	21.50	NR
1985	MISSED A BUTTON, M. Hague, 10 days	21.50	NR

		ISSUE	CURRENT
1985	TENDER LOVING BEAR, M. Hague, 10 days	21.50	NR
1985	SUNDAY STROLL, M. Hague, 10 days	21.50	NR

Puppy Playtime

1987	DOUBLE TAKE—COCKER SPANIELS, Jim Lamb, 14 days	24.50	30.00
1987	FUN AND GAMES—POODLE, Jim Lamb, 14 days	24.50	NR
1988	CATCH OF THE DAY—GOLDEN RETRIEVER, Jim Lamb, 14 days	24.50	NR
1988	CABIN FEVER—BLACK LABRADOR, Jim Lamb, 14 days	24.50	NR
1988	WEEKEND GARDENER—LLASA APSOS, Jim Lamb, 14 days	24.50	NR
1988	GETTING ACQUAINTED—BEAGLES, Jim Lamb, 14 days	24.50	NR
1988	HANGING OUT—GERMAN SHEPHERD, Jim Lamb, 14 days	24.50	30.00
1988	A NEW LEASH ON LIFE, Jim Lamb, 14 days	24.50	NR

Remington Bronze

1977	BRONCO BUSTER, Roger Brown, 15,000	55.00	70.00
1978	COMING THROUGH THE RYE, Roger Brown, 15,000	60.00	NR
1980	CHEYENNE, Roger Brown, 15,000	60.00	NR
1981	THE MOUNTAIN MAN, Roger Brown, 15,000	60.00	NR

Rockwell Cats

1982	JENNIE AND TINA, Norman Rockwell, 9,500	39.50	NR

Rockwell Four Freedoms

1981	FREEDOM OF SPEECH, Norman Rockwell, 17,000	65.00	100.00
1982	FREEDOM OF WORSHIP, Norman Rockwell, 17,000	65.00	125.00
1982	FREEDOM FROM FEAR, Norman Rockwell, 17,000	65.00	200.00
1982	FREEDOM FROM WANT, Norman Rockwell, 17,000	65.00	425.00

Rockwell Good Old Days

1982	OLD OAKEN BUCKET, Norman Rockwell	24.50	NR
1982	BOY FISHING, Norman Rockwell	24.50	NR
1982	BAREFOOT BOY, Norman Rockwell	24.50	NR

Rockwell Single Issues

1979	SPRING FLOWERS, Norman Rockwell, 17,000	75.00	145.00
1980	LOOKING OUT TO SEA, Norman Rockwell, 17,000	75.00	195.00
1981	GRANDPA'S GUARDIAN, Norman Rockwell, 17,000	80.00	NR
1982	GRANDPA'S TREASURES, Norman Rockwell, 17,000	80.00	NR

Signs of Love

1981	A KISS FOR MOTHER, Yin-Rei Hicks, <1 year	18.50	BR
1981	A WATCHFUL EYE, Yin-Rei Hicks, <1 year	21.50	BR
1982	A GENTLE PERSUASION, Yin-Rei Hicks, <1 year	21.50	BR
1983	A PROTECTIVE EMBRACE, Yin-Rei Hicks, <1 year	23.50	BR
1983	A TENDER COAXING, Yin-Rei Hicks, <1 year	23.50	BR
1984	A REASSURING TOUCH	23.50	BR
1985	A TRUSTING HUG	26.50	BR
1985	A LOVING GUIDANCE	26.50	BR

		ISSUE	CURRENT

Timberlake's Christmas after Christmas

1982	KAY'S DOLL, Bob Timberlake, 9,500	75.00	NR

Vignette

1981	THE BROKEN WINDOW, Norman Rockwell, 22,500	19.50	NR
1982	SUNDAY BEST, Norman Rockwell, 22,500	19.50	NR

We the Children (Hamilton Collection)

1987	THE FREEDOM OF SPEECH, Don Crook, 14 days	24.50	NR
1988	RIGHT TO VOTE, Don Crook, 14 days	24.50	NR
1988	UNREASONABLE SEARCH AND SEIZURE, Don Crook, 14 days	24.50	NR
1988	RIGHT TO BEAR ARMS, Don Crook, 14 days	24.50	NR
1988	TRIAL BY JURY, Don Crook, 14 days	24.50	NR
1988	SELF-INCRIMINATION, Don Crook, 14 days	24.50	NR
1988	CRUEL AND UNUSUAL PUNISHMENT, Don Crook, 14 days	24.50	NR
1988	QUARTERING OF SOLDIERS, Don Crook, 14 days	24.50	NR

A Protective Embrace
Photo courtesy of *Collectors News*

The Freedom of Speech
Photo courtesy of *Collectors News*

ROCKFORD EDITIONS UNITED STATES

Little Mothers

1985	LOVE IS BLIND, Bessie Pease Gutmann	29.95	NR
1985	FIRST STEP, Bessie Pease Gutmann	29.95	NR

ROCKWELL COLLECTORS CLUB UNITED STATES

Christmas

1978	CHRISTMAS STORY, Norman Rockwell, 15,000	24.50	NR

ROCKWELL MUSEUM UNITED STATES

(Museum Collections, Nostalgia Collectibles)

American Family I

		ISSUE	CURRENT
1979	BABY'S FIRST STEP, Norman Rockwell, 9,900	28.50	50.00
1979	HAPPY BIRTHDAY, DEAR MOTHER, Norman Rockwell, 9,900	28.50	45.00
1979	SWEET SIXTEEN, Norman Rockwell, 9,900	28.50	35.00
1979	FIRST HAIRCUT, Norman Rockwell, 9,900	28.50	60.00
1979	FIRST PROM, Norman Rockwell, 9,900	28.50	35.00
1979	WRAPPING CHRISTMAS PRESENTS, Norman Rockwell, 9,900	28.50	35.00
1979	THE STUDENT, Norman Rockwell, 9,900	28.50	35.00
1979	THE BIRTHDAY PARTY, Norman Rockwell, 9,900	28.50	35.00
1979	LITTLE MOTHER, Norman Rockwell, 9,900	28.50	35.00
1979	WASHING OUR DOG, Norman Rockwell, 9,900	28.50	35.00
1979	MOTHER'S LITTLE HELPERS, Norman Rockwell, 9,900	28.50	35.00
1979	BRIDE AND GROOM, Norman Rockwell, 9,900	28.50	35.00

American Family II

1980	NEW ARRIVAL, Norman Rockwell, 22,500	35.00	55.00
1980	SWEET DREAMS, Norman Rockwell, 22,500	35.00	NR
1980	LITTLE SHAVER, Norman Rockwell, 22,500	35.00	40.00
1980	WE MISSED YOU, DADDY, Norman Rockwell, 22,500	35.00	NR
1981	HOME RUN SLUGGER, Norman Rockwell, 22,500	35.00	NR
1981	GIVING THANKS, Norman Rockwell, 22,500	35.00	55.00
1981	LITTLE SALESMAN, Norman Rockwell, 22,500	35.00	NR
1981	ALMOST GROWN UP, Norman Rockwell, 22,500	35.00	NR
1981	COURAGEOUS HERO, Norman Rockwell, 22,500	35.00	NR
1981	AT THE CIRCUS, Norman Rockwell, 22,500	35.00	NR
1981	GOOD FOOD, GOOD FRIENDS, Norman Rockwell, 22,500	35.00	NR

Children at Christmastime

NA	CHRISTMAS PRAYERS, Norman Rockwell, 1 year	NA	NA

Christmas Collectibles

1979	THE DAY AFTER CHRISTMAS, Norman Rockwell, 1 year	75.00	NR
1980	CHECKING HIS LIST, Norman Rockwell, 1 year	75.00	NR
1981	RINGING IN GOOD CHEER, Norman Rockwell, 1 year	75.00	NR
1982	WAITING FOR SANTA, Norman Rockwell, 1 year	75.00	NR
1983	HIGH HOPES, Norman Rockwell, 1 year	75.00	NR
1984	SPACE AGE SANTA, Norman Rockwell, 1 year	55.00	75.00

Classic Plate

1981	PUPPY LOVE, Norman Rockwell, 60 days	24.50	NR
1981	WHILE THE AUDIENCE WAITS, Norman Rockwell, 60 days	24.50	NR
1981	OFF TO SCHOOL, Norman Rockwell, 60 days	24.50	NR
1982	THE COUNTRY DOCTOR, Norman Rockwell, 60 days	24.50	NR
1982	SPRING FEVER, Norman Rockwell, 60 days	24.50	NR
1982	A DOLLHOUSE FOR SIS, Norman Rockwell, 60 days	24.50	NR

Elvis Presley Collection

1985	HOUND DOG, limited	15.00	NR
1985	LONESOME TONIGHT, limited	15.00	NR

		ISSUE	CURRENT
1985	TEDDY BEAR, limited	15.00	NR
1985	DON'T BE CRUEL, limited	15.00	NR
	Set of 4	60.00	NR

Gene Autry Collection (Nostalgia Collectibles)

1984	AMERICA'S FAVORITE COWBOY, Norman Rockwell, 25,000	45.00	NR

James Dean Collection (Nostalgia Collectibles)

1985	EAST OF EDEN, limited	15.00	NR
1985	REBEL WITHOUT A CAUSE, limited	15.00	NR
1985	GIANT, limited	15.00	NR
1985	JIM AND SPYDER, limited	15.00	NR
	Set of 4	60.00	NR

Mother's Day

1982	A TENDER MOMENT, Norman Rockwell, 5,000	70.00	NR

Shirley Temple Collectibles

1982	BABY TAKE A BOW, 22,500	75.00	100.00
1982	BABY TAKE A BOW, sgd, 2,500	100.00	160.00
1982	STAND UP AND CHEER, 22,500	75.00	100.00
1982	STAND UP AND CHEER, sgd, 2,500	100.00	NR
1982	CURLY TOP, 22,500	75.00	100.00
1982	CURLY TOP, sgd, 2,500	100.00	150.00

Shirley Temple Classic Collection

1983	CAPTAIN JANUARY, William Jacobson, 25,000	35.00	NR
1984	HEIDI, William Jacobson, 25,000	35.00	NR
1984	LITTLE MISS MARKER, William Jacobson, 25,000	35.00	NR
1984	BRIGHT EYES, William Jacobson, 25,000	35.00	NR
1985	THE LITTLE COLONEL, William Jacobson, 25,000	35.00	NR
1985	REBECCA OF SUNNYBROOK FARM, William Jacobson, 25,000	35.00	NR
1986	POOR LITTLE RICH GIRL, William Jacobson, 25,000	35.00	NR
1986	WEE WILLIE WINKIE, William Jacobson, 25,000	35.00	NR

Touch of Rockwell

1984	SONGS OF PRAISE, Norman Rockwell, 1 year	14.95	NR
1984	BEDTIME PRAYERS, Norman Rockwell, 1 year	14.95	NR
1984	FIRST DAY OF SCHOOL, Norman Rockwell, 1 year	14.95	NR
1984	SUPRISE TREAT, Norman Rockwell, 1 year	14.95	NR
1984	THE RUNAWAY, Norman Rockwell, 1 year	14.95	NR

World of Children Bas-Relief

1982	DOWNHILL RACER, Norman Rockwell, 15,000	45.00	NR
1982	VACATION OVER, Norman Rockwell, 15,000	45.00	NR
1982	LITTLE PATIENT, Norman Rockwell, 15,000	45.00	NR
1982	BICYCLE BOYS, Norman Rockwell, 15,000	45.00	NR

Special Commemorative Issues

1985	ELVIS PRESLEY—THE ONCE AND FOREVER KING, William Jacobson, 10,000	40.00	NR
1985	JAMES DEAN—AMERICA'S REBEL, William Jacobson, 10,000	45.00	NR

Rebecca of Sunnybrook Farm
Photo courtesy of *Collectors News*

Norman Rockwell Remembered
Photo courtesy of *Collectors News*

Single Issues

		ISSUE	CURRENT
1979	NORMAN ROCKWELL REMEMBERED, Norman Rockwell, 30 days	45.00	NR
1982	CELEBRATION, Norman Rockwell, 9,900	55.00	NR
1983	A TRIBUTE TO JOHN F. KENNEDY, Norman Rockwell	39.50	NR
1983	WITH THIS RING, Norman Rockwell, 1 year	50.00	NR

ROCKWELL SOCIETY UNITED STATES
(Edwin Knowles)

Christmas

1974	SCOTTY GETS HIS TREE, Norman Rockwell, 1 year	24.50	90.00
1975	ANGEL WITH A BLACK EYE, Norman Rockwell, 1 year	24.50	50.00
1976	GOLDEN CHRISTMAS, Norman Rockwell, 1 year	24.50	30.00
1977	TOY SHOP WINDOW, Norman Rockwell, 1 year	24.50	35.00
1978	CHRISTMAS DREAM, Norman Rockwell, 1 year	24.50	NR
1979	SOMEBODY'S UP THERE, Norman Rockwell, 1 year	24.50	30.00
1980	SCOTTY PLAYS SANTA, Norman Rockwell, 1 year	24.50	NR
1981	WRAPPED UP IN CHRISTMAS, Norman Rockwell, 1 year	25.50	NR
1982	CHRISTMAS COURTSHIP, Norman Rockwell, 1 year	25.50	30.00
1983	SANTA IN THE SUBWAY, Norman Rockwell, 1 year	25.50	30.00
1984	SANTA IN HIS WORKSHOP, Norman Rockwell, 1 year	27.50	30.00
1985	GRANDPA PLAYS SANTA	27.50	NR
1986	DEAR SANTY CLAUS	27.90	NR
1987	SANTA'S GOLDEN GIFT	29.90	NR
1988	SANTA CLAUS	29.90	NR
1989	JOLLY OLD ST. NICK	29.90	35.00
1990	A CHRISTMAS PRAYER	29.90	NR
1991	SANTA'S HELPERS	32.90	NR
1992	THE CHRISTMAS SURPRISE	32.90	NR
1993	THE TREE BRIGADE	32.90	RI
1994	CHRISTMAS MARVEL	32.90	RI

		ISSUE	CURRENT
1995	FILLING THE STOCKINGS	32.90	RI
1996	AND TO ALL A GOODNIGHT	34.95	RI

Coming of Age

		ISSUE	CURRENT
1990	BACK TO SCHOOL, Norman Rockwell, 150 days	29.90	45.00
1990	HOME FROM CAMP, Norman Rockwell, 150 days	29.90	35.00
1990	HER FIRST FORMAL, Norman Rockwell, 150 days	32.90	65.00
1990	THE MUSCLEMAN, Norman Rockwell, 150 days	32.90	NR
1990	A NEW LOOK, Norman Rockwell, 150 days	32.90	NR
1991	A BALCONY SEAT, Norman Rockwell, 150 days	32.90	BR
1991	MEN ABOUT TOWN, Norman Rockwell, 150 days	34.90	BR
1991	PATHS OF GLORY, Norman Rockwell, 150 days	34.90	BR
1991	DOORWAY TO THE PAST, Norman Rockwell, 150 days	34.90	BR
1991	SCHOOL'S OUT!, Norman Rockwell, 150 days	34.90	45.00

Innocence and Experience

		ISSUE	CURRENT
1991	THE SEA CAPTAIN, Norman Rockwell, 150 days	29.90	BR
1991	THE RADIO OPERATOR, Norman Rockwell, 150 days	29.90	NR
1991	THE MAGICIAN, Norman Rockwell, 150 days	32.90	50.00
1992	THE AMERICAN HEROES, Norman Rockwell, 150 days	32.90	BR

The Sea Captain
Photo courtesy of *Collectors News*

Mending Time
Photo courtesy of *Collectors News*

A Mind of Her Own

		ISSUE	CURRENT
1986	SITTING PRETTY, Norman Rockwell, 150 days	24.90	BR
1987	SERIOUS BUSINESS, Norman Rockwell, 150 days	24.90	BR
1987	BREAKING THE RULES, Norman Rockwell, 150 days	24.90	NR
1987	GOOD INTENTIONS, Norman Rockwell, 150 days	27.90	NR
1988	SECOND THOUGHTS, Norman Rockwell, 150 days	27.90	NR
1988	WORLDS AWAY, Norman Rockwell, 150 days	27.90	NR
1988	KISS AND TELL, Norman Rockwell, 150 days	29.90	BR
1988	ON MY HONOR, Norman Rockwell, 150 days	29.90	NR

Mother's Day

		ISSUE	CURRENT
1976	A MOTHER'S LOVE, Norman Rockwell, 1 year	24.50	60.00
1977	FAITH, Norman Rockwell, 1 year	24.50	50.00
1978	BEDTIME, Norman Rockwell, 1 year	24.50	35.00
1979	REFLECTIONS, Norman Rockwell, 1year	24.50	NR
1980	A MOTHER'S PRIDE, Norman Rockwell, 1 year	24.50	NR
1981	AFTER THE PARTY, Norman Rockwell, 1 year	24.50	BR
1982	THE COOKING LESSON, Norman Rockwell, 1 year	25.50	BR
1983	ADD TWO CUPS AND A MEASURE OF LOVE, Norman Rockwell, 1 year	25.50	BR
1984	GRANDMA'S COURTING DRESS, Norman Rockwell, 1 year	25.50	BR
1985	MENDING TIME, Norman Rockwell, 1 year	27.50	BR
1986	PANTRY RAID, Norman Rockwell, 1 year	27.50	BR
1987	GRANDMA'S SURPRISE, Norman Rockwell, 1 year	29.90	BR
1988	MY MOTHER, Norman Rockwell, 1 year	29.90	BR
1989	SUNDAY DINNER, Norman Rockwell, 1 year	29.90	BR
1990	EVENING PRAYERS, Norman Rockwell, 1 year	29.90	BR
1991	BUILDING OUR FUTURE, Norman Rockwell, 1 year	32.90	BR
1991	GENTLE REASSURANCE, Norman Rockwell, 1 year	32.90	NR
1992	A SPECIAL DELIVERY, Norman Rockwell, 1 year	32.90	NR

Rockwell Commemorative Stamps

		ISSUE	CURRENT
1994	TRIPLE SELF PORTRAIT, Norman Rockwell, 95 days	29.90	RI
1994	FREEDOM FROM WANT, Norman Rockwell, 95 days	29.90	RI
1994	FREEDOM FROM FEAR, Norman Rockwell, 95 days	29.90	RI
1995	FREEDOM OF SPEECH, Norman Rockwell, 95 days	29.90	RI
1995	FREEDOM OF WORSHIP, Norman Rockwell, 95 days	29.90	RI

Rockwell Heritage

		ISSUE	CURRENT
1977	TOY MAKER, Norman Rockwell, 1 year	14.50	60.00
1978	THE COBBLER, Norman Rockwell, 1 year	19.50	35.00
1979	THE LIGHTHOUSE KEEPER'S DAUGHTER, Norman Rockwell, 1 year	19.50	35.00
1980	THE SHIP BUILDER, Norman Rockwell, 1 year	19.50	30.00
1981	THE MUSIC MASTER, Norman Rockwell, 1 year	19.50	25.00
1982	THE TYCOON, Norman Rockwell, 1 year	19.50	25.00
1983	THE PAINTER, Norman Rockwell, 1 year	19.50	NR
1984	THE STORYTELLER, Norman Rockwell, 1 year	19.50	NR
1985	THE GOURMET, Norman Rockwell, 1 year	19.50	NR
1986	THE PROFESSOR	22.90	NR
1987	THE SHADOW ARTIST	22.90	NR
1988	THE VETERAN	22.90	BR
1989	THE BANJO PLAYER	24.90	BR
1990	THE OLD SCOUT	24.90	BR
1991	THE YOUNG SCHOLAR	24.90	NR
1992	THE FAMILY DOCTOR	27.90	40.00
1993	THE JEWELER	27.90	RI
1994	HALLOWEEN FROLIC	27.90	RI
1995	THE APPRENTICE	29.90	RI
1996	THE MASTER VIOLINIST	29.90	RI
1997	THE DREAMER	29.95	RI

Rockwell on Tour

		ISSUE	CURRENT
1983	WALKING THROUGH MERRIE ENGLANDE, Norman Rockwell, 150 days	16.00	NR
1983	PROMENADE A PARIS, Norman Rockwell, 150 days	16.00	30.00

		ISSUE	CURRENT
1983	WHEN IN ROME, Norman Rockwell, 150 days	16.00	NR
1984	DIE WALK AM RHEIN, Norman Rockwell, 150 days	16.00	NR

Rockwell's American Dream

1985	A YOUNG GIRL'S DREAM, Norman Rockwell, 150 days	19.90	BR
1985	A COUPLE'S COMMITMENT, Norman Rockwell, 150 days	19.90	NR
1985	A FAMILY'S FULL MEASURE, Norman Rockwell, 150 days	22.90	NR
1986	A MOTHER'S WELCOME, Norman Rockwell, 150 days	22.90	NR
1986	A YOUNG MAN'S DREAM, Norman Rockwell, 150 days	22.90	NR
1986	THE MUSICIAN'S MAGIC, Norman Rockwell, 150 days	22.90	30.00
1987	AN ORPHAN'S HOPE, Norman Rockwell, 150 days	24.90	30.00
1987	LOVE'S REWARD, Norman Rockwell, 150 days	24.90	30.00

Love's Reward
Photo courtesy of *Collectors News*

Standing in the Doorway
Photo courtesy of *Collectors News*

Rockwell's Christmas Legacy (Norman Rockwell Gallery)

1992	SANTA'S WORKSHOP, Norman Rockwell, 150 days	49.90	75.00
1993	MAKING A LIST, Norman Rockwell, 150 days	49.90	RI
1993	WHILE SANTA SLUMBERS	54.90	RI
1993	VISIONS OF SANTA	54.90	RI
1993	FILLING EVERY STOCKING	54.90	RI
1993	SANTA'S MAGICAL VIEW	54.90	RI

Rockwell's Colonials

1985	UNEXPECTED PROPOSAL	27.90	NR
1986	WORDS OF COMFORT	27.90	NR
1986	LIGHT FOR THE WINTER	30.90	NR
1987	PORTRAIT FOR A BRIDEGROOM	30.90	NR
1987	THE JOURNEY HOME	30.90	NR
1987	CLINCHING THE DEAL	30.90	NR
1988	SIGN OF THE TIMES	32.90	NR
1988	YE GLUTTON	32.90	NR

Rockwell's Golden Moments

		ISSUE	CURRENT
1987	GRANDPA'S GIFT, Norman Rockwell, 150 days	19.90	NR
1987	GRANDMA'S LOVE, Norman Rockwell, 150 days	19.90	25.00
1988	END OF DAY, Norman Rockwell, 150 days	22.90	30.00
1988	BEST FRIENDS, Norman Rockwell, 150 days	22.90	BR
1989	LOVE LETTERS, Norman Rockwell, 150 days	22.90	30.00
1989	NEWFOUND WORLDS, Norman Rockwell, 150 days	22.90	BR
1989	KEEPING COMPANY, Norman Rockwell, 150 days	24.90	BR
1989	EVENING'S REPOSE, Norman Rockwell, 150 days	24.90	BR

Rockwell's Light Campaign

1983	THE ROOM THAT LIGHT MADE, Norman Rockwell, 150 days	19.50	BR
1984	GRANDPA'S TREASURE CHEST, Norman Rockwell, 150 days	19.50	30.00
1984	FATHER'S HELP, Norman Rockwell, 150 days	19.50	BR
1984	EVENING'S EASE, Norman Rockwell, 150 days	19.50	BR
1984	CLOSE HARMONY, Norman Rockwell, 150 days	21.50	NR
1984	THE BIRTHDAY WISH, Norman Rockwell, 150 days	21.50	NR

Rockwell's Rediscovered Women

1981	DREAMING IN THE ATTIC, Norman Rockwell, 100 days	19.50	BR
1982	WAITING ON THE SHORE, Norman Rockwell, 100 days	22.50	BR
1983	PONDERING ON THE PORCH, Norman Rockwell, 100 days	22.50	BR
1983	MAKING BELIEVE AT THE MIRROR, Norman Rockwell, 100 days	22.50	BR
1983	WAITING AT THE DANCE, Norman Rockwell, 100 days	22.50	NR
1983	GOSSIPING IN THE ALCOVE, Norman Rockwell, 100 days	22.50	BR
1983	STANDING IN THE DOORWAY, Norman Rockwell, 100 days	22.50	NR
1983	FLIRTING IN THE PARLOR, Norman Rockwell, 100 days	22.50	BR
1983	WORKING IN THE KITCHEN, Norman Rockwell, 100 days	22.50	30.00
1984	MEETING ON THE PATH, Norman Rockwell, 100 days	22.50	NR
1984	CONFIDING IN THE DEN, Norman Rockwell, 100 days	22.50	NR
1984	REMINISCING IN THE QUIET, Norman Rockwell, 100 days	22.50	NR

Rockwell's the Ones We Love

1988	TENDER LOVING CARE, Norman Rockwell, 150 days	19.90	BR
1989	A TIME TO KEEP, Norman Rockwell, 150 days	19.90	NR
1989	THE INVENTOR AND THE JUDGE, Norman Rockwell, 150 days	22.90	NR
1989	READY FOR THE WORLD, Norman Rockwell, 150 days	22.90	NR
1989	GROWING STRONG, Norman Rockwell, 150 days	22.90	NR
1990	THE STORY HOUR, Norman Rockwell, 150 days	22.90	NR
1990	THE COUNTRY DOCTOR, Norman Rockwell, 150 days	24.90	NR
1990	OUR LOVE OF COUNTRY, Norman Rockwell, 150 days	24.90	NR
1990	THE HOMECOMING, Norman Rockwell, 150 days	24.90	NR
1991	A HELPING HAND, Norman Rockwell, 150 days	24.90	NR

Rockwell's Treasured Memories

1991	QUIET REFLECTIONS, Norman Rockwell, 150 days	29.90	BR
1991	ROMANTIC REVERIE, Norman Rockwell, 150 days	29.90	NR
1991	TENDER ROMANCE, Norman Rockwell, 150 days	32.90	BR
1991	EVENING PASSAGE, Norman Rockwell, 150 days	32.90	BR
1991	HEAVENLY DREAMS, Norman Rockwell, 150 days	32.90	BR
1991	SENTIMENTAL SHORES, Norman Rockwell, 150 days	32.90	BR

ROMAN, INC. UNITED STATES
(March of Dimes)

Abbie Williams Collection

		ISSUE	CURRENT
1987	THE CHRISTENING, Abbie Williams, open	29.50	NR
1990	THE DEDICATION, Abbie Williams, open	29.50	NR
1990	THE DEDICATION, Abbie Williams, miniature	5.00	NR
1990	THE BAPTISM, Abbie Williams, open	29.50	NR
1991	LEGACY OF LOVE, Abbie Williams	29.50	NR
1991	BLESS THIS CHILD, Abbie Williams, 14 days	29.50	NR
NA	FIRST COMMUNION, BOY, Abbie Williams	19.50	NR
NA	FIRST COMMUNION, GIRL, Abbie Williams	19.50	NR

Anniversary Commemoratives

1997	25TH ANNIVERSARY, Ellen Williams	39.50	RI
1997	GENERAL ANNIVERSARY, Ellen Williams	39.50	RI

Baby Keepsakes

1997	ON THE DAY YOU WERE BORN	29.50	RI

Catnippers

1986	CHRISTMAS MOURNING, Irene Spencer, 9,500	34.50	NR
1992	HAPPY HOLIDAZE, Irene Spencer, 9,500	34.50	NR

Cats

1984	GRIZABELLA, 30 days	29.50	NR
1984	MR. MISTOFFELEES, 30 days	29.50	NR
1984	RUM TUM TUGGER, 30 days	29.50	NR
1985	GROWLTIGER, 30 days	29.50	NR
1985	SKIMBLESHANKS, 30 days	29.50	NR
1985	MUNGOJERRIE AND RUMPELTEAZER, 30 days	29.50	NR

Child's Play (Edwin M. Knowles)

1982	BREEZY DAY, Frances Hook, 30 days	29.95	40.00
1982	KITE FLYING, Frances Hook, 30 days	29.95	40.00
1984	BATHTUB SAILOR, Frances Hook, 30 days	29.95	35.00
1984	THE FIRST SNOW, Frances Hook, 30 days	29.95	35.00

Child's World

1980	LITTLE CHILDREN, COME TO ME, Frances Hook, 15,000	45.00	NR

Fontanini Annual Christmas Plate

1986	A KING IS BORN, E. Simonetti, 1 year	60.00	NR
1987	O COME, LET US ADORE HIM, E. Simonetti, 1 year	60.00	NR
1988	ADORATION OF THE MAGI, E. Simonetti, 1 year	70.00	NR
1989	FLIGHT INTO EGYPT, E. Simonetti, 1 year	75.00	85.00

Frances Hook Collection—Set I

1982	I WISH, I WISH, Frances Hook, 15,000	24.95	75.00
1982	BABY BLOSSOMS, Frances Hook, 15,000	24.95	35.00

		ISSUE	CURRENT
1982	DAISY DREAMER, Frances Hook, 15,000	24.95	35.00
1982	TREES SO TALL, Frances Hook, 15,000	24.95	35.00

Frances Hook Collection—Set II

1983	CAUGHT IT MYSELF, Frances Hook, 15,000	24.95	NR
1983	WINTER WRAPPINGS, Frances Hook, 15,000	24.95	NR
1983	SO CUDDLY, Frances Hook, 15,000	24.95	NR
1983	CAN I KEEP HIM?, Frances Hook, 15,000	24.95	NR

Frances Hook Legacy (Edwin M. Knowles)

1985	FASCINATION, Frances Hook, 100 days	19.50	35.00
1985	DAYDREAMING, Frances Hook, 100 days	19.50	35.00
1985	DISCOVERY, Frances Hook, 100 days	22.50	35.00
1985	DISAPPOINTMENT, Frances Hook, 100 days	22.50	35.00
1985	WONDERMENT, Frances Hook, 100 days	22.50	35.00
1985	EXPECTATION, Frances Hook, 100 days	22.50	35.00

Daydreaming
Photo courtesy of *Collectors News*

Baby's First Step
Photo courtesy of *Collectors News*

God Bless You Little One

1991	BABY'S FIRST BIRTHDAY (GIRL), Abbie Williams, open	29.50	NR
1991	BABY'S FIRST BIRTHDAY (BOY), Abbie Williams, open	29.50	NR
1991	BABY'S FIRST SMILE, Abbie Williams, open	19.50	NR
1991	BABY'S FIRST WORD, Abbie Williams, open	19.50	NR
1991	BABY'S FIRST STEP, Abbie Williams, open	19.50	NR
1991	BABY'S FIRST TOOTH, Abbie Williams, open	19.50	NR

Ice Capades Clown

1983	PRESENTING FREDDIE TRENKLER, George B. Petty, 30 days	24.50	NR

Jesus Loves Me

1997	BOY	25.00	RI

			ISSUE	CURRENT
1997	GIRL		25.00	RI

Legendary Santas

1996	KRISS KRINGLE, Galleria Lucchese, open	39.50	RI
1996	ST. NICHOLAS, Galleria Lucchese, open	39.50	RI

Lord's Prayer

1986	OUR FATHER, Abbie Williams, 10 days	24.50	NR
1986	THY KINGDOM COME, Abbie Williams, 10 days	24.50	NR
1986	GIVE US THIS DAY, Abbie Williams, 10 days	24.50	NR
1986	FORGIVE OUR TRESPASSES, Abbie Williams, 10 days	24.50	NR
1986	AS WE FORGIVE, Abbie Williams, 10 days	24.50	NR
1986	LEAD US NOT, Abbie Williams, 10 days	24.50	NR
1986	DELIVER US FROM EVIL, Abbie Williams, 10 days	24.50	NR
1986	THINE IS THE KINGDOM, Abbie Williams, 10 days	24.50	NR

Love's Prayer

1988	LOVE IS PATIENT AND KIND, Abbie Williams, 14 days	29.50	NR
1988	LOVE IS NEVER JEALOUS OR BOASTFUL, Abbie Williams, 14 days	29.50	NR
1988	LOVE IS NEVER ARROGANT OR RUDE, Abbie Williams, 14 days	29.50	NR
1988	LOVE DOES NOT INSIST ON ITS OWN WAY, Abbie Williams, 14 days	29.50	NR
1988	LOVE IS NEVER IRRITABLE OR RESENTFUL, Abbie Williams, 14 days	29.50	NR
1988	LOVE REJOICES IN THE RIGHT, Abbie Williams, 14 days	29.50	NR
1988	LOVE BELIEVES ALL THINGS, Abbie Williams, 14 days	29.50	NR
1988	LOVE NEVER ENDS, Abbie Williams, 14 days	29.50	NR

Magic of Childhood

1985	SPECIAL FRIENDS, Abbie Williams, 10 days	24.50	NR
1985	FEEDING TIME, Abbie Williams, 10 days	24.50	NR
1985	BEST BUDDIES, Abbie Williams, 10 days	24.50	NR
1985	GETTING ACQUAINTED, Abbie Williams, 10 days	24.50	NR
1986	LAST ONE IN, Abbie Williams, 10 days	24.50	NR
1986	A HANDFUL OF LOVE, Abbie Williams, 10 days	24.50	NR
1986	LOOK ALIKES, Abbie Williams, 10 days	24.50	NR
1986	NO FAIR PEEKING, Abbie Williams, 10 days	24.50	NR

Masterpiece Collection

1979	ADORATION, Fra Filippo Lippi, 5,000	65.00	NR
1980	MADONNA WITH GRAPES, P. Mignard, 5,000	87.50	NR
1981	THE HOLY FAMILY, G. Delle Notti, 5,000	95.00	NR
1982	MADONNA OF THE STREETS, Robert Feruzzi, 5,000	85.00	NR

Millennium Series, Oxolyte

1992	SILENT NIGHT, Ennio Morcaldo/Alfonso Lucchesi, 5,000	49.50	NR
1993	THE ANNUNCIATION, Ennio Morcaldo/Alfonso Lucchesi, 5,000	49.50	RI
1994	PEACE ON EARTH, Ennio Morcaldo/Alfonso Lucchesi, 5,000	49.50	RI
1995	CAUSE OF OUR JOY, Ennio Morcaldo/Alfonso Lucchesi, 5,000	49.50	RI
1996	PRINCE OF PEACE, Ennio Morcaldo/Alfonso Lucchesi, 5,000	49.50	RI
1997	GENTLE LOVE, Sister Mary Jean Dorcy, 1 year	49.50	RI

Precious Children

1993	BLESS BABY BROTHER, Abbie Williams	29.50	RI

		ISSUE	CURRENT
1993	BLOWING BUBBLES, Abbie Williams	29.50	RI
1993	DON'T WORRY, MOTHER DUCK, Abbie Williams	29.50	RI
1993	TREETOP DISCOVERY, Abbie Williams	29.50	RI
1993	THE TEA PARTY, Abbie Williams	29.50	RI
1993	MOTHER'S LITTLE ANGEL, Abbie Williams	29.50	RI
1993	PICKING DAISIES, Abbie Williams	29.50	RI
1993	LET'S SAY GRACE, Abbie Williams	29.50	RI

Pretty Girls of the Ice Capades

1983	ICE PRINCESS, George B. Petty, 30 days	24.50	NR

Promise of a Savior (Bradford Exchange)

1993	AN ANGEL'S MESSAGE, 95 days	29.90	RI
1993	GIFTS TO JESUS, 95 days	29.90	RI
1993	THE HEAVENLY KING, 95 days	29.90	RI
1993	ANGELS WERE WATCHING, 95 days	29.90	RI
1993	HOLY MOTHER & CHILD, 95 days	29.90	RI
1993	A CHILD IS BORN, 95 days	29.90	RI

Remembrances

1997	CELEBRATIONS, Timothy Botts	35.00	RI

Richard Judson Zolan Collection

1992	THE BUTTERFLY NET, Richard Judson Zolan, 100 days	29.50	NR
1994	THE RING, Richard Judson Zolan, 100 days	29.50	RI
1994	TERRACE DANCING, Richard Judson Zolan, 100 days	29.50	RI

Roman Memorial

1984	THE CARPENTER, Frances Hook, 1 year	100.00	135.00

Seraphim Classics™ Faro Collection

1994	ROSALYN—RAREST OF HEAVEN, Ennio Morcaldo/Alfonso Lucchesi, 7,200	65.00	RI
1995	HELENA—HEAVEN'S HERALD, Ennio Morcaldo/Alfonso Lucchesi, 7,200	65.00	RI
1996	FLORA—FLOWER OF HEAVEN, Ennio Morcaldo/Alfonso Lucchesi, 7,200	65.00	RI
1997	EMILY—HEAVEN'S TREASURE, Ennio Morcaldo/Alfonso Lucchesi, 1 year	65.00	RI
1998	ELISE—HEAVEN'S GLORY, Ennio Morcaldo/Alfonso Lucchesi, 1 year	65.00	RI

Seraphim Classics™ Sculpted Oval Plate

1996	CYMBELINE—PEACEMAKER, Seraphim Studios, 2 years	49.95	RI
1996	ISABEL—GENTLE SPIRIT, Seraphim Studios, 2 years	49.95	RI
1996	LYDIA—WINGED POET, Seraphim Studios, 2 years	49.95	RI
1996	PRISCILLA—BENEVOLENT GUIDE, Seraphim Studios, 2 years	49.95	RI

Sweetest Songs

1986	A BABY'S PRAYER, Irene Spencer, 30 days	39.50	45.00
1986	THIS LITTLE PIGGIE, Irene Spencer, 30 days	39.50	NR
1988	LONG, LONG AGO, Irene Spencer, 30 days	39.50	NR
1989	ROCKABYE, Irene Spencer, 30 days	39.50	NR

Tender Expressions

1992	THOUGHTS OF YOU ARE IN MY HEART, Barbi Sargent, 100 days	29.50	NR

		ISSUE	CURRENT

Tidings of Joy

1997	THE FIRST BREAKFAST	24.95	RI

Visions of Our Lady

1994	OUR LADY OF LOURDES, Hector Garrido, 95 days	29.90	RI
1994	OUR LADY OF MEDJUGORJE, Hector Garrido, 95 days	29.90	RI
1994	OUR LADY OF FATIMA, Hector Garrido, 95 days	29.90	RI
1994	OUR LADY OF GUADELOUPE, Hector Garrido, 95 days	29.90	RI
1994	OUR LADY OF GRACE, Hector Garrido, 95 days	29.90	RI
1994	OUR LADY OF MOUNT CARMEL, Hector Garrido, 95 days	29.90	RI
1994	OUR LADY OF LASALETTE, Hector Garrido, 95 days	29.90	RI
1994	OUR LADY OF THE POOR, Hector Garrido, 95 days	29.90	RI
1994	VIRGIN WITH THE GOLDEN HEART, Hector Garrido, 95 days	29.90	RI
1994	OUR LADY OF HOPE, Hector Garrido, 95 days	29.90	RI
1994	OUR LADY OF SILENCE, Hector Garrido, 95 days	29.90	RI
1994	OUR LADY OF THE SNOW, Hector Garrido, 95 days	29.90	RI

Visions of Our Lady—Oxolyte

1994	OUR LADY OF FATIMA	39.90	RI
1994	OUR LADY OF GRACE	39.90	RI
1994	OUR LADY OF LOURDES	39.90	RI
1994	OUR LADY OF GUADALUPE	39.90	RI

Visions of Our Lady—Three-Dimensional

1997	OUR LADY OF FATIMA	39.50	RI
1997	OUR LADY OF LOURDES	39.50	RI
1997	OUR LADY OF GRACE	39.50	RI
1997	OUR LADY OF MEDJUGORJE	39.50	RI

Single Issues

1983	THE KNEELING SANTA	29.50	NR
1985	FAIREST FLOWER OF PARADISE	45.00	NR
1995	CHILDHOOD DREAMS, Richard Judson Zolan, miniature, open	7.50	RI

Love Is Patient and Kind
Photo courtesy of *Collectors News*

A Baby's Prayer
Photo courtesy of *Collectors News*

RORSTRAND SWEDEN

Christmas

		ISSUE	CURRENT
1968	BRINGING HOME THE TREE, Gunner Nylund, 1 year	12.00	475.00
1969	FISHERMEN SAILING HOME, Gunner Nylund, 1 year	13.50	25.00
1970	NILS WITH HIS GEESE, Gunner Nylund, 1 year	13.50	NR
1971	NILS IN LAPLAND, Gunner Nylund, 1 year	15.00	NR
1972	DALECARLIAN FIDDLER, Gunner Nylund, 1 year	15.00	NR
1973	FARM IN SMALAND, Gunner Nylund, 1 year	16.00	60.00
1974	VADSLENA, Gunner Nylund, 1 year	19.00	40.00
1975	NILS IN VASTMANLAND, Gunner Nylund, 1 year	20.00	30.00
1976	NILS IN UPPLAND, Gunner Nylund, 1 year	20.00	30.00
1977	NILS IN VARMLAND, Gunner Nylund, 1 year	29.50	NR
1978	NILS IN FJALLBACKA, Gunner Nylund, 1 year	32.50	40.00
1979	NILS IN VAESTERGOETLAND, Gunner Nylund, 1 year	38.50	NR
1980	NILS IN HALLAND, Gunner Nylund, 1 year	55.00	NR
1981	NILS IN GOTLAND, Gunner Nylund, 1 year	55.00	BR
1982	NILS AT SKANSEN, Gunner Nylund, 1 year	47.50	NR
1983	NILS IN OLAND, Gunner Nylund, 1 year	42.50	55.00
1984	NILS IN ANGERMANLAND, Gunner Nylund, 1 year	42.50	NR
1985	CHRISTMAS, Gunner Nylund, 1 year	42.50	BR
1985	NILS IN JAMTLAND, Gunner Nylund, 1 year	42.50	70.00
1986	NILS IN KARLSKRONA, Gunner Nylund, 1 year	42.50	NR
1987	DALSLAND, FORGET-ME-NOT, Gunner Nylund, 1 year	47.50	150.00
1988	NILS IN HALSINGLAND, Gunner Nylund, 1 year	55.00	NR
1989	NILS VISITS GOTHENBORG, Gunner Nylund, 1 year	60.00	NR
1990	NILS IN KVIKKJOKK, Gunner Nylund, 1 year	75.00	NR
1991	NILS IN MEDELPAD, Gunner Nylund, 1 year	85.00	NR
1992	GASTRIKLAND, LILY OF THE VALLEY, Gunner Nylund, 1 year	92.50	NR
1993	NARKE'S CASTLE, Gunner Nylund, 1 year	92.50	RI

Father's Day

		ISSUE	CURRENT
1971	FATHER AND CHILD, 1 year	15.00	NR
1972	MEAL AT HOME, 1 year	15.00	25.00
1973	TILLING THE FIELDS, 1 year	16.00	25.00
1974	FISHING, 1 year	18.00	30.00
1975	PAINTING, 1 year	20.00	30.00
1976	PLOWING, 1 year	20.00	30.00
1977	SAWING, 1 year	27.50	NR
1978	IN THE STUDIO, 1 year	27.50	NR
1979	RIDING IN THE BUGGY, 1 year	27.50	NR
1980	MT ETCH-NOOK, 1 year	27.50	NR
1981	ESBJORN WITH PLAYMATE, 1 year	27.50	NR
1982	HOUSE SERVANTS, 1 year	36.00	NR
1984	FATHER WORKING, 1 year	42.50	NR

Jubilee

		ISSUE	CURRENT
1980	1980, 1 year	47.50	NR

Julpoesi Series

		ISSUE	CURRENT
1979	SILENT NIGHT, Julpoesi, 1 year	38.50	NR
1980	ADORATION, Julpoesi, 1 year	47.50	NR

Mother's Day

		ISSUE	CURRENT
1971	MOTHER AND CHILD, 1 year	15.00	30.00
1972	SHELLING PEAS, 1 year	15.00	30.00
1973	OLD-FASHIONED PICNIC, 1 year	16.00	30.00
1974	CANDLE LIGHTING, 1 year	18.00	25.00
1975	PONTIUS ON THE FLOOR, 1 year	20.00	NR
1976	APPLE PICKING, 1 year	20.00	NR
1977	KITCHEN, 1 year	27.50	NR
1978	AZALEA, 1 year	27.50	NR
1979	STUDIO IDYLL, 1 year	27.50	NR
1980	LISBETH, 1 year	27.50	NR
1981	KARIN WITH BRITA, 1 year	27.50	NR
1982	BRITA, 1 year	36.00	NR
1983	LITTLE GIRL, 1 year	42.50	NR
1984	MOTHER SEWING, 1 year	42.50	NR

ROSENTHAL GERMANY

(Hibel Studios)

Christmas

1910	WINTER PEACE	NA	550.00
1911	THREE WISE MEN	NA	325.00
1912	STARDUST	NA	255.00
1912	CHRISTMAS LIGHTS	NA	235.00
1914	CHRISTMAS SONGS	NA	350.00
1915	WALKING TO CHURCH	NA	180.00
1916	CHRISTMAS DURING WAR	NA	240.00
1917	ANGEL OF PEACE	NA	200.00
1918	PEACE ON EARTH	NA	200.00
1919	ST. CHRISTOPHER WITH THE CHRIST CHILD	NA	225.00
1920	THE MANGER IN BETHLEHEM	NA	325.00
1921	CHRISTMAS IN THE MOUNTAINS	NA	200.00
1922	ADVENT BRANCH	NA	200.00
1923	CHILDREN IN THE WINTER WOODS	NA	200.00
1924	DEER IN THE WOODS	NA	200.00
1925	THE THREE WISE MEN	NA	200.00
1926	CHIRSTMAS IN THE MOUNTAINS	NA	195.00
1927	STATION ON THE WAY	NA	135.00
1928	CHALET CHRISTMAS	NA	185.00
1929	CHRISTMAS IN THE ALPS	NA	225.00
1930	GROUP OF DEER UNDER THE PINES	NA	225.00
1931	PATH OF THE MAGI	NA	225.00
1932	CHRIST CHILD	NA	185.00
1933	THROUGH THE NIGHT TO LIGHT	NA	190.00
1934	CHRISTMAS PEACE	NA	190.00
1935	CHRISTMAS BY THE SEA	NA	190.00
1936	NURNBERG ANGEL	NA	175.00
1937	BERCHTESGADEN	NA	195.00
1938	CHRISTMAS IN THE ALPS	NA	195.00
1939	SCHNEEKOPPE MOUNTAIN	NA	195.00
1940	MARIEN CHURCH IN DANZIG	NA	200.00
1941	STRASSBURG CATHEDRAL	NA	200.00

		ISSUE	CURRENT
1942	MARIANBURG CASTLE	NA	300.00
1943	WINTER IDYLL	NA	300.00
1944	WOOD SCAPE	NA	300.00
1945	CHRISTMAS PEACE	NA	400.00
1946	CHRISTMAS IN AN ALPINE VALLEY	NA	240.00
1947	THE DILLINGEN MADONNA	NA	985.00
1948	MESSAGE TO THE SHEPHERDS	NA	875.00
1949	THE HOLY FAMILY	NA	185.00
1950	CHRISTMAS IN THE FOREST	NA	185.00
1951	STAR OF BETHLEHEM	NA	450.00
1952	CHRISTMAS IN THE ALPS	NA	195.00
1953	THE HOLY LIGHT	NA	195.00
1954	CHRISTMAS EVE	NA	195.00
1955	CHRISTMAS IN A VILLAGE	NA	195.00
1956	CHRISTMAS IN THE ALPS	NA	195.00
1957	CHRISTMAS BY THE SEA	NA	195.00
1958	CHRISTMAS EVE	NA	195.00
1959	MIDNIGHT MASS	NA	75.00
1960	CHRISTMAS IN A SMALL VILLAGE	NA	195.00
1961	SOLITARY CHRISTMAS	NA	100.00
1962	CHRISTMAS EVE	NA	75.00
1963	SILENT NIGHT	NA	75.00
1964	CHRISTMAS MARKET IN NURNBERG	NA	225.00
1965	CHRISTMAS IN MUNICH	NA	185.00
1966	CHRISTMAS IN ULM	NA	275.00
1967	CHRISTMAS IN REGINBURG	NA	185.00
1968	CHRISTMAS IN BREMEN	NA	195.00
1969	CHRISTMAS IN ROTHENBURG	NA	220.00
1970	CHRISTMAS IN COLOGNE	NA	175.00
1971	CHRISTMAS IN GARMISCH	42.00	100.00
1972	CHRISTMAS IN FRANCONIA	50.00	95.00
1973	LUBECK-HOLSTEIN	77.00	105.00
1974	CHRISTMAS IN WURZBURG	85.00	100.00

Classic Rose Christmas

1974	MEMORIAL CHURCH IN BERLIN, Helmut Drexel	84.00	160.00
1975	FREIBURG CATHEDRAL, Helmut Drexel	75.00	NR
1976	CASTLE OF COCHEM, Helmut Drexel	95.00	BR
1977	HANOVER TOWN HALL, Helmut Drexel	125.00	NR
1978	CATHEDRAL AT AACHEN, Helmut Drexel	150.00	NR
1979	CATHEDRAL IN LUXEMBOURG, Helmut Drexel	165.00	NR
1980	CHRISTMAS IN BRUSSELS, Helmut Drexel	190.00	NR
1981	CHRISTMAS IN TRIER, Helmut Drexel	190.00	NR
1982	MILAN CATHEDRAL, Helmut Drexel	190.00	NR
1983	CHURCH AT CASTLE WITTENBERG, Helmut Drexel	195.00	NR
1984	CITY HALL OF STOCKHOLM, Helmut Drexel	195.00	NR
1985	CHRISTMAS IN AUGSBURG, Helmut Drexel	195.00	NR

Fantasies and Fables

1976	ORIENTAL NIGHT MUSIC, 10,000	50.00	NR
1977	MANDOLIN PLAYERS, 1 year	75.00	NR

Harvest Time

		ISSUE	CURRENT
1976	PUMPKINS, John Falter, 5,000	70.00	NR
1977	HONEST DAY'S WORK, John Falter, 4,000	70.00	NR

Lorraine Trester Series

1975	SUMMERTIME, Lorraine Trester, 5,000	60.00	135.00
1977	ONE LOVELY YESTERDAY, Lorraine Trester, 5,000	70.00	90.00

Runci Classic

1977	SUMMERTIME, Edward Runci, 5,000	95.00	NR
1978	SPRINGTIME, Edward Runci, 5,000	95.00	NR

Tribute to Classical Greek Beauty

1980	DIANA, Edna Hibel, 3,000	350.00	360.00

Wiinblad Christmas

1971	MARIA AND CHILD, Bjorn Wiinblad, 8,000	100.00	750.00
1972	CASPAR, Bjorn Wiinblad, 10,000	100.00	290.00
1973	MELCHIOR, Bjorn Wiinblad, 10,000	125.00	335.00
1974	BALTHAZAR, Bjorn Wiinblad, 10,000	125.00	300.00
1975	THE ANNUNCIATION, Bjorn Wiinblad, 1 year	195.00	200.00
1976	ANGEL WITH TRUMPET, Bjorn Wiinblad, 1 year	195.00	200.00
1977	ADORATION OF SHEPHERDS, Bjorn Wiinblad,1 year	225.00	NR
1978	ANGEL WITH HARP, Bjorn Wiinblad, 1 year	275.00	295.00
1979	EXODUS FROM EGYPT, Bjorn Wiinblad, 1 year	310.00	NR
1980	ANGEL WITH GLOCKENSPIEL, Bjorn Wiinblad,1 year	360.00	NR
1981	THE CHRIST CHILD VISITS THE TEMPLE, Bjorn Wiinblad, 1 year	375.00	NR
1982	CHRISTENING OF CHRIST, Bjorn Wiinblad, 1 year	375.00	NR

Wiinblad Crystal

1976	THE MADONNA, Bjorn Wiinblad, 2,000	150.00	400.00
1977	THE ANNUNCIATION, Bjorn Wiinblad, 2,000	195.00	285.00
1978	THREE KINGS, Bjorn Wiinblad, 2,000	225.00	270.00
1980	ANGEL WITH SHEPHERDS, Bjorn Wiinblad, 1 year	290.00	300.00
1981	ADORATION OF THE SHEPHERDS, Bjorn Wiinblad, 1 year	295.00	NR

ROWE POTTERY WORKS UNITED STATES

Annual

1995	CHRISTMAS COLLECTIBLE PLATE, 1 year	24.50	RI
1996	CHRISTMAS ANGEL, 1 year	24.50	RI
1997	SANTA, 1 year	35.00	RI

ROYAL BAYREUTH GERMANY

(Kern Collectibles)

Anniversary

1980	YOUNG AMERICANS, Leo Jansen, 5,000	125.00	NR

Antique American Art

		ISSUE	CURRENT
1976	FARMYARD TRANQUILITY, 3,000	50.00	70.00
1977	HALF DOME, 3,000	55.00	65.00
1978	DOWN MEMORY LANE, 3,000	65.00	NR

Christmas

		ISSUE	CURRENT
1972	CARRIAGE IN THE VILLAGE, 4,000	15.00	80.00
1973	SNOW SCENE, 4,000	16.50	NR
1974	THE OLD MILL, 4,000	24.00	NR
1975	FOREST CHALET "SERENITY," 4,000	27.50	NR
1976	CHRISTMAS IN THE COUNTRY, 5,000	40.00	NR
1977	PEACE ON EARTH, 5,000	40.00	NR
1978	PEACEFUL INTERLUDE, 5,000	45.00	NR
1979	HOMEWARD BOUND, 5,000	50.00	NR

L. Henry Series

		ISSUE	CURRENT
1976	JUST FRIENDS, 5,000	50.00	60.00
1977	INTERRUPTION, 5,000	55.00	NR

Mother's Day

		ISSUE	CURRENT
1973	CONSOLATION, Leo Jansen, 4,000	16.50	50.00
1974	YOUNG AMERICANS, Leo Jansen, 4,000	25.00	130.00
1975	YOUNG AMERICANS II, Leo Jansen, 5,000	25.00	105.00
1976	YOUNG AMERICANS III, Leo Jansen, 5,000	30.00	70.00
1977	YOUNG AMERICANS IV, Leo Jansen, 5,000	40.00	60.00
1978	YOUNG AMERICANS V, Leo Jansen, 5,000	45.00	50.00
1979	YOUNG AMERICANS VI, Leo Jansen, 5,000	60.00	65.00
1980	YOUNG AMERICANS VII, Leo Jansen, 5,000	65.00	75.00
1981	YOUNG AMERICANS VIII, Leo Jansen, 5,000	65.00	NR
1982	YOUNG AMERICANS IX, Leo Jansen, 5,000	65.00	NR

Sun Bonnet Babies

		ISSUE	CURRENT
1974	MONDAY—WASHING DAY, 15,000	—	—
1974	TUESDAY—IRONING DAY, 15,000	—	—
1974	WEDNESDAY—MENDING DAY, 15,000	—	—
1974	THURSDAY—SCRUBBING DAY, 15,000	—	—
1974	FRIDAY—SWEEPING DAY, 15,000	—	—
1974	SATURDAY—BAKING DAY, 15,000	—	—
1974	SUNDAY—FISHING DAY, 15,000	—	—
	Set of 7	120.00	230.00

ROYAL COPENHAGEN DENMARK

America's Mother's Day

		ISSUE	CURRENT
1988	WESTERN TRAIL, Sven Vestergaard, 1 year	34.50	NR
1989	INDIAN LOVE CALL, Sven Vestergaard, 1 year	37.00	NR
1990	SOUTHERN BELLE, Sven Vestergaard, 1 year	39.50	NR
1991	MOTHER'S DAY AT THE MISSION, Sven Vestergaard, 1 year	42.50	NR
1992	TURN OF THE CENTURY BOSTON, Sven Vestergaard, 1 year	45.00	NR

Christmas

		ISSUE	CURRENT
1908	MADONNA AND CHILD, Christian Thomsen, 1 year	1.00	1,900.00
1909	DANISH LANDSCAPE, Stephn Ussing, 1 year	1.00	75.00
1910	THE MAGI, Christian Thomsen, 1 year	1.00	159.00
1911	DANISH LANDSCAPE, Oluf Jensen, 1 year	1.00	100.00
1912	ELDERLY COUPLE BY THE CHRISTMAS TREE, Christian, Thomsen, 1 year	1.00	165.00
1913	SPIRE OF FREDERIK CHURCH, Arthur Boesen, 1 year	1.50	100.00
1914	HOLY SPIRIT CHURCH, Arthur Boesen, 1 year	1.50	165.00
1915	DANISH LANDSCAPE, Arnold Krog, 1 year	1.50	75.00
1916	THE SHEPHERDS IN THE FIELD, Richard Bocher, 1 year	1.50	115.00
1917	THE TOWER OF OUR SAVIOUR'S CHURCH, Oluf Jensen, 1 year	2.00	100.00
1918	THE SHEPHERDS AND SHEEP, Oluf Jensen, 1 year	2.00	105.00
1919	IN THE PARK, Oluf Jensen, 1 year	2.00	120.00
1920	MARY WITH THE CHILD JESUS, Oluf Jensen, 1 year	2.00	110.00
1921	AABENRAA MARKETPLACE, Oluf Jenen, 1 year	2.00	75.00
1922	THREE SINGING ANGELS, Ellinor Selschau, 1 year	2.00	70.00
1923	DANISH LANDSCAPE, Oluf Jensen, 1 year	2.00	70.00
1924	CHRISTMAS STAR OVER THE SEA, Benjamin Olsen, 1 year	2.00	130.00
1925	STREET SCENE FROM CHRISTIANSHAVN, Oluf Jensen, 1 year	2.00	110.00
1926	CHRISTIANSHAVN CANAL, Richard Bocher, 1 year	2.00	110.00
1927	THE SHIP'S BOY AT THE TILLER CHRISTMAS NIGHT, Benjamin Olsen, 1 year	2.00	130.00
1928	THE VICAR FAMILY ON THE WAY TO CHURCH, Gotfred Rode, 1 year	2.00	105.00
1929	THE GRUNDTVIG CHURCH, COPENHAGEN, Oluf Jensen, 1 year	2.00	95.00
1930	FISHING BOATS, Benjamin Olsen, 1 year	2.50	90.00
1931	MOTHER AND CHILD, Gotfred Rode, 1 year	2.50	100.00
1932	FREDERIKSBERG GARDENS WITH STATUE OF FREDERIK VI, Oluf Jensen, 1 year	2.50	115.00
1933	THE GREAT BELT FERRY, Benjamin Olsen, 1 year	2.50	65.00
1934	THE HERMITAGE CASTLE, Oluf Jensen, 1 year	2.50	135.00
1935	FISHING BOAT OFF KRONBORG CASTLE, Benjamin Olsen, 1 year	2.50	225.00
1936	ROSKILKDE CATHEDRAL, Richard Bocher, 1 year	2.50	150.00
1937	CHRISTMAS SCENE IN COPENHAGEN, Nils Thorsson, 1 year	2.50	195.00
1938	THE ROUND CHURCH IN OSTERLARS, Herne Nielsen, 1 year	3.00	175.00
1939	EXPEDITIONARY SHIP IN THE PACK ICE OF GREENLAND, Svend Nicolai Nielsen, 1 year	3.00	300.00
1940	THE GOOD SHEPHERD, Kai Lange, 1 year	3.00	250.00
1941	DANISH VILLAGE CHURCH, Theodor Kjolner, 1 year	3.00	300.00
1942	BELL TOWER OF OLD CHURCH IN JUTLAND, Nils Thorsson, 1 year	4.00	300.00
1943	THE FLIGHT OF THE HOLY FAMILY TO EGYPT, Nils Thorsson, 1 year	4.00	625.00
1944	TYPICAL DANISH WINTER SCENE, Viggo Olsen, 1 year	4.00	225.00
1945	A PEACEFUL MOTIF, Richard Bocher, 1 year	4.00	300.00
1946	ZEALAND VILLAGE CHURCH, Nils Thorsson, 1 year	4.00	240.00
1947	THE GOOD SHEPHERD, Kai Lange, 1 year	4.50	175.00
1948	NODEBO CHURCH, Theodor Kjolner, 1 year	4.50	145.00
1949	OUR LADY'S CATHEDRAL COPENHAGEN, Hans Henrik Hansen, 1 year	5.00	180.00
1950	BOESLUNDE CHURCH, Viggo Olsen, 1 year	5.00	200.00
1951	CHRISTMAS ANGEL, Richard Bocher, 1 year	5.00	175.00
1952	CHRISTMAS IN THE FOREST, Kai Lange, 1 year	5.00	180.00
1953	FREDERIKSBERG CASTLE, Theodor Kjolner, 1 year	6.00	170.00
1954	AMALIENBORG PALACE, COPENHAGEN, Kai Lange, 1 year	6.00	150.00
1955	FANO GIRL, Kai Lange, 1 year	7.00	145.00
1956	ROSENBORG CASTLE, Kai Lange, 1 year	7.00	200.00
1957	THE GOOD SHEPHERD, Hans Henrik Hansen, 1 year	8.00	125.00
1958	SUNSHINE OVER GREENLAND, Hans Henrik Hansen, 1 year	9.00	165.00

		ISSUE	CURRENT
1959	CHRISTMAS NIGHT, Hans Henrik Hansen, 1 year	9.00	90.00
1960	THE STAG, Hans Henrik Hansen, 1 year	10.00	120.00
1961	THE TRAINING SHIP *DANMARK*, Kai Lange, 1 year	10.00	130.00
1962	THE LITTLE MERMAID AT WINTERTIME, Kai Lange, 1 year	11.00	140.00
1963	HOJSAGER MILL, Kai Lange, 1 year	11.00	40.00
1964	FETCHING THE CHRISTMAS TREE, Kai Lange, 1 year	11.00	40.00
1965	LITTLE SKATERS, Kai Lange, 1 year	12.00	40.00
1966	BLACKBIRD AND CHURCH, Kai Lanage, 1 year	12.00	30.00
1967	THE ROYAL OAK, Kai Lange, 1 year	13.00	25.00
1968	THE LOST UMIAK, Kai Lange, 1 year	13.00	20.00
1969	THE OLD FARMYARD, Kai Lange, 1 year	14.00	20.00
1970	CHRISTMAS ROSE AND CAT, Kai Lange, 1 year	14.00	30.00
1971	HARE IN WINTER, Kai Lange, 1 year	15.00	NR
1972	IN THE DESERT, Kai Lange, 1 year	16.00	NR
1973	TRAIN HOMEWARD BOUND, Kai Lange, 1 year	22.00	NR
1974	WINTER TWILIGHT, Kai Lange, 1 year	22.00	30.00
1975	QUEEN'S PALACE, Kai Lange, 1 year	27.50	BR
1976	DANISH WATERMILL, Kai Lange, 1 year	27.50	NR
1977	IMMERVAD BRIDGE, Kai Lange, 1 year	32.50	BR
1978	GREENLAND SCENERY, Kai Lange, 1 year	35.00	NR
1979	CHOOSING A CHRISTMAS TREE, Kai Lange, 1 year	42.50	BR
1980	BRINGING HOME THE CHRISTMAS TREE, Kai Lange, 1 year	49.50	NR
1981	ADMIRING THE CHRISTMAS TREE, Kai Lange, 1 year	52.50	BR
1982	WAITING FOR CHRISTMAS, Kai Lange, 1 year	54.50	60.00
1983	MERRY CHRISTMAS, Kai Lange, 1 year	54.50	60.00
1984	JINGLE BELLS, Kai Lange, 1 year	54.50	NR
1985	SNOWMAN, Kai Lange, 1 year	54.50	NR
1986	CHRISTMAS VACATION, Kai Lange, 1 year	54.50	NR
1987	WINTER BIRDS, Sven Vestergaard, 1 year	59.50	NR
1988	CHRISTMAS EVE IN COPENHAGEN, Sven Vestergaard, 1 year	59.50	NR
1989	THE OLD SKATING POND, Sven Vestergaard, 1 year	59.50	75.00
1990	CHRISTMAS AT TIVOLI, Sven Vestergaard, 1 year	64.50	120.00
1991	THE FESTIVAL OF SANTA LUCIA, Sven Vestergaard, 1 year	69.50	100.00
1992	THE QUEEN'S CARRIAGE, Sven Vestergaard, 1 year	69.50	NR

Danish Watermill

Immervad Bridge

		ISSUE	CURRENT
1993	CHRISTMAS GUESTS, Sven Vestergaard, 1 year	69.50	RI
1994	CHRISTMAS SHOPPING, Sven Vestergaard, 1 year	72.50	RI
1995	CHRISTMAS AT THE MANOR HOUSE, Sven Vestergaard, 1 year	72.50	RI
1996	LIGHTING THE STREET LAMPS, Sven Vestergaard, 1 year	74.50	RI
1997	ROSKILDE CATHEDRAL, Sven Vestergaard, 1 year	69.50	RI

Christmas in Denmark

1991	BRINGING HOME THE TREE, Hans Henrik Hansen, 1 year	72.50	NR
1992	CHRISTMAS SHOPPING, Hans Henrik Hansen, 1 year	72.50	NR
1993	THE SKATING PARTY, Hans Henrik Hansen, 1 year	74.50	RI
1994	THE SLEIGH RIDE, Hans Henrik Hansen, 1 year	74.50	RI

Christmas Jubilee

1983	CHRISTMAS MEMORIES, Kai Lange, 1 year	95.00	NR

First Bing & Grøndahl

1996	CHRISTMAS EVE AT THE STATUE OF LIBERTY, C. Masgadine, 1 year	47.50	RI

Hans Christian Andersen Fairy Tales

1983	SHEPHERDESS AND CHIMNEY SWEEP, Sven Vestergaard, 1 year	39.50	NR
1984	THUMBELINA, Sven Vestergaard, 1 year	39.50	NR
1985	MERMAID, Sven Vestergaard, 1 year	44.50	NR

Historical

1975	R. C. BICENTENNIAL, 1 year	30.00	NR
1976	U. S. BICENTENNIAL, 1 year	35.00	NR
1977	ELECTROMAGNETISM, 1 year	35.00	NR
1978	CAPTAIN COOK, 1 year	37.50	BR
1979	ADAM OEHLENSCHLEGER, 1 year	42.00	BR
1980	AMAGETORV, 1 year	57.50	BR
1983	ROYAL COPENHAGEN 75TH ANNIVERSARY, 1 year	95.00	NR

Jingle Bells
Photo courtesy of *Collectors News*

Mother Robin with Babies
Photo courtesy of *Collectors News*

Motherhood

		ISSUE	CURRENT
1982	MOTHER ROBIN WITH BABIES, Sven Vestergaard, 1 year	29.50	50.00
1983	MOTHER CAT AND KITTENS, Sven Vestergaard, 1 year	29.50	45.00
1984	MARE AND FOAL, Sven Vestergaard, 1 year	29.50	45.00
1985	MOTHER AND BABY RABBIT, Sven Vestergaard, 1 year	32.00	NR

Mother's Day

1971	AMERICAN MOTHER, Kamma Svensson, 1 year	12.50	130.00
1972	ORIENTAL MOTHER, Kamma Svensson, 1 year	14.00	65.00
1973	DANISH MOTHER, Arne Ungermann, 1 year	16.00	60.00
1974	GREENLAND MOTHER, Arne Ungermann, 1 year	16.00	60.00
1975	BIRD IN NEST, Arne Ungermann, 1 year	20.00	60.00
1976	MERMAIDS, Arne Ungermann, 1 year	20.00	55.00
1977	TWINS, Arne Ungermann, 1 year	24.00	55.00
1978	MOTHER AND CHILD, Ib Spang Olsen, 1 year	26.00	NR
1979	A LOVING MOTHER, Ib Spang Olsen, 1 year	29.50	NR
1980	AN OUTING WITH MOTHER, Ib Spang Olsen, 1 year	37.50	50.00
1981	REUNION, Ib Spang Olsen, 1 year	37.50	45.00
1982	CHILDREN'S HOUR, Ib Spang Olsen, 1 year	37.50	45.00

National Parks of America

1978	YELLOWSTONE, 5,000	75.00	NR
1979	SHENANDOAH, 5,000	75.00	NR
1981	MT. MCKINLEY, 5,000	75.00	NR
1981	THE EVERGLADES, 5,000	75.00	NR
1981	GRAND CANYON, 5,000	75.00	NR
1981	YOSEMITE, 5,000	75.00	NR

Nature's Children

1993	THE ROBINS, Jørgen Nielsen, 1 year	39.50	NR
1994	THE FAWN, Jørgen Nielsen, 1 year	39.50	NR
1997	THE SWANS, Jørgen Nielsen, 1 year	39.50	NR

Special Issues

1967	VIRGIN ISLANDS, 1 year	12.00	25.00
1969	DANISH FLAG, 1 year	12.00	25.00
1969	APOLLO II, 1 year	15.00	NR
1970	REUNION, 1 year	12.00	25.00
1970	STATUE OF LIBERTY	15.00	25.00
1972	MUNICH OLYMPIAD	25.00	NR
1972	KING FREDERIK IX	25.00	NR

ROYAL CORNWALL UNITED STATES

(Haviland, Schumann, Wedgwood and Woodmere)

Alice in Wonderland

1979	ALICE AND THE WHITE RABBIT, Lawrence W. Whittaker, 27,500	45.00	NR
1979	ADVICE FROM A CATERPILLAR, Lawrence W. Whittaker, 27,500	45.00	NR
1980	THE CHESHIRE CAT'S GRIN, Lawrence W. Whittaker, 27,500	45.00	NR
1980	MAD HATTER'S TEA PARTY, Lawrence W. Whittaker, 27,500	45.00	NR
1980	QUEEN'S CROQUET MATCH, Lawrence W. Whittaker, 27,500	45.00	NR

		ISSUE	CURRENT
1980	WHO STOLE THE TARTS?, Lawrence W. Whittaker, 27,500	45.00	NR

Beauty of Bouguereau

1979	LUCIE, William A. Bouguereau, 19,500	35.00	45.00
1980	MADELAINE, William A. Bouguereau, 19,500	35.00	NR
1980	FRÈRE ET SOEUR, William A. Bouguereau, 19,500	35.00	NR
1980	SOLANGE ET ENFANT, William A. Bouguereau, 19,500	35.00	NR
1980	COLETTE, William A. Bouguereau, 19,500	35.00	65.00
1980	JEAN ET JEANETTE, William A. Bouguereau, 19,500	35.00	NR

Bethlehem Christmas

1977	FIRST CHRISTMAS EVE, Gerald R. Miller, 10,000	29.50	85.00
1978	GLAD TIDINGS, Robert Ahlcrona, 10,000	34.50	75.00
1979	THE GIFT BEARERS, B. Higgins Bond, 10,000	34.50	NR

Classic Christmas

1978	CHILD OF PEACE, 10,000	55.00	85.00
1978	SILENT NIGHT, 10,000	55.00	70.00
1978	MOST PRECIOUS GIFT, 10,000	55.00	65.00
1978	WE THREE KINGS, 10,000	55.00	65.00

Classic Collection

1980	ROMEO AND JULIET, J. C. Leyendecker, 17,500	55.00	65.00
1980	YOUNG GALAHAD, J. C. Leyendecker, 17,500	55.00	65.00
1980	AT LOCKSLEY HALL, J. C. Leyendecker, 17,500	55.00	NR
1980	ST. AGNES EVE, J. C. Leyendecker, 17,500	55.00	NR

Courageous Few

1982	THE FALL OF JERICHO, Yiannis Koutsis, 19,500	59.50	NR
1982	GIDEON'S FIVE HUNDRED, Yiannis Koutsis, 19,500	59.50	NR
1982	DESTRUCTION OF THE TEMPLE, Yiannis Koutsis, 19,500	59.50	NR
1982	RUTH AT THE HARVEST, Yiannis Koutsis, 19,500	59.50	NR
1982	DAVID AND GOLIATH, Yiannis Koutsis, 19,500	59.50	NR
1982	SOLOMON'S DECISION, Yiannis Koutsis, 19,500	59.50	NR
1982	BUILDING OF THE TEMPLE, Yiannis Koutsis, 19,500	59.50	NR
1982	ELIJAH AND HEAVEN'S CHARIOT, Yiannis Koutsis, 19,500	59.50	NR
1982	JOB'S REWARD, Yiannis Koutsis, 19,500	59.50	NR
1983	PSALM OF DAVID, Yiannis Koutsis, 19,500	59.50	NR
1983	DANIEL AND THE LIONS, Yiannis Koutsis, 19,500	59.50	NR
1983	JONAH AND THE WHALE, Yiannis Koutsis, 19,500	59.50	NR

Creation

1977	IN THE BEGINNING, Yiannis Koutsis, 10,000	37.50	90.00
1977	IN HIS IMAGE, Yiannis Koutsis, 10,000	45.00	55.00
1978	ADAM'S RIB, Yiannis Koutsis, 10,000	45.00	55.00
1978	BANISHED FROM EDEN, Yiannis Koutsis, 10,000	45.00	NR
1978	NOAH AND THE ARK, Yiannis Koutsis, 10,000	45.00	NR
1980	TOWER OF BABEL, Yiannis Koutsis, 10,000	45.00	75.00
1980	SODOM AND GOMORRAH, Yiannis Koutsis, 10,000	45.00	NR
1980	JACOB'S WEDDING, Yiannis Koutsis, 10,000	45.00	NR
1980	REBEKAH AT THE WELL, Yiannis Koutsis, 10,000	45.00	75.00
1980	JACOB'S LADDER, Yiannis Koutsis, 10,000	45.00	75.00

		ISSUE	CURRENT
1980	JOSEPH'S COAT OF MANY COLORS, Yiannis Koutsis, 10,000	45.00	75.00
1980	JOSEPH INTERPRETS PHARAOH'S DREAM, Yiannis Koutsis, 10,000	45.00	75.00

Crystal Maidens

1979	STRAWBERRY SEASON (SPRING), 2,500	57.50	80.00
1979	SUNSHINE SEASON (SUMMER), 2,500	57.50	80.00
1979	SCENIC SEASON (FALL), 2,500	57.50	80.00
1979	SNOWFLAKE SEASON (WINTER), 2,500	57.50	80.00

Dorothy's Day

1980	BRAND-NEW DAY, Bill Mack, 15,000	55.00	NR
1980	ALL BY MYSELF, Bill Mack, 15,000	55.00	NR
1981	OFF TO SCHOOL, Bill Mack, 15,000	55.00	NR
1981	BEST FRIENDS, Bill Mack, 15,000	55.00	NR
1981	HELPING MAMMY, Bill Mack, 15,000	55.00	NR
1981	BLESS ME TOO!, Bill Mack, 15,000	55.00	NR

Exotic Birds of Tropique

1981	SCARLET MACAWS, Konrad Hack, 19,500	49.50	NR
1981	TOCO TOUCAN, Konrad Hack, 19,500	49.50	NR
1981	GREATER SULFUR-CRESTED COCKATOO, Konrad Hack, 19,500	49.50	NR
1981	ROSY FLAMINGOS, Konrad Hack, 19,500	49.50	NR
1982	ULTRAMARINE KING, Konrad Hack, 19,500	49.50	NR
1982	RED-FAN PARROT, Konrad Hack, 19,500	49.50	NR
1982	GOLDIE'S BIRD OF PARADISE, Konrad Hack, 19,500	49.50	NR
1982	ANDEAN COCK-OF-THE-ROCK, Konrad Hack, 19,500	49.50	NR
1982	SEVEN-COLORED TANAGER, Konrad Hack, 19,500	49.50	NR
1982	SCARLET IBIS, Konrad Hack, 19,500	49.50	NR
1982	QUETZAL, Konrad Hack, 19,500	49.50	NR
1982	LONG-TAILED SYLPH, Konrad Hack, 19,500	49.50	NR

Five Perceptions of Weo Cho

1979	SENSE OF TOUCH, 19,500	55.00	125.00
1979	SENSE OF SIGHT, 19,500	55.00	85.00
1980	SENSE OF TASTE, 19,500	55.00	75.00
1980	SENSE OF HEARING, 19,500	55.00	75.00
1980	SENSE OF SMELL, 19,500	55.00	75.00

Golden Age of Cinema

1978	THE KING AND HIS LADIES, Lawrence W. Whittaker, 22,500	45.00	NR
1978	FRED AND GINGER, Lawrence W. Whittaker, 22,500	45.00	NR
1978	JUDY AND MICKEY, Lawrence W. Whittaker, 22,500	45.00	NR
1978	*THE PHILADELPHIA STORY*, Lawrence W. Whittaker, 22,500	45.00	NR
1979	*THE THIN MAN*, Lawrence W. Whittaker, 22,500	45.00	NR
1979	*GIGI*, Lawrence W. Whittaker, 22,500	45.00	NR

Golden Plates of the Noble Flower Maidens

1982	IRIS MAIDEN, Kitagawa Utamaro, 19,500	65.00	NR
1982	PLUM BLOSSOM, Kitagawa Utamaro, 19,500	65.00	NR
1982	QUINCE MAIDEN, Kitagawa Utamaro, 19,500	65.00	NR
1982	CHERRY BLOSSOM MAIDEN, Kitagawa Utamaro, 19,500	65.00	NR

		ISSUE	CURRENT
1982	CRYSANTHEMUM MAIDEN, Kitagawa Utamaro, 19,500	65.00	NR
1982	AUGUST LILY MAIDEN, Kitagawa Utamaro, 19,500	65.00	NR

Impressions of Yesteryear

1982	MOON MIST, Dominic Mingolla, 19,500	59.50	NR
1982	FALL FLOWERS, Dominic Mingolla, 19,500	59.50	NR
1982	WISHING WELL, Dominic Mingolla, 19,500	59.50	NR
1982	THE LETTER, Dominic Mingolla, 19,500	59.50	NR
1982	SLEDDING, Dominic Mingolla, 19,500	59.50	NR
1982	RED TREE, Dominic Mingolla, 19,500	59.50	NR
1982	SWANS, Dominic Mingolla, 19,500	59.50	NR
1982	SAILBOAT, Dominic Mingolla, 19,500	59.50	NR
1982	WINTER PARK, Dominic Mingolla, 19,500	59.50	NR
1983	SEASHORE, Dominic Mingolla, 19,500	59.50	NR
1983	RED BALLOON, Dominic Mingolla, 19,500	59.50	NR
1983	SNOWMAN, Dominic Mingolla, 19,500	59.50	NR

Kitten's World

1979	JUST CURIOUS, Rudy Droguett, 27,500	45.00	80.00
1979	HELLO, WORLD, Rudy Droguett, 27,500	45.00	NR
1979	ARE YOU A FLOWER?, Rudy Droguett, 27,500	45.00	NR
1980	TALK TO ME, Rudy Droguett, 27,500	45.00	NR
1980	MY FAVORITE TOY, Rudy Droguett, 27,500	45.00	NR
1980	PURR-FECT PLEASURE, Rudy Droguett, 27,500	45.00	NR

Legend of the Peacock Maidens

1982	DANCE OF THE PEACOCK MAIDENS, 19,500	69.50	NR
1982	PROMISE OF LOVE, 19,500	69.50	NR
1982	THE BETRAYAL, 19,500	69.50	NR
1982	THE PRINCE AND THE PYTHON, 19,500	69.50	NR
1982	RETURN OF THE BRACELET, 19,500	69.50	NR
1982	THE MARRIAGE, 19,500	69.50	NR

Legendary Ships of the Sea

1980	*THE FLYING DUTCHMAN*, Alan D'Estrehan, 19,500	49.50	90.00
1981	*THE REFANU*, Alan D'Estrehan, 19,500	49.50	NR
1981	*THE GASPEE BAY*, Alan D'Estrehan, 19,500	49.50	NR
1981	*THE RESCUE*, Alan D'Estrehan, 19,500	49.50	NR
1981	*THE COPENHAGEN*, Alan D'Estrehan, 19,500	49.50	NR
1981	*THE PALATINE*, Alan D'Estrehan, 19,500	49.50	NR
1981	*THE PRIDE*, Alan D'Estrehan, 19,500	49.50	NR
1981	*THE FOOCHOW SEA JUNK*, Alan D'Estrehan, 19,500	49.50	NR
1981	*THE ROTH RAMHACH*, Alan D'Estrehan, 19,500	49.50	NR
1981	*THE FRIGORIFIQUE*, Alan D'Estrehan, 19,500	49.50	NR

Little People

1980	OFF TO THE PICNIC, Seima, 19,500	34.50	NR
1981	DECORATING THE TREE, Seima, 19,500	34.50	NR
1981	CRUISING DOWN THE RIVER, Seima, 19,500	34.50	NR
1981	THE SWEETEST HARVEST, Seima, 19,500	34.50	NR
1981	THE HAPPY CHORUS, Seima, 19,500	34.50	NR
1981	PAINTING THE LEAVES, Seima, 19,500	34.50	NR

		ISSUE	CURRENT

Love's Precious Moments

		ISSUE	CURRENT
1981	LOVE'S SWEET VOW, Robert Gunn, 17,500	55.00	NR
1981	LOVE'S SWEET VERSE, Robert Gunn, 17,500	55.00	NR
1981	LOVE'S SWEET OFFERING, Robert Gunn, 17,500	55.00	NR
1981	LOVE'S SWEET EMBRACE, Robert Gunn, 17,500	55.00	NR
1981	LOVE'S SWEET MELODY, Robert Gunn, 17,500	55.00	NR
1981	LOVE'S SWEET KISS, Robert Gunn, 17,500	55.00	NR

Memories of America by Grandma Moses

		ISSUE	CURRENT
1980	BRINGING IN THE MAPLE SUGAR, Grandma Moses, 5,000	120.00	NR
1980	THE OLD AUTOMOBILE, Grandma Moses, 5,000	120.00	NR
1981	HALLOWEEN, Grandma Moses, 5,000	120.00	NR
1981	THE RAINBOW, Grandma Moses, 5,000	120.00	NR

Memories of the Western Prairies

		ISSUE	CURRENT
1983	PICKING DAISIES, Rosemary Calder, 1 year	49.50	NR
1984	FEEDING THE COLT, Rosemary Calder, 1 year	49.50	NR

Mingolla Christmas

		ISSUE	CURRENT
1977	WINTER WONDERLAND, Dominic Mingolla, 5,000	65.00	NR

Most Precious Gifts of Shen Lung

		ISSUE	CURRENT
1981	FIRE, Sharleen Pederson, 19,500	49.00	NR
1981	WATER, Sharleen Pederson, 19,500	49.00	NR
1981	SUN, Sharleen Pederson, 19,500	49.00	NR
1981	MOON, Sharleen Pederson, 19,500	49.00	NR
1981	EARTH, Sharleen Pederson, 19,500	49.00	NR
1981	SKY, Sharleen Pederson, 19,500	49.00	NR

Promised Land

		ISSUE	CURRENT
1979	PHARAOH'S DAUGHTER FINDS MOSES, Yiannis Koutsis, 24,500	45.00	NR
1979	THE BURNING BUSH, Yiannis Koutsis, 24,500	45.00	NR
1979	LET MY PEOPLE GO, Yiannis Koutsis, 24,500	45.00	NR
1979	THE PARTING OF THE RED SEA, Yiannis Koutsis, 24,500	45.00	NR
1980	MIRIAM'S SONG OF THANKSGIVING, Yiannis Koutsis, 24,500	45.00	NR
1980	MANNA FROM HEAVEN, Yiannis Koutsis, 24,500	45.00	NR
1980	WATER FROM THE ROCK, Yiannis Koutsis, 24,500	45.00	NR
1980	THE BATTLE OF AMALEK, Yiannis Koutsis, 24,500	45.00	NR
1980	THE TEN COMMANDMENTS, Yiannis Koutsis, 24,500	45.00	NR
1980	THE GOLDEN CALF, Yiannis Koutsis, 24,500	45.00	NR
1980	MOSES SMASHES THE TABLET, Yiannis Koutsis, 24,500	45.00	NR
1980	THE GLORIOUS TABERNACLE, Yiannis Koutsis, 24,500	45.00	NR

Puppy's World

		ISSUE	CURRENT
1982	FIRST BIRTHDAY, Rudy Droguett, 19,500	49.50	NR
1982	BEWARE OF DOG, Rudy Droguett, 19,500	49.50	NR
1982	TOP DOG, Rudy Droguett, 19,500	49.50	NR
1982	NEED A FRIEND?, Rudy Droguett, 19,500	49.50	NR
1982	DOUBLE TROUBLE, Rudy Droguett, 19,500	49.50	NR
1982	JUST CLOWNING, Rudy Droguett, 19,500	49.50	NR
1982	GUEST FOR DINNER, Rudy Droguett, 19,500	49.50	NR
1982	GIFT WRAPPED, Rudy Droguett, 19,500	49.50	NR

Remarkable World of Charles Dickens

		ISSUE	CURRENT
1980	OLIVER TWIST AND FAGIN, Konrad Hack, 19,500	60.00	NR
1980	SCROOGE AND MARLEY'S GHOST, Konrad Hack, 19,500	60.00	NR
1980	BOB CRATCHIT AND TINY TIM, Konrad Hack, 19,500	60.00	NR
1980	DAVID COPPERFIELD AND GREAT-AUNT BETSY TROTWOOD, Konrad Hack, 19,500	60.00	NR
1980	MICAWBER DENOUNCING URIAH HEEP, Konrad Hack, 19,500	60.00	NR
1980	LITTLE NELL, Konrad Hack, 19,500	60.00	NR
1981	MADAME DEFARGE, Konrad Hack, 19,500	60.00	NR
1981	MR. PICKWICK AND FRIENDS, Konrad Hack, 19,500	60.00	NR
1981	NICHOLAS NICKLEBY, Konrad Hack, 19,500	60.00	NR
1982	LITTLE DORRIT, Konrad Hack, 19,500	60.00	NR
1982	BARKIS AND PEGGOTTY, Konrad Hack, 19,500	60.00	NR
1982	PIP AND MISS HAVISHAM, Konrad Hack, 19,500	60.00	NR

Treasures of Childhood

1979	MY CUDDLIES COLLECTION, Charlotte Jackson, 19,500	45.00	NR
1980	MY COIN COLLECTION, Charlotte Jackson, 19,500	45.00	NR
1980	MY SHELL COLLECTION, Charlotte Jackson, 19,500	45.00	NR
1980	MY STAMP COLLECTION, Charlotte Jackson, 19,500	45.00	NR
1980	MY DOLL COLLECTION, Charlotte Jackson, 19,500	45.00	NR
1980	MY ROCK COLLECTION, Charlotte Jackson, 19,500	45.00	NR

Two Thousand Years of Ships

1982	U.S.S. *CONSTITUTION*, Alan D'Estrehan	39.50	NR
1982	*SANTA MARIA*, Alan D'Estrehan	39.50	NR
1983	*MAYFLOWER*, Alan D'Estrehan	39.50	NR
1983	*DRAKAR*, Alan D'Estrehan	39.50	NR
1983	*CUTTY SARK THERMOPYLAE*, Alan D'Estrehan	39.50	NR
1983	HMS *ROYAL SOVEREIGN*, Alan D'Estrehan	39.50	NR
1983	*VASA*, Alan D'Estrehan	39.50	NR
1983	HMS *VICTORY*, Alan D'Estrehan	39.50	NR
1983	*ROYAL BARGE*, Alan D'Estrehan	39.50	NR
1984	*AMERICA*, Alan D'Estrehan	39.50	NR
1984	*GOLDEN HIND*, Alan D'Estrehan	39.50	NR

Windows on the World

1980	THE GOLDEN GATE OF SAN FRANCISCO, B. Higgins Bond, 19,500	45.00	NR
1981	THE SNOW VILLAGE OF MADULAIN, B. Higgins Bond, 19,500	45.00	NR
1981	RAINY DAY IN LONDON, B. Higgins Bond, 19,500	45.00	NR
1981	WATER FESTIVAL IN VENICE, B. Higgins Bond, 19,500	45.00	NR
1981	SPRINGTIME IN PARIS, B. Higgins Bond, 19,500	45.00	NR
1981	HARVESTIME IN THE UKRAINE, B. Higgins Bond, 19,500	45.00	NR
1981	LUNCHTIME IN MICHELSTADT, B. Higgins Bond, 19,500	45.00	NR
1981	FLAMENCO OF MADRID, B. Higgins Bond, 19,500	45.00	NR
1981	GREAT TUSKS OF THE SERENGETI, B. Higgins Bond, 19,500	45.00	NR
1981	CARNIVAL TIME IN RIO, B. Higgins Bond, 19,500	45.00	NR
1981	TOKYO AT CHERRY BLOSSOM TIME, B. Higgins Bond, 19,500	45.00	NR
1981	PALACE OF THE WINDS, JAIPUR, B. Higgins Bond, 19,500	45.00	NR
1982	CARNIVAL TIME IN RIO, B. Higgins Bond, 19,500	45.00	NR

ROYAL DELFT NETHERLANDS

Christmas (Large)

		ISSUE	CURRENT
1915	CHRISTMAS BELLS, 1 year	2.25	6,250.00
1916	STAR—FLORAL DESIGN, 1 year	4.25	720.00
1916	CRADLE WITH CHILD, 1 year	4.25	370.00
1917	SHEPHERD, 1 year	6.00	450.00
1917	CHRISTMAS STAR, 1 year	4.25	290.00
1918	SHEPHERD, 1 year	7.50	375.00
1918	CHRISTMAS STAR, 1 year	5.50	275.00
1919	CHURCH, 1 year	12.50	400.00
1920	CHURCH TOWER, 1 year	12.50	390.00
1920	HOLLY WREATH, 1 year	7.50	290.00
1921	CANAL BOATMAN, 1 year	12.50	425.00
1921	CHRISTMAS STAR, 1 year	6.25	315.00
1922	LANDSCAPE, 1 year	10.00	425.00
1922	CHRISTMAS WREATH, 1 year	6.25	290.00
1923	SHEPHERD, 1 year	10.00	440.00
1924	CHRISTMAS STAR, 1 year	6.25	290.00
1924	SHEPHERD, 1 year	10.00	415.00
1925	TOWNGATE IN DELFT, 1 year	10.00	465.00
1925	CHRISTMAS STAR, 1 year	6.25	265.00
1926	WINDMILL LANDSCAPE, 1 year	12.50	465.00
1926	CHRISTMAS STAR, 1 year	6.25	290.00
1927	CHRISTMAS STAR, 1 year	6.25	300.00
1927	SAILBOAT, 1 year	10.00	475.00
1928	LIGHTHOUSE, 1 year	10.00	375.00
1928	CHRISTMAS POINSETTIA, 1 year	6.25	315.00
1929	CHRISTMAS BELL, 1 year	6.25	390.00
1929	SMALL DUTCH TOWN, 1 year	10.00	390.00
1930	CHURCH ENTRANCE, 1 year	10.00	350.00
1930	CHRISTMAS ROSE, 1 year	6.25	325.00
1931	CHRISTMAS STAR, 1 year	5.00	300.00
1931	SNOW LANDSCAPE, 1 year	8.00	375.00
1932	FIREPLACE, 1 year	8.00	440.00
1932	CHRISTMAS STAR, 1 year	5.00	390.00
1933	INTERIOR SCENE, 1 year	7.88	450.00
1934	INTERIOR SCENE, 1 year	7.75	475.00
1935	INTERIOR SCENE, 1 year	8.25	475.00
1936	INTERIOR SCENE, 1 year	8.25	490.00
1937	INTERIOR SCENE, 1 year	8.25	490.00
1938	INTERIOR SCENE, 1 year	8.25	485.00
1939	INTERIOR SCENE, 1 year	8.25	490.00
1940	CHRISTMAS TREE, 1 year	8.75	490.00
1941	INTERIOR SCENE, 1 year	8.75	440.00
1955	CHURCH TOWER, 200	24.00	440.00
1956	LANDSCAPE, 200	23.50	325.00
1957	LANDSCAPE, 225	23.50	325.00
1958	LANDSCAPE, 225	25.00	325.00
1959	LANDSCAPE, 250	26.25	325.00
1960	STREET IN DELFT, 250	25.00	350.00
1961	VILLAGE SCENE, 260	30.00	370.00
1962	TOWER IN LEEUWARDEN, 275	30.00	370.00
1963	TOWER IN ENKHUISEN, 275	35.00	370.00

		ISSUE	CURRENT
1964	TOWER IN HOORN, 300	35.00	370.00
1965	CORN MILL IN RHOON, 300	35.00	370.00
1966	SNUFF MILL IN ROTTERDAM, 325	40.00	370.00
1967	TOWER IN AMSTERDAM 350	45.00	370.00
1968	TOWER IN AMSTERDAM, 350	60.00	365.00
1969	CHURCH IN UTRECHT, 400	60.00	340.00
1970	CATHEDRAL IN VEERE, 500	60.00	340.00
1971	"DOM" TOWER IN UTRECHT, 550	60.00	340.00
1972	CHURCH IN EDAM, 1,500	70.00	340.00
1973	"DE WAAG" IN ALKAMAR, 1,500	75.00	415.00
1974	KITCHEN IN HINDELOOPEN, 1,500	160.00	400.00
1975	FARMER IN LAREN, 1,500	250.00	390.00
1976	FARM IN STAPHORST, 1,500	220.00	375.00
1977	FARM IN SPAKENBURG, 1,500	277.00	370.00
1978	WINTER SKATING SCENE, 1,000	277.00	300.00
1979	CHRISTMAS RHENEN, 500	260.00	270.00
1980	WINTER SCENE, 500	245.00	260.00
1981	WINTER SCENE, 500	245.00	260.00
1982	WINTER SCENE, 500	245.00	NR
1983	EVENING TWILIGHT, 500	230.00	NR
1984	THE HOMECOMING, Jan Dessens, 500	230.00	NR
1985	CHURCH AT T'WOUDT, Mar de Bruijn, 500	270.00	NR
1986	ST. DIONYSIUS, Mar de Bruijn, 500	324.00	NR

Christmas (9")

1955	CHRISTMAS STAR, 1 year	11.75	175.00
1956	CHRISTMAS BELLS, 1 year	11.75	340.00
1957	FLOWER DESIGN, 1 year	11.75	140.00
1957	CHRISTMAS STAR, 1 year	12.25	140.00
1958	CHRISTMAS STAR, 1 year	12.25	140.00

Christmas (7")

1915	CHRISTMAS STAR, 1 year	1.50	3,630.00
1926	BELL TOWER, 1 year	3.00	225.00
1927	CHURCH TOWER, 1 year	3.00	300.00
1928	MILL, 1 year	3.00	325.00
1929	CHURCH SPIRE, 1 year	3.00	325.00
1930	SAILING BOAT, 1 year	3.00	225.00
1931	CHURCH TOWER, 1 year	3.00	300.00
1932	BELL TOWER, 1 year	3.00	300.00
1959	LANDSCAPE WITH MILL, 400	9.50	140.00
1960	LANDSCAPE, 400	11.25	170.00
1961	SNOW LANDSCAPE, 500	12.00	165.00
1962	TOWN VIEW, 500	12.00	165.00
1963	MILL IN ZEDDAM, 500	12.25	165.00
1964	TOWNGATE IN KAMPEN, 600	14.75	165.00
1966	TOWNGATE IN MEDEMBLIK, 600	14.75	165.00
1967	MILL IN HAZERSWOUDE, 700	16.75	165.00
1968	MILL IN SCHIEDAM, 700	18.00	165.00
1969	MILL NEAR GORKUM, 800	26.25	140.00
1970	MILL NEAR HAARLEM, 1,500	26.25	140.00
1971	TOWNGATE AT ZIERIKZEE, 3,500	30.00	140.00
1972	TOWNGATE AT ELBURG, 3,500	42.50	125.00
1973	TOWNGATE AT AMERSFOORT, 4,500	47.50	125.00

		ISSUE	CURRENT
1974	WATERGATE AT SNEEK, 4,500	52.50	165.00
1975	TOWNGATE AT AMSTERDAM, 1,000	65.00	165.00
1976	TOWNGATE IN GORINCHEM, 4,500	72.50	165.00
1977	DROMEDARIS TOWER, 4,500	77.50	150.00
1978	CHRISTMAS FISHERMAN, 1,500	77.50	140.00
1979	GOLF PLAYERS ON THE ICE, 1,000	97.50	130.00
1980	ICE SAILING, 1,000	117.50	130.00
1981	HORSE SLEDDING, 1,000	117.50	130.00
1982	ICE SKATING, 1,000	125.00	NR
1983	CAKE AND SOMETHING TO DRINK, 1,000	120.00	NR
1984	FIGURE SKATING, Jan Dessens, 1,000	120.00	NR
1985	THE FARMHOUSE, Mar de Bruijn, 1,000	140.00	NR
1986	FARMHOUSE, Mar de Bruijn, 1,000	168.00	NR

Easter

1973	DUTCH EASTER PALM, 3,500	75.00	150.00
1974	DUTCH EASTER PALM, 1,000	110.00	145.00
1975	DUTCH EASTER PALM, 1,000	125.00	180.00
1976	DUTCH EASTER PALM, 1,000	175.00	205.00

Father's Day

1972	FATHER AND SON, VOLENDAM, 1,500	40.00	75.00
1973	FATHER AND SON, HINDELOOPEN, 2,000	40.00	70.00
1974	FATHER AND SON, ZUID-BEVELAND, 1 year	80.00	105.00
1975	FATHER AND SON, SPAKENBURG, 1 year	140.00	BR

Mother's Day

1971	MOTHER AND DAUGHTER, VOLENDAM, 2,500	50.00	75.00
1972	MOTHER AND DAUGHTER, HINDELOOPEN, 2,500	40.00	80.00
1973	MOTHER AND DAUGHTER, MARKEN, 3,000	50.00	75.00
1974	MOTHER AND DAUGHTER, ZUID-BEVALAND, 1 year	80.00	100.00
1975	MOTHER AND DAUGHTER, SPAKENBURG, 1 year	100.00	120.00
1976	MOTHER AND DAUGHTER, SCHEVENINGEN, 1 year	115.00	125.00

Special Bicentenary

1976	GEORGE WASHINGTON, 2,500	350.00	NR
1976	EAGLE PLATE, 5,000	150.00	NR

Stars, Satellites and Space

1910	HALLEY'S COMET	22.50	750.00
1957	FIRST EARTH SATELLITE	22.50	90.00
1968	APOLLO 8	22.50	40.00
1969	APOLLO II	22.50	40.00
1974	SKYLAB AND COMET KOHOUTEK, 1,000	80.00	NR
1975	APOLLO SOYUZ	140.00	BR
1972	OLYMPIAD	70.00	BR

Valentine

1973	VALENTINE "ENDURING BEAUTY," 1,500	75.00	150.00
1974	VALENTINE, 1,000	125.00	135.00

		ISSUE	CURRENT
1975	VALENTINE, 1,000	125.00	NR
1976	VALENTINE, 1,000	175.00	NR

Single Issue

1987	50TH WEDDING ANNIVERSARY OF PRINCESS JULIANA AND PRINCE BERNHARD, Mar de Bruijn, 500	337.50	350.00

ROYAL DEVON UNITED STATES

(Hamilton Collection)

Norman Rockwell Christmas

1975	DOWNHILL DARING, Norman Rockwell, 1 year	24.50	30.00
1976	THE CHRISTMAS GIFT, Norman Rockwell, 1 year	24.50	35.00
1977	THE BIG MOMENT, Norman Rockwell, 1 year	27.50	50.00
1978	PUPPETS FOR CHRISTMAS, Norman Rockwell, 1 year	27.50	NR
1979	ONE PRESENT TOO MANY, Norman Rockwell, 1 year	31.50	NR
1980	GRAMPS MEETS GRAMPS, Norman Rockwell, 1 year	33.00	NR

ROYAL DOULTON GREAT BRITAIN

All God's Children

1978	A BRIGHTER DAY, Lisette DeWinne, 10,000	75.00	NR
1980	VILLAGE CHILDREN, Lisette DeWinne, 10,000	65.00	NR
1981	NOBLE HERITAGE, Lisette DeWinne, 10,000	85.00	NR
1982	BUDDIES, Lisette DeWinne, 10,000	85.00	NR
1983	MY LITTLE BROTHER, Lisette DeWinne, 10,000	95.00	NR
1984	SISTERLY LOVE, Lisette DeWinne, 10,000	95.00	NR

American Tapestries

1978	SLEIGH BELLS, C. A. Brown, 15,000	70.00	NR
1979	PUMPKIN PATCH, C. A. Brown, 15,000	70.00	NR
1980	GENERAL STORE, C. A. Brown, 15,000	95.00	NR
1981	FOURTH OF JULY, C. A. Brown, 15,000	95.00	NR

Behind the Painted Masque

1982	PAINTED FEELINGS, Ben Black, 10,000	95.00	175.00
1983	MAKE ME LAUGH, Ben Black, 10,000	95.00	175.00
1984	MINSTREL SERENADE, Ben Black, 10,000	95.00	175.00
1985	PLEASING PERFORMANCE, Ben Black, 10,000	95.00	175.00

Beswick Christmas

1972	CHRISTMAS IN ENGLAND, Harry Sales, 15,000	35.00	NR
1973	CHRISTMAS IN MEXICO, Chavela Castrejon, 15,000	37.50	NR
1974	CHRISTMAS IN BULGARIA, Dimitri Yordanov, 15,000	37.50	45.00
1975	CHRISTMAS IN NORWAY, Alton S. Tobey, 15,000	45.00	NR
1976	CHRISTMAS IN HOLLAND, Alton S. Tobey, 15,000	50.00	BR
1977	CHRISTMAS IN POLAND, Alton S. Tobey, 15,000	50.00	70.00
1978	CHRISTMAS IN AMERICA, Alton S. Tobey, 15,000	55.00	NR

		ISSUE	CURRENT

Celebration of Faith

		ISSUE	CURRENT
1982	ROSH HASHANAH, James Woods, 7,500	250.00	300.00
1983	YOM KIPPUR, James Woods, 7,500	250.00	300.00
1984	PASSOVER, James Woods, 7,500	250.00	300.00
1985	CHANUKAH, James Woods, 7,500	250.00	300.00

Character Plates

		ISSUE	CURRENT
1979	OLD BALLOON SELLER, closed 1983	100.00	NR
1980	BALLOON MAN, closed 1983	125.00	NR
1981	SILKS AND RIBBONS, closed 1983	125.00	NR
1982	BIDDY PENNY FARTHING, closed 1983	125.00	NR

Charles Dickens Plates

		ISSUE	CURRENT
1980	ARTFUL DODGER, closed 1984	65.00	NR
1980	BARKIS, closed 1984	80.00	NR
1980	CAP'N CUTTLE, closed 1984	80.00	NR
1980	FAGIN, closed 1984	65.00	NR
1980	FAT BOY, closed 1984	65.00	NR
1980	MR. MICAWBER, closed 1984	80.00	NR
1980	MR. PICKWICK, closed 1984	80.00	NR
1980	OLD PEGGOTY, closed 1984	65.00	NR
1980	POOR JO, closed 1984	80.00	NR
1980	SAIREY GAMP, closed 1984	80.00	NR
1980	SAM WELLER, closed 1984	65.00	NR
1980	SERGEANT BUZ FUZ, closed 1984	80.00	NR
1980	TONY WELLER, closed 1984	65.00	NR

Childhood Christmas

		ISSUE	CURRENT
1983	SILENT NIGHT, Neil Faulkner, 1 year	39.95	NR
1984	WHILE SHEPHERDS WATCHED, Neil Faulkner, 1 year	39.95	NR
1985	OH LITTLE TOWN OF BETHLEHEM, Neil Faulkner, 1 year	39.95	NR
1986	WE SAW THREE SHIPS A-SAILING, Neil Faulkner, 1 year	39.95	NR
1987	THE HOLLY AND THE IVY, Neil Faulkner, 1 year	39.95	NR

Children of the Pueblo

		ISSUE	CURRENT
1983	APPLE FLOWER, Mimi Jungbluth (She Cloud), 15,00	60.00	100.00
1984	MORNING STAR, Mimi Jungbluth (She Cloud), 15,000	60.00	100.00

Christmas Around the World

		ISSUE	CURRENT
1972	OLD ENGLAND, 15,000	35.00	NR
1973	MEXICO, 15,000	37.50	NR
1974	BULGARIA, 15,000	37.50	NR
1975	NORWAY, 15,000	45.00	NR
1976	HOLLAND, 15,000	50.00	NR
1977	POLAND, 15,000	50.00	NR
1978	AMERICA, 15,000	55.00	NR

Christmas Plates

		ISSUE	CURRENT
1993	ROYAL DOULTON—TOGETHER FOR CHRISTMAS, J. James, 1 year	45.00	RI
1993	ROYAL ALBERT—SLEIGH RIDE, 1 year	45.00	RI

		ISSUE	CURRENT
1994	ROYAL DOULTON—HOME FOR CHRISTMAS, J. James, 1 year	45.00	RI
1994	ROYAL DOULTON—COACHING INN, 1 year	45.00	RI
1995	ROYAL DOULTON—SEASON'S GREETINGS, J. James, 1 year	45.00	RI
1995	ROYAL ALBERT—SKATING POND, 1 year	45.00	RI
1996	ROYAL DOULTON—NIGHT BEFORE CHRISTMAS, J. James, 1 year	45.00	RI
1996	ROYAL ALBERT—GATHERING WINTER FUEL, 1 year	45.00	RI

Commedia Dell' Arte

1974	HARLEQUIN, LeRoy Neiman, 15,000	50.00	175.00
1975	PIERROT, LeRoy Neiman, 15,000	60.00	160.00
1977	COLUMBINE, LeRoy Neiman, 15,000	70.00	80.00
1978	PUNCHINELLO, LeRoy Neiman, 15,000	70.00	75.00

Encore

1985	GABRIELLA, Francisco Masseria, 10,000	95.00	NR

Family Christmas Plates

1991	DAD PLAYS SANTA, 1 year	60.00	NR

Festival Children of the World

1983	MARIANI, Brenda Burke, 15,000	65.00	NR
1983	MICHIKO, Brenda Burke, 15,000	65.00	NR
1983	MAGDALENA, Brenda Burke, 15,000	65.00	NR
1983	MONIKA, Brenda Burke, 15,000	65.00	NR

Flower Garden

1975	SPRING HARMONY, Hahn Vidal, 15,000	60.00	80.00
1976	DREAMING LOTUS, Hahn Vidal, 15,000	65.00	90.00
1977	FROM THE POET'S GARDEN, Hahn Vidal, 15,000	70.00	75.00
1978	COUNTRY BOUQUET, Hahn Vidal, 15,000	70.00	75.00
1979	FROM MY MOTHER'S GARDEN, Hahn Vidal, 15,000	85.00	90.00

Grandest Gift

1984	REUNION, MaGo, 10,000	75.00	100.00
1985	STORYTIME, MaGo, 10,000	75.00	100.00

Grandparents

1984	GRANDFATHER AND CHILDREN, MaGo, 15,000	95.00	NR

I Remember America

1977	PENNSYLVANIA PASTORALE, Eric Sloane, 15,000	70.00	90.00
1978	LOVE JOY BRIDGE, Eric Sloane, 15,000	70.00	80.00
1979	FOUR CORNERS, Eric Sloane, 15,000	75.00	NR
1981	MARSHLANDS, Eric Sloane, 15,000	95.00	NR

Jungle Fantasy

1979	THE ARK, Gustavo Novoa, 10,000	75.00	NR
1981	COMPASSION, Gustavo Novoa, 10,000	95.00	NR
1982	PATIENCE, Gustavo Novoa, 10,000	95.00	NR
1983	REFUGE, Gustavo Novoa, 10,000	95.00	NR

Leroy Neiman Special

		ISSUE	CURRENT
1980	WINNING COLORS, LeRoy Neiman, 10,000	85.00	NR

Log of the *Dashing Wave*

		ISSUE	CURRENT
1976	SAILING WITH THE TIDE, John Stobart, 15,000	65.00	NR
1977	RUNNING FREE, John Stobart, 15,000	70.00	150.00
1978	ROUNDING THE HORN, John Stobart, 15,000	70.00	NR
1979	HONG KONG, John Stobart, 15,000	75.00	NR
1981	BORA BORA, John Stobart, 15,000	95.00	NR
1984	JOURNEY'S END, John Stobart, 15,000	95.00	150.00

Portraits of Innocence

		ISSUE	CURRENT
1980	PANCHITO, Francisco Masseria, 15,000	75.00	125.00
1981	ADRIEN, Francisco Masseria, 15,000	85.00	120.00
1982	ANGELICA, Francisco Masseria, 15,000	95.00	120.00
1983	JULIANA, Francisco Masseria, 15,000	95.00	120.00
1985	GABRIELLA, Francisco Masseria, 15,000	95.00	115.00
1986	FRANCESCA, Francisco Masseria, 15,000	95.00	115.00

Ports of Call

		ISSUE	CURRENT
1975	SAN FRANCISCO, Doug Kingman, 15,000	60.00	90.00
1976	NEW ORLEANS, Doug Kingman, 15,000	65.00	80.00
1977	VENICE, Doug Kingman, 15,000	70.00	NR
1978	PARIS, Doug Kingman, 15,000	70.00	NR

Reflections on China

		ISSUE	CURRENT
1976	GARDEN OF TRANQUILITY, Chen Chi, 15,000	70.00	90.00
1977	IMPERIAL PALACE, Chen Chi, 15,000	70.00	80.00
1978	TEMPLE OF HEAVEN, Chen Chi, 15,000	75.00	NR
1980	LAKE OF MISTS, Chen Chi, 15,000	85.00	NR

Rollinson's Portraits of Nature

		ISSUE	CURRENT
1988	OTTER PAIR ON THE RIVERBANK, Rollinson	NA	NA

Victorian Childhood

		ISSUE	CURRENT
1991	THE ORIGINAL "IN DISGRACE"	29.00	35.00
1991	BREAKFAST IN BED, Charles Burton-Barber	29.00	75.00
1992	SAY, "PLEASE"	32.00	85.00
1992	MY PRECIOUS BUNDLE	32.00	40.00
1992	THE CONCERT, Charles Burton-Barber	32.00	50.00
1992	IN GOOD HANDS	34.00	50.00
1992	TEMPTING FARE	34.00	NR
1992	A RIVAL ATTRACTION	34.00	50.00

Victorian Era Christmas

		ISSUE	CURRENT
1977	WINTER FUN, 1 year	25.00	55.00
1978	CHRISTMAS DAY,1 year	25.00	55.00
1979	CHRISTMAS, 1 year	39.95	BR
1980	SANTA'S VISIT, 1 year	42.00	BR
1981	CHRISTMAS CAROLERS, 1 year	37.50	NR
1982	SANTA ON BICYCLE, 1 year	39.95	NR

		ISSUE	CURRENT

Victorian Era Valentines

		ISSUE	CURRENT
1976	VICTORIAN BOY AND GIRL, 1 year	25.00	NR
1977	MY SWEETEST FRIEND, 1 year	25.00	NR
1978	IF I LOVED YOU, 1 year	25.00	NR
1979	MY VALENTINE, 1 year	29.95	NR
1980	ON A SWING, 1 year	32.95	NR
1981	SWEET MUSIC, 1 year	35.00	NR
1982	FROM MY HEART, 1 year	35.00	NR
1983	CHERUB'S SONG, 1 year	40.00	NR

Single Issue

		ISSUE	CURRENT
1981	COMMEMORATIVE WEDDING OF THE PRINCE OF WALES AND LADY DIANA SPENCER, 1,500	195.00	225.00

Mariani

Journey's End

Otter Pair on the Riverbank

Breakfast in Bed

Photos courtesy of *Collectors News*

ROYALE GERMANY

Christmas

		ISSUE	CURRENT
1969	CHRISTMAS FAIR, factory artist, 6,000	12.00	125.00
1970	VIGIL MASS, factory artist, 10,000	13.00	110.00
1971	CHRISTMAS NIGHT, factory artist, 8,000	16.00	50.00
1972	ELKS, factory artist, 8,000	16.00	45.00
1973	CHRISTMAS DAWN, factory artist, 6,000	20.00	40.00
1974	VILLAGE CHRISTMAS, factory artist, 5,000	22.00	60.00
1975	FEEDING TIME, factory artist, 5,000	26.00	35.00
1976	SEAPORT CHRISTMAS, factory artist, 5,000	27.50	NR
1977	SLEDDING, factory artist, 5,000	30.00	NR

Father's Day

1970	U.S. FRIGATE *CONSTITUTION*, factory artist, 5,000	13.00	80.00
1971	MAN FISHING, factory artist, 5,000	13.00	35.00
1972	MOUNTAINEER, factory artist, 5,000	16.00	55.00
1973	CAMPING, factory artist, 4,000	18.00	45.00
1974	EAGLE, factory artist, 2,500	22.00	35.00
1975	REGATTA, factory artist, 2,500	26.00	35.00
1976	HUNTING, factory artist, 2,500	27.50	35.00
1977	FISHING, factory artist, 2,500	30.00	NR

Game Plates

1972	SETTERS, J. Poluszynski, 500	180.00	200.00
1973	FOX, J. Poluszynski, 500	200.00	250.00
1974	OSPREY, J. Poluszynski, 250	250.00	NR
1975	CALIFORNIA QUAIL, J. Poluszynski, 250	265.00	NR

Mother's Day

1970	SWAN AND YOUNG, 6,000	12.00	80.00
1971	DOE AND FAWN, 9,000	13.00	55.00
1972	RABBITS, 9,000	16.00	40.00
1973	OWL FAMILY, 6,000	18.00	40.00
1974	DUCK AND YOUNG, 5,000	22.00	40.00
1975	LYNX AND CUBS, 5,000	26.00	40.00
1976	WOODCOCK AND YOUNG, 5,000	27.50	35.00
1977	KOALA BEAR, 5,000	30.00	NR

Single Issue

1969	APOLLO MOON LANDING, 2,000	30.00	80.00

ROYALE GERMANIA GERMANY

Christmas Annual

1970	ORCHID, 600	200.00	650.00
1971	CYCLAMEN, 1,000	200.00	325.00
1972	SILVER THISTLE, 1,000	250.00	290.00
1973	TULIPS, 600	275.00	310.00
1974	SUNFLOWERS, 500	300.00	320.00
1975	SNOWDROPS, 350	450.00	500.00

			ISSUE	CURRENT
1976	FLAMING HEART, 350		450.00	NR

Mother's Day Crystal

1971	ROSES, 250	135.00	650.00
1972	ELEPHANT AND YOUNGSTER, 750	180.00	250.00
1973	KOALA BEAR AND CUB, 600	200.00	225.00
1974	SQUIRRELS, 500	240.00	250.00
1975	SWAN AND YOUNG, 350	350.00	360.00

ROYAL GRAFTON GEAT BRITAIN

(Collector's Treasury)

Beauty of Polar Wildlife (Collector's Treasury)

1990	BABY SEALS, Mike Jackson, 150 days	27.50	BR
1990	POLAR BEAR CUBS, Mike Jackson, 150 days	27.50	BR
1991	ARCTIC FOX CUBS, Mike Jackson, 150 days	30.50	BR
1991	ARCTIC HARE FAMILY, Mike Jackson, 150 days	30.50	BR
1991	ARCTIC WOLF FAMILY, Mike Jackson, 150 days	30.50	BR
1991	DALL SHEEP, Mike Jackson, 150 days	32.50	BR
1991	EMPEROR PENGUINS, Mike Jackson, 150 days	32.50	BR
1992	REINDEER YOUNG, Mike Jackson, 150 days	32.50	BR

Braithwaite Game Birds

1987	PHEASANTS IN FLIGHT	24.50	30.00
1987	RED-LEGGED PARTRIDGE	24.50	BR
1988	BLACK GROUSE	27.50	BR
1988	FLOCK OF PTARMIGAN	27.50	NR
1988	QUAIL ON THE WING	27.50	NR
1988	CAPERCAILLIE	27.50	BR
1989	RED GROUSE	29.50	BR

Twelve Days of Christmas

1976	PARTRIDGE ON PEAR TREE, 3,000	17.50	NR
1977	TWO TURTLE DOVES, 3,000	17.50	NR
1978	THREE FRENCH HENS, 3,000	21.50	NR
1979	FOUR CALLING BIRDS, 3,000	26.50	NR
1980	FIVE GOLDEN RINGS, 3,000	35.00	NR

ROYAL LIMOGES FRANCE

Christmas

1972	NATIVITY, 5,000	25.00	40.00
1973	THREE WISE MEN, 5,000	27.50	40.00

ROYAL OAKS LIMITED UNITED STATES

Love's Labor

1983	THE INTRUDER, James Landenberger, 15,000	50.00	NR

ROYAL ORLEANS UNITED STATES

(Hoyle Products)

Coca-Cola: The Classic Santa Claus

		ISSUE	CURRENT
1983	GOOD BOYS AND GIRLS, Haddon Sundblom, 15,000	55.00	NR
1984	A GIFT FOR SANTA, Haddon Sundblom, 15,000	65.00	NR
1985	SANTA, PLEASE PAUSE HERE, Haddon Sundblom, 15,000	65.00	NR

Dynasty

1986	KRYSTLE, Shell Fisher	35.00	NR

Elvis in Concert

1984	ALOHA FROM HAWAII, Rick Grimes, 20,000	35.00	NR
1985	LAS VEGAS, Rick Grimes, 20,000	35.00	NR

Famous Movies

1985	*CAT ON A HOT TIN ROOF*, Rick Grimes, 20,000	35.00	NR

Marilyn—An American Classic

1983	*THE SEVEN YEAR ITCH*, Twentieth Century-Fox, 20,000	35.00	NR
1984	*GENTLEMEN PREFER BLONDES*, Twentieth Century-Fox, 20,000	35.00	NR
1985	*NIAGARA*, Twentieth Century-Fox, 20,000	35.00	NR
1986	*HOW TO MARRY A MILLIONAIRE*, Twentieth Century-Fox, 20,000	35.00	NR

Pink Panther Christmas Collection

1982	SLEIGH RIDE, D. DePatie, 10,000	18.50	NR
1983	HAPPY LANDINGS, D. DePatie, 10,000	18.50	NR
1984	DOWN THE CHIMNEY, D. DePatie, 10,000	18.50	NR
1985	PASS THE BLAST, D. DePatie, 10,000	18.50	NR

How to Marry a Millionaire
Photo courtesy of *Collectors News*

The M*A*S*H *Plate*
Photo courtesy of *Collectors News*

		ISSUE	CURRENT

In Trompe L'Oeil

1984	UP TO MISCHIEF, Carol Eytinge, 10,000	25.00	NR

TV

1983	THE *M*A*S*H* PLATE, J. LaBonte, 1 year	25.00	NR
1983	*DYNASTY*, Shell Fisher, 1 year	35.00	NR

Yorkshire Brontes

1984	*WUTHERING HEIGHTS*, 30 days	35.00	NR
1985	*JANE EYRE*, 30 days	35.00	NR

ROYAL PORCELAIN—KINGDOM OF THAILAND THAILAND

Love Story of Siam

1991	THE BETROTHAL	29.92	BR
1991	THE MAGIC BOW	29.92	NR
1991	THE WEDDING DANCE	32.92	NR
1992	THE CORONATION PREPARATIONS	32.92	NR
1992	THE EXILE	32.92	NR
1992	THE RETURN TO THE THRONE	32.92	50.00

ROYAL PRINCESS

Christmas

1973	THREE WISE MEN	10.00	NR

ROYAL TETTAU GERMANY

Christmas

1972	CARRIAGE IN THE VILLAGE	12.50	NR

Papal Series

1971	POPE PAUL VI, 5,000	100.00	175.00
1972	POPE JOHN XXIII, 5,000	100.00	150.00
1973	POPE PIUS XII, 5,000	100.00	125.00

ROYALWOOD UNITED STATES

Leyendecker

1978	CORNFLAKE BOY, J. C. Leyendecker, 10,000	25.00	NR
1978	CORNFLAKE GIRL, J. C. Leyendecker, 10,000	25.00	NR

Single Issue

1977	DOCTOR AND DOLL, Norman Rockwell, 1 year	21.50	NR

ROYAL WORCESTER GREAT BRITAIN

(Hamilton Collection)

American History

		ISSUE	CURRENT
1977	WASHINGTON'S INAUGURATION, 1,250	65.00	300.00

Audubon Birds

1977	WARBLER AND JAY, 5,000, set of 2	150.00	NR
1978	KINGBIRD AND SPARROW, 10,000, set of 2	150.00	NR

Birth of a Nation

1972	BOSTON TEA PARTY, Prescott W. Baston, 10,000	45.00	275.00
1973	THE RIDE OF PAUL REVERE, Prescott W. Baston, 10,000	45.00	250.00
1974	INCIDENT AT CONCORD BRIDGE, Prescott W. Baston, 10,000	50.00	120.00
1975	SIGNING THE DECLARATION OF INDEPENDENCE, Prescott W. Baston, 10,000	65.00	125.00
1976	WASHINGTON CROSSING THE DELAWARE, Prescott W. Baston, 10,000	65.00	125.00
1977	WASHINGTON'S INAUGURATION, 1,250	65.00	275.00

Currier & Ives

1974	ROAD IN WINTER, Prescott W. Baston, 5,570	59.50	NR
1975	OLD GRIST MILL, Prescott W. Baston, 3,200	59.50	NR
1976	WINTER PASTIME, Prescott W. Baston, 1,500	59.50	NR
1977	HOME TO THANKSGIVING, Prescott W. Baston, 546	59.50	NR

Doughty Birds

1972	REDSTART AND BEECH, D. Doughty, 2,750	150.00	NR
1973	MYRTLE WARBLER AND CHERRY, D. Doughty, 3,000	175.00	NR
1974	BLUE-GREY GNATCATCHERS, D. Doughty, 3,000	195.00	210.00
1975	BLACKBURNIAN WARBLER, D. Doughty, 3,000	195.00	NR
1976	BLUE-WINGED SIVAS AND BAMBOO, D. Doughty, 3,000	195.00	NR
1977	PARADISE WYDAH, D. Doughty, 3,000	195.00	NR
1978	BLUETITS AND WITCH HAZEL, D. Doughty, 3,000	195.00	NR
1979	MOUNTAIN BLUEBIRD AND PINE, D. Doughty, 3,000	195.00	NR
1980	CERULEAN WARBLERS AND BEECH, D. Doughty, 3,000	315.00	NR
1981	WILLOW WARBLER, D. Doughty, 3,000	315.00	NR
1982	RUBY-CROWNED KINGLETS, D. Doughty, 3,000	330.00	NR
1983	WREN AND JASMINE, D. Doughty, 3,000	330.00	NR

English Christmas

1979	CHRISTMAS EVE, 1 year	60.00	NR
1980	CHRISTMAS MORNING, Ewnece, 1 year	65.00	NR
1980	CHRISTMAS DAY	70.00	NR

Fabulous Birds

1976	PEACOCKS, 10,000	65.00	NR
1978	PEACOCKS II, 10,000	65.00	NR

Kitten Classics (Hamilton Collection)

1985	CAT NAP, Pam Cooper, 14 days	29.50	35.00
1985	PURRFECT TREASURE, Pam Cooper, 14 days	29.50	NR

		ISSUE	CURRENT
1985	WILD FLOWER, Pam Cooper, 14 days	29.50	NR
1985	BIRDWATCHER, Pam Cooper, 14 days	29.50	NR
1985	TIGER'S FANCY, Pam Cooper, 14 days	29.50	NR
1985	COUNTRY KITTY, Pam Cooper, 14 days	29.50	NR
1985	LITTLE RASCAL, Pam Cooper, 14 days	29.50	NR
1985	FIRST PRIZE, Pam Cooper, 14 days	29.50	NR

Kitten Encounters

1987	FISHFUL THINKING, P. Cooper, 14 days	29.50	NR
1987	PUPPY PAL, P. Cooper, 14 days	29.50	35.00
1987	JUST DUCKY, P. Cooper, 14 days	29.50	35.00
1987	BUNNY CHASE, P. Cooper, 14 days	29.50	NR
1987	FLUTTER BY, P. Cooper, 14 days	29.50	NR
1987	BEDTIME BUDDIES, P. Cooper, 14 days	29.50	NR
1988	CAT AND MOUSE, P. Cooper, 14 days	29.50	NR
1988	STABLEMATES, P. Cooper, 14 days	29.50	50.00

Water Birds of North America

1985	MALLARDS, J. Cooke, 15,000	55.00	NR
1985	CANVASBACKS, J. Cooke, 15,000	55.00	NR
1985	WOOD DUCKS, J. Cooke, 15,000	55.00	NR
1985	SNOW GEESE, J. Cooke, 15,000	55.00	NR
1985	AMERICAN PINTAILS, J. Cooke, 15,000	55.00	NR
1985	GREEN-WINGED TEALS, J. Cooke, 15,000	55.00	NR
1985	HOODED MERGANSERS, J. Cooke, 15,000	55.00	NR
1985	CANADA GEESE, J. Cooke, 15,000	55.00	NR

Single Issue

1976	SPIRIT OF 1776, 10,000	65.00	NR

SABINO FRANCE

Annual Crystal

1970	KING HENRY IV AND MARIA DE MEDICI, 1,500	65.00	75.00
1971	MILO AND THE BEASTS, 1,500	65.00	75.00

SANGO JAPAN

Christmas

1974	SPARK OF CHRISTMAS, Marvin Nye, 5,000	25.00	NR
1975	CHRISTMAS EVE IN COUNTRY, Marvin Nye, 5,000	27.50	NR
1976	MADONNA AND CHILD, Marvin Nye, 5,000	25.00	NR
1976	UNDESIRED SLUMBER, Marvin Nye, 7,500	25.00	55.00
1977	TOGETHERNESS, Marvin Nye, 7,500	25.00	40.00

Living American Artists

1976	SWEETHEARTS, Norman Rockwell, 10,000	30.00	60.00
1977	APACHE GIRL, Gregory Perillo, 5,000	35.00	290.00
1978	NATURAL HABITAT, 5,000	40.00	NR

		ISSUE	CURRENT

Mother's Day

1976	SPRING DELIGHT, Leslie De Mille, 7,500	20.00	NR
1977	BROKEN WINGS, Leslie De Mille, 5,000	22.50	NR

SANTA CLARA SPAIN

Christmas

1970	CHRISTMAS MESSAGE, 10,000	18.00	40.00
1971	THREE WISE MEN, 10,000	18.00	35.00
1972	CHILDREN ON WOODS PATH, 10,000	20.00	40.00
1974	ARCHANGEL, 5,000	25.00	50.00
1974	SPIRIT OF CHRISTMAS, 5,000	25.00	NR
1975	CHRISTMAS EVE, 5,000	27.50	35.00
1976	MADONNA AND CHILD, 5,000	25.00	35.00
1977	MOTHER AND CHILD, 10,000	27.50	35.00
1978	ANGEL WITH FLOWERS, 10,000	32.00	NR
1979	MADONNA AND ANGELS, 10,000	34.50	NR

Mother's Day

1971	MOTHER AND CHILD, 10,000	12.00	30.00
1972	MOTHER AND CHILDREN, 12,000	12.00	40.00

SARAH'S ATTIC UNITED STATES

Classroom Memories

1991	CLASSROOM MEMORIES, S. Schultz, closed	80.00	NR

SARNA INDIA

Christmas

1975	HOLY FAMILY, 4,000	17.50	NR

SAVACOU GALLERY UNITED STATES

Foundations of African American Heritage

1993	GENERATIONS OF NECKBONE, Leroy Campbell, 20 days	39.95	RI
1994	SPIRIT OF SANKOFA, Frank Frazier, 20 days	39.95	RI
1995	FOUR HUNDRED YEARS OF OUR PEOPLE, Michael Escoffery, 20 days	45.00	RI
1996	MEN OF TRIUMPH, Ray Isaac, 20 days	45.00	RI
1996	WOMEN OF COURAGE, Ray Isaac, 20 days	45.00	RI
1997	SOUL SERENADE, James Denmark, 20 days	45.00	RI
1997	AMAZING GRACE, Brenda Joysmith, 20 days	45.00	RI

Men of Triumph
Photo courtesy of *Collectors News*

Soul Serenade
Photo courtesy of *Collectors News*

SCHMID GERMANY

(Anri, Lowell Davis Farm Club, Goebel)

Beatrix Potter

		ISSUE	CURRENT
1978	PETER RABBIT, Beatrix Potter, 5,000	50.00	NR
1979	JEMIMA PUDDLEDUCK, Beatrix Potter, 5,000	50.00	NR
1980	TALE OF BENJAMIN BUNNY, Beatrix Potter, 5,000	50.00	NR

Berta Hummel Christmas

		ISSUE	CURRENT
1971	ANGEL IN A CHRISTMAS SETTING, Berta Hummel, 1 year	15.00	NR
1972	ANGEL WITH FLUTE, Berta Hummel, 1 year	15.00	BR
1973	THE NATIVITY, Berta Hummel, 1 year	15.00	55.00
1974	THE GUARDIAN ANGEL, Berta Hummel, 1 year	18.50	BR
1975	CHRISTMAS CHILD, Berta Hummel, 1 year	25.00	BR
1976	SACRED JOURNEY, Berta Hummel, 1 year	27.50	BR
1977	HERALD ANGEL, Berta Hummel, 1 year	27.50	BR
1978	HEAVENLY TRIO, Berta Hummel, 1 year	32.50	BR
1979	STARLIGHT ANGEL, Berta Hummel, 1 year	38.00	BR
1980	PARADE INTO TOYLAND, Berta Hummel, 1 year	45.00	BR
1981	A TIME TO REMEMBER, Berta Hummel, 1 year	45.00	BR
1982	ANGELIC PROCESSION, Berta Hummel, 1 year	45.00	BR
1983	ANGELIC MESSENGER, Berta Hummel, 1 year	45.00	BR
1984	A GIFT FROM HEAVEN, Berta Hummel, 1 year	45.00	BR
1985	HEAVENLY LIGHT, Berta Hummel, 1 year	45.00	BR
1986	TELL THE HEAVENS, Berta Hummel, 1 year	45.00	NR
1987	ANGELIC GIFTS, Berta Hummel, 1 year	47.50	BR
1988	CHEERFUL CHERUBS, Berta Hummel, 1 year	53.00	65.00
1989	ANGELIC MUSICIAN, Berta Hummel, 1 year	53.00	BR
1990	ANGEL'S LIGHT, Berta Hummel, 1 year	53.00	BR
1991	A MESSAGE FROM ABOVE, Berta Hummel, 1 year	60.00	BR
1992	SWEET BLESSINGS, Berta Hummel, 1 year	65.00	NR

Angelic Messenger
Photo courtesy of *Collectors News*

Mother's Little Athlete
Photo courtesy of *Collectors News*

Berta Hummel Mother's Day

		ISSUE	CURRENT
1972	PLAYING HOOKY, Berta Hummel, 1 year	15.00	NR
1973	THE LITTLE FISHERMAN, Berta Hummel, 1 year	15.00	35.00
1974	THE BUMBLEBEE, Berta Hummel, 1 year	18.50	NR
1975	MESSAGE OF LOVE, Berta Hummel, 1 year	25.00	NR
1976	DEVOTION FOR MOTHER, Berta Hummel, 1 year	27.50	NR
1977	MOONLIGHT RETURN, Berta Hummel, 1 year	27.50	NR
1978	AFTERNOON STROLL, Berta Hummel, 1 year	32.50	NR
1979	CHERUB'S GIFT, Berta Hummel, 1 year	38.00	NR
1989	MOTHER'S LITTLE HELPERS, Berta Hummel, 1 year	45.00	55.00
1981	PLAYTIME, Berta Hummel, 1 year	45.00	55.00
1982	THE FLOWER BASKET, Berta Hummel, 1 year	45.00	NR
1983	SPRING BOUQUET, Berta Hummel, 1 year	45.00	55.00
1984	A JOY TO SHARE, Berta Hummel, 1 year	45.00	NR
1985	A MOTHER'S JOURNEY, Berta Hummel, 1 year	45.00	NR
1986	HOME FROM SCHOOL, Berta Hummel, 1 year	45.00	55.00
1987	MOTHER'S LITTLE LEARNER, Berta Hummel, 1 year	47.50	NR
1988	YOUNG READER, Berta Hummel, 1 year	52.50	80.00
1989	PRETTY AS A PICTURE, Berta Hummel, 1 year	53.00	75.00
1990	MOTHER'S LITTLE ATHLETE, Berta Hummel, 1 year	53.00	NR
1991	SOFT AND GENTLE, Berta Hummel, 1 year	55.00	NR

Carousel Fantasies

1983	A FAIRY TALE PRINCESS, Jessica Zemsky and Jack Hines, 7,500	50.00	NR

Ferràndiz Beautiful Bounty

1982	SUMMER'S GOLDEN HARVEST, Juan Ferràndiz, 10,000	40.00	NR
1982	AUTUMN BLESSING, Juan Ferràndiz, 10,000	40.00	NR
1982	A MIDWINTER'S DREAM, Juan Ferràndiz, 10,000	40.00	NR
1982	SPRING BLOSSOMS, Juan Ferràndiz, 10,000	40.00	NR

Ferràndiz Mother and Child

		ISSUE	CURRENT
1977	ORCHARD MOTHER AND CHILD, Juan Ferràndiz, 10,000	65.00	NR
1978	PASTORAL MOTHER AND CHILD, Juan Ferràndiz, 10,000	75.00	NR
1979	FLORAL MOTHER AND CHILD, Juan Ferràndiz, 10,000	95.00	NR
1980	AVIAN MOTHER AND CHILD, Juan Ferràndiz, 10,000	100.00	NR

Ferràndiz Music Makers

1981	THE FLUTIST, Juan Ferràndiz, 10,000	25.00	NR
1981	THE ENTERTAINER, Juan Ferràndiz, 10,000	25.00	NR
1982	MAGICAL MEDLEY, Juan Ferràndiz, 10,000	25.00	NR
1982	SWEET SERENADE, Juan Ferràndiz, 10,000	25.00	NR

Ferràndiz Wooden Jubilee

1979	SPRING DANCE, Juan Ferràndiz, 2,500	500.00	NR
1982	RIDING THRU THE RAIN, Juan Ferràndiz, 2,500	550.00	NR

Friends of Mine

1989	SUN WORSHIPPERS, Lowell Davis, 7,500	53.00	NR
1990	SUNDAY AFTERNOON TREAT, Lowell Davis, 7,500	53.00	NR
1991	WARM MILK, Lowell Davis, 7,500	55.00	NR
1992	CAT AND JENNY WREN, Lowell Davis, 7,500	55.00	NR

Gift of Happiness

1984	LILIES OF THE FIELD, Pati Bannister, 7,500	125.00	NR
1984	MORNING GLORIES, Juan Ferràndiz, 2,500	125.00	NR

Golden Moments

1978	TRANQUILITY, 15,000	250.00	NR
1981	SERENITY, 15,000	250.00	NR

Good Ol' Days

1984	WHEN MINUTES SEEM LIKE HOURS, Lowell Davis, 5,000	—	—
1984	WAITING FOR HIS MASTER, Lowell Davis, 5,000	—	—
	Set of 2	60.00	NR

Littlest Night

1993	THE LITTLEST NIGHT, Berta Hummel, 1 year	25.00	RI

My Name Is Star

1981	STAR'S SPRING, Jessica Zemsky, 10,000	30.00	NR
1981	STAR'S SUMMER, Jessica Zemsky,10,000	30.00	NR
1982	STAR'S AUTUMN, Jessica Zemsky, 10,000	30.00	NR
1982	STAR'S WINTER, Jessica Zemsky, 10,000	30.00	NR

Prairie Women

1982	THE MAIDEN, Jack Hines, 12,500	35.00	NR
1982	THE COURTSHIP BLANKET, Jack Hines, 12,500	35.00	NR
1982	MOTHER NOW, Jack Hines, 12,500	35.00	NR
1982	THE PASSING OF THE MOONS, Jack Hines, 12,500	35.00	NR

		ISSUE	CURRENT

Reflections of Life

1980	QUIET REFLECTIONS, Juan Ferràndiz, 10,000	85.00	NR
1981	TREE OF LIFE, Juan Ferràndiz, 10,000	85.00	NR

Schmid Crystal Desevres

1978	THE SEA, 1,500	60.00	NR
1979	THE SKY, 1,500	80.00	NR
1980	THE EARTH, 1,500	90.00	NR

Schmid Design

1971	FAMILY PORTRAIT, 5,000	13.00	NR
1972	ON HORSEBACK, 5,000	15.00	NR
1973	BRINGING HOME TREE, 5,000	20.00	NR
1974	DECORATING TREE, 5,000	25.00	NR
1975	OPENING PRESENTS, 5,000	27.00	NR
1976	BY FIRESIDE, 5,000	28.50	NR
1977	SKATING, 5,000	28.50	NR
1978	FAMILY PICKING TREE, 5,000	36.00	NR
1979	BREAKFAST BY TREE, 5,000	45.00	NR
1980	FEEDING ANIMALS, 5,000	55.00	NR

Schmid Father's Day

1975	BAVARIAN FATHER'S DAY	27.50	NR

Schmid Pewter Christmas Plates

1977	SANTA, 6,000	50.00	NR
1978	BEAUTIFUL SNOW, 6,000	50.00	NR
1979	I HEAR AMERICA SING, 6,000	50.00	NR
1980	A COUNTRY SLEIGH RIDE, 6,000	50.00	NR

Single Issues

1983	THE CRITICS, Lowell Davis, 12,500	45.00	65.00
1983	CHRISTMAS KINGDOM, Juan Ferràndiz, 10,000	45.00	NR
1986	HOME FROM MARKET, Lowell Davis, 7,000	55.00	NR

SCHMID JAPAN

Disney Bicentennial

1976	BICENTENNIAL PLATE, Disney Studios	13.00	NR

Disney Characters Collection

1983	SNEAK PREVIEW, Disney Studios, 20,000	22.50	NR
1984	COMMAND PERFORMANCE, Disney Studios, 20,000	22.50	NR
1985	SNOW BIZ, Disney Studios, 20,000	22.50	NR
1986	TREE FOR TWO, Disney Studios, 20,000	22.50	NR
1987	MERRY MOUSE MEDLEY, Disney Studios, 20,000	25.00	NR
1988	WARM WINTER RIDE, Disney Studios, 20,000	25.00	NR
1989	MERRY MICKEY CLAUS, Disney Studios, 20,000	32.50	60.00
1990	HOLLY JOLLY CHRISTMAS, Disney Studios, 20,000	32.50	NR
1991	MICKEY AND MINNIE'S ROCKIN' CHRISTMAS, Disney Studios, 20,000	37.00	NR

Disney Christmas

		ISSUE	CURRENT
1973	SLEIGH RIDE, Disney Studios, 1 year	10.00	150.00
1974	DECORATING THE TREE, Disney Studios, 1 year	10.00	55.00
1975	CAROLING, Disney Studios, 1 year	12.50	25.00
1976	BUILDING A SNOWMAN, Disney Studios, 1 year	13.00	NR
1977	DOWN THE CHIMNEY, Disney Studios, 1 year	13.00	20.00
1978	NIGHT BEFORE CHRISTMAS, Disney Studios, 1 year	15.00	20.00
1979	SANTA'S SURPRISE, Disney Studios, 15,000	17.50	25.00
1980	SLEIGH RIDE, Disney Studios, 15,000	17.50	30.00
1981	HAPPY HOLIDAYS, Disney Studios, 15,000	17.50	25.00
1982	WINTER GAMES, Disney Studios, 15,000	18.50	25.00

Disney Four Seasons of Love

1983	TICKETS ON THE FIFTY YARD LINE, Disney Studios, 10,000	17.50	NR
1983	LET IT SNOW, Disney Studios, 10,000	17.50	NR
1983	SPRING BOUQUET, 10,000	17.50	NR
1983	SHADES OF SUMMER, 10,000	17,50	NR

Disney Mother's Day

1974	FLOWERS FOR MOTHER, Disney Studios, 1 year	10.00	45.00
1975	SNOW WHITE AND THE SEVEN DWARFS, Disney Studios, 1 year	12.50	50.00
1976	MINNIE MOUSE AND FRIENDS, Disney Studios, 1 year	13.00	25.00
1977	PLUTO'S PALS, Disney Studios, 1 year	13.00	20.00
1978	FLOWERS FOR BAMBI, Disney Studios, 1 year	15.00	40.00
1979	HAPPY FEET, Disney Studios, 10,000	17.50	NR
1980	MINNIE'S SURPRISE, Disney Studios, 10,000	17.50	30.00
1981	PLAYMATES, Disney Studios, 10,000	17.50	35.00
1982	A DREAM COME TRUE, Disney Studios, 10,000	18.50	40.00

Disney Special Edition

1978	MICKEY MOUSE AT FIFTY, Disney Studios, 15,000	25.00	80.00
1980	HAPPY BIRTHDAY, PINOCCHIO, Disney Studios, 7,500	17.50	45.00
1981	ALICE IN WONDERLAND, Disney Studios, 7,500	17.50	NR
1982	HAPPY BIRTHDAY, PLUTO, Disney Studios, 7,500	17.50	40.00
1982	GOOFY'S GOLDEN JUBILEE, Disney Studios, 7,500	18.50	30.00
1987	SNOW WHITE GOLDEN ANNIVERSARY, Disney Studios, 5,000	47.50	NR
1988	MICKEY MOUSE AND MINNIE MOUSE 60TH, Disney Studios, 10,000	50.00	110.00
1989	SLEEPING BEAUTY 30TH ANNIVERSARY, Disney Studios, 5,000	80.00	95.00
1990	FANTASIA—SORCERER'S APPRENTICE, Disney Studios, 5,000	59.00	80.00
1990	PINOCCHIO'S FRIEND, Disney Studios, 1 year	25.00	NR
1990	FANTASIA RELIEF PLATE, Disney Studios, 20,000	25.00	40.00

Disney Valentine's Day

1979	HANDS AND HEART, Disney Studio, 1 year	17.50	NR
1981	BE MINE, Disney Studios, 1 year	17.50	NR
1982	PICNIC FOR TWO, Disney Studios, 1 year	17.50	NR

Golden Anniversary

1987	SNOW WHITE AND THE SEVEN DWARFS, Disney Studios, 5,000	47.50	NR

Kitty Cucumber Annual

1989	RING AROUND THE ROSIE, M. Lillemoe, 20,000	25.00	45.00

		ISSUE	CURRENT
1990	SWAN LAKE, M. Lillemoe, 20,000	25.00	45.00
1991	TEA PARTY, M. Lillemoe, 2,500	25.00	45.00
1992	DANCE 'ROUND THE MAYPOLE, M. Lillemoe, 2,500	25.00	RI

Nature's Treasures

1984	TULIP NEST—ROBIN, Mitsuko Gerhart, 5,000	45.00	NR
1984	ROSE HAVEN—CHIPPING SPARROW, Mitsuko Gerhart, 5,000	45.00	NR
1984	LEAFY BOWER—SPOTTED ORIOLE, Mitsuko Gerhart, 5,000	45.00	NR
1984	NESTING COMPANION—MOCKINGBIRD, Mitsuko Gerhart, 5,000	45.00	NR

Paddington Bear Annual

1979	PYRAMID OF PRESENTS, 25,000	12.50	30.00
1980	SPRINGTIME, 25,000	12.50	25.00
1981	SANDCASTLES, 25,000	12.50	25.00
1981	BACK TO SCHOOL, 25,000	12.50	NR

Paddington Bear Annual Christmas

1983	A BEAR'S NOEL, 10,000	22.50	NR
1984	HOW SWEET IT IS, 10,000	22.50	NR

Paddington Bear Musician's Dream

1982	THE BEAT GOES ON, 10,000	17.50	25.00
1982	KNOWING THE SCORE, 10,000	17.50	NR
1983	PERFECT HARMONY, 10,000	17.50	NR
1983	TICKLING THE IVORY, 10,000	17.50	NR

Peanuts Annual

1983	PEANUTS IN CONCERT, Charles Schulz, 20,000	22.50	NR
1984	SNOOPY AND THE BEAGLESCOUTS, Charles Schulz, 20,000	22.50	NR
1985	CLOWN CAPERS, Charles Schulz, 20,000	22.50	NR
1986	LION TAMER SNOOPY, Charles Schulz, 20,000	22.50	NR
1987	BIG TOP BLAST OFF, Charles Schulz, 20,000	17.50	NR

Mickey and Minnie's Rockin' Christmas
Photo courtesy of *Collectors News*

Rose Haven—Chipping Sparrow
Photo courtesy of *Collectors News*

Peanuts Christmas

		ISSUE	CURRENT
1972	SNOOPY GUIDES THE SLEIGH, Charles Schulz, 20,000	10.00	50.00
1973	CHRISTMAS EVE AT THE DOGHOUSE, Charles Schulz, 1 year	10.00	95.00
1974	CHRISTMAS EVE AT THE FIREPLACE, Charles Schulz, 1 year	10.00	60.00
1975	WOODSTOCK, SANTA CLAUS, Charles Schulz, 1 year	12.50	NR
1976	WOODSTOCK'S CHRISTMAS, Charles Schulz, 1 year	13.00	25.00
1977	DECK THE DOGHOUSE, Charles Schulz, 1 year	13.00	30.00
1978	FILLING THE STOCKING, Charles Schulz, 1 year	15.00	35.00
1979	CHRISTMAS AT HAND, Charles Schulz, 15,000	17.50	40.00
1980	WAITING FOR SANTA, Charles Schulz, 15,000	17.50	150.00
1981	A CHRISTMAS WISH, Charles Schulz, 15,000	17.50	45.00
1982	PERFECT PERFORMANCE, Charles Schulz, 15,000	18.50	60.00

Peanuts Mother's Day

1972	LINUS, Charles Schulz, 15,000	10.00	NR
1973	MOM?, Charles Schulz, 8,000	10.00	NR
1974	SNOOPY AND WOODSTOCK ON PARADE, Charles Schulz, 1 year	10.00	NR
1975	A KISS FOR LUCY, Charles Schulz, 1 year	12.50	NR
1976	LINUS AND SNOOPY, Charles Schulz, 1 year	13.00	35.00
1977	DEAR MOM, Charles Schulz, 1 year	13.00	30.00
1978	THOUGHTS THAT COUNT, Charles Schulz, 1 year	15.00	25.00
1979	A SPECIAL LETTER, Charles Schulz, 10,000	17.50	NR
1980	A TRIBUTE TO MOM, Charles Schulz, 10,000	17.50	NR
1981	MISSION FOR MOM, Charles Schulz, 10,000	17.50	NR
1982	WHICH WAY TO MOTHER?, Charles Schulz, 10,000	18.50	NR

Peanuts Special Edition

1976	BICENTENNIAL, Charles Schulz, 1 year	13.00	30.00
1989	PEANUTS 30TH BIRTHDAY, Charles Schulz, 15,000	27.50	NR

Peanuts Valentine's Day

1977	HOME IS WHERE THE HEART IS, Charles Schulz, 1 year	13.00	35.00
1978	HEAVENLY BLISS, Charles Schulz, 1 year	13.00	30.00
1979	LOVE MATCH, Charles Schulz, 1 year	17.50	30.00
1980	FROM SNOOPY, WITH LOVE, Charles Schulz, 1 year	17.50	25.00
1981	HEARTS-A-FLUTTER, Charles Schulz, 1 year	17.50	NR
1982	LOVE PATCH, Charles Schulz, 1 year	17.50	NR

Peanuts World's Greatest Athlete

1983	GO DEEP, Charles Schulz, 10,000	17.50	25.00
1983	THE PUCK STOPS HERE, Charles Schulz, 10,000	17.50	NR
1983	THE WAY YOU PLAY THE GAME, Charles Schulz, 10,000	17.50	NR
1983	THE CROWD WENT WILD, Charles Schulz, 10,000	17.50	NR

Prime Time

1984	*LOVE BOAT*, Shelly Mathers, limited	30.00	NR
1984	*DALLAS*, Shelly Mathers, limited	30.00	NR

Raggedy Ann Annual

1980	THE SUNSHINE WAGON, 10,000	17.50	80.00
1981	THE RAGGEDY SHUFFLE, 10,000	17.50	45.00
1982	FLYING HIGH, 10,000	18.50	NR

		ISSUE	CURRENT
1983	WINNING STREAK, 10,000	22.50	NR
1984	ROCKING RODEO, 10,000	22.50	NR

Raggedy Ann Bicentennial

1976	BICENTENNIAL PLATE, 1 year	13.00	45.00

Raggedy Ann Christmas

1975	GIFTS OF LOVE, 1 year	12.50	45.00
1976	MERRY BLADES, 1 year	13.00	40.00
1977	CHRISTMAS MORNING, 1 year	13.00	25.00
1978	CHECKING THE LIST, 1 year	15.00	20.00
1979	LITTLE HELPER, 15,000	17.50	NR

Raggedy Ann Mother's Day

1976	MOTHERHOOD, 1 year	13.00	NR
1977	BOUQUET OF LOVE, 1 year	13.00	NR
1978	HELLO MOM, 1 year	15.00	NR
1979	HIGH SPIRITS, 1 year	17.50	NR

Raggedy Ann Valentine's Day

1978	AS TIME GOES BY, 1 year	13.00	25.00
1979	DAISIES DO TELL, 1 year	17.50	NR

SCHOFIELD GALLERY UNITED STATES

Clowns, Klowns, Klonz

1986	PAINTING ON A SMILE, Mildred Schofield, 7,500	47.50	NR
1986	KEYSTONE KOP, Mildred Schofield, 7,500	47.50	NR

SCHUHAMANN GERMANY

Hidden Treasures of the Wood

1991	WILD STRAWBERRIES IN THE MOSS	29.72	NR
1991	BLUEBERRIES AMONGST THE UNDERGROWTH	29.72	40.00
1991	RASPBERRIES AMONGST THE GORSE	32.72	45.00
1992	BLACKBERRIES AMONGST THE HERBS	32.72	60.00
1992	CRANBERRIES AMONGST THE GENTIAN	32.72	50.00

SCHUMANN GERMANY

Christmas

1971	SNOW SCENE, 10,000	12.00	NR
1972	DEER IN SNOW, 15,000	12.00	NR
1973	WEIHNACHTEN, 5,000	12.00	NR
1974	CHURCH IN SNOW, 5,000	12.00	NR
1975	FOUNTAIN, 5,000	12.00	NR

Composers

1970	BEETHOVEN	12.00	NR

		ISSUE	CURRENT
1972	MOZART	12.00	NR

Imperial Christmas (Royal Cornwall)

1979	LIEBLING, Marianne Stuwe, 10,000	65.00	100.00
1980	HALLELUJAH, Marianne Stuwe, 10,000	65.00	80.00
1981	STILLE NACHT, Marianne Stuwe, 10,000	75.00	80.00
1982	WINTER MELODIE, Marianne Stuwe, 10,000	75.00	80.00

SEBASTIAN UNITED STATES

America's Favorite

1978	MOTIF #1, 10,000	75.00	NR
1979	GRAND CANYON, 10,000	75.00	NR

SEELEY'S CERAMIC SERVICE UNITED STATES

Antique French Doll Collection

1979	THE BRU, Mildred Seeley, 5,000	39.00	200.00
1979	THE E. J., Mildred Seeley, 5,000	39.00	75.00
1979	THE A. T., Mildred Seeley, 5,000	39.00	55.00
1980	ALEXANDRE, Mildred Seeley, 5,000	39.00	45.00
1981	THE SCHMITT, Mildred Seeley, 5,000	39.00	45.00
1981	THE MARQUE, Mildred Seeley, 5,000	39.00	45.00
1983	BEBE HALO, Mildred Seeley, 5,000	39.00	NR
1984	BRU'S FAITH, Mildred Seeley, 5,000	39.00	NR
1984	STEINER'S EASTER, Mildred Seeley, 5,000	39.00	NR

Antique French Doll Collection II

1983	THE SNOW ANGEL, Mildred Seeley, 5,000	39.00	NR
1984	MARQUE'S ALYCE, Mildred Seeley, 5,000	39.00	NR
1984	JUMEAU'S GAYNELL, Mildred Seeley, 5,000	39.00	NR

Goldie
Photo courtesy of *Collectors News*

Elise
Photo courtesy of *Collectors News*

		ISSUE	CURRENT

Old Baby Doll Collection

1982	JDK HILDA, Mildred Seeley, 9,500	43.00	NR
1982	GOLDIE, Mildred Seeley, 9,500	43.00	NR
1983	LORI, Mildred Seeley, 9,500	43.00	NR
1983	BYE-LO, Mildred Seeley, 9,500	43.00	NR
1983	LAUGHING BABY, Mildred Seeley, 9,500	43.00	NR

Old German Dolls

1981	DEAR GOOGLY, Mildred Seeley, 7,500	39.00	NR
1981	LUCY, Mildred Seeley, 7,500	39.00	NR
1981	THE WHISTLER, Mildred Seeley, 7,500	39.00	NR
1982	APRIL, Mildred Seeley, 7,500	39.00	NR
1982	ELISE, Mildred Seeley, 7,500	39.00	NR

SELANDIA

Christmas

1972	WAY TO BETHLEHEM, sgd, 250	100.00	NR
1972	WAY TO BETHLEHEM, 4,750	30.00	50.00
1973	THREE WISE MEN, sgd, 200	100.00	NR
1973	THREE WISE MEN, 4,750	35.00	NR

SELTMANN VOHENSTRAUSS GERMANY

Romantic Village Views

1990	BY THE MILL STREAM	32.50	NR
1991	THE BAKEHOUSE	32.50	NR
1991	WASHDAY ON THE RIVER	34.50	NR
1991	BY THE OLD BRIDGE	35.50	NR
1991	DRINKING HORSES	35.50	NR
1992	THE VILLAGE POND	35.50	NR

SEVEN SEAS UNITED STATES

Christmas Carols

1970	I HEARD THE BELLS, 4,000	15.00	25.00
1971	OH TANNENBAUM, 4,000	15.00	20.00
1972	DECK THE HALLS, 1,500	18.00	25.00
1973	O HOLY NIGHT, 2,000	18.00	25.00
1974	JINGLE BELLS, 1,200	25.00	NR
1975	WINTER WONDERLAND, 1,500	25.00	NR
1976	TWELVE DAYS OF CHRISTMAS, 1,500	25.00	NR
1977	UP ON THE HOUSETOP, 1,500	25.00	NR
1978	LITTLE TOWN OF BETHLEHEM, 1,500	25.00	NR
1979	SANTA CLAUS IS COMING TO TOWN, 1,500	25.00	NR
1980	FROSTY THE SNOWMAN, 1,500	25.00	NR

Historical Events

1969	MOON LANDING—NO FLAG, 2,000	13.50	175.00

		ISSUE	CURRENT
1969	MOON LANDING—WITH FLAG, 2,000	13.50	70.00
1970	YEAR OF CRISIS, 4,000	15.00	20.00
1971	FIRST VEHICULAR TRAVEL, 3,000	15.00	35.00
1972	LAST MOON JOURNEY, 2000	15.00	35.00
1973	PEACE, 3,000	15.00	35.00

Mother's Day

1970	GIRL OF ALL NATIONS, 5,000	15.00	20.00
1971	SHARING CONFIDENCES, 1,400	15.00	20.00
1972	SCANDINAVIAN GIRL, 1,600	15.00	20.00
1973	ALL-AMERICAN GIRL, 1,500	15.00	30.00

New World

1970	HOLY FAMILY, 3,5000	15.00	20.00
1971	THREE WISE MEN, 1,500	15.00	30.00
1972	SHEPHERDS WATCHED, 1,500	18.00	NR

Single Issue

1970	OBERAMMERGAU, 2,500	18.00	25.00

SEYMOUR MANN, INC. UNITED STATES

Connoisseur Collection™

1995	DOVE DUO CLT-1, Bernini, 25,000	45.00	RI
1995	HUMMINGBIRD DUO CLT-4, Bernini, 25,000	45.00	RI
1995	CARDINAL CLT-7, Bernini, 25,000	45.00	RI
1995	CANARY CLT-10, Bernini, 25,000	45.00	RI
1995	BLUEBIRD CLT-13, Bernini, 25,000	45.00	RI
1995	ROBIN CLT-16, Bernini, 25,000	45.00	RI
1995	SWAN DUO CLT-50, Bernini, 25,000	45.00	RI
1995	PINK ROSE CLT-70, Bernini, 25,000	45.00	RI
1995	MAGNOLIA CLT-76, Bernini, 25,000	45.00	RI
1996	CHICKADEES CLT-300, Bernini, 25,000	50.00	RI
1996	DOVES CLT-305, Bernini, 25,000	50.00	RI
1996	CARDINALS CLT-310, Bernini, 25,000	50.00	RI
1996	HUMMINGBIRDS/MORNING GLORY, PINK CLT-320, Bernini, 25,000	45.00	RI
1996	HUMMINGBIRDS/MORNING GLORY, BLUE CLT-320b, Bernini, 25,000	45.00	RI
1996	BUTTERFLY/LILY CLT-330, Bernini, 25,000	45.00	RI
1996	ROSES/FORGET-ME-NOT CLT-340, Bernini, 25,000	45.00	RI
1997	DOVE/MAGNOLIA CLT-350, Bernini, 25,000	45.00	RI
1997	BLUBIRD/LILY CLT-390, Bernini, 25,000	45.00	RI
1997	CARDINAL/DOGWOOD CLT-405, Bernini, 25,000	45.00	RI

Connoisseur Collection™ 3-D

1996	BEAUTY ROSE, Bernini, 25,000	50.00	RI
1997	RED ROSES, Bernini, 5,000	45.00	RI

Doll Art™ Collection

1996	HOPE, GUARDIAN ANGEL OF THE WORLD CLT-800P, E. Mann, 25,000	25.00	RI

SIGNATURE COLLECTION UNITED STATES

(Artaffects)

		ISSUE	CURRENT
Grandma's Scrapbook			
1983	COURTING, Robert L. Berran, 12,500	45.00	NR
Legends			
1983	PAUL BUNYAN, Carl Cassler, 10,000	45.00	NR
1983	RIP VAN WINKLE, Carl Cassler, 10,000	45.00	NR
Very Special Edition			
1984	THE WEDDING, Rob Sauber	50.00	NR
1984	HAPPY BIRTHDAY, Rob Sauber	50.00	NR

Courting
Photo courtesy of *Collectors News*

SILVER CITY

Christmas			
1969	WINTER SCENE	37.00	NR
1970	WATER MILL	25.00	NR
1971	SKATING SCENE	25.00	NR
1972	LOGGING IN WINTER	30.00	NR
1973	ST. CLAUDENS	20.00	NR
Single Issue			
1972	INDEPENDENCE HALL	13.50	NR

SILVER CREATIONS UNITED STATES

Americana			
1973	CLYDESDALES	150.00	NR
History			
1972	CHURCHILLIAN HERITAGE, proof	550.00	575.00

		ISSUE	CURRENT
1972	CHURCHILLIAN HERITAGE	150.00	200.00
1973	YALTA CONFERENCE, proof	550.00	575.00
1973	YALTA CONFERENCE	150.00	NR

SILVER DEER LTD.

Christmas

1970	H. C. ANDERSEN HOUSE, G. Sausmark, 1 year	14.50	NR
1971	LITTLE MATCH GIRL, Mads Stage, 1 year	15.00	NR
1972	MAID OF COPENHAGEN, Edvard Eriksen, 1 year	16.50	NR
1973	THE FIR TREE, Svend Otto, 1 year	22.00	NR
1974	THE CHIMNEY SWEEP, Svend Otto, 1 year	25.00	NR
1975	THE UGLY DUCKLING, Svend Otto, 1 year	27.50	NR
1976	THE SNOW QUEEN, Mads Stage, 1 year	27.50	NR
1977	SNOWMAN, Svend Otto, 1 year	29.50	NR
1978	LAST DREAM OF THE OLD OAK TREE, Svend Otto, 1 year	32.00	NR
1980	WILLIE WINKIE, Svend Otto, 1 year	36.50	NR
1981	UTTERMOST PARTS OF THE SEA, Svend Otto, 1 year	42.50	NR
1982	TWELVE BY THE MAILCOACH, Svend Otto, 1 year	49.50	NR
1983	THE STORY OF THE YEAR, Svend Otto, 1 year	54.50	NR
1984	THE NIGHTINGALE, Svend Otto, 1 year	54.50	NR
1985	KRONBERG CASTLE, Svend Otto, 1 year	54.50	NR
1986	THE BELL, Svend Otto, 1 year	60.00	NR
1987	THUMBELINA, Svend Otto, 1 year	60.00	NR
1988	THE BELL DEEP, Svend Otto, 1 year	60.00	NR
1989	THE OLD HOUSE, Svend Otto, 1 year	60.00	NR
1990	GRANDFATHER'S PICTURE BOOK, Svend Otto, 1 year	64.50	NR
1991	THE WINDMILL, Svend Otto, 1 year	64.50	NR

Mother's Day

1970	BOUQUET FOR MOTHER, 1 year	14.50	NR
1971	MOTHER'S LOVE, 1 year	15.00	NR
1972	GOOD NIGHT, 1 year	16.50	NR
1973	FLOWERS FOR MOTHER, 1 year	20.00	NR
1974	DAISIES FOR MOTHER, 1 year	25.00	NR
1975	SURPRISE FOR MOTHER, 1 year	27.50	NR
1976	THE COMPLETE GARDENER, 1 year	27.50	NR
1977	LITTLE FRIENDS, 1 year	29.50	NR
1978	DREAMS, 1 year	32.00	NR
1979	PROMENADE, 1 year	36.50	NR
1980	NURSERY SCENE, 1 year	42.50	NR
1981	DAILY DUTIES, 1 year	49.50	NR
1982	MY BEST FRIEND, 1 year	54.50	NR
1983	AN UNEXPECTED MEETING, 1 year	54.50	NR
1984	WHO ARE YOU?, Mads Stage, 1 year	54.50	NR
1986	MEETING ON THE MEADOW, Mads Stage, 1 year	60.00	NR
1987	THE COMPLETE ANGLER, Svend Otto, 1 year	60.00	NR
1988	THE LITTLE BAKERY, Svend Otto, 1 year	60.00	NR
1989	SPRINGTIME, Svend Otto, 1 year	60.00	NR
1990	THE SPRING EXCURSION, Svend Otto, 1 year	64.50	NR
1991	WALKING AT THE BEACH, Svend Otto, 1 year	64.50	NR

SMITH GLASS UNITED STATES

Americana

		ISSUE	CURRENT
1971	MORGAN SILVER DOLLAR, 5,000	10.00	NR

Christmas

1971	FAMILY AT CHRISTMAS	10.00	NR
1972	FLYING ANGEL	10.00	NR
1973	ST. MARY'S IN MOUNTAINS	10.00	NR

Famous Americans

1971	KENNEDY, 2,500	10.00	NR
1971	LINCOLN, 2,500	10.00	NR
1972	DAVIS, 5,000	11.00	NR
1972	LEE, 5,000	11.00	NR

SOUTHERN LIVING GALLERY UNITED STATES

Game Birds of the South

1983	BOBWHITE QUAIL, Antony Heritage, 19,500	39.95	NR
1983	MOURNING DOVE, Antony Heritage, 19,500	39.95	NR
1983	GREEN-WINGED TEAL, Antony Heritage, 19,500	39.95	NR
1983	RING-NECKED PHEASANT, Antony Heritage, 19,500	39.95	NR
1983	MALLARD DUCK, Antony Heritage, 19,500	39.95	NR
1983	AMERICAN COOT, Antony Heritage, 19,500	39.95	NR
1983	RUFFED GROUSE, Antony Heritage, 19,500	39.95	NR
1983	PINTAIL DUCK, Antony Heritage, 19,500	39.95	NR
1983	AMERICAN WOODCOCK, Antony Heritage, 19,500	39.95	NR
1983	CANADA GOOSE, Antony Heritage, 19,500	39.95	NR
1983	WILD TURKEY, Antony Heritage, 19,500	39.95	NR
1983	WOOD DUCK, Antony Heritage, 19,500	39.95	NR

Songbirds of the South

NA	AMERICAN GOLDFINCH, A. E. Ruffing, 19,500	39.95	NR
NA	TUFTED TITMOUSE, A. E. Ruffing, 19,500	39.95	NR
NA	RED-WINGED BLACKBIRD, A. E. Ruffing, 19,500	39.95	NR
NA	MOCKINGBIRD, A. E. Ruffing, 19,500	39.95	NR
NA	CARDINAL, A. E. Ruffing, 19,500	39.95	NR
NA	BLUEJAY, A. E. Ruffing, 19,500	39.95	NR
NA	ROBIN, A. E. Ruffing, 19,500	39.95	NR

Southern Forest Families

NA	EASTERN COTTONTAIL RABBIT, Sy and Dorothea Barlowe, 19,500	39.95	NR
NA	WHITE-TAILED DEER, Sy and Dorothea Barlowe, 19,500	39.95	NR
NA	RACCOON, Sy and Dorothea Barlowe, 19,500	39.95	NR
NA	STRIPED SKUNK, Sy and Dorothea Barlowe, 19,500	39.95	NR
NA	BOBCAT, Sy and Dorothea Barlowe, 19,500	39.95	NR
NA	FOX SQUIRREL, Sy and Dorothea Barlowe, 19,500	39.95	NR
NA	RED FOX, Sy and Dorothea Barlowe, 19,500	39.95	NR
NA	BLACK BEAR, Sy and Dorothea Barlowe, 19,500	39.95	NR
NA	OPOSSUM, Sy and Dorothea Barlowe, 19,500	39.95	NR

		ISSUE	CURRENT
NA	CHIPMUNK, Sy and Dorothea Barlowe, 19,500	39.95	NR
NA	BEAVER, Sy and Dorothea Barlowe, 19,500	39.95	NR
NA	MINK, Sy and Dorothea Barlowe, 19,500	39.95	NR

Story of Christmas (Royal Windsor)

NA	FLIGHT INTO EGYPT, Garri Katz, 19,500	NA	NA

Flight Into Egypt
Photo courtesy of *Collectors News*

Wildflowers of the South

NA	WILD HONEYSUCKLE, R. Mark, 19,500	39.95	NR
NA	FROST ASTER, R. Mark, 19,500	39.95	NR
NA	FLOWERING DOGWOOD, R. Mark, 19,500	39.95	NR
NA	BEE BALM, R. Mark, 19,500	39.95	NR
NA	QUEEN ANNE'S LACE, R. Mark, 19,500	39.95	NR
NA	BLUEBONNET, R. Mark, 19,500	39.95	NR
NA	SOUTHERN MAGNOLIA, R. Mark, 19,500	39.95	NR
NA	BIRDSFOOT VIOLET, R. Mark, 19,500	39.95	NR
NA	REGAL LILY, R. Mark, 19,500	39.95	NR
NA	LADY SLIPPER ORCHID, R. Mark, 19,500	39.95	NR
NA	BLACK-EYED SUSAN, R. Mark, 19,500	39.95	NR
NA	BUTTERCUP, R. Mark, 19,500	39.95	NR

SPODE GREAT BRITAIN

(Royal Worcester)

American Songbirds

1970	RUFUS-SIDED TOWHEE, Ray Harm, 5,000	—	—
1970	WINTER WREN, Ray Harm, 5,000	—	—
1971	EASTERN BLUEBIRD, Ray Harm, 5,000	—	—
1971	STELLAR'S JAY, Ray Harm, 5,000	—	—
1971	EASTERN MOCKINGBIRD, Ray Harm, 5,000	—	—
1971	BARN SWALLOW, Ray Harm, 5,000	—	—
1971	ROSE-BREASTED GROSBEAK, Ray Harm, 5,000	—	—

		ISSUE	CURRENT
1971	CARDINAL, Ray Harm, 5,000	—	—
1972	WESTERN TANAGER, Ray Harm, 5,000	—	—
1972	WOODPECKER, Ray Harm, 5,000	—	—
1972	CHICKADEE, Ray Harm, 5,000	—	—
1972	AMERICAN GOLDFINCH, Ray Harm, 5,000	—	—
	Set of 12	350.00	765.00

Christmas

1970	PARTRIDGE, Gillian West, 1 year	35.00	NR
1971	ANGELS SINGING, Gillian West, 1 year	35.00	NR
1972	THREE SHIPS A-SAILING, Gillian West, 1 year	35.00	NR
1973	WE THREE KINGS OF ORIENT, Gillian West, 1 year	35.00	NR
1974	DECK THE HALLS, Gillian West, 1 year	35.00	NR
1975	CHRISTBAUM, Gillian West, 1 year	45.00	NR
1976	GOOD KING WENCESLAS, Gillian West, 1 year	45.00	NR
1977	HOLLY AND IVY, Gillian West, 1 year	45.00	NR
1978	WHILE SHEPHERDS WATCHED, Gillian West, 1 year	45.00	NR
1979	AWAY IN A MANGER, Gillian West, 1 year	50.00	BR
1980	BRINGING IN THE BOAR'S HEAD, P. Wood, 1 year	60.00	BR
1981	MAKE WE MERRY, P. Wood, 1 year	65.00	BR

Christmas Pastimes

1982	SLEIGH RIDE	75.00	NR

Maritime (Royal Worcester)

1980	U.S.S. *UNITED STATES* AND H.M.S *MACEDONIAN*, 2,000	150.00	NR
1980	U.S.S. *PRESIDENT* AND H.M.S *LITTLE BELT*, 2,000	150.00	NR
1980	H.M.S. *SHANNON* AND U.S.S *CHESAPEAKE*, 2,000	150.00	NR
1980	U.S.S. *CONSTITUTION* AND H.M.S G*UERRIERE*, 2,000	150.00	NR
1980	U.S.S. *CONSTITUTION* AND H.M.S *JAVA*, 2,000	150.00	NR
1980	H.M.S. *PELICAN* AND U.S.S *ARGUS*, 2,000	150.00	NR

Noble Horse

1988	ENGLISH THOROUGHBRED	29.00	BR
1988	AUSTRIAN LIPIZZANER	29.00	BR
1988	THE AMERICAN QUARTERHORSE	32.00	BR
1988	THE ARABIAN	32.00	NR
1989	THE HANOVERIAN	32.00	NR
1989	THE CLEVELAND BAY	32.00	NR
1989	THE HACKNEY	34.00	NR
1990	THE APPALOOSA	34.00	NR

Single Issues

1969	PRINCE OF WALES, 1,500	65.00	NR
1970	DICKENS	70.00	80.00
1970	*MAYFLOWER*, 2,500	70.00	130.00
1970	LOEWSTOFT	70.00	BR
1971	IMPERIAL PERSIA, 10,000	125.00	NR
1971	CHURCHILL, 5,000	110.00	120.00
1972	PASSOVER, 5,000	59.00	BR
1972	*CUTTY SARK*	59.00	80.00
1973	DICKEN'S LONDON	70.00	BR

SPORTS ACCESSORIES & MEMORABILIA UNITED STATES

Single Issue

		ISSUE	CURRENT
1996	A MAGIC NIGHT IN CAMDEN YARDS, Andrew Allen, 6 days	39.95	RI

SPORTS IMPRESSIONS

(Celebrity Impressions, Enesco, Hamilton Collection)

Baseball

1996	NOLAN RYAN FAREWELL NOLAN RYAN, 1161-04, Robert Tanenbaum, 2,500, 10¼" d	100.00	RI
1996	NOLAN RYAN ALL-TIME NO-HITTER MAN, 1226-04, T. Treadway, 2,500, 10¼" d	100.00	RI
1996	NOLAN RYAN ALL-TIME NO-HITTER MAN, 1226-02, T. Treadway, open, 4¼" d	10.00	RI
1996	NOLAN RYAN STILL STRONG, 1146-03, Joseph Catalano, 7,500, 8½" d	30.00	RI
1996	NOLAN RYAN NO HITTER, 1131-03, 5,000, 8½" d	30.00	RI
1996	NOLAN RYAN A CAREER TO REMEMBER, 1226-03, 5,000, 8½" d	30.00	RI
1996	HANK AARON, 1227-04, T. Treadway, 2,500, 10¼" d	100.00	RI
1996	HANK AARON, 1227-03, 5,000, 8½" d	30.00	RI
1996	HANK AARON, 1227-02, open, 4¼" d	10.00	RI
1996	BABE RUTH SULTAN OF SWAT, 1130-03, Joseph Catalano, 5,000, 8½" d	30.00	RI
1996	BABE RUTH SULTAN OF SWAT, 1130-02, Joseph Catalano, open, 4¼" d	10.00	RI
1996	MIKE SCHMIDT, 1166-04, Robert Tanenbaum, 2,500, 10¼" d	100.00	RI
1996	MIKE SCHMIDT, 1166-03, Joseph Catalano, 7,500, 8½" d	30.00	RI
1996	MIKE SCHMIDT, 1166-02, Joseph Catalano, open, 4½" d	10.00	RI
1996	DON MATTINGLY, 1162-04, Robert Tanenbaum, 2,500, 10¼" d	100.00	RI
1996	DON MATTINGLY, 1162-03, C. Hayes, 7,500, 8½" d	30.00	RI
1996	DON MATTINGLY, 1162-02, Robert Tanenbaum, open, 4½" d	10.00	RI

Basketball

1996	DREAM TEAM II, 5512-04, Robert Tanenbaum, 1,994, 10¼" d	100.00	RI
1996	DREAM TEAM II, 5512-03, 5,000, 8¼" d	30.00	RI
1996	LARRY BIRD, 4043-04, Robert Tanenbaum, 2,500, 10¼" d	100.00	RI
1996	LARRY BIRD, 4043-02, Robert Tanenbaum, open, 4" d	10.00	RI
1996	LARRY BIRD, 4086-03, C. Hayes, 5,000, 8¼" d	30.00	RI
1996	LARRY BIRD, 4086-02, C. Hayes, open, 4" d	10.00	RI
1996	GRANT HILL, 4076-03, C. Hayes, 5,000, 8¼" d	30.00	RI
1996	GRANT HILL, 4076-02, C. Hayes, open, 4¼" d	10.00	RI
1996	CHARLES BARKLEY, 4017-04, 2,500, 10¼" d	100.00	RI
1996	CHARLES BARKLEY, 4017-02, open, 4¼" d	10.00	RI
1996	CHARLES BARKLEY, 4074-03, C. Hayes, 5,000, 8¼" d	30.00	RI
1996	CHRIS WEBBER, 4065-04, Robert Tanenbaum, 2,500, 10¼" d	100.00	RI
1996	CHRIS WEBBER, 4065-03, C. Hayes, 5,000, 8¼" d	30.00	RI
1996	CHRIS WEBBER, 4065-64, Robert Tanenbaum, 2,500, 10" d	100.00	RI
1996	CHRIS WEBBER, 4087-02, Robert Tanenbaum, open, 4¼" d	10.00	RI
1996	SHAWN KEMP, 4072-04, Robert Tanenbaum, 2,500, 10¼" d	100.00	RI
1996	SHAWN KEMP, 4072-02, Robert Tanenbaum, open, 4¼" d	10.00	RI
1996	SHAWN KEMP, 4072-03, C. Hayes, 5,000, 8¼" d	100.00	RI
1996	SCOTTIE PIPPEN, 4060-03, 7,500, 8¼" d	30.00	RI
1996	SCOTTIE PIPPEN, 4060-04, Robert Tanenbaum, 2,500, 10¼" d	100.00	RI
1996	SCOTTIE PIPPEN, 4060-02, Robert Tanenbaum, 4¼" d	10.00	RI

		ISSUE	CURRENT
1996	ALONZO MOURNING, 4055-04, Robert Tanenbaum, 2,500, 10¼" d	100.00	RI
1996	ALONZO MOURNING, 4055-02, C. Hayes, open, 4¼" d	10.00	RI
1996	ALONZO MOURNING, 4055-03, 7,500, 8¼" d	30.00	RI
1996	SHAQUILLE O'NEAL, 4053-04, 2,500, 10¼" d	100.00	RI
1996	SHAQUILLE O'NEAL, 4053-03, C. Hayes, 7,500, 8¼" d	30.00	RI

Best of Baseball (Hamilton Collection)

1993	THE LEGENDARY MICKEY MANTLE, Robert Tanenbaum, 28 days	29.50	RI
1993	THE IMMORTAL BABE RUTH, Robert Tanenbaum, 28 days	29.50	RI
1993	THE GREAT WILLIE MAYS, Robert Tanenbaum, 28 days	29.50	RI
1993	THE UNBEATABLE DUKE SNIDER, Robert Tanenbaum, 28 days	29.50	RI
1993	THE EXTRAORDINARY LOU GEHRIG, Robert Tanenbaum, 28 days	29.50	RI
1993	THE PHENOMENAL ROBERTO CLEMENTE, Robert Tanenbaum, 28 days	29.50	RI
1993	THE INCREDIBLE NOLAN RYAN, Robert Tanenbaum, 28 days	29.50	RI
1993	THE EXCEPTIONAL BROOKS ROBINSON, Robert Tanenbaum, 28 days	29.50	RI
1993	THE UNFORGETTABLE PHIL RIZZUTO, Robert Tanenbaum, 28 days	29.50	RI
1995	THE INCOMPARABLE REGGIE JACKSON, Robert Tanenbaum, 28 days	29.50	RI

Classics Collection

1996	'57 CORVETTE, 101478, 8¼" d	30.00	RI
1996	'57 CORVETTE, 111201, 4¼" d	7.50	RI
1996	'65 SILVER BLUE CORVETTE, 174858, C. Hayes, 8" d	30.00	RI
1996	'65 SILVER BLUE CORVETTE, 174890, C. Hayes, 4" d	7.50	RI
1996	'53 WHITE CORVETTE, 174831, 8" d	30.00	RI
1996	'53 WHITE CORVETTE, 174882, 4" d	7.50	RI
1996	'57 CHEVY BEL AIR, 101508, 8¼" d	30.00	RI
1996	'57 CHEVY BEL AIR, 111317, 4¼" d	7.50	RI
1996	'56 THUNDERBIRD, 101494, 8¼" d	30.00	RI
1996	'56 THUNDERBIRD, 111252, 4¼" d	7.50	RI
1996	'65 MUSTANG, 101486, 8¼" d	30.00	RI
1996	'65 MUSTANG, 111376, 4¼" d	7.50	RI
1996	'59 PINK CADILLAC, 174866, 8" d	30.00	RI
1996	'59 PINK CADILLAC, 174904, 4" d	7.50	RI
1996	'56 FORD TRUCK, 174874, 8" d	30.00	RI
1996	'56 FORD TRUCK, 174912, 4" d	7.50	RI

Collectors' Club—Members Only

1993	1927 YANKEES	60.00	RI

Collectoval Plates

1990	KINGS OF K, Joseph Catalano, 1,000	195.00	NR
1990	LIFE OF A LEGEND, T. Fogarty, 1,968	195.00	NR
1990	FENWAY TRADITION, Brian Johnson, 1,000	195.00	NR
1990	GOLDEN YEARS, M. Petronella, 1,000	195.00	NR

Football

1996	EMMITT SMITH, 3054-04, 2,500, 10¼" d	100.00	RI
1996	EMMITT SMITH, 3054-02, 4¼" d	10.00	RI
1996	TROY AIKMAN, 3051-03, 7,500, 8¼" d	30.00	RI
1996	TROY AIKMAN SUPER BOWL, 3041-02, Robert Tanenbaum, 4¼" d	10.00	RI
1996	STAUBACH / LANDRY, 3055-04, Robert Tanenbaum, 2,500, 10¼" d	100.00	RI
1996	STAUBACH / LANDRY, 3055-02, Robert Tanenbaum, 4¼" d	10.00	RI
1996	STAUBACH / LANDRY, 3055-03, 7,500, 8¼" d	30.00	RI

		ISSUE	CURRENT
1996	JOE MONTANA, 3049-04, Robert Tanenbaum, 2,500, 10¼" d	100.00	RI
1996	JOE MONTANA, 3049-02, Robert Tanenbaum, 4¼" d	10.00	RI
1996	JOE MONTANA, 3048-03, 7,500, T. Treadway, 8¼" d	30.00	RI
1996	JOE MONTANA, 3052-03, 7,500, Joseph Catalano, 8¼" d	30.00	RI

Gold Edition Plates

1986	DON MATTINGLY, Brian Johnson, closed	125.00	NR
1986	KEITH HERNANDEZ, Robert Stephen Simon, closed	125.00	150.00
1986	LARRY BIRD, Robert Stephen Simon, closed	125.00	275.00
1986	MICKEY MANTLE AT NIGHT, sgd, Robert Stephen Simon, closed	125.00	200.00
1986	WADE BOGGS, sgd, Brian Johnson, closed	125.00	150.00
1987	AL KALINE, E. Lapere, 1,000	125.00	NR
1987	CARL YASTRZEMSKI, Robert Stephen Simon, 3,000	60.00	NR
1987	CARL YASTRZEMSKI, sgd, Robert Stephen Simon, closed	125.00	BR
1987	DARRYL STRAWBERRY, Robert Stephen Simon, 2,000	60.00	NR
1987	DARRYL STRAWBERRY, Robert Stephen Simon, sgd, 1,000	200.00	NR
1987	DARRYL STRAWBERRY #1, Robert Stephen Simon, closed	125.00	BR
1987	DON MATTINGLY PLAYER OF THE YEAR, Brian Johnson, 5,000	60.00	NR
1987	GARY CARTER "THE KID," Robert Stephen Simon, 2,000	60.00	NR
1987	GARY CARTER "THE KID," Robert Stephen Simon, 1,000	125.00	NR
1987	KEITH HERNANDEZ, Robert Stephen Simon, 2,000	60.00	NR
1987	KEITH HERNANDEZ, Robert Stephen Simon, sgd, 1,000	100.00	NR
1987	LARRY BIRD, Robert Stephen Simon, 5,000	60.00	NR
1987	LENNY DYKSTRA, Robert Stephen Simon,1,000	60.00	NR
1987	LENNY DYKSTRA, Robert Stephen Simon, sgd, 1,000	100.00	NR
1987	MANTLE, "MICKEY AT NIGHT," Robert Stephen Simon, 3,500	60.00	NR
1987	MANTLE, "MICKEY AT NIGHT," Robert Stephen Simon, sgd, 1,500	100.00	NR
1987	MICKEY, WILLIE AND THE DUKE, sgd, Robert Stephen Simon, 1,500	150.00	NR
1987	TED WILLIAMS, sgd, Robert Stephen Simon, closed	125.00	495.00
1987	WADE BOGGS, Brian Johnson, 2,000	60.00	NR
1987	WADE BOGGS, Brian Johnson, sgd, 1,000	100.00	NR
1988	BOB FELLER, E. Lapere, 2,500	125.00	NR
1988	BROOKS ROBINSON, sgd, Robert Stephen Simon, closed	125.00	150.00
1988	DUKE SNIDER, Brian Johnson, 1,500	125.00	NR
1988	JOSE CANSECO, Joseph Catalano, 2,500	125.00	NR
1988	LARRY BIRD, Robert Stephen Simon, closed	125.00	275.00
1988	MAGIC JOHNSON, Robert Stephen Simon, closed	125.00	350.00
1988	MICKEY, WILLIE AND THE DUKE, 1041-59, sgd, Robert S. Simon, 2,500	150.00	NR
1988	PAUL MOLITOR, T. Fogarty, 1,000	125.00	NR
1988	YANKEE TRADITION, Joseph Catalano, closed	150.00	225.00
1989	DARRYL STRAWBERRY #2, T. Fogarty, closed	125.00	100.00
1989	DWIGHT GOODEN, T. Fogarty, 5,000	125.00	NR
1989	KIRK GIBSON, M. Petronella, 2,500	125.00	NR
1989	FRANK VIOLA, T. Fogarty, 2,500	125.00	NR
1989	ALAN TRAMMELL, E. Lapere, 1,000	125.00	NR
1989	GREATEST CENTERFIELDERS, R. Lewis, 5,000	150.00	NR
1989	MICKEY MANTLE THE GREATEST SWITCH HITTER, Joseph Catalano, sgd, 2,401, 10¼" d	150.00	225.00
1989	OREL HERSHISER, Joseph Catalano, 2,500, 10¼" d	125.00	NR
1989	WILL CLARK, Joseph Catalano, closed	125.00	195.00
1990	ANDRE DAWSON, R. Lewis, closed	150.00	NR
1990	LIVING TRIPLE CROWN WINNERS, R. Lewis, closed	150.00	NR
1990	NOLAN RYAN 300 GOLD, 1091-04, T. Fogarty, 1,990	150.00	NR
1990	NOLAN RYAN 5,000 K's, Joseph Catalano, 1,990	150.00	NR

		ISSUE	CURRENT
1990	RICKEY HENDERSON, R. Lewis, closed	150.00	NR
1990	TOM SEAVER, R. Lewis, closed	150.00	NR
1991	DREAM TEAM (1st TEN CHOSEN), L. Salk, closed	150.00	300.00
1991	HAWKS DOMINIQUE WILKINS, Joseph Catalano, closed	150.00	NR
1991	LARRY BIRD, Joseph Catalano, closed	150.00	195.00
1991	MAGIC JOHNSON, W. C. Mundy, closed	150.00	235.00
1991	MAGIC JOHNSON LAKERS GOLD, 4007-04, W. C. Mundy, 1,991, 10¼" d	150.00	NR
1991	MAGIC JOHNSON LAKERS PLATINUM, 4007-03, M. Petronella, 5,000, 8¼" d	60.00	NR
1991	MICHAEL JORDAN GOLD, 4002-04, Joseph Catalano, 1,991, 10¼" d	150.00	200.00
1991	MICHAEL JORDAN PLATINUM, 4002-03, M. Petronella, 1,991, 8¼" d	60.00	NR
1991	MICKEY MANTLE, 7-B, Robert Stephen Simon, closed	150.00	NR
1992	CHICAGO BULLS '92 WORLD CHAMPIONS, C. Hayes, 1,992	150.00	NR
1992	DREAM TEAM, Robert Tanenbaum, closed	150.00	175.00
1992	DREAM TEAM 1992, 5507-03, C. Hayes, 7,500, 8¼" d	60.00	NR
1992	DREAM TEAM 1992 GOLD, 5509-04, Robert Tanenbaum, 1,992, 10¼" d	150.00	NR

Emmitt Smith

Mickey, Willie, & The Duke

Michael Jordan

Dream Team

Photos courtesy of *Collectors News*

		ISSUE	CURRENT
1992	MAGIC JOHNSON LAKERS GOLD, 4042-04, R. Tanenbaum, 1,992, 10¼" d	150.00	175.00
1992	MICHAEL JORDAN, Robert Tanenbaum, closed	150.00	225.00
1992	MICHAEL JORDAN BULLS, 4032-04, Robert Tanenbaum, 1,991, 10¼" d	150.00	NR
1992	NBA 1ST TEN CHOSEN PLATINUM, 5502-03, J. Catalano, 7,500, 8¼" d, blue	60.00	NR
1992	NBA 1ST TEN CHOSEN PLATINUM, 5503-03, W. C. Mundy, 7,500, 8¼" d, red	60.00	NR
1992	TEAM USA BASKETBALL, L. Salk, closed	150.00	NR
1993	CHICAGO BULLS 1993 WORLD CHAMPIONSHIP GOLD, 4062-04, B. Vann, 1,993, 10¼" d	150.00	RI
1993	MAGIC JOHNSON, T. Fogarty, closed	150.00	RI
1993	MICHAEL JORDAN BULLS GOLD, 4046-04, T. Fogarty, 2,500, 10¼" d	150.00	RI
1993	SHAQUILLE O'NEAL GOLD, T. Fogarty, 2,500, 10¼" d	150.00	RI
1994	CHARLES BARKLEY, 2,500, 10¼" d	150.00	RI
1994	SHAQUILLE O'NEAL, ROOKIE OF THE YEAR, open	100.00	RI
NA	A's JOSE CANSECO GOLD, 1028-04, Joseph Catalano, 2,500, 10¼" d	125.00	RI
NA	ROBERTO CLEMENTE, 1090-03, R. Lewis, 10,000	75.00	RI
NA	JACKIE ROBINSON, M. Petronella, closed	150.00	RI

Golden Years

1990	DUKE SNIDER, M. Petronella, 5,000	60.00	NR
1990	MICKEY MANTLE, M. Petronella, 5,000	60.00	NR
1990	WILLIE MAYS, M. Petronella, 5,000	60.00	NR

Mickey Mantle

1996	THE LEGEND, 1148-04, Robert Tanenbaum, 2,500, 10¼" d	100.00	RI
1996	THE LEGEND, 1148-02, Robert Tanenbaum, open, 4¼" d	10.00	RI
1996	YANKEE FOREVER, 1148-03, open, 8½" d	37.50	RI
1996	YANKEE TRADITION, 1234-03, Joseph Catalano, open, 8" d	30.00	RI
1996	MICKEY AT NIGHT, 1235-03, Robert S. Simon, open, 8" d	30.00	RI
1996	MICKEY IN THE 50's, 1120-02, open, 4¼" d	10.00	RI
1996	LEGENDARY MICKEY MANTLE, 12346-03, open, 8" d	30.00	RI
1995	MICKEY MANTLE THE GREATEST SWITCH HITTER / TRIPLE CROWN 40TH ANNIVERSARY, 176923, T. Treadway, 2,401, double plate set	75.00	RI
1995	MICKEY MANTLE MY GREATEST YEAR 1956, 1229-04, B. Vann, 1,956, 10" d	100.00	RI
1995	PROFILES IN COURAGE, 1231-03, M. Petronella, open, 8" d	30.00	RI

Miniature Plates

1989	MICKEY MANTLE THE GREATEST SWITCH HITTER, Joseph Catalano	19.95	NR
1989	OREL HERSHISER, Joseph Catalano	19.95	NR

NFL Gold Edition

1990	BOOMER ESIASON, Joseph Catalano, closed	150.00	NR
1990	DAN MARINO, Joseph Catalano, closed	150.00	NR
1990	JOE MONTANA 49ERS, Joseph Catalano, closed	150.00	NR
1990	JOHN ELWAY, Joseph Catalano, closed	150.00	NR
1990	LAWRENCE TAYLOR, Joseph Catalano, closed	150.00	NR
1990	RANDALL CUNNINGHAM, Joseph Catalano, closed	150.00	NR

NFL Platinum Edition

1990	BOOMER ESIASON, M. Petronella, 5,000	49.95	NR
1990	DAN MARINO, M. Petronella, 5,000	49.95	NR
1990	JOE MONTANA, M. Petronella, 5,000	49.95	NR
1990	JOHN ELWAY, M. Petronella, 5,000	49.95	NR

		ISSUE	CURRENT
1990	LAWRENCE TAYLOR, M. Petronella, 5,000	49.95	NR
1990	RANDALL CUNNINGHAM, M. Petronella, 5,000	49.95	NR

NFL Superstar Set 2

1996	TROY AIKMAN, 3008-03, Joseph Catalano, 5,000, 8¼" d	30.00	RI

Race Cars

1996	JEFF GORDON DUPONT AUTOMOTIVE FINISHES, 8101-03, 5,000, 8½" d	30.00	RI
1996	JEFF GORDON DUPONT AUTOMOTIVE FINISHES, 8101-04, Robert Tanenbaum, 2,500, 10¼" d	100.00	RI
1996	JEFF GORDON DUPONT AUTOMOTIVE FINISHES, 8101-02, Robert Tanenbaum, open, 4¼" d	10.00	RI
1996	RUSTY WALLACE MILLER GENUINE DRAFT, 8105-03, 5,000, 8½" d	30.00	RI
1996	RUSTY WALLACE MILLER GENUINE DRAFT, 8105-04, Robert Tanenbaum, 2,500, 10¼" d	100.00	RI
1996	RUSTY WALLACE MILLER GENUINE DRAFT, 8105-02, Robert Tanenbaum, open, 4¼" d	10.00	RI
1996	GEOFF BODINE EXIDE BATTERIES, 8121-03, 5,000, 8½" d	30.00	RI
1996	GEOFF BODINE EXIDE BATTERIES, 8121-04, R. Tanenbaum, 2,500, 10¼" d	100.00	RI
1996	GEOFF BODINE EXIDE BATTERIES, 8121-02, R. Tanenbaum, open, 4¼" d	10.00	RI
1996	DARRELL WALTRIP WESTERN AUTO, 8103-03, 5,000, 8½" d	30.00	RI
1996	DARRELL WALTRIP WESTERN AUTO, 8103-04, Robert Tanenbaum, 2,500, 10¼" d	100.00	RI
1996	DARRELL WALTRIP WESTERN AUTO, 8103-02, R. Tanenbaum, open, 4¼" d	10.00	RI

Regular Edition

1989	OREL HERSHISER, Joseph Catalano, 10,000	49.50	NR
NA	JOSE CANSECO, Joseph Catalano, 10,000	49.50	NR
NA	WHO'S ON FIRST, Joseph Catalano, 10,000	49.50	NR
NA	WILL CLARK, Joseph Catalano, 10,000	49.50	NR
NA	YANKEE TRADITION, Joseph Catalano, 10,000	49.50	NR
NA	FRANK VIOLA, T. Fogarty, 10,000	49.50	NR
NA	KIRK GIBSON, T. Fogarty, 10,000	49.50	NR
NA	PAUL MOLITOR, T. Fogarty, 10,000	49.50	NR
NA	BABE RUTH, Brian Johnson, 10,000	49.50	NR
NA	DON MATTINGLY, Brian Johnson, 10,000	49.50	NR
NA	DUKE SNIDER, Brian Johnson, 10,000	49.50	NR
NA	LOU GEHRIG, Brian Johnson, 10,000	49.50	NR
NA	WADE BOGGS, Brian Johnson, 10,000	49.50	NR
NA	AL KALINE, E. Lapere, 10,000	49.50	NR
NA	ALAN TRAMMEL, E. Lapere, 10,000	49.50	NR
NA	BOB FELLER, E. Lapere, 10,000	49.50	NR
NA	ANDRE DAWSON, R. Lewis, 10,000	49.50	NR
NA	CY YOUNG, R. Lewis, 10,000	49.50	NR
NA	HONUS WAGNER, R. Lewis, 10,000	49.50	NR
NA	LIVING TRIPLE CROWN WINNERS, R. Lewis, 10,000	49.50	NR
NA	NOLAN RYAN, R. Lewis, 10,000	49.50	NR
NA	ROBERTO CLEMENTE, R. Lewis, 10,000	49.50	NR
NA	TY COBB, R. Lewis, 10,000	49.50	NR
NA	BROOKS ROBINSON, Robert Stephen Simon, 10,000	49.50	NR
NA	CARL YASTRZEMSKI, Robert Stephen Simon, 10,000	49.50	NR
NA	GARY CARTER, Robert Stephen Simon, 10,000	49.50	NR
NA	DARRYL STRAWBERRY, Robert Stephen Simon, 10,000	49.50	NR

		ISSUE	CURRENT
NA	DEM BUMS, Robert Stephen Simon, 10,000	49.50	NR
NA	K. HERNANDEZ, Robert Stephen Simon, 10,000	49.50	NR
NA	LARRY BIRD, Robert Stephen Simon, 10,000	49.50	NR
NA	LENNY DYKSTRA, Robert Stephen Simon, 10,000	49.50	NR
NA	MICKEY MANTLE, Robert Stephen Simon, 10,000	49.50	NR
NA	MICKEY, WILLIE AND THE DUKE, Robert Stephen Simon, 10,000	49.50	NR
NA	TED WILLIAMS, Robert Stephen Simon, 10,000	49.50	NR
NA	THURMAN MUNSON, Robert Stephen Simon, 10,000	49.50	NR

Today's Stars

1996	EMMITT SMITH, 3031-03, Brian Johnson, 7,500, 8¼" d	30.00	RI
1996	EMMITT SMITH, 3031-02, Brian Johnson, 4¼" d	10.00	RI

FRANZ STANEK

Single Issues

1969	MOON LANDING, 150	250.00	1,100.00
1972	MAYFLOWER, 60	250.00	650.00
1972	SANTA MARIA, 60	250.00	600.00
1973	EAGLE, 400	250.00	NR

STEIFF UNITED STATES

Bicentennial

1972	DECLARATION OF INDEPENDENCE, 10,000	50.00	NR
1974	BETSY ROSS, 10,000	50.00	NR
1975	CROSSING DELAWARE, 10,000	50.00	NR
1976	*SERAPIA* AND *BON HOMME*, 10,000	50.00	NR

STERLING AMERICA UNITED STATES

Christmas Customs

1970	YULE LOG, 2,500	18.00	30.00
1971	HOLLAND, 2,500	18.00	30.00
1972	NORWAY, 2,500	18.00	NR
1973	GERMANY, 2,500	20.00	NR
1974	MEXICO, 2,500	24.00	NR

Mother's Day

1971	MARE AND FOAL, 2,500	18.00	25.00
1972	HORNED OWL, 2,500	18.00	25.00
1973	RACCOONS, 2,500	20.00	NR
1974	DEER, 2,500	24.00	NR
1975	QUAIL, 2,500	24.00	NR

Twelve Days of Christmas

1970	PARTRIDGE, 2,500	18.00	25.00
1971	TURTLE DOVES, 2,500	18.00	25.00
1972	FRENCH HENS, 2,500	18.00	25.00

		ISSUE	CURRENT
1973	CALLING BIRDS, 2,500	18.00	25.00
1974	FIVE RINGS, 2,500	24.00	NR
1975	SIX GEESE, 2,500	24.00	NR
1976	SEVEN SWANS, 2,500	24.00	NR
1977	EIGHT MAIDS, 2,500	28.00	BR

STRATFORD COLLECTION UNITED STATES

Famous Clowns

1982	EMMETT LOOKING OUT TO SEE, Robert Blottiaux, 10,000	35.00	NR
1982	JACK THUM AND CHILD, Robert Blottiaux, 10,000	35.00	NR

Four Seasons of the Unicorn

1983	UNICORN IN WINTER, Michele Livingstone, 10,000	45.00	NR

Real Children

1982	MICHAEL'S MIRACLE, Nancy Turner, 19,500	39.50	NR
1983	SUSAN'S WORLD, Nancy Turner, 19,500	45.00	NR

Young Wildlife

1982	SIBERIAN CUB AT PLAY, Robert Blottiaux, 15,000	35.00	NR
1982	CURIOUS RACCOON, Robert Blottiaux, 15,000	35.00	NR

STUART DEVLIN SILVER UNITED STATES

Americana

1972	GASPEE INCIDENT, 1,000	130.00	145.00

STUART INTERNATIONAL UNITED STATES

Annual

NA	JENNY, Nancy Turner, 5,500	49.50	NR
NA	JENNY, Nancy Turner, gold edition, 250	NA	NA

Jenny
Photo courtesy of *Collectors News*

		ISSUE	CURRENT

Childhood Secrets

1983	BILLY'S TREASURE, Nancy Turner, 19,500	39.50	NR

Spring Flowers

1984	MEGAN, Lisette DeWinne, 5,500	55.00	NR
1984	DANIELLE, Lisette DeWinne, 5,500	55.00	NR

STUDIO COLLECTION

Santa's Animal Kingdom

1994	SANTA'S ANIMAL KINGDOM, T. Rubel, 5,000	30.00	RI

STUDIO DANTE DI VOLTERADICI ITALY

Benvenuti's Muses

1985	ERATO, Sergio Benvenutí	50.00	BR
1985	CLIO, Sergio Benvenutí	50.00	NR
1986	TERPSICHORE, Sergio Benvenutí	55.00	NR
1986	EUTERPE, Sergio Benvenutí	55.00	NR

Erato
Photo courtesy of *Collectors News*

O Come All Ye Faithful
Photo courtesy of *Collectors News*

Christmas Crèche

1987	JOY TO THE WORLD	55.00	BR
1987	HARK, THE HERALD ANGELS SING	55.00	NR
1988	O, COME ALL YE FAITHFUL	60.00	BR
1989	WE THREE KINGS	60.00	NR
1990	SILENT NIGHT, HOLY HIGHT	60.00	150.00
1991	ANGELS WE HAVE HEARD ON HIGH, Ennio Furiesi	60.00	90.00

Gates of Paradise

		ISSUE	CURRENT
1989	GOD CREATES ADAM	75.00	BR
1990	THE CREATION OF EVE	75.00	80.00
1990	THE ANGELS VISIT ABRAHAM	80.00	BR
1990	ISAAC BLESSING JACOB	80.00	95.00
1991	MOSES RECEIVES THE LAW	80.00	115.00
1991	SOLOMON AND THE QUEEN OF SHEBA	80.00	120.00

Ghiberti Doors

1983	ADORATION OF THE MAGI, Alberto Santangela	50.00	BR
1984	THE NATIVITY, Alberto Santangela	50.00	BR
1985	THE ANNUNCIATION, Alberto Santangela	50.00	BR
1985	CHRIST AMONG THE DOCTORS, Alberto Santangela	55.00	BR
1986	CHRIST WALKS ON THE WATER, Alberto Santangela	55.00	BR
1986	THE EXPULSION OF THE MONEY CHANGERS, Alberto Santangela	55.00	BR
1987	CHRIST'S ENTRY INTO JERUSALEM	55.00	BR
1987	THE RAISING OF LAZARUS	55.00	BR

Grand Opera

1976	RIGOLETTO, Gino Ruggeri, 1 year	35.00	NR
1977	MADAME BUTTERFLY, Gino Ruggeri, 1 year	35.00	BR
1978	CARMEN, Gino Ruggeri, 1 year	40.00	BR
1979	AIDA, Gino Ruggeri, 1 year	40.00	BR
1980	BARBER OF SEVILLE, Gino Ruggeri, 1 year	40.00	BR
1981	TOSCA, Gino Ruggeri, 1 year	40.00	BR
1982	I PAGLIACCI, Gino Ruggeri, 1 year	40.00	NR

Living Madonnas

1978	MADONNA PENSOSA (PENSIVE MADONNA), Ado Santini	45.00	BR
1979	MADONNA SERENA (SERENE MADONNA), Ado Santini	45.00	NR
1980	MADONNA BEATA (BEATIFIC MADONNA), Ado Santini	45.00	NR
1981	MADONNA PROFETICA (PROPHETIC MADONNA), Ado Santini	45.00	BR
1982	MADONNA MODESTA (DEMURE MADONNA), Ado Santini	45.00	NR
1983	MADONNA SAGGIA (WISE MADONNA), Ado Santini	45.00	60.00
1984	MADONNA TENERA (TENDER MADONNA), Ado Santini	45.00	BR

Masterpiece Madonnas

1990	RAPHAEL'S MADONNA	60.00	NR
1990	DELLA ROBBIA'S MADONNA	60.00	NR
1991	MICHELANGELO'S MADONNA	65.00	80.00
1991	BOTTICELLI'S MADONNA	65.00	BR
1991	LEONARDO'S MADONNA	65.00	75.00
1991	TITIAN'S MADONNA	65.00	100.00

Renaissance Madonnas: Gifts of Maternal Love

1986	THE GIFT OF WISDOM	65.00	NR
1987	THE GIFT OF FAITH	65.00	NR
1987	THE GIFT OF COMFORT	70.00	BR
1987	THE GIFT OF PATIENCE	70.00	NR
1988	THE GIFT OF DEVOTION	70.00	85.00
1988	THE GIFT OF TENDERNESS	70.00	80.00

		ISSUE	CURRENT
1988	THE GIFT OF VIGILANCE	70.00	80.00
1988	THE GIFT OF SOLICITUDE	70.00	95.00

STUMAR GERMANY

Christmas

1970	ANGEL, 10,000	8.00	35.00
1971	THE OLD CANAL, 10,000	8.00	25.00
1972	COUNTRYSIDE, 10,000	10.00	25.00
1973	FRIENDSHIP, 10,000	10.00	20.00
1974	MAKING FANCY, 10,000	10.00	20.00
1975	CHRISTMAS, 10,000	10.00	20.00
1976	CHRISTMAS, 10,000	15.00	NR
1977	JOYFUL EXPECTATIONS, 10,000	15.00	NR
1978	CHRISTMAS, 10,000	19.50	NR

Egyptian

1977	ANCIENT EGYPTIAN TRILOGY, 5,000	45.00	NR
1978	CHARIOTEER, 5,000	54.00	NR

Mother's Day

1971	AMISH MOTHER AND DAUGHTER, 10,000	8.00	35.00
1972	CHILDREN, 10,000	8.00	25.00
1973	MOTHER SEWING, 10,000	10.00	20.00
1974	MOTHER, CRADLE, 10,000	10.00	20.00
1975	BAKING, 10,000	10.00	20.00
1976	READING TO CHILDREN, 10,000	15.00	NR
1977	COMFORTING CHILD, 10,000	15.00	NR
1978	TRANQUILITY, 10,000	19.50	NR

TIRSCHENREUTH GERMANY

(Edwin M. Knowles)

Band's Songbirds of Europe (Edwin M. Knowles)

1985	BLUE TITMOUSE, Ursula Band, 100 days	19.50	NR
1986	FIRECREST, Ursula Band, 100 days	19.50	NR
1986	CORSICAN NUTHATCH, Ursula Band, 100 days	22.50	NR
1986	GOLDEN ORIOLE, Ursula Band, 100 days	22.50	BR
1986	GREAT TITMOUSE, Ursula Band, 100 days	22.50	BR
1986	RED ROBIN, Ursula Band, 100 days	22.50	NR
1986	CHAFFINCH, Ursula Band, 100 days	24.50	BR
1986	REDSTART, Ursula Band, 100 days	24.50	NR

Christmas

1969	HOMESTEAD, 3,500	12.00	25.00
1970	CHURCH, 3,500	12.00	NR
1971	STAR OF BETHLEHEM, 3,500	12.00	NR
1972	ELK, 3,500	13.00	NR
1973	CHRISTMAS, 3,500	14.00	NR

TOPSY TURVY UNITED STATES

		ISSUE	CURRENT

Storybook

1982	HARES AND HOUNDS, 10,000	19.50	NR
1982	OSTRICH AND ELEPHANT, 10,000	19.50	NR

TOWLE SILVERSMITHS UNITED STATES

Christmas

1972	WISE MEN, 2,500	250.00	NR

Valentines

1972	SINGLE HEART, 1 year	10.00	NR
1973	ENTWINED HEARTS, 1 year	10.00	NR

TUDOR MINT, INC.

Collector Plates

1992	MEETING OF UNICORNS, 4401, J. Mulholland, closed	27.10	NR
1992	CAULDRON OF LIGHT, 4402, J. Mulholland, closed	27.10	NR
1992	THE GUARDIAN DRAGON, 4403, J. Mulholland, closed	27.10	NR
1992	THE DRAGON'S NEST, 4404, J. Mulholland, closed	27.10	NR

UNITED STATES BICENTENNIAL SOCIETY

American Revolutionary Patriots

1974	BENJAMIN FRANKLIN, David Martin, 2,500	25.00	NR
1974	JOHN PAUL JONES, Charles Willson Peale, 2,500	25.00	NR
1974	ALEXANDER HAMILTON, John Trumball, 2,500	25.00	NR
1974	THOMAS PAINE, John Wesley Jarvis, 2,500	25.00	NR
1974	JOHN MARSHALL, Rembrandt Peale, 2,500	25.00	NR
1974	THOMAS JEFFERSON, John Trumball, 2,500	25.00	NR
1974	PATRICK HENRY, Thomas Sully, 2,500	25.00	NR
1974	NATHANIAL GREENE, Charles Willson Peale, 2,500	25.00	NR
1974	GEORGE WASHINGTON, Charles Willson Peale, 2,500	25.00	NR
1974	JOHN HANCOCK, Edward Savage, 2,500	25.00	NR

UNITED STATES GALLERY OF ART UNITED STATES

Single Issue

1984	INNOCENCE, Jack Woodson	19.50	NR

U.S. HISTORICAL SOCIETY UNITED STATES

Annual Historical

1977	GREAT EVENTS, 5,000	60.00	NR
1978	GREAT EVENTS, 10,000	75.00	NR

Annual Spring Flowers

		ISSUE	CURRENT
1983	FLOWERS IN A BLUE VASE, J. Clark, 10,000	135.00	150.00
1984	SPRING FLOWERS, M. Wampler	135.00	NR

Annual Stained Glass and Pewter Christmas

		ISSUE	CURRENT
1978	THE NATIVITY—CANTERBURY CATHEDRAL, 10,000	97.00	175.00
1979	FLIGHT INTO EGYPT—ST. JOHN'S, NEW YORK, 10,000	97.00	175.00
1980	MADONNA AND CHILD—WASHINGTON CATHEDRAL, 10,000	125.00	175.00
1981	THE MAGI—ST. PAUL'S, SAN FRANCISCO, 10,000	125.00	175.00
1982	FLIGHT INTO EGYPT—LOS ANGELES CATHEDRAL, 10,000	135.00	175.00
1983	SHEPHERDS AT BETHLEHEM—ST. JOHN'S, NEW ORLEANS, 10,000	135.00	150.00
1984	THE NATIVITY—ST. ANTHONY'S, ST. LOUIS, 10,000	135.00	NR
1985	GOOD TIDINGS OF GREAT JOY—BOSTON, 10,000	160.00	NR
1986	THE NATIVITY—OLD ST. MARY'S CHURCH, PHILADELPHIA, 10,000	160.00	NR
1987	O COME, LITTLE CHILDREN, 10,000	160.00	NR

The Nativity—Old St. Mary's Church, Philadelphia
Photo courtesy of *Collectors News*

Deck the Halls with Boughs of Holly
Photo courtesy of *Collectors News*

Audubon's Birds

		ISSUE	CURRENT
1986	AUDUBON AND THE BLUEJAY, Jack Woodson, 10,000	135.00	NR

Buffalo Bill's Wild West

		ISSUE	CURRENT
1984	PONY EXPRESS, Jack Woodson, 5,000	55.00	NR
1984	ANNIE OAKLEY, Jack Woodson, 5,000	55.00	NR
1984	SITTING BULL, Jack Woodson, 5,000	55.00	NR
NA	BUFFALO HUNTER, Jack Woodson, 5,000	55.00	NR
NA	FAREWELL APPEARANCE, Jack Woodson, 5,000	55.00	NR
NA	DEADWOOD STAGE, Jack Woodson, 5,000	55.00	NR
NA	CONGRESS OF THE ROUGH RIDERS, Jack Woodson, 5,000	55.00	NR
NA	ROYAL VISIT, Jack Woodson, 5,000	55.00	NR

		ISSUE	CURRENT

Christmas Carol

1982	DECK THE HALLS WITH BOUGHS OF HOLLY, Joan Landis, 10,000	55.00	65.00
1983	O CHRISTMAS TREE, Jack Woodson, 10,000	55.00	65.00
1984	WINTER WONDERLAND, Jack Woodson, 10,000	55.00	NR
1985	HERE WE COME A-CAROLING, Jack Woodson, 10,000	55.00	NR
1986	THE CHRISTMAS SONG, Jack Woodson, 10,000	55.00	NR
1987	I HEARD THE BELLS ON CHRISTMAS DAY, Jack Woodson, 10,000	55.00	NR

Dacey Series

1984	MELODIES OF STEPHEN FOSTER, Robert Dacey	19.50	NR

Easter

1987	THE GOOD SHEPHERD, Jack Woodson, 5,000	160.00	NR

Great American Sailing Ships

1983	*OLD IRONSIDES*, Jack Woodson, 10,000	135.00	150.00
1984	*CHARLES W. MORGAN*, Jack Woodson, 10,000	135.00	NR
1985	*FLYING CLOUD*, Jack Woodson, 10,000	135.00	NR

Stained Glass Cathedral Christmas

1978	CANTERBURY CATHEDRAL, 10,000	87.00	95.00
1979	FLIGHT INTO EGYPT, 10,000	97.00	NR
1980	MADONNA AND CHILD, 10,000	125.00	150.00
1981	THE MAGI, 10,000	125.00	NR
1982	FLIGHT INTO EGYPT, 10,000	125.00	NR
1983	SHEPHERDS AT BETHLEHEM, 10,000	150.00	NR

Stained Glass Mother's Day

1987	A MOTHER'S LOVE, Nancy A. Noël, 5,000	160.00	NR

Stained Glass and Pewter Special Issues

1986	TEXAS SESQUICENTENNIAL COMMEMORATIVE, Jack Woodson, 10,000	135.00	NR
1986	STATUE OF LIBERTY, Jack Woodson, 10,000	135.00	NR

Two Hundred Years of Flight

1984	MAN'S FIRST FLIGHT, Jack Woodson, 5,000	48.75	NR
1984	MIRACLE AT KITTY HAWK, Jack Woodson, 5,000	48.75	NR
1984	CHINA CLIPPER, Jack Woodson, 5,000	48.75	NR
1984	MAN IN SPACE, Jack Woodson, 5,000	48.75	NR

Young America

1972	YOUNG AMERICA OF WINSLOW HOMER, Winslow Homer, 2,500, set of 6	425.00	1,100.00

VAGUE SHADOWS UNITED STATES

(Artaffects, Curator Collection)

Arabians

1986	SILVER STREAK, Gregory Perillo, 3,500	95.00	125.00

Arctic Friends

		ISSUE	CURRENT
1982	SIBERIAN LOVE and SNOW PALS, Gregory Perillo, 7,500, set of 2	100.00	175.00

Chieftains I (Artaffects)

1979	CHIEF SITTING BULL, Gregory Perillo, 7,500	65.00	325.00
1979	CHIEF JOSEPH, Gregory Perillo, 7,500	65.00	80.00
1980	CHIEF RED CLOUD, Gregory Perillo, 7,500	65.00	120.00
1980	CHIEF GERONIMO, Gregory Perillo, 7,500	65.00	85.00
1981	CHIEF CRAZY HORSE, Gregory Perillo, 7,500	65.00	100.00

Chieftains II (Artaffects)

1983	CHIEF PONTIAC, Gregory Perillo, 7,500	70.00	85.00
1983	CHIEF VICTORIO, Gregory Perillo, 7,500	70.00	150.00
1983	CHIEF TECUMSEH, Gregory Perillo, 7,500	70.00	150.00
1983	CHIEF COCHISE, Gregory Perillo, 7,500	70.00	80.00
1983	CHIEF BLACK KETTLE, Gregory Perillo, 7,500	70.00	150.00

Child's Life

1983	SIESTA, Gregory Perillo, 10,000	45.00	NR
1984	SWEET DREAMS, Gregory Perillo, 10,000	45.00	NR

Indian Nations (Artaffects)

1983	BLACKFOOT, Gregory Perillo, 7,500	35.00	85.00
1983	CHEYENNE, Gregory Perillo, 7,500	35.00	85.00
1983	APACHE, Gregory Perillo, 7,500	35.00	85.00
1983	SIOUX, Gregory Perillo, 7,500	35.00	85.00
	Set of 4	140.00	350.00

Legends of the West

1982	DANIEL BOONE, Gregory Perillo, 10,000	65.00	NR
1983	DAVY CROCKETT, Gregory Perillo, 10,000	65.00	NR
1983	KIT CARSON, Gregory Perillo, 10,000	65.00	NR
1983	BUFFALO BILL, Gregory Perillo, 10,000	65.00	NR

Masterpieces of Impressionism (Curator Collection)

1980	WOMAN WITH PARASOL, Claude Monet, 17,500	35.00	60.00
1981	YOUNG MOTHER SEWING, Mary Cassatt, 17,500	35.00	50.00
1982	SARA IN GREEN BONNET, Mary Cassatt,17,500	35.00	50.00
1983	MARGOT IN BLUE, Mary Cassatt, 17,500	35.00	45.00

Masterpieces of Rockwell (Curator Collection)

1980	AFTER THE PROM, Norman Rockwell, 17,500	42.50	90.00
1980	THE CHALLENGER, Norman Rockwell, 17,500	50.00	NR
1982	GIRL AT THE MIRROR, Norman Rockwell, 17,500	50.00	75.00
1982	MISSING TOOTH, Norman Rockwell, 17,500	50.00	NR

Masterpieces of the West (Curator Collection)

1980	TEXAS NIGHT HERDER, Frank T. Johnson, 17,500	35.00	55.00
1981	INDIAN TRAPPER, Frederic Remington, 17,500	35.00	45.00
1982	COWBOY STYLE, William R. Leigh, 17,500	35.00	NR
1982	INDIAN STYLE, Gregory Perillo, 17,500	35.00	75.00

		ISSUE	CURRENT

Motherhood (Artaffects)

		ISSUE	CURRENT
1983	MADRE, Gregory Perillo, 10,000	50.00	75.00
1984	MADONNA OF THE PLAINS, Gregory Perillo, 10,000	50.00	75.00
1985	ABUELA, Gregory Perillo, 3,500	50.00	75.00
1986	NAP TIME, Gregory Perillo, 3,500	50.00	75.00

Nature's Harmony (Artaffects)

		ISSUE	CURRENT
1982	PEACEABLE KINGDOM, Gregory Perillo, 12,500	100.00	125.00
1982	ZEBRA, Gregory Perillo, 12,500	50.00	NR
1982	BENGAL TIGER, Gregory Perillo, 12,500	50.00	60.00
1982	BLACK PANTHER, Gregory Perillo, 12,500	50.00	70.00
1982	ELEPHANT, Gregory Perillo, 12,500	50.00	80.00

Perillo Santas (Artaffects)

		ISSUE	CURRENT
1980	SANTA'S JOY, Gregory Perillo, 1 year	29.95	40.00
1981	SANTA'S BUNDLE, Gregory Perillo, 1 year	29.95	40.00

Plainsmen

		ISSUE	CURRENT
1978	BUFFALO HUNT, Gregory Perillo, bronze, 2,500	350.00	375.00
1979	THE PROUD ONE, Gregory Perillo, bronze, 2,500	350.00	550.00

Pride of America's Indians (Artaffects)

		ISSUE	CURRENT
1986	BRAVE AND FREE, Gregory Perillo, 10 days	24.50	35.00
1986	DARK-EYED FRIENDS, Gregory Perillo, 10 days	24.50	45.00
1986	NOBLE COMPANIONS, Gregory Perillo, 10 days	24.50	35.00
1987	KINDRED SPIRITS, Gregory Perillo, 10 days	24.50	35.00
1987	LOYAL ALLIANCE, Gregory Perillo, 10 days	24.50	75.00
1987	SMALL AND WISE, Gregory Perillo, 10 days	24.50	35.00
1987	WINTER SCOUTS, Gregory Perillo, 10 days	24.50	NR
1987	PEACEFUL COMRADES, Gregory Perillo, 10 days	24.50	40.00

Princesses (Artaffects)

		ISSUE	CURRENT
1982	LILY OF THE MOHAWKS, Gregory Perillo, 7,500	50.00	175.00
1982	POCAHONTAS, Gregory Perillo, 7,500	50.00	100.00
1982	MINNEHAHA, Gregory Perillo, 7,500	50.00	100.00
1982	SACAJAWEA, Gregory Perillo, 7,500	50.00	100.00

Professionals

		ISSUE	CURRENT
1979	THE BIG LEAGUER, Gregory Perillo, 15,000	29.95	45.00
1980	BALLERINA'S DILEMMA, Gregory Perillo, 15,000	32.50	45.00
1981	QUARTERBACK, Gregory Perillo, 15,000	32.50	50.00
1981	RODEO JOE, Gregory Perillo, 15,000	35.00	40.00
1982	MAJOR LEAGUER, Gregory Perillo, 15,000	35.00	50.00
1983	THE HOCKEY PLAYER, Gregory Perillo, 15,000	35.00	50.00

Special Issues (Artaffects)

		ISSUE	CURRENT
1981	APACHE BOY, Gregory Perillo, 5,000	95.00	175.00
1981	PERILLO LITHO BOOK, Gregory Perillo, 3,000	95.00	NR
1983	PAPOOSE, Gregory Perillo, 3,000	100.00	125.00
1984	NAVAJO GIRL, Gregory Perillo, 3,500	95.00	175.00
1986	NAVAJO BOY, Gregory Perillo, 3,500	95.00	175.00

Navajo Boy
Photo courtesy of *Collectors News*

Cinderella
Photo courtesy of *Collectors News*

Storybook Collection

		ISSUE	CURRENT
1980	LITTLE RED RIDING HOOD, Gregory Perillo, 18 days	29.95	45.00
1981	CINDERELLA, Gregory Perillo, 18 days	29.95	45.00
1981	HANSEL AND GRETEL, Gregory Perillo, 18 days	29.95	45.00
1982	GOLDILOCKS AND THE THREE BEARS, Gregory Perillo, 18 days	29.95	45.00

Thoroughbreds (Artaffects)

1984	WHIRLAWAY, Gregory Perillo, 9,500	50.00	250.00
1984	SECRETARIAT, Gregory Perillo, 9,500	50.00	350.00
1984	MAN-OF-WAR, Gregory Perillo, 9,500	50.00	150.00
1984	SEABISCUIT, Gregory Perillo, 9,500	50.00	150.00

Tribal Ponies

1984	ARAPAHO, Gregory Perillo, 3,500	65.00	100.00
1984	COMANCHE, Gregory Perillo, 3,500	65.00	100.00
1984	CROW, Gregory Perillo, 3,500	65.00	150.00

War Ponies

1983	SIOUX, Gregory Perillo, 7,500	60.00	115.00
1983	NEZ PERCE, Gregory Perillo, 7,500	60.00	135.00
1983	APACHE, Gregory Perillo, 7,500	60.00	110.00

VAL ST. LAMBERT BELGIUM

American Heritage

1969	PILGRIM FATHERS, 500	200.00	450.00
1970	PAUL REVERE'S RIDE, 500	200.00	225.00
1971	WASHINGTON ON DELAWARE, 500	200.00	225.00

Annual Old Masters

1969	REUBENS and REMBRANDT, 5,000, set of 2	50.00	90.00

		ISSUE	CURRENT
1969	VAN GOGH and VAN DYCK, 5,000, set of 2	50.00	85.00
1970	DA VINCI and MICHELANGELO, 5,000, set of 2	50.00	90.00
1971	EL GRECO and GOYA, 5,000, set of 2	50.00	85.00
1972	REYNOLDS and GAINSBOROUGH, 5,000, set of 2	50.00	70.00

Single Issue

1970	REMBRANDT	25.00	40.00

VENETO FLAIR ITALY

American Landscape

1979	HUDSON VALLEY, 7,500	75.00	NR
1980	NORTHWEST CASCADE, 7,500	75.00	NR

Bellini Series

1971	MADONNA, Vincente Tiziano, 500	45.00	400.00

Birds

1972	OWL, 2,000	37.50	100.00
1973	FALCON, 2,000	37.50	NR
1974	MALLARD, 2,000	45.00	NR

Cats

1974	PERSIAN, 2,000	40.00	55.00
1975	SIAMESE, 2,000	45.00	55.00
1976	TABBY, 2,000	45.00	55.00

Children's Christmas

1979	THE CAROLERS, Vincente Tiziano, 7,500	60.00	NR
1980	HEADING HOME, Vincente Tiziano, 7,500	75.00	NR
1981	THE NIGHT BEFORE, Vincente Tiziano, 7,500	95.00	NR
1982	A VISIT TO SANTA, Vincente Tiziano, 7,500	95.00	NR

Christmas

1971	THREE KINGS, Vincente Tiziano, 1,500	55.00	NR
1972	SHEPHERDS, Vincente Tiziano, 1,500	55.00	NR
1973	CHRIST CHILD, Vincente Tiziano, 1,500	55.00	NR
1974	ANGEL, Vincente Tiziano, 1,500	55.00	NR

Christmas Card

1975	CHRISTMAS EVE, Vincente Tiziano, 4,000	37.50	NR
1976	OLD NORTH CHURCH, Vincente Tiziano, 4,000	37.50	NR
1977	LOG CABIN CHRISTMAS, Vincente Tiziano, 4,000	37.50	NR
1978	DUTCH CHRISTMAS, Vincente Tiziano, 4,000	40.00	NR

Dogs

1972	GERMAN SHEPHERD, Vincente Tiziano, 2,000	37.50	75.00
1973	POODLE, Vincente Tiziano, 2,000	37.50	45.00

		ISSUE	CURRENT
1974	DOBERMAN, Vincente Tiziano, 2,000	37.50	NR
1975	COLLIE, Vincente Tiziano, 2,000	40.00	NR
1976	DACHSHUND, Vincente Tiziano, 2,000	45.00	NR

Easter

1973	RABBITS, 2,000	50.00	90.00
1974	CHICKS, 2,000	50.00	NR
1975	LAMB, 2,000	50.00	NR
1976	COMPOSITE, 2,000	50.00	NR

Flower Children

1978	ROSE, 3,000	45.00	NR
1979	ORCHID, 3,000	60.00	NR
1980	CAMELIA, 3,000	65.00	NR

Four Seasons

1972	FALL, silver plate, 2,000	75.00	NR
1972	FALL, sterling silver, 2,000	125.00	NR
1973	SPRING, silver plate, 300	75.00	NR
1973	SPRING, sterling silver, 750	125.00	NR
1973	WINTER, silver plate, 2,000	75.00	NR
1973	WINTER, sterling silver, 250	125.00	NR
1974	SUMMER, silver plate, 300	75.00	NR
1974	SUMMER, sterling silver, 750	125.00	NR

Goddesses

1973	POMONA, 1,500	75.00	125.00
1974	DIANA, 1,500	75.00	NR

La Belle Femme

1978	LILY, 9,500	70.00	NR
1979	GIGI, 9,500	76.50	NR
1980	DOMINIQUE, 9,500	76.50	NR
1980	GABRIELLE, 9,500	76.50	NR

Lamincia Annual

1981	YOUNG LOVE, Franco Lamincia, 7,500	95.00	NR

Last Supper

1972	THREE APOSTLES, Vincente Tiziano, 2,000	100.00	NR
1973	THREE APOSTLES, Vincente Tiziano, 2,000	70.00	NR
1974	THREE APOSTLES, Vincente Tiziano, 2,000	70.00	NR
1975	THREE APOSTLES, Vincente Tiziano, 2,000	70.00	NR
1976	JESUS CHRIST, Vincente Tiziano, 2,000	70.00	85.00

Mosaic

1973	JUSTINIAN, Vincente Tiziano, 500	50.00	75.00
1974	PELICAN, Vincente Tiziano, 1,000	50.00	NR
1977	THEODORA, Vincente Tiziano, 500	50.00	NR

Noah and the Dove
Photo courtesy of *Collectors News*

Mother and Child

		ISSUE	CURRENT
1981	LOONS, Guilio Gialletti and Franco Lamincia, 5,000	95.00	NR
1981	POLAR BEAR, Guilio Gialletti and Franco Lamincia, 5,000	95.00	NR
1981	KOALAS, Guilio Gialletti and Franco Lamincia, 5,000	95.00	NR
1981	BUFFALOS, Guilio Gialletti and Franco Lamincia, 5,000	95.00	NR
1981	LIONS, Guilio Gialletti and Franco Lamincia, 5,000	95.00	NR
1981	ELEPHANTS, Guilio Gialletti and Franco Lamincia, 5,000	95.00	NR

Mother's Day

		ISSUE	CURRENT
1972	MADONNA AND CHILD, Vincente Tiziano, 2,000	55.00	85.00
1973	MADONNA AND CHILD, Vincente Tiziano, 2,000	55.00	NR
1974	MOTHER AND SON, Vincente Tiziano, 2,000	55.00	NR
1975	DAUGHTER AND DOLL, Vincente Tiziano, 2,000	45.00	NR
1976	SON AND DAUGHTER, Vincente Tiziano, 2,000	55.00	NR
1977	MOTHER AND CHILD, Vincente Tiziano, 2,000	50.00	NR

St. Mark's of Venice

		ISSUE	CURRENT
1984	NOAH AND THE DOVE	60.00	NR
1985	MOSES AND THE BURNING BUSH	60.00	NR
1986	ABRAHAM AND THE JOURNEY	60.00	NR
1986	JOSEPH AND THE COAT	63.00	NR

Valentine's Day

		ISSUE	CURRENT
1977	VALENTINE BOY, 3,000	45.00	60.00
1978	VALENTINE GIRL, 3,000	45.00	55.00
1979	HANSEL, 3,000	60.00	NR
1980	GRETEL, 5,000	67.50	NR

Wildlife

		ISSUE	CURRENT
1971	DEER, Vincente Tiziano, 500	37.50	450.00
1972	ELEPHANT, Vincente Tiziano, 1,000	37.50	275.00
1973	PUMA, Vincente Tiziano, 2,000	37.50	65.00
1974	TIGER, Vincente Tiziano, 2,000	40.00	50.00

VERNONWARE UNITED STATES

Christmas

		ISSUE	CURRENT
1971	PARTRIDGE, 1 year	15.00	60.00
1972	JINGLE BELLS, 1 year	17.50	30.00
1973	THE FIRST NOEL, 1 year	20.00	35.00
1974	UPON A MIDNIGHT CLEAR, 1 year	20.00	30.00
1975	O HOLY NIGHT, 1 year	20.00	30.00
1976	HARK! THE HERALD ANGELS, 1 year	20.00	30.00
1977	AWAY IN THE MANGER, 1 year	30.00	NR
1978	WHITE CHRISTMAS, 10,000	30.00	NR
1979	LITTLE DRUMMER BOY, 10,000	30.00	NR

Corvette Collector

1986	PACE CAR CONVERTIBLE, Bill Seitz, 2,000	29.95	NR
1987	'63 SPLIT WINDOW COUPE, Bill Seitz, 2,000	29.95	NR

VILETTA CHINA UNITED STATES

(R. J. Ernst Enterprises, Hamilton Collection, Pemberton & Oakes)

Alice in Wonderland

1980	ALICE AND THE WHITE RABBIT, Robert Blitzer, 28 days	25.00	NR
1980	ADVICE FROM A CATERPILLAR, Robert Blitzer, 28 days	25.00	NR
1980	END OF A DREAM, Robert Blitzer, 28 days	25.00	NR
1981	MAD HATTER'S TEA PARTY, Robert Blitzer, 28 days	25.00	NR
1981	ALICE AND CHESHIRE CAT, Robert Blitzer, 28 days	25.00	NR
1981	ALICE AND CROQUET MATCH, Robert Blitzer, 28 days	25.00	NR

Boys Town

1986	REV. EDWARD J. FLANAGAN, FOUNDER OF BOYS TOWN, Michael Engstrom, 5,000	32.00	NR

Carefree Days (Hamilton Collection)

1982	AUTUMN WANDERER, Thornton Utz, 10 days	24.50	NR
1982	BEST FRIENDS, Thornton Utz, 10 days	24.50	NR
1982	FEEDING TIME, Thornton Utz, 10 days	24.50	NR
1982	BATHTIME VISITOR, Thornton Utz, 10 days	24.50	NR
1982	FIRST CATCH, Thornton Utz, 10 days	24.50	NR
1982	MONKEY BUSINESS, Thornton Utz, 10 days	24.50	NR
1982	TOUCHDOWN, Thornton Utz, 10 days	24.50	NR
1982	NATURE HUNT, Thornton Utz, 10 days	24.50	NR

Childhood Memories (Collector's Heirloom)

1978	JENNIFER BY CANDLELIGHT, William Bruckner, 5,000	60.00	NR
1979	BRIAN'S BIRTHDAY, William Bruckner, 5,000	60.00	NR

Children's Series

1979	LAST OF THE NINTH, 5,000	45.00	NR

Rev. Edward J. Flanagan,
Founder of Boys Town

Friends Forever
Photo courtesy of *Collectors News*

Christmas Annual

		ISSUE	CURRENT
1978	EXPRESSION OF FAITH, 7,400	49.95	NR
1979	SKATING LESSON, 7,400	49.95	NR
1980	BRINGING HOME THE TREE, 7,400	49.95	NR

Coppelia Ballet (Hamilton Collection)

1980	FRANZ'S FANTASY LOVE, Renée Faure, 28 days	25.00	NR
1980	THE CREATION OF A DOLL, Renée Faure, 28 days	25.00	NR
1981	THE SECRET IS UNLOCKED, Renée Faure, 28 days	25.00	NR
1981	SWANILDA'S DECEPTION, Renée Faure, 28 days	25.00	NR
1981	AN UNEASY SLEEP, Renée Faure, 28 days	25.00	NR
1981	COPPELIA AWAKENS, Renée Faure, 28 days	25.00	NR
1982	A SHATTERED DREAM, Renée Faure, 28 days	25.00	NR
1982	THE WEDDING, Renée Faure, 28 days	25.00	NR

Days of the West

1978	COWBOY CHRISTMAS, 5,000	50.00	60.00

Disneyland

1976	SIGNING THE DECLARATION, 3,000	15.00	100.00
1976	CROSSING THE DELAWARE, 3,000	15.00	100.00
1976	BETSY ROSS, 3,000	15.00	100.00
1976	SPIRIT OF '76, 3,000	15.00	100.00
1979	MICKEY'S 50TH ANNIVERSARY, 5,000	37.00	50.00

Great Comedians (Warwick)

1978	THE LITTLE TRAMP, 7,500	35.00	NR
1978	OUTRAGEOUS GROUCHO, 7,500	35.00	NR

In Tribute to America's Great Artists

1978	DEGRAZIA, J. Marco, 5,000	65.00	NR

Joys of Motherhood (Collector's Heirlooms)

		ISSUE	CURRENT
1978	CRYSTAL'S JOY, William Bruckner, 7,500	60.00	BR

Making Friends

		ISSUE	CURRENT
1978	FEEDING THE NEIGHBOR'S PONY, Irish McCalla, 5,000	45.00	NR
1979	COWBOYS 'N INDIANS, Irish McCalla, 5,000	47.50	NR
1980	SURPRISE FOR CHRISTY, Irish McCalla, 5,000	47.50	NR

Nutcracker Ballet (Hamilton Collection)

		ISSUE	CURRENT
1978	CLARA AND THE NUTCRACKER, Shell Fisher, 28 days	19.50	30.00
1979	GIFT FROM GODFATHER, Shell Fisher, 28 days	19.50	NR
1979	SUGARPLUM FAIRY, Shell Fisher, 28 days	19.50	30.00
1979	SNOW KING AND QUEEN, Shell Fisher, 28 days	19.50	40.00
1980	WALTZ OF FLOWERS, Shell Fisher, 28 days	19.50	25.00
1980	CLARA AND THE PRINCE, Shell Fisher, 28 days	19.50	35.00

Olympics (Ghent Collection)

		ISSUE	CURRENT
1980	WINTER OLYMPICS, 13 days	24.50	NR
1980	SUMMER OLYMPICS, <1 year	29.50	NR

The Performance (R. J. Ernst Enterprises)

		ISSUE	CURRENT
1979	ACT I, Bonnie Porter, 5,000	65.00	NR

Portraits of Childhood (Hamilton Collection)

		ISSUE	CURRENT
1981	BUTTERFLY MAGIC, Thornton Utz, 28 days	24.95	NR
1982	SWEET DREAMS, Thornton Utz, 28 days	24.95	NR
1983	TURTLE TALK, Thornton Utz, 28 days	24.95	NR
1984	FRIENDS FOREVER, Thornton Utz, 28 days	24.95	NR

Precious Moments

		ISSUE	CURRENT
1979	FRIEND IN THE SKY, Thornton Utz, 28 days	21.50	50.00
1980	SAND IN HER SHOE, Thornton Utz, 28 days	21.50	35.00
1980	SNOW BUNNY, Thornton Utz, 28 days	21.50	30.00
1980	SEASHELLS, Thornton Utz, 28 days	21.50	30.00
1981	DAWN, Thornton Utz, 28 days	21.50	30.00
1982	MY KITTY, Thornton Utz, 28 days	21.50	30.00

Rufus and Roxanne (R. J. Ernst Enterprises)

		ISSUE	CURRENT
1980	LOVE IS..., C. Kelly, 19,000	14.95	NR

Seasons of the Oak

		ISSUE	CURRENT
1979	LAZY DAYS, Ralph Homan, 5,000	55.00	NR
1980	COME FLY WITH ME, Ralph Homan, 5,000	55.00	NR

Tender Moments

		ISSUE	CURRENT
1978	OLD-FASHIONED PERSUASION, Eugene Christopherson, 7,500	40.00	NR
1980	DANDELIONS, Eugene Christopherson, 7,500	40.00	NR

Unicorn Fantasies

		ISSUE	CURRENT
1979	FOLLOWERS OF DREAMS, K. Chin, 5,000	55.00	NR

		ISSUE	CURRENT
1980	TWICE UPON A TIME, K. Chin, 5,000	55.00	NR
1981	FAMILIAR SPIRIT, K. Chin, 5,000	55.00	NR
1982	NOBLE GATHERING, K. Chin, 5,000	55.00	NR

Weddings Around the World

1979	HAWAIIAN WEDDING, Elke Sommer, 5,000	75.00	NR
1980	DUTCH WEDDING, Elke Sommer, 5,000	75.00	NR

Women of the West (R. J. Ernst Enterprises)

1979	EXPECTATIONS, Donald Putnam, 10,000	39.50	BR
1979	SILVER DOLLAR SAL, Donald Putnam, 10,000	39.50	BR
1980	FIRST DAY, Donald Putnam, 10,000	39.50	BR
1980	DOLLY, Donald Putnam, 10,000	39.50	BR
1982	SCHOOL MARM, Donald Putnam, 10,000	39.50	BR

Single Issues

1980	MAIL ORDER BRIDE, Irish McCalla, 5,000	60.00	NR
1980	THE DUKE (R. J. Ernst Enterprises), 27,500	29.75	NR
1983	PRINCESS GRACE, Thornton Utz, 21 days	75.00	NR

VILLEROY AND BOCH GERMANY

(Heinrich Studio)

Christmas

1977	HOLY FAMILY, 10,000	175.00	200.00
1978	THREE HOLY KINGS, 20,000	175.00	200.00
1979	MARY WITH CHILD, 10,000	198.00	NR
1980	MADONNA IN GLORY, 10,000	200.00	NR

Dreams of Katharina

1985	KATHARINA RECEIVES A PROMISE OF LOVE, Gero Trauth, 19,900	NA	NA

Katharina Receives a Promise of Love
Photo courtesy of *Collectors News*

Katharina's Blossoming Love
Photo courtesy of *Collectors News*

Fortunata and the Hen
Photo courtesy of *Collectors News*

Monkeys in the Garden
Photo courtesy of *Collectors News*

		ISSUE	CURRENT
1986	KATHARINA'S AURA AND HER EARTHLY LAMENTS, Gero Trauth, 19,900	NA	NA
1986	KATHARINA'S DREAM CASTLE, Gero Trauth, 19,900	NA	NA
1986	KATHARINA'S BLOSSOMING LOVE, Gero Trauth, 19,900	NA	NA
1986	PROPOSAL OF MARRIAGE FOR KATHARINA, Gero Trauth, 19,900	NA	NA
1987	KATHARINA'S HOUR OF BLISS, Gero Trauth, 19,900	NA	NA

French Fairy Tales

NA	FORTUNATA AND THE HEN, Edmund Dulac, 19,750	70.00	NR
NA	THE KING OF THE PEACOCKS, Edmund Dulac, 19,750	70.00	NR
NA	THE KING AND PUSS IN BOOTS, Edmund Dulac, 19,750	70.00	NR

Once Upon a Rhyme

NA	ROSES ARE RED, Renée Faure	NA	NA

Statue of Liberty—Ellis Island Foundation Commemorative

NA	STATUE OF LIBERTY, Renée Faure	NA	NA

Single Issue

NA	MONKEYS IN THE GARDEN	NA	NA
NA	PRINCESS RADIANT AND THE PHOENIX	NA	NA
NA	PRINCE AHMED AND PERI BANU	NA	NA

VINOGRADOFF PORCELAIN

Russian Legends

1988	RUSLAN AND LUDMILLA, Gleb V. Lubimov, 195 days	29.87	BR
1988	THE PRINCESS AND THE SEVEN BOGATYRS, Aleksandr I. Kovalev, 195 days	29.87	BR
1988	THE GOLDEN COCKEREL, Vladmir A. Vleshko, 195 days	32.87	BR
1988	LUKOMORYA, R. Belousov, 195 days	32.87	BR
1989	THE FISHERMAN AND THE MAGIC GOLD FISH, N. Lopatin, 195 days	32.87	BR
1989	TSAR SALTAN, Galina Zhiryakova, 195 days	32.87	BR

		ISSUE	CURRENT
1989	THE PRIEST AND HIS SERVANT BALDA, O. An, 195 days	34.87	BR
1990	STONE FLOWER, V. Bolshakova, 195 days	34.87	BR
1990	SADKO, E. Populor, 195 days	34.87	NR
1990	THE TWELVE MONTHS, N. Lopatin, 195 days	36.87	NR
1990	SILVER HOOF, S. Adeyanor, 195 days	36.87	45.00
1990	MOROZKO, N. Lopatin, 195 days	36.87	60.00

WALDENBURG PORCELAIN CANADA

Punkinhead, The Happy Little Bear

1983	PUNKINHEAD AND HIS FRIENDS, 4,000	34.50	NR
1983	PUNKINHEAD AND SANTA CLAUS, 4,000	34.50	NR

WARNER BROS. STUDIO UNITED STATES

Single Issue

1997	THAT'S ALL FOLKS, 2,500	55.00	RI
1997	SPACE JAM, 5,000	35.00	RI
1998	ORIGINS OF BATMAN, Bob Kane, 2,500	35.00	RI

WATERFORD-WEDGWOOD USA
(Avon)

Avon Americana

1973	BETSY ROSS, 1 year	15.00	25.00
1974	FREEDOM, 1 year	15.00	25.00

Avon Christmas

1973	CHRISTMAS ON THE FARM, 1 year	15.00	40.00
1974	COUNTRY CHURCH, 1 year	16.00	30.00
1975	SKATERS ON POND, 1 year	18.00	25.00
1976	BRINGING HOME THE TREE, 1 year	18.00	NR
1977	CAROLERS IN THE SNOW, 1 year	19.50	NR
1978	TRIMMING THE TREE, 1 year	21.50	NR
1979	DASHING THROUGH THE SNOW, 1 year	24.00	NR
1995	TRIMMING THE TREE, Peggy L. Toole, 1 year	25.00	RI
1996	SANTA'S LOVING TOUCH, 1 year	24.99	RI

Avon Mother's Day

1974	TENDERNESS, 1 year	15.00	20.00
1975	GENTLE MOMENTS, 1 year	17.00	30.00

Avon North American Songbirds

1974	CARDINALS, Don Eckelberry, 1 year	18.00	NR
NA	BLUEBIRD, Don Eckelberry, 1 year	NA	NA
NA	YELLOW BREASTED CHAT, Don Eckelberry, 1 year	NA	NA
NA	BALTIMORE ORIOLE, Don Eckelberry, 1 year	NA	NA

Avon Single Issues

		ISSUE	CURRENT
1973	BETSY ROSS	NA	15.00
1974	FREEDOM	NA	15.00
1974	TENDERNESS	NA	15.00
1975	GENTLE MOMENTS	NA	15.00

Bicentennial

		ISSUE	CURRENT
1972	BOSTON TEA PARTY, 1 year	40.00	NR
1973	PAUL REVERE'S RIDE, 1 year	40.00	115.00
1974	BATTLE OF CONCORD, 1 year	40.00	55.00
1975	ACROSS THE DELAWARE, 1 year	40.00	105.00
1975	VICTORY AT YORKTOWN, 1 year	45.00	55.00
1976	DECLARATION SIGNED, 1 year	45.00	NR

Blossoming of Suzanne

		ISSUE	CURRENT
1977	INNOCENCE, Mary Vickers, 7,000	60.00	NR
1978	CHERISH, Mary Vickers, 7,000	60.00	NR
1979	DAYDREAM, Mary Vickers, 7,000	65.00	NR
1980	WISTFUL, Mary Vickers, 7,000	70.00	NR

Calendar

		ISSUE	CURRENT
1971	VICTORIAN ALMANAC, 1 year	12.00	NR
1972	THE CAROUSEL, 1 year	12.95	NR
1973	BOUNTIFUL BUTTERFLY, 1 year	12.95	NR
1974	CAMELOT, 1 year	14.00	75.00
1975	CHILDREN'S GAMES, 1 year	15.00	NR
1976	ROBIN, 1 year	25.00	NR
1977	TONATIUH, 1 year	30.00	NR
1978	SAMURAI, 1 year	30.00	NR
1979	SACRED SCARAB, 1 year	35.00	NR
1980	SAFARI, 1 year	42.50	NR
1981	HORSES, 1 year	47.50	NR
1982	WILD WEST, 1 year	52.00	NR
1983	THE AGE OF THE REPTILES, 1 year	54.00	NR
1984	DOGS, 1 year	54.00	NR
1985	CATS, 1 year	54.00	NR
1986	BRITISH BIRDS, 1 year	54.00	NR
1987	WATER BIRDS, 1 year	54.00	NR
1988	SEA BIRDS, 1 year	54.00	NR

Cathedrals Christmas

		ISSUE	CURRENT
1986	CANTERBURY CATHEDRAL, 1 year	40.00	NR

Child's Birthday

		ISSUE	CURRENT
1981	PETER RABBIT, Beatrix Potter, 1 year	24.00	NR
1982	MRS. TIGG-WINKLE, Beatrix Potter, 1 year	27.00	NR
1983	PETER RABBIT AND BENJAMIN BUNNY, Beatrix Potter, 1 year	29.00	NR
1984	PETER RABBIT, Beatrix Potter, 1 year	29.00	NR
1985	PETER RABBIT, Beatrix Potter, 1 year	29.00	NR
1986	PETER RABBIT, Beatrix Potter, 1 year	29.00	NR
1987	OAKAPPLE WOOD, J. Partridge, 1 year	29.00	NR
1988	OAKAPPLE WOOD, J. Partridge, 1 year	29.00	NR

Child's Christmas

		ISSUE	CURRENT
1979	CHILDREN AND SNOWMAN, 1 year	35.00	NR
1980	COLLECTING THE CHRISTMAS TREE, 1 year	37.50	NR
1981	CHILDREN SLEDDING, 1 year	40.00	NR
1982	SKATERS, 1 year	40.00	NR
1983	CAROL SINGING, 1 year	40.00	NR
1984	MIXING THE CHRISTMAS PUDDING, 1 year	40.00	NR

Children's Story

		ISSUE	CURRENT
1971	THE SANDMAN, 1 year	7.95	25.00
1972	THE TINDER BOX, 1 year	7.95	NR
1973	THE EMPEROR'S NEW CLOTHES, 1 year	9.00	NR
1974	THE UGLY DUCKLING, 1 year	10.00	NR
1975	THE LITTLE MERMAID, 1 year	11.00	NR
1976	HANSEL AND GRETEL, 1 year	12.00	NR
1977	RUMPELSTILTSKIN, 1 year	15.00	NR
1978	THE FROG PRINCE, 1 year	15.00	25.00
1979	THE GOLDEN GOOSE, 1 year	15.00	NR
1980	RAPUNZEL, 1 year	16.00	NR
1981	TOM THUMB, 1 year	18.00	NR
1982	THE LADY AND THE LION, 1 year	20.00	NR
1983	THE ELVES AND THE SHOEMAKER, 1 year	20.00	NR
1984	KING ROUGHBEARD, 1 year	20.00	NR
1985	THE BRAVE LITTLE TAILOR, 1 year	20.00	NR

Christmas

		ISSUE	CURRENT
1969	WINDSOR CASTLE, Tom Harper, 1 year	25.00	70.00
1970	TRAFALGAR SQUARE, Tom Harper, 1 year	30.00	BR
1971	PICCADILLY CIRCUS, Tom Harper, 1 year	30.00	NR
1972	ST. PAUL'S CATHEDRAL, Tom Harper, 1 year	35.00	NR
1973	TOWER OF LONDON, Tom Harper, 1 year	40.00	NR
1974	HOUSES OF PARLIAMENT, Tom Harper, 1 year	40.00	60.00
1975	TOWER BRIDGE, Tom Harper, 1 year	45.00	NR
1976	HAMPTON COURT	50.00	NR
1977	WESTMINSTER ABBEY	55.00	BR
1978	HORSE GUARDS, Tom Harper, 1 year	60.00	BR
1979	BUCKINGHAM PALACE, 1 year	65.00	BR
1980	ST. JAMES'S PALACE, 1 year	70.00	BR
1981	MARBLE ARCH, 1 year	75.00	BR
1982	LAMBETH PALACE, 1 year	80.00	NR
1983	ALL SOULS, LANGHAM PALACE, 1 year	80.00	NR
1984	CONSTITUTION HILL, 1 year	80.00	NR
1985	THE TATE GALLERY, 1 year	80.00	NR
1986	THE ALBERT MEMORIAL, 1 year	80.00	110.00
1987	GUILDHALL, 1 year	80.00	NR
1988	THE OBSERVATORY/GREENWICH, 1 year	80.00	90.00
1989	WINCHESTER CATHEDRAL, 1 year	80.00	90.00

Colin Newman's Country Panorama

		ISSUE	CURRENT
1987	MEADOWS AND WHEATFIELDS, Colin Newman	29.00	NR
1987	THE MEANDERING STREAM, Colin Newman	29.00	NR
1987	VILLAGE IN THE VALLEY, Colin Newman	32.00	NR
1988	ROLLING HILLS AND GRASSLANDS, Colin Newman	32.00	NR

		ISSUE	CURRENT
1988	THE BEECHWOOD, Colin Newman	32.00	NR
1988	THE FARM COTTAGE, Colin Newman	32.00	NR
1988	THE HAYFIELD, Colin Newman	34.00	NR
1988	THE LAKESIDE, Colin Newman	34.00	NR

Legends of King Arthur

1986	ARTHUR DRAWS THE SWORD, Richard Hook	39.00	NR
1986	ARTHUR CROWNED KING	39.00	NR
1987	EXCALIBUR	42.00	NR
1987	WEDDING OF KING ARTHUR AND GUINEVERE	42.00	NR
1987	KNIGHTS OF THE ROUND TABLE	42.00	50.00
1987	LANCELOT AND GUINEVERE	42.00	60.00
1988	MORGAN LE FAY AND MORDRED	44.00	75.00
1988	ARTHUR IS TAKEN TO AVALON	44.00	80.00

Mother's Day

1971	SPORTIVE LOVE, 1 year	20.00	NR
1972	THE SEWING LESSON, 1 year	20.00	NR
1973	THE BAPTISM OF ACHILLES, 1 year	20.00	NR
1974	DOMESTIC EMPLOYMENT, 1 year	30.00	NR
1975	MOTHER AND CHILD, 1 year	35.00	NR
1976	THE SPINNER, 1 year	35.00	NR
1977	LEISURE TIME, 1 year	35.00	NR
1978	SWAN AND CYGNETS, 1 year	40.00	NR
1979	DEER AND FAWN, 1 year	45.00	NR
1980	BIRDS, 1 year	47.50	NR
1981	MARE AND FOAL, 1 year	50.00	NR
1982	CHERUBS WITH SWING, 1 year	55.00	NR
1983	CUPID AND BUTTERFLY, 1 year	55.00	NR
1984	MUSICAL CUPIDS, 1 year	55.00	NR
1985	CUPIDS AND DOVES, 1 year	55.00	NR
1986	CUPIDS FISHING, 1 year	55.00	NR
1987	ANEMONES, 1 year	55.00	NR
1988	TIGER LILY, 1 year	55.00	NR
1989	IRISES, 1 year	65.00	NR
1991	PEONIES, 1 year	65.00	NR

My Memories

1981	BE MY FRIEND, Mary Vickers	27.00	NR
1982	PLAYTIME, Mary Vickers	27.00	NR
1983	OUR GARDEN, Mary Vickers	27.00	50.00
1984	THE RECITAL, Mary Vickers	27.00	50.00
1985	MOTHER'S TREASURES, Mary Vickers	27.00	35.00
1986	RIDING HIGH, Mary Vickers	29.00	NR

Peter Rabbit Christmas

1981	PETER RABBIT, Beatrix Potter, 1 year	27.00	NR
1982	PETER RABBIT, Beatrix Potter, 1 year	27.00	NR
1983	PETER RABBIT, Beatrix Potter, 1 year	29.00	NR
1984	PETER RABBIT, Beatrix Potter, 1 year	29.00	NR
1985	PETER RABBIT, Beatrix Potter, 1 year	29.00	NR
1986	PETER RABBIT, Beatrix Potter, 1 year	29.00	NR
1987	PETER RABBIT, Beatrix Potter, 1 year	29.00	NR

		ISSUE	CURRENT

Portraits of First Love

		ISSUE	CURRENT
1986	THE LOVE LETTER, Mary Vickers	27.00	NR

Queen's Christmas

		ISSUE	CURRENT
1980	WINDSOR CASTLE, A. Price, 1 year	24.95	NR
1981	TRAFALGAR SQUARE, A. Price, 1 year	24.95	NR
1982	PICCADILLY CIRCUS, A. Price, 1 year	32.50	NR
1983	ST. PAUL'S, A. Price, 1 year	32.50	NR
1984	TOWER OF LONDON, A. Price, 1 year	35.00	NR
1985	PALACE OF WESTMINSTER, A. Price, 1 year	35.00	NR
1986	TOWER BRIDGE, A. Price, 1 year	35.00	NR

Street Sellers of London

		ISSUE	CURRENT
1986	THE BAKED POTATO MAN, John Finnie	25.00	NR

Valentine's Day

		ISSUE	CURRENT
1993	VALENTINE'S DAY PLATE, 1 year	60.00	RI

Waterford Wedgwood

		ISSUE	CURRENT
1989	MOSS ROSE	NA	NA

WENDELL AUGUSTE FORGE UNITED STATES

Christmas

		ISSUE	CURRENT
1974	CAROLER, bronze, 2,500	25.00	NR
1974	CAROLER, pewter, 2,500	30.00	NR
1975	CHRISTMAS IN COUNTRY, bronze, 2,500	30.00	NR
1975	CHRISTMAS IN COUNTRY, pewter, 2,500	35.00	NR
1976	LAMPLIGHTER, bronze, 2,500	35.00	NR
1976	LAMPLIGHTER, pewter, 2,500	40.00	NR
1977	COVERED BRIDGE, bronze, 2,500	40.00	NR
1977	COVERED BRIDGE, pewter, 2,500	45.00	NR

Collectors Guild Members Only

		ISSUE	CURRENT
1995	HOLIDAY EXPRESS, Len Youngo, 1 year	NA	RI
1996	FIRST LOVE, Len Youngo, 5,000	39.00	RI

Great Americans

		ISSUE	CURRENT
1971	KENNEDY, pewter, 500	40.00	NR
1971	KENNEDY, silver, 500	200.00	NR
1972	LINCOLN, pewter, 500	40.00	NR
1972	LINCOLN, silver, 500	200.00	NR

Great Moments

		ISSUE	CURRENT
1972	LANDING OF PILGRIMS, pewter, 5,000	40.00	NR
1972	LANDING OF PILGRIMS, silver, 500	200.00	NR
1973	FIRST THANKSGIVING, pewter, 5,000	40.00	NR
1972	FIRST THANKSGIVING, silver, 500	200.00	NR

		ISSUE	CURRENT
1974	PATRICK HENRY, pewter, 5,000	40.00	NR
1974	PATRICK HENRY, silver, 500	200.00	NR
1975	PAUL REVERE, pewter, 5,000	45.00	NR
1975	PAUL REVERE, silver, 500	200.00	NR
1976	SIGNING OF DECLARATION, pewter, 5,000	45.00	NR
1976	SIGNING OF DECLARATION, silver, 500	200.00	NR

Norman Rockwell's Finest Moments

1996	FIRST LOVE, Len Youngo/Rockwell-inspired, 5,000, bronze	65.00	RI
1996	FIRST LOVE, Len Youngo/Rockwell-inspired, 5,000, pewter	85.00	RI
1996	FIRST LOVE, Len Youngo/Rockwell-inspired, 5,000, sterling silver	450.00	RI

Peace

1973	PEACE DOVES, 2,500	250.00	275.00

Wildlife

1977	ON GUARD, aluminum, 1,900	35.00	NR
1977	ON GUARD, bronze, 1,500	45.00	NR
1977	ON GUARD, pewter, 1,500	55.00	NR
1977	ON GUARD, silver, 100	250.00	NR
1978	THUNDERBIRD, aluminum, 1,900	40.00	NR
1978	THUNDERBIRD, bronze, 1,500	50.00	NR
1978	THUNDERBIRD, pewter, 1,500	60.00	NR
1978	THUNDERBIRD, silver, 100	250.00	NR

Wings of Man

1971	COLUMBUS' SHIPS, pewter, 5,000	40.00	NR
1971	COLUMBUS' SHIPS, silver, 500	200.00	NR
1972	CONESTOGA WAGON, pewter, 5,000	40.00	NR
1972	CONESTOGA WAGON, silver, 500	200.00	NR

WESTERN AUTHENTICS CANADA

Guns at Sea

1986	H.M.C.S. *HAIDA*, Robert Banks, 5,000	39.95	NR
1986	H.M.C.S. *BONAVENTURE*, Robert Banks, 5,000	39.95	NR

Iron Pioneers

1986	CPR NO. 374, Robert Banks, 15,000	39.95	NR
1986	COUNTESS OF DUFFERIN, Robert Banks, 15,000	39.95	NR

Tunes of Glory

1986	THE PIPER, Robert Banks, 15,000	42.50	NR
1986	PIPER AND DRUMMER, Robert Banks, 15,000	42.50	NR

Single Issues

1986	DOUGLASS DC-3, Robert Banks, 7,500	39.95	NR
1986	SCARLET AND GOLD, Robert Banks, 19,500	49.95	NR

WESTMINSTER COLLECTIBLES UNITED STATES

Holiday

		ISSUE	CURRENT
1976	ALL HALLOWS EVE, 5,000	38.50	NR
1977	CHRISTMAS, 5,000	38.50	NR

WEXFORD GROUP UNITED STATES

Grandmother's World

1982	LITTLE TOY FRIENDS, Cynthia Knapton, 12,500	45.00	NR
1983	THE PROMENADE, Cynthia Knapton, 12,500	45.00	NR
1983	AFTERNOON TEA, Cynthia Knapton, 12,500	45.00	NR

Storyland Dolls

1984	MARY HAD A LITTLE LAMB, Cynthia Knapton, 5,000	39.50	NR

Little Toy Friends
Photo courtesy of *Collectors News*

WILDLIFE INTERNATIONALE UNITED STATES

(Armstrong's)

Owl Family

1983	SAW-WHET OWL FAMILY, John Ruthven, 5,000	55.00	NR
1983	GREAT HORNED OWL FAMILY, John Ruthven, 5,000	55.00	NR
1983	SNOWY OWL FAMILY, John Ruthven, 5,000	55.00	NR
1983	BARRED OWL FAMILY, John Ruthven, 5,000	55.00	NR

Waterfowl

1983	WOOD DUCKS, John Ruthven, 5,000	65.00	NR

WILD WINGS UNITED STATES

Broken Silence

		ISSUE	CURRENT
1997	ELK, Rosemary Millette, 14 days	49.50	RI
1997	MULE DEER, Rosemary Millette, 14 days	49.50	RI

Dog Plates

1997	BLACK LAB, Robert K. Abbett, 14 days	49.50	RI
1997	BRITTANY, Robert K. Abbett, 14 days	49.50	RI
1997	YELLOW LAB, Robert K. Abbett, 14 days	49.50	RI
1997	CHOCOLATE LAB, Robert K. Abbett, 14 days	49.50	RI
1997	GOLDEN RETRIEVER, Robert K. Abbett, 14 days	49.50	RI

Single Issues

1996	BLACK GHOST, Michael Sieve, 14 days	49.50	RI
1996	DAY'S END, Lee Stroncek, 14 days	49.50	RI
1996	DUCK INN, Sam Timm, 14 days	49.50	RI
1996	SNOWFALL HORSES, Chris Cummings, 14 days	49.50	RI
1996	SONG OF THE NORTH, 14 days	49.50	RI

WILLITTS DESIGNS UNITED STATES

Amish Heritage

1995	KATIE'S FIRST QUILT, Barbara Bradley, 25 days	30.00	RI

Ebony Visions Collection

1998	THE PROTECTOR, Thomas Blackshear, 7,500	35.00	RI

Single Issue

1997	THE MADONNA, Thomas Blackshear, 28 days	35.00	RI

WILTON ARMETALE

Christmas Carol

1996	JOLLY OLD ST. NICHOLAS, open	50.00	RI

WINDBERG ENTERPRISES

Single Issues

1975	AUTUMN'S WAY, D. Windberg	650.00	NR
1975	THE MOUNTAIN'S MAJESTY, D. Windberg	NA	NA

WINDEMERE COLLECTION ENTERPRISES UNITED STATES

Single Issue

1984	PIANO MOODS, Robert Olson, 7,500	60.00	NR

WINSTON ROLAND CANADA

(Danbury Mint, Zolan Fine Arts)

		ISSUE	CURRENT
Angel (Zolan Fine Arts)			
1996	HARP SONG, Donald Zolan, 2,000, 8¼"	29.90	RI
Best of Loates			
1988	THE LOON FAMILY, Glen Loates	38.50	NR
1988	THE WOOD DUCK, Glen Loates	38.50	NR
1988	THE PACIFIC LOON, Glen Loates	38.50	NR
1988	THE MERGANSER, Glen Loates	38.50	NR
Big Wheels Keep On Rolling			
1992	I THINK I CAN, Lance Nowther, 10,000	59.00	NR
1992	SHOOTING THE MOON, Lance Nowther, 10,000	59.00	NR
1992	THE BLUE PETE, Lance Nowther, 10,000	59.00	NR
1992	DUSTY ROADS, Lance Nowther, 10,000	59.00	NR
Big Wheels II			
1997	THE BIG MACK, Lance Nowther	59.00	RI
Brush with Life			
1988	LYNX IN WINTER, Glen Loates	42.25	NR
1988	TIMBER WOLVES, Glen Loates	42.25	NR
1988	RACCOON FAMILY, Glen Loates	42.25	NR
1988	FAWN AT REST, Glen Loates	42.25	NR
Canada Geese (Canadian Geo Society)			
1992	THE MARCHING BAND, Herbert Pikl	45.00	NR
1992	EARLY ARRIVALS, Herbert Pikl	45.00	NR

The Blue Pete
Photo courtesy of Winston Roland Ltd.

Kittie's Breakfast
Photo courtesy of Winston Roland Ltd.

Children and Pets

		ISSUE	CURRENT
1993	KITTIE'S BREAKFAST, Shirley Deaville, 5,000	39.99	RI
1993	TAKING TURNS, Shirley Deaville, 5,000	39.99	RI

Cloud Companions

1992	408 SQUADRON, Rich Thistle	55.00	NR

Cottage Wildlife C.W.F. Plate

1994	QUIET WATER (LOONS), Christine Wilson	45.00	RI
1994	FOREST MISCHIEF (CHIPMUNKS), Christine Wilson	45.00	RI
1994	SILENT SUNSET (BLUE HERON), Christine Wilson	45.00	RI
1994	FAMILY OUTING (RACCOONS), Christine Wilson	45.00	RI

Country Memories (Danbury Mint)

1992	SO GOOD TO BE HOME, Rudi Reichardt	26.95	NR
1992	BY THE OLD MILL, Rudi Reichardt	26.95	NR
1995	NATURE'S SWEET SYRUP, Rudi Reichardt	26.95	RI
1995	SUMMERTIME, Rudi Reichardt	26.95	RI
1995	PEACEFUL RETREAT, Rudi Reichardt	26.95	RI
1995	RUSTIC BEAUTY, Rudi Reichardt	26.95	RI
1995	SNUG HARBOUR, Rudi Reichardt	26.95	RI
1995	EARLY SNOWFALL, Rudi Reichardt	26.95	RI

Deere Memories

1990	GOD'S GOLDEN HARVEST, Peter Sawatsky, 10,000	59.00	NR
1990	TAKIN' A BREAK, Peter Sawatzky, 10,000	59.00	NR

Deere Memories III

1997	A CHIP OFF THE OLD BLOCK, Ross Logan, 10,000	59.00	RI
1997	NOTHING RUNS LIKE A DEERE, Ross Logan, 10,000	59.00	RI

Dodd's Annual

1994	CHRISTMAS CABIN, Kevin Dodds, 1,000	49.00	RI
1995	MEMORIES OF HOME, Kevin Dodds, 1,000	49.00	RI
1996	WINTER'S EVE, Kevin Dodds, 1,000	49.00	RI

Eagles Across America (Danbury Mint)

1995	PRIDE OF AMERICA, Rudi Reichardt, 75 days	29.90	RI
1995	CATCH OF THE DAY, Rudi Reichardt, 75 days	29.90	RI
1995	KING OF THE CANYON, Rudi Reichardt, 75 days	29.90	RI
1995	TRYING THEIR WINGS, Rudi Reichardt, 75 days	29.90	RI
1995	EVERGLADE SUNRISE, Rudi Reichardt, 75 days	29.90	RI
1995	PERFECT HARMONY, Rudi Reichardt, 75 days	29.90	RI
1995	SPIRIT OF ALASKA, Rudi Reichardt, 75 days	29.90	RI
1995	THE GUARDIANS, Rudi Reichardt, 75 days	29.90	RI

Enchanted Garden (Danbury Mint)

1995	FLOWER GIRL, Mary Baxter-St. Clair, 75 days	29.90	RI
1995	GOLDEN BUTTERFLY, Mary Baxter-St. Clair, 75 days	29.90	RI
1995	UNDER THE RAINBOW, Mary Baxter-St. Clair, 75 days	29.90	RI
1995	BALANCING ACT, Mary Baxter-St. Clair, 75 days	29.90	RI

		ISSUE	CURRENT
1995	SWEET DREAMS, Mary Baxter-St. Clair, 75 days	29.90	RI
1995	SPRINGTIME SERENADE, Mary Baxter-St. Clair, 75 days	29.90	RI
1995	GOOD MORNING, MISS LADYBUG, Mary Baxter-St. Clair, 75 days	29.90	RI
1995	GENTLE FRIENDS, Mary Baxter-St. Clair, 75 days	29.90	RI

Extraordinary Landscapes

1988	THROUGH THE MIST, Edwin Matthews	38.50	NR
1988	EARLY SNOW (WINTER HAZE), Edwin Matthews	38.50	NR
1988	EVENING GLOW, Edwin Matthews	38.50	NR
1988	FOGGY MORNING, Edwin Matthews	38.50	NR

Faithful Companions

1990	EVENING WATCH, Shirley Deaville	49.90	NR
1990	PATIENTLY WAITING, Shirley Deaville	49.90	NR
1990	COMPANY'S COMING, Shirley Deaville	49.90	NR
1990	GOLDEN DAYS, Shirley Deaville	49.90	NR

Faithful Companions II

1994	TOO POOPED TO PLAY, Shirley Deaville	49.90	RI

God Bless America (Danbury Mint)

1993	WHERE EAGLES SOAR, Rudi Reichardt, 75 days	26.95	RI
1993	ICE-CAPPED MAJESTY, Rudi Reichardt, 75 days	26.95	RI
1993	PROUD GUARDIAN, Rudi Reichardt, 75 days	26.95	RI
1993	PEACEFUL SOLITUDE, Rudi Reichardt, 75 days	26.95	RI
1993	AFTER THE STORM, Rudi Reichardt, 75 days	26.95	RI
1993	VIGILANT BEACON, Rudi Reichardt, 75 days	26.95	RI
1993	SUNLIT RETREAT, Rudi Reichardt, 75 days	26.95	RI
1993	FLYING FREE, Rudi Reichardt, 75 days	26.95	RI
1993	TRANQUIL BEAUTY, Rudi Reichardt, 75 days	26.95	RI
1993	FROSTY MORNING, Rudi Reichardt, 75 days	26.95	RI
1993	UNTAMED GLORY, Rudi Reichardt, 75 days	26.95	RI
1993	CASCADING THUNDER, Rudi Reichardt, 75 days	26.95	RI

Golden Age of Flight

1995	KINDRED SPIRITS, Rich Thistle, 10 days	44.95	RI
1995	HANGAR FLYING, Rich Thistle, 10 days	44.95	RI
1995	LOVE AT FIRST SIGHT, Rich Thistle, 10 days	44.95	RI

Halvorson's Horses

1998	REFLECTIONS OF SUMMER, Adeline Halvorson	34.95	RI

Halvorson's Puppies

1998	PEACE AND QUIET, Adeline Halvorson	34.95	RI

Here Today Gone Tomorrow

1992	SIBERIAN TIGER, Spencer Hodge	49.50	NR
1992	AFRICAN ELEPHANT, Spencer Hodge	49.50	NR
1992	LEOPARD, Spencer Hodge	49.50	NR
1992	BLACK RHINO, Spencer Hodge	49.50	NR

		ISSUE	CURRENT

Hockey in Canada

		ISSUE	CURRENT
1988	NIGHT GAME, Gary McLaughlin, 10,000	33.75	NR
1988	THE LAST RUSH, Gary McLaughlin, 10,000	33.75	NR
1988	THE PUCK STOPS HERE, Gary McLaughlin, 10,000	33.75	NR
1988	FACING OFF, Gary McLaughlin, 10,000	33.75	NR

In Praise of Hummingbirds

1993	RUBY THROATED HUMMINGBIRD, Peter Sheeler	42.99	RI
1993	RUFUS HUMMINGBIRD, Peter Sheeler	42.99	RI

International Harvester

1996	HORSEPOWER, Rich Thistle, 7,500	59.00	RI
1996	HEY MOM, IT'S HERE, Rich Thistle, 7,500	59.00	RI
1996	DAD NEEDS A BREAK, Rich Thistle, 7,500	59.00	RI
1996	BIG RED, Rich Thistle, 7,500	59.00	RI

Horsepower
Photo courtesy of Winston Roland Ltd.

Legendary Aircraft

1989	THE MYNARSKI LANCASTER, Reg Griffin	55.25	NR
1989	THE CANADIAN MEMORIAL FLY PAST, Reg Griffin	55.25	NR

Little Farm Hands

1997	TRACTOR RIDE, Donald Zolan, 75 days	29.90	RI
1997	CLEAN AND SHINY, Donald Zolan, 75 days	29.90	RI
1997	TUG O' WAR, Donald Zolan, 75 days	29.90	RI
1997	PITCHING IN, Donald Zolan, 75 days	29.90	RI
1997	BUMPER CROP, Donald Zolan, 75 days	29.90	RI
1997	MORNING SONG, Donald Zolan, 75 days	29.90	RI
1997	TOO BUSY TO PLAY, Donald Zolan, 75 days	29.90	RI
1997	PIGLET ROUNDUP, Donald Zolan, 75 days	29.90	RI

Looking Back

1998	HARVEST TIME, Ross Logan	29.90	RI
1998	TIL THE COWS COME HOME, Ross Logan	29.90	RI

		ISSUE	CURRENT

Look to the Rainbow

1988	SEARCHING FOR GOLD, Muriel Hughes	42.90	NR
1988	SHAKY BEGINNINGS, Muriel Hughes	42.90	NR
1988	PRACTICE MAKES PERFECT, Muriel Hughes	42.90	NR
1988	END OF THE RAINBOW, Muriel Hughes	42.90	NR

Man's Best Friend

1998	THE ROTTWEILER, Ross Logan	34.95	RI
1998	THE GOLDEN RETRIEVER, Ross Logan	34.95	RI
1998	THE GERMAN SHEPHERD, Ross Logan	34.95	RI

Max's Memories

1995	MILE 'O' KVR, Max Jacquiard	52.00	RI

Memories Are Made of This

1990	JUST FOR MOM, Gary McLaughlin	43.00	NR
1990	READING, WRITING AND ROMANCES, Gary McLaughlin	43.00	NR

Monarchs of the Sky

1992	MAGNIFICENT OBSESSION, Rudi Reichardt, 5,000	47.00	NR
1992	SPIRITS OF THE WIND, Rudi Reichardt, 5,000	47.00	NR

More Deere Memories

1992	FARMER'S PRIDE, Ross Logan, 10,000	59.00	NR
1992	WATERLOO BOY, Ross Logan, 10,000	59.00	NR
1992	EARTH'S BOUNTY, Ross Logan, 10,000	59.00	NR
1992	BREAKING NEW GROUND, Ross Logan, 10,000	59.00	NR

Nature's Majesty

1989	A TIMELESS VIEW, Rudi Reichardt	47.00	NR
1989	A PINPOINT LANDING, Rudi Reichardt	47.00	NR
1989	A VANISHING REFUGE, Rudi Reichardt	47.00	NR
1989	A NOBLE VISTA, Rudi Reichardt	47.00	NR

Old Duffer Collection

1991	TE'ED OFF, Ross Logan	47.00	NR
1991	WADE A MINUTE, Ross Logan	47.00	NR
1991	BREAKS LEFT, Ross Logan	47.00	NR
1991	NINE TO THE GREEN, Ross Logan	47.00	NR

Olde Country Cottages

1989	SPRINGTIME IN THE GREENWOOD, Dawn Karr	45.50	NR
1989	AUTUMN GRANDEUR, Dawn Karr	45.50	NR
1989	WINTER SOLACE, Dawn Karr	45.50	NR
1989	SUMMER SPLENDOUR, Dawn Karr	45.50	NR

Outside My Window

1991	CARDINAL, Glen Loates	45.00	NR
1991	GOLDFINCH, Glen Loates	45.00	NR
1991	BLUE JAY, Glen Loates	45.00	NR
1991	MOURNING DOVE, Glen Loates	45.00	NR

		ISSUE	CURRENT
Professionals			
1997	A HELPING HAND (TEACHER), Adeline Halvorson, 7,500	34.95	RI
1997	IN GOOD HANDS, Adeline Halvorson, 12,000	34.95	RI
Reichardt's Annual			
1990	WARM LIGHTS, WINTER'S NIGHT, Rudi Reichardt	65.00	NR
1990	HEARTS CONTENT, Rudi Reichardt	65.00	NR
Reichardt's Eagle			
1991	A SACRED TRUST, Rudi Reichardt	80.00	NR
Reichardt's Game Birds			
1991	GAMBLE QUAIL, Rudi Reichardt	49.00	NR
1991	SPRUCE GROUSE, Rudi Reichardt	49.00	NR
Reichardt's Loon			
1991	TRANQUILITY, Rudi Reichardt	69.50	NR
Remember When			
1989	THE WELCOME (WARM & WONDERFUL), Shirley Deaville, 10,000	42.25	NR
1989	WHO DO YOU LOVE, Shirley Deaville, 10,000	42.25	NR
1989	FROSTY AND FRIENDS, Shirley Deaville, 10,000	42.25	NR
1989	SUMMER COOLER, Shirley Deaville, 10,000	42.25	NR
Reminiscing			
1997	HAYING TIME, Kevin Dodds	49.00	RI
Sawatsky's Steam			
1989	THE BEST SHOW IN TOWN, Peter Sawatsky	49.50	NR
1989	THE WATER STOP, Peter Sawatsky	49.50	NR
1989	KOOTENAY LIFELINE, Peter Sawatsky	49.50	NR
1989	THE TIE THAT BINDS, Peter Sawatsky	49.50	NR
Sawatsky's Steam II			
1992	STATION BREAK (PRINCE GEORGE), Peter Sawatsky	52.00	NR
1992	A LITTLE BOY'S DREAM, Peter Sawatsky	52.00	NR
Sheeler's Wolves			
1993	A CRY IN THE WILDERNESS, Peter Sheeler, 5,000	39.99	RI
Shirley Temple Signature Series (Danbury Mint, Zolan Fine Arts)			
1995	PRECIOUS, Donald Zolan, 75 days	32.85	RI
1996	AMBASSADOR OF SMILES, Donald Zolan, 75 days	32.85	RI
1996	SOMETHING SPECIAL, Donald Zolan, 75 days	32.85	RI
1996	ONE IN A MILLION, Donald Zolan, 75 days	32.85	RI
1996	SIMPLY IRRESISTIBLE, Donald Zolan, 75 days	32.85	RI
1996	PRIDE AND JOY, Donald Zolan, 75 days	32.85	RI
1996	AMERICA'S SWEETHEART, Donald Zolan, 75 days	32.85	RI
1996	LITTLE ANGEL, Donald Zolan, 75 days	32.85	RI

			ISSUE	CURRENT

Sky Warriors of Desert Storm

1994	BLACK DAWN (STEALTH FIGHTER), Rich Thistle	45.00	RI

Someone to Watch Over Me

1989	LADIES OF THE LAKE, Janette O'Neil	47.00	NR
1989	A QUIET CONVERSATION, Janette O'Neil	47.00	NR

Sunrise…Sunset

1988	THE APPRENTICE, Nori Peter	50.00	NR
1988	TENDING THE LAMP, Nori Peter	50.00	NR
1988	GRANDMA'S TASK, Nori Peter	50.00	NR
1988	BUILDING FOR TODAY, Nori Peter	50.00	NR

Taking Responsibility

1995	ONE DOWN, James Majury, 5,000	42.50	RI
1995	CAT TAILS, James Majury, 5,000	42.50	RI

Valour Over Dangerous Seas

1991	INTO THE WIND, Rich Thistle	55.00	NR
1991	PRESS ON REGARDLESS, Rich Thistle	55.00	NR
1991	DIEPPE DAWN, Rich Thistle	55.00	NR
1991	QUARRY IN TO THE MOONPATH, Rich Thistle	55.00	NR

War Birds

1989	SPITFIRE, Reg Griffin	45.00	NR
1989	HALIFAX, Reg Griffin	45.00	NR
1989	HURRICANE, Reg Griffin	45.00	NR
1989	MOSQUITO, Reg Griffin	45.00	NR

The Way We Were

1992	WONDERLAND IN WHITE, Kevin Dodds, 7,500	49.00	NR
1992	LAZY DAYS, Kevin Dodds, 7,500	49.00	NR
1992	OUR CUP RUNNETH OVER, Kevin Dodds, 7,500	49.00	NR
1992	SIGNS OF SPRING, Kevin Dodds, 7,500	49.00	NR

Wild and Free

1988	THE LOONS, Fred Neubacher	38.50	NR
1988	THE MOOSE, Fred Neubacher	38.50	NR
1988	THE EAGLE, Fred Neubacher	38.50	NR
1988	THE BEAVER, Fred Neubacher	38.50	NR
1988	THE WOLVES, Fred Neubacher	38.50	NR
1988	THE TRUMPETER SWANS, Fred Neubacher	38.50	NR

World of Dolls

1990	MY FIRST DOLL, Tammy Laye	38.50	NR
1990	A DOLL'S DELIGHT, Tammy Laye	38.50	NR
1990	AS GOOD AS NEW, Tammy Laye	38.50	NR
1990	AFTERNOON TEA, Tammy Laye	38.50	NR

Young Hopefuls

		ISSUE	CURRENT
1989	DAWN, Elaine MacPherson	46.75	NR
1989	BREEZY, Elaine MacPherson	46.75	NR
1989	WESTWARD, Elaine MacPherson	46.75	NR
1989	MISTY, Elaine MacPherson	46.75	NR

Single Issue

1991	A LIGHT IN THE FOREST, Shirley Deaville, 7,500	45.00	NR
1993	HORNETS OVER THE GULF, Rich Thistle	62.50	RI
1993	UNITED, Eddie LePage	42.00	RI
1994	AMERICAN CLASSICS, Rich Thistle	39.99	RI
1995	PROUD SERVICE, Rich Thistle	35.00	RI
1997	DREAM MACHINE 'THE AVRO ARROW,' Rich Thistle	49.90	RI
1997	THE GOOD EARTH, Adeline Halvorson, 7,500	29.90	RI
1997	THROUGH FIELDS OF GOLD, Adeline Halvorson, 7,500	29.90	RI

WOODMERE CHINA UNITED STATES

(Hamilton Collection, River Shore)

Field Trials

NA	FIRST IMPRESSIONS, Diana L. Charles, 10 days	NA	NA

WORLD BOOK ENCYCLOPEDIA

Christmas

1979	SILENT NIGHT, Betsy Bates	NA	NA
1980	CHRISTMAS MORNING, Betsy Bates	NA	NA
1981	CHRISTMAS ON THE FARM, Betsy Bates	NA	NA
1982	HOME FOR CHRISTMAS, Betsy Bates	NA	NA
1983	VILLAGE INN, Betsy Bates	NA	NA
1984	VILLAGE CHURCH, Betsy Bates	NA	NA
1985	VILLAGE SCHOOL, Betsy Bates	NA	NA
1986	VILLAGE ANTIQUE, Betsy Bates	NA	NA
1987	CHRISTMAS AT HARBOR, Betsy Bates	NA	NA
1988	CHRISTMAS BY THE MILLSTREAM, Betsy Bates	NA	NA
1989	COUNTRY CHRISTMAS, Betsy Bates	NA	NA
1990	HOLIDAY, Betsy Bates	NA	NA

ZANOBIA

African Violet Miniatures

1985	HALF PINT, Zanobia, 5,000	29.50	NR
1985	LUVKINS, Zanobia, 5,000	29.50	NR

Violet Portraits

1987	CANADIAN SUNSET, Zanobia, 5,000	34.50	NR
1987	KISS'T, Zanobia, 5,000	34.50	NR

ZOLAN FINE ARTS / WINSTON ROLAND UNITED STATES

Angel Songs—Miniature

		ISSUE	CURRENT
1997	HARP SONG, Donald Zolan, 15 days, $3\frac{5}{8}$"	19.90	RI
1997	HEAVENLY SONG, Donald Zolan, 15 days, $3\frac{5}{8}$"	19.90	RI
1997	LOVE SONG, Donald Zolan, 15 days, $3\frac{5}{8}$"	19.90	RI

Country Friends

1998	LITTLE GARDENER, Donald Zolan, 15 days, $3\frac{5}{8}$"	19.90	RI
1998	GIGGLES AND WIGGLES, Donald Zolan, 15 days, $3\frac{5}{8}$"	19.90	RI
1998	LET'S PLAY, Donald Zolan, 15 days, $3\frac{5}{8}$"	19.90	RI

Harp Song
Photo courtesy © Zolan Fine Arts, Ltd.

Little Gardener
Photo courtesy © Zolan Fine Arts, Ltd.

Donald Zolan Society Free Mini Plate

1997	A CHILD'S FAITH, Donald Zolan, 15 days, $3\frac{5}{8}$"	gift	RI

Donald Zolan Society Members Only Gift

1998	REACH FOR THE SKY, Donald Zolan, $3\frac{5}{8}$"	gift	RI

Donald Zolan Society Members Only Product

1997	RAINED OUT, Donald Zolan, <1 year, $3\frac{5}{8}$"	19.90	RI
1998	SUMMER THUNDER, Donald Zolan, 3,000, $3\frac{5}{8}$"	19.90	RI

Symphony of Seasons

1996	WINTER WONDER, Donald Zolan, 15 days, $3\frac{5}{8}$"	19.90	RI
1997	SUMMERTIME FRIENDS, Donald Zolan, 15 days, $3\frac{5}{8}$"	19.90	RI
1997	PUDDLES 'N SPLASHES, Donald Zolan, 15 days, $3\frac{5}{8}$"	19.90	RI
1997	COUNTRY PUMPKINS, Donald Zolan, 15 days, $3\frac{5}{8}$"	19.90	RI

Single Issues

1998	DOWNHILL DELIGHT, Donald Zolan, 15 days, $3\frac{5}{8}$"	19.90	RI

Artist Index

– S –

– T –

Series Index

– J –

– K –

– L –

– M –

– N –

– U –

– V –

– W –

– X, Y, Z –